EVALUATION FOR THE 21st CENTURY

A HANDBOOK

EDITORS
ELEANOR CHELIMSKY
WILLIAM R. SHADISH

SAGE Publications
International Educational and Professional Publisher
Thousand Oaks   London   New Delhi

For information address:

SAGE Publications, Inc.
2455 Teller Road
Thousand Oaks, California 91320
E-mail: order@sagepub.com

SAGE Publications Ltd.
6 Bonhill Street
London EC2A 4PU
United Kingdom

SAGE Publications India Pvt. Ltd.
M-32 Market
Greater Kailash I
New Delhi 110 048 India

Printed in the United States of America

Library of Congress Cataloging-in-Publication Data

Main entry under title:

Evaluation for the 21st century: A handbook / editors, Eleanor
    Chelimsky and William R. Shadish.
        p.   cm.
    Includes bibliographical references and index.
    ISBN 0-7619-0610-X (acid-free paper). – ISBN 0-7619-0611-8 (pbk.:
acid-free paper)
        1. Evaluation research (Social action programs).   I. Chelimsky,
Eleanor.   II. Shadish, William R.
    H62.E8473   1997
    001.4–dc20   96-25373

97 98 99 00 01 02 03 10 9 8 7 6 5 4 3 2 1

Acquiring Editor:	C. Deborah Laughton
Editorial Assistant:	Eileen Carr
Production Editor:	Astrid Virding
Production Assistant:	Denise Santoyo
Typesetter/Designer:	Christina Hill
Indexer:	Teri Greenberg
Cover Designer:	Lesa Valdez
Print Buyer:	Anna Chin

EVALUATION FOR THE 21st CENTURY

In Memoriam

As this book goes to press, we are deeply saddened to hear of the passing of Donald T. Campbell in May 1996. We publish here the last paragraph of some remarks made about his work at an evaluation conference 5 years ago that remain entirely pertinent:

"Looking back over Campbell's work, it is clear that he has consistently tried to integrate opposite poles in evaluative thinking, to bridge the gaps between them. This effort of his was crucial to evaluation's survival over the past decade, when it was under attack, and it promises Campbell an enduring place, not only in the annals of applied social science research but also in whatever pantheon we have in America for people who can understand both sides of an issue and integrate them into a larger—but always elegant—framework."

Contents

PREFACE   *xi*

1. The Coming Transformations in Evaluation   1
    Eleanor Chelimsky

PART I: EVALUATION—YESTERDAY AND TODAY   *27*

2. Lessons Learned in Evaluation Over the Past 25 Years   30
    Thomas D. Cook

3. The Political Environment of Evaluation and
   What It Means for the Development of the Field   53
    Eleanor Chelimsky

PART II: AUDITING AND EVALUATION   *69*

4. Evaluation as an Essential Component of "Value-for-Money"   72
    L. Denis Desautels

5. Auditing and Evaluation in Sweden   80
    Inga-Britt Ahlenius

6. Performance Auditing: Travelers' Tales   86
   Christopher Pollitt and *Hilkka Summa*

7. Evaluation and Auditing in State Legislatures:
   Meeting the Client's Needs   109
   Roger A. Brooks

PART III: PERFORMANCE MEASUREMENT AND EVALUATION   121

8. Trends in Performance Measurement:
   Challenges for Evaluators   124
   Joseph S. Wholey

9. Performance Measurement in the United Kingdom
   (1985–1995)   134
   Caroline Mawhood

PART IV: INTERNATIONAL EVALUATION   145

10. Evaluating Global Issues in a Community Setting   149
    Masafumi Nagao

11. The Development of Evaluation in the
    People's Republic of China   170
    Hong Hougi and *Ray C. Rist*

12. Critical Comments on Evaluation Research in Denmark   177
    Finn Hansson

13. Evaluation, Markets, and Institutions in the Reform Agenda
    of Developing Countries   189
    Eduardo Wiesner

14. Evaluation in the World Bank: Antecedents, Instruments,
    and Concepts   201
    Robert Picciotto

PART V: NEW TOPICS FOR EVALUATION   *215*

15. Evaluating Human Rights Violations   221
   Ignacio Cano

16. Lessons of Immigration Policy and the Role of Research   234
   John Nieuwenhuysen

17. Tracing Gender Issues Through Institutional Change
   and Program Implementation at the World Bank   251
   Josette Murphy

18. Understanding the Impact of Development Projects on Women:
   The Tunisia Institutional Development Fund Project   260
   Michael Bamberger

19. The Analysis and Evaluation of Foreign Aid   272
   Kristina Svensson

20. Evaluating the U.S. Nuclear Triad   284
   Kwai-Cheung Chan and Jonathan R. Tumin

21. Evaluation, Nuclear Power Plant Remediation and
   Redesign, and Russian Policy Making After Chernobyl   299
   Vladimir Novikov

22. The Independent Evaluation of the Global Environment
   Facility Pilot Phase   311
   W. Haven North

23. Environmental Changes and Their Measurement:
   What Data Should We Collect and What Collaborative
   Systems Do We Need for Linking Knowledge to Action?   329
   Charles A. Zraket and William Clark

**PART VI: A SAMPLER OF THE CURRENT
   METHODOLOGICAL TOOL KIT**   *337*

24. Multimethod Evaluations: Using Case Studies Together
   With Other Methods   344
   Lois-ellin Datta

25. Cross-Design Synthesis: Concept and Application   360
    Judith A. Droitcour

26. Research Synthesis for Public Health Policy:
    Experience of the Institute of Medicine   373
    Michael A. Stoto

27. Empowerment Evaluation and Accreditation in
    Higher Education   381
    David M. Fetterman

28. Cluster Evaluation   396
    James R. Sanders

29. An Introduction to Scientific Realist Evaluation   405
    Ray Pawson and *Nick Tilley*

30. Single-Case Evaluation in British Social Services   419
    Mansoor A. F. Kazi

31. Twenty-One Years Old and Counting:
    The Interrupted Time Series Comes of Age   443
    Robert G. Orwin

**PART VII: AN ENDURING ARGUMENT ABOUT THE
PURPOSE OF EVALUATION**   **467**

32. Advocacy in Evaluation: A Necessary Evil?   470
    Robert E. Stake

33. Truth and Objectivity in Evaluation   477
    Michael Scriven

INDEX   **501**

ABOUT THE EDITORS   **521**

ABOUT THE CONTRIBUTORS   **523**

Preface

For the past 30 years, we have witnessed the development of a discipline and a profession of evaluation. Less than 4 years from now, we will be witnessing the passing of the millennium, which leads naturally to the question, What will evaluation be like in the 21st century? Our crystal ball is undoubtedly fallible, but in this book we present some of the features of the professional landscape that we suspect will become increasingly salient as the end of the 20th century comes and goes. We call this a handbook because it is our hope that as evaluators begin to encounter these developing features, they will recognize them from our description, be able to place them into context, and perhaps even return to read about them in more detail once these features impinge more strongly on their professional practice.

Evaluation is becoming increasingly international, but in ways that go beyond previous conceptions of what *international* means. *International* is no longer used only to describe the efforts of particular evaluators in individual countries around the world—although it certainly is still used this way, as in the descriptions of evaluation in China and in Denmark included in this book. Today, evaluation is also becoming international in the sense of being at the same time more indigenous, more global, and more transnational. By *indigenous,* we mean that evaluators in different countries around the world are developing their own infrastructures to support their endeavors as well as their own preferred theoretical and methodological approaches. By *global,* we mean that developments in one part of the globe frequently affect people, institutions, and programs all around the world. An example in this volume is the description of how the evaluation of community development in a small town in Japan is influenced by policies and people in and from other nations. By *transnational,* we mean that the problems and programs that we are called upon to evaluate today often extend beyond the boundaries of any one nation, any one continent, or even one hemisphere. As is noted in Chapter 1, these include problems of pollution, of the economics of developing countries, and of the role of women in society. We cannot say exactly what the best responses to these internationalizing developments will be for evaluators, but we do know that recognizing the developments is the first step toward accommodating to them.

Evaluation is becoming increasingly diverse in what it is asked to evaluate. Michael Scriven once said that it is possible to evaluate anything (including evaluation itself). That observation looks prophetic in the context of the contents of this book. Today, the diverse array of things being evaluated is nearly bewildering—not just programs, personnel, and products, not only medical and military technology, but also foreign aid, defense policy, environmental interventions, nuclear power plant accidents, massive human rights violations, and World Bank loan programs. This diversity will undoubtedly challenge evaluators to develop new methods, new organizational strategies, and new conceptualizations of what they can and should be doing.

Evaluation is becoming increasingly self-conscious about its own identity. To be sure, we will continue to ask the question, What is evaluation? The now-classic answer is that evaluation is about determining merit or worth—although it is far from clear that we have consensus on that answer across the diversity of the evaluation profession. The more interesting development may be the increasing frequency with which we are asking the question, What makes evaluation different from other disciplines? For example, the increasingly close ties between the evaluation profession and the auditing profession prompt many thoughtful questions about the differences and similarities between the two that are explored in this book. Certainly we have much to learn from each other. Similarly, evaluators are asking more subtle questions about exactly which activities have priority in evaluation, under what circumstances, for what purposes. Examples in this book concern the relative priority assigned to advocacy versus truth in evaluation and to evaluating programs versus empowering people to evaluate their own programs.

Evaluation continues to become ever more methodologically diverse. It is by now well established that the full array of social science methods belongs in the evaluator's methodological tool kit—tools from psychology, statistics, education, sociology, political science, anthropology, and economics. Clearly we must also include the logical tools given to us by philosophers who study the nature of evaluation. Further, evaluators continue to invent interesting constellations of methods, or strategies for approaching evaluation, such as cluster evaluation and empowerment evaluation. But even evaluators who accept all this diversity may be surprised by the tools they may still need to learn about, to judge from the chapters in this book—the methods of auditors who have extended their work from auditing financial records to auditing program performance, of evaluators who synthesize studies done quite differently, and perhaps even of physical scientists whose global questions make locally constrained methods impractical.

It is often uncomfortable to stir oneself from familiar cultural, topical, conceptual, and methodological niches. But if there is a moral to the present book, it is this: Evaluation in the next century will be far more diverse than it is today. So we must face the discomfort of stirring ourselves if we are to avoid being left behind.

Finally, evaluators, in whatever field of evaluation they may be, are likely to find themselves, at least sometimes, at odds with the political actors, systems, and processes in their countries that militate against the free flow of information required by evaluation. This means that as the world becomes more politically diverse and complex in the 21st century, evaluators will be called upon to exhibit considerable courage in the normal pursuit of their work. Because they are examples of admirable courage in using research to speak truth to power, we want to dedicate this book to six men of the 20th century: Vaclav Havel, C. Everett Koop, Jean Monnet, Daniel Patrick Moynihan, Gunnar Myrdal, and Elliot Richardson. Their strength and vision have paved the way for the next generations.

Eleanor Chelimsky
William R. Shadish

1

The Coming Transformations in Evaluation

Eleanor Chelimsky

The joint International Evaluation Conference held in Vancouver, Canada, during the first week of November 1995 was, in one participant's words, "a watershed event."[1] It marked the first time that five evaluation associations and more than 1,600 evaluators from 66 countries and five continents had come together.[2] The purpose was to take stock of where evaluation is today and where it is likely to be going in the next century.

The conference focused on three topics intended to reflect international experience in evaluation to date: first, global issues (centering on transnational problems rather than national or local ones); second, lessons learned from evaluation theory and practice of the past; and third, evaluation's changing characteristics (especially changes related to the adaptation of traditional methods and the use of nontraditional methods in different parts of the world).

There were 363 panels, workshops, and other sessions (each with a number of presenters); there were five plenary speakers; there were

1

preconference workshops focusing on a variety of evaluation methods; and throughout the conference—in the corridors and over coffee—spontaneous debates arose, inspired by particular sets of papers, perhaps, but bringing to bear a wonderful variety of evaluative experiences from far-flung places.

This book, of necessity, can present only selected papers from the conference and therefore gives a somewhat attenuated reflection of its extraordinary richness, spirit, and vitality. The hope is that what it must lose in diversity it will gain in focus as the scope is narrowed to just one subject—current changes in evaluation. In this chapter, I will discuss four themes that are related to those changes:

■ the new political and policy context as we move into the 21st century

■ new actors, topics, and nations in the field of evaluation

■ new versions of old arguments about the purposes of evaluation and the implications of those purposes for methodology, for the use of findings, and for the role of the evaluator

■ new and old lessons from the continuing evaluation experience

Although these are certainly not the unique themes of the chapters in this volume, they are very important ones. In this chapter, then, I will try to confront, as objectively as possible, the principal elements and controversies with respect to these themes, using the 33 chapters in this book as data for the discussion.

■ *A New Political and Policy Context for Evaluation*

The mere fact of examining the evaluative questions confronting, say, continents rather then nations, and facing outward toward worldwide challenges rather than inward toward domestic problems, brings three issues immediately to the fore that have not been traditional ones in evaluation.

First, evaluation must now deal with a number of global political forces that are transforming all societies—developing and developed nations alike—and at fairly high rates of speed. One of these forces is certainly the worldwide adoption of new technologies—for example, automated workplaces or genetically engineered crops—with all the changes they imply for the old factory- and field-based ways of doing things and employing people. Another force is the steadily increasing demographic imbalance between developed and developing countries: Many poor nations are seeing population explosions that are generating increased migration, while rich nations can barely replace the populations they have, even as they are beset by job insecurities that make immigration seem threatening. Forces such as these (and others as well, such as the globalization of national and local economies, the spread of terrorism, and the "small" wars that have followed the collapse of the Soviet Union) are bearing down on affluent and deprived regions alike, challenging citizens everywhere to try to understand what is happening; to adapt to a whole new set of changing economic and cultural circumstances; and to do, politically, what appears to be in their own self-interest. In many industrialized nations around the world, there is talk of self-protection, and less attention is being paid both to the sufferings of "outsiders" and to the problem of exclusion within societies. The focus today is much more on differences between people than on the common heritage of the human family.

Second, as developing nations struggle to raise their citizens' quality of life in the face of these forces, it seems that the broader global questions that should be of great concern to all nations are suffering in consequence. These are the questions of environmental protection; sustainable development; regional or continental cooperation (along with the international legal framework needed for assuring it); the rights of women, children, and the elderly; the treatment of political prisoners; the advent of massive human rights violations; and more. Yet despite their importance, all of these questions appear to be relegated to a much lower priority than are questions directly related, for example, to economic gains to an individual nation or to specific groups within that nation.

In Chapter 14 of this book, Picciotto remarks that "with the end of the Cold War, the developing world has become more volatile and violent conflict more common. Increasingly, [World Bank] resources for development assistance are mortgaged to meet the needs of peacemaking and peacekeeping." In Chapter 10, Nagao examines from a community perspective "the global economic movement toward an increasingly borderless world, as represented by the opening of national economies to international markets." He focuses on the social costs of this movement for rural and urban places, observing, first, the occurrence in rural communities worldwide of a continuing "crisis of identity and intergenerational succession" brought on by the out-migration of these communities' youth, the aging of their societies, and their sense that in the future, they might "cease to be viable economic entities." He then points to corresponding effects on urban centers from rural out-migration, especially in developing countries, where sizable flows of people are leading to "excessive population concentration on the receiving end of the cities, causing massive poverty and degradation of the environment." Similarly, Nieuwenhuysen, in his discussion of immigration policy in Chapter 16, quotes Castles and Miller (1993), who note that "the perspective of the 1990s and the early part of the next century is that migration will continue to grow [and] . . . ecological demographic pressures may force many people to seek refuge outside their own countries" (pp. 3-4).

It is not by accident that world planners and policy makers are substituting sustainable development for the unbounded growth desired in the past. As Zraket and Clark note in Chapter 23:

> By the year 2050, the global population is projected to increase by a factor of 2, agricultural consumption by a factor of 4, energy consumption by a factor of 6, and economic turnover by a factor of 8. The cumulative impacts of these estimates in terms of chemical flows are that carbon dioxide emissions will increase by 25%, sulfur emissions by 100%, sediment flows by 300%, water withdrawals by 400%, lead use by 18,000%, and synthetic organic compounds by 70,000%. In terms of ecosystems, fertile soils will decrease by 10%, forested land by 20%, and wetlands by 50%, not to mention unknown impacts upon biodiversity.
>
> Our challenge is to navigate successfully the transition from unbounded growth to sustainability, through research, technology and policy assessment, and critical ex post evaluation of our successes and failures to date.

In all of these areas, evaluation has an important role to play, not only in determining past successes and failures, but in identifying, empirically describing, and monitoring problems; in increasing public awareness of the current and likely future impacts of these problems; and in developing and comparatively assessing proposed solutions. However, it is also the case that evaluation will need to adapt to new conditions, such as greatly modified geographic scope and time periods. For example, assessing changes in air pollution involves measuring levels and flows across great distances, and evaluating the policy impacts of crop-breeding research on hunger may require as many as 20 years across quite tenuously connected components of the research and technology transfer processes.

The third issue is that, partly because of all these changes and the personal and community insecurities they have engendered, but also because of a late-20th-century social climate that has featured strong grassroots and national movements against taxation in developed countries, citizens everywhere appear intent on contributing less to government and international institutions, and on keeping more of their resources to spend at their own discretion. As a consequence, parsimony in public life and a need for evaluation to justify past expenditures to parliaments, donors, and taxpayers have become common characteristics of the new public management discourse. In Chapter 4 of this volume, for example, Desautels refers to the international "move toward more affordable forms of government" and the "growing public demand for accountability for the results that are being achieved with our tax dollars." Picciotto also speaks of new "poles of resistance among employers and employees in developed regions who feel vulnerable to the winds of international competition." "With the end of superpower confrontation," he writes, "the ideological case for resource transfers to poor countries has evaporated, and the electorates of the industrial countries, preoccupied by fiscal and employment problems of their own, have become far more skeptical and demanding," calling for "improved performance," and "documented results" through evaluation. In the same way, Wholey views performance measurement and evaluation as means to rebuild lost public trust in government (see Chapter 8).

In short, the political and policy context in which evaluations are performed is changing. The movement worldwide is toward reduced taxation, reduced deficits, reduced fund transfers from the rich to the poor, and reduced government size. Because of this movement, evaluation takes on greater public importance as the need grows to measure policy and program cost-effectiveness.

But accountability and good management are not the only reasons for conducting evaluations. As the world gets smaller through spreading communications technology and demographic shifts, the opportunity also exists to use evaluation to gain greater understanding and outreach among peoples; better knowledge of the specific problems they confront; more thoroughgoing dissemination of existing evaluation findings with regard to proposed policy solutions; increased institutional capacity, integrity, and responsiveness; and stronger encouragement of local initiatives— aided by international research, as in Nagao's example of a Japanese town in Chapter 10—in creating innovative solutions to help counteract the new problems of people and communities.

In this sense, evaluation—not only for the purposes of accountability and good management, but also for knowledge building and sharing, for institutional learning and development, for governmental and democratic reform through the serious examination of public policy—has become a precious and unique tool as we prepare to deal with the new socioeconomic, political, and infrastructure needs of the next century. Perhaps it is this more widely glimpsed utility that accounts for the current expansion in many areas now being seen in the evaluation field.

■ *New Actors, New Topics, and New National Evaluation Systems*

Increasing interest by auditors in the use of evaluation for assessing performance led to the 1992 adoption of evaluation as a key work area for the national audit agencies of 188 independent states worldwide, including both developed and developing nations. One important reason for this interest has been the increase in policy demands on auditors everywhere to determine the results of programs—that is, their merit or worth. In consequence, auditors have recognized the need for nonauditing methods that allow the acquisition of information, as Desautels puts it in Chapter 4, "on the more difficult issues (such as attribution) surrounding the outcomes of programs and activities—which is where evaluation has a unique contribution to make."

In the same way, practitioners of performance measurement (the "new public management," as it is called in Europe), with its emphasis on assessment and measurement of institutional performance (and citizen satisfaction with that performance), count on evaluation to help achieve governmental or agency reform. In Chapter 9, Mawhood discusses the use being made of evaluation techniques in the United Kingdom to achieve more direct government accountability. For example:

- The continued employment and pay of many top public sector managers now depend on the achievement of stated performances, which must often be validated by external agencies.

- A "Citizen's Charter" was introduced in 1991 that aims to make the executive more directly accountable to consumers of public services by setting a range of targets for good service. Before the Charter, parents had no formal right to information about their children's progress or about schools' performance in public examinations. Now all parents must receive annual reports on their children and can compare the examination results achieved at their children's schools with those of other schools in their areas. Since June 1994 in England and Wales, comparative information has been published on the performance of hospitals and ambulance services against six key indicators.

- Most public services now conduct regular user surveys and publish the results. The best organizations do more. For example, some police services are making follow-up visits to victims of crime to find out how they feel about how their cases have been handled.

Like auditors, the planners and implementers of performance measurement expect that evaluation will be most important for attributional purposes (i.e., to tie outcomes to achievements) through the "sophisticated program evaluation studies" recommended by Wholey in Chapter 8. Such studies might be expected to use techniques such as interrupted time series and to explore plausible competing hypotheses that could equally well have accounted for the results claimed. In the United Kingdom, where performance measurement is already widely implemented, practitioners have in fact relied on external evaluation to validate achievement findings, as already noted. In addition, evaluation has been used to answer some of the more complex policy questions. Mawhood notes that the British Department of Health examined strategies for providing long-term community care by carrying out a "detailed and rigorous evaluation" that compared health outcomes between community institutions and hospitals.

In development assistance, as in auditing and performance measurement, administrators look toward evaluation to respond to the requirements of their donors for accountability. In Chapter 19, Svensson notes that the reporting of results has assumed an increasingly prominent position in foreign aid policy: "An open and honest results report is necessary to a donor's willingness to give aid over the long term." International organizations also use evaluation to help with capacity building, which has largely been focused on strengthening borrower (or recipient) institutions. As Picciotto writes in Chapter 14, "There is scarce tolerance for the assignment of resources to countries that mismanage their economies."

The development assistance focus goes still further, to the organizational learning process itself and how it works. Svensson remarks that evaluation is needed to examine "those factors that affect the willingness of the entire system to change, such as leadership, incentives, human resources management, division of responsibilities, organizational structure, and institutional competition." She notes that "the readiness for change in recipient countries is decisive for the results of aid, such change being the ultimate aim of aid." The call here, then, is for the evaluation and strengthening of institutions, and this issue is developed and amplified in Wiesner's discussion in Chapter 13 of special interests and their damaging effects on governmental reform in developing nations.

Not only are there many new actors in evaluation, there are many new topics as well, reflecting both the preoccupations of these actors and the global issues discussed earlier. As a result, evaluators will find in this book a wide variety of subjects that have not been familiar ones in evaluation, such as the effects of the nuclear disaster at Chernobyl, the data required for evaluating environmental programs, the use of evaluation to establish a research agenda in immigration policy, the determination of the cost-effectiveness of a $350 billion cross-service defense program, the assessment of results achieved by foreign aid, and the use of evaluation techniques to understand numbers and trends in human rights violations. Other unusual topics in this volume include those already discussed in terms of their practitioners (i.e., evaluation in auditing, in public management, and in development assistance). Finally, Hong and Rist (Chapter 11) and Hansson (Chapter 12) discuss approaches to evaluation in China and Denmark, respectively, and show two ways of thinking about establishing new evaluation systems.

As these new actors came together with longtime evaluators at the Vancouver conference, two points of persistent tension emerged among them that need to be confronted here, because of the ramifications they have for evaluation's ability to meet the varied demands that will be made on it over the coming years. These tensions relate to (a) differing purposes and perspectives in evaluation, along with the differing methodological emphases they imply; and (b) differing views about the uses of evaluations and about evaluators' role in conducting them. Although these tensions are long-standing, they take on new significance in the global political context we now face, which combines increasing evaluation opportunities with increasing cutbacks in public funds and resources generally,

■ New Versions of Old Arguments

□ Differing Purposes, Perspectives, and Methods

What, then, are our purposes in doing evaluations? Looking only at the different purposes already invoked in this chapter, a list would have to include at least the following: to measure and account for the results of public policies and programs; to determine the efficiency of programs, projects, and their component processes; to gain explanatory insights into social and other public problems and into past and present efforts to address them; to understand how organizations learn; to strengthen institutions and improve managerial performance; to increase agency responsiveness to the public; to reform governments through the free flow of evaluative information; and to expand results or efficiency measurement from that of local or national interventions to that of global interventions such as reducing poverty and hunger or reversing patterns of environmental degradation.

All of these purposes are, of course, clearly legitimate and worthwhile reasons for conducting evaluations, but they differ with regard to the questions they address and the kinds of methods needed to answer those questions. For example, consider the first purpose mentioned above: the evaluative effort to measure and account for results. Whether those results are local, national, or worldwide, the evaluator is faced with answering the question of whether a particular intervention *caused* a particular result, or (put another way) whether a change observed is attributable to the intervention. This kind of cause-and-effect question usually calls for methods that allow findings or estimates to be linked to interventions as closely and conclusively as possible. One example of such a method is the randomized controlled clinical trial, commonly used to measure the effectiveness of medical interventions (see Droitcour, Chapter 25).

On the other hand, for other purposes mentioned above—such as strengthening institutions, improving agency performance, or helping managers think through their planning, evaluation, and reporting tasks—evaluators are faced with a different type of question, in particular, whether others can be assisted to develop a culture of evaluation that will build capacity for better performance. This kind of question calls for formative types of evaluation using developmental methods, such as the participatory analyses described by Fetterman (see Chapter 27). These methods usually have the goal of empowering agency people rather than determining the results of agency programs, but the latter may also be a part of the developmental focus. In such a case (see Wholey, Chapter 8, and Mawhood, Chapter 9), independent evaluators employing different methods can be (and have been) asked to validate the findings established by these internal collaborations of evaluators and agency (or program) actors.

Other purposes noted above involve gaining greater understanding, whether about public problems, or programs, or the processes by which they come about. Here the evaluator is faced with the complex question of trying to learn about and explain what lies behind the issues confronting public policy. As Cook puts it in Chapter 2, these knowledge-seeking kinds of evaluations often "change the way social issues and programs are framed; they change the level of realism about what might be expected to result from a certain type of program; or they foster generalizations about how programs operate." As in scientific research generally, the effort to gain such explanatory insights requires strong designs and methods, usually involving both quantitative and qualitative approaches, and advanced levels of both substantive and methodological expertise.

These different purposes, along with the questions they seek to address, seem to fall naturally into three general perspectives:

■ evaluation for accountability (e.g., the measurement of results or efficiency)

■ evaluation for development (e.g., the provision of evaluative help to strengthen institutions)

■ evaluation for knowledge (e.g., the acquisition of a more profound understanding in some specific area or field)

Although these perspectives are neither exhaustive nor mutually exclusive with regard to methods, they do present notable differences on a variety of dimensions; they may be needed at particular times or policy points and not at others (e.g., an evaluation for knowledge or one for development may need to precede an evaluation for accountability); and they appear to have considerable explanatory power with regard to the current tensions in the evaluation field. Let us try to characterize them a little further.

☐ *The Accountability Perspective in Evaluation*

From the standpoints of auditors, government sponsors of evaluation studies, donors to international organizations, and many others, evaluation is done to establish accountability. This involves the provision of information to decision makers, whether they are in the public or private sector. Specific cause-and-effect questions about results in an accountability perspective might be, for example: What happened to poverty levels among the very poor as a result of development assistance provided? Did a policy of capital punishment affect crime rates? Did welfare cases decrease in number because of the introduction of mandated work programs? Sometimes, questions about results from an accountability perspective may involve merely documentation of whether or not anything has changed after something new has been tried. Normally, however, the ability to say that something is in fact a "result" hinges on the ability to establish that it came about because of something else. As for questions about efficiency, these usually concern costs per value received and also comparative costs for the same (or a similar) program or product.

Many methods are used to answer these kinds of accountability questions, including, as already noted, the randomized designs used for clinical trials, when they are applicable; quasi-experimental designs (an example of such a design, using interrupted time series analysis, is discussed by Orwin in Chapter 31); controlled designs (see Bamberger, Chapter 18, on the gender effects of development assistance projects in Tunisia); cost-effectiveness designs (see Chapter 20, by Chan and Tumin, on nuclear weapons); and research synthesis (see Droitcour, Chapter 25, and Stoto, Chapter 26, for examples). Occasionally, case study designs are employed to examine results (see Kazi, Chapter 30, and examples in the literature of cross-site and replicated case designs).[3] However, case studies are used more often to examine processes rather than results, and the same is true of process evaluations. Although the latter—especially in their stand-alone guise—are not generally considered methods of choice for gathering information on results, still, in combination with some kind of outcome study, a process evaluation can greatly assist researchers in understanding the outcome findings. For the most part, process evaluations have been used to inform on what is happening in (rather than what has been achieved by) a program (see, for example, Chapter 22, by North, on the process evaluation of the Global Environment Facility). But it is also the case that information on what has happened in, say, the implementation of a program, is indispensable for an evaluation of its results. Thus, process evaluations can be necessary adjuncts for accountability studies, but they probably have their greatest importance and use in an institution-building, developmental perspective.

☐ *The Developmental Perspective in Evaluation*

For government reformers, public managers, capacity builders, and others, evaluation is done to improve institutional performance. It serves as a flexible tool that works both prospectively and retrospectively to set a research agenda in an agency; to improve the design of projects and demonstrations; to measure and recommend changes in organization activities; to develop the indicators and performance targets needed to improve institutional effectiveness and responsiveness (see again Wholey, Chapter 8; Mawhood, Chapter 9); to monitor, in an ongoing way, how projects are being implemented across a number of different sites (see Sanders, Chapter 28, on cluster evaluation); to see how cooperation is occurring (or not occurring) across independent agencies collaborating on a program; to determine what data systems are needed to understand what is happening in a program; and/or to find out how beneficiaries feel about an agency and its programs, and whether spending is going according to plan or not (see again North, Chapter 22).

To some accountability- or knowledge-perspective evaluators, developmental evaluators may seem more like evaluation "consultants" than evaluators (see Scriven, Chapter 33), but those who do developmental work are convinced that building evaluation capability is as important an evaluation function as evaluation itself and that indeed, in some cases, evaluation cannot be done without it.

Specific questions asked of evaluators in a developmental perspective might include the following: What is the best research evidence with respect to formulating a new program or modifying an old one? How can demonstrations be structured so that they produce evidence on the value of the intervention being tested? What is the most appropriate research agenda for an agency? How can managers improve their own performance and that of their organization? What data systems are needed to monitor trends in problems being tracked, in program accomplishments, and in agency performance?

Both process and outcome designs may be used in a developmental perspective, depending on the evaluation question posed. In addition to the outcome approaches mentioned earlier, the formative methods typically used include monitoring, case studies (often combined with other methods; see Datta, Chapter 24), internal evaluation and empowerment evaluation (see Fetterman, Chapter 27), cluster evaluation (see Sanders, Chapter 28), performance measurement (see Wholey, Chapter 8), and research synthesis of both qualitative and quantitative types. Some of these methods are quite similar to one another. Consider, for example, the steps outlined by Wholey (Chapter 8) for doing performance measurement—strategic planning, performance planning, and performance reporting—and compare these with the steps for doing empowerment evaluation detailed by Fetterman in Chapter 27: "(a) taking stock . . . ; (b) focusing on establishing goals . . . ; (c) developing strategies and helping participants determine their own strategies to accomplish . . . goals and objectives; and (d) helping . . . participants determine the type of evidence required to document progress credibly toward their goals."

☐ *The Knowledge Perspective in Evaluation*

In the view of many researchers working independently in universities and other evaluators in scientific institutions, evaluation is done to generate understanding and explanation. The specific questions may not be especially important to analyze here, given that it is the evaluator who decides what will be asked and answered, and the topic generally follows from the researcher's prior work. This means that the evaluations associated with individual academic researchers, or those of research teams, will be more likely to continue in-depth cumulative inquiry into particular areas or sectors of research than to be concerned—as are accountability and developmental evaluations—with applying systematic research methods to a variety of sectors. Questions that have been addressed by different knowledge-perspective evaluators are, for example: How do organizations learn? Why is a technology successful in Asia but not in Africa? What are the different reasons for persons' being homeless? Which teenagers become addicted, which do not, and why? Which policies and programs might best address problems of alcoholic violence, based on which theory?

The larger purpose of the knowledge perspective is to increase understanding about the factors underlying public problems, about the "fit" between these factors and the policy or program solutions proposed, and about the theory and logic (or their lack) that lie behind an implemented intervention. These evaluations may employ any of the methods discussed above, separately or in conjunction with each other, but the purpose of knowledge gain leads logically to the use of the strongest designs (to promote conclusiveness and generalizability in the findings) as well as the greatest clarity possible in explication and documentation of methods (to facilitate replication or later use in research synthesis and policy formulation).

☐   *Some Commonalities and Differences*
    Among the Perspectives

The three perspectives described above have multiple methodological interactions and points of overlap. For example, evaluability assessment is a method often used by accountability evaluators to investigate the underpinnings (i.e., the theory, logic, and policy origins) of particular programs or interventions, often a preoccupation of the knowledge perspective. Knowledge evaluators may borrow cost-effectiveness or cost-benefit approaches from accountability evaluators when they decide to "follow the money," as Cook suggests. Also, developmental evaluators may use case studies or research synthesis in ways very similar to those of knowledge or accountability evaluators.

However, accountability evaluators will only rarely be able to duplicate the substantive and methodological understanding of knowledge evaluators on a particular topic, or that of developmental evaluators with respect to the workings of particular institutions. Also, not all methods are interchangeable. For example, developmental evaluators have made wide use of such methods as self-evaluation and internal evaluation, which have been criticized by accountability and knowledge evaluators because of their greater potential for allowing the introduction of bias in an evaluation, the loss of control they engender for the evaluator, and the consequent uncertainty about the quality of the information produced using these methods (see Hansson, Chapter 12).

These three perspectives can be further characterized and the similarities and differences among them further confronted through an examination of how they compare with respect to use (i.e., whether and how their findings are used) and to the kinds of roles they engender for evaluators in carrying out their professional responsibilities.

☐ *Differing Views About Use and the Evaluator's Role*

The Relation Between Purpose and Use

Questions about how evaluations should be used—and whether or not they are—have been a source of controversy in evaluation for a very long time, as Cook points out in Chapter 2:

> Twenty-five years ago, many evaluators naively anticipated that their results would be routinely used as the central input into policy decisions . . .
>
> [However,] experience quickly taught evaluators that decisions are not so easily made in the political world. . . .
>
> Such empirical observations led to a crisis in evaluation. If the field could not be justified in terms of instrumental use, how could it be justified?

As Cook notes, "enlightenment" use was then proposed as a substitute for "instrumental" or "policy" use to justify evaluations, but given that evaluation perspectives are not the same, it seems unlikely that one kind of use—of whatever type—could be appropriate for all kinds of findings and purposes. This is especially the case because use is an integral part of some perspectives but not of others.

For example, to measure or account for something, say, or to learn something, is a purpose that can be fulfilled without recourse to an external user. The measurement of effectiveness is often done for its own sake, as in the case of the execution of a mandate in the law to show value received for resources expended (see Pollitt & Summa, Chapter 6). Similarly, the knowledge purpose is achieved when new learning (whether substantive or methodological) can be demonstrated (see Droitcour, Chapter 25). And although policy or enlightenment uses of both types of findings are certainly desirable—indeed, devoutly to be wished—such use is not always possible, and it is not needed to fulfill these evaluation purposes. Put another way, accountability- and knowledge-perspective evaluations typically seek and accommodate appropriate policy or enlightenment use, but do not require it as a justification.

On the other hand, to develop organizational capacity in some area, to improve agency performance, and to strengthen institutions are all purposes that need use to be achieved. As discussed above, the developmental perspective in evaluation is conceived as a participatory enterprise that renounces imposition of change from the top down (or based on judgments by distant evaluators) in favor of a situation in which the evaluator is part of a team; prospective and retrospective evaluation approaches may be used together to reach consensus on goals and their measurement; there may be no evaluation report or findings per se; and the immediate purpose of the effort is to achieve agreed-upon organizational change (see again Wholey, Chapter 8; Mawhood, Chapter 9; Fetterman, Chapter 27). In such developmental evaluation efforts, use is a part of the process: If it does not occur, the purpose is not attained.

In other cases, although *findings* are not used, things change anyway because an evaluation is anticipated. The purpose of reforming government can sometimes be achieved through deterrence, whenever the evaluation function has an institutionally independent position and evaluations are conducted regularly and credibly. That is, the mere presence of the function and the likelihood of a persuasive evaluation can prevent or stop a host of undesirable government practices. But these effects are neither policy nor enlightenment use of findings.

Further, with respect to both accountability and knowledge evaluations, it is often the case that they are—and should be—undertaken without any hope of use, even though use may in fact occur later as evidence accumulates and the political environment changes (see Chelimsky, Chapter 3). Indeed, such *expected* nonuse is a characteristic of some of the noblest types of evaluations: those that question accepted beliefs in a time of ideology or that threaten powerful entrenched interests. It is such evaluations that, over the long term, carry the greatest promise for democratic reform, even though no policy or enlightenment use was intended.

In short, it may be important to reexamine the criterion of some kind of use as a necessity for all evaluations. This is not to argue that use is unimportant to evaluation, or that evaluators should not plan for and build into the design, conduct, and reporting of their evaluations the relevance, expertise, objectivity, and persuasiveness that can increase the likelihood that their findings will be appropriately used. Of course evaluators should do that. But, as already noted, many evaluations are important in their own right, even though their findings may fail to please their sponsors and hence receive little or no attention. In these and other cases, the idea that all evaluations should be used may be a constraining rather than an enabling one; it can push evaluators toward excessive preoccupation with the acceptability of their work to users, and can thereby encourage banality, the reiteration of the status quo, and even the stifling of important insights out of concern for users' reactions. In Chapter 16, Nieuwenhuysen, quoting Castles and Miller (1993), gives a good example of what can happen when there is unwillingness to challenge the conventional wisdom. In this instance, if researchers had made available the information they had on migratory processes to the architects of the postwar European "guest-worker systems," the latter would

> never have held the naive belief that they could turn flows of migrant labour on and off as if with a tap. They would have understood the movement of workers almost always leads to family reunion and permanent settlement. The very fears of permanent ethnic minorities held by some governments turned into self-fulfilling prophecies: by denying legitimacy to family reunion and settlement, government made sure that these processes would take place under the most unfavourable circumstances, leading to the creation of minorities and to deep divisions in society. (p. 123)

With respect to the three perspectives examined here, use is a reasonable criterion for developmental evaluation, because it is a part of the evaluation process itself. Although such use may be difficult to measure when it cannot be represented as a discrete event and when the users are a part of the evaluation, it is nonetheless integrally related to the purpose of developmental evaluations.

On the other hand, knowledge-perspective evaluators, who choose their own questions to examine and who tend to be somewhat isolated from the policy process, may be disadvantaged with regard to policy use because the connection with these users may be tenuous from the very beginning of a study. Enlightenment use also may be hard to achieve, even for some very strong studies, yet this is hardly a reason not to conduct them.

Accountability-perspective evaluations are more favored with regard to use (policy or other) if they are expertly done, because they often respond to questions originating with the users themselves and because the evaluators can keep in touch with the users throughout the conduct of their studies. For these reasons (and others), accountability evaluations are typically used in policy making. However, nonuse or deferred use also occurs for a variety of reasons, for example, when findings are unexpected (i.e., they disagree with past findings on some important point), when the evaluation uses a new methodology, when the topic is politically controversial, or when ideological fervor, say, makes a study's conclusions unacceptable.

In sum, the purpose of an evaluation conditions the use that can be expected of it; use is integrally a part only of developmental evaluation, and although it is more likely to occur in accountability than in knowledge evaluations, this has more to do with the institutional arrangements of the two perspectives than with anything else. Indeed, it is probably time to recognize not only that many uses of evaluation are good and reasonable uses (as Cook notes in Chapter 2), but also that justifying all evaluations by any kind of use may be overly limiting and restrictive for nondevelopmental evaluations.

A particular evaluation perspective thus affects the way findings may be used; it also affects the way evaluators see their jobs.

The Role of the Evaluator

In the developmental perspective, the evaluator is a partner, or a "critical friend" (see Fetterman, Chapter 27), but in the accountability and knowledge perspectives, it has long been accepted that the evaluator must maintain independence and a certain distance in order to be an objective assessor of fact, value, merit, and worth (see Scriven, Chapter 33). However, this latter view of the evaluator's role is now under fire. Stake, for example, argues that advocacy for program participants is potentially acceptable in a knowledge (not a developmental) perspective of evaluation (see Chapter 32), whereas Scriven warns that advocacy opens up some life-threatening questions about bias and credibility: "Tempering validity with mercy (or the like) is a violation of validity—and validity is the highest professional imperative of the evaluator" (Chapter 33).

Stake's claim for the legitimacy of advocacy, if it were accepted, would certainly have some major implications for evaluation generally and for those evaluators who would decide to lobby for their clients. They would be moving away from the traditional position of independence that universities have tried hard to protect to a position somewhere between that of developmental evaluators (who are very close to their clients) and accountability evaluators (who keep their distance). Indeed, there is a certain similarity between Fetterman's "critical friend" and Stake's view of the evaluator's role. Stake comments: "We saw ourselves as guests in the schools we visited, inquiring sometimes into the teachers' personal affairs. We wanted to do our work with empathy and care, with discretion." Still, with the very next sentence, Stake returns to the traditional knowledge perspective:

> Yet we are evaluators. We work to find and understand quality. We do not come to assist in remediation. We do not think of ourselves as collaborators in reform. We promised to help the Academy staff understand itself, particularly in terms of the quality of its operations. We provided details of merit and shortcoming. We interpreted and discussed the issues.

The case for advocacy seems to be based on the idea that, as all groups create their own realities and no one can be completely objective, one reality is as good as another, and advocacy is hence permissible as a countervailing force. To this the reply has been that even if absolute objectivity is not achievable, that hardly excuses deliberate subjectivity and partisanship. And there is real concern that lowering standards of validity, even on the part of just a few evaluators, could hurt the entire field.

It is already the case that some accountability evaluators hold a dim view of knowledge-perspective objectivity. For example, Ahlenius (see Chapter 5) believes that evaluations always support the use of more government resources for programs and have no interest in reducing government expenditures. (Although this may be a fair assessment for some individual evaluations, it does not square very well with the experience in the United States of many evaluation reports that have been both negative with respect to program accomplishments and far indeed from proposing funding increases; further, when evaluations have proposed major reductions in program expenditures—see Chan and Tumin, Chapter 20, for example—special interest groups have successfully impeded the logical policy use of the recommendations.) The point here, however, is not whether this alleged advocacy is true but rather that it is perceived to be true and is used to make the case that evaluation is not to be trusted when the time comes to cut programs.

At the same time that evaluators are being told by some that advocacy for clients is acceptable, they are being asked by others (see Scriven, Chapter 33, for example) to maintain the highest standards with respect to objectivity and also to use their knowledge to intervene more in public discussions relevant to their research. Cook observes in Chapter 2, "Our voices are not heard in major policy debates as regularly as they might be." He believes this is at least partly because the evaluation field has not taken on the task of preparing summaries or syntheses of what is known and what works in such areas as preschool education, family maintenance, homelessness, and job training. Without such syntheses, each evaluator working in a university remains "peripheral to public debates about what to do to improve programs and lives." However, knowledge and accountability evaluators working in institutions or think tanks may be better able to reach relevant audiences, not only because of the summaries and syntheses they have available, but also because of their channels to policy makers and the media and their excellent dissemination strategies.

Both knowledge and accountability evaluators can be extremely effective in policy debates, both by saying what the data show and do not show and by being persistent in stating their case. Developmental evaluators, on the other hand, may have some disadvantage in speaking out because they are often part of a group. Thus the degree to which they can be credible in appearing nonpartisan is affected by the degree of their independence from their clients and their control over what they can say on the record.

To summarize the discussion in this section, then, Table 1.1 lays out the three perspectives and their positions with regard to a number of the dimensions that have been examined here. This matrix helps to illustrate the places where important differences exist.

TABLE 1.1 The Three Perspectives and Their Respective Positions Along
Nine Dimensions

Dimensions	Accountability Perspective	Knowledge Perspective	Developmental Perspective
Purpose	to measure results or value for funds expended; to determine costs; to assess efficiency	to generate insights about public problems, policies, programs and processes; to develop new methods and to critique old ones	to strengthen institutions; to build agency or organizational capability in some evaluative area
Need for use to fulfill purpose	no	no	yes
Typical uses	policy use; debate and negotiation; enlightenment; governmental/ agency reform; public use	enlightenment use; policy; research and replication; education; knowledge base construction	institutional or agency use as part of the evaluative process; public and policy use
Evaluator role re client	distant	distant or close, depending on evaluation design and methods	close: the evaluator is a "critical friend" or may be part of a team
Independence	a prerequisite	critical	little need
Advocacy	unacceptable	unacceptable, but now being debated	often inevitable, but correctable through independent, outside review
Acceptability to clients or users	often difficult but may be helped by negotiation	clients may ignore or shelve findings they do not like	easy: no threat is posed
Objectivity	high	high (when advocacy is not present)	uncertain (based on independence and control)
Position under policy debate	can be strong (depending on leadership)	can be strong (if consolidated and dissemination channels exist)	uncertain (based on independence and control)

□ Complementarity and Blurring of the Perspectives

Looking at Table 1.1, one can see that the differences among the three perspectives suggest some complementarity among them. That is, the perspectives represent different ways to think about evaluation, and each tends to solve particular evaluative problems while complicating others. None of them, however, can solve all of the problems or answer all of the questions posed to evaluation; hence their complementarity. Thus one reason for the tensions in evaluation today may be the failure to recognize that all three perspectives exist, that all have become necessary to the evaluation field, and that what is highly relevant for one perspective may be inappropriate for another.

Moreover, by treating evaluation as a single entity, we allow a certain blurring of the perspectives to occur that further raises tensions, as, for example, when claims are made about the universal applicability of a particular evaluation approach that in fact addresses the questions of one perspective much better than it does those of the others.

Examples of such blurring abound. Although self-evaluations and some other types of developmental methods are admittedly not the best choices for answering accountability questions about results, findings from these methods have sometimes been used to do just that, without any explanation of limitations. Again, stakeholder evaluation has been suggested as a replacement for all other methods in evaluation, but although it helps in understanding the different mind-sets that underlie policy and program issues, it is not clear to accountability and knowledge evaluators how arraying together on an equal plane the differing views and interests of all stakeholders in a program can answer questions such as, Is the program meeting its goals? Some knowledge evaluators have argued that for all evaluation findings, enlightenment use is the only use attainable, even though accountability evaluators achieve policy use regularly. Knowledge and accountability evaluators have sometimes dismissed the developmental perspective as "consultancy," assuming that only knowledge- and accountability-perspective inquiries into merit and worth are viable for evaluation, despite the fact that strengthening institutions is what allows merit and worth to be determined in some places. The partnerships and close relationships that are needed in a developmental perspective are dangerous in the accountability and knowledge perspectives; similarly, the "threat" represented by the latter is not a problem for developmental evaluators. The use of evaluation findings, an integral part of developmental evaluation, has been viewed as a requirement for all evaluation, even though too much zeal about use can render accountability and knowledge evaluations bland and innocuous when they should be challenging the status quo. It has been argued by some developmental evaluators who have difficulty assessing merit and worth while working closely with clients that goal-attainment questions cannot be answered, even though accountability and knowledge evaluators answer such questions every day.

In short, many of the tensions experienced recently in evaluation may have come about because (a) we have been seeing only one piece of the elephant and generalizing widely from that piece, and (b) we have become enamored of our methods, recommending them to all, for all purposes, without restriction. This is especially curious in evaluation, because we are trained to worry about precisely these issues, and because a fair number of the methodological problems we face would be curable if we broadened our vision and became a little more skeptical about our methods. For example, to correct the potential biases of self-evaluation and performance measurement, we can employ independent evaluation review, which would resolve the problem of using self-evaluation to establish merit or worth; we can carefully and comprehensively review the relevant body of theory and practice in evaluation before claiming that one method is superior to another or that goal-attainment and cause-and-effect relationships cannot be measured; and we can learn to rely on a number of methods so that the specific deficiencies of some of them can be balanced by the specific strengths of others.

Evaluation, as it goes global, needs all the help it can get. More than anything else, it needs honesty of the sort illustrated by Sanders in his discussion of cluster evaluation (Chapter 28), in which he presents no exaggerated claims and clearly spells out the method's limitations. Evaluators need to stop talking past each other and begin a constructive dialogue in which we seek to correct weaknesses, not exacerbate them. But we cannot correct weaknesses unless we first identify them, and the place to start is with the evaluation purpose and the question that has been asked—whether we have chosen it ourselves or it was posed by a decision maker. Evaluative purposes and questions determine the choice of methods, and methods are neither good nor bad per se; surveys answer some questions well but not others, and the same is true for the case study, the randomized controlled study, the research synthesis, or any existing method. What counts is not the method used but how well we answer the question or achieve the purpose, and whether or not we use our experience to construct better theory and practice. This is what makes evaluation meaningful and keeps it vital in changing environments.

■ *New and Old Lessons From the Evaluation Experience for the Next Century*

That the environment for evaluation is changing—has already changed— is evident from the chapters of this book and the new topics, actors, and arguments they represent. International comparisons, just by being readily available, change the sense of what some problems and processes mean in evaluation. This statement by Novikov (Chapter 21), for example, about program implementation in the former Soviet Union, will set American evaluators dreaming:

> This development was facilitated and encouraged by . . . the fact that centrally planned economies favor consistent program implementation; nuclear programs especially benefited from this. In such economies, once the technical and economic studies have been performed and the political decisions made, the government authorities in all the related economic sectors have the obligation to support the implementation of the approved policy and programs.

Further, the fact that Russian analysts are less familiar with political debate on technical issues than are their Western counterparts is shown by a single laconic sentence—his final point—in which Novikov contrasts what should have been done with what was done: "This is a clear case in which pragmatic policy decisions have been made that run counter to the technical analysis conducted." In a similar way, the term *high-stakes event* as used by Fetterman in Chapter 27 ("This accreditation study was considered a high-stakes event in higher education for all parties involved") undergoes a metamorphosis when Cano (Chapter 15) uses it to describe massive human rights violations involving torture and death.

As we move toward transnational boundaries and a borderless world, there are many adaptations that evaluation will need to make, including, for example, the much broader scope and longer duration of evaluations and the ability of various methods to be deployed on a large enough scale. Also, there are a number of outside influences that will determine whether evaluations can be done successfully, such as the capabilities of institutions to conduct evaluations and manage them well and the willingness of political institutions to tolerate and profit from the free flow of information.

Further, based on the past 30 years of evaluation experience, we have learned some important lessons that will likely continue to be important:

- We need to think of evaluation as an "eclectic enterprise" (see Cook, Chapter 2), with a rich tool kit of methods and many legitimate perspectives, purposes, questions, and uses.

- We need to be inclusive—that is, to welcome prospective as well as retrospective studies, to use quantitative as well as qualitative methods, to develop cross-disciplinary linkages, and to create channels for the effective dissemination of evaluation findings.

- We need to remember that purpose and question dictate method, and not vice versa.

- We need to establish credibility (i.e., of both expertise and objectivity) if evaluation findings are to be used either for enlightenment or in policy making.

- We need to recognize the importance of strengthening institutions in both developing and developed nations as evaluation assumes global responsibilities; before assessments of merit and worth can proceed, there must be infrastructure in place that allows them to be conducted.

- We need to let evaluation be evaluation—that is, to keep its skepticism about the conventional wisdom, its meticulousness about measuring achievements, its willingness to be persistent about getting the information out, and its dedication to democratic reform on the basis of knowledge.

The evaluator's role in the 21st century should include not only the assessment of what has been experienced and observed, but also a constant questioning of his or her own objectivity and sensitivity in reporting on precisely what has been experienced and observed. In this effort to testify truthfully and, at the same time, to judge the truth of the testimony, the evaluator is a little like Bernard Malamud's "blind man slowly evolving insight into sight," or Muriel Sparks's Job, who not only argued the problem of suffering, but suffered the problem of argument. Although this has always been true of evaluation's tortuous and self-critical methods that build bit by bit on what has gone before, the challenge now is to face both inward and outward, to be aware that resolving one problem usually opens up another, and to marshal the forces, energies, and resources needed to tackle the new problems as they arise.

■ *Notes*

1. This description comes from Michael Scriven, speaking at a reception for participants at the Vancouver conference, November 1, 1995.
2. The conference was cosponsored by the American Evaluation Association, the Australasian Evaluation Society, the Canadian Evaluation Society, the Central-American Evaluation Association, and the European Evaluation Society.
3. Six types of case study evaluation in an accountability perspective are discussed in U.S. General Accounting Office (1990, especially pp. 45-52).

■ *References*

Castles, S., & Miller, M. (1993). *The age of migration: International population movements in the modern world.* London: Macmillan.
U.S. General Accounting Office. (1990). *Case study evaluations* (GAO/PEMD-10.1.9). Washington, DC: Author.

PART I

Evaluation—
Yesterday and Today

*W*e paint a picture in this book of some possibilities for evaluation in the 21st century, a picture that we hope will both challenge experienced evaluators to expand their traditional horizons and entice new evaluators to join the enterprise. Yet any such forecasting of future possibilities benefits from a grounding in the past and present of evaluation. The two chapters in Part I provide such a grounding. These chapters are authored by two experienced evaluators whose work has exposed them to very different parts of evaluation, but their analyses of many important issues are surprisingly similar.

Thomas Cook begins Chapter 2 by listing a set of lessons learned over the short history of evaluation. The first lesson is that the broad set of qualitative methods, such as case studies and participant observation, are now firmly entrenched as part of the methodological repertoire of evaluators, alongside the more quantitative methods that evaluators began with, such as surveys and experimentation (see also Chapter 24). Like many others, however, Cook expresses some surprise and dismay at the disputes that occasionally flare up about quantitative and qualitative methods, disputes that distract us from more important intellectual issues. The second lesson is that evaluation has come to rely more on the results of syntheses of multiple evaluations on the same question than on the results of any single study (examples of this may be found in Chapters 25 and 26). This dependence stems partly from the increased understanding of the fallibility of any single study no matter what method is used, and partly from the opportune development of quantitative methods for research synthesis over the past 15 years. Cook notes an apparent contradiction between the results of these summaries, which usually suggest modest program effectiveness, compared with the pessimism of current political rhetoric that nothing works. The third lesson is that evaluations get used in many different ways, including both instrumentally, to provide information about the merits of specific changes that could be made, and conceptually, to change the ways stakeholders think about problems and solutions, both now and in the future. Fourth, Cook notes that evaluation is practiced by people who belong to many different professions and associations, which results in undue fractionation, given lack of channels for mutual communication about the crucial issues in the field. Cook ends his chapter with a call for a metaphorical three-legged stool as a foundation for a future profession of evaluation. Only the first leg of that stool—methodology—has received much attention in evaluation over the past several decades. The second leg is big-picture analysis of evaluation theory, work that turns a critical eye to what we have learned about evaluation in the interests of integrating it into a common set of disciplinary assumptions and assertions that we can all agree on as a foundation for the field. The third leg is the systematic synthesis of what is known about important policy issues of our time, for such synthesis is something that evaluators have the methodological expertise to do, and that would raise the stature of the profession of evaluation in the policy world.

In Chapter 3, Eleanor Chelimsky begins by noting many of the same lessons that Cook describes, especially the accomplished use of a wide methodological repertoire to do evaluations that actually have impacts on public policy and local decision making. She also points to the growing international use of evaluation, accompanied by the growth of professional evaluation societies and journals throughout the world, as an auspicious development for the future of the profession. But the bulk of Chelimsky's chapter is about the political environment of evaluation and the implications of that environment for the profession. After all, the work of most evaluators is conducted either directly in highly political environments or on topics that are themselves highly politicized. In either case, the evaluator cannot escape *the inevitable ideological disputes that take place among stakeholders from all parts of the political spectrum. In such an environment, Chelimsky sees six implications for the conduct of evaluation. The first is that evaluations must not only be credible, they must also be seen as credible by the various stakeholders in the political debate. By contrast, she notes, even the mere appearance of advocacy for a particular point of view can spell the death of an otherwise good evaluation. Second, evaluators need the courage to speak out on controversial issues and, just as important, the courage to insist on the independence they need to do so, especially in the face of both rewards and punishments that the political system offers for saying what certain stakeholders want to hear. Third, evaluators must persist in disseminating their findings, especially when those findings are sound and the issue important, for the attention span of a highly politicized environment is often short, and frequent reminders of what we know are usually needed to have an impact. Fourth, the problems and programs studied by evaluators require interdisciplinary skills, and, within disciplines, they require knowledge from both basic and applied research. This need is, unfortunately, not matched by any coherent organization that would bring together evaluators with all these backgrounds and skills. Fifth, a growing concern is the classification of some data as secret, typically in agencies such as the Department of Defense, where a justification for secrecy often exists, but also increasingly in areas such as health care, where few national security interests would seem to be present. Evaluators who want to work in a political environment must do more to redress this situation. Sixth, Chelimsky calls for increased political realism in the training of evaluation students. In summary, Chelimsky envisions the evaluator's job as one of gathering data that are useful to all political parties. Readers who find this chapter interesting will also benefit from reading the chapters by Stake and Scriven at the end of the book, for the issues they raise of advocacy versus truth in evaluation are part of the same intellectual challenge presented in Chelimsky's work.*

William R. Shadish

2

Lessons Learned in Evaluation Over the Past 25 Years

Thomas D. Cook

Paul Wortman has told the story of how, 20 years ago, when the plan was announced to begin an organization called the Evaluation Research Society of America, I objected to the inclusion of *America* in the proposed name. I supposedly said that evaluation is an intellectual and policy enterprise for all nations, and so a name should be chosen that is not geographically restricting and invites all nations under the same institutional tent. Apparently I carried the day and the society became simply the Evaluation Research Society. Frankly, I can't remember any of this, but it's something I'd like to believe happened. Though evaluation practice has to respect local context and so be tailored to some national realities, there are many other things about evaluation writ large that are supranational.

It is unfortunate that nearly all of my evaluation experience has been in the United States. Even worse is that most of my experience has been at the federal rather than the state or local level, and then more in education, social service, and social welfare than in, say, defense, economic development, or international trade. These national, federal, and sectoral experiences have clearly influenced what I have to say, and I would like to apologize in advance for those occasions when my remarks reflect experiences that are irrelevant to different countries, government levels, or sectors.

It is impossible to discuss all, or even most, of the lessons learned in evaluation over the past 25 years. My account will be highly personal. I ask you to consider me as a catalyst to the field rather than as one of evaluation's historians. I am not a historian, and I am certainly not a disinterested commentator on the field's past, in which some of my friends have played significant roles. But I will try to identify some major lessons I have learned that, I believe, constitute distinct progress for the field, for I am in general delighted at our progress. I will also try to outline some lessons we still need to learn. The discussion will revolve around the following four themes.

1. Initially, evaluation was almost always portrayed as a quantitative enterprise. This is no longer the case, and I want to discuss the qualitative/quantitative debate that has raged in the field for the past 15 years or so. The debate has been very helpful, and the qualitative advocates have deservedly won full equality in today's evaluation enterprise. However, the debate is now diverting intellectual energy from more urgent tasks, and we need to move on.

2. Knowledge claims in evaluation are increasingly based on the results of research syntheses rather than individual studies, and these syntheses usually present a more positive (but still modest) view of the effectiveness of social programs. This leads to an apparent contradiction that I will discuss. Reviews are associated with guardedly optimistic conclusions about program effects, but the current political rhetoric in the United States and some other market-oriented economies suggests that "nothing works" in the public sector.

3. It was originally believed that evaluation results would feed directly into policy decisions, but claims were made that such "instrumen-

tal" use is rare and that most use is of a more diffuse type called "enlightenment." Evaluation then came to be justified in terms of enlightenment. But instrumental use does occur, and more often than was noted in earlier reports. It is self-defeating for evaluators to justify one concept or approach by denigrating others, as happened not just with instrumental versus enlightenment use, but also with qualitative versus quantitative methods and experiments versus quasi-experiments. Discourse that denigrates one alternative to foster another tends to violate the eclectic character of evaluation, undermining public perceptions of its unity and utility.

4. Within the United States, members of the American Evaluation Association (AEA) are mostly trained in psychology and education, and they evaluate programs with a corresponding disciplinary flavor. Economist and political science evaluators tend to be in the Association for Public Policy Analysis and Management (APPAM) and concentrate on policies more than programs and on cash-transfer programs more than other sorts of social service programs. Most evaluators in the American Public Health Association (APHA) examine policies and programs designed to improve physical health. This disciplinary fractionalization is not necessary, and we need to build more bridges. We also need to enlarge the scope of evaluation. Today, American evaluation is most aptly characterized in terms of its concern with the methodological tools needed to assess policies and programs. A firmer foundation would complement this emphasis on method with improved evaluation theory and with regular summaries of what is known about effective policies and programs in various sectors. Nearly all scholarly disciplines have their own theories, their own sets of methods, and their own stores of useful empirical findings. Evaluation should too.

■ *Quantitative and Qualitative Methods*

In the 1960s, qualitative methods were given short shrift in evaluation. They were rarely if ever mentioned. At that time, the key evaluation issue was the black-box task of generating unbiased, precise estimates of the causal consequences of programs or their major constituent parts. The preferred designs for doing this were experimental, and the preferred analytic techniques were quantitative (Suchman, 1967). Indeed, the quantitative preference was so strong that nonexperimental quantitative strategies were preferred over nonexperimental qualitative ones under the assumptions that (a) statistical controls are adequate substitutes for the design controls that experimenters emphasize, such as comparison groups, pretests, and longitudinal pretests; and (b) qualitative methods provide neither the design nor statistical controls needed for ruling out alternatives to the notion that the program under study is responsible for any observed relationships between the program and outcome changes.

In the 1970s and 1980s, the dominance of quantitative methods came under intense attack in evaluation, as in all the other social sciences except economics (Jessor, Colby, & Shweder, 1996). The struggle to legitimate qualitative methods within evaluation was probably the product of two influences. One was the long-standing debate, especially in sociology, about the utility of qualitative methods and the limitations of quantitative methods. Sociologists brought these debates with them when they entered evaluation in the 1970s (Patton, 1980), feeling slighted when they detected that inferior status was deliberately or inadvertently assigned to qualitative work. The second influence was from scholars trained in quantitative methods—particularly in education—who rejected their formal training as epistemologically inadequate and expressed a qualitative preference (Guba & Lincoln, 1981; Stake, 1980). Both of these streams ran together within evaluation to form a larger river; or—if one prefers a different metaphor—both sets of renegades from the orthodoxy joined forces to go to war for their shared faith. This war has been the prime intellectual agenda in evaluation for the past 15 years or so.

It has been a strange war, however. The advocates of qualitative methods have fought hard, attacking the assumptions and accomplishments of quantitative research and making a powerful case for the utility of what they prefer. But for the most part, the quantitative advocates have not fought back. Thus it would be more appropriate to describe the war as a long-lasting guerrilla skirmish than as an all-out war. Although this failure to engage could be interpreted as another indication of the hubris of the quantitative orthodoxy, I suspect there was another reason for it. Most quantitative types believe that the advocates of qualitative methods deserve to win the war so long as they march under the banner that there is a legitimate and central role for qualitative methods within evaluation. Few quantitative researchers would disagree with such maxims as these: Qualitative methods are very useful for making explicit the theory behind a program; for understanding the context in which a program operates; for describing what is actually implemented in a program; for assessing the correspondence between what the program theory promised and what is actually implemented; for helping elucidate the processes that might have brought about program effects; for identifying some likely unintended consequences of the program; for learning how to get the program results used; or for synthesizing the wisdom learned about a program or a set of programs with somewhat similar characteristics. Almost all quantitative researchers would acknowledge that these are central evaluation tasks and that qualitative methods are therefore totally legitimate.

But the rationale for qualitative methods is sometimes expressed more sweepingly. Some advocates have marched to war under the banner that qualitative methods can answer the same questions about generalization and descriptive causal relationships to which quantitative methods are primarily addressed. I suspect few advocates of quantitative methods would disagree with this in principle. The key to answering causal questions is, for instance, that all other alternative interpretations of the cause need to be ruled out, and Campbell (1974, 1978) has demonstrated that this can be done in any type of study if the background conditions warrant ruling out enough alternative interpretations a priori. We can all point to qualitative work showing that a program is probably effective by various criteria, to work showing that a program is not likely to be effective in light of the low quality of program implementation, and to work providing valuable clues about how to improve a program. There is no doubt of the relevance of qualitative work to reducing uncertainty about both causal propositions and generalization to specific populations, particularly when generalization is construed in ways that do not make it inevitably depend on formal sampling theory (Cook, 1993). Quantitative types would probably disagree with the strongest version of the argument above that contends that qualitative methods are as good as formal sampling methods when it comes to generalizing and as good as experimental methods when it comes to describing causal relationships. But very few qualitative advocates make this very strong claim. Their usual objection is to treating qualitative methods as irrelevant to generalization or causation, which they are not.

The one version of the war banner that has unleashed counterattacks from both quantitative (e.g., Cook & Reichardt, 1979; Shadish, 1995) and qualitative researchers (e.g., Heap, 1995) is the assertion that the ontological and epistemological bases of quantitative work are so inherently flawed that such work has no value and so only qualitative work has value. In this argument, findings from metascience are used to justify the rejection of all things quantitative on the grounds that (a) quantitative work assumes that there is a real world, and this cannot be "proven," and (b) testing theories about this world assumes both a "paradigm commensurability" and a "theoretical neutrality of observations," neither of which is logically warranted. Many quantitative types have crafted reasoned rejoinders to both of these criticisms that accept their validity (e.g., Campbell, 1986; Cook, 1985), but these counterpositions are ignored by scholars who persist in attacking a caricature of what sophisticated scientists actually believe about the nature of reality and the ways in which scientists know (Guba & Lincoln, 1989). The case for qualitative methods does not depend on attacking the foundations of quantitative methods; it rests on their utility for answering important evaluation questions either when used alone or when used together with quantitative methods. Practitioners of qualitative evaluation methods need not be defensive now as they were 25 years ago. They are full brothers and sisters in evaluation.

But as there is no peace treaty yet, I want to offer some guidelines for one. I suspect most quantitative researchers agree with propositions such as the following: (a) Evaluation is richer for qualitative research; (b) qualitative research is empirical; (c) qualitative research can serve multiple functions, not just discovery ones; (d) the results of qualitative research are potentially generalizable; (e) they can in principle be used to probe descriptive causal propositions; and (e) qualitative work can be designed to achieve all of the research designs and data manipulations that characterize quantitative research. But there are other propositions that would likely prolong the conflict, especially if advocates of qualitative methods insist that (a) their methods are generally as good as quantitative methods for generalizing and describing causal relationships or (b) the basic assumptions of all quantitative work are wrong (Heap, 1995; Shadish, 1995). The two method types are not interchangeable, however. Qualitative methods are not good for generating quantitative estimates, whereas quantitative methods are not good for exploring program processes unless considerable prior information about the program is available or its theoretical underpinnings are unusually explicit.

Once one has escaped from the belief that a single type of question should be dominant in evaluation, one finds that we usually need to use both types of method. The limitations to this are financial and logistical, but not logical. So, let's metaphorically craft a peace document and go on to more productive battles in evaluation. We grow through our battles, but sometimes they just go on too long and start to generate intolerable opportunity costs.

■ *Syntheses and Individual Studies*

One of the greatest changes in evaluation over the past 25 years has been the growth in the use of research syntheses and in the theory justifying such syntheses (Cooper & Hedges, 1994). There is increasing recognition that, however they are carried out, syntheses are more valid with respect to inferences about program implementation, program impact, the generalizability of effects, and the identification of contingency conditions that moderate when a particular pattern of effects is obtained (Light & Pillemer, 1984; Cook et al., 1992). Syntheses may well also have more credibility with potential users looking for the most valid general conclusions about a program.

Twenty-five years ago the belief was rampant that single large studies could achieve major evaluation goals. But experience taught us many sobering lessons: that the same source of bias could be inadvertently built into such studies; that such individual studies were rarely as statistically powerful as the original designers had hoped; that program realizations were inevitably less faithful than had been originally anticipated; and that program realizations were more variable from site to site than had been originally anticipated. I could go on and on. The point is that we came to see the leverage of individual studies in a new light, given the manifestly better prospects implicit in literature reviews. We need individual studies, and nothing about the advocacy of syntheses reduces the need for them. They are, after all, what is synthesized! Indeed, the emphasis on reviews has been used to highlight which individual studies make more of a contribution—usually those that fill in demonstrated holes in the available literature; those that provide textured insights into program and policy realities; and those in which the methodology is so superior to the past that the new results will partially validate older findings.

Reviews became a staple of one of the most consistent and highest-quality evaluation organizations—the Program Evaluation and Methodology Division (PEMD) of the U.S. General Accounting Office. PEMD used reviews regularly to assess the effects of many different types of programs about which Congress requested information. The motto was something like: Get a congressional commission for a study; find out what has been done already on the topic; obtain the studies as quickly as possible; synthesize them as carefully as possible using colleagues, consultants, the phone, and reanalysis if called for; and write a report that is reviewed by others, including those responsible for administering the program under review. Few of the PEMD studies involved the systematic quantitative synthesis of prior evaluation results in the way that meta-analysis has made famous. But the systematic way of thinking about the reviewing that meta-analysis introduced may have influenced PEMD procedures, especially as concerns the search for fugitive reports, the coding of studies by topical relevance and methodological quality (among other attributes), the use of indicators of effectiveness other than statistical significance tests, the search for contingency variables that specify the conditions under which a program is implemented one way or another or has one pattern of effects rather than another, and the need to use the review to highlight the missing gaps in the available literature. Whenever I went to PEMD to consult, I was always surprised at how quickly analysts with no background in a particular substantive area could identify relevant studies and undertake their analysis.

This may not be as true in other countries, where the backlog of relevant reports might be smaller—I am not sure. But in this regard, I have to say how astonished I have been by the large number of studies there are in both the Spanish-language and German-language psychotherapy meta-analyses, though I know how long it took the authors (Navarro, 1990; Wittmann & Matt, 1986) to collect the many relevant studies. Unfortunately, I have no idea of what is available in these same regions in other substantive areas, especially regarding the evaluation of government programs. My suspicion, however, is that we would all be surprised how much there is. A lot of social science is buried under rocks, making reviews possible.

Perhaps the most striking discovery with meta-analyses is how frequently we find that interventions have positive impacts on lives. To be sure, the size of the average impact is often less than we would like, and the long-term consequences have not been explored as well as the short-term ones, but positive impacts are still the norm. Lipsey and Wilson

(1993) have provided the most detailed evidence of this in a large number of different social service areas, and these results—as well as other recent syntheses (Cook et al., 1992)—clearly dispel the conventional wisdom from the 1970s (Lipton, Martinson, & Wilkins, 1975) and repeated in the 1990s that "nothing works." This incorrect conclusion probably arose because we took individually underpowered studies and, in reviewing them, counted how many of them provided statistically significant results, inevitably inclining the study toward a no-difference finding; or else we overgeneralized from individual highly visible studies, like the New Jersey Income Maintenance Experiment (Watts & Rees, 1977) or the first evaluation of Head Start (Cicirelli et al., 1969). We did not fully realize at the time just how pioneering these efforts were and how much they were destined to become empirical exercises in mistake learning. In any event, when we now go to conferences on mental health, let us say, we do not have to waste time debating whether mental health services can make a difference. Thanks to meta-analytic reviews, we know they can.

That is not to say that they routinely do. If one looks at Lipsey and Wilson's massive, careful, and hope-inspiring review of meta-analyses in the social services, broadly construed, one is struck by how many of the original studies were small-scale, carefully controlled, local studies of services designed to be faithful to a particular theoretical model of some intervention. This tendency was, I suspect, propelled by the ease with which demonstration projects lend themselves to the experimental designs most readily meta-analyzed and by the need graduate students have to do doctoral theses on theoretical topics. But whatever the source of these preferences for the small and the theory "testing," a key issue for today is to assess whether the positive results associated with meta-analyses continue to hold in that subset of studies where the research context is manifestly within the range of normal professional practice. This is a topic Will Shadish and Georg Matt are currently addressing.

If there is a striking mismatch between the contexts built into much past research and the contexts of desired application, this might explain the obvious disparity between the guarded optimism about modest positive effects that meta-analyses provide and the widespread popular perception, in the United States at least, that few social programs are effective. Of course, politics and ideology play important roles in promoting the "nothing works" scenario—so do unrealistically high expectations about the size of effects we should expect to obtain, and the unrealistic assumption that programs designed to improve material well-being should also improve social and moral behavior. But why should improving material welfare through social programs necessarily reduce societal violence, or increase commitments to family, or improve minority group commitment to values that many believe are alien (Jencks & Mayer, 1995)? Also relevant to why we have such pessimistic rhetoric about "nothing works" is the way journalists are trained and the types of issues and modes of presentation that do and do not sell newspapers and advertising time. Sober reviews of a social science literature do not sell newspapers the way dramatic stories, stereotypes, atypical lives and events, and stark value confrontations can.

But we social scientists are also partly at fault for the rhetoric of "nothing works." We do not do many formal evaluations of the largest social programs that capture most attention and dollars, programs in the United States such as social security, Medicare, Medicaid, AFDC, food stamps, and the Earned Income Tax Credit. These are the central focus of public discussion, but they are not the programs we evaluate. We should learn better "to follow the money" when deciding what to evaluate, even while examining any variations within these programs that might be particularly amenable to future modification. If we did follow the money better, I suspect we would then be in a better position to confront the misinformation and stereotypes that surface in public debates. Take today's debates in the United States as an example. Poverty rates have not dramatically changed over the past 25 years, and syntheses show that material welfare is almost everywhere on the rise, including among poorer Americans, who are living in increasingly better houses, having more space per person, eating better food, owning more appliances, and so on (Jencks & Mayer, 1995). We have also learned a lot from many studies about patterns of fraud, abuse, and error in most of these larger social programs. Little of the existing fraud and abuse is due to service recipients (Matt & Cook, 1993), but that is not the message one would pick up from newspapers and television reports. We have also learned from accumulated qualitative studies that relatively few recipients of AFDC use their money to avoid work, as most of them have sources of off-the-books income from various forms of work (Edin & Jencks, 1992; Jencks & Edin, 1990). Public rhetoric about social programs is more global, pessimistic, and poor bashing than is warranted by the cumulative social science evidence, yet there is no countervailing voice from the evaluation community, myself included. Should we not play a special role in public debates like these, given the close correspondence between the issues being debated and evaluation's core function of generating cumulative knowledge about social programs?

■ *The Political Context of Programs and Policies*

Twenty-five years ago, many evaluators naively anticipated that their results would be routinely used as the central input into policy decisions. The advocacy of experimentation at that time probably fed into this naïveté, because the decision logic underlying experimentation seems to mirror the rational actor model from public policy. In this model, a problem or need is first clearly defined (in experiments, the analogue involves specifying outcome criteria), alternatives for solving the problem are then determined and implemented (the various treatments are put in place), the outcome criteria are then monitored (in experiments, data are collected), and finally a decision is made from the data about which alternative is best for solving the problem (a statistical test is conducted to assess which treatments are most effective).

Experience quickly taught evaluators that decisions are not so easily made in the political world, just as it also taught us that experiments are not so easily implemented outside of laboratories. There are many reasons policy decisions do not routinely follow as was hoped. Evaluation results are rarely so definitive, and doubts always remain about the policy relevance of the particular alternatives examined, about the quality of program implementation, about the relevance of the outcomes examined, and about the utility of placing such a high priority on examining program outcomes rather than program theory, program context, program implementation, or many other process factors. We also learned not to avoid the tricky normative questions. Should social science information play such an instrumental, decision-creating role in a democracy where value concerns are supposed to be paramount and managerial efficiency is a less crucial desideratum? We also learned more about naked political realities: that the politician's prime goal is to be reelected rather than to respect technical evidence; that personal and party political ideology often entail that evidence is used in markedly selective ways; and that politicians experience a greater need to be part of budget allocation than of program review. Indeed, in announcing his retirement from U.S. congressional politics, Senator Nunn recently observed that too much attention is paid to budget making and not enough to evaluating what has happened because of prior budget expenditures. Finally, we also learned anew that there are alternative cultural models of truth seeking. In the United States, a premium is placed on an adversarial, debate-centered, judicial model of eliciting the "truth," and the assumptions of this model are quite different from those built into the rational decision model and its experimental analogue.

Such empirical observations led to a crisis in evaluation. If the field could not be justified in terms of instrumental use, how could it be justified? Several other possibilities were discussed, primary among them being the notion that results are used to create enlightenment—that is, they change the way social issues and programs are framed; they change the level of realism about what might be expected to result from a certain type of program; or they foster generalizations about how programs operate. This perspective emphasizes the task of creating generalizations about program design, implementation, and context, perhaps making these more important than the description of individual program effects. This only raises the issue: Would those who pay for evaluation be satisfied if it created enlightenment but did not feed more directly into specific decisions? I'm not sure they would.

Fortunately, no such dire confrontation is required, for in the past decade it has become clearer that instrumental use does occur and that prior accounts of its demise were exaggerated. In the United States, Chelimsky (1987a, 1987b) has pointed to relevant instances from among the work PEMD conducted for Congress. It might be argued that PEMD is a special context, because someone in Congress has requested the information, often for use in specific policy debates, and there can be more interaction between the evaluators and those who commission their work, allowing changing knowledge needs to be built into an evaluation that has already begun. However, I know of many other instances where evaluation results were cited as part of the evidence base for expanding and contracting programs, though the results were never the sole determinants of the decisions in question. It is surely time in evaluation to stop shooting ourselves in the foot by denigrating the frequency of instrumental use. Instrumental and enlightenment use should exist side by side as justifications for evaluation. They are not necessary alternatives.

Nor are they exhaustive of how evaluations are productively used. Evaluation results seem to be cited more and more in the textbooks used to train the next generation of professionals in a number of fields (Leviton & Cook, 1983). I am now reading a manuscript on social welfare in the United States that may well be used to train economists and social workers and that is packed with the results of evaluations at the federal and state level (Blank, 1997). The same is true of books in education and of articles in psychology, such as Lipsey and Wilson's (1993) work. Evaluations provide major sources of information for describing to graduate students what seems to "work" and for probing the theories of practice that undergird any professional field. As we consider the multiple ways in which evaluations are used, we ought to be as inclusive as possible. When we roughly calculate our utility, we ought to include educational use along with instrumental and enlightenment use, for evaluation itself has to be just as accountable as any other activity that makes claims on the public purse.

But we must not be sanguine about the good we are doing in the policy world. Our voices are not heard in major policy debates as regularly as they might be. There are lobbyists for financial interests, broadly understood, but there is no lobby for the best approximation to the truth at a given time, and there is little public recognition that such a lobby is needed. This is not to say that all truth-seeking social scientists speak with a common voice. They do not and should not. But I do believe that in any area there will be some "facts" and even some "interpretations" that most parties will agree to, even if they disagree on others. Let me give you a concrete example. When it existed, the National Institute of Education commissioned six meta-analyses of the effects of racial school desegregation on the academic achievement of African American children. Two of the analysts were thought to be conservatives, opposed to desegregation; two were thought to be liberals, in favor of it; and the others were thought to be neutral. The enterprise was restricted to quasi-experimental studies that included one group of students who had moved from segregated to desegregated schools and another group who had not moved. All the analysts agreed closely in their estimate of the size of the effects attributable to desegregation, though they radically disagreed about the practical utility of the magnitude of the effects obtained. But surely it helped to know that everybody agreed as to the magnitude of effects, even if all the analysts did not agree in judging them to be important. My suspicion is that, on almost every topic investigated by evaluators, some points of important and helpful agreement will be uncovered and disagreements can be sharpened. That is all I want to see in public debates, though such information will rarely be dramatic, will rarely speak clearly to ideologies even though it illuminates them, will often render issues more rather than less complex, and will only occasionally lend itself to easy sound bites. We have to struggle some more with these issues in order to provide even more useful inputs into even more public debates.

What I would appreciate seeing less of in evaluation is the type of discourse used in the debate about instrumental versus enlightenment use. This debate was limited to two options, and a central assumption was that enlightenment use was better justified the less instrumental use could be demonstrated. As we saw earlier, this form of discourse also characterized the qualitative/quantitative debate, and it is also the form that characterizes the debate about randomized experiments versus quasi-experiments. But when one examines all of these cases, it is immediately apparent that many more options could have been examined, and that the use of disparaging contrast to gain rhetorical advantage was not needed. Evaluation needs both instrumental and enlightenment use as part of its justification; evaluation needs both qualitative and quantitative methods to probe the many different types of issues evaluators need to raise; and evaluation needs both randomized experiments and quasi-experiments (particularly the better ones) for those many occasions when random assignment is not possible. In all of these cases a clear justification can be established without denigrating any alternative. Evaluation is an eclectic enterprise; let's not undertake unnecessary fights, creating factions and making the field look more disoriented to outsiders than it really is.

■ *What Next?*
Does Evaluation Need a Three-Legged Stool?

□ *Leg 1: Evaluation and Method Concerns*

The topics I have just discussed are primarily methodological. This may reflect my own parochial research interests, but it may also be that today's evaluation could be grossly characterized as a field that uses a broad array of quantitative and qualitative social science tools to examine social programs. This characterization assigns a centrality to method. I am proud that evaluators take method so seriously, so long as the field is not parochial about a particular set of method preferences. Indeed, the interest in method is one source of potential unity in a field where evaluators work in different substantive areas and have been trained in many different disciplines. However, the interest in method has not been systematically exploited for the promotion of unity, and the method research that takes place among members of AEA, APPAM, or APHA does not circulate easily from one of these professional networks to the others.

Evaluation is probably not unique in defining itself largely through methods. Earls (Lawrence-Lightfoot, 1995) has claimed that this is also the case in epidemiology, though we will shortly see that this is not a completely accurate depiction of that field. But my claim is that so long as evaluation is without empirical substance that can guide social change attempts, and so long as the field does not have lively theories of evaluation practice that are broader than theories of method choice, evaluation will probably not play as central a role as it deserves within the policy sciences. We need the method leg we already have on our stool, but it is hard to balance on this alone. We need other legs.

☐ *Leg 2: More and Better Evaluation Theory*

All disciplines require their own theoretical bases. In evaluation's case, we need theories of what evaluation means and of how it might be carried out to generate the best approximations to the truth about important social programs. Until about 10 years ago there was vigorous and fruitful theoretical debate in the field, summarized in Shadish, Cook, and Leviton (1991) where the advantages of such theory are also explicated.

Ten years ago, Scriven had already developed his incisive and comprehensive decision-theoretic logic that is also coincidentally used in economics and cognitive psychology as well as in popular evaluation outlets such as *Consumer Reports,* though none of these have the subtlety of Scriven's work. His major writings are the sine qua non for understanding evaluation in all areas of application, not just social welfare writ large. I cringe inside whenever I talk to evaluators who haven't read his writings. Not to know Scriven is to be illiterate in evaluation, even though

I don't think we should all agree with him on all matters. But at the very least, we need to engage ourselves with the central issues Scriven raises about the nature of bias and objectivity, about whether evaluation goals are needed, and about the logic of decision making.

Twenty-five years ago, Donald Campbell was writing about the "experimenting society," his personal vision of a massive societal transformation toward a set of values commensurate with an open democracy and a caring society. In Campbell's utopia it would be politically ordinary to be forthright in acknowledging social problems; it would be politically ordinary to confess one does not know how to solve these problems; it would be politically normal to be energetic in testing multiple possibilities for solving these problems—usually in demonstration projects that sometimes examine options so bold that they could not currently be considered as likely policy; and it would be politically normal to be comprehensive and critical in the scrutiny of findings from such projects. His work was not an apology for experimental methods. Indeed, it depended mostly on lay understandings of experimentation that emphasize playing with different ways of meeting a need and assessing the results of this serious play as best one can. His work only lent itself to experimentation in the traditional methodological sense because experiments provide the best answers to questions about responsible experimenting in the lay sense. Campbell's emphasis was more on a cultural revolution about political honesty and public truth seeking than on a technical revolution designed to increase the use of formal experiments.

The emphasis Scriven and Campbell placed on the ultimate priority of summarizing what a program or possible future program had achieved was vigorously opposed in the 1970s. Joseph Wholey argued that ongoing social programs are not like demonstration projects, that they can usually be revised only at the margins, and that such revision sometimes comes about merely through the assessment of how a program might be evaluated, for the assessment of evaluability can reveal where a program is theoretically deficient or requires different resources from those actually available. He also suggested that inexpensive audits of program implementation quality can be very instructive and do not require the costly and time-consuming resources of most outcome studies. In all of this he was guided by his empirical experience of how programs are actually developed, funded, implemented, and protected in the political and administrative world.

Carol Weiss independently arrived at this last emphasis, arguing that decision-oriented models of evaluation neglect the fact that information is rarely used in government as the sole or major input into decisions. Decisions accrete and are not made, she noted. She further noted that the information social scientists provide is always contested, even by social scientists themselves. It is sometimes not accorded even the same weight as anecdotes and personal experience. And she also pointed out that policy makers are highly rational in the pursuit of political survival and are less securely attached to making the best technical decisions. Like Wholey, Weiss contextualized social program evaluation, and she clearly saw it as only one element within a larger public policy framework.

Lee Cronbach (1982; Cronbach et al., 1980) produced two major theoretical works that also took on the decision-theoretic model, arguing that evaluation should be most concerned with generating general knowledge applicable to many programs and policies rather than with summarizing what is known about a particular program at a particular time. His preferred method for generating such transfer was through identifying that part of a program's process that is most responsible for producing changes in the lives of program participants. The crucial assumption here is that, if one learns why a program works, this knowledge can often be used in the design of future programs or in the modification of existing ones. Obviously, learning about such transfer depends on, and extends, substantive theory, so that Cronbach's work increases the relevance of evaluation for developing and probing theories from substantive disciplines.

Peter Rossi surveyed this theoretical cacophony and tried to create a theory of comprehensive evaluation that would incorporate all these different perspectives. And through most of this period we had Eleanor Chelimsky building at the federal level a unit for conducting evaluations that depended primarily on the critical examination of existing knowledge bases in order to answer sharply focused questions posed by members of the U.S. Congress. This was an action theory of how to institutionalize evaluation, a theory developed in the crucible of actually doing the work for government. And the theory so developed had to be flexible enough to handle evaluations from many different sectors, with the list of sectors seeming to grow year by year until even evaluating weapons testing systems fell under her purview. This was a model in action of how evaluation can be productive and routine.

The evaluation field is not as concerned now with big-picture theory about the nature, conduct, and institutionalization of evaluation and the stimulation of use of its results. Many of the previously mentioned theorists are not now active in evaluation, and the younger scholars wanting to tackle such issues head-on are few in number. There are many younger scholars willing to write about methodology, to report on particular evaluations, to offer wisdom from the field about how to deal with some aspect or another of the evaluation enterprise, or to proclaim a new paradigm for evaluation. But when I look at the most recent claims in this last regard, they seem weak. In the family preservation field, there is a so-called new evaluation paradigm that reads like Joe Wholey rediscovered, and his work is not even cited. And a recent volume on new approaches to the evaluation of community development initiatives again reads like a rehash of both Joe Wholey's work on the utility of program theory and the literature on selection bias. Moreover, it almost entirely omits the wisdom gained in epidemiology and behavioral medicine from more than two decades of evaluating community health promotion campaigns. I suspect that past theoretical efforts in evaluation are not being closely read now, and are not taken to heart and recognized as stepping-stones for creating new theories of evaluation. I hope I am wrong in this, but my fear is that the upcoming generation neither knows nor cares about evaluation theory.

We need to encourage those scholars who still have interest in the topic, both those of the older generation, like Scriven and House, and those of the younger generation, like Smith, Kirkhart, Shadish, and Chen. We need people willing to be as bold as Cronbach or Weiss, taking on the received wisdom of the day. We also need successful practitioners to write about evaluation theory using their experience and reading, as Wholey did and I hope Chelimsky will do. We have one theory of how to construct evaluation theory, for which Shadish is largely responsible (Shadish et al., 1991). But this work needs even more criticism than it has received, and it does not develop in detail its own theory of evaluation. It develops only a theory of evaluation theory. I'm not sure why there is a lack of intellectual fervor about core concepts in evaluation. Perhaps evaluation theory is too hard today, given that the major overarching positions were staked out by the pioneers between 1965 and 1985—I'm not sure. But without active theoretical debates about core issues in evaluation that transcend method, the field may not grow, even if it does not atrophy.

□ *Leg 3: A Substantive Base in Disciplinary Theories
and Syntheses of Past Findings*

I suspect that the power associated with economics within government arises partly because the subject matter of economics is money, and
power goes with money. Also important, however, is the generality of the
discipline's substantive theories, which permits the application of those
theories to all kinds of specific contexts—whether accurately or not.
When one thinks of the power of management consulting firms in the
private sector—the closest single analogue I can think of to evaluators in
the public sector—one is struck by the consultants' ability to use a wide
variety of qualitative and quantitative techniques for evaluating how a
business is performing and also to use standard economic theories, theories of business strategy and organizational behavior, and their own and
their colleagues' past experience as eclectic sources of ideas about improving the situation in which a particular business finds itself. Management consultants are expected to evaluate and prescribe, using the wisdom
in their specialized field supplemented by knowledge from the many
social science disciplines that feed into their field. Like economists, they
are never far from grounded presumptions about "what works to improve
things," and these presumptions depend on a wider theoretical and empirical evidence base than the program they are examining. Something
similar is also true of epidemiology, where many scholars strive to
synthesize knowledge of what seems to work to impede or improve
physical health, creating a temporary compendium of cause-and-effect
knowledge that eventually comes to be reproduced in textbooks together
with the usual litany of preferred methods.

My impression, perhaps mistaken, is that we evaluators are less
deliberate and systematic than others in accumulating substantive findings and in drawing inferences about the programs and classes of programs that seem to work best. If this is true, there are many reasons for it.
One is that evaluators are usually commissioned to evaluate specific
programs rather than to review the literature on the classes of programs
targeting a given problem; and evaluators cover a more heterogeneous
collection of substantive areas than, say, epidemiologists. But even within
a more homogeneous subarea such as education in schools there have now
been 30 years of evaluations covering a wide array of programs. I think I
know to whom I would turn for advice on what seems most effective in a

given area in education, but few of these persons would think of themselves primarily as evaluators, even though they make use of evaluation reports. And I suspect that many education evaluators do not consider themselves to be substantive experts on anything, but instead move from one commission to the next, rarely having the luxury (or support) to cast a wide-angle view over educational reform writ large.

The most important compendia of "what works, when, and for whom" are probably the two books by Lisbeth Schorr (1988) and Joy Dryfoos (1990). These two writers seem to have capitalized on the widespread hunger among the public, policy makers, and foundation officials to have some research-based overview of what improves children's lives. Whether Schorr and Dryfoos meet the standards of evidence you or I might prefer is irrelevant to the point I want to make: Is there an ongoing need to summarize what seems to work in given areas? And given that establishing what seems to work is one of the major questions evaluators ask, is it appropriate for evaluators to place greater emphasis on generating consumer-oriented research syntheses than on generating the knowledge that goes into others' syntheses? Speaking very personally, I think many interest groups want the type of comparative summary information that *Consumer Reports* delivers in the United States. They want more evaluators with the ambition to do what Mark Lipsey has done for many different types of intervention in the social welfare domain.

If evaluation, as a field, were "somehow" more responsible for synthesizing the knowledge base in particular areas, then evaluators assessing individual projects could use this information and be in an even better position to recommend program modifications, as management consultants now routinely do. And our field would grow beyond a methods-based discipline to become a discipline, like epidemiology, that is known for its substantive knowledge base as well as its methodological sophistication. No longer would introductory evaluation texts be restricted to telling us how to identify a program theory, to deal with multiple stakeholders, and to conduct surveys, focus groups, ethnography, participant observation, randomized experiments, and quasi-experiments. Instead, general textbooks on evaluation would also contain sections on some subset of the following issues: This is what we know about what works in preschool education, in elementary education, in high school education, in family maintenance, in dealing with homelessness, in job training, and so on.

But just enumerating this small subset of topics reveals the immensity of the task I am suggesting, particularly if there is no external funding base. Yet if some part of this task is not undertaken, evaluation runs the risk of being nothing more than applied social science methods, and evaluators will be peripheral to public debates about what to do to improve programs and lives, however much others might use evaluation results in these debates. Of course, no individual can do all of the synthesizing required to make evaluation more relevant as a repository for accumulated substantive knowledge; but small committees might be able to do some of the substantive synthesizing I am calling for and that is absolutely required, I think, if evaluation is to be seen as a social science discipline in its own right.

■ *Conclusions*

We have learned from the qualitative/quantitative debate that qualitative research is indispensable, but the long debate about this issue is now getting repetitive and may be preventing us from going on to other topics. We have learned from the literature on research syntheses how much more prevalent these are becoming, how useful they are from both validity and credibility perspectives, and how they paint a somewhat more optimistic picture of what government interventions can achieve in the social welfare field than much current political rhetoric suggests is the case. Further, we have learned that evaluations are used in many different ways, and that putting one form of use onto the evaluation map does not necessarily require denigrating other forms of use. Finally, if evaluation is to be an even more useful field, I at least have learned that its emphasis on the applied use of social science methods needs to be complemented by more vigorous debates about evaluation theory and by the publication of compendia of policies, programs, projects, and project components that seem to work—not that they invariably work, but that they often work.

Evaluation sitting on a stool with three legs—called method, theory, and compendia of substantive findings—would be an even more vigorous and self-renewing field than it is now. But don't get me wrong—I think we have made a lot of progress over the past 25 years. It's just that I'm greedy for more. I want to see a field that is much more than social science methods applied to the study of social interventions.

■ References

Blank, R. M. (1997). *It takes a nation: A new agenda for fighting proverty.* Princeton, NJ: Princeton University Press.

Campbell, D. T. (1974). *Qualitative knowing in action research.* Kurt Lewin Award Address, Society for the Psychological Study of Social Issues, presented at the 82nd Annual Meeting of the American Psychological Association, New Orleans.

Campbell, D. T. (1978). Qualitative knowing in action research. In M. Brenner, P. Marsh, & M. Brenner (Eds.), *The social context of methods.* London: Croom Helm.

Campbell, D. T. (1986). Science's social system of validity-enhancing collective belief change and the problems of the social sciences. In D. W. Fiske & R. A. Shweder (Eds.), *Metatheory in social science: Pluralisms and subjectivities.* Chicago: University of Chicago Press.

Chelimsky, E. (1987a). The politics of program evaluation. In D. S. Cordray, H. S. Bloom, & R. J. Light (Eds.), *Evaluation practice in review.* San Francisco: Jossey-Bass.

Chelimsky, E. (1987b). What have we learned about the politics of program evaluation? *Evaluation News, 8,* 5-22.

Cicirelli, V. G., & Associates. (1969). *The impact of Head Start: An evaluation of the effects of Head Start on children's cognitive and affective development* (2 vols.) (Report to the Office of Economic Opportunity). Athens: Ohio University and Westinghouse Learning Corporation.

Colby, J., & Shweder, R. A. (Eds.). (1995). *Qualitative research.* Chicago: University of Chicago Press

Cook, T. D. (1985). Postpositivist critical multiplism. In L. Shotland & M. M. Mark (Eds.), *Social science and social policy.* Beverly Hills, CA: Sage.

Cook, T. D. (1993). A quasi-sampling theory of the generalization of causal relationships. In L. Sechrest & A. G. Scott (Eds.), *Understanding causes and generalizing about them.* San Francisco: Jossey-Bass.

Cook, T. D., Cooper, H., Cordray, D. S., Hartmann, H., Hedges, L. V., Light, R. J., Louis, T. A., & Mosteller, F. (1992). *Meta-analysis for explanation: A casebook.* New York: Russell Sage Foundation.

Cook, T. D., & Reichardt, C. S. (Eds.). (1979). *Qualitative and quantitative methods in evaluation research.* Beverly Hills, CA: Sage.

Cooper, H., & Hedges, L. V. (Eds.). (1994). *The handbook of research synthesis.* New York: Russell Sage Foundation.

Cronbach, L. J. (1982). *Designing evaluations of educational and social programs.* San Francisco: Jossey-Bass.

Cronbach, L. J., & Associates. (1980). *Toward reform of program evaluation.* San Francisco: Jossey-Bass.

Dryfoos, J. (1990). *Adolescents at risk: Prevalence and prevention.* New York: Oxford University Press.

Edin, K., & Jencks, C. (1992). Reforming welfare. In C. Jencks, *Rethinking social policy: Race, poverty, and the underclass* (pp. 204-235). Cambridge, MA: Harvard University Press.

Guba, E. G., & Lincoln, Y. S. (1981). *Effective evaluation: Improving the usefulness of evaluation results through responsive and naturalistic approaches.* San Francisco: Jossey-Bass.

Guba, E. G., & Lincoln, Y. S. (1989). *Fourth generation evaluation.* Newbury Park, CA: Sage.

Heap, J. L. (1995). Constructionism in the rhetoric and practice of fourth generation evaluation. *Evaluation and Program Planning, 18,* 51-61.

Jencks, C., & Edin, K. (1990, Winter). The real welfare problem. *American Prospect,* pp. 31-50.

Jencks, C., & Mayer, S. (1995, November 9). War on poverty: No apologies please. *New York Times.*

Jessor, R., Colby, A., & Shweder, R. A. (Eds.). (1996). *Ethnography and human development: Context and meaning in social inquiry.* Chicago, IL: University of Chicago Press.

Lawrence-Lightfoot, S. (1995). *I've known rivers: Lives of loss and liberation.* New York: Penguin.

Leviton, L. C., & Cook, T. D. (1983). Evaluation findings in education and social work textbooks. *Evaluation Review, 7,* 497-518.

Light, R. J., & Pillemer, D. B. (1984). *Summing up: The science of reviewing research.* Cambridge, MA: Harvard University Press.

Lipsey, M. W., & Wilson, D. B. (1993). The efficacy of psychological, educational and behavioral treatment: Confirmation from meta-analysis. *American Psychologist, 48*(12).

Lipton, D., Martinson, R., & Wilkins, J. (1975). *The effectiveness of correctional treatment: A survey of treatment evaluation studies.* New York: Praeger.

Matt, G. E., & Cook, T. D. (1993). The war on fraud and error in the food stamp program: An evaluation of its effects in the Carter and Reagan administrations. *Evaluation Review, 17,* 503-520.

Navarro, A. M. (1990). Eficacia de las terapias psicologicas: Meta-analisis de estudios en paises de habla hispana [Effectiveness of psychological therapies: Meta-analysis of outcome studies in Spanish-speaking countries]. *Revista de Psicologia Social y Personalidad, 6,* 87-99.

Patton, M. Q. (1980). *Qualitative evaluation methods.* Beverly Hills, CA: Sage.

Schorr, L. B., with Schorr, D. (1988). *Within our reach: Breaking the cycle of disadvantage.* Garden City, NY: Anchor.

Shadish, W. R. (1995). Philosophy of science and the quantitative-qualitative debates: 13 common errors. *Evaluation and Program Planning, 18,* 63-75.

Shadish, W. R., Cook, T. D., & Leviton, L. C. (1991). *Foundations of program evaluation.* Newbury Park, CA: Sage.

Stake, R. E. (1980). Program evaluation, particularly responsive evaluation. In W. B. Dockrell & D. Hamilton (Eds.), *Rethinking educational research.* London: Hodder & Stoughton.

Suchman, E. (1967). *Evaluation research.* New York: Russell Sage Foundation.

Watts, H. W., & Rees, A. (1977). *Labor supply responses. The New Jersey Income Maintenance Experiment* (Vol. 2). New York: Academic Press.

Wittmann, W. W., & Matt, G. E. (1986). Meta-Analyse als Integration von Forschungsergebnissen am Beispie deutschsprächiger Arbeiten zur Effektivität von Psychotherapie. *Psychologische Rundschau, 37.*

3

The Political Environment of Evaluation and What It Means for the Development of the Field

Eleanor Chelimsky

The future of the evaluation profession seems very different today from what we thought it was 20 years ago, when we came together in Boston to explore whether the field was sufficiently advanced to warrant the founding of a professional society. What changes we see today!

First, the question we worried about so much then—whether we could, in fact, routinely produce methodologically strong evaluations that would also be timely enough and policy relevant enough to have practical value to decision makers—worries us no longer: We have shown quite conclusively that we can do that.

Second, over the past 20 years, we have developed (through invention, or through begging, borrowing, and stealing) an extraordinary wealth of methods, styles, and reporting formats that are available to us today for use in evaluation.

Third, we have seen our findings incorporated into policy making—sometimes imperfectly, sometimes incorrectly, but often very well indeed—even in ferocious political debates that leave little room for open-minded discussion of what may have been learned through evaluation.

Fourth, the practice of evaluation is now spreading to the far corners of the globe. For example, evaluation was adopted in 1992 as a key work area for the national audit agencies of 188 independent states worldwide. Indeed, the 1995 Vancouver conference was honored by the presence of auditors from many different regions of the world, intent on delving deeper into the language and practice of evaluation. As a second example, international institutions such as the United Nations' Development and Environmental Programs, the European Commission, the World Bank and its related international banks, and the Kellogg and Rockefeller Foundations have been notably increasing their use of evaluation, mostly to examine the results—and especially the cumulative results—of their amazingly far-flung projects. These projects may be designed to decrease hardship and poverty on a continentwide basis, or to improve agricultural productivity in arid climates, or to increase environmental awareness and protection worldwide, or to strengthen managerial learning by delivering training to midcareer leaders in the seven most populated countries of the world. All of this work, and a great deal more besides, is now becoming operational on a truly breathtaking scale.

Fifth, associations that bring together evaluators, policy analysts, auditors, and researchers involved in knowledge production and diffusion are multiplying internationally (I believe the most recent of these are the European and British Evaluation Societies, now just over one year old). Also, newsletters and other periodicals on the theory and practice of evaluation have been springing up—let me particularly mention the new international journal called *Evaluation,* published jointly by Sage and the Tavistock Institute. Indeed, the panels, plenary speakers, and participants at the 1995 Vancouver conference—in which five evaluation associations were involved—presented specific data attesting to evaluation's global progress to date.

So yes, we have indeed come a long way, but if we rejoice in these achievements, it is not only because evaluation is our life's work and we love it, but because evaluation is so important to any democratic society. It benefits those who make decisions about policy, and it benefits the citizens who have to live with those decisions, once made. Evaluation's voice may be the only one raised, sometimes, to question the reality of certain images and perceptions widely believed to be true. The *measures* we use to represent concepts such as justice or fairness or well-being can shed new light on policy failures of the past. Also, the *data* we provide can lead public decision making away from the deceptive war story, the anecdote, or the outlier, and instead focus needed attention on the size and direction of an issue or trend.

Evaluation is important also because it is not just a top-down tool for high-ranking policy makers with ample resources. People at all levels of government—from cops on the beat to budget analysts—can benefit from learning what works in community policing or victim services, or how to target local programs to different types of homeless people, or why it is important to make distinctions between social drinkers and alcoholics in efforts to reduce drunken driving. School districts have for years been using evaluation effectively for humble but very important things such as determining the least costly way to bring kids to school.

But if there is very good reason to celebrate the fact that evaluation is at last hitting its stride, we must also recognize that this did not happen without mistakes and misunderstandings. Indeed, I believe that it is precisely our past errors and defeats that have brought us to our present successes.

T. S. Eliot (1943) has written, "Time present and time past are both perhaps present in time future, and time future contained in time past." So, because our future meaningfulness depends heavily on how well we understand our past and the lessons it contains, I want to address here the political environment of our work and what it means for the development of our field. As new institutions and organizations take up the challenge of making evaluations useful to public policy, I think it is time to recognize, not just theoretically but also in our practice and in the training we give to new evaluators, that our ability to serve policy depends as much on what we understand about how politics works as it does on the quality and appropriateness of our methods.

Understanding Our Political Environment

Some of you may remember Lee Cronbach, in 1980, telling us that a theory of evaluation has to be as much a theory of political interaction as a theory of how to determine facts or how knowledge is constructed (Cronbach et al., 1980). Even so, 16 years later, we still don't seem to understand political processes very well, and especially their dynamic nature. For example, it is conventional in evaluation circles to talk about ideology as a sort of static political phenomenon, and some of us believe that evaluation has no place in an ideological scheme of things. In my view, this is a misconception, and it has led to a widespread but mistaken picture of a political spectrum that moves from "good" Democratic incrementalism on the left to "bad" Republican ideology on the right. Although I would agree that the spectrum does range from incrementalism to ideology, I would argue, first, that as typically happens with any spectrum, the outlier situation is pretty rare: most of the time, in most political environments represented on the spectrum, incrementalism and ideology are almost inextricably bound together, and evaluators must therefore always be prepared to confront them both. I would argue, second, that the ideological and incrementalist outliers, when they do occur, can each be as characteristic of Democratic thinking as of Republican.

Let me use Aaron Wildavsky (1964) here to define incrementalism as a noncomprehensive, fragmented, data-based way of examining facts, budgets, policies, or programs. Incrementalism in politics usually starts from last year's base and adds to, or subtracts from, that base. The theory behind it is that we can solve problems step-by-step, learning as we go, rather than by making grandiose, radical changes. The Nixon and Eisenhower administrations, for example, show how incrementalist domestic Republican politics can be.

Ideology, on the other hand, does make grandiose, radical changes: It is comprehensive, it is thoroughgoing, it can be overwhelming. But in the same way, if we use Everett Ladd's (1972) definition of ideology as involving the application of an overarching framework of beliefs and opinions to the events and decisions of public life, and we look back a few years, then it becomes clear that ideology cannot be synonymous with the political right alone. Indeed, we have experienced some mighty swings of the political pendulum over the past 60 years or so in the United States, and I believe that the New Deal euphoria of the 1930s and the Great Society euphoria of the 1960s were as opinion-ridden, as unsupported by evidence and knowledge about the likely effects of their actions, as the Reagan Revolution euphoria of the 1980s and that of today's "Contract with America." Senator Moynihan is right, of course, when he tells today's Republican ideologues, "Don't pretend that you know what you don't know. . . . Do not hurt children on the basis of an unproven theory, an untested hypothesis" (statement on the Senate floor, quoted in the *New York Review of Books,* October 19, 1995, p. 72). Yet it is also the case, as the senator himself has documented (in *Maximum Feasible Misunderstanding,* 1969) that Democratic ideologues have been equally pretentious about what was, in fact, known, and equally encumbered by unproven theories and untested hypotheses.

In short, both ideology and incrementalism can be on the left as well as on the right; the two occur *together* in most political environments, and evaluators deal with them every day, whether they know it or not. Further, it is the *fact* of ideology, not the political direction in which it leans, that evokes the professional responsibility of evaluators. This is because, when the political environment shifts to ideology at its most euphoric, evaluators are not likely to be asked for a lot of help. Not only should this not stop us from doing our work, it sets up our public duty to do evaluations that oppose evidence to the myths, the personal beliefs and opinions, and, above all, the selectively presented data dear to ideologues.

Let me note in passing that some of the best use of findings in policy making that I experienced while running GAO's evaluation division came from presenting evidence publicly at precisely those times when the political environment was most unreceptive to it. I am thinking here of the work we did on chemical warfare, on bilingual education, on the evidence supporting the Women's, Infants and Children's (WIC) Program, on the effects of trying to save money in Medicare, on the cost-effectiveness of America's strategic nuclear "triad," and so on. All of these findings involved us in major battles; all of them were very well used.

So it is up to us to make objective information available, especially in a hostile political environment, and also when the relevant public groups are unaware of the facts. It is up to us, as well, to see that those data are known and disseminated. Why is it up to us? Because we know the data, because we believe in the value of knowledge, and because we are noneuphoric by training. Vaclav Havel (1995), who has some understanding and experience of what ideology means for public policy, said recently:

Improvements and changes should be made according to whatever has been proven to be good, practical, desirable and meaningful, without the arrogant presumption that we have understood everything about this world and thus know everything there is to know about how to change it for the better. . . . People should proceed with the utmost caution and sensitivity, step by step, always paying attention to what each change actually has brought about. (p. 36)

But what Havel is describing here, of course, is a kind of pure incrementalism, devoutly to be wished for from an enlightenment perspective, perhaps, but rarer than rare in everyday politics.

So, because we don't often see a political environment in which Havel's kind of caution, step-by-step learning, and sensitivity are possible, we need to be realistic about the political environments we do have—in particular, the perennial presence of ideological agendas as we plan, conduct, and report our evaluations. We should not imagine that stakeholders in any political environment are likely to be open-minded, or willing to change their value positions or to share power, except in extraordinary circumstances. Rather, the norm is that political actors never forget their agendas—indeed, they were elected to remember them, not forget them—and so evaluators need to work with those agendas, concentrating on securing the one thing that is most important for evaluation in any political environment, and that is the independence necessary to conduct their evaluations and state their conclusions without political interference.

But what, then, are the other effects on evaluators of having to work in a political environment? Does it make any difference for evaluation practice if we recognize the responsibility to say what the data are, no matter what the political climate? I think the fact of working in a political environment has a number of important implications for evaluation, for its theory and practice, for its practitioners, and for its future. In the next section I briefly address six of them.

■ *Implications of the Political Environment for Evaluation*

☐ *Credibility*

The first and most critical implication I see is the overriding need for evaluation credibility. By credibility, I mean a judgment by others—

including reviewers, lay readers, researchers, journalists, sponsors, users, policy makers—that the evaluation is both competent and objective.

To be listened to by various stakeholders in even an ordinary political debate requires a great deal of effort by evaluators not only to *be* competent and objective, but to appear so. Although all of us realize that we can never be entirely objective, that is hardly an excuse for skewed samples, or for grandiloquent conclusions or generalizations that go far beyond the data, or for any of the numerous indications to a careful reader that a particular result was more desired than documented.

There are, in fact, a great many things we can do to foster both objectivity and its appearance, not just technically, in the steps we take to make and explain our evaluative decisions, but also intellectually, in the effort we put forth to look at all sides and stakeholders of an evaluation.

As for competence, I believe most of us now understand the possibility that we will need to defend our work against attack in most political environments, and I believe we understand also that the hotter the debate, the stronger the defense of the chosen methodology will need to be. But I'm not sure we always take the necessary practical steps, during the design phase of a study and throughout its conduct, to be truly ready to make a serious defense if and when it is needed. What seems least well understood, in my judgment, is the dramatically negative and long-term impact on credibility of the appearance of advocacy in an evaluation. There is a vast cemetery out there of unused evaluation findings that have been loudly or quietly rejected because they didn't "seem" objective. In short, evaluators' survival in a political environment depends heavily on their credibility, as does the use of their findings in policy.

□   *Courage*

A second implication for evaluators of a political environment is the need for courage. Although this seems fairly obvious, somehow we don't talk about it much. Yet speaking out (in situations that may include numerous political adversaries, all with different viewpoints and axes to grind), and also insisting on the right to independence in speaking out, takes a strong stomach. Even in ordinary times—that is, in the political environments occurring toward the middle of the spectrum—the normal skepticism of the evaluator is unwelcome amid the ambient enthusiasm for one program or another. But as we move down the spectrum toward ideology, doubting the conventional wisdom becomes a hanging offense, and everything must be a matter of absolute certainty, easily expressed in sound bites. Often evaluators are told bluntly that they must become members of "the team," and that loyalty to the head of their agency or to the party line is a lot more important—and certainly more "career enhancing"—than their evidence or data. But because evaluation findings can be inconclusive, too complex for sound bites, and at odds with the prevailing "team" or agency or political view, evaluators can be (and feel) quite isolated.

It also takes internal fortitude and strong resistance not to succumb to political blandishments of one sort or another. These blandishments move from the siren song that lures evaluators into wanting to become political "players" on the national scene, through the temptation to avoid battles by "helping" policy makers, to the promise of glorious career rewards as compensation for obedience.

So it takes courage to refuse sponsors the answers they want to hear, to resist becoming a "member of the team," to challenge the myths that everyone is comfortable with, to fight inappropriate intrusion into the evaluation process. In a political environment, courage is as important as credibility. Goethe said, "Possessions lost, nothing lost. Principles lost, something lost. Courage lost, everything lost" (quoted in "Visions of Public Service," 1986, p. 12).

☐ *Dissemination of Strong Findings*

A third implication of the political environment is that, when evaluators have unambiguous data and evidence, the short memory of the political process obliges them to be persistent to the point of obstinacy in bringing what has been learned to the attention of policy makers. We do, after all, occasionally have findings that are clear, corroborated, and policy relevant; think, for example, of what we have learned about the effects of smoking on lung cancer, or the effects of drinking-age laws on traffic fatalities, or the effects of some types of agricultural research on crop yields, or the cost-effectiveness of some vaccines. When we have such findings, we have a duty to share them, to see that concerned groups and individuals hear about them. The fact that the political process loses sight of findings almost from one week to another means that the evaluator's job in a political environment does not end with publication. There is a need to summarize findings, to incorporate them with other findings, in short, to disseminate them in order to keep the most important facts at the forefront of public debate.

We have not paid a lot of attention to dissemination, and it took us a very long time to get the facts out about smoking—although not so long as the time it took between the development of porcelain and lacquer in China's Chou dynasty and the decline in dysentery due to their spreading use during the Han period: that was about 500 years. We are doing better than that today, perhaps, but we can do much better than we are doing. The recent debate on health care policy, which was much more focused on economics than on health, would have greatly benefited, for example, from a succinct and credible summary, intelligently disseminated, of what we know (and what we don't know) about the quality of our health care; about the national, regional, and local impediments hindering access to that care; and about the known past results of efforts to cut the costs of that care.

We also need to consider targeted dissemination of strong findings that may have had the misfortune to run up against special interests (the gun lobby, say, or the tobacco industry), or the misfortune to thwart or contradict agency policy, or simply to run counter to prevailing political winds. Although the policy use of findings will surely be reduced in such situations if opponents are powerful enough, still—once evaluations with important findings have been published, no matter how reluctantly—it is evaluators' duty to bring their knowledge forward.

In the same way, we simply must challenge rhetoric and hyperbole in areas where we know the facts. Remember the speaker who was introduced as having made a hundred million dollars in oil in California? "Well, it wasn't California," he said, "it was Pennsylvania; and it wasn't oil, it was coal; it wasn't a hundred million, it was one million; it wasn't me, it was my brother; and he didn't make it, he lost it." We really should get the information out when we have it.

☐ *Linkages Across Disciplines and With Basic Research*

A fourth implication of the political environment and the credibility requirements it lays on evaluators is the need for stronger links across applied sciences and especially with basic research. As things stand now in the United States, there is no single association that brings together evaluators from all disciplines and in all topical areas. We have one association for educational evaluators, another for evaluators in health care, another for political science and policy evaluators, another for budget analysts, and so on. Yet it would be so much easier and faster for evaluators to answer questions credibly if we had stronger networks, better access to evaluative data, more comprehensive clearinghouses of completed evaluations and other studies across applied disciplines and topical areas. To use the research synthesis method properly, for example, an evaluator needs to know all the studies that have been done on a given topic. But the lack of a clearinghouse and our embryonic development in networking means that initial syntheses can be unnecessarily long and difficult to do. For new countries or agencies beginning their evaluation enterprises, the lesson from our experience is clearly to be as *inclusive* as possible in crossing disciplinary lines.

We also suffer from being largely separated from basic research. Yet it is hardly a secret that evaluators rely heavily on what basic research has to say about the theoretical assumptions underlying public programs, whereas basic researchers look to evaluation to test the validity of those assumptions. There is a two-way street here, unacknowledged though it may still be by those who should be most concerned with assuring a free flow of traffic. Evaluators expect basic researchers to inform them on the causes of public problems, on the processes of problem development, and on the predictability of problems. We know we are ill equipped, for the most part, to answer policy questions of the more fundamental sort, such as, Who gets addicted to drugs and who doesn't? Which offenders are likely to recidivate? Who becomes homeless and by what process? Basic researchers, on the other hand, often use evaluators' unanswered questions to set up politically salient agendas for their work. In short, both evaluators and basic researchers would benefit from stronger links and a much more cooperative relationship, because of the greater amount of information that would be available to them and the greater resulting credibility of their work in a political environment.

We have in fact paid a heavy price for the lack of such relationships in learning about the environment and applying reasonable policy solutions to our problems, but we may now be starting to see some progress in this area. "Hard" and "soft" scientists are working together under United Nations and other international sponsorship to increase both knowledge of the environment and measurement of efforts to protect it. In the same way, "hard" and "soft" scientists are regularly brought together in the United States by the Agency for Health Care Policy and Research, by the Public Health Service, by the Department of Defense, and by the Department of Justice, among other government agencies. But even if stronger links may now be forming, these are mostly quite limited and project specific, and a major effort is needed if we are to expand our dialogue to the many areas of study for which evaluation credibility requires the expertise of multiple disciplines and types of research.

☐ *Access to Information*

A fifth implication of a political environment is that it may impose constraints—sometimes going as far as the total restriction or classification of information—on evaluators' access to data. Whether the climate is ideological or incrementalist, classification of information is a fact of life in some agencies, and it constitutes a serious problem for evaluators in that, if they ignore the classified literature, they risk coming to manifestly false conclusions. When we started our chemical warfare work at GAO, for example, we found that all the open literature had been written by so-called doves, whereas the classified reports had been signed by people usually referred to as hawks. This meant that doing a research synthesis in this area forced the inclusion of classified data and the consequent restrictions that imposed on publication.

Another problem for evaluators has to do with what is classified. The temptation is, of course, for an agency to hide under a blanket of secrecy whatever might show up its warts and foibles. For example, we found in our review of operational test and evaluation at the Department of Defense that once we had examined all the classified information, it was clear that what had been released to the public on an unclassified basis "resulted in a more favorable presentation to the Congress of test adequacy and system performance than was warranted by the facts" (U.S. General Accounting Office, 1988, p. 3). In other words, unclassified information may be favorable to a system for which funding or approval is sought only because the unfavorable data have been classified or suppressed. Classification, then, by its selective release of data, puts evaluators in a difficult position. We can tell the truth and go to jail for revealing classified information; we can tell only truths that are palatable to the agency; or we can take so narrow an approach on such unimportant policy issues that nobody cares, not even the agency.

Of course, no one contests the idea that some information, such as the design of nuclear weapon systems, *should* be classified. But because of the wonderfully sanitizing properties of secrecy, we are now seeing its spread beyond the Department of Defense into such policy domains as health care reform and public safety, where no national security issue can be invoked. Evaluators—for that matter, all researchers—need to do more to redress this situation, because it precludes the presentation of all the facts, leads to bad public policy, and drastically reduces and distorts the flow of factual information to the public.

☐ *More Realistic Training of Evaluation Students*

The last implication I want to mention of having to conduct evaluations under dynamic political conditions is that we need to focus more on how we train new evaluators to work under those conditions. Fewer students are being specifically trained in evaluation today, which is unfortunate given the steady expansion of the field. Still, many students come to evaluation from other fields, and I would like to propose five ways in which our political environment ought to influence the training of evaluators.

First, it is clear that we need to go beyond social problems and policy in evaluation education. The techniques developed for the evaluation of social programs are not limited to those programs, and the political demand for evaluation is equally great in areas such as defense, transportation, agriculture, energy, and the environment, to name only a few. Also, nonsocial programs may have tremendous social effects and social programs may have nonsocial effects, all of which are worthy of important involvement by the evaluation profession. So we should try to ensure that evaluation techniques are also taught in the relevant nonsocial area courses, like agricultural research and development, defense policy, and environmental protection.

Second, we should help students learn how to design studies that are credible in a political environment, and also help them gain actual experience in using evaluation methods. This holds not just for evaluation students but also for students of accounting and business, who should learn how to perform the complete evaluation function, including data collection and analysis. Understanding the logic or theory behind evaluation methods is necessary, but students should also have some real experience in using those methods if we are to cut down on overpromising and unwarranted optimism in our evaluation designs.

Third, many modern evaluation methods require evaluators to work in groups, to sequence and manage their work efficiently, and to write in a clear, concise style that policy makers, if not politicians, will read. Students need to be better prepared in these management and user-focused facets of evaluation.

Fourth, the different methods for valuing and comparing costs, so familiar to auditors and accountants and economists, should be seriously studied by evaluation students. No matter how elegant or sophisticated our work is in establishing, say, a cause-and-effect relationship, the quintessential question in a political environment, whether incremental, ideological, or mixed, is, What is the program or system's cost-effectiveness, compared with other programs or systems?

Finally, a bit more realism needs to creep into the training of evaluators; they should, for example, have a better understanding of what is reasonable to expect in a political environment with regard to the use of findings in policy making. Immediate success in influencing policy based on evaluative evidence is pretty rare. Usually it takes strong and repeated evaluations as well as a happy concatenation of circumstances before anything happens at all.

To sum up, I have argued here that there are six important implications for evaluators that derive from the political environment in which evaluation must make its case. These include needs for the following:

- the production of credible and defensible evaluation reports
- the courage to fight hard for independence and for freedom from political pressure
- the dissemination of strong evaluation findings
- the development of linkages across disciplines and with basic research
- the achievement of better access to data
- the insertion of political realism into evaluation training

Conclusion

In conclusion, let me suggest that what I am proposing here is in the tradition of the British civil service, whose policy researchers try to collect data and gather information that is useful to all political parties (Blackstone & Plowden, 1988). This is critical if evaluation is to continue to have a meaningful role in public policy. Political environments are volatile, power changes hands, and evaluations need to be defensible across the spectrum of political mixes, and also over time as mixes change.

Real cumulative benefit accrues to courage and persistence in the defense and dissemination of strong findings. As one fighter in the tobacco wars, David Spain (1960), put it sadly, "Having only recently emerged scarred and non-victorious from the battlefield of cigarette smoking versus cancer of the lung, I can testify that the dairy and beef trusts, as well as the hamburger and custard stands, will not willingly give up their vested and powerful interests" (p. 831). Yes, but in 1996, at least in the United States, we are beginning to see some policy progress and some successes in terms of smoking outcomes, thanks to the obstinacy of a small band of researchers.

I can personally attest to the difficulties and the importance of fighting special interests, having run up against the gun lobby, the medical devices lobby, the Air Force lobby, the Navy lobby, the beer lobby, and the dairy lobby, among others, in the course of my work over the past 15 years. It was an especial joy to me to see the recent announcement by the Health Care Financing Administration that henceforth, eye surgeons will need to show that the removal of a cataract is medically necessary before Medicare will pay for such an operation ("Plan Proposes," 1995). GAO's work had shown that medical necessity had not been apparent or demonstrated for cataract surgery in about one-quarter of the 2 million Medicare patients who received it in 1991. We reported that this surgery was therefore questionable for those patients and involved an inappropriate expenditure of about $200 million for that year (U.S. General Accounting Office, 1993, pp. 2-4). The reaction of America's ophthalmologists to this finding was, or course, entirely predictable, but nonetheless impressive. I came away from the Senate hearing on our study feeling every bit as battle scarred and bruised as David Spain. Yet now, only 2 years later, thanks to our work and the work of the Agency for Health Care Policy and Research, and also to the Republican cost-cutting euphoria that finally gave HCFA the courage to face up to the ophthalmologists, we see the right results occurring. Now, that's 498 years less than for porcelain and lacquer. To me, this suggests not only that it is worth fighting for important findings, and that, if we do, they may eventually be used appropriately in policy making, but also—depending on the findings—that ideology can be a help as well as a hindrance.

The major point I want to make here is that we evaluators have a role to play, even (and especially) if we must work in a political environment dominated by ideology. All values are always present in any democratic society, and unless there is actual censorship (such as the kind I mentioned earlier that is imposed by classification), our work, our role, our function continues to be very precious indeed.

I have made the argument here from an evaluative viewpoint (that is, whether or not there has been careful, skeptical examination of the facts underlying beliefs and opinions) that one can lump together, as ideological, both the Democratic enthusiasm for program building and the Republican enthusiasm for program cutting. Both enthusiasms impose overarching frameworks of values upon the events and decisions of public life. But this is not to say that these ideologies are the same, except from a researcher's standpoint. On the contrary, they are diametrically opposed systems of values, and moving from one to the other can be a bumpy journey, quite devastating in the shifts they entail of money and power from one group of people to another, but also quite normal in the American experience. Will Rogers pointed this out in 1934, after Franklin Roosevelt and the New Deal swept the Democrats back into office:

> Now where has that Republican Party gone? Such extermination . . . has never before been recorded. History tells us they were rather a kindly people, good to their young, and thrifty. Controlled most of the money. They had foresight and would take over the reins of government about the time things were going good. And when they saw pestilence and famine was about to be visited on the land, they'd slip it back to the Democrats. The Democrats were a kind of semi-heathen tribe, a nomad race. They could live on little because they'd never had much. But they didn't live on little when they got in office. . . . they had a certain native shrewdness. They figured out that the way to get the money away from the Republicans was to tax 'em. The theory is that while the Republicans are smart enough to make money, the Democrats are smart enough to get in office every two or three times a century and take it away from 'em. So the whole thing's just a revolving wheel. (in Dudden, 1975, pp. 406-407)

Our job, on the other hand, is not revolving but cumulative. We must, as a profession, deal with the fact that what we report in one political environment—static though it may seem at the time—will be seen later on from the viewpoint of another. It is true that when policy is made in any political environment, neither the policy nor the evidence we bring to support it is likely to be perfect. But policy and evidence don't need to be perfect. Instead, they are iterative and should be correctable, as part of a political process that requires feedback and corroboration. No one is asking us to be sublime—only serious, credible, and persistent.

The challenge for us is to understand the strengths and vulnerabilities of both politics and evaluation, and to use both to help us contribute to public policy in meaningful and enduring ways.

■ *References*

Blackstone, T., & Plowden, W. (1988). *Inside the think tank.* London: Heinemann.

Cronbach, L. J., & Associates. (1980). *Toward reform of program evaluation.* San Francisco: Jossey-Bass.

Dudden, A. P. (1975). *Pardon us, Mr. President.* Cranbury, NJ: A. S. Barnes.

Eliot, T. S. (1943). *Four quartets.* New York: Harcourt Brace Jovanovich.

Havel, V. (1995, June 22). The responsibility of intellectuals (Address at Victoria University, Wellington, New Zealand). *New York Review of Books.*

Ladd, E. C. (1972). *Ideology in America.* New York: W. W. Norton.

Moynihan, D. P. (1969). *Maximum feasible misunderstanding.* New York: Free Press.

Plan proposes less coverage for cataracts. (1995, October 8). *New York Times.*

Spain, D. M. (1960). Problems in the study of coronary arteriosclerosis in population groups. *Annals of the New York Academy of Sciences, 84,* 831.

U.S. General Accounting Office. (1988). *Weapons testing: Quality of DOD operational testing and reporting* (GAO/PEMD-88-32BR). Washington, DC: Author.

U.S. General Accounting Office. (1993). *Cataract surgery* (GAO/PEMD-93-14). Washington, DC: Author.

Visions of public service. (1986, Fall/Winter). *JFK School of Government Bulletin.*

Wildavsky, A. (1964). *The politics of the budgetary process.* Boston: Little, Brown.

PART II

Auditing and Evaluation

*T*here seems to be a good deal of consensus today, reflected in the four
chapters in Part II, that auditing (in its "performance" guise) and
evaluation have moved, and are continuing to move, closer together with
regard to understanding and to methodological approach. L. Denis Desautels, the auditor general of Canada, distinguishes clearly, in Chapter 4,
between auditing and evaluation, but notes the importance of the latter to
auditors from an accountability perspective (i.e., the measurement of results)
and discusses the different evaluation methods and techniques that Canadian
auditors are now using, not only to gather and analyze information, but also
to critique the many evaluations conducted in various government offices. In
Canada, all government departments and agencies are required "to establish
an evaluation function and to evaluate systematically the efficiency and
effectiveness of their programs and activities." Not only has Canada been a
pioneer in formalizing evaluation as a function of government, but the ability
of agencies, and of officials such as Desautels, to provide the infrastructure
for its conduct and to routinize its practice has been remarkable.

Inga-Britt Ahlenius, auditor general of Sweden, focuses in Chapter 5 on a critique of evaluation as it has occurred in Sweden. She points out the narrowness of the questions that evaluators tend to ask, and especially their silence with respect to the comparative effectiveness of programs. She notes, for example, that evaluators have often looked only at programs or parts of programs and that "the conclusion has been, for example, that funds in program A should be reviewed in order to better reach goal B within the framework program C. But the question of whether we can afford program C, or whether it is more important to use funds to reach goal B instead of another goal in another area, is not asked." Although she does not generalize about whether auditors are equally—or even more—narrow in their questions, the point she raises is an important one: Looking only at goal-attainment questions, whether it is auditors or evaluators who do so, can result in ever better performance of the wrong tasks. Also, the sense we get from Ahlenius that she believes evaluators are biased in favor of programs—a view that was widely shared in the United States by members of the Reagan administration—has some implications for the dangers implicit in advocacy (see Chapters 1, 32, and 33), even when that advocacy is merely perceived.

In Chapter 6, Christopher Pollitt and Hilkka Summa, through a fascinating set of observations—which they call "travelers' tales"—on the relation between auditing and evaluation, take us through the history of each of the professions and then settle down to a careful examination of their common functions, including choosing study topics, getting resources for the work, assembling credible study teams, using appropriate methods, and reporting findings. The observations here are focused more on academic evaluators than on developmental or accountability evaluators, which means that, when the latter are included, some of the comparisons with auditing may hold up less well. For example, the assumption is that evaluators have little statutory power, but of course that changes when evaluators are housed with auditors and have the same statutory power, as in the U.S. General Accounting Office, for example. An important conclusion of this chapter is that the methods and approaches of auditors and evaluators are coming closer to each other. Indeed, the authors state, "There are only marginal differences in the tool kits potentially available to performance auditors and evaluators."

Finally, Roger Brooks, in Chapter 7, describes the relation of auditing and evaluation as one in which the separate characteristics of each—with regard to both culture and method—are blended together as a resource pool for decision makers to use. Brooks believes this "blended approach" to the assessment of public programs has been successful because it responds to the diverse needs of legislative bodies for all kinds of information. He notes that "legislators are less concerned with the methods of professionals than with the products they can deliver," and also mentions three key factors in the success—for both auditors and evaluators—of the blended approach: professionalism, responsiveness to a wide range of questions, and flexibility in trying new approaches. What is perhaps most interesting and encouraging about the blending initiative now being pursued in Minnesota is its willingness to let both auditors and evaluators be themselves, and yet to capitalize on and benefit from the range of methods and capacities presented by both professions.

Eleanor Chelimsky

4

Evaluation as an Essential Component of "Value-for-Money"

L. Denis Desautels

Evaluation is a topic that has been of growing interest and concern to me since I was appointed auditor general of Canada a little more than 5 years ago. I have become convinced during this time that (a) evaluation offers one important way of getting at the bottom line of many government programs, and (b) the information evaluation can provide about the results of policies and programs is as essential to accountability and to informed decision making as is financial information. Having put those cards on the table, let me now make it clear that, unlike some other audit offices around the world, we in the Office of the Auditor General of Canada do not ourselves carry out program evaluations that question the rationale or

AUTHOR'S NOTE: Copyright © held by Her Majesty the Queen in Right of Canada 1996 as represented by the Auditor General of Canada.

72

continued relevance of federal government policies and programs, nor do we generally carry out evaluations of policy effectiveness.

Those who drafted the Auditor General Act in the late 1970s believed that if the Office of the Auditor General were to carry out policy evaluations, this would inevitably lead to the office's becoming embroiled in political debates. In other words, there would be a real risk that the office would be drawn into partisan issues, and that would compromise the independence and credibility that are absolutely essential to an audit office.

The Auditor General Act suggests no restrictions with respect to the audit of *economy* and *efficiency,* so that my office can, and frequently does, measure and report directly on these matters. In the case of *effectiveness,* however, the act "suggests" reporting instances where satisfactory procedures have not been established to measure and report the effectiveness of programs, where such procedures could be reasonably expected. I use the word *suggests* here because some would argue that, strictly speaking, the act does not prevent us from doing measurements on effectiveness if we feel they are necessary.

Anyway, I believe, at least, that this puts the responsibility for evaluation where it should be—with the government. It becomes our role, among other things, to see that the government's responsibility to measure and report on the effectiveness of its programs and activities is carried out. Let me now turn to the four questions that each of us on this panel has been asked to address.

■ *What Role Does Evaluation Play in the Work of the Office of the Auditor General of Canada?*

Although we do not conduct evaluations of government policies and programs, evaluation nevertheless plays a very important role in the Office of the Auditor General. In particular, in carrying out value-for-money (or VFM) audit work, it has a significant influence on what we do, as well as on how we do it.

In recent years, the emphasis throughout the public sector has shifted from processes to results. Maintaining essential systems and procedures continues to be a key responsibility of government, but the systems and procedures are not ends in themselves. They are there to ensure desired results, and have to be judged in those terms. In auditing, as well as in management, it has become clear that it is more cost-effective to put greater emphasis on results. Therefore, we now carry out results-based audits wherever possible. The change in our emphasis from process- to results-oriented auditing is important. We no longer look at evaluations just as one important element of management control. Instead, we are much more concerned with what evaluations show about the value for money being achieved by the programs we are auditing.

Obviously, taking a results-based approach means that we have to rely on evaluations, as well as on other forms of performance measurement done by departments. Unfortunately, in too many cases, we are still finding that no information—or no useful information—on results is available. One of the techniques we have used in these circumstances is to undertake a form of "evaluation synthesis" to see what evaluations of similar programs in other jurisdictions have revealed. This allows us to get a better understanding of the implications (the "so what," if you will) of the failure to evaluate.

I said earlier that evaluation also has a significant influence on how we do our audits. What I have in mind is that many of the techniques of evaluation are used in VFM auditing, especially for data gathering and analysis. For example, our audits are making increasing use of surveys, focus groups, and structured interviews for gathering information. We also rely on many of the analytic tools familiar to evaluators, including regression analysis, simulation and modeling, and content analysis of qualitative data.

■ How Do Our Auditors Obtain Information About the Effectiveness of Government Programs and Activities?

I believe I have answered much of this question in addressing the first one. In the main, our auditors obtain information on the effectiveness of government programs and activities by relying on evaluations and other reviews conducted by the departments and agencies we audit. I should add that before we can rely on these evaluations, we have to satisfy ourselves that they have indeed produced valid and reliable findings. This, in turn, means that we have to have evaluation expertise within the office. Where effectiveness information is not available from existing departmental evaluations, our first recourse is to encourage the departments to evaluate their programs and activities. However, where practical, we will also undertake the kind of evaluation syntheses I described earlier. Whether or not effectiveness information is available from the organizations we audit, we will typically gather related evidence from a variety of other sources, including, for example, consultations with experts in Canada and elsewhere, as well as review of research publications.

Finally, I should note that there are cases where we will do some evaluation ourselves. To date, this has mainly been in the area of operational, as distinct from program or policy, effectiveness. Our assessments of operational effectiveness focus on such issues as the quantity, quality, or cost of outputs produced in relation to targets, or on the immediate goals that must be met if the policy or program is to achieve its ultimate purposes.

■ *How Have We Encouraged the Development of Evaluation in the Federal Government, and What Influence Have We Had?*

This is, of course, a question that begs an evaluation in order to provide a fully satisfactory answer. I will admit that we have not undertaken this evaluation, and that my views on the nature and extent of our influence are therefore somewhat subjective. In evaluators' terms, there may be problems of attribution here. Nevertheless, I would argue that it is hardly a coincidence that in 1977, the year that the Auditor General Act went into effect, the Canadian federal government issued a policy requiring all departments and agencies to establish an evaluation function and to evaluate systematically the efficiency and effectiveness of their programs and activities. Since 1977, the Office of the Auditor General has been a persistent advocate of stronger evaluation functions in departments, of good leadership from the central agencies concerned, and, ultimately, of better evaluations. We have consistently argued the case for evaluation as a means to support management for results, better-informed resource allocation decisions, and meaningful accountability within government and to Parliament.

In 1977, we launched our first governmentwide study of program evaluation. We completed another one in 1983, and reported that the basic infrastructure for evaluation was in place across government. Our 1993 annual report included three chapters on program evaluation. Although we were able to point to several instances of good evaluation, we concluded that the performance of the evaluation function had fallen short of its potential and of the expectations set for it. Among the problems we noted were limited coverage, lack of timeliness and relevance, uneven quality, and a focus on operational issues as distinct from the tougher questions relating to outcomes or impacts.

Since those three chapters were published, a great deal has happened. A parliamentary committee, the Standing Committee on Public Accounts, considered the chapters at public hearings in June and October 1994. In November 1994, the Public Accounts Committee issued a strong report on these deliberations—with a number of recommendations directed mainly at the Treasury Board Secretariat, the central agency that is responsible for federal program evaluation policy. Among other things, the committee called for the president of the Treasury Board to issue an annual performance report on program evaluation, starting in the fall of 1995. It also called on my office to report, no later than the spring of 1996, on the extent to which the Treasury Board Secretariat had complied with the committee's recommendations and lived up to the commitments it had made in the course of the two meetings. As of the time of this writing, we are in the process of carrying out the audit work required to meet the committee's request, as well as to follow up on some of the key findings and recommendations we made in 1993. The results of this audit will be reported in May 1996.

Our focus on evaluation does not stop, however, with the governmentwide audits we have conducted and reported. We have also placed emphasis on the organization and products of evaluation functions in the course of carrying out VFM audits in specific departments and agencies. And as I have already described, our emphasis on the importance of evaluation, as well as other forms of performance measurement, is growing as we move increasingly toward results-based auditing. Auditing, by its very nature, tends to concentrate on the negative, by pointing out weaknesses. But our criticisms reflect a commitment to the inherent value and potential of having good information on results.

I want to be very clear about my intentions. My aim, as was the case with my predecessors in this office, is to continue doing what I can to support, strengthen, and promote good evaluation in the Canadian federal government. It is my aim as well to promote the use of results information for management and accountability at all levels. In 1993, we sought to make the case for evaluation, and our audit identified numerous instances that demonstrated the contribution evaluation can make. Overall, however, we were disappointed in the inability of evaluators to demonstrate the value added by their activities. I believe the case for evaluation still needs to be made, and I call on you as evaluators to find ways to make it.

■ *What Are My Views on the Future of Evaluation and the Role of Evaluation in Legislative Audit Offices?*

First of all, I certainly see the focus on results continuing and even strengthening throughout public administration in the foreseeable future, fueled in part by the difficult decisions that remain to be made in the face of continuing budgetary deficits and high levels of public debt. A related factor here is the move toward more affordable forms of government. These include greater decentralization of responsibility and authority within government, as well as a variety of new arrangements for delivering government programs—such as joint ventures, partnerships, and contracting out. The reduced central control and diffused responsibilities need to be counterbalanced by improved accountability for results.

Service quality, an increasingly important aspect of modern management in the public and private sectors, and a growing public concern as governments seek ways to reduce expenditures also create pressures for results information. There is, in general, growing public demand for accountability for the results that are being achieved with tax dollars. Although I am most familiar with the Canadian federal government scene, I see these forces at work in most of the jurisdictions with which I am familiar. The picture is consistent in depicting fertile ground for all kinds of results measurement, including evaluation. By way of example, I note the strong public commitment to results, and the measurement of results, by the present federal government. This includes putting in place a revised expenditure management system that emphasizes the use of results information for making strategic and tactical decisions and the enhanced reporting of such information to the executive and to Parliament.

Although I am encouraged by what is clearly a growing demand for results information at all levels, I am uneasy when I look at the supply side. For one thing, with all of the downsizing that has taken place in recent years, much of it in the overhead areas of government, my sense is that a lot of the analytic capability of the government has been lost. At the same time, budgets for consulting are severely limited. So we may have a situation now that is the exact opposite of what we had a few years ago, which was that of a supply-driven system with little interest on the part of would-be users of information.

At the federal level, there has been considerable change in the functions that are responsible for producing much of the results information in departments and agencies. It is not uncommon now for a variety of review functions—such as internal audit, program evaluation, and management review—to be integrated within one organizational unit. Although in some cases these units still produce outputs that can be identified as internal audits or program evaluations, in other cases the products are identifiable only as reviews.

What we are seeing in results measurement within the Canadian federal government is a growing interest in ongoing performance measurement systems and recourse to reviews that are less time-consuming, less costly, and not bound by evaluation or internal audit standards. The results available from these performance measurement systems and reviews focus more on outputs and service quality, for example, and less on the more difficult issues (such as attribution) surrounding the outcomes of programs and activities—which is where evaluation has a unique contribution to make. These developments recognize that results include more than outcomes and objective achievement, that there are a variety of tools available for measuring results, and that there are many sources of information on results. They reflect, as well, a pragmatic response to the changing government environment and the immediacy of demands for results information.

However, I am concerned that in these circumstances it is less likely than ever that departments will, of their own accord, tackle the tough questions relating to outcomes that evaluations can address, but that require the investment of considerable time and resources if credible answers are to be obtained. At the same time, I believe that these tough questions do need to be addressed, and in ways that are practical and useful. Program evaluations cannot be seen as academic or purely technical exercises. Findings have to be communicated to legislators and policy makers in clear, convincing, and nontechnical language. Evaluations also need to be selective and strategic. The question is, How can these things be done? Part of the answer lies with you, the evaluators, and part of the answer is in the commitment that the government has made to carry out centrally led evaluations, mainly in governmentwide or multidepartmental areas where there are key strategic issues. My office will certainly be looking at the government's performance in this regard in the years to come. And we will also continue to advocate and look for strong evaluations of tax policies, as well as major expenditures such as those involved in social, industrial assistance, and debt management programs.

In conclusion, let me simply say that I am encouraged by the recent developments I have just described and I am confident that we will make further advances in our quest for better accountability for results.

5

Auditing and Evaluation in Sweden

Inga-Britt Ahlenius

The German political scientist Hans Ullrich Derlien maintains that three countries followed the efforts in the field of policy evaluations in the United States earlier than other countries: Sweden, Canada, and West Germany. Derlien's picture of developments thus puts Sweden in a favorable light. Why this early interest in evaluation?

■ *The Development of Evaluation in Sweden*

The early Swedish adoption of the modern evaluation tradition should be seen as an expression of an interest in the effect of policies—an interest that has its roots further back in time. For example, counterfactual com-

AUTHOR'S NOTE: This chapter was written while the author was employed by the Swedish government and belongs in the public domain.

parisons are discussed in reports of Swedish government commissions as early as the 1930s, and government commissions of the 1950s and 1960s asked questions about the effects one measure or another actually had. There are several reasons for this process. One reason is that there was a relatively broad consensus at the time in Sweden on goals; focus was placed on the means to those goals, on the relative effectiveness of different means, and thus on empirics. There was also an institution to channel this interest, namely, the Swedish commission system. I will come back to this institution shortly. Another reason is that the interest in the effects of policies reflected belief in the government's ability to solve problems. Exactly as in the United States, therefore, the interest in evaluations reflected the wish to expand central government at that time. There was both a broad consensus on goals and, over time, a belief in the ability of government to deal successfully with the problems confronting society.

Traditionally in Sweden, policy decisions with more fundamental implications have in most cases been prepared by specially appointed ad hoc policy commissions, a tradition that goes back to the 17th century. The Swedish commission system has played a central role in the preparation of political decisions during the whole of the 20th century. It celebrated its greatest triumphs, however, in the 1960s and 1970s, with more than 300 commissions working annually. Practically every question of any significance was prepared in a commission. What is significant in this respect is the great importance attached to the collection of various kinds of factual material. The commission system is a major channel for introducing knowledge of the current state of research in various fields into the political decision-making process. Thus evaluations were used as a tool to determine the emphasis of the major reform programs in education, social welfare, housing, and so on. Evaluations were an integral part of the strategy in construction of the welfare state. The interest in evaluations grew as a result of the wish to expand central government as a means of reaching specific goals. Sector representatives and stakeholders were actively interested in evaluations and even in promoting them.

The aims and focuses of evaluations during the 1950s, 1960s, and 1970s were different from those of today. Today's problems are ones of failing growth, financial scarcity, and imbalances. Questions asked then were associated with the external perspective, which starts after public services have been produced: What were and would be the effects of the measures taken in the different programs? What means should be used? The questions of how much it cost to produce the services a program comprised and if they could have been produced in better ways were rarely or never asked. Now that we work with these matters in the Swedish National Audit Office, we consider it important to combine these two perspectives and traditions: the tradition that concerns the external perspective of central government operations (effects/external efficiency) and the tradition that concerns the internal production perspective (internal efficiency/productivity). The combination of both perspectives is important. Focusing only on the easier part of it—that is, internal efficiency/productivity—is dangerous, as it may result in ever better performance of the wrong tasks.

■ *Evaluation and the Swedish National Audit Office*

How does the Swedish model work today? The role played by the Swedish National Audit Office where evaluations are concerned necessitates a short discussion of how the Swedish central government machinery works. The Swedish administration consists of small ministries and large independent agencies that have the operational task of transforming the decisions and ambitions of the Swedish government and Parliament into reality. The government is responsible for policy formulation, and implementation lies with the agencies. Another characteristic of the Swedish system is the principle of public access to official documents and records. This is significant because this principle has the effect that almost all information concerning results is public.

The Swedish National Audit Office works in an environment in which there are a number of other organizations that produce information through evaluations. In several areas there are special sector organizations that work a great deal with evaluations. Our system, with special ad hoc policy commissions that often sit for 2 or 3 years, often means that researchers, among others, are commissioned to perform evaluations and other analyses. Many government agencies also have the responsibility to perform special evaluations within their respective sectors. The government sometimes commissions special evaluations, as does the Swedish Parliament. Evaluations have been an integral part of the reforms of the public sector. It has quite simply been a case of organizational integration.

If we look at the institutional setting for evaluations, we see a pluralistic structure with many producers. The evaluations have not remained tucked away in the desk drawers of the researchers; rather, the researchers have been part of the structure and culture. One of these evaluation institutions is the Swedish National Audit Office. This office has a special role, as opposed to all other evaluation institutions—a special and overall focus on Swedish central government finances. The selection of the areas we study and the questions we choose to ask are ultimately subordinated to this purpose: to improve central government finances. In our work on evaluations, the National Audit Office is in an extremely enviable situation when it comes to access to information. The Swedish National Audit Office is an important producer of analyses, and many of these analyses could be called evaluations. But in fact one of our main tasks is also to influence the institutional conditions for making evaluations. We try to influence agencies to perform different types of evaluations. We have an important role in the development of the overall structure and functioning of those processes, not least the budget process, in which different types of information about results can be used. We are also active in the work of developing and spreading methods and techniques. In this work we naturally ask ourselves questions that are common in all discussions on the organization of evaluations. What shall our independent agencies—those that implement policies—evaluate, and what shall be assigned to others? How shall we create a situation in which the information on results produced by evaluations is also considered relevant by different decision makers? And how shall we direct evaluation projects toward areas in which we can make significant savings?

■ *Evaluation During Fiscal Expansion Versus Contraction*

I think that there is a very relevant question to be put in this context: How can it be possible to have a large number of evaluations and yet wretched government finances? Much has been evaluated in Sweden by many different institutions over a long period of time. Sweden should thus appear to be a fairly orderly, rationalistic part of the world. Despite this, economic developments of the past two decades have led us into a situation in which we have a large and growing national debt, expenditures that amount to close to 70% of the gross domestic product, high rates of taxation, modest economic growth even during an economic upswing, and still very high levels of unemployment. How is it possible to reconcile these two sides of Sweden? The question may be all the more important to ask because there is good reason to suspect that no other country can demonstrate any particular distinct, positive connections between evaluation activities and government finances.

There are two possible answers: First, it is evident from the above that evaluations have not had the aim of reducing central government expenditure. The results of evaluations have rather been used as justification for the use of more resources. Second, evaluations have often been made of programs or parts of programs. The conclusion has been, for example, that funds in program A should be reviewed in order to better reach goal B within the framework program C. But the question of whether we can afford program C, or whether it is more important to use funds to reach goal B instead of another goal in another area, is not asked. Evaluations have thus become a means to generate new arguments for change, which often also cost more money.

There is now another side to the issue. Parliament and the government need evaluation not for new reforms but to reach decisions on reductions in public expenditure. In this situation the traditional evaluation system has hitherto not managed to make a very impressive contribution. Commissions composed of politicians have often had problems agreeing on reductions or terms of reference for evaluations. The conclusion is possibly that the consensus model is not so effective in times when reductions have to be made. In such times discussions tend to focus and get stuck on the goals rather than the means—and they even get stuck on old goals set up decades ago.

The government has then sought new ways to deal with this problem. The Expert Group on Public Finance is an effective and internationally well-known institution. It is formally a committee under the government, but in reality it is a drafting committee that, for more than a decade and without any formal restrictions, has commissioned and guaranteed the quality of a number of evaluations, many very controversial. Furthermore, a number of independent central government agencies have developed or been transformed into evaluation institutions, for example, the National School Board, the National Board of Health and Welfare, and the National Council for Crime Prevention. It is also evident that the Ministry of Finance during the past decade has been the great agent for change and evaluation, rather than the sector ministries, as the Ministry of Finance has had the difficult position of identifying and formulating economic problems. Finally, the Audit Office is an important agent of change through the delivery of evaluations and audit results.

An Example of an Evaluation From the Audit Office

How can the Audit Office evaluate policy programs? We have raised the perspective from program objectives to overall economic goals and priorities. We evaluate program goals as to their compatibility or effects on superior overriding goals. From this perspective we have, for example, evaluated the early retirement scheme. The program objectives in this field are as follows:

- People with reduced working capacity are entitled to early retirement pensions.
- The decisions are made by the central agency responsible, according to a set of prerequisites; doctors are involved and so on.
- Over time, we have evolved a very "liberal" interpretation of the law and the rules (10% of the labor force is actually under the early retirement scheme).

It is natural to evaluate this system against the overall ambition of rapid economic growth, increased labor participation, formulated in the official objective of priority, that is, the work-first principle. The early retirement scheme fulfills its own program objectives but it jeopardizes the overall objective. That was our conclusion, and we accordingly presented proposals for changes.

Conclusion

The great Roman Cicero has been quoted as stating: "Mankind consists of two kinds of people: Those who go first and do things and those who come after and criticize"—the first quotation ever on evaluation (a word of Latin origin). Cicero may have been less fortunate with his auditors, who at that time probably had nothing in common with today's well-trained, creative, and analytic young men and women that I know in the evaluation and audit functions of my office.

6

Performance Auditing
Travelers' Tales

Christopher Pollitt
Hilkka Summa

■ *Expeditions and Stories of Expeditions*

Both performance audit and evaluation can be viewed through the analogies of exploring and storytelling. Both auditors and evaluators have to attempt the exploration of unknown or only partly known territory—the specific activities of the organizations or programs they intend to investigate. Using the tools available to them, they must locate the relevant pieces of territory, convince superiors that their expeditions will be worthwhile, travel to the areas of interest, investigate them, and then bring back convincing stories of what they found.

There may be many pitfalls on the way. The territory may prove inaccessible—for example, an evaluator may be denied access to crucial information. Fierce creatures (politicians or professional groups) may attempt to frighten them off. Or they may reach their destination, only to find that their equipment is not precise enough to dig up the ore they came looking for. Or they may get drawn into swamps and delayed. Most frustrating of all, they may find that—after all the traveling and hard work—the stories they bring back are untimely or unwelcome to those who sent them, or are disputed by the native inhabitants of the explored territory.

The stories told by auditors and evaluators are special in that they are supposed to provoke change. They are meant to carry recommendations that will make things better. For example, auditors in the Swedish National Audit Office have recently been described as "change agents" with a "strategic competence" (Holmquist & Barklund-Larsson, 1995). However, because change usually threatens current practices—and therefore practitioners—every audit or evaluation may be vulnerable to stonewalling, reinterpretation, or outright rejection by some of the stakeholders involved. Both auditors and evaluators have to seek to persuade their audiences that their particular framing of "the problem" is the appropriate one, paying attention to the performative as well as the epistemological dimension of their work (Fischer & Forester, 1993, p. 5). All these hazards are commonly recognized in the published material on evaluation, but they are less frequently acknowledged in the audit literature. One of the purposes of this chapter is to bring these aspects of performance auditing out of the shade.

Thus our main aim is to seek a better interpretive understanding of the activity of performance audit by examining its similarities to and differences from evaluation. Our use of the commonplace analogies of journeying and storytelling is intended to provide an unencumbered focus on the common tasks—basic to both activities—of finding out, devising a text that sets out these findings, and persuading others to believe in it.

The main evidential basis for this chapter is the general literature on audit and evaluation, including published reports of state audit institutions (SAIs). We also refer to casework research and interviews each of us has undertaken in, respectively, the U.K. National Audit Office (NAO), the U.K. Audit Commission, and the Finnish State Audit Office (SAO). We will use examples from the work of these institutions to highlight how the different phases of an audit project differ from or are similar to those of an evaluation. The institutional roles and positions of the three SAIs referred to here differ from each other—the Finnish SAO, for example, is a part of the executive, with no direct link to the legislature, whereas the U.K. NAO reports to the Parliamentary Committee of Public Accounts. These differences obviously have implications for their respective practices and cultures as performance auditors, but in this chapter our focus will be on their similarities with and contrast to evaluators.

■ Audit and Evaluation

Many of the major points of contrast between audit and evaluation are established in a definitive article by Chelimsky (1985). We draw on that source, but also go beyond it. Chelimsky's article, in the main, contrasts evaluation with traditional financial audit, whereas we shall focus on performance audit. Chelimsky's model remains relevant, however, because much of the culture and authority of state audit institutions are still deeply influenced by their history as guardians of regularity in the use of public finance.

We will compare the activities of SAIs with external evaluations, not with internal evaluations or the self-evaluating organization. A tendency of the past decade or more has been for external evaluations to be commissioned by state executive bodies, and for many of these to have adopted a managerialist approach (Pollitt, 1993).

Chelimsky (1985) identifies significant differences in the origins of audit and evaluation. The former is older, and grew out of the practical concerns of early modern bookkeeping. Evaluation, as a labeled and self-conscious set of activities, appeared in the 1960s, mainly in the United States, as part of the postwar growth in the social sciences. Unlike audit, it was concerned with theory and explanation rather than regularity and compliance. For many of its practitioners, evaluation is still more a "science" than an administrative practice. In audit, the idea is to apply fixed criteria to a set of accounts and to report the results of this comparison to a clearly identified audience. In evaluation, both the criteria and the client to be addressed are less certain. The selection of criteria is in most cases part of the problem to be solved, and instead of a singular client a variety of audiences may demand consideration—the body(ies) paying for the evaluation, but also the professional peer group, governments, and even the wider public.

From the mid-1970s, a new school of evaluation developed that laid great stress on evaluators' need to form cooperative and interactive relationships with those being evaluated, in order to maximize the chances that their evaluations' recommendations would be accepted and implemented. The emphasis on the need to learn from and convince evaluees replaced the earlier image of evaluators as objective outsiders. The model of evaluation as interactive learning reached a peak in Guba and Lincoln's (1989) notion of "fourth-generation evaluation." Such an approach contrasts starkly with the assumptions of traditional financial audit, particularly with the view of the independent auditor who derives his or her knowledge only from the black print of formal documents.

Audit and evaluation also seem to address different questions. Audit is interested in whether what has been done conforms—a "what" question. Evaluators endeavor to understand what produces certain desired or undesired effects—a "why" question. Whereas auditors might claim to increase the transparency and accountability of public bodies, evaluators could hold out the vision of an "experimenting society" (Shadish, Cook, & Leviton, 1991, chap. 4). Also, evaluators frequently claim that one of their major contributions is the reformulation of issues, encouraging stakeholders to see problems in different ways. The implementation of specific recommendations may be less important (Greenberg & Mandell, 1991).

Both audit and evaluation may claim to contribute to increasing collective control over public programs and organizations, but whereas audit constitutes "a distinct mentality of administrative control" (Power, 1994, p. 4), evaluation offers a more positive kind of control—that achieved through a deeper understanding and application of superior methods and techniques. Audit is also inherently retrospective, concerned with the detection of errors past—whereas many evaluative techniques can be applied retrospectively, concurrently, or prospectively. One of the recent developments in evaluation involves the viewing of evaluation as part of the formulation of the activity itself (Monnier, 1992, p. 2).

In one important respect the SAIs have a major advantage over their new evaluator cousins. They possess statutory clout of a kind that evaluation organizations rarely if ever achieve. Evaluators may, for example, be denied access to an organization or to crucial documents, whereas auditors usually wield rights of access to defined categories of organizations and papers. The evaluation literature of the 1970s and 1980s is full of musings about why the results of evaluations are neglected by decision makers. For SAIs the situation is often different: There may be statutory procedures to ensure that auditors' reports are at least formally acknowledged. Of course, the result of these may be only a show of polite consideration.

What is interesting about the recent expansion of performance audit—as distinct from traditional financial audit—is that SAIs appear to want to retain their distinctive (sometimes coercive) authority, although they are now moving out into much less certain territories and using a wider range of analytic tools. However, the basis for this authority is beginning to be questioned (e.g., Power, 1994). In the remainder of this chapter we will dissect the process of performance audit step-by-step, and compare the problems faced by auditors with those that have already been documented by evaluators.

■ *Finding a Promising Destination*

This is the first step. SAIs usually do not choose topics at random, but devise programs of activity, using defined criteria of choice. One of the most common criteria is the volume of public resources involved in an activity, priority being given to high-cost programs. For example, in the United Kingdom, schools are usually the biggest item in local authority budgets, and they soon became the focus of a special study by the newly created Audit Commission (Henkel, 1991). In the SAO, economic importance is one of the four criteria that guide topic choice for performance audits (State Audit Office, 1994).

A second common criterion for choosing the territory is the risk to public funds. For example, new high-technology investments are likelier to present risks than are routine licensing operations. This is one reason the procurement of advanced military equipment and facilities is a frequent focus of SAIs (e.g., National Audit Office, 1994b, 1994c). High-tech civil R&D may also come under scrutiny (National Audit Office, 1994d).

The political salience of an activity is a third criterion, though one that SAIs are sometimes uneasy about or may even deny, yet pressure to explore territory of current political interest is known to most SAIs. For example, a U.K. NAO study of the Trident Works Programme was promoted straight to the preliminary study stage when the costs of the project began to receive hostile comment in the press and from members of Parliament, even though it had not previously been particularly salient in the NAO's strategic plan (National Audit Office, 1994c). However, the opportunity for direct political input to the choice of topic varies considerably according to the institutional position of the SAI in question. Direct input is unlikely in the case of the SAO, which is part of the executive and "far" from politicians, but is explicitly provided for through the Public Accounts Committee in the case of the NAO.

Fourth, SAIs often strive to make a "systematic coverage of the audit field over a period of years" (Comptroller and Auditor General, 1993, para. 4). For example, the NAO study *Creating and Safeguarding Jobs in Wales* (1991) emerged from a strategic planning process that envisaged a series of NAO investigations of government bodies in Wales (Roberts & Pollitt, 1994, p. 532).

Finally, there is a likelihood that investigation of a particular topic will yield useful new knowledge that could contribute to improvements or be applied to other areas of state activity. The SAO's criteria of choice include that of the potential "fruitfulness" of a topic (State Audit Office, 1994, p. 4).

Even if there are a number of fairly common and defensible criteria by which SAIs choose their topics, it would be an exaggeration to claim that such choices are usually "scientific" or even predictably formulaic. The U.K., Canadian, and Australian cases studied by Sloan (1995) demonstrate that the preferences of individuals within SAIs are frequently influential. Our own work with the NAO and the SAO reinforces this impression.

In finding promising destinations, auditors experience both advantages and disadvantages compared with evaluators. SAIs can and do develop programs of audits more or less systematically covering particular sectors or topics over a period of years. Very few evaluators can do this. Evaluations are usually more ad hoc affairs. An evaluation team is hired to analyze a topic or program that has been chosen by someone else. However, evaluators may enjoy greater freedom to define the objects and theoretical frameworks of their investigations. Whereas auditors usually must delimit their investigations to particular spending programs or organizations, evaluators may use a broader approach and direct their studies toward problems or theoretical issues rather than particular programs. Yet, in the real world, evaluators get to exercise their greater theoretical freedom only rarely (Hellstern, 1991, p. 302). Often, commissioning bodies will define both the objects and the frameworks of evaluations, constraining evaluators even more than auditors may be constrained.

Like any other activity, audits take time and cost money. SAIs have to cost their activities and demonstrate that they themselves embody the principle of value for money (VFM). The NAO has a global annual savings target and claims to save £7 for every £1 it spends (National Audit Office, 1994a, p. 2). The average cost of an NAO VFM audit is currently around £180,000. Auditors are judged by their own top managers, by their ability to complete audits on time and within budget, while pointing to substantial savings or efficiency gains wherever possible. Likewise, the SAO has a systematic annual planning procedure. The auditor general establishes "results agreements" with heads of units. The number of planned workdays is spelled out for each investigation, and the costs and results achieved are compared to targets and annually reported (State Audit Office, 1994, 1995a).

Usually the situation of evaluators is somewhat different. At the outset they need to "sell" their product to the commissioning body, and pricing the evaluation is very much part of that process (especially where, as is increasingly the case in the United Kingdom, evaluations are the subject of competitive tendering procedures). Often the commissioner will already have a maximum figure in mind, so the "package" of people and methods to be employed in the evaluation will be adjusted to that figure. Even though SAIs are usually working with fixed global budgets, they seem to possess a greater degree of freedom than most evaluators in the resourcing and dimensioning of their investigations. They are in a "portfolio" situation, where in principle they could choose to make project A bigger by scrapping or downsizing projects B and C. Evaluation units may be able to do something similar, for example, by offering projects at cost or as "loss leaders" to important new clients. However, most European evaluation units are not large enough or well enough established to be able to maneuver within a broad portfolio.

Assembling a Team With Appropriate Skills

Performance audits call for more than conventional accountancy skills. It may be necessary for auditors to cooperate with a host of specialists in order not to get lost in the new territory and to avoid accusations of having misunderstood what they have found. For example, when the U.K. Audit Commission carried out a study of the National Health Service (NHS) pathology laboratories it consulted with the Royal College of Pathologists and the Association of Medical Laboratory Officers. Also, specialists in management techniques and organizational development with experience of working in the NHS were hired for the project (Audit Commission, 1993; Longdon, 1995).

Similarly, the NAO frequently employs expert consultants for its studies, and there have been occasions when these have influenced the design and/or contents of particular investigations. The co-option of experts has two-way advantages in that it offers safeguards to the SAIs and assures the professional groups that their voices will be heard. This raises the question of whether the brought-in experts can have too much influence on audit results. During the conduct of the Audit Commission study published under the title *Towards Better Management of Secondary Education* (1986), there was a debate between members of the team with audit background and the educationalists brought in from local education authorities. The first draft of the report was written by a consultant, but later the controller of the Audit Commission himself intervened and insisted on important changes (Henkel, 1991, pp. 36-41).

Of course, evaluators also have to assemble appropriately skilled teams to tackle specialized problems. However, academic evaluators tend to be linked to the social science community, and therefore to bear assumptions about expertise particular to certain scientific methodologies. Auditors, by contrast, constitute a distinct occupational group with specific professional qualifications and widely accepted standards. Such standards carry a status that is foreign to most of the contemporary, postpositivist world of the social sciences. Management consultants, who became increasingly involved in public sector evaluations during the 1980s, are probably culturally closer to SAI staff than to academic social scientists. Nevertheless, they frequently put together multidisciplinary teams in order to bid for particular evaluations, albeit teams that tend to be weighted toward the disciplines of economics, management, accountancy, and operations research and away from sociology, social policy, and political science.

◼ Contacting the Natives

One of the most sensitive phases of the expedition takes place when the explorers come into contact with the natives of the territories to be investigated, who usually regard the explorers with a mixture of curiosity and anxiety. The natives are usually contacted early on. Often there is a period of prior negotiations, aimed at securing the acquiescence and support of the locals. This is what happened when Commonwealth departments initially resisted the proposal of the Australian National Audit Office to investigate performance-related pay in the Australian Public Service but eventually gave way to the ANAO's determination (Australian National Audit Office, 1993; Sloan, 1995).

In interviews, SAO officials have argued that direct resistance from auditees has not been part of their experience. This is no surprise, as the SAO is an example of an organization with strong statutory rights of access to any territory in its audit field, and to any documents that are necessary for the SAO's purposes (State Audit Act, Section 6, para. 7). However, the SAO staff have emphasized the importance for an auditor of establishing a good dialogue with the auditees at an early stage. They consider this necessary to secure cooperation and support. Often the auditees may even play a role in the investigation itself. An audit by the SAO of state subsidies to technology development was conducted with the help of a sample of more than 800 subsidized projects, for which the staff of the audited body did most of the data collecting and processing (State Audit Office, 1991). In a U.K. Audit Commission's investigation of medical records, a group of doctors, nurses, health care managers, and other "locals" was recruited to draft a set of principles of good practice that subsequently became a centerpiece of the final report (Audit Commission, 1995). One may see parallels here with the acquisition of native bearers by 19th century imperialist explorers.

The co-option of local experts serves several purposes. It helps the auditors to know where to look and whom to contact during the expedition. It hinders the local inhabitants from uniting in resistance, given that "some of their own" have already joined the explorers. It also reduces the probability of the auditors' making mistakes that can come from a lack of thorough acquaintance with the territory under investigation. In short, it provides both legitimacy and expertise.

Many of these issues are also faced by evaluators. It is essential for them, too, to secure the support of those to be evaluated. Evaluation designs are, like audits, frequently modified as a result of early discussions with natives. Sensible evaluators take on board experts from the territory they are about to explore—all these features are common. The biggest difference between auditors and evaluators at this phase of the expedition is their different status: Evaluators have to negotiate access, and may be refused, whereas auditors usually have the right to insist on the delivery of necessary information. Another difference has to do with the "continuity" aspect of the evaluator-evaluee relationship. An evaluator is often performing one particular evaluation, with no previous or renewed contact with the agency or program in question. SAIs, by contrast, usually have continuing relationships with major state bodies within their audit fields. They may therefore be concerned about preserving good relations for audits yet to come.

This difference, combined with the possibly weaker status of evaluators, may either help or hinder investigations. The natives may be more cautious in speaking to the auditor and may feel less inhibited with a one-off visiting academic. Alternatively, if the natives see the evaluation as unlikely to carry much clout, they may dismiss visiting academics after minimal provision of information.

■ *Seeing the Lay of the Land*

Performance audits are by definition journeys into the unknown or partly known. Unforeseen difficulties may emerge. An SAI usually builds in a preliminary investigation phase before committing to a full study. Occasionally, expeditions are actually abandoned or scaled down at this stage. This is said to be rare in the NAO, but it appears less so in the SAO. In 1993 the SAO dropped about 16% of its investigations on the basis of prestudies. The decision to abort is typically made because the preliminary results indicate a low probability of making important findings if the study is continued.

Two types of territory that tend to pose difficulties are those marked "policy" or "professional" (Henkel, 1991, pp. 34-70). An example of a political "no-go area" is the NAO audit of the Pergau Dam project in

Malaysia. This dam was financed through U.K. overseas aid funds, despite earlier information indicating that it would not be a good investment. The NAO report pointed this out (National Audit Office, 1993c, p. 11). The subsequent parliamentary hearings led to the disclosure that evidently aid for the dam had been used to persuade the Malaysian government to buy a large quantity of British military hardware (see, e.g., Hencke, 1994). Although the NAO auditors must have uncovered the "leads" to this larger network of decisions, the report stuck to the procedural question of whether the aid conformed to aid guidelines and whether the financing had been fashioned in the most economical way. The boundary for the no-go territory was signposted by the following wording in the report's conclusions: "It is not for the National Audit Office to question the merits of this policy decision" (National Audit Office, 1993c, p. 11).

Professional no-go areas are perhaps less clearly marked. Bold SAIs can and do penetrate professional territories, usually with relevant professionals co-opted onto their teams. For example, the NAO has reported on medical audit (National Audit Office, 1993d) and the Audit Commission has tackled a whole series of topics of great sensitivity to both the teaching and medical professions. On the whole, the SAO seems to have been rather more cautious than either the NAO or the Audit Commission in exploring professional territory. Their emphasis is on financial management, which keeps them away from those issues of service quality that can prove particularly sensitive for professionals. In its recent medium-term plan, the SAO (1995b) states very clearly, "The audited topic must always be approached from a financial point of view. Argumentation connected to this basic task of the SAO must be clearly explicated both in the definition of objectives and in the reporting of findings of each audit" (p. 2; translation, HS).

Despite this tighter financial focus, the SAO sometimes comes up against vigorous professional criticism. For example, SAO auditors pointed out a record of declining productivity in Finnish prisons (a falling prison population but no fall in total resources consumed), but were confronted by prison professionals who claimed that the auditors had failed to see the improvement of quality and effectiveness in prison care. The auditors then proposed that the prison administrators should include measures of effectiveness to their system of performance indicators, possibly based on rates of recidivism. The prison administrators fiercely questioned this recommendation by pointing out that recidivism rates depend principally on factors beyond their control. However, after this debate, the prison service engaged in the development of performance indicators (Summa, 1996).

One topical issue is whether the audit is to be, in audit jargon, systemic or substantive. Systemic audits, rather than focusing on the activity itself, concentrate on the control systems governing those activities. The optimal balance between the two types of investigation is a matter of controversy within the audit profession. Some argue that performance auditors should confine themselves to systemic reviews, which are said to be less vulnerable to political objections and, one may say, to the limitations of auditors' expertise. Others believe that SAIs need to keep a firm footing in particularistic, substantive studies. Others still argue that in practice the line between the two types of audit is less than clear, and that the relationship between them is complementary rather than substitutive.

Inspection of the published output of both the NAO and the Audit Commission suggests that they carry out both systemic and substantive work. In the case of the SAO, performance audits are usually substantive, but the SAO's annual financial audits include a systemic component focusing on the quality of performance information produced by the audited bodies.

In terms of our analogy, systemic audits represent a kind of aerial mapping of the main topographic features of the chosen territory, whereas substantive audits are more like hacking through the jungle on foot. The arguments against concentrating exclusively on aerial surveys suggest that this approach will tempt auditees to polish what is seen from above. According to Power (1994), systemic audits "burden the auditee with the need to invest in mechanisms of compliance" (p. 48). It has also been argued that there is an advantage "from having more respect for non-standard and tacit kinds of knowledge which are complex and close to their products" (p. 46).

Evaluators are perhaps less preoccupied with the systemic/substantive distinction. On the whole, they evaluate what they are asked to evaluate, though reserving the right to reformulate the issues somewhat as they go along. Many evaluations seem to be hybrids, examining both substantive activity and control systems (e.g., Packwood, Keen, & Buxton, 1991). On the wider question of no-go territories, evaluators are generally in a weaker position than are performance auditors. They lack statutory rights of access and must depend upon the power of the commissioning authority, plus the legislation on freedom of information—if there is any—in the country concerned. Independent academic researchers, in particular, may have little to offer ministries and agencies in return for access. They can be regarded as a waste of time or, worse, as a potential embarrassment. The willingness of public bodies voluntarily to submit to independent investigation may have diminished as time and cost pressures have increased and the "luxury" of talking to academics has been regarded as less and less justifiable (see, e.g., Pollitt, Harrison, Hunter, & Marnoch, 1990). On the other hand, evaluators commissioned by, for example, a central ministry or department to investigate a subordinate body may find themselves in a position more akin to that of an SAI auditor.

■ *The Tools for the Job*

Nowadays few explorers can rely solely on impressionistic judgments of a territory or its inhabitants. If their account is to carry authority, it must be based on the use of generally accepted tools or methods. With the advent of performance audits, SAIs have widened the range of tools that they commonly employ. For example, the NAO's reports of the past decade or so appear to be methodologically considerably more adventurous than those of the previous period. They include, *inter alia,* the use of customer satisfaction surveys for national museums and for the issuing of driving licenses (National Audit Office, 1993a, 1993b), surveys of opinion among participants in government subsidy schemes (National Audit Office, 1991, 1994d), and construction of economic models showing estimates of displacement, deadweight, and additionality for a system of regional subsidies (National Audit Office, 1991).

Most of these techniques might equally have been used by evaluators working on the same topics. There seems to be considerable overlap between the tools used by evaluators and those used, at least sometimes, by performance auditors. Nevertheless, at least four differences are apparent. First, although SAIs use interviews quite extensively, they usually do not document these in the way academic evaluators do. Interview schedules and the numbers and types of interviews are frequently unrecorded. Problems of validating interview data are not discussed. Second, SAIs appear to be more cautious than evaluators about entering into comparative analysis that goes beyond the organizations under investigation. The idea of comparing comes quickly to most social science-trained evaluators, but the NAO seldom adopts this tactic. Third, SAI reports differ from academic evaluations in that they make less reference to other work on similar topics. A typical academic evaluation is festooned with references to other studies and may well include some kind of formal literature review, conveying a sense of the evaluators adding to some cumulative and collective body of knowledge. SAI reports read more as stand-alone products.

The fourth difference is more fundamental. Audit teams usually "plan" their audits in a fairly pragmatic way. Evaluators, by contrast, "design" their projects in a more methodologically self-conscious fashion. In the latter case, tools are selected as part of a theoretically and methodologically integrated project. In the former, tool selection may well take place on primarily functional rather than theoretical criteria. These are quite dissimilar cultures.

■ *Delays and Delayers*

Some delays may be due simply to difficult terrain. Others, however, stem from recalcitrant behavior by local inhabitants. An SAI may have to sustain its expedition in the field for quite a long time, during which the natives may be more or less cooperative. They may be tardy in producing requested information or slow to arrange meetings. As the final report begins to be drafted, they may raise a host of detailed objections. Most SAIs lay considerable stress on checking their facts with auditees.

Evaluators are probably even more exposed to environmental hazards that may delay the completion of their explorations. Their terms of reference may be modified in midstudy, as the interests of the commissioner shift with current political tides. They may encounter recalcitrant natives who simply refuse to talk to them. Powerful ministers may reject the very need to evaluate their pet reforms (Robinson & Le Grand, 1994,

p. 1). The need to confirm factual information is only one entry on a long list of potential delays.

■ *What Baggage Can Be Carried Back?*

One important feature of any audit is the "clearance" arrangements through which draft reports are checked out with auditees. The precise rules and understandings around this vary among SAIs, the NAO being quite conservative. Although not obliged to do so by statute, the NAO clears each report, line by line, with the audited body. This is mainly because the NAO has received guidance from the Parliamentary Public Accounts Committee to the effect that it should submit only agreed-upon texts to Parliament. The knowledge that this process will have to be gone through at the end of the expedition causes NAO auditors to think very carefully before embarking on a line of investigation that could be deemed speculative.

Also, the SAO offers auditees an opportunity to contest the draft findings. Unlike the NAO, where disagreement seems to be excluded or fudged, SAO reports may explicitly include auditee comments in the text, so that final reports may proceed on a "thesis-antithesis-synthesis" basis. Performance auditors in the SAO are less constrained than their counterparts at the NAO in terms of freedom to write their reports. They will clear facts with auditees, but they have no need to reach consensus over the conclusions or recommendations.

It is common for auditors to be told informally about aspects of local affairs that may appear to possess explanatory potential, but that the auditors' cultural norms of objectivity and facticity will not permit them to use. This seems to be closely connected to an underlying epistemology of audit. Like auditors, evaluators may frequently find themselves the repositories of anecdotal and other information that cannot be embodied in their final reports. This will be particularly true for evaluators working with hard, quantitative designs. For those employing pluralistic or naturalistic assumptions, matters may be less constricted. Reporting fears, feelings, and perceptions is a natural part of the work for the fourth-generation evaluator, whereas this is precisely the type of information an auditor will feel obliged to exclude from a report. As a generalization, it might be said that whereas value analysis and cognitive mapping are accepted parts of pluralistic evaluation, information of this type is usually avoided by performance auditors.

■ *Is the Story Fit for Public Consumption?*

Finally, the auditors arrive back at base, having cleared their story with the auditees and ready to tell it to the wider public. However, its impact will often depend partly on the chance factor of what other stories are being told at that particular time. If the territory the auditors had set off to investigate is now fashionable, their report may gain great attention, but if the political and media spotlight has moved on to other topics, it may have little public effect. There may be sensitive decisions to make, both about the timing of the release of reports and about their "slant" or emphasis.

In 1995, shortly before the parliamentary elections in Finland, the SAO had some experience of how important timing may be in the publishing of an audit report. In February 1995, the SAO published a report on the system of rating the financial capacity of municipalities. The report suggested that the system was wasteful and led to inequitable results in the allocation of state subsidies to the municipalities. Shortly thereafter, the then minister of the interior, who was in charge of the subsidy system in question, arranged a press conference at which he accused the auditors of taking advantage of hindsight to point out issues that were already under revision, and of politicking by releasing the report close to the elections. The following month, the SAO published a report that was critical of the system of subsidies to the shipping industry, after which the then minister of transport also resorted to a press conference to attack the auditors' conclusions and defend the prevailing system. Neither in these nor in other cases have the SAO's conclusions been changed. Nor has the auditor general reacted to the accusations.

Besides problems of timing, there may also be some tension between the requirements of different audiences. General politicians and the lay public may want a diet of dramatic stories—tales of waste, corruption, and inefficiency, replete with "good guys" and "bad guys." However, the audited bodies themselves may respond best to careful, modulated presentations that make recommendations for nondramatic, incremental improvements.

In all these respects there is little difference between audit reports and evaluations. Both are at the mercy of the unpredictable movements of the political spotlight and of the attention of the mass media. Both SAIs and evaluation units need to think about how to strike a balance between, on the one hand, generating popular interest and support and, on the other, convincing and enrolling insiders.

■ *Stories of Improvement*

Audit reports are supposed to make things better. They are also supposed to be authoritative, unbiased, above mere political argument, objective, and conclusive. These are very demanding specifications, and the shift from financial audit to performance auditing has made these expectations still more difficult to meet. The traditional criteria of procedural correctness have been supplemented by more complex and slippery criteria of economy, efficiency, effectiveness, and quality. The positivist myth that there is only one true story to be told is more and more obviously unsustainable. Whereas in traditional financial auditing accounts are certified as constituting "true and fair accounts," no such epistemological claim is made on the surface of performance audits. As the British Comptroller and Auditor General has acknowledged, "There can be no such thing as an objective appraisal of whether a programme has a positive or a negative impact" (Bourn, 1992, p. 44).

The question of what criteria to use has always been central to evaluators, but it has become an issue for auditors only as performance auditing has gradually moved them beyond the solid criteria of procedural accounting correctness. Inspection of NAO, Audit Commission, and SAO reports reveals a variety of audit criteria, both explicit and implicit. Unsurprisingly, economy and efficiency are frequently mentioned, though not always operationally defined. Quality is a concept deployed in several recent NAO reports, and seems to be loosely equated with customer satisfaction, "good practice," or both (National Audit Office, 1993a, 1993b). "Good practice" is a particularly interesting criterion. It is seldom much explicated other than by reference to peer opinion (e.g., Audit Commission, 1995; National Audit Office, 1993a).

This list confirms that auditors are now operating far beyond their traditional sphere of competence as accountants. They have become interpreters of the expectations, objectives, good practice, and general principles of a range of other groups—policy makers, administrators, managers, and professionals.

The gradual move away from the underlying objectivist epistemology is also seen in the discussion on the auditors' models of feedback. As a senior Dutch auditor has pointed out, the model underlying traditional audit, and to some extent inherited by performance audit, is both mechanistic and naive (Leeuw, 1995). It apparently supposes that, once the audit team has reported, (a) the auditee will read and listen to the recommendations, (b) the auditee will take action to meet the recommendations, (c) these actions will lead to the realization of the formal goals of the audit, but (d) the same actions will not lead to any unintended or undesired side effects. In such a model, auditors can retain their distance from the auditees. Unfortunately, it has few other virtues. In the real world each assumption can be easily faulted, and the impact of performance audit thereby put in doubt.

Alternative models are, however, emerging. They generally require auditors to take a supportive role toward auditees and to negotiate and sell their recommendations, rather as do management consultants. The first steps toward such a relationship may be seen in a number of SAI practices, such as the SAO guidelines recommending that auditors enter into open dialogue with auditees (State Audit Office, 1995b, p. 3). Such an approach is favored by some SAIs because it increases the probability of their having impacts on auditee behavior. Yet it also decreases the distance between auditor and auditee and makes the auditor's storytelling more like a conversation between partners in a joint enterprise of improvement. Such a conversational form tends to work best when the parties are both closer to each other and more equal in status than SAIs have traditionally felt comfortable with vis-à-vis departments and agencies.

These issues are familiar to students of evaluation. In the United States, early experimental paradigms of evaluation gave ground, during the 1970s and 1980s, to conceptions that stressed the need to convince audiences to use evaluation findings (Palumbo, 1988). It was more and more widely recognized that having a scientific basis was not enough to ensure that a piece of knowledge would actually be applied to solve problems (Lindblom & Cohen, 1979, pp. 40-42). The result has been the development of a more diverse and differentiated range of evaluation models and theories. Within audit, change has been slower to come, but there are now signs that SAIs are becoming more conscious of the need to convince and persuade their audiences, not merely to be "right."

■ *Concluding Reflections*

In the above discussion our central focus has been on the essential character of performance auditing, viewed through a comparison with external evaluation. In this context it has been possible only to touch upon a number of related issues, such as the differences between SAIs and the varied types of performance audit.

There are many similarities and shared contingencies between performance audit and evaluation. Both auditors and evaluators study formal documentation, carry out interviews, undertake surveys, hire expert consultants, use economic concepts, undertake statistical analysis, and so on. There are only marginal differences in the tool kits potentially available to performance auditors and evaluators.

Furthermore, evaluators usually need to negotiate access, whereas auditors commonly find it prudent to do so; both seek to avoid antagonizing their auditees/evaluees, consult over the nature of their final reports, and present these reports in ways that are likely to capture the attention of and convince their audiences. Also, both auditors and evaluators may become political actors, if not directly, then in the sense of contributing to political agenda setting and in framing the problems and issues in the areas they choose as their targets.

However, there are also important differences between performance audit and evaluation. Their institutional homes offer sharp contrasts. SAIs are august bodies with a strong sense of institutional and collective solidarity. They house a coherent, well-defined professional community, buttressed by internationally accepted standards and strong statutory powers. The home institution is acutely concerned with the way in which the findings of individual expeditions will reflect on its broader standing. Henkel (1991) stresses how the Audit Commission "must present itself as a national body fulfilling a significant mandate and possessing credentials to succeed" (p. 63).

Evaluation units can seldom offer their staffs such a firmly founded— or firmly funded—base for their tale-telling. Their institutional histories are shorter, their statutory powers nonexistent, their staffs less homogeneous and more prone to rapid turnover. Unlike the SAIs, they have rivals and competitors. Of course, evaluation units do their best to promote and defend their reputations, but in a different sense from the SAIs. Evaluation units want to be known for good work, exciting ideas, original insights, clever staffs, and, of course, influence (Weiss, 1992). The last of these is usually achieved only by getting close to political leaders or top officials—a procedure that is still regarded with a degree of reserve by SAIs.

A further difference occurs in the processes of choosing routes and destinations. Auditors have real independence in this regard, whereas evaluation units are driven principally by what is demanded by those with the resources to commission studies. This constrains the territories that evaluators can penetrate, as does their limited ability to disperse the fog of official secrecy. The contrast is not absolute—a determined university evaluation team working with pure academic funding can go a long way—but it is nonetheless significant.

The differences "back at base" and in the ability to choose destinations are reflected in the tones of the reports themselves. Performance auditors tend to present their material as definitive, factual, and value-neutral. Furthermore, the emphasis of the published texts of SAIs is still mainly corrective. Helping the natives may be a secondary objective, but it is pursued only insofar as it can be reconciled with the primary purpose of public accountability.

Evaluation units lack the statutory authority of SAIs, and must distinguish their stories on a different basis. Their claim is less one of special authority than of superior methodology or expertise. Their stories should be believed because they are more carefully put together than other stories. Their answers may not be the right ones, but they are more rigorous, defensible, or creative than anyone else's. The methodology may be scientific or naturalistic, but in either case it is displayed and defended as the most appropriate one for the particular case. Their emphasis is less one of correction than of exploration—for example, probing causal and correlational relationships in scientific approaches or mapping stakeholders' perceptions, expectations, and tolerances in naturalistic approaches.

Finally, even if the methods and approaches of auditors and evaluators are coming closer to each other as performance auditing becomes more common, the significance and reception of the results of their work remains different. A story always derives its significance from the particular context in which it is told. Despite convergent tool kits, SAIs and external evaluation units tell their tales from different positions on the map of power.

■ *References*

Audit Commission. (1986). *Towards better management of secondary education.* London: Author.

Audit Commission. (1993). *Critical path: An analysis of pathology services.* London: Author.

Audit Commission. (1995). *Setting the records straight: A study of hospital medical records.* London: Author.

Australian National Audit Office. (1993). *Pay for performance.* Canberra: Author.

Bourn, J. (1992). Evaluating the performance of central government. In C. Pollitt & S. Harrison (Eds.), *Handbook of public services management* (pp. 25-46). Oxford: Blackwell Business.

Chelimsky, E. (1985). Comparing and contrasting auditing and evaluation: Some notes on their relationship. *Evaluation Review, 9,* 485-503.

Comptroller and Auditor General (U.K.). (1993). *National Audit Office Programme for 1993-94 and areas for consideration for 1994/95* (memorandum, House of Commons). London: Author.

Fischer, F., & Forester, J. (Eds.). (1993). *The argumentative turn in policy analysis and planning.* Durham, NC: Duke University Press.

Greenberg, D., & Mandell, M. (1991). Research utilization in policy making: A tale of two series (of social experiments). *Journal of Policy Analysis and Management, 10,* 633-656.

Guba, E. G., & Lincoln, Y. S. (1989). *Fourth generation evaluation.* Newbury Park, CA: Sage.

Hellstern, G.-M. (1991). Generating knowledge and refining experience: The task of evaluation. In F.-X. Kaufmann (Ed.), *The public sector: Challenge for coordination and learning* (pp. 271-307). New York: Walter De Gruyter.

Hencke, D. (1994, February 16). Thatcher's secret arms deal: Malaysia offered cheap loans. *Guardian,* p. 1.

Henkel, M. (1991). *Evaluation, government and change.* London: Jessica Kingsley.

Holmquist, J., & Barklund-Larsson, U. (1995, June). *New public management, performance auditing and how the auditors can contribute to performance improvement.* Paper presented at the Symposium on Performance Auditing and Performance Improvement in Government, Public Management Service, Organization for Economic Cooperation and Development.

Leeuw, F. (1995, June). *Performance auditing, new public management and performance improvement: Questions and challenges.* Paper presented at the Symposium on Performance Auditing and Performance Improvement in Government, Public Management Service, Organization for Economic Cooperation and Development.

Lindblom, C., & Cohen, D. (1979). *Usable knowledge: Social science and social problem-solving.* New Haven, CT: Yale University Press.

Longdon, P. (1995, June). *A case study in performance auditing: The Audit Commission (England and Wales).* Paper presented at the Symposium on Performance Auditing and Performance Improvement in Government, Public Management Service, Organization for Economic Cooperation and Development.

Monnier, E. (1992). *Evaluations de l'action des pouvoirs publics.* Paris: Economica.

National Audit Office (U.K.). (1991). *Creating and safeguarding jobs in Wales* (HC 666). London: Her Majesty's Stationery Office.

National Audit Office (U.K.). (1993a). *Department of National Heritage, National Museums and Galleries: Quality of service to the public* (HC841). London: Her Majesty's Stationery Office.

National Audit Office (U.K.). (1993b). *The Driving and Vehicle Licensing Agency: Quality of service to customers* (HC105). London: Her Majesty's Stationery Office.

National Audit Office (U.K.). (1993c). *Pergau hydro-electric project* (HC908). London: Her Majesty's Stationery Office.

National Audit Office (U.K.). (1993d). *Repeat prescribing by general medical practitioners in England* (HC897). London: Her Majesty's Stationery Office.

National Audit Office (U.K.). (1994a). *Annual report 1994.* London: Author.

National Audit Office (U.K.). (1994b). *Ministry of Defence: Defence procurement in the 1990s* (HC390). London: Her Majesty's Stationery Office.

National Audit Office (U.K.). (1994c). *Ministry of Defence: Management of the Trident Works Programme* (HC621). London: Her Majesty's Stationery Office.

National Audit Office (U.K.). (1994d). *The Renewable Energy Research, Development and Administration Programme* (HC156). London: Her Majesty's Stationery Office.

Packwood, T., Keen, J., & Buxton, M. (1991). *Hospitals in transition: The resource management experiment,* Milton Keynes, Open University Press.

Palumbo, D. (Ed.). (1988). *The politics of program evaluation.* London: Sage.

Pollitt, C. (1993). Occasional excursions: A brief history of policy evaluation in the UK. *Parliamentary Affairs, 46,* 353-362.

Pollitt, C., Harrison, S., Hunter, D. J., & Marnoch, G. (1990). No hiding place: On the discomforts of researching the contemporary policy process. *Journal of Social Policy, 19,* 169-190.

Power, M. (1994). *The audit explosion.* London: Demos.

Roberts, S., & Pollitt, C. (1994). Audit or evaluation? A National Audit Office value-for-money study. *Public Administration, 72,* 527-549.

Robinson, R., & Le Grand, J. (1994). *Evaluating the NHS reforms.* London: King's Fund Institute.

Shadish, W. R., Cook, T. D., & Leviton, L. C. (1991). *Foundations of program evaluation.* Newbury Park, CA: Sage.

Sloan, N. (1995). *Performance audit and other evaluative studies compared.* Unpublished master's thesis, Brunel University, Uxbridge.

State Audit Office (Finland). (1991). *Teollisuuden tutkimus—ja tuotekehitystoiminnan edistamen, Valitiontalouden tarkastusvirasto* [Audit report on state subsidies to industry for technology and product development] (Tarkastuskertomus nro 291/54/90). Helsinki: Author.

State Audit Office (Finland). (1994). *Valtiontalouden tarkastusviraston toimintasuunnitelma 1994* [State Audit Office plan of operations for 1994] (VTV 180/04/93). Helsinki: Author.

State Audit Office (Finland). (1995a). *Annual report: The State Audit Office of Finland.* Helsinki: Painatuskeskus Oy.

State Audit Office (Finland). (1995b). *Valtiontalouden tarkastusviraston toiminta—ja talous-suunnitelma vuosille 1996-1999* [State Audit Office plan of action and finances for 1996-1999] (VTV 260/20/95). Helsinki: Author.

Summa, H. (1996). Giving up orthodoxy in performance measurement: From effectiveness to process measures in the case of Finnish prison administration. In A. Halachmi & D. Grant (Eds.), *Performance measurement and re-engineering in criminal justice and social programs*. Perth: Western Australia Ministry of Justice.

Weiss, C. (Ed.). (1992). *Organizations for policy analysis: Helping government think*. London: Sage.

7

Evaluation and Auditing in State Legislatures

Meeting the Client's Needs

Before the 1970s, most observers considered state governments passé, and many thought state legislatures were weak and ineffectual backwaters. Most of the growth and innovation in the public sector was occurring in the federal government, and although the states collaborated in the im- plementation of many new programs, especially in health and welfare, they consistently played the role of junior partner. Within most state governments, governors dominated legislatures. Legislatures lacked any real organizational capacity, and most met only a few weeks out of the year. They were governed by hidebound rules, and they were understaffed.

But things began to change in the late 1960s. More and more legis- latures became full-time institutions, adding staff and becoming "pro- fessionalized." Legislatures began to streamline their internal operations and to develop a greater capacity to perform their constitutional and political functions. The impetus for these changes was complex, but ironically it was partly due to federal government actions, such as the creation of Medicaid and block grants, that made states active participants in new and growing programs. It was also due to a national movement, sponsored by several large foundations, to reform and reinvigorate state legislatures.

An important aspect of the transformation of state legislatures over the past 30 years has been the development of legislative auditing and evaluation functions. In 1969, the New York State Legislature created the Legislative Commission on Expenditure Review, the first state legislative research unit dedicated to overseeing the expenditure of public funds. Other states soon followed suit. The Minnesota Legislature transformed the state's internal, preaudit function (which before 1973 reported to the governor) into an external, postaudit function reporting to the legislature, enabling it to conduct more independent, arms-length audits of the executive and judicial branches. Minnesota, like other states, also added a program evaluation unit that could investigate a wide range of issues of interest to the legislature. By 1980, more than 40 states had established some kind of legislative oversight function, employing a total of more than 600 staff members (Botner, 1986; Brown, 1984, 1988; Funkhouser, 1984; Green, 1984; Jones, 1987; Wheat, 1991).

Today, according to the National Legislative Program Evaluation Society, there are 61 state auditing and evaluation units, at least 1 in each of the 50 state legislatures. Collectively, they employ almost 1,100 staff members trained in fields such as accounting, business, economics, political science, sociology, statistics, law, and journalism. Each unit is nonpartisan and organizationally independent from the entities that it audits and evaluates. Most units report to bipartisan committees of their legislatures, sometimes to standing committees, which typically select topics for evaluation and receive the completed reports. In other respects, the offices differ from one another, largely because of local circumstances and the preferences of decision makers.

One factor differentiating auditing and evaluation units within state legislatures is their organizational location within the legislature. There are three main patterns:

■ affiliation with a financial audit office

- attachment to a budget committee
- existence as a freestanding unit

Of the 61 individual state auditing and evaluation units in existence in 1995, 42% were attached to financial audit offices, 16% were attached to legislative budget or finance committees, and 43% were freestanding units. As might be expected, the organizational location has some effect on the type of work performed, the way the services of traditional auditors and evaluators are utilized, and the way staff members adapt their training to the job at hand.

Staffing is a second differentiating factor. In some states, staff members were trained as financial auditors and retrained to do performance auditing. In other states, staff were trained in the social sciences or public affairs. This single factor, for obvious reasons, determines the kind of approach taken in conducting work. But even in those places where traditional auditors predominate, increasingly there are mixes of backgrounds represented on the staff rosters. The average office (which has between 12 and 15 staff members) boasts of staff trained in a variety of fields, from accounting to sociology, mostly at the graduate level.

One telling factor that differentiates among state auditing and evaluation units is whether or not the units accept the National State Auditors Association (NSAA) peer review process. The NSAA, which offers the only widely accepted peer review process, establishes whether an office's work is conducted in a manner consistent with the standards of the U.S. Comptroller General's *Government Auditing Standards* (1994), or the "yellow book," a basic guide used by government financial auditors as well as performance auditors. Several units, such as those in Mississippi, Virginia, Minnesota, and Wisconsin, although accepting the general principles contained within the yellow book, consider the NSAA peer review inappropriate because of its emphasis on traditional audit process standards. Many other auditing and evaluation units embrace the NSAA peer review.

Despite these differences, the 61 auditing and evaluation units share many characteristics and, as we shall see, have come to adopt a more or less common perspective. Although the titles of the offices vary, each unit considers itself part of a national network of state legislative program evaluation (or performance audit) research offices.

◼ The Professions of Auditing and Evaluation

As state legislatures have gained more experience with their auditing and evaluation units, they have begun to learn more about what services auditors and evaluators can and cannot deliver. And auditors and evaluators, for their part, have learned to adapt their work to meet the requirements of their clients.

Auditing and evaluation, of course, arise from completely different traditions. Emerging from the realm of accounting in the 19th century, auditing has traditionally emphasized the process of checking or verifying records to find out whether they are consistent with agreed-upon standards. Auditors compare "what should be" with "what actually is."

The Office of the Comptroller General of the United States (1994) distinguishes between financial auditing, or checking on the accuracy of financial statements, and "performance auditing," which is defined as

> an objective and systematic examination of evidence for the purpose of providing an independent assessment of the performance of a government organization, program, activity, or function in order to provide information to improve public accountability and facilitate decision-making by parties with responsibility to oversee or initiate corrective action. (p. 14)

This definition suggests the increasingly close interface between auditing and evaluation.

Program evaluation has a shorter history as an organized activity than does auditing, and it lacks the formal organizational underpinnings that help to define accounting and auditing. The formal discipline of evaluation has developed mainly since World War II as a response to the growing complexity of social programs and the increasing need of decision makers for information on those programs. Because the need has arisen in many different contexts at the same time, evaluation has developed eclectically and has not fully coalesced as a unified profession in the way auditing has.

Evaluation may be defined as "the systematic application of social research procedures in assessing the conceptualization and design, implementation, and utility of social intervention programs" (Rossi & Freeman, 1985, p. 19). Fundamentally, this involves judging the merit or value of an activity based on a formal, agreed-upon set of procedures that are grounded in the principles of social science.

But evaluation is not just an academic exercise. It supplies information to decision makers who have responsibility for designing, funding, and implementing programs. A basic assumption of evaluation is that wise decision making requires good, reliable information about how well programs are being managed and how effectively they are accomplishing their goals.

■ *Blending Two Cultures*

Although it is still important to distinguish between the auditing approach and the evaluation approach to the assessment of government performance, there are signs that the two approaches are coming closer to each other. No state legislative auditing and evaluation unit follows either a pure auditing approach or a pure evaluation approach. Instead, a kind of amalgamated approach has emerged that draws upon the characteristics of both auditing and evaluation.

Some indicators suggest that the traditional auditing approach is becoming "liberalized" throughout the profession. For one thing, there is an increasing tendency for offices that have taken a traditional auditing approach, such as the Texas State Auditor's Office and the Nevada State Auditor's Office, to hire new staff who have training in the social sciences and public affairs. Also, the government auditing standards have been changed recently to acknowledge the validity of nonstandard audits (Comptroller General, 1994). The traditional auditing approach has simply proved too limited in its ability to respond to the needs of important clients such as state legislatures.

But the approach of evaluators, at least the use by evaluators of the standard approach and protocols of social science research, has also sometimes proven to be ill suited to the state legislative setting. Some work of evaluators has been too concerned with methodological perfection and has been insensitive to the rhythms of the legislative client and the language of policy making. Brandl (1980) observes that this is not a question of legislators' parochialism, but rather a mismatch between the logic used by evaluators and that used by politicians: "Legislators know that evaluations do not yield truth. They sense that there is some arbitrariness to all scientific work, including evaluation [whose] logical scaffolding rests on assumptions that cannot be verified; evaluations mix dispassionate analysis with political judgments that politicians can make on their own" (p. 41).

Instead of adopting either the traditional auditing approach or the social science-based evaluation approach in its pure form, many state legislative auditing and evaluation units have developed a middle course. This middle course, or what may be called the "blended approach," has the following characteristics:

- It places a high value on independence—from the client as well as from the entity under examination. Legislative auditors and evaluators have learned that their credibility rests on a kind of aloofness as well as technical prowess. This aloofness would be anathema to many evaluators working in other settings.

- It stresses painstaking research documentation retained in carefully organized "working papers" and extensive internal review procedures. These, too, add credibility and reassure those whose performance is being reviewed that professional, not political, standards apply.

- It uses multiple methodologies, including shortcuts and quick analysis techniques that provide information quickly to clients who are often pressured to make decisions under less-than-ideal conditions.

- It addresses issues of wide scope, often providing users with contextual information and broad analyses of whole programs, rather than narrow functional issues.

- It is suitable for answering almost any kind of question—normative and descriptive questions as well as those that focus on causality. Legislators typically want to know such things as, What is going on within government programs and agencies? How did the money that we appropriated get spent? Was the program implemented as we directed? Is the program being managed well? Is the program reaching its goals? What can be done to improve the program? These questions touch on matters of accountability and good management as well as program design and policy alternatives.

The first two of these characteristics derive from the auditing approach, the next two derive from the evaluation approach, and the last draws upon both approaches. As noted earlier, there are still important differences among state legislative auditing and evaluation units, and it would be misleading to imply that the blended approach describes the perspective of all. But there is a perceptible trend toward a common approach that relies on elements from both auditing and evaluation traditions.

■ *Why a New Approach Is Emerging*

From the vantage point of the state legislatures, the reasons for this evolutionary development are plain. They are rooted in the institution of the legislature itself and flow naturally from the diverse roles that legislatures play in state governmental systems.

Like any client who looks for professional assistance in solving a problem, legislators are less concerned with the methods of professionals than with the products they can deliver. As the Association of Governmental Accountants has pointed out:

> Policy makers [want] reliable facts and sound, independent professional judgment, and they care little about . . . terminology. They use terms like performance auditing and program evaluation interchangeably. Their greatest concern is that they get answers to their most pressing questions about the performance of government programs and agencies. ("AGA Task Force Report," 1993, p. 13)

State legislative auditors and evaluators have begun to adopt a blended approach to their work, stressing elements of both auditing and evaluation, because state legislatures need and want the products that derive from both auditing and evaluation. Although state legislatures existed for almost two centuries without much help from professional auditors or evaluators, today these professionals play an important role in assisting state legislatures with their most vital functions—making policy, allocating public money, and overseeing the implementation of public programs. In each of these areas, state auditors and evaluators have found ways to provide information and analyses that, over the past 25 years, legislatures have come to depend upon.

Because of local preferences and organizational location, some state units have stressed their ability to help legislatures with one of these fundamental roles more than another. But perhaps the most successful state auditing and evaluation units are those that have emphasized assisting in all three areas.

□ *Legislative Oversight*

Of the three legislative functions, state auditors and evaluators play their most significant role in legislative oversight. Mirroring the structure of the federal government, each state government is organized into three more or less coequal branches that share state powers. Within this general scheme, state legislatures have the power and responsibility to check on the actions of the other two branches. This arrangement reflects a fundamental tenet of American political philosophy—that concentrated power eventually leads to tyranny and needs to be checked.

Traditionally, state legislatures have exercised control over the executive mainly by giving and withholding money or by approving and disapproving personnel appointments. But legislators have long been dissatisfied with their ability to oversee the other branches and hold them accountable. They have been at a particular disadvantage in their ability to do fact-finding and technical analysis. Public hearings are not particularly well suited for these purposes, mainly because of the difficulty of receiving balanced and objective testimony that can be verified. Also, public hearings are subject to abuse by legislatures themselves and, unless conducted with judiciousness and discernment, can be less than credible to the parties involved.

The creation of specialized audit and evaluation staff offices has helped to address this shortcoming in most states. As a result, legislators have an alternative method of gathering information on which to base decisions; they can now dispatch auditors and evaluators to examine agency files, interview program clients, evaluate program performance, examine management's track record, and check records to see how appropriated money has been spent. According to Rosenthal (1983), this has contributed to a major shift in the balance of power between governors and legislators. Legislatures have now become the "first branch of state government," clearly the "dominant partner" in many states.

State legislative auditors and evaluators have been able to perform this role for several reasons. They possess a range of technical skills, are afforded adequate time and resources to probe, have privileged access in some areas to data on public programs (often buttressed by the power of subpoena), and enjoy a standing with legislative bodies that derives from their nonpartisanship, independence, and track records.

Staff who are trained in the traditional auditing approach are comfortable with legislative oversight assignments because a great deal of oversight involves checking to see if public officials are in compliance with laws, regulations, and legislative intent. The traditional auditing approach, with its emphasis on answering normative questions and verifying compliance with standards, is well suited to helping legislatures exercise legislative oversight.

☐ *Budget Making*

In some places, state legislative auditors and evaluators have also carved out a prominent role as legislative budget analysts. In some states, auditors and evaluators work under the direction of legislative fiscal or budget committees, sometimes for just one house of the legislature and other times for both houses. In these cases, auditors and evaluators have a direct role in influencing state budgets. In other states, the relationship between the budget process and auditors and evaluators is more informal.

Budget making is often considered the most important legislative function because it involves setting public priorities and deciding how resources will be distributed to various public programs. Budget committees of the legislature are considered more powerful than standing policy committees because most programs can function only with tangible resources.

In those states where legislative auditing/evaluation is structurally a part of the legislature's budget or fiscal committees, staff members operate near the heart of the legislative budget process. They assist by determining what happened to past appropriations and analyzing the cost-effectiveness of budget alternatives. The kinds of analyses performed in these situations are often somewhat limited, given the way budget committees operate, but the "interim" between legislative sessions offers an opportunity for longer-term studies and the use of methodologies other than straight cost-benefit analysis.

In those states where there are no formal ties between auditing and evaluation units and budget committees, the role of auditors and evaluators in budget making is less direct. But in recent years, budget committees nevertheless have tried to get auditors and evaluators to address two kinds of budget-relevant questions: Where can savings be found to help balance the budget or reduce spending? and What is the likely fiscal impact of alternative courses of state action? Interestingly, many legislative auditing and evaluation offices have justified their own future funding based on their track records in identifying cost savings from executive branch agencies.

☐ *Policy Making*

Finally, state legislative auditors and evaluators have begun to help legislatures perform their policy-making function. Although some legislators do not welcome legislative staff's becoming involved in policy questions, partly because they perceive policy making to be the exclusive domain of elected officials, many see a valid role for evaluators. Increasingly, legislative auditors and evaluators have provided background and contextual information about programs or agencies, identified and highlighted issues, and offered analyses of alternative policy decisions.

But auditors and evaluators seldom make recommendations favoring one policy alternative over another, mainly because they lack the political standing to do so. When such recommendations are made, it is common for them to be made contingent. In Minnesota, for example, legislative program evaluators studied the impacts of various factors on workers' compensation premium rates and concluded that high benefits contributed the most to making Minnesota's rates among the nation's highest. Evaluators recommended that, if the legislature wanted to lower premiums, it could do so by reducing certain benefits (Minnesota Office of the Legislative Auditor, 1988).

But there are clearly limits to the application and effectiveness of this policy role. As Brandl (1980) has pointed out, legislators know that "all truth cannot be captured by an evaluation and that truth in any event does not always carry necessary implications for policy" (p. 41). While acknowledging the key role of evaluators to confront politicians with "explicit statements of what is going on," Brandl implies that evaluators will wear out their welcome if they do not recognize that policy making is fundamentally a *political* process, not a *rational* one.

Legislative auditors and evaluators also have difficulty in playing a high-profile policy advocacy role because they are internal to a process that is dominated by their bosses. Their main stock-in-trade—their independence and credibility—enhances their effectiveness in addressing policy questions, but may itself be jeopardized if they take sides in political disputes.

Today's legislative auditors and evaluators are somewhat like baseball's "switch hitters," capable of responding to the occasion. When legislators call for an oversight study, a budget review, or a policy analysis, they can respond. Even when a study involves a variety of diverse questions—including normative, descriptive, and cause-and-effect questions—and requires the use of a complex, multimethod research design, most state legislative auditing and evaluation units can rise to the occasion.

They have also developed close working relationships with their respective legislative bodies. Individual staff work closely with individual members and committees of the legislature, at least for the duration of particular studies. This "personalization" of the auditing and evaluation process strengthens ties between researcher and client, improving the overall level of responsiveness to the client.

■ *Conclusion: Lessons for Others*

Emerson argues that there is no false logic in nature. Likewise, there is a certain inescapability in the development of auditing and evaluation within the state legislatures because it has arisen from the nature of the legislative institution itself. Where local conditions vary, so does the complexion of auditing and evaluation.

To be sure, the separate "cultures" of auditing and evaluation still exist. Particularly when comparing approaches across states, one can still observe important differences. But the gap between auditors and evaluators is narrowing, mostly because of the liberalization of traditional auditing. Key factors in the success of state legislative auditors and evaluators include the following:

- *Professionalism:* Adoption of professional standards and adherence to widely accepted protocols have lent credibility and weight to the work of auditors and evaluators operating within state legislatures, even though these environments are volatile and highly political.
- *Responsiveness:* State legislative auditors and evaluators have adapted their work to match the complex roles played by legislative institutions.

They have developed an ability to respond to a wide range of questions and to generate a variety of products.

■ *Flexibility:* State legislative auditors and evaluators have been willing to try new approaches. The two groups have learned from each other, freely borrowing techniques and perspectives from one another, and have gradually forged an approach that suits the changing needs of legislatures.

The environment of state legislative auditing and evaluation can be volatile and the stakes can be high. Fundamentally, it is a political environment. But by stressing professionalism, remaining responsive to the needs of the institutions within which they work, and remaining flexible and open to alternative ways of operating, legislative auditors and evaluators have thrived. Their work may become more important and visible as the states continue to become more significant partners in the federal system.

■ **References**

AGA Task Force report on performance auditing. (1993). *Government Accountants Journal, 42*(2).

Botner, S. B. (1986, Winter). Trends and developments in state postauditing. *State and Local Government Review,* pp. 13-19.

Brandl, J. (1980). *Policy evaluation and the work of legislatures.* San Francisco: Jossey-Bass.

Brown, J. R. (1984). Legislative program evaluation: Defining a legislative service and a profession. *Public Administration Review, 44,* 258-260.

Brown, J. R. (1988). *State evaluation in a legislative environment: Adapting evaluation to legislative needs.* San Francisco: Jossey-Bass.

Comptroller General of the United States. (1994). *Government auditing standards, 1994 revision.* Washington, DC: U.S. General Accounting Office.

Funkhouser, M. (1984). Current issues in legislative program evaluation. *Public Administration Review, 44,* 261-264.

Green, A. (1984). The role of evaluation in legislative decision making. *Public Administration Review, 44,* 265-267.

Jones, R. (1987, July). Keeping an eye on state agencies. *State Legislatures,* pp. 20-23.

Minnesota Office of the Legislative Auditor, Program Evaluation Division. (1988, February). *Workers' Compensation Program.* St. Paul: Author.

Rosenthal, A. (1983). Legislative oversight and the balance of power in state government. *State Government, 53*(3), 90-98.

Rossi, P. H., & Freeman, H. F. (1985). *Evaluation: A systematic approach* (3rd ed.). Beverly Hills, CA: Sage.

Wheat, E. M. (1991). The activist auditor: A new player in state and local politics. *Public Administration Review, 51,* 385-393.

PART III

Performance Measurement and Evaluation

---

*W*hereas auditing developed mostly as a separate enterprise from evaluation, the topic of the chapters in the present section—performance measurement—has a long history in evaluation, especially in such fields as mental health (e.g., Attkisson, Hargreaves, Horowitz, & Sorenson, 1978). Recently, the topic has been given new life in the United States by the Government Performance and Results Act of 1993 (U.S. Congress, 1993), which requires agencies to articulate goals and to report results achieved, and in the United Kingdom by similar efforts, such as the Financial Management Initiative of 1982. The task is one that brings evaluators into much closer contact with auditors, as the latter group has frequently been asked to advise on how to meet the mandates required by law. The two chapters in Part III provide some perspective on current thinking about evaluation and performance measurement in both the United States and the United Kingdom.

After a brief review of past evaluative policies that set the stage for today's interest in performance measurement, Joseph Wholey—a longtime pioneer in this sort of approach to evaluation in the United States—provides in Chapter 8 some details about the nature of the legislative mandate for performance measurement in the Government Performance and Results Act (GPRA). He notes that GPRA provides an important new source of funding for evaluators in a time when other funding is becoming more difficult to locate in many areas. He also points out that evaluators are particularly well suited to fill this need, given the skills they have in such central performance monitoring techniques as evaluability assessment, outcome monitoring, interrupted time series studies, and qualitative evaluations of the effectiveness of public programs and of the reform efforts themselves. But Wholey also points out that the activities mandated under GPRA are worth doing only to the extent that they are cost-effective—it should not cost more to do these evaluations than their fiscal, social, and political benefits merit. So he calls for evaluators not only to do the activities required by GPRA, but also to generate case studies that evaluate various responses to GPRA. We support this latter call wholeheartedly. The development of evaluation as a profession depends critically on its ability not only to present methods and strategies for doing evaluation, but also to present reasoned and empirically supported arguments about which methods and strategies ought to be chosen in which situations, and why.

In Chapter 9, Caroline Mawhood describes performance measurement in the United Kingdom. Like Wholey, she notes that a driving pressure behind performance measurement comes from the demands of budgeting when resources are getting tighter. Because this pressure is now experienced in many Western democracies, we can expect to see performance measurement initiatives proliferate in such countries. In the United Kingdom, this has led to a host of performance measurement activities, such as the Financial Management Initiative of 1982 and the Next Steps Executive Agencies, Citizen's Charter, and Competing for Quality programs. Some of these focus on improving policy making, and others on improving the operations of specific programs. Mawhood describes all of them from her perspective in the U.K. National Audit Office, providing one more example of the increasingly overlapping interests of auditors and evaluators in performance measurement. As in the United States, Mawhood believes, performance measurement is a feature of evaluation that has come to the United Kingdom to stay; it is necessary for the improvement of public sector performance and demanded by both the electorate and their elected bodies for accountability purposes. In part because she believes that there will be increased use of such measures *in the near future, Mawhood identifies the critical need in this area as being better measures for validation of performance. This latter point is crucial, and both these chapters provide us with many similar lessons about what needs to be done to improve performance measurement if it is to be as useful to public sector learning as it has the potential to be.*

Performance
Measurement
and Evaluation
123

William R. Shadish

■ *References*

Attkisson, C. C., Hargreaves, W. A., Horowitz, M. J., & Sorenson, J. E. (Eds.). (1978). *Evaluation of human service programs.* New York: Academic Press.

U.S. Congress, Senate, Committee on Governmental Affairs. (1993). *Government Performance and Results Act of 1993* (Report 103-58, 103rd Congress, 1st sess.). Washington, DC: Government Printing Office.

8

Trends in Performance Measurement

Challenges for Evaluators

Joseph S. Wholey

The current public management environment in the United States is more than challenging. Not only is there little public understanding of the purpose and value of government, but also, and correspondingly, public confidence in government is very low. Both the lack of public trust and continuing federal budget deficits constrain needed government action, inhibit economic growth, and reduce future living standards and quality of life.

Current public management reform initiatives seek to improve public management, increase program efficiency and effectiveness, and improve public confidence in government. The Government Performance and Results Act provides a legislative base for many of the most important reform efforts, asking agencies to articulate goals and to report results achieved. In this chapter I will explore the Government Performance and Results Act and related initiatives and suggest ways in which evaluators can help government managers respond to the reform initiatives and help find solutions to the problems we face in American society.

Context and Theory

Over the past 30 years, a series of public management reforms have had their time in the sun. In the 1960s, policy analysis and program evaluation began to affect policy and management decisions (see Rivlin, 1971). In the 1970s, management by objectives and zero-base budgeting each had its day (see Anthony, 1977; Malek, 1978; Pyhrr, 1973). In the 1980s and early 1990s, as "top-down" reforms became less prominent, total quality management and related "reinventing government" approaches captured the attention of managers and policy makers alike (see Gore, 1993; Osborne & Gaebler, 1992). Though many of these reform efforts have subsided, each of the earlier reforms left a residue that helped support subsequent attempts to introduce greater rationality into public sector decision making.

Since the 1960s, the use of periodic (at least annual) measurement of program performance has gained a foothold in many localities, states, and federal agencies in the United States and in many of the industrialized democracies abroad. In recent years, inspired by the growing use of performance measurement in countries such as Australia and the United Kingdom as well as in localities and states such as Sunnyvale, California, and Florida—and encouraged by the support of public interest groups such as the National Academy of Public Administration and the American Society for Public Administration—Congress enacted legislation requiring annual measurement of program performance under the Chief Financial Officers Act of 1990 (P.L. 101-576) and significantly expanded those requirements through the Government Performance and Results Act (P.L. 103-62) and the Government Management Reform Act of 1994 (P.L. 103-356).

Introduced in 1990, passed by the Senate under unanimous consent in 1992, and then reintroduced and enacted with strong administration support in 1993, the Government Performance and Results Act (GPRA) provides a broad legislative framework for many of the current reform efforts. Finding that "waste and inefficiency in federal programs undermine the confidence of the American people in the government" and that managers and policy makers are handicapped by insufficient attention to program goals and inadequate information on performance, Congress prescribed planning that would clarify agency and program goals and annual reporting on program performance. GPRA also authorized waivers of administrative controls in return for increases in program performance.

☐ *Strategic Plans*

Under GPRA, through "strategic planning," each agency is to solicit and consider the views of Congress and other affected or interested parties; develop a mission statement covering the agency's major functions and operations; establish and periodically update long-term goals and objectives, including outcome-related goals and objectives; describe how those goals and objectives are to be achieved, including the resources and activities required to meet the goals and objectives; describe how annual program performance goals will be related to the agency's long-term goals and objectives; and identify key external factors that could significantly affect the achievement of the long-term goals and objectives.

☐ *Performance Plans*

Through "performance planning," which will become part of each year's budget process, each agency and the federal government as a whole are to prepare annual performance plans that will define "performance goals" for each fiscal year (target levels of outputs and outcomes to be achieved by key agency programs), briefly describe the resources and activities required to meet those performance goals, establish performance indicators to be used in assessing relevant program outputs and outcomes, and provide a basis for comparing actual program results with the performance goals. (Performance goals may be stated in descriptive terms if the Office of Management and Budget determines that it is not feasible to express a program's performance goals in quantitative terms.) In addition, agency performance plans may include proposals to waive administrative procedural requirements in return for improved levels of program performance.

☐ *Program Performance Reports*

Through "program performance reports" after the close of each fiscal year, each agency is to report actual program results compared with the performance goals for that fiscal year, report actual program results for prior fiscal years, explain why any performance goals were not met and what action is then recommended, assess the effectiveness of any waiver of administrative requirements, and summarize the findings of program evaluations completed during that fiscal year.

☐ *Purposes*

Together, strategic planning, performance planning, and performance reporting are intended to

> improve the confidence of the American people in the capability of the federal government by systematically holding federal agencies accountable for achieving program results . . . ; improve federal program effectiveness and public accountability by promoting a new focus on results, service quality, and customer satisfaction; help federal managers improve service delivery by requiring that they plan for meeting program objectives and by providing them with information on program results and service quality; improve congressional decisionmaking by providing more objective information on achieving statutory objectives and on the relative effectiveness and efficiency of federal programs and spending; and improve internal management of the federal government. (Government Performance and Results Act, Sec. 2)

Implicit in GPRA is the assumption that all of this can be done at reasonable cost.

■ *Changes in the Use of Performance Measurement at the Federal Level*

Implementation of GPRA began with a series of pilot projects in performance planning and reporting for fiscal years 1994, 1995, and 1996. Though GPRA required only 10 performance measurement pilot projects reflecting a representative range of government functions, more than 70 such projects were implemented. These performance measurement pilot projects cover 450,000 staff and almost every major function of the federal government (Groszyk, 1995).

During the same period, the Office of Management and Budget (OMB) focused increasing attention on the use of performance information in the budget process, moving toward full-scale implementation of

GPRA well before the statutory deadlines in 1997 and beyond. A month after GPRA was signed, the Clinton administration's National Performance Review urged rapid implementation of strategic planning and performance measurement as means toward "a government that works better and costs less" (Gore, 1993). As OMB director Alice Rivlin (1995) explains:

> GPRA fit well with the Administration's approach to reinventing government. . . . Under GPRA, and much more rapidly in today's political climate, every agency must present a clear picture of its goals, the links between those goals and how it spends its money, and its performance—what it produces for the American people. . . . GPRA gives agencies the chance to tell their story in a credible way—to communicate the value of agency and program activities to OMB, to Congress, and to the public. (p. 3)

In the FY 1996 budget process, performance information influenced some of the administration's budget decisions as well as some of the proposals for legislation that would have transformed many federal grant-in-aid programs into "performance partnerships"—consolidated programs that would increase state and local flexibility in return for accountability for results (see Office of Management and Budget, 1995).

Performance measurement efforts have also expanded in federal agencies in response to National Performance Review initiatives such as the establishment of customer service standards, development of performance agreements between agency heads and the president, and use of performance agreements within agencies.

■ *Are the Changes Likely to Endure?*

Just as earlier public management reform efforts have had continuing influence, so will the current performance measurement efforts. Policy makers, executives, managers, and public interest groups will continue to support the use of performance information to improve policy and management decision making. Furthermore, the Chief Financial Officers Act, the Government Performance and Results Act, and the Government Management Reform Act are laws of the land that are likely to outlast any administration. Though Congress may enact block grant legislation that lacks the accountability and incentive provisions that would have been included in the Clinton administration's proposed performance partnerships, GPRA will provide an enduring framework for the management of federal programs. Even as Congress debated the extent to which performance planning and performance reporting requirements should be included in block grant legislation that would transform much of the system of federal grants-in-aid to states and localities, plans were being developed to set performance goals and measure performance in those programs in response to GPRA requirements.

Though there has been a good deal of performance measurement activity in federal agencies, much remains to be done to ensure that performance measurement is useful enough to justify its cost. Reflecting on early experiences in GPRA pilot projects, the National Academy of Public Administration (1994) noted fragmentation among performance-related initiatives and pointed to the need to involve House and Senate Appropriations Committees in the use of performance information, the need to involve agency leadership and program managers in strategic planning and performance measurement, and the need for training in performance measurement.

A major, and so far unaddressed, issue is the cost of performance measurement. When GPRA was before the Congress, representatives of both the Office of Management and Budget and the General Accounting Office testified that the proposed legislation could be implemented without significant additional cost. But new performance measurement efforts will in fact have significant costs, as the Congressional Budget Office noted when the legislation was before Congress: "We estimate that implementing the bill would cost at least $50 million annually in fiscal years 1996-1998, and more than that in subsequent years. The costs could be in the hundreds of millions of dollars per year if the executive branch aggressively pursues performance management" (U.S. Congress, 1993). GPRA calls for production of information on the outcomes of government programs, and outcome information often requires additional costs for surveys and other follow-up efforts.

■ *Implications for Evaluation Practice*

At a time of severely constrained resources and declining public trust, the Government Performance and Results Act and related performance initiatives offer exciting opportunities for evaluators to help improve government performance and help restore public confidence in government. In times of limited resources, all agencies will be called upon to articulate key program goals and to measure the extent to which program performance meets those goals. Current reform efforts will increase the demand for training, technical assistance, and technical support that evaluators can supply—in particular, for evaluability assessment, outcome monitoring, interrupted time series studies, and qualitative evaluations of the effectiveness of public programs and of the reform efforts themselves. These demands will present exciting political, bureaucratic, and technical challenges for evaluators.

☐ *Planning*

"Performance" is not an objective reality. Agencies must therefore achieve some level of agreement on what performance means before they attempt to measure it. Requirements to clarify agency and program goals create demands that evaluators can meet—demands for help in clarifying stakeholder expectations and priorities, demands for help in identifying possible performance indicators (especially outcome indicators) for agency programs, demands for help in assessing the feasibility and likely utility of alternative performance measurement systems, and demands for help in determining the "right" set of performance indicators and performance goals on which agencies and programs should be held accountable. Using their evaluation design skills and such techniques as process evaluation and evaluability assessment, evaluators can help meet these demands (Scheirer, 1994; Wholey; 1994).

☐ *Measuring Program Performance*

Requirements to measure and report on program performance create demands for annual or more frequent monitoring of program results in comparison with performance goals as well as for more sophisticated program evaluation studies that explore variations in program outcomes. Using their evaluation skills and such techniques as outcome monitoring, qualitative evaluation, and interrupted time series analysis, evaluators can help managers meet these demands (Affholter, 1994; Caudle, 1994; Marcantonio & Cook; 1994; Miller, 1994).

In the end, the key issue will be whether the cost of performance measurement is justified by the use of performance information—to improve management, to improve program efficiency and effectiveness, to improve budget decision making, to improve public confidence in government. As the Congressional Budget Office has noted: "Over the long term, the procedures required by GPRA could save money by leading to more effective management of government agencies" (U.S. Congress, 1993). Through case studies and cross-case syntheses, evaluators can test the theory underlying GPRA and related reforms, assessing whether and when strategic planning and performance measurement contribute to improved management, increased program efficiency and effectiveness, and improved public confidence in government. Unless performance information is used, the current wave of reform should and will subside.

To give executives and managers a sense of what it takes to do strategic planning and performance measurement, and to throw light on the extent to which strategic planning and performance measurement are useful, case studies of strategic planning and performance measurement efforts are needed (see Koskinen, 1995). The American Society for Public Administration's Government Accomplishment and Accountability Task Force has undertaken an effort to develop case studies of the use of outcome information in government (Olsen, 1995).

Case studies should focus on the extent to which strategic planning and performance measurement are actually useful. Case studies of strategic planning should explore the context for agency strategic planning efforts, summarize and present significant elements of the agency's strategic plan, trace the use and impact of strategic planning, document the agency's strategic planning process, suggest "lessons learned" from the strategic planning effort, and document the most significant political, bureaucratic, and financial costs of the strategic planning effort. Case studies of performance measurement should explore the context for efforts to develop and use performance indicators (in particular, outcome indicators), present outcome indicators and other performance indictors that are in use, trace the use and impact of performance information, describe how and why performance indicators were developed, suggest "lessons learned" from the performance measurement experience, and document the most significant political, bureaucratic, and financial costs of the development and use of performance indicators. Through case studies and cross-case "lessons learned" analyses, evaluators can help answer the big questions of public management and public administration: questions of how to break the micromanagement cycle, how to motivate people, and how to use performance measurement to improve program performance (Behn, 1995), as well as broader questions of what instruments of collective action best achieve which societal goals and how processes of societal learning can be improved (Kirlin, 1995).

Working in learning networks that include public managers, evaluators should help create forums in which managers and evaluators will be able to explore individual cases of strategic planning or performance measurement and begin to develop cross-case "lessons learned." The Office of Personnel Management, the American Society for Public Administration, and the National Academy of Public Administration will invite agency presentations that should help initiate the production of strategic planning and performance measurement case studies. Using agency products as starting points, evaluators should help complete case studies of strategic planning and performance measurement, synthesize cross-case "lessons learned," and disseminate the resulting products. Dissemination of case studies, cross-case "lessons learned" reports, and follow-up training and development efforts should help answer the big questions of public administration, help improve the performance of government, help communicate those improvements to the public and to elected leaders, and help rebuild the public trust needed for the continuation of civilized society.

■ References

Affholter, D. P. (1994). Outcome monitoring. In J. S. Wholey, H. P. Hatry, & K. E. Newcomer (Eds.), *Handbook of practical program evaluation*. San Francisco: Jossey-Bass.

Anthony, R. N. (1977, April 27). Zero-base budgeting is a fraud. *Wall Street Journal*.

Behn, R. B. (1995). The big questions of public management. *Public Administration Review, 55,* 313-324.

Caudle, S. L. (1994). Using qualitative approaches. In J. S. Wholey, H. P. Hatry, & K. E. Newcomer (Eds.), *Handbook of practical program evaluation*. San Francisco: Jossey-Bass.

Gore, A. (1993). *From red tape to results: Creating a government that works better and costs less.* New York: Plume/Penguin.

Groszyk, W. (1995, November). *Using performance measurement in government.* Paper presented at the Public Management Service Activity Meeting of the Organization for Economic Cooperation and Development, Paris.

Kirlin, J. J. (1995). *The big questions of public administration.* Manuscript submitted for publication.

Koskinen, J. A. (1995, December 21). *Strategic planning and performance measurement: Learning as we go* (memorandum to members of the President's Management Council). Washington, DC: Office of Management and Budget.

Malek, F. V. (1978). *Washington's hidden tragedy: The failure to make government work.* New York: Free Press.

Marcantonio, R. J., & Cook, T. D. (1994). Convincing quasi-experiments: The interrupted time series and regression-discontinuity designs. In J. S. Wholey, H. P. Hatry, & K. E. Newcomer (Eds.), *Handbook of practical program evaluation.* San Francisco: Jossey-Bass.

Miller, T. I. (1994). Designing and conducting surveys. In J. S. Wholey, H. P. Hatry, & K. E. Newcomer (Eds.), *Handbook of practical program evaluation.* San Francisco: Jossey-Bass.

National Academy of Public Administration. (1994, November). *Toward useful performance measurement: Lessons learned from initial pilot performance plans prepared under the Government Performance and Results Act.* Washington, DC: Author.

Office of Management and Budget. (1995). *Budget of the United States government, fiscal year 1996.* Washington, DC: Executive Office of the President.

Olsen, R. (1995, December 14). *GAA status report and action items* (memorandum to members of the Government Accomplishment and Accountability Task Force). Washington, DC: American Society for Public Administration.

Osborne, D., & Gaebler, T. (1992). *Reinventing government: How the entrepreneurial spirit is transforming the public sector.* Reading, MA: Addison-Wesley.

Pyhrr, P. (1973). *Zero-base budgeting: A practical management tool for evaluating expenses.* New York: John Wiley.

Rivlin, A. M. (1971). *Systematic thinking for social action.* Washington, DC: Brookings Institution.

Rivlin, A. M. (1995). Linking resources to results: Management and budgeting in a time of resource constraints. *Public Manager, 24*(2), 3-6.

Scheirer, M. A. (1994). Designing and using process evaluation. In J. S. Wholey, H. P. Hatry, & K. E. Newcomer (Eds.), *Handbook of practical program evaluation.* San Francisco: Jossey-Bass.

U.S. Congress, Senate, Committee on Governmental Affairs. (1993). *Government Performance and Results Act of 1993* (Report 103-58, 103rd Congress, 1st sess.). Washington, DC: Government Printing Office.

Wholey, J. S. (1994). Assessing the feasibility and likely usefulness of evaluation. In J. S. Wholey, H. P. Hatry, & K. E. Newcomer (Eds.), *Handbook of practical program evaluation.* San Francisco: Jossey-Bass.

9

Performance Measurement in the United Kingdom (1985–1995)

The economic difficulties that most Western democracies have faced in recent years, and particularly the need to keep a grip on the financing of the public sector, have meant that many nations with different administrative traditions have focused attention on the size, remit, and structure of the public sector. Frequently the reaction has been to privatize or contract out services, or to introduce some form of commercialization and decentralization where activity has remained within the public sector. The scale of change and the degree of enthusiasm for the mechanisms of the market vary from country to country, but performance measurement has been a central theme throughout.

Modern performance measurement in the U.K. central government has its origins in the early 1980s, beginning with the narrowly based departmental reviews of efficiency referred to as "Rayner scrutinies"

134

(after their creator) and the Financial Management Initiative (FMI) of 1982, which was much broader in its approach to public sector efficiency.

These were the successors to the short-lived initiatives of the 1960s, when departments experimented with "output budgeting" and Program Analysis and Review (PAR). However, unlike the experiments of the 1960s, sustained political commitment at the highest levels helped to establish the FMI as the permanent and powerful vehicle for changing the culture in Whitehall.

The FMI and subsequent management reforms have given increasing prominence to value for money (VFM), including the responsibility of managers at all levels to make the best use of resources and the need for good output and performance information both inside departments and for publication. The FMI emphasized (a) managerial control over resources, (b) the need to work within tight budgets, (c) the need for improved financial information systems, and (d) the requirement to measure departmental output and performance.

Since the 1980s, the traditional command-and-control hierarchical structure of bureaucratic government has been increasingly replaced by decentralized agencies that concentrate on serving specific client needs and are motivated by commercial disciplines. Public administration has been replaced by public sector management, and a key part of this has been a subtle shift away from established forms of policy evaluation toward the measurement of effectiveness and efficiency by setting specific output measures, performance indicators, and targets.

The increasingly commercial focus of government has been driven by the need for improved efficiency and a desire to reduce the size of the public sector. This is now reflected in the development of what has become known in the United Kingdom as "new public management":

- focusing on outputs rather than inputs
- driving by goals and not by rules and regulations
- redefining clients as customers
- decentralizing authority
- using market rather than bureaucratic mechanisms
- catalyzing public, private, and voluntary sectors
- empowering citizens
- introducing private finance

Departments, executive agencies, and other central government bodies have all embraced performance measurement to some degree. This has also been the case in many other parts of the public sector. For example, in April 1995, the Audit Commission (responsible for the audit of U.K. local government) published a major series of statistics showing the comparative performance of every local authority in England and Wales, across a wide range of dimensions and services. In the health field league, tables have been published on the performance of hospitals across a wide range of activities.

These developments have come about not least because increased competition between public sector bodies for available funds has led to funding agencies' paying more attention to indicators of value for money and effectiveness. In addition, the continued employment and pay of many top public sector managers now depend on the achievement of stated performance, which must often be validated by external agencies.

■ *Policies, Programs, and Operations*

In the United Kingdom there has never been a history of differentiation between performance measurement at policy, program, and operational levels. Early attempts at measurement were mainly financially based, with managers tending to produce and publish statistics as an end in itself. A much wider range of measures now exists, and there is more thought in their application, but there is no neat classification of differing levels of administration.

In policy terms, it is a government requirement that all cabinet papers proposing new policies should state clearly what is to be achieved, by whom, at what cost, and how the polices are to be measured and evaluated. In support of this, Her Majesty's Treasury published *Policy Evaluation: A Guide for Managers* (1988), which provides the framework for evaluating policies and programs.

In reality, the implementation of these guidelines has been patchy. It is not uncommon for new policies to be introduced as "ministerial initiatives," leaving little time for thorough appraisal of the direct effects of the policies and often with no consideration of their potential interactions with policies within other departments.

There have, however, been notable examples of detailed and rigorous evaluations. For example, the Department of Health carried out an examination of the policy of providing "Care in the Community." This is a policy for the provision of care for people with long-term needs (mental health problems, learning difficulties, and the elderly) within their local communities rather than in hospitals. The evaluation cost about £800,000 for a program expenditure of £28 million.

At other levels, the development of performance measurement in the U.K. public sector has gone hand in hand with the implementation of several major initiatives. The Next Steps Executive Agencies, the Citizen's Charter, and Competing for Quality programs all embrace performance measurement to some degree.

■ *Next Steps Executive Agencies*

Next Steps was launched in 1988 with a report from the Prime Minister's Efficiency Unit. The aim was to deliver services for the benefit of customers, taxpayers, and staff. The chief distinguishing feature of Next Steps was the creation of a large number of executive "agencies" from the operational arm of government, on the assumption that "policy" and "operational" issues could be separated and clearly distinguished. Such differentiation required performance information, so that those responsible for service delivery were able to feed back information on its implementation to policy makers.

Consequently, the creation of agencies required a fundamental reappraisal of objectives and the setting of aims, measures, and key targets within a formal planning framework. In particular, Her Majesty's Treasury's *Executive Agencies: A Guide to Setting Targets and Measuring Performance* (1992) required a range of measures covering financial performance output, quality of service, and efficiency. It also attempted to establish a linkage between operations and policy. For example, driver testing and licensing were not done just for their own sake but because they contributed to wider government objectives relating to road safety, pollution control, and crime prevention and detection.

The impact of performance measurement on the Next Steps program was considered by Sylvie Trosa (1994) in a paper for the Office of Public Service and Science. Her main findings were as follows:

■ Targets tended to be set around what agencies could measure, which may not always have been the most important areas of activity.

■ Even where agencies had a range of different targets, those that measured financial performance tended to have the highest priority.

■ There was still much to do to clarify the issues concerning quality of service and the relationship between quality and efficiency generally.

■ *The Citizen's Charter*

The Citizen's Charter, introduced in 1991, aimed to make the executive more directly accountable to consumers of public services by setting a range of targets for good service and by finding more effective and efficient ways of organizing and delivering those services.

For example, before the Charter, parents had no formal right to information about their children's progress in school or about schools' performance in public examinations. Now all parents must receive annual reports on their children, and they can compare the examination results achieved at their children's schools with those of other schools in their areas. Since June 1994 in England and Wales comparative information has been published for the first time on the performance of hospitals and ambulance services against six key indicators.

The Citizen's Charter also promised that there would be greater openness about how the business of government is conducted. Since April 1994 a new code of practice, policed by the Parliamentary Ombudsman, has required government departments to publish the facts and analysis behind major policies when they are announced and to give factual information in response to specific requests.

Under the Citizen's Charter, public services need to take more account of the needs and wishes of individual users. Some of the results so far have been as follows:

■ Most public services now conduct regular user surveys and publish the results. The best organizations do more. For example, some police services are making follow-up visits to the victims of crime to find out how they feel about the ways in which their cases were handled.

- Many services are making special efforts to take account of the views of customers with special needs, for example, people with disabilities.
- Response times for dealing with complaints are being monitored and reduced.
- Complaints adjudicators are being appointed to bring a measure of independence to decisions about individuals' grievances.

The drive for improved quality of service exemplified by the Charter has contributed to the development of performance regimes across the public sector. Monitoring performance against published standards has given feedback to managers with the responsibility for achieving program outcomes. The report *The Citizen's Charter: The Facts and Figures,* published by the Office of Public Service (1995), cites a number of examples of the program's delivering improved services to the public, including the following:

- In 1990 there were more than 200,000 patients waiting more than a year for operations. In March 1995, the figure was around 32,000.
- In 1990-1991, Royal mail delivered 85.5% of U.K. first-class letters by the next working day. The figure in 1994-1995 was 92%.
- It used to take up to 95 working days to process a passport application; now it takes a maximum of 15.

These are unaudited figures, and the relative newness of the charter scheme means that to date there has been only limited objective assessment of its real performance. However, the National Audit Office is currently investigating the performance of the U.K. Contributions Agency (which pays national insurance benefits) against the standards for customer service set out for it by the secretary of state.

■ Competing for Quality

With the pressure to raise public services to higher standards, the government has a continuing commitment to increase competition and private sector involvement. The Competing for Quality program, also launched in 1991, required departments and agencies to open many of their functions to competition from private sector or other public sector contractors. The consequent introduction of contracts and service-level agreements with defined standards of performance has required performance information.

■ *Lessons for Performance Measurement: An Audit Viewpoint*

Performance in the public domain is an elusive concept. Different bodies attach different meanings to performance, and interpretation can vary from citizen to citizen. Performance can be subject to political argument, for example, the extent to which environmental factors should be taken into account in the assessment of a highways program, or social factors in the assessment of an educational program. Other problems for performance measurement in the public sector include the following:

■ It is difficult to find satisfactory measures to assess policy—which reflects the fact that the relationships among inputs, outputs, and outcomes are not necessarily clear.

■ There is a need for a wide variety of measures, because performance in the public sector has many dimensions, none of which can be considered irrelevant.

■ The validity and interpretation of measures can be open to public debate, as different interests lay different emphases, and it cannot be assumed that all have the same requirements of performance.

In addition, the production and use of performance indicators has a cost; it takes time, effort, and resources to collect the raw data from which performance information can be produced. Also, performance measures are not neutral in their behavioral impacts. As soon as something becomes the subject of measurement, it is likely to change its form.

In the United Kingdom it is generally accepted that the three Es— economy, efficiency, and effectiveness—are the initial criteria against which performance may be judged. For many years the National Audit Office (NAO) has conducted "value-for-money" investigations in central government, and performance measurement has been a regular theme. For example, in 1986 it published a review of the FMI and in 1989 reported on the initial stages of the Next Steps program.

In 1991, the NAO study *Creating and Safeguarding Jobs in Wales* examined the extent to which the Welsh Office and associated bodies had attempted to assess the effectiveness of its job creation programs and initiatives. The report concludes:

> The bodies have been slow to make forecasts for and assess the achievements of the initiatives by measuring and verifying actual jobs achieved and by undertaking more regular and commonly devised evaluation studies. The bodies, therefore, are not able to compare on a consistent basis, and against their own criteria, their forecasts of jobs to be created or safeguarded with what is actually achieved either in gross or net terms. Moreover, they are not in a position to measure the net benefits in relation to the costs to public funds in order to determine whether those funds are being used in the most cost-effective way. (pp. 4-5)

Most recently, the NAO (1995) published a report on the Meteorological Office, with an evaluation of its performance regime. The report explores the target-setting process and shows how targets are set with little attention to past performance. The NAO found that three key corporate targets the Meteorological Office reported as being met were in fact missed—and that the office regularly reported results on bases different from its targets. For example, in 1993–1994 the Meteorological Office's achievement against its overall target for customer satisfaction, forecast accuracy, and timeliness proved to be 74%, lower than the 82% reported at the time and below the target of 80%.

There has also been a tendency for measures to be focused on efficiency rather than effectiveness, and for these to concentrate on "hard" rather than "soft" measures. Indeed, performance indicators have been criticized generally for being based on too limited a definition of performance, preoccupied with a narrow concept of efficiency and value for money, with insufficient concern for the quality or impact of public services. Yet commercial companies use surveys of consumer wants and consumer satisfaction to inform their investment decisions, so there is scope for improvement in this area.

Given the complexities of performance indicators and performance regimes, therefore, it is essential to be clear about their value.

■ *Accountability and Control or Management and Improvement?*

Performance measurement is an important part of accountability, but it can also inform management decisions. This may involve the need for two different types of measures: one for external consumption, such as an organization's performance against a published target or standard, and another for internal use, concentrating directly on the parameters under the control of individual managers.

Professors John Stewart and Kieron Walsh (1995) argue that the purpose of performance assessment is to gain an understanding of how successful performance has been and how it can be improved. Performance indicators are a means to that end. Full assessment of performance is not simply a matter of devising ever more subtle performance indicators, but a matter of judgment that can be informed by indicators, but cannot be determined by them. Indicators are therefore likely to be more useful where (a) they are seen as being relevant, but not decisive; (b) the need for a set of indicators is recognized; (c) tension between indicators is seen as desirable, reflecting the complexities of public sector delivery and where the political context is recognized; and (d) problems of technical measurement, including weightings to be applied to indicators, are recognized.

■ *Future Developments*

The consensus among commentators is that performance measurement is now an integral feature of U.K. government and is likely to remain so. Target setting and the reporting of achievements against target is now an established part of accountability, as evidenced by the Office of Public Service's annual reporting of executive agencies' performance.

Performance information is vital to public sector managers in responding to the challenge of new public management; using performance information can lead to changes in resource allocation and impacts upon decision making that should lead to overall improvements in effectiveness.

A key development in the United Kingdom will be the introduction of resource budgeting at the end of the century. This will move parliamentary funding from a cash to an accruals basis, which will radically alter the accounting for public expenditure and the financial procedures of the House of Commons. It will offer Parliament more useful information from the executive and improvements in the way it sanctions departmental expenditure. It will also provide an explicit link between the analysis of input costs and departmental objectives and outputs. Specifically, it will produce a more systematic analysis of the costs incurred by departments in pursuit of each of their main aims and objectives and the outputs from each departmental program, and performance against objective.

It is also intended to have a separate schedule of specific performance measures included in each resource budget. Performance against these measures will therefore be considered as part of the annual expenditure cycle and will be exposed directly to parliamentary scrutiny. In such circumstances there is the separate issue of validation—it is one thing to produce a range of measures, but another to ensure that they are worthwhile and robust, accurate, and complete. The government proposals on resource accounting and budgeting do not require a performance audit. The National Audit Office, however, believes that it should prepare for the possibility that this may be needed in the future and has therefore begun a two-year study into performance validation, with the aim of providing guidance to its VFM auditors.

■ *Summary*

Performance measurement in the United Kingdom has developed markedly over the past 10-15 years. Although it is not the practice in the United Kingdom to discriminate formally among policies, programs, and operations, several broad conclusions can be reached:

- At a policy level, performance measurement has been part of a move away from public administration toward public sector management.
- At a program level, performance measures have been an integral part of the Next Steps, Citizen's Charter, and Market Testing initiatives, and these have included a wide range of operational performance information.

The value of such measures has improved as people have come to appreciate the importance of defining their purpose and recognizing the need to use them to link inputs, outputs, and impacts.

Nevertheless, there is still scope for further development, and by incorporating performance measurement into key new initiatives such as resource accounting, the government has shown its continuing wish for performance information. However, this will be of real value only if there is a proper means of validating the information produced.

■ *References*

Her Majesty's Treasury. (1988). *Policy evaluation: A guide for managers.* London: Author.

Her Majesty's Treasury. (1992). *Executive agencies: A guide to setting targets and measuring performance.* London: Author.

National Audit Office (U.K.). (1991). *Creating and safeguarding jobs in Wales.* London: Her Majesty's Stationery Office.

National Audit Office (U.K.). (1995). *The Meteorological Office Executive Agency: Evaluating performance.* London: Her Majesty's Stationery Office.

Office of Public Service. (1995). *The Citizen's Charter: The facts and figures.* London: Her Majesty's Stationery Office.

Stewart, J., & Walsh, K. (1995). *Studies in public service management.* London: CIPFA.

Trosa, S. (1994). *Next Steps: Moving on.* London: Her Majesty's Stationery Office.

PART IV

International Evaluation

![black rectangle]

O ne of the most important developments in evaluation in recent years has been its rapid expansion into a wide array of international arenas. In venues as diverse as the World Bank and the United Nations, as well as in many developing nations, the methods and ideas of evaluation are rapidly spreading. In part, of course, these new venues have the advantage of benefiting from the accumulated wisdom of evaluators in nations with three decades of evaluation experience, saving considerable reinventing of the wheel. But perhaps more important, the evaluation issues in many of these new international venues are not always the same as those encountered in the past, so that much inventing of new wheels is required as well. The chapters in Part IV provide a wide array of apt illustrations. Whereas some of these chapters describe the evaluation efforts of single nations (e.g., Chapter 11 on China and Chapter 12 on Denmark), others address topics that span many national boundaries, and approach being global in scope. Examples include the role of evaluation in developing countries and the evaluation of gender issues in the lending practices of multinational institutions.

In Chapter 10, Masafumi Nagao shows how evaluation of community development in the small Japanese town of Oguni is confronted with global issues that necessarily influence the way the evaluation must be conducted. Some of the influences he documents include increased geographic scope that crosses township, region, and even international boundaries, and a more rapid time schedule for the evaluation, as decision makers are more quickly affected by developments elsewhere. Nagao also shows how differing value perspectives become increasingly salient as evaluations cross international boundaries where, for example, traditions of pluralistic versus central decision making differ even within the general group of Western democracies. These value differences need much more exploration, and Nagao's thoughtful examples are a very useful start. Nagao also speculates about the interplay of freer international communication via routes such as the Internet with the increased production of evaluative information. The combination of these influences will have unknown effects on the participation of citizens in the social and political development of their countries, but the influences will undoubtedly be profound. Nagao sees them as increasing the likelihood of democratization of governments throughout the world.

In Chapter 11, Hong Houqi and Ray Rist describe the development of evaluation in the People's Republic of China. They point out that the driving force for evaluation in China is the massive and sustained surge in national development and economic growth. Most of China's evaluation studies are a combination of performance measurement, cost-benefit assessments, implementation monitoring, and technical and engineering studies; few systematic impact studies of large-scale national projects have been done. Organizationally, most evaluation is coordinated by central state agencies, but both Chinese banks and multilateral agencies such as the World Bank are also prime forces in the trend toward doing more evaluation. All these agencies currently place a good deal of emphasis on development of the infrastructure for evaluation—the trained personnel, technical guides and manuals, and studies of how other countries organize their evaluation systems. In the case of the last of these, it is probably worth noting that such studies should examine not only the current status of the systems, but how those systems have changed over time. In the United States, for example, a simple snapshot of current U.S. evaluation would not convey the historical importance of some offices that now no longer exist (e.g., the Office of Technology Assessment) or a sense of the reasons evaluation dollars and infrastructure tend to expand or contract over time within a given country.

A very different view from a very different national perspective is provided in Chapter 12 by Finn Hansson, who discusses the development of evaluation in Denmark. As is the case in China (Chapter 11), Sweden (Chapter 19), and the United Kingdom (Chapter 9), the development of evaluation in the past decade in Denmark was also prompted in significant part by economic pressures posed by proportionally smaller budgets available to meet proportionally larger demands. Hansson asserts that most Danish evaluations fall into one of four categories: survey-based evaluations of the effects and efficiency of programs and projects; the development of theory in evaluations, especially in the fields of education and research evaluations; evaluations based on action research; and internal evaluations. He intertwines all this with discussion of philosophies and methodologies common in these four categories. Interestingly, one can discern in Hansson's chapter the beginnings of a Danish version of the quantitative/qualitative debates that have generated so much heat and light in U.S. evaluation. Perhaps the lessons already learned about this matter in U.S. evaluation— especially the lesson that evaluation needs both kinds of methods (see, e.g., Cook, Chapter 2, and Datta, Chapter 24, this volume)—can help provide some guideposts and warn of booby traps and pitfalls ahead as evaluators in Denmark and other countries debate this issue.

In Chapter 13, Eduardo Wiesner, former minister of finance for Colombia, outlines the role he sees for evaluation as part of the reform agenda of developing countries. These reform efforts have three main thrusts: privatization drives, fiscal and political decentralization, and new spending priorities that emphasize social and equity issues. All three of these thrusts aim to foster competition in hopes of improving overall outcome. Implementing these reforms requires the adept and efficient use of public and private institutions, in concert with the economic marketplace. But these efforts can succeed only if accurate information is available about which programs and policies are working. Providing that information is the role evaluation should play. But Wiesner is not optimistic that performance measurement techniques such as those outlined in Part III of this book will be useful in developing countries, partly because his experience is that they are too easily manipulated by those skilled at capturing benefits from the government, and partly because he is skeptical of their validity (the latter point is, of course, acknowledged by both Wholey and Mawhood, even in developed countries). He prefers to see evaluators focus on three key tasks: sorting out those who are complying with regulations only on a nominal basis from those whose *compliance reflects actual performance success; assessing institutional, program, and project success in outcomes; and conducting strategically targeted evaluation in some of the most critical reform areas where information is needed most quickly. This is an ambitious agenda, and, as Wiesner notes, a key obstacle to its successful implementation is the paucity of trained evaluation capacity to do the tasks required.*

Robert Picciotto, director general of operations evaluation at the World Bank, provides in Chapter 14 a detailed overview of how evaluations are conducted at the World Bank. The World Bank is a large, international source of funding for loans to developing countries. Within the World Bank, the Operations Evaluation Department (OED) is charged with evaluating World Bank activities, distilling lessons of development experience, and overseeing self-evaluation processes (see Murphy, Chapter 17, for an example of the latter). The OED carries out this task using many methods, including ratings of program performance at the end of loan disbursement, performance audits of program performance, and impact evaluation of the long-term results of a program. The results of such evaluations are summarized in many ways, including an annual review of all completed evaluations. Picciotto describes how the evaluation function at the World Bank has evolved over the years in response to very rapidly changing political and economic conditions. From its initial focus on efficacy (the achievement of project goals) and efficiency (the effectiveness of resource use), World Bank evaluators now give increasing attention to relevance (the degree to which project goals reflect country assistance priorities). Picciotto points out that World Bank evaluators now pay particular attention to the Bank's areas of special emphasis—poverty reduction, the environment, private enterprise development, and human capital formation—as they seek to assess economic, social, technological, cultural, environmental, and institutional impacts of individual interventions against the backdrop of country policies and a rapidly changing global economy. Finally, the development of sustainable capacities in developing countries to evaluate programs is a high priority for World Bank funding.

William R. Shadish

10

Evaluating Global Issues in a Community Setting

Masafumi Nagao

This chapter focuses on how, today, global issues find their way into community life, how this is changing the perspectives and behaviors of ordinary people, and how all this poses challenges to evaluation and evaluators.

The underlying phenomenon, to be referred to here as *globalization of the local community,* has been observed for quite some time as rela-

AUTHOR'S NOTE: The original version of this chapter was delivered at a plenary session of Evaluation '95, an international evaluation conference jointly organized by the Canadian Evaluation Society and the American Evaluation Association (November 1-5, 1995, Vancouver). I want to express my gratitude to Michael Q. Patton (Utilization-Focused Information and Training) and Akira Iriyama (the Sasakawa Peace Foundation) for their encouragement to make the plenary speech and for commenting on a draft of the speech. This chapter could not have been written without the cooperation of Mayor Nobutoshi Miyazaki and the staff of Oguni Town, Kumamoto Prefecture, Japan, who provided me not only with the relevant materials, including some photos of the town, but also the inspiration to consider the subject of this chapter.

tively self-contained and often formalistic activities in the form of international sister-city relations, multinational associations of local governments, and the like. Its impact has been limited mostly to the participating parties. More recently, however, the dynamic nature of interactions among cities across national boundaries has begun to receive attention among the academically concerned, most notably Kanter (1995), as well as by more action-minded experts of urban planning, such as Perlman (1993) and her Mega-Cities Group. This chapter shows that globalization is having a much greater impact, reaching even smaller communities at the level of towns and villages, and examines evaluation issues in such a community setting. Before going into the discussion, however, it will perhaps be useful to glimpse an actual community undergoing globalization. A good example is provided by the Japanese town of Oguni.

■ *A Small Town Named Oguni*

Oguni is a remote mountain community located in the Western part of Japan (see Photo 10.1). Its isolated setting is signified by its name, which means literally "Little Country." Oguni has a long history, dating back many centuries, and a noted forestry tradition that started in the middle of the 18th century. Roughly four-fifths of its area comprises mountainous woodlands, of which three-fourths is covered with planted cedar, the result of an active reforestation program undertaken since the turn of the century. The area is also known for its hot springs, which attract many tourists. The principal economic activity, however, has been logging and farming—mainly production of rice, horticulture, and animal husbandry. As such, Oguni is like any other rural community in Japan.

The township of Oguni was incorporated in 1935 with the merging of six local districts. The town's economy grew with the development of its timber resources against the background of postwar reconstruction and increased housing and construction demand all over Japan. In 1960, its population reached a peak of 16,000 people, but since then it has experienced a gradual decline, to the level of around 10,000 today. Like most other rural communities in Japan, Oguni became a reservoir of industrial labor to fill the needs of rapidly growing manufacturing industries in more urban locations. The outflow of youth leaving for factory employment caused a rapid aging of the community. Many of the old people today live

Photo 10.1. Oguni Township, Kumamoto Prefecture, Japan

alone or just with their spouses, quite a drastic change from the community tradition of large family systems with 6, 7, or even 10 people to a household. This drastic alteration of age structure, combined with the decline in the size of the population, also led to considerable weakening of the area's economic base.

In 1970, Oguni was officially designated a "depopulated area" by the central government, entitling the township to special subsidies and other favorable treatment provided by the law enacted to support such areas. Oguni's farming also enjoyed various support schemes of the government, including aid for rice and cattle production. However, all these support measures were not sufficient to reverse the declining trend in the local economy, which was hurt further by the sharp downturn in forestry industry production since around 1980 as it lost competitiveness to timber imported from Southeast Asia.

From such a sketch of the town, no one would, or could, have imagined the changes and new developments that have taken place in

Oguni during the past 10 years.[1] The turning point was the announcement made in 1984 by the National Railway of its decision to abolish the Miyanohara Line, which served the area. This sent a shock wave throughout the town, as the railway line represented the physical as well as psychological link between the town and the rest of the world. In 1985, on the occasion of its 50th anniversary, Oguni decided to embark on a new community-building project called the Yuki Village Development Scheme (*yuki* means "serene woodlands"). The project aimed at building a "prosperous and lively" community, taking maximum advantage of the local resources, including historical, cultural, geographic, and other assets unique to the area.

The township authorities took the initiative in constructing a series of public buildings with unique designs produced with the collaboration of independent architects. These included a bus terminal built on the spot where the railway station had stood; a dome-shaped gymnasium with a wooden frame for holding concerts, theatrical presentations, and athletic events (see Photo 10.2); a seminar house used for youth training as well as educational, cultural, and recreational activities and all kinds of town meetings (see Photo 10.3); a play-and-study house for children; and an art museum with a permanent exhibit featuring the works of a famous Oguni-born painter (see Photo 10.4). The designs for these buildings not only maximized the use of local cedar but also embodied a unified theme to shape a scenery of serene woodlands. Moreover, in order to implement the designs for the large-scale wooden structures, the architect team invented a new technique using timber from thinning, which won wide acclaim in architectural design circles.

These publicly organized developments induced private sector initiatives for construction with corresponding design innovations and for utilization of locally produced materials. The local farm association used local cedar to build a pyramid-shaped restaurant where top-quality beef, ham, sausages, and natural cheese manufactured in the town are served, and fruit preserves and other processed food items are sold. A group of young local businessmen constructed a commercial center consisting of a chain of wooden houses (see Photo 10.5). A private gas station renovated its shop after the image of the wooden dome (see Photo 10.6). A local liquor store owner redid the store's interior, inspired by the town's wooden structures. And even the branch office of the regional bank modified the design of its front in harmony with the town's scenery.

Photo 10.2. Oguni's New Multiuse Gymnasium

Photo 10.3. Oguni's Seminar House

As part of Oguni's development scheme, numerous projects and events were organized for social, cultural, educational, and even recreational purposes. Since 1989, Oguni has organized an annual classical music festival featuring baroque music played with original wind instruments, attracting musicians from Europe. The first concert was held in the amphitheater of the town's cattle market. The women volunteers organized a day-long forum to talk about the problems women face living in rural areas, out of which sprung many women's groups and initiatives for improving women's status in the town's community life (see Photo 10.7). Many theatrical and music groups have been invited to give performances at the dome, including some from abroad, such as the Calgary Stampede. For the past several years, the town has been sending its youth for overseas observation missions in Switzerland and the United States, to learn about the development of mountain communities there, and return visits from citizens of these countries are also encouraged to create opportunities for the local people to experience international exchanges. During the past

Photo 10.4. Oguni's Art Museum

few years, Oguni has organized a series of international seminars on
community planning, with the participation of visiting researchers from
abroad (see Photo 10.8).

The Yuki Village Development Scheme was conceived and put into
implementation with the strong and tenacious leadership of Oguni's
mayor, who is in his third four-year term. The fact that he was not opposed
in the last two elections is perhaps an indication of the popular support he
commands for his policy initiatives. He is said to have particularly strong
backing from the younger generations and from women, who variously
contribute to the implementation of the town's development scheme.

Global Issues as Observed in Oguni

It is perhaps clear even from this brief and rather sketchy introduction that
Oguni is a very innovative and dynamic community, particularly for its

Photo 10.5. Oguni's Commercial Center

size. Because of these qualities, the town also provides fertile ground for tracing global issues and concerns and their reflections on the working of the microcosm. In this section I will analyze Oguni's globalization from three different viewpoints: global changes that affect life in small communities like Oguni, community concerns facing Oguni that are shared by many communities around the world, and global perspectives being developed by Oguni as part of its community development effort.

□ *Global Changes Affecting Life in Small Communities*

Despite its remote location, Oguni is not free from the global economic movement toward an increasingly borderless world, as represented by the opening of national economies to international markets. Even before the onset of the Uruguay Round, the local cattle industry faced liberalization of beef imports. Now under the new regime of the World Trade Organization, local agricultural production may lose out because

Photo 10.6. A Renovated Gas Station

of high production costs, as the many-layered protection now accorded it will have to be gradually removed. Even today, full-time farmers account for less than 15% of Oguni's farming population of 1,000. Successors to farming will be hard to find, given such a poor prospect. What exists of manufacturing industry in Oguni, being of the labor-intensive type and far from high-technology based, will also face increasing competition from imports originating in East and Southeast Asian economies with lower average wages. In sum, rural communities such as Oguni will increasingly be affected by the ongoing integration of the national economy into the global economic movement and might cease to be viable economic entities.

Although it is still true that global changes, and global economic issues in particular, belong to the domain of capital-based diplomats and bureaucrats for negotiating appropriate international arrangements, the growing international interdependence is transforming even remote communities into relevant actors, whether they figure as active ones, like Oguni, or more passive ones, like most Japanese communities. Although

Photo 10.7. Meeting of an Oguni Women's Group

individually they may be without much power, collectively they could yield considerable influence. The communities' reactions might even affect the direction and pace of global negotiations. The government can no longer ignore the social costs involved in the adjustments it makes to global economic changes. Needless to say, the reference to remote communities here is not restricted to Japan. There is a great need for governments to understand the impacts of global change on such communities and their reactions to it everywhere.

☐ *Concerns Shared by Many Communities Around the World*

In the drastic socioeconomic transformation that Japan experienced during the high economic growth of the postwar decades, the progression of urbanization and increased dependence of the rural periphery on income transfers from urban centers, through both public and private

Photo 10.8. An International Seminar on Community Planning Held in Oguni

channels, was accepted by people as inevitable. The urban centers represented the frontiers of the country's advance in every way—social, cultural, economic, and political, including international contacts. As such,
they cast a magnetic pull on ideas, money, and talent. The young and the
ambitious were naturally attracted to urban centers. The rural areas, on
the other hand, represented the old, the traditional, and the less advanced.
The elders could not and did not keep their youth from leaving the
communities. Rural communities such as Oguni now face a crisis of
identity and of intergenerational succession. This is a concern shared by
many communities around the world, especially in the developing countries that are experiencing rapid rural-to-urban migration. In their case,
the problem may be even more acute, because such migration leads to
excessive population concentration on the receiving end of the cities,
causing massive poverty and degradation of the environment.

The experiences being accumulated by the people of Oguni as they
pursue their community-building efforts may be of much significance to

other communities facing similar problems of rural-urban imbalance and a crisis of intergenerational succession. As Oguni townspeople are eager to learn from other communities, they are also quite open to sharing their experience, information, and ideas with others. Every year, more than 100,000 people visit Oguni's seminar house to be briefed on the Yuki Village Development Scheme. This number includes more than 100 from abroad. These numbers are each significant in their own right. No other community of Oguni's size and location in Japan attracts 100,000 visitors from within Japan, nor 100 visitors from abroad, for inquiries about township-building schemes. To the extent that the problems faced by Oguni constitute global concerns, there is a significant scope for international learning at the level of the community.

☐   *A Global Perspective for Community Initiatives*

A third category of global issues observed in Oguni is an outgrowth of its own initiative, and it has to do with the development of a global orientation in the community-building effort itself. Oguni's global outlook found concrete expression in the plan to shape the town as a "recycling town," with reduced wastes and recycled materials. Adoption of this plan showed the community's appreciation of the globally shared concern for protection of the environment and preservation of resources and demonstrated its intent to contribute an approach that, if pursued collectively, would have significant impact.

Another example is the annually held classical music festival mentioned above. One may find some difficulty in linking baroque music played on original instruments, a genuinely Western tradition, with a remote mountainous community in the Far East with no Western classical music tradition. The link was actually made by a Japanese classical music instrumentalist who came upon Oguni while seeking a "truly serene" environment that would approximate the conditions for music making in baroque times. Although Oguni township was doubtful at the beginning about the festival's continuation, it is now convinced, after several successful years, that a new community tradition has taken root and that the community is contributing its small share to the preservation of global cultural traditions.

Oguni township has also been cooperating with an international research project on the problems faced by remote mountainous communities carried out by a team of Japanese, American, and Swiss researchers. Oguni has been selected as one of two communities for case studies, and the town administration is providing data and logistical support as well as financial support for local costs. This research partnership developed out of the town's participation in an overseas youth training project conducted by the researchers' universities. The town recently added an international exchange with a Swiss community to this spectrum of international cooperation activities.

What these examples from Oguni's case signify is the emergence of local communities as actors on the international scene. Conducting international relations is no longer the exclusive domain of governments and multinational enterprises. Today, nongovernmental organizations (private, usually nonprofit, organizations with citizen involvement), township administrations, local associations, and even individuals participate in all sorts of international exchanges and joint undertakings. While governments and big enterprises still operate in the context of international interdependence among states, agents from local communities have already begun to experiment with the theme of international interactions. They may not be as adept with symbols and concepts as the symbol analysts and new knowledge creators championed by Drucker (1989) and Reich (1991), but they are joining the new "transnational" communities of people. The greatly improved transport and telecommunication access among localities and regions is favoring their emergence on the international scene. As a result, not only have local communities today acquired a more global perspective, they have also begun to globalize their activities. And this has given rise to a tremendous increase in issue-based international networking activities, mutual learning exchanges, and joint project experiments of all kinds. The Oguni phenomenon is a mere reflection of this new global trend.

■ Challenges Posed for Evaluation

What, then, does the foregoing discussion of global issues and concerns in the community setting mean for evaluation practice? First and foremost, it probably means that evaluation conducted in community settings or any other localized contexts will have to have increasingly wider spatial or geographic scope, going beyond the national boundaries. Growing international interdependence, increased sharing of common concerns on an interregional basis, and globalization of local actions all combine to make this inevitable. Although it may not require any alteration of evaluation methods to be employed, the broadening of the spatial context for a particular evaluation exercise may pose new difficulties for evaluators. Take, for example, the evaluation of an international leadership training project for Japanese rural youth in which the Oguni township participates. This project is set up to put 10 trainees through a 1-week domestic workshop and a 12-day overseas training course, followed by a 3-day reflection seminar at the site of the domestic workshop after 6 months. A thorough evaluation of this project would involve considerable logistic and technical complications, including the translation of relevant data and information needed for evaluation.

Such complications may be even greater in the case, for example, of an international collaboration project between two communities from different countries. The task of setting up an evaluation framework may call for much preparatory work, because undertaking such a project, even when it starts with completely agreed-upon objectives and implementation methods as well as shared expectations of outcome, normally requires adjustments and modifications along the way. Evaluators may even find halfway through such a project that the conceptual framework they had agreed upon at the start of the project has actually meant different things to different people. To begin to address such complications, be they logistical, technical, semantic, or conceptual, the key consideration should be information availability. To assure information availability in the right quantity and quality and at the right time, given a wider geographic scope, evaluators will have to resort to some kind of information sharing as an evaluation strategy.

A second way in which the effects of global changes on community life may affect evaluation relates to the time dimension of its practice. As local communities are internationalized, they also become more susceptible to changes in the surrounding context. Because the pace of change in the latter is quickening, the time horizon for decision making with respect to individual local actions tends to become shorter. Under such circumstances, the importance of prospective evaluation should increase relative to retrospective evaluation, and undertaking experimental projects should increase in order to defuse political risks. In the extreme case, evaluation will have to become a continual function of the project-implementing agent.

In the case of Oguni, the town administration makes frequent use of local meetings and informal seminars with outside experts for monitoring and assessing projects being carried out. This is a way to cope with the multiplicity of projects and the loose manner in which the overall objective of the community-building effort has been defined. It also represents the community's answer to the absence of a project evaluation tradition in Japan. As mentioned earlier, Oguni is itself investing in a study being conducted by an international team of researchers to obtain "objective views and outsiders' insights." But the townspeople's questions and the researchers' do not necessarily coincide. In the meantime, the challenge still remains for evaluators to conceive an effective evaluation scheme for an innovative development program of global scope, such as the one developed by Oguni.

Finally, there is a third challenge posed by cross-cultural evaluation that also involves the question of value premises for evaluation exercises. Oguni's mechanism for elaborating the Yuki Village Development Scheme provides a useful illustration of this question. Oguni's planning is done at two levels, the township level and the district level. Township-level planning is done in the elected town council, whereas district-level planning is carried out by a special planning team established in each of the six districts. Selection of members for this team was based on local tradition—the "elders" of each district decided how many and who should be included on the team. To the extent that the district planning scheme has aimed at breaking with the district's past, giving control of the planning exercise to the elders was somewhat of a contradiction. Besides, it was not consistent with the democratic procedures followed at the township level. To a Western evaluator with the value premise of democratic rule, this may be a less-than-desirable situation, or at least a problematic situation for a fair evaluation. However, in Oguni, people do not question the validity of the combined planning mechanism; in fact, most observers of Oguni's development effort laud this dual approach as a practical one.

Perhaps at the community level, this is not a problem; or, at most, it is a problem of manageable proportions. But a similar approach followed at the national level could mean a diplomatic crisis. In U.S.-Japanese trade negotiations, both governments are in total accord regarding the need to maintain the free trade system and keep the national economies open to outside involvement, but at the level of individual industries, each side has its own real-life situation to reckon with. On the Japanese side, most of the major industries have evolved, in the process of catching up with their Western counterparts, various institutional arrangements that are still instrumental in running the industries domestically but that may act as nontariff barriers to trade internationally. Such is the case of the very cohesive ancillary production structure for auto parts developed over many years into a system called *keiretsu* in Japan, which is perceived by Americans as an obstacle to the import of U.S.-made auto parts. There is a very uneasy parallel between this situation and the dual approach of Oguni's planning mechanism.

At the root of these considerations obviously lies the important problem of value premises for evaluation. In any local evaluation context, there are problems of differing and competing values and information needs for different stakeholders. Globalization of local communities certainly adds to this complication. The importance of cross-cultural factors for the comprehension of the nature of global competitions and conflicts has been highlighted by recent debates surrounding the ideas of Huntington (1993) and Fukuyama (1995). Growing interactions among diverse actors throughout the world are causing friction and conflicts among different cultures and value systems. There appears to be no escape from it even in a community setting in which all the relevant actors come within punching distance of each other.

Here is an illustration. The international research program mentioned earlier in reference to Oguni also included a study on a second Japanese town with similarly dynamic features. In that study, the Swiss team found that the long list of innovative projects the town had carried out for "greater autonomy" had been made possible by a special fiscal facility of the central government that allowed the town to float public bonds to be redeemed later by subsidy grants from the central government. According to the Swiss idea of autonomy in a local community (or commune), accumulation of debts, accompanied by continued, if not increased, dependence on higher authorities, cannot lead to greater autonomy. For the people of that town, however, the central government facility had been there for more than three decades for all disadvantaged, depopulated communities to utilize, and as such constituted an integral part of "initial conditions" for any community-building effort, for greater autonomy or otherwise. Least of all did they think that being autonomous immediately or even soon should be a necessary condition for achieving greater autonomy over the longer term. In order for all the parties concerned to arrive at the realization that for the same terms, *autonomy* and *autonomous*, different perceptions were at work, it took many long discussions, preceded, of course, by lengthy explanatory sessions on the complicated fiscal scheme. This illustration highlights the important role that user-conscious evaluators could play in a cross-cultural setting. The question, or the challenge, is whether evaluation can serve as an instrument of cross-cultural communication. It points to the importance of the capacity of evaluators to handle the difficult task of measuring and comparing the impact of different cultures and value systems on the project in question.

A closely related question concerns the capacity of the evaluator to communicate the outcome of the analysis and its implications to the parties affected by the project. The delicate and difficult nature of cross-cultural communication, especially for transmitting messages that are negative or critical to the ears of the stakeholders, remains, no matter how well trained or well prepared the evaluator may be, because the question ultimately would also hinge on the particular interpersonal relations involved. Added to this is the intriguing question of which language is to be used in the communication process. Because language and culture go hand in hand, in some cases the use of foreign language may be advantageous for transmission of messages without cultural overtones. This, however, may be the case only where evaluation practice is not yet firmly established. In the longer run, internationalization or international transfer of evaluation practice should cast a wider net over all these issues.

■ *Internationalization of Evaluation Practice*

The challenge to evaluation in this increasingly borderless world is, indeed, quite formidable. In order to project how evaluation practice and evaluators should cope with this challenge, it is necessary to consider the increasing importance of international information brokering.

That decision making in any localized setting should require both relevant information and sound understanding of the global context bearing on the decision would suggest increased importance of information trading across national and community boundaries. In this connection, the communication facility afforded by the Internet has been receiving much attention. The problems of limited accessibility and language constraints aside, the spread of computer-aided communication should greatly facilitate information flow. However, the quantitative expansion of information flow may be a necessary but not sufficient condition for sound decision making. For information that is critical to a decision, a credibility test is needed. And it is here that evaluators may be called upon to play a role. Information trading needs to be upgraded to information brokering through evaluation practice. As a prerequisite of that, evaluation practice itself needs to be internationalized in a credible way.

One important issue to be addressed is how to ascertain communicability of evaluation. In Japan, project evaluation is still in its early stages of acceptance. The principal reason for this is that the state has assumed for a long time a near monopoly control over organized public interest activities, to the exclusion of private nonprofits, or the so-called Third Sector.[2] This control is so extensive and institutionalized that the need for project evaluation does not arise. Taxpaying citizens, of course, ask how their money is spent, so there is an independent system for financial audit on government projects and projects carried out with government money, but not for substantive evaluation. Only now, with the emergence of the Third Sector, is there a need felt for exposure to evaluation practice and its subsequent buildup. But before project evaluation as an occupation can be addressed, basic learning schemes and curricula have to be developed and reading materials prepared. And there is talk among the Japanese foundations about forming a study group on project evaluation.

The global wave of democratization should be encouraging people in developing countries to cast a critical eye on development projects carried out by their governments and international donors. Here they must have benefited from project evaluation carried out by foreign experts. In the circle of aid-giving agencies, there is even joint evaluation attempted. The Canadian International Development Agency and the Japan International Cooperation Agency have been carrying out a joint evaluation exercise on aid projects in developing countries for the purpose of learning from each other's aid objectives and implementation methods. It is not clear how the recipient countries figure in this exercise. However, given all the challenging circumstances raised by growing international interactions today, it is probably more than ever true that practice of sound project evaluation should require a sound local project evaluator first. Only then can we begin to talk about the communicability of evaluation across national borders and cultural frontiers.

A second major hurdle for the internationalization of evaluation practice from the viewpoint of communicability of evaluation is the task of establishing a credibility-building mechanism. As amply demonstrated by the example of Oguni, there is an increasing need for international sharing of information and learning on a wide range of global issues and concerns that affect community life. Already international networking arrangements have been instituted for research, action, advocacy, and information exchange on a multitude of issues, such as human rights, environment, development, AIDS, drugs, and refugee relief. Evaluators should examine what kind of role they have actually been playing in respect to the various concerns of communities and networking groups. In particular, they should ask if their work has served the international information-brokering function with the element of credibility testing. In places like North America, where there is a long-standing tradition of project evaluation, there should be an understandable emphasis in the profession on the specific user focus. What I am suggesting here is the possibility that in places with no or only limited local evaluation traditions, public sharing of the results of evaluation may contribute to the cultivation of evaluation practice among the users as well as potential practitioners of evaluation.

Finally, internationalization of evaluation practice should not be regarded simply as the spreading of a tool, a method, or a practice. It should also mean the transfer of a value-creating process, because project evaluation practice, if accepted and pursued with discipline, will promote diversity of views in the society. In this age of continuous and dynamic interactions, projects and programs come and go, but not their effects and impacts. They show up with different time spans and in many different, and not always predictable, ways. In this sense, whatever object is chosen for evaluation never really ends—or it may end in a totally confused state for the stakeholders. Project evaluation attempts to sort out all the factors, catch the essence of moving forces, approximate the gap between the reality and a desired state, and suggest promising steps to take to fill that gap. This is a rather bold enterprise. It should be encouraged so that society may benefit from the many and different ways of viewing social phenomena and appreciate the diversity within as a value to be cherished.

The practical beneficiary of the international transfer of evaluation practice will be the emerging Third Sector in societies undergoing democratization. To go back to Oguni for a moment, many initiatives have been taken by voluntary groups and associations in the town to promote the Yuki Village Development Scheme. Among them, women's groups now count 31. However, Oguni's 16-member town council, which is the formal decision-making body, as yet includes no female council members. The various activities organized by Oguni women are beginning to have impacts on the town, but not yet of the kind that can either legitimate their groups in the eyes of the community or elect the first Oguni councilwoman. Democracy is still on its way, or may be farther down the road, in male-dominated Oguni. In the meantime, project evaluation conducted on the women's groups' activities, problems, and aspirations may establish them in a new light. Even without the town's sanction, such an evaluation would give a tremendous moral boost to the women themselves. As such, promotion of evaluation would acquire a certain capacity to inspire and even energize the stakeholders concerned. The result, then, could be a kind of evaluation aimed at creating inspirational values.

When all is said and done, internationalization of evaluation practice should start with concrete actions by evaluators themselves. There is much scope for international collaboration and cooperation among evaluators. To discuss such possibilities and challenges is, indeed, the very purpose of an international evaluation conference.

■ *Notes*

1. The remainder of this section relies on the information provided by the Oguni township authorities in Japanese. Oguni's mayor, Mr. Nobutoshi Miyazaki, gave a brief account of the town's recent experience in a paper (written in English) titled "Autonomy for a Little Country, Oguni," which was presented at a colloquium, Exploring Best Practices in Public Policy for the Sustainable Development of Remote Depopulated Mountainous Areas, held at the University of Oregon, Eugene, on April 2-4, 1992.

2. *Third Sector* refers to the residual segment of the society after the government (First Sector) and the enterprises (Second Sector). It does not have the standing of a sector relative to the other two, so it is private and nonprofit in character but does not yet form a private, nonprofit sector per se.

■ References

Drucker, P. (1989). *The new realities.* New York: Harper & Row.

Fukuyama, F. (1995). *Trust: The social virtues and the creation of prosperity.* New York: Free Press.

Huntington, S. (1993). The clash of civilizations? *Foreign Affairs, 72,* 22-49.

Kanter, R. M. (1995). *World class: Thriving locally in the global economy.* New York: Simon & Schuster.

Perlman, J. (Ed.). (1993). *Selected readings on innovation transfer and replication.* Document prepared for the Seventh Mega-Cities Coordinators' Meeting, Jakarta, Indonesia.

Reich, R. (1991). *The work of nations: Preparing ourselves for 21st-century capitalism.* New York: Alfred A. Knopf.

11

The Development of Evaluation in the People's Republic of China

Evaluation is relatively new in the People's Republic of China (PRC)—
indeed, before the early 1980s, it was unknown there. This unfamiliarity
with evaluation reflected the orientation of the social sciences at that time,
the virtual absence of any evaluation literature published in Chinese, and
the lack of systematic contacts by Chinese with those practicing evaluation in other parts of the world. Some activities under way, however,
within the PRC did come to resemble evaluation, including some policy
analysis, economic and management studies, survey research, project
completion reviews, and what was broadly termed *experience summari-
zation.* But these were not called *evaluation,* nor were they systematic or
focused on the issues now encompassed in our understanding of evaluation.

In the 1950s, the PRC established policy and economic research institutes in national and ministerial, provincial, and county governments. Over the past 40 years, these institutes have undertaken a wide variety of studies using an array of methods. Early work was largely economic, but the later work has branched out into studies of financial systems, social affairs, environmental protection, and sustainable development, to name four.

Although there are few formal studies of use of material from these institutes in national planning, a general consensus is that the institutes have been helpful. The policy community is aware of their work and sees them increasingly as sources of pertinent data and analysis. The material is largely anecdotal, but some important findings from the institutes directly affect government decision making, especially after the economic reforms and openings to the world in 1978. As the reform movement in the PRC has grown over the past nearly 20 years, a number of studies in agriculture, fiscal and tax policy, financial policy, foreign trade, and enterprise management have contributed significantly to the formulation of reform policies.

As the impetus for development grew from the 1950s to now, the PRC built methodological experience in how to study development projects and programs. It focused on the technology, engineering, and cost-effectiveness of development initiatives—and most initiatives were infrastructure and construction projects, such as dams, highways, bridges, power plants, highways, telecommunications, irrigation, heavy industry, and railroads. Studies of these projects examined quality control, financial accountability, and compliance with development objectives.

As the 1978 reforms took hold, more capital and development assistance came into the PRC. As researchers built contacts elsewhere, comprehensive and regular evaluations were more often undertaken. The past 15 years have seen a growing capability in and understanding of technological and engineering analysis, financial systems analysis, economic analyses and modeling, social impact analysis, environmental impact analysis, sustainability analysis, and implementation studies. Building skill and experience in these areas for the PRC has been undertaken via a two-way flow of information and expertise—many persons from China have gone elsewhere to study these techniques, and many consultants and experienced researchers in these areas have traveled to China.

■ The Present Situation

The driving force for evaluation in China is the massive and sustained surge in national development and economic growth. The attention and capability of the country to address evaluation questions comes from this concern with development. Although most evaluation is ex-post project and program assessment, there is recognition that evaluation issues are also embedded in all stages of the development project cycle. For this reason, there is a growing awareness within China that the evaluation function is applicable at all stages of the project cycle. There is now interest in linking evaluation to project and program formulation, implementation, and accountability, though explicitly doing so is still infrequent.

The major national agency in China for project and program evaluation is the State Planning Commission (SPC), which issues evaluation directives, establishes policies and guidelines for evaluation, and plans what projects or programs need to be evaluated and when. The major executing agency for the SPC is the China International Engineering Consulting Company (CIECC). The CIECC, located in Beijing, undertakes many large, nationally funded evaluation projects for the SPC. The CIECC focuses its efforts on large national projects rather than provincial or local projects. The CIECC is systematically studying the policies and methods of evaluation, training staff from multiple ministries and agencies, and publishing in Chinese manuals and handbooks on evaluation practice.

By 1995, the CIECC had completed evaluations of 33 national government projects, with another 6 project evaluations under way. These studies are generally a combination of performance measurement, cost-benefit assessments, implementation monitoring, and technical and engineering analysis. The CIECC to date has done few systematic ex-post or impact studies of large-scale national projects.

A smaller sector influencing the development of evaluation in China is banking. Many banks in China also evaluate projects they themselves have financed. The People's Construction Bank of China (PCBC), for example, has evaluated more than 70 projects within its portfolio. In the banks, evaluations largely assess financial benefits, management performance, and compliance with terms of loans. There is little in the way of evaluation of outcomes or impacts, studies of stakeholder satisfaction, and performance monitoring. The banks evaluate against criteria they have as lending institutions, and not against criteria relevant to other sectors. They set their own evaluation policies largely independently of the SPC.

The third key set of actors in evaluation within the PRC is made up of the bilateral and multilateral development organizations, most notably the World Bank, the Asian Development Bank, and the United Kingdom Overseas Development Administration. These three organizations in particular have demonstrated sustained support for the development of an evaluation capability within China. With their support, China has undertaken the following activities to strengthen its evaluation infrastructure:

- It has conducted studies of how other countries in both the developed and developing world have established their national evaluation systems.
- It has drafted evaluation guidelines, manuals, and handbooks.
- It has sent senior Chinese officials on trips to both developing and developed countries to study their evaluation systems.
- It has provided training in evaluation to several hundred officials, professionals, and researchers.
- It has organized a ministry-level seminar on evaluation.

Many of these activities have been carried out within the past 2 to 4 years, and there have already been notable results. First, the CIECC and the State Development Bank have set up internal units to focus exclusively on ex-post evaluation. Second, the PCBC, similar banks, and some sectoral ministries have established evaluation divisions. Third, the Ministry of Finance and the State Planning Commission have set up units responsible for project benefit analysis and ex-post evaluations, respectively. Further, those trained have now themselves begun training others in their own and other central agencies.

■ *Where to From Here?*

China has just begun to (a) establish an evaluation culture that legitimates serious inquiry into public sector performance, (b) build the necessary expertise to undertake evaluation studies, (c) cultivate understanding and recognition in the program and policy communities of the utility of evaluation information, (d) find appropriate means to convey evaluation findings to the policy community, and (e) create the development of evaluation as a sustainable effort. China is building the foundation. However, there is no grand edifice in place; indeed, there is no edifice at all. In the Chinese governmental structure and administrative hierarchy, five key tasks must be undertaken.

First, it is vital for the PRC to have a strong central organization for overall evaluation management and coordination. Further, given the magnitude and diversity of the national administration, such a central organization would also set comprehensive national evaluation policies and guidelines so that any national organizational unit undertaking an evaluation will have a common understanding of policies and methods necessary. In addition, there is a strong need for alignment among the key organizations involved in evaluation so that they share a common understanding and build a common set of approaches to different evaluation tasks. This coordination has not existed to date, but many in these different sectors see the need to establish it.

Second, it is important that the PRC establish formal evaluation functions, policies, and guidelines in the sectoral ministries, provinces, and banks. These are now required to evaluate their own projects and programs. Such evaluations are a basis for discussions and decisions at the central level as to whether further evaluations are required.

Third, the PRC needs to set up an auditing function in the State Audit Administration so that there can be ongoing oversight and auditing of the evaluations undertaken within the sectoral ministries, provinces, and banks. Evaluation units need to be accountable and must adhere to standards of high performance. This oversight responsibility would be like that performed by the U.S. General Accounting Office, The Netherlands Court of Audit, the Swedish National Audit Office, and the Office of the Auditor General in Canada.

Fourth, the PRC needs to develop advanced evaluation methods across these units and organizational entities. Much evaluation work to date has not been informed by such methods. Learning new approaches and bringing them into evaluation at the national level requires training, building curricula, translation of materials, and mentoring from those more experienced in evaluation.

Finally, the PRC needs to develop a supply of well-trained evaluators for the many national sectors, ministries, provinces, and banks moving into the evaluation arena. The supply at present is far too small to meet demand. Indeed, demand will probably outstrip supply for some considerable time in the future. Building training centers, recruiting talented students and government employees, legitimating the professional status of evaluators, creating means of sharing experiences and developments through journals and conferences, and linking evaluation skills to subject matter expertise will take considerable time and effort. But if China is to build the necessary capacity and expertise, all these efforts need careful, sustained attention.

One task viewed within the Chinese government as the initial step to the achievement of the evaluation goals set out above is the creation of a steering committee and board made up of major government ministers and officials in the relevant banks. There is also a need for an executive office to support this board, which would have oversight in the following areas:

- drafting of guidelines and procedures for the ministries in the area of evaluation
- coordination of training, development of materials, and use of consultants
- development and maintenance of data banks for itself, sectoral ministries, provinces, banks, and the State Audit Administration
- building of evaluator networks
- building of the capacity for the future supply of persons trained in evaluation
- dissemination of evaluation findings
- guidance of the executive office responsible for administration and coordination of these functions

Given the movement in China toward a national evaluation system, the creation of such a board is an essential first step. At present, there is no national coordination or oversight to ensure the best use of resources, prevent duplication, and set high standards.

The experiences of developed and developing countries suggest that establishing a national evaluation system is a long and difficult process. It takes system coordination and alignment that is not easily achieved, even in small countries with relatively sophisticated public sectors. China is not small, and its public sector is still developing.

China can best approach this undertaking through a number of pilot projects targeted at sectoral ministries, provinces, and banks with a good understanding of what careful evaluation work requires. This select group could test activities related to capacity strengthening, the building of methodological skills, development of reporting formats, and training. The emphasis would be on piloting different approaches to the institutionalization of evaluation in the public sector. In the beginning, the emphasis would be more on organizational learning than on organizational accountability. If the system begins with an emphasis on accountability, there may be a reluctance to test out new approaches—something essential in a pilot phase. As lessons emerge from these pilot efforts, the system can expand to other ministries and levels of government. Over time, the balance between learning and accountability can be worked through.

The demand for evaluation in China is great. One source is the economic, social, technological, and environmental development of the country, which is moving at a high and sustained level. Tracking the changes and assessing the impacts associated with this development will necessitate a large evaluation infrastructure, considerable expertise in both the subject matter and evaluation, and development of routes for conveying evaluation findings into the policy communities. The second source of demand comes from development assistance given by the bilateral and multilateral lending organizations. The loan portfolio of the PRC now represents billions of dollars. China is the largest borrower from the World Bank. The emphasis by both the lenders and the Chinese government upon portfolio performance, indicators, and evaluation of outcomes drives still more need for evaluation capability.

Finally, as China moves into the international arena, its policy communities will encounter new evaluation developments, approaches, and forms of utilization that will apply to China. There will be encouragement to bring these developments home and test them out in the Chinese context.

The major concern in the public policy community is whether the initiatives and efforts described in these pages can be sustained. Building a national evaluation system in China will take decades. The infrastructure has to be built piece by piece across ministries, provinces, and local jurisdictions. The first steps we have described above are being taken, but sustaining this marathon effort will take financial support, technical assistance, the perseverance of officials, and patience.

12

Critical Comments on Evaluation Research in Denmark

Finn Hansson

The use of evaluation research has grown rapidly in Denmark in the past 10 years in the public sector and in private organizations and institutions. Evaluation research has established itself as a much-needed instrument for political and organizational development, control, monitoring, and modernization. At any point in time, many evaluations are being conducted in all areas of Danish society, with a majority in different parts of the public sector, in the social and cultural sector, and in the labor market. In this chapter I will chiefly consider evaluations in the public sector, using examples from the social and labor market area.

Evaluation research in Denmark also covers many different areas—from evaluation of public services and institutions to evaluation of social projects, experiments, and policy programs. A majority of these evaluations are, as I will discuss later, often conducted with the use of very traditional methods of data collection.

Considering the amount of evaluation research conducted in Denmark in the past 10 years and the international evaluation research debate, it is astonishing that discussions and debates on evaluation theory and methods in Denmark are so few. Debates on the scientific foundations and assumptions associated with evaluation research, have, in the past 10 years or so, been growing rapidly in international, and especially American, evaluation research. A critical discussion about the institutionalization and professionalization of evaluation research can be found in the work of House (1993), and the concept of metaevaluation (evaluation of evaluations and auditing procedures for quality control in evaluation research) has been discussed by Schwandt and Halpern (1988). Both House and Schwandt and Halpern point to the growing social importance of the uses of evaluation research. The work of Albæk and Winter (1990) is still the best and almost only Danish contribution to this discussion. In recent years, with different concepts of theory and its usage, American evaluation research has demonstrated a growing interest in debating questions of the use of theory to improve evaluations (Chen & Rossi, 1992). Much of this debate has focused primarily on the more technical aspects of evaluation research: on questions of reliability and validity (issues that are common to other areas of applied social research). Parts of this discussion take up arguments and positions from the 25-year-old critical discussion of instrumental positivism in American sociology and discussions in Europe on critical theory and positivism. General questions on the relation between theory and methods and on the relation between "data" and representation versus interpretation are, in evaluation research as elsewhere, extremely complicated though much debated (Guba & Lincoln, 1994; House, 1993). The debate is abstruse because it raises questions concerning the theory of knowledge as well as epistemology and philosophy and concepts of causality. However, it is beyond the scope of this chapter to pursue this important discussion further.

I will attempt to analyze major trends in Danish evaluation research based on the assumption that evaluation research is of growing importance in the overall field of applied or practical social research. Evaluation research has two specific features that distinguish it from other kinds of applied social research: It inquires into programs and processes within a short time span, and it normally involves researchers in closer relations with stakeholders (Patton, 1982) than can be found in other kinds of applied social research. These two features of evaluation research are strong arguments for considering evaluation research as crucial to the development of modern social theory (House, 1993).

■ *Social Policy and Social Science in Denmark*

To be able to explain why evaluation research emerged so late in Denmark compared with the United States, I need to give a short presentation of the development of applied social research in Denmark. The administrative and political use of social statistics and systematic investigations of social problems were institutionalized in Danish politics around 1930, with the employment of a social statistics consultant in the Ministry of Social Affairs. By the late 1950s, this function had grown to become an important instrument in policy planning and implementation, and it was decided to form a special institute for applied social research, SFI (the Danish National Institute for Social Research). Today SFI is the largest institute for applied social research in Denmark and is still economically and politically linked to government and public administration. Throughout the 1960s and 1970s, the institute grew rapidly and specialized in large-scale surveys of social problem areas, often closely integrated in the development of social reform policies, and even took part in preparing specific legislation, as can be seen in the many large-scale surveys of social and labor market problems carried out in preparation for extensive welfare policy reform in 1974 (*bistandsloven*). At the end of the 1970s, the institute had established a large apparatus for interview-based surveys and other types of quantitative data collection and analysis, and it produced an enormous amount of empirical data describing social problems. But SFI hardly ever conducted evaluations of the effects of the reforms.

As to why evaluation research emerged at this period, and so much later than in the United States, is a complex question. House (1993) gives a general description of the very uneven development in closely related Western societies of the systematic use of evaluations. With a focus on organizational learning, Leeuw, Rist, and Sonnichsen (1994) present a series of case studies on the use of evaluations in government and public organizations in different countries. Albæk (1995) and Albæk and Winter (1990) have attempted to apply such parameters to the Danish case.

According to these researchers, a major reason is that the Danish (and Scandinavian) construction of the welfare state in the 1960s and 1970s occurred very rapidly, on a very large scale, and, most of the time, in conditions of economic growth and a climate of general political consensus concerning the central features of the welfare state. The lack of economic pressure for cuts in state expenditure and the general political consensus between the major political parties can probably explain in part why there was so little public interest in evaluation of many welfare reforms and programs.

Also, the development of the welfare state in Denmark was based primarily on a policy of planning and regulation according to political programs and ideology. Many welfare state reforms were initiated on the basis of political-ideological agreements between the Social Democratic Party and the trade unions, especially in the area of the labor market. The need for more systematic knowledge of the effects and outcomes, in the form of evaluations of these reforms and programs, became more evident during the 1980s, with economic recession, stagnation, and increasing political protest against high taxation and hence demands for state budget cuts. Given this, the necessity for systematic information to increase efficiency and goal orientation in social policy was unavoidable. The size of the public sector, and especially the social sector, stood out as a problem in itself. The economic recession required budget cuts, and the social problems stemming from the economic crises, particularly unemployment, grew.

◼ Major Features in the Development of Danish Evaluation Research

In this section I will attempt to present major trends in Danish evaluation research during the period after evaluation research had been established and recognized as a professional social science activity. The few existing studies (e.g., Albæk & Winter, 1990) seem to agree on a general tendency in Danish evaluation research not to discuss problems of methodology and, especially, not to discuss the use of theory in evaluations. These studies conclude that Danish evaluation research generally is weak in evaluation theory and methodology, and that more critical and theoretical evaluation research probably would result in better and more usable evaluations.

In the rest of this section I will present Danish evaluation research in four major fields—based on specific features of the kind of evaluation in each field. The first three groups belong to what could be called the realm of professional evaluation—external evaluations conducted by institutions or individuals with a professional social science background. The first group consists of mostly large-scale, survey-based evaluations of the effects and efficiency of programs and projects. The second group deals with the development of theory in evaluations, especially in the fields of education and research evaluations. The third group consists of evaluations based on action research, and the last group comprises internal evaluations.

Survey-based evaluations are very often conducted in the social policy and labor market policy fields and performed by the major applied social science institutes, the Institute of Local Government Studies (AKF) and SFI. This group includes evaluations of current policy programs and projects and is, in terms of volume, cost, and efficiency, the predominant kind of evaluation research conducted in Denmark. In a sense, growth in this type of evaluations tends to help concentrate the means of social science production in what Bryant (1985, pp. 133-173) calls instrumental positivism. To clarify such a critique, I will examine some evaluations in more detail.

The evaluation of the SUM program (Social Development Programme, 1988-1991, total of $60 million U.S.) with the purpose of strengthening local initiatives and promoting restructuralization and preventive work in the social sector is, as of today, the largest evaluation performed in Denmark ($3 million U.S.). At the early stages in the formulation of the design for this evaluation, critical questions on how to integrate and use existing social theory were raised but put aside by the management of the evaluation program. The many individual evaluations of this large program were summarized in four major evaluation reports (Boll Hansen, 1992; Flex & Koch-Nielsen, 1992; Jæger, 1992; Jensen, 1992), based on data from a survey, from a database in the Ministry of Social Affairs, and from some structured interviews with key personnel in local administration where the experiments took place. But none of the four reports takes up discussions of theoretical or methodological problems in evaluation research in the field of social experiments and social work except for short discussions of technical and statistical problems. Central or fundamental questions of methodology in social science or evaluation research today, like questions about quantitative or qualitative methods, are not discussed at all. Discussions of social or social policy theory and concepts can be found only, and very briefly, in the work of Boll Hansen (1992). These evaluations are all organized primarily to provide answers to five questions concerning the outcome of the SUM project put forward by the politically elected steering group (Flex & Koch-Nielsen, 1992, p. 16). Based on this limited background the quantitative data are analyzed with the help of some simple statistical measures, and the summarized evaluation amounts to nothing more than an empirical-statistical description of the overall development of the program.

The main report maintains that it "has been difficult to document secure and reliable results" in the evaluations (Jensen, 1992, p. 14) because of great variations in the quality of the collected material. The author does not ask, however, if this could have anything to do with the fact that none of the evaluations in this project tried to establish any kind of conceptual or theoretical foundation for the evaluation of the social experiments and program. Critical comments had already been raised very early by some of the independent researchers involved in specific parts of the program with regard to this omission. They have shown that the omission resulted in a lack of specification and formulation of relevant evaluation questions, with the unfortunate consequence that important questions concerning the social experiment were impossible to evaluate due to lack of information.

In a way, it is surprising that large-scale evaluations have been conducted without central questions being raised about the quality of the empirical data. There seems to be a continued belief in quantitative methodology, even 25 years after the very intense and radical critique of neopositivism by the student movement in social science in Denmark, not to mention the international literature on the subject. It is difficult to find any outright supporters of neopositivism today in an epistemological or philosophical sense. But the use of methodologies associated with neopositivism and causal explanations based on data supposed to represent "reality" has not disappeared in evaluation research. In an article on qualitative program evaluations, Jennifer Greene (1994) calls this kind of evaluation research "postpositivist," to underline that these attitudes toward empirical research are still dominant in evaluation research: "Postpositivist evaluators retain a strong position amidst theorists and methodologists and a still-dominant position among evaluation practitioners and, perhaps most notably, evaluation audiences" (p. 532). According to Greene, this kind of evaluation is closely linked to traditional ideas of efficiency and accountability, output control, and result orientation. The SUM evaluations can be seen as an example of this dominant postpositivist tradition in Danish evaluation research and an example of a genre that has produced a rather meager outcome in terms of new knowledge and relevant information.

If we move away from survey-based evaluations to the second type, *theory-oriented evaluations,* the field is much smaller. Probably the most interesting evaluations in this field in Denmark have been conducted in the area of research evaluation. The growing public and political interest in publicly financed research has resulted in some successful attempts to develop reflexive and theoretical evaluations. Foss Hansen (1994) and others have succeeded in combining evaluations in the field of research with organizational theory and have turned the focus in the discussion of research evaluation from individual results or productivity to the organizational setting and environment for research (universities, institutes, working groups, networks).

The third major group of evaluation research in Denmark is rather difficult to label; it consists of *evaluations with a more explicit user or stakeholder involvement.* Often this kind of evaluation has an action research background or affiliation, as action research in Danish sociology has grown over the past 25 years to become the dominant kind of active, engaged sociology, though not with the same dominance as in Norwegian sociology and evaluation research. In Denmark, evaluations inspired by action research can be found in the field of education and in work studies, such as occupational risk studies, implementation of new technology and organizational change, and technology assessment. With a more direct inspiration from the concept of fourth-generation evaluation (Guba & Lincoln, 1989) and its demand for participation in evaluation, a growing number of evaluations of programs and experiments can be found in the social and cultural sector. Some evaluation research in this area attempts to formulate problems of theory and theoretical development, but much of this type of evaluation can be criticized for not being able to distinguish systematically between the researcher's own values and the values of those he or she investigates—a critique often raised concerning action research.

To sum up this presentation of three major areas of Danish evaluation research, the crucial issue seems to be that the vast majority of evaluations are conducted within the use of predominantly empirical positivist methods. More reflexive and critical discussions and commentary are few in Danish applied social science. Despite the radical critique of neopositivism in the social sciences by the student movement, positivists still dominate Danish evaluation research and all other areas of applied social science. Part of the explanation for this can be found in the political and organizational framework of the two large research institutes, AKF and SFI. They have a long tradition of doing large-scale empirical research and do not seem to be under political pressure to change. Also, these institutions have published the very few Danish books on how to conduct evaluation research, described as a mainly technical collection of data.

The fourth and last group in this presentation of Danish evaluation research has not been included in the short summary above. *Internal evaluation* is a rather new phenomenon in evaluation research internationally and does not follow the same traditions of evaluation practice (Sonnichsen, 1994). It is difficult to define precisely, but this group of studies consists of evaluations performed inside organizations as an integral part of organizational activity, as opposed to evaluations conducted by independent institutes or persons, as is the case in the other three groups. Here, in principle, we can expect to find evaluations of all kinds and methods, but they are not implemented in a professional evaluation setting.

The Danish minister of finance, Mogens Lykketoft, formulated the offensive political strategy for the government with a focus on using evaluations and user studies as instruments in modernization and quality control of institutions and organizations in the public sector. The general impression, and my own experience from the library sector, gives reason to believe that internal evaluations (or in-house evaluations), as part of administrative control, information management, and organizational learning, are a fast-growing type of evaluation activity in Denmark. This observation is in agreement with Sonnichsen's (1994) study of internal evaluation in the United States, but specific information concerning the amount and rate of increase of this kind of evaluation is almost non-existent.

This rather new evaluation activity poses a lot of questions for evaluation research. House (1993) formulates maybe the most fundamental question, concerning the evaluators' independence in internal evaluations. The demand for independent evaluations can easily be subordinated to organizational or management interests. Furthermore, parts of such evaluations can be used in order to legitimate particular decisions or can be steered according to political interests and hence result in purely symbolic actions to ensure the reputation of the organization or institution vis-à-vis the public (Albæk, 1995). The more positive role for internal evaluations, especially as an instrument in organizational learning, as put forward by Leeuw et al. (1994), has to confront the question of control but also other problems concerning the quality of the knowledge produced by internal evaluations. Questions are raised about the quality of the results due to the possible lack of a professional evaluation research background by those who conduct internal evaluations. For evaluation research in general, it would be problematic if a growing proportion of evaluations were to be performed outside the professional realm of evaluation, outside the professional discussions and critical networks that are considered crucial for ensuring the development of quality in evaluations. Accounts by internal evaluators and my own experience both indicate the conflict of interest between what evaluators will consider sufficiently stringent theory and methodology for an inside evaluation and management's short-term interest in the most cost-effective production of information using traditional (positivist) methods.

■ Conclusions: Danish Evaluation Research at a Crossroads

This presentation of Danish evaluation research has focused, critically, on the development in the past 10 years of mainly publicly funded evaluation research as a special field or tradition within applied sociological or social research. The many different tendencies or traditions have been grouped into four major types of evaluations, based on their particular evaluation research features or characteristics: survey-based evaluations, theory-

driven evaluations, action research-based evaluations, and internal evaluations. The result of this descriptive analysis is a picture of Danish
evaluation research standing at a crossroads.

On the one hand, general and political interest in evaluation research
has never been more widespread and positive in Denmark than it is today;
the demand for specific evaluations is emphasized again and again, taken
up by the media and subject to much public discussion. Policy makers
view evaluation research as an integral tool in the modernization of
institutions and especially of the public sector. On the other hand, the
mainstream of Danish evaluation research is, as we have seen, still deeply
anchored in positivist (or neopositivist) empiricist data collection in
which survey research predominates.

It is almost impossible for this kind of social research, with its long
tradition of conceiving social relations as just facts to be collected by
questionnaires and analyzed using statistical methods, to produce socially
usable and relevant knowledge on the growing complexity and changes
in social relations in complex modern or postmodern industrial societies.
This kind of social research cannot, as Alvesson and Skjöldberg (1996)
have shown, produce information on social relations that can be interpreted in a historical-cultural context and integrated in a reflexive interpretation of the social processes analyzed.

In some fields, alternative traditions in evaluation research can be
located, from action research and fourth-generation evaluations to theory-
driven evaluations and, especially, evaluations aiming at theory development. Even if some of these attempts seem very promising, they still are
only a marginal activity in the total picture of evaluation research in
Denmark, given the dominance of survey-based evaluations.

Applied social research in Denmark has a long tradition of quantitative empirical research often based on survey methods, and evaluation
research has followed this tradition and developed it in a postpositivist
direction (Greene, 1994).

Another important aspect of developments in evaluation research, not
only in Denmark, is the rapid growth in internal evaluations. Internal
evaluations are essentially an instrument in organizational development,
management information, and control, and raise many important questions for evaluation research. The criticisms made of professional Danish
evaluation research for its continuation of a traditional use of positivist
methods, and for its lack of professional discussion of evaluation theory

and methods, are even more important when we consider the growth in internal evaluations.

It cannot be assumed that internal evaluations will be performed only or mainly by professional evaluators, so the system of control performed by the professional networks and the system of scientific communication and control will be much weaker or nonexistent in the case of internal evaluation. And as Greene (1994) has shown, the kind of positivist methods criticized above probably have a strong position among managers and political decision makers. Because traditional empiricist methods, based on a positivist conception of social "facts," predominate in leadership and management studies, there is ample reason to fear a revival of positivist methods in internal evaluations. The risk of close political or managerial control and intervention in internal evaluations, both in the selection of topics and methods and in the execution of the evaluation process, is much greater than in traditional evaluations. Such a development can reduce internal evaluations to merely technical or administrative instruments for control and information in an organization. The development of internal evaluation and its possible change in methods and analysis from what traditionally has been described as evaluation theory and method can be explained in many ways. Political influence on evaluations and the use of evaluations as a part of organizational culture (Albæk, 1995) are only aspects of a more profound change.

■ References

Albæk, E. (1995). Between knowledge and power: Utilization of social science in public policy making. *Policy Science, 28,* 79-100.

Albæk, E., & Winter, S. (1990). Evaluation research in Denmark: The state of the art. In R. C. Rist (Ed.), *Program evaluation and the management of government: Pattern and prospects across eight nations.* New Brunswick, NJ: Transaction.

Alvesson, M. (1995). Leadership studies: From procedure and abstraction to reflexivity and situation. In J. Christiansen (Ed.), *Proceedings of the 13th Nordic Conference on Business Studies* (Vol. 1, pp. 237-258). Copenhagen.

Alvesson, M., & Skjöldberg, K. (1996). *Toward a reflexive methodology.* London: Sage.

Boll Hansen, E. (1992). *Forandring og fornyelse gennem SUM.* Copenhagen: AKF.

Bryant, C. (1985). *Positivism in social theory and research.* London: Polity.

Chen, H.-T., & Rossi, P. H. (Eds.). (1992). *Using theory to improve program and policy evaluations.* Westport, CT: Greenwood.

Flex, K., & Koch-Nielsen, I. (1992). *Kommunerne og SUM-programmet* (Social-forskningsinstituttet Rapport 92:11). Copenhagen: SFI.

Foss Hansen, H. (1994, November 25-26). *Evaluation of research: Performance, control, organizational learning and/or politics?* Paper presented at the symposium Studies in Research Evaluation, Copenhagen.

Greene, J. C. (1994). Qualitative program evaluation: Practice and promise. In N. K. Denzin & Y. S. Lincoln (Eds.), *Handbook of qualitative research* (pp. 530-544). Newbury Park, CA: Sage.

Guba, E. G., & Lincoln, Y. S. (1989). *Fourth generation evaluation.* Newbury Park, CA: Sage.

Guba, E. G., & Lincoln, Y. S. (1994). Competing paradigms in qualitative research. In N. K. Denzin & Y. S. Lincoln (Eds.), *Handbook of qualitative research* (pp. 105-117). Newbury Park, CA: Sage.

House, E. (1993). *Professional evaluation: Social impact and political consequences.* Newbury Park, CA: Sage.

Jæger, B. (1992). *Formidling på kryds og tværs, -evaluering af SUM-programmets formidlingsenheder-.* Copenhagen: AKF.

Jensen, M. K. (1992). *Slut-SUM. En sammenfatning af projekterfaringerne fra Socialministeriets Udviklingsprogram* (Socialforskningsinstituttet Rapport 92:18). Copenhagen: SFI.

Leeuw, F. L., Rist, R. C., & Sonnichsen, R. C. (1994). *Can government learn? Comparative perspectives on evaluation and organizational learning.* New Brunswick, NJ: Transaction.

Patton, M. Q. (1982). *Practical evaluation.* Beverly Hills, CA: Sage.

Schwandt, T. A., & Halpern, E. S. (1988). *Linking auditing and metaevaluation.* Newbury Park, CA: Sage.

Sonnichsen, R. C. (1994). Effective internal evaluation: An approach to organizational learning. In F. L. Leeuw, R. C. Rist, & R. C. Sonnichsen, *Can government learn? Comparative perspectives on evaluation and organizational learning* (pp. 125-144). New Brunswick, NJ: Transaction.

13

Evaluation, Markets, and Institutions in the Reform Agenda of Developing Countries

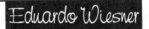

Eduardo Wiesner

Since the late 1980s, several developing countries, particularly in Latin America, have adopted ambitious reform programs that include trade and financial liberalization, privatization, fiscal and political decentralization, greater emphasis on social spending, and new modalities of intervention and regulation. In brief, they seek more efficient public sectors and a greater role for markets and competition in the determination of resource allocation. But reform design is one thing, and effective achievement of the ultimate results sought is another. When, for instance, countries privatize public entities, they may fail to realize that a simple change in ownership does not guarantee greater efficiency. When they give greater priority to social spending, they should be aware that larger budgets alone seldom improve social conditions. Finally, when countries decentralize resources and decision making, this, by itself, does not assure better resource allocation efficiency or improved local public choices.

In sum, it is not enough to decree what, in principle, may appear to be the right modernizing policies. Beyond that, the reform agenda needs to be complemented with the strategically combined actions of other factors, such as evaluation, markets, and institutions. These must be aligned to produce enhanced competition in both the private and the public markets. Without competition in these markets, better public sector performance will prove to be elusive. My purpose in this chapter is to discuss how these factors can be used to strengthen the effectiveness of public sector reforms. Through this discussion, new challenges for evaluation may emerge.

■ *The Role of Evaluation in the Reform Agenda of Developing Countries*

For many developing countries, the experience of the 1980s suggests that although macroeconomic stability is a necessary condition for growth, such stability alone cannot ensure growth. Structural change and public sector reform appear to be the next two steps toward establishing sufficient conditions for sustainable growth and for social and political development. In this "sequence of reform approach," evaluation comes into play as a powerful tool for public sector reform as well as for policy assessment. Evaluation thus acquires special policy relevance in the reform agenda of developing countries. This is what Guerrero (1993) calls "the use of evaluation as an input for policy reform."

More specifically, the reform agenda that many developing countries have adopted includes the following three fronts of action: privatization drives, fiscal and political decentralization, and new spending priorities. The question that arises is, What role should evaluation play in the design and implementation of this reform agenda? The short answer is that evaluation can be used prospectively to assess whether the basic "macroinstitutional and policy framework" constitutes the propitious enabling environment for the achievement of the reform goals. By revealing, at an early point in time, what is wrong or what can go wrong with a given policy approach, evaluation can contribute significantly to the success of the reform agenda of developing countries. But how precisely would evaluation accomplish this role?

The role of evaluation in assessing the achievements of individual and specific programs and projects is well known. What appears to be needed is an expansion of that role to ensure that markets and institutions are aligned to produce competition. This is the critical condition—that is, that competition be brought into the design and into the implementation and evaluation of the reform program.

☐ *Privatization*

Some developing countries are discovering that after all their efforts to privatize public utilities, or state-owned enterprises, performance has not improved as they had originally anticipated. They had thought that changes in ownership would automatically bring state-of-the-art technology and greater efficiency, but this has not happened. What has gone wrong? Their expectations have been based on a simple non sequitur. What brings about efficiency is not public or private ownership, but competition. The private sector is not in the business of increasing competition—that is not its role. Instead, inducing and preserving competition are two of the major roles of governments.

Assuming that this dictum is accepted, how does evaluation enter the process? Evaluation enters the process through the emergence of regulation to protect competition as a new and rapidly expanding form of intervention. But most reforming countries have no special expertise in regulation and even less in evaluating the results of their incipient regulation activities. Regulation is a complex topic. Even in developed countries, regulatory policy oscillates between the two major theoretical paradigms of regulatory behavior—that is, the public interest theory and the so-called capture or special interest theory. Under the first, regulators have the public interest—or their view of it—as their main leitmotiv. Under the latter, regulators are motivated, principally, by their narrow self-interested goals.

In reforming countries that are just beginning to develop technical and institutional expertise in regulation, "rent-seekers" are often able to insert restrictions and ad hoc performance criteria into the regulatory legal framework.[1] In this fashion they are able to obstruct the role of competition. In this case, it is not so much the regulators who "capture" benefits as it is the legislators who "distribute" benefits among their constituencies and friends.

□ *Fiscal and Political Decentralization*

Several developing countries, particularly in Latin America, have embarked on political and fiscal decentralization drives. They have done so in search of a "local public choice model" that will yield better resource allocation and more political participation by the local citizenry. This is a laudable goal. However, although the theoretical arguments in favor of decentralization are strong, converting these into reality can be very difficult (Proud'homme, 1994). Part of that reality has not materialized because the policy frameworks of some of those decentralization drives end up discouraging local fiscal response. By making transfers virtually automatic, Colombia, for instance, is not obtaining the right local fiscal response, particularly in medium and small municipalities (Wiesner, 1994). Another deleterious consequence of largely unconditional grants is that interjurisdictional competition can hardly develop. The basic premise of decentralization is that competition within the government will improve public service provision, but this has not happened, basically, because the incentive structure has not induced competition.

□ *New Spending Priorities*

The reform agendas of many developing countries are increasingly emphasizing attention to social and equity issues. Social development is seen as the new priority, particularly in Latin America. Most countries are implementing this policy by increasing budget allocations for primary education and for health. The assumption seems to be that larger budgets will yield greater social welfare. The experience in most cases, however, is that policies are more important than resources and that the benefits of greater educational spending may accrue more to teachers, suppliers, politicians, and others than to students. If the consumer of education or health has little to do with the way in which the supply allocates the additional resources, not much will be gained in terms of efficiency and equity in the social sectors. On the contrary, if competition for the additional resources is assured, much will be accomplished.

■ Markets, Institutions, and Organizational Structure

One of the reasons Professor G. Stigler was awarded the Nobel Prize was his work on the importance of information for the development of markets (Stigler, 1961). More recently, Alchian and Demsetz (1972) as well as Stiglitz (1991) have gone even further to say that without information, markets do not work. The key link between information and markets appears to be institutions. Nobel Prizes have gone to Douglas North (1981) and Ronald Coase (1960), who think that institutions matter. In other words, considerable thought has been given to the question of how to ensure that competition and the markets function. What these scholars are conveying is a warning that markets tend to be weak, that institutions are not always interested in the general welfare, and that, as Williamson (1990) has put it, "Bureaucracy is a seriously neglected topic."

These views are summarized in what is called *neoinstitutional economics*. This school of thought holds not only that institutions matter but that institutions are susceptible to analysis. They can also be subject to specific evaluations of their performance (Ostrom, Schroeder, & Wynne, 1993). With specific regard to the evaluation of institutions, Quesnel (1994) has pointed out that evaluations can reveal the relevance and efficiency of single institutions as well as of the public sector in general. The message is that evaluation should address the complex issues that arise from the interactions among institutions, markets, regulation, and policy performance. Evaluation, particularly in countries attempting to reform the role of the state and their public sectors, can be a very useful instrument for revealing the "empty spaces" in the neoclassical model and seeing that they are properly remedied.[2]

In the examples discussed above, ex ante and ex post evaluations of institutions would have warned the Colombian government that simply increasing budget allocations for primary education would benefit the teachers' union more than the students (Wiesner, 1995). Evaluation of the "organizational structure" of the power sector in Colombia might have helped the country escape the electricity rationing that took place in 1992. At that time, the "property rights" applying to water—the main source of hydroelectricity—were not clearly defined. The result was that the opportunity cost of water was underestimated and rationing became inevitable when the rains did not come.

■ Trends in Evaluation

Throughout the world, both developed and developing, major efforts are under way to stimulate improved government performance. These efforts can take many forms, but the underlying common thread is the use of market and quasi-market forces to design policies and to allocate resources. This global trend acquires special relevance in those countries trying to change the role of the state and that want, precisely, to give a greater role to the markets. In these countries, evaluation may well be one of the most powerful instruments for reform (Wiesner, 1993).

While this healthy trend is followed in many developing countries, another less salubrious practice is evolving in some developing countries through the development of what could be called *interventionist evaluations*. These can be defined as the introduction of ad hoc performance indicators into the legislation that develops policy decisions. Compliance with these alleged performance criteria is supposed to assure the government and the public at large that some programs or projects are being well managed. In reality, it is just process compliance and has little connection with the results sought by the reforming policies. At least two questions arise from this trend. First, were these performance indicators the result of independent evaluations? Second, is the performance measured through those ad hoc indicators validated by external benchmarking? By performance observed in a competitive environment?

This practice arises from a combination of two causes: (a) efforts by rent-seekers to protect the benefits they normally capture from most government interventions, and (b) well-intentioned but rather naive beliefs by people who honestly think that only direct and active government intervention will correct market failures. It is the deliberate or fortuitous alliance of these two groups of people that makes it so difficult for the markets and competition to function. The challenge for evaluation is to unmask the interests of rent-seekers and to inform the public about the options for correcting market failures.

■ Challenges for Evaluation

Chelimsky (1995) notes that "awareness is broadening of the potential of evaluation for improving decision making and . . . today, evaluators feel ready to move on to topics of more global interest than those they previously studied." It is precisely within this expanding dimension of evaluation that I argue for a greater role for evaluation in support of the reform agendas of many developing countries. More specifically, I submit that evaluation, with all its arsenal of theory, instruments, and experience, should be used more intensively to study and to assess what could be called the *macroinstitutional policy framework* under which many developing countries are trying to restructure their economics and reform their public sectors. These reform processes pose formidable challenges for these countries and also for evaluation. In effect, what I propose is nothing less than the use of evaluation to improve the effectiveness of policies and programs in areas where most developing countries are just beginning to learn the intricacies. Such is the case of regulation.

Another difficult challenge for evaluation in developing countries arises from social and developmental programs that involve several institutions from different ministries. Often programs in rural areas, or those addressed to people living below the poverty line, involve multiple objectives and multiple agencies. Evaluating performance within such fragmented interinstitutional frameworks can be very difficult. And yet, because substantial resources are allocated to these programs and because they constitute major social priorities, they cannot be excluded from evaluation policy.

There are many aspects derived from the macroinstitutional policy framework that evaluation might examine, but three areas in particular should be singled out:

1. nominal or legal process compliance versus compliance with independent performance indicators or with market-derived benchmarks
2. the evaluation of market and marketlike conditions to assess institutional, program, and project performance
3. the realization of strategic evaluations of key policies and of selected institutional structures in the reform process

In sum, the specific issue that evaluation needs to address is whether market, or marketlike, conditions constitute the external environment within which policies, programs, or projects are being evaluated.

☐ *Nominal Performance Compliance Versus Real Evaluations*

One way in which rent-seekers protect their interests is by building into legislation alleged performance indicators that, if met—and they have to be met by legal mandate—are supposed to guarantee desirable institutional or program performance. In this fashion, independent evaluations are virtually excluded. What is more important, external evaluations in the form of competition or marketlike evaluations—through regulation, for instance—are also avoided.

Colombia's Law 60 of 1993, which establishes the framework for the decentralization drive, and Law 115 of 1994, which deals with educational policy, are two examples of situations in which real evaluation of performance is extremely difficult. This legislation has established, ex ante, rigorous and detailed procedures for the distribution of funds in such a way that, in the end, the interests of the teachers' union and of other intermediaries are protected, whereas external evaluations and competition are left out. These laws have built into them legislation performance indicators that are linked to process compliance and not to outcomes that could be validated by evaluation.

☐ *Evaluation of the External Competitive Environment*

The effectiveness of evaluation is also confined by political economy restrictions arising from ad hoc financing practices such as earmarking of funds for special programs and institutions. Earmarking, in most cases, defeats a basic purpose of evaluations—that is, linking performance with budgets. In Colombia, close to $2 billion is, de facto if not de jure, earmarked for specific expenditures. This is a large proportion of the available resources. It is equivalent to about 3% of the country's GDP and to more than 30% of its national tax revenues. Around these funds, strong institutional and political interests have developed. One of the institutions involved is the Instituto Colombiano de Bienestar Familiar. Under its current management, this institution is adopting a performance-based evaluation system that the National Planning Department (DNP) is sponsoring. These efforts are laudable. The question remains, however: How much real additional improvement is possible from what could be called "micro-intrainstitutional" evaluations if the financing will not be significantly affected by the evaluation results?[3]

☐ *Strategic Evaluations*

As countries implement their reform agendas, they need to learn quickly from their experiences and to feed lessons back promptly into their reforming policies. One way to do this is to conduct strategic evaluations of some of the most critical areas. Evaluation analysis would indicate how to select the strategic priorities to be conducted and what methodologies to use. Colombia has adopted a program of strategic evaluations of a few selected policies, programs, and projects. These evaluations are beginning to offer valuable results and, in some specific cases, such as the decentralization drive, they have led to a consensus that the policy framework needs substantial revision. The evaluations are conducted under the aegis of the DNP, and, as Ocampo (1995) has indicated, they offer great potential for evaluating Colombia's National Development Plan. Colombia's "National System of Evaluation" contemplates budget incentives for improved performance (Escobar, 1993).

■ *A Comprehensive Approach*

The theoretical argument for a comprehensive approach—that is, one that integrates markets, evaluation, and institutions—is more easily postulated as a normative nostrum than developed into specific steps or actions. In fact, conventional wisdom posits that one of the "macro" requirements of a reform agenda is that it needs to take place within a policy and institutional environment that is market-friendly. The problem and the challenge are to go beyond this nostrum. No two countries are really alike. Nevertheless, some guidelines can be offered. These could be summarized in the following three questions:

1. Is the sectoral environment within which the reform process takes place one in which competition has been given a major role?
2. What are the intrinsic complexities of the specific components of the reform agenda?
3. What specific demands arise from those complexities in terms of evaluation and in terms of assessing whether competition is allowed to play its role?

The answers to these questions do not come easily. They are more empirical than conceptual and can be answered only through empirical evaluations. That is, problems *begin* when developing countries discover, for instance, that the legislation needed to accompany privatization is extremely complex; that the costs of privatized public services seldom come down; that advanced technical expertise is necessary for the regulation of natural monopolies; and that such expertise must be assembled institutionally in ways in which they have little experience. In short, they discover that even when the demand for evaluation is there, supply is inelastic in the short run. They also discover that a goodly number of imponderable factors play roles in changing traditional public sector management practices. Among these factors, perhaps the most crucial one is political leadership, and this is primarily fortuitous. Yet the outlook is not hopeless. The probability of a *gradual* process of improvement is not low as long as it is clear in the minds of the reformers—and built into the reform process—that competition must be given a major role.

Recognizing that there are evaluation capacity restrictions, one possible course of action is to conduct selected strategic evaluations. These would assess whether markets, institutions, and policies are consistent and conducive to the objectives in mind. These strategic evaluations have to be independent and should, in most cases, be supported by microinstitutional performance evaluations. Colombia is following this practice.

■ *Summary and Conclusions*

Better public sector performance in developing countries results largely from the right mix of evaluation, markets, and institutions. When these countries embark on the restructuring of their public sectors, they could benefit from adopting an integrated approach to pursue those reforms. Such a comprehensive approach would comprise the combination of specific modalities of evaluation, a larger role for the markets, and a propitious institutional enabling environment. These factors must be aligned to produce enhanced competition in both the private and the public markets. Without competition in these markets, better performance will prove to be elusive.

The range for potential improvement in public sector reform, based on results-oriented management programs, is predetermined by the specific macroinstitutional policy framework under which those programs are being implemented. The challenge is to find ways in which "microprogram" evaluations can induce a macroinstitutional policy framework that is conducive to enhanced public sector performance.

Evaluation priorities should be adjusted not only to public expenditure and policy priorities but to the intrinsic exigencies of, for example, decentralization, social expenditures, regulation of natural monopolies, and privatization. Evaluation capacity development, therefore, should be selective and strategically strengthened to respond to the specific demands of the reform path chosen.

Strategic evaluations have great potential to contribute significantly to the proper alignment of markets, institutions, and performance-based management systems. In some developing countries, some spurious evaluation practices are being built into legislation more to protect rent-seekers than to protect the public interest. The emphasis in these situations is more on process compliance than on results validated by external verification. This development poses a major problem to evaluation. In addition, most efforts to strengthen the demand for evaluation will ultimately fail if public sector budgets continue to finance projects and programs independently of evaluation results.

The challenge for evaluation is to identify what is wrong or missing in the reform agenda of developing countries, whether it is market failure, institutional failure, or government failure, and advise accordingly. In brief, although evaluation is no panacea, it can play a major role in outlining the path of public sector reform that offers the greatest potential for effectiveness.

■ Notes

1. The term *rent-seekers,* which was developed by Tullock (1967) and Krueger (1974), refers to actions by individuals who seek to capture rents and revenues from government through nonmarket choices on contracts, tariffs, regulation, quotas, and earmarking in general.

2. The neoclassical model assumes, among other things, perfect information, full rational choice, unambiguous property rights, and the enforceability of those rights. However, this is not exactly reality. Thus to use this model for understanding reality requires both the accommodation of erosion from the ideal and constant vigilance for it to function.

3. It is interesting to note that Colombia's new 1991 Constitution, which seeks to eradicate earmarking practices, establishes through its Article 343 the legal obligation to develop a national evaluation system.

■ References

Alchian, A., & Demsetz, H. (1972). Production, information costs, and economic organization. *American Economic Review, 62,* 777-795.
Coase, R. (1960). The problem of social cost. *Journal of Law and Economics, 3,* 1-44.

Chelimsky, E. (1995). New dimensions in evaluation. In R. Picciotto & R. C. Rist (Eds.), *Evaluating country development policies and programs: New approaches for a new agenda.* San Francisco: Jossey-Bass.

Escobar, S. (1993). *Colombia: Evaluación de resultados de la gestión pública.* Paper presented at the Primer Seminario de Evaluación de Centroamerica, Panama y República Centroamericana, San Jose, Costa Rica.

Guerrero, P. (1993). *Desarrollo de la capacidad nacional de evaluación: Resumen de la experiencia y posible acción.* Paper presented at the Seminario Regional sobre Seguimiento y Evaluación en America Latina, Quito, Ecuador.

Krueger, A. (1974). The political economy of the rent-seeking society. *American Economic Review, 64,* 291-303.

North, D. (1981). *Structure and change in economic history.* New York: W. W. Norton.

Ocampo, J. A. (1995). *La descentralización, el gasto social y la gobernabilidad en Colombia.* Bogotá, Colombia: DNP, ANIF, and FINDETER.

Ostrom, E., Schroeder, L., & Wynne, S. (1993). *Institutional incentives and sustainable development.* Boulder, CO: Westview.

Proud'homme, R. (1994). *On the dangers of decentralization* (Research Working Paper No. 1253). Washington, DC: World Bank.

Quesnel, J. (1994, December). *Evaluación y la modernización del estado.* Paper presented at the Seminario de Evaluación de Centroamerica, Panama y República Dominicana, Banco Internacional de Desarrollo.

Stigler, G. J. (1961). The economics of information. *Journal of Political Economy, 69,* 213-225.

Stiglitz, J. (1991). *The invisible hand and modern welfare economics* (Working Paper No. 3641). Washington, DC: National Bureau of Economic Research.

Tullock, G. (1967). The welfare costs of tariffs monopolies and theft. *Western Economic Journal, 5,* 224-232.

Wiesner, E. (1993). From macroeconomic correction to public sector reform. In *The critical role of evaluation* (Discussion Paper No. 214). Washington, DC: World Bank.

Wiesner, E. (1994). *Fiscal decentralization and social spending in Latin America: The search for efficiency and equity* (Working Paper No. 199). Washington, DC: Inter-American Development Bank.

Wiesner, E. (1995). *La descentralización, el gasto social y la gobernabilidad en Colombia.* Bogotá, Colombia: DNP, ANIF, and FINDETER.

Williamson, O. E. (1990). Political institutions: The neglected side of the story. *Journal of Law, Economics and Organization, 6.*

14

Evaluation in the World Bank

Antecedents, Instruments, and Concepts

The evaluation of policies, programs, and projects in the zones of turmoil and development where 85% of the world's population lives poses special problems. To illustrate these problems, I will outline in this chapter the origins, methods, and challenges of the World Bank's independent evaluation function. First, I will sketch the nature of the World Bank and the scope of its evaluation activities. I will then describe the shifting context for development activities and note the implications of the new development agenda for the World Bank's evaluation criteria.

■ The World Bank

A global development institution, the World Bank has special features that have influenced the design of its evaluation system. First, evaluation has been called upon to illuminate allocative decisions for the considerable resources the Bank lends ($20-25 billion annually) and those it spends on administration and nonlending services (about $1.5 billion annually).

Second, evaluation has had to deal with a wide variety of development activities. World Bank loans are used to implement specific projects of reconstruction and development in a wide range of sectors and to improve policies and programs in highly diverse low- and middle-income countries. Third, evaluation has had to take account of the cooperative character of the institution and of shared responsibilities for operational outcomes: World Bank-financed projects are owned and managed by borrowers and usually involve participation by other development agencies and/or nongovernmental organizations. (The collaborative character of the institution also derives from the fact that the Bank itself is owned by governments, with shares allocated broadly in proportion to the wealth of individual member countries.)

Finally, the market-based characteristics of the World Bank have shielded it from political interference and enhanced the rigor of its operational policies (the benchmarks for evaluation). The bulk of World Bank funds derives from long-term bonds floated in private capital markets. Because these bonds enjoy AAA rating, the Bank is able to pass on long-term funds to its developing country members on terms that they cannot secure on their own accounts. For very poor countries, the World Bank operates a soft loan window, the International Development Association.

The World Bank has become the largest single provider of financial and technical assistance to developing countries. More than 100 new members have joined the World Bank since its creation 50 years ago. Today, more than 1,800 Bank-financed projects involving $140 billion in commitments are being implemented throughout the developing world. Every year sees about 250 new projects funded. Beyond its financial intermediation role, the World Bank generates knowledge about development and acts as a transmission belt for ideas and skills. It conducts a large development research program and provides training to development policy makers through its Economic Development Institute. Its large concentration of development know-how, its field office network, its global professional contacts, and the strategic alliances it has built with a wide variety of development agencies all help it to accomplish its mission. These features, in turn, provide wide scope for evaluative work.

■ Origins and Scope of the Function

The World Bank's evaluation function is almost as old as the evaluation profession itself. In 1970, World Bank president Robert McNamara created an evaluation group as part of the Planning and Budgeting Department. Though the function has evolved with time, many of the ideas that animate today's evaluation activities date from this early phase. In 1975, at shareholders' request, the evaluation function was made independent of management, and the Operations Evaluation Department (OED) was placed under the aegis of a director general, with the rank of a vice president, reporting to the Board of Executive Directors, with a broad mandate to evaluate World Bank activities, distill lessons of development experience, and oversee self-evaluation processes (OED, 1994a). A standing committee of the Board of Executive Directors satisfies itself that the operations evaluation system is adequate and efficient, reviews OED's annual program, takes note of the policy implications of evaluation products, and oversees the use of evaluation findings by management.

The director general is not concerned with the functions of the World Bank's external auditor, who is appointed by the executive directors to examine and report on the annual financial statements of the Bank and its affiliates. The director general does, however, maintain contact with the auditor general on matters affecting the Bank's effectiveness and efficiency. The director general also provides advice, as needed, to the World Bank's independent Inspection Panel, recently established to investigate claims by local stakeholders that the Bank may have failed to adhere to its operational policies and procedures in the design, appraisal, or implementation of ongoing or new operations.

The evaluation function has kept pace with the growth, diversification, and reorientation of World Bank activities. In 1994, OED carried out reviews and performance audits for some 350 completed development operations worth more than $20 billion in commitments. These operations span a remarkable variety of sectors (including agriculture, energy, finance, transport, water supply, urban development) and instruments (including investment projects, sector operations, financial intermediation schemes, and adjustment loans). Beyond its project-level evaluation activities, OED devotes a growing share of its resources to cross-cutting studies, including process and impact evaluations, country program assessments, and global/regional policy reviews—200 at last count.

■ *Evaluation Instruments*

It was Mr. McNamara's intention to have every World Bank-financed project evaluated at the completion of loan disbursements. This principle has been observed ever since. Today, OED rates the performance of each project at the completion of loan/credit disbursements. The resulting evaluation database now includes design and performance characteristics for about 4,000 development projects. All implementation completion reports produced by the regional departments are evaluated by OED, which assesses and reports on their quality, collects evaluation data for aggregate analysis, extracts findings and recommendations useful for new operations, and selects operations to be audited.

In selecting operations for *performance audit,* preference is given to those that are innovative, large, or complex; those for which executive directors request audits; and those that, individually or as part of a cluster, are likely to generate important lessons. Thus projects, topics, and analytic approaches for the performance audit work program are chosen to provide inputs for evaluation studies. To prepare performance audits, OED staff examine project files and other documents, interview operations staff, and, in most cases, visit the borrowing country for on-site discussions. The operational staff concerned, and subsequently the borrowers, receive draft audits. Borrowers' comments are incorporated into the document that is sent to the Bank's board. When an audit report is released to the board by the director general, it is also widely distributed within the Bank and to concerned authorities in member countries.

The ultimate test of the Bank's programs is their long-term effects on people, policies, and domestic capacities. Accordingly, OED impact evaluations take an independent second look at projects 5 to 10 years after completion to assess what lasting contributions the Bank is making to borrower countries' development. Impact evaluations assess projects against a broad set of criteria that relate to social dynamics, income distribution, effects on women and families, institutional development, and the environment. They examine what has happened to the infrastructure created under the project, the experience with production of goods and services aided by the project, the distribution of the benefits created, and the performance of the implementing organizations. Most impact evaluations to date have used relatively formal study methods—in particular, field surveys that use key questions to gather opinions of stakeholders, including the ultimate beneficiaries. OED also uses low-cost evaluation methods of the rapid appraisal type, including interviews, direct observation, informal surveys, and reviews of existing information. Even though they may be relatively costly to execute, impact evaluations allow unique insights into the conditions needed to sustain benefit flows over the long term. They provide evidence of the Bank's development impact, which represents the true worth of the Bank's portfolio.

OED uses findings from completion, audit, and impact evaluation reports, supplemented by further investigation, including staff fieldwork and surveys, to prepare evaluation studies. These studies assess the effectiveness of Bank policies, processes, and practices from the perspective of operational experience. The work program for the studies is planned so as to feed into the Bank's reviews of its operational policies.

Sector studies address such issues as the effectiveness of dialogue between borrowers and the Bank on sector policies or on project selection, design, and implementation; the socioeconomic impacts of sector policies and programs; institutional development; and human resources needs. Many of these studies compare experiences across countries, whereas others are in-depth reviews of particular sectors in individual countries.

Evaluating the Bank's *business processes* from a development perspective is part of OED's mandate. Process studies examine how well the Bank applies its policies, as well as the efficiency and effectiveness of the Bank's business practices in reaching intended development goals. Examples of recent process evaluations include studies of loan supervision, the monitoring and evaluation components of projects, and the economic analysis of new loan proposals.

Country assistance reviews are, in essence, countrywide impact evaluations that concentrate on the impact and development effectiveness of the Bank's whole program of assistance to each country. They have essentially the same relationship to the Bank's overall assistance program that performance audits have to individual lending operations. They provide opportunities to assess lending and nonlending services in the context of overall country assistance strategies. Country assistance reviews have recently been completed for Mexico and Ghana.

OED synthesizes the findings of all its evaluations in its *Annual Review of Evaluation Results,* which is discussed by the Bank's board and is published. The review summarizes the findings of evaluations done during the preceding calendar year and reports on trends in the Bank's operational performance. Using evidence from evaluation work, it also analyzes selected topics (such as experience with adjustment lending, the effects of Bank operations on the environment, and support for institutional development).

Finally, each year the director general reports to the executive directors and the president on the status of evaluation in the Bank. This annual report on evaluation activities includes information on the effectiveness of evaluation, dissemination, and feedback processes for lending and nonlending services.

■ *The New Evaluation Challenge*

For evaluation at the World Bank, the frame of reference is evolving fast. The demands on evaluation have escalated, and the goals, standards, and methods of evaluation have had to adapt.

Development is now defined as equitable and sustainable growth achieved through good economic governance; suitable attention to human capital formation through better nutrition, health services, and education; environment-friendly policies; and private sector development. The development agenda has thus become multidimensional. Beyond generating economic growth, it seeks to create more equitable and harmonious societies and to protect humankind's environmental legacy for the use of future generations. It embodies principles of economic management that provide ample room for private entrepreneurship and civil society.

The art of development assistance practiced by World Bank operations professionals consists in adapting these broad policy directions to specific country circumstances. This is done through the fashioning of country assistance programs that are aligned with the new priorities and capable of producing satisfactory development impacts "on the ground."

To judge these diverse, multifaceted, decentralized projects and programs, World Bank evaluators have had to adjust their methods and standards. Evaluators now pay particular attention to the Bank's areas of special emphasis—poverty reduction, the environment, private enterprise development, and human capital formation. And they seek to assess economic, social, technological, cultural, environmental, and institutional impact of individual interventions against the backdrop of country policies and a rapidly changing global economy.

■ *A New Context*

Technology, trade, and investment flows point to ever-greater economic interdependence, and today, more than ever, developing countries can tap large benefits from connecting to the competitive requirements of the global market place. Hence World Bank assistance increasingly supports policy reform in borrowing countries. At the same time, with the end of the Cold War, the developing world has become more volatile and violent conflict more common. Increasingly, resources for development assistance are mortgaged to meet the needs of peacemaking and peacekeeping.

The collapse of states, though occurring in relatively few countries, is obscuring the overall achievements of development assistance. Attention is riveted to the trouble spots pictured on television screens. The general public is only dimly aware that the world's engine of economic growth is now in the developing world, that economic expansion in poor countries has been running substantially ahead of growth in developed countries, and that socioeconomic indicators have improved dramatically in the developing world, especially in the most populous nations (Lateef, 1995).

Many of the countries that received financial assistance from the World Bank in the 1950s have graduated to high-income status. Examples of these include Finland, Greece, Spain, and Japan. And many middle-income country borrowers, especially in East Asia, have enjoyed rapid economic growth and made major strides in reducing poverty.

■ *Growing Demands*

Ironically, the very success of development assistance is inducing poles of resistance among employers and employees in developed regions, who feel vulnerable to the winds of international competition. With the end of superpower confrontation, the ideological case for resource transfers to poor countries has evaporated, and the electorates of the industrial countries, preoccupied by fiscal and employment problems of their own, have become far more skeptical and demanding with respect to development assistance. Public support for development assistance has shrunk, and the demands for economically sound, socially responsive, and environmentally responsible policies and programs as a basis for development assistance have risen dramatically. To be sure, a substantial reservoir of public compassion exists with respect to poverty, malnutrition, the status of women, and other social problems, but there is also greater sensitivity to issues of governance, militarization, human rights violations, unfair trade practices, and loose environmental standards. There is scarce tolerance for the assignment of resources to countries that mismanage their economies, to projects that involve undue social or environmental risks, or to studies that add little of value to people's well-being.

Just as the development agenda has become more demanding, improved performance on the ground (rather than the traditional focus on public investment) is now the acid test for development assistance. Accountability for lean, responsive, effective, results-based assistance has become a fundamental imperative for the World Bank and its development partners. Efficiency, transparency, and documented results are at a premium. A rigorous, relevant, independent evaluation function has become essential to institutional credibility.

Beyond accountability, evaluation is required to contribute to organizational learning. Accordingly, OED shapes its work in recognition of the considerable delegation of authority to individual units within the World Bank and the fundamental role of borrowers in achieving development results.

■ Evolving Criteria

Conceptually, the World Bank's evaluation function has evolved to reflect the changes in development priorities just described. In the 1960s and 1970s, the dominant paradigm was the production function. Input-output tables drove resource allocation, and cost-benefit analysis governed evaluation. Central planning and public investment were seen as the major determinants of economic growth, and evaluation focused on the economic justification of the projects that made up the economic plan. As a result, evaluation methods were highly sector specific and sought to tie the economic contribution of individual projects to the goals set by planners for the overall economy. Then, as now, ex ante methods of economic appraisal were identical to those used in retrospective evaluations. Rate-of-return methodology was the standard tool used in both project analysis and ex post evaluation, and much attention was devoted to estimating (and reestimating) the shadow prices used to correct for distortions in the market value of products and factors of production (principally labor, foreign exchange, and capital).

In the 1980s, as disillusionment with state-led approaches to development set in, development economics shifted its focus from physical planning to economic policy, and from a predilection for centrally planned investments to the creation of market-friendly, people-friendly, and environment-friendly policy frameworks. In response, development evaluation has had to reshape its approach, diversify its instruments, and broaden the focus of its concerns.

For projects that deal with policies and institutions, or for those that center on indirect benefits and costs, there is no straightforward way to calculate meaningful rates of return. This is why only a third of World Bank-financed projects today are justified based on such calculations. Accordingly, the economic evaluation of projects has become far more comprehensive and multidisciplinary than it used to be. The main "unit of account" in the Bank's operational work has now in fact shifted from the project to the country. Portfolios of projects, and increasingly the full mix of lending and nonlending services that make up country assistance programs, have become the dominant preoccupation of development policy makers. As a result, World Bank evaluators have had to broaden their traditional concentration on individual projects. Individual project evaluations—the performance audits described above—have not been abandoned, but their scope and focus have been adapted to make them useful as "building blocks" for evaluating programs and, in particular, for relating the outcomes of individual projects to the achievement of broader country assistance goals. Today, projects are judged not only in cost-benefit terms as freestanding investments, but also as vehicles for policy reform and capacity building.

Hence, over and above the traditional focus on efficacy (the achievement of project goals) and efficiency (the effectiveness of resource use), World Bank evaluators have given increasing attention to relevance (the degree to which project goals reflect country assistance priorities). The outcomes of projects are rated by OED according to these three main determinants of development effectiveness (OED, 1996).

■ *Sustainability*

Sustainability has emerged as another fundamental criterion in World Bank evaluation. Since 1989, the sustainability of projects has been rated systematically. Among the many possible definitions of sustainability, the one used by the Bank is pragmatic: It connotes the ability of a development intervention to sustain the flow of its benefits over time. Threats to sustainability abound. A project may make excessive use of scarce and nonrenewable natural resources, or a volatile policy environment may endanger project benefits and sink the rate of return below the demanding threshold of 10% set by the World Bank to rate a project's outcome as acceptable. This has happened in several projects centered on production of farm and plantation crops for export (see, for example, OED, 1993a, 1994b, 1994c). Project institutions may be too weak to operate and maintain facilities properly. Poor financial management may threaten the quality of operations and thus the sustainability of benefits. In urban water supply, for example, the Bank has often found that it is relatively easy to install physical facilities, but that the development of agencies and policies takes sustained effort and assistance over many years. Many water companies have failed to build up the financial and institutional bases needed to operate and maintain their facilities well, let alone make new investments, and hence to sustain the services they provide (OED, 1992, 1994e).

For evaluators, a dilemma arises out of the fact that sustaining a policy or program may require frequent adjustments in investment patterns and forms of organization, especially in the framework of an integrated and volatile global economy. In other words, just as Joseph Schumpeter (1942) characterizes capitalism as "creative destruction," a sustainable policy or program may be conceived as a cluster of multiple initiatives endowed with varying life spans, which replace one another through an evolutionary, natural selection process. From this perspective, there can be a trade-off between sustainability at the project level and sustainability at the program level.

☐ *The Role of Institutions*

Evaluation evidence indicates that sustainability is closely correlated with effective institutional development impact (OED, 1995b, 1996). This is not surprising, given that most institutions seek to preserve themselves, and the achievement of sustainability calls for decision-making protocols and social arrangements that can trigger recovery mechanisms in response to unexpected challenges. Institutional development may involve a wide variety of activities, ranging from the development of new skills or attitudes to changes in the regulatory, contractual, or ownership framework, to the establishment of new public, private, or voluntary capacities. Institutional development does not always connote capacity building within existing organizational frameworks; sometimes agencies must be "reinvented," restructured, or altogether abandoned to make way for other organizations better adapted to the necessary policy environment.

In India and Pakistan, for example, the Bank in the 1970s supported the development of seed industries that would help increase production of the staple foods wheat and rice. At first, the projects supported the monopolistic national parastatal seed companies—the countries' only seed companies at the time. Meanwhile, however, they also encouraged the freeing of policies toward the seed industry and the development of state and provincial seed companies. Staff trained in the original companies, lured by promotion prospects, moved out into the local public companies and into private companies that began to establish themselves. Twenty years later, an OED impact evaluation found thriving private seed industries in these countries. It judged that the organizational framework that the projects supported is now obsolete, but that without this support the private seed industry could not have developed as it has (OED, 1995c).

The World Bank's comparative advantage lies in its nonpartisan stance and its ability to provide technical assistance toward improved economic governance, defined as the encouragement of accountability, transparency, and the rule of law. This assistance is typically combined with complementary lending activities designed to improve economic policies. In this context, the promotion of evaluation capacity in developing countries has emerged as a priority within the World Bank's public sector management activities (OED, 1994d).

■ Participation

The new social and environmental emphases of the development agenda imply a participatory mode in the design and operation of investment projects. Accordingly, evaluators have been called upon to assess participation and, in particular, the role of decentralized modes of governance in area development projects (OED, 1993b) and of beneficiary involvement in building and maintaining community infrastructure. Conversely, participatory development has created a larger and more demanding market for evaluation services and induced experiments with participatory modes of evaluation (OED, 1995a). Self-evaluation combined with independent evaluation is the approach adopted by the World Bank because it adds the rigor of performance auditing to the learning advantages of utilization-based evaluation processes. Greater use of beneficiary surveys, adaptation of rapid rural appraisal techniques, more systematic use of focus groups, and computer-based modes of beneficiary consultation have begun to influence evaluation products and processes.

The exposure of government officials to such activities and the resulting feedback from beneficiaries help to make development more participatory. Ultimately, however, the solution lies in building within the developing countries the initiatives needed for effective governance, including a vibrant civil society and independent evaluation organizations.

■ References

Lateef, S. (1995). *The evolving role of the World Bank: Helping meet the challenge of development.* Washington, DC: World Bank.

Operations Evaluation Department (OED), World Bank. (1992, June). Urban water supply and sanitation. *OED Precis,* 29.

Operations Evaluation Department (OED), World Bank. (1993a, January). Rural development in Sri Lanka. *OED Precis, 37.*

Operations Evaluation Department (OED), World Bank. (1993b, September). Area development projects. *Lessons & Practices, 3.*

Operations Evaluation Department (OED), World Bank. (1994a). *Assessing development effectiveness: Evaluation in the World Bank and International Finance Corporation.* Washington, DC: World Bank.

Operations Evaluation Department (OED), World Bank. (1994b, June). Interplay of adjustment and investment operations: Agriculture in Madagascar. *OED Precis, 64.*

Operations Evaluation Department (OED), World Bank. (1994c, June). Revitalizing treecrops: Rubber in Thailand. *OED Precis, 66.*

Operations Evaluation Department (OED), World Bank. (1994d, November). Building evaluation capacity. *Lessons & Practices, 4.*

Operations Evaluation Department (OED), World Bank. (1994e, November). Managing urban water supply and sanitation: Operation and maintenance. *Lessons & Practices, 5.*

Operations Evaluation Department (OED), World Bank. (1995a). *Evaluation and development: Proceedings of the 1994 World Bank Conference.* Washington, DC: World Bank.

Operations Evaluation Department (OED), World Bank. (1995b). *Evaluation results, 1993.* Washington, DC: World Bank.

Operations Evaluation Department (OED), World Bank. (1995c, June 30). *Impact evaluation: Seed projects in Bangladesh, India, and Pakistan* (Report No. 1476-IN). Washington, DC: World Bank.

Operations Evaluation Department (OED), World Bank. (1996). *Evaluation results, 1994.* Washington, DC: World Bank.

Schumpeter, J. A. (1942). *Capitalism, socialism, and democracy.* New York: Harper.

PART V

New Topics for Evaluation

---

*I*n the United States, the development of evaluation had its historical roots in such diverse topics as agricultural experiments, medical trials, and defense planning and budgeting processes, and it had its great professional expansion concurrent with the expansion of social programming during the 1960s, in education, mental health, income maintenance, and other fields. To judge from the contents of Part V, evaluation in the 21st century can anticipate a continued expansion of the topics to which evaluation is applied.

In Chapter 15, Ignacio Cano argues for applying evaluation methodologies and concepts to a very novel topic indeed: massive human rights violations. Although this topic is often conceptualized—and rightly so—as a problem of prosecuting individual cases with standard judicial practices, Cano points out that in the case of massive violations, such individually tailored investigations are rarely feasible on a large scale. In such cases, evaluation can play an important role in documenting the existence of problems, the effectiveness of interventions to improve human rights, and general improvement of human rights situations. Cano shows how the same problems that occur in any evaluation occur with this topic, but often

multiplied many times as stakeholder opinions take on life-and-death mean-
ing, as some important stakeholders refuse any cooperation at all, and as the
systematic destruction of records and people thwarts careful documentation
of events. His description of biases in identifying and reporting abuses is
particularly enlightening. Many of the tasks that Cano describes sound like
standard evaluation problems, such as determining the credibility of a source,
deciding how to aggregate data, and deciding when an episode ends. But in
this context, they take on meanings that are so extreme as to seem fantastic.
Can the victim recall events that occurred under such extreme duress? Is an
episode a single torture session or a sequence of abuses that one person
experiences over many years? Does the episode end when the torture session
ends or when the victim is removed from the possibility of further torture?
When the populations of entire villages have been killed, is there anyone left
who can provide a veridical firsthand account? It is a truism that evaluation
is itself a political act, but that truism takes on poignant meaning with this
highly charged topic. Cano's chapter is, perhaps, the most emotionally
engrossing in this book.

In Chapter 16, John Nieuwenhuysen discusses the role that evaluation
has played in immigration policy in Australia. In the first part of his chapter,
he describes the development of Australian immigration policy, with occa-
sional comments on how research information played a part in that develop-
ment. The second part of the chapter is devoted to the role that research might
play in driving and informing immigration policy. Nieuwenhuysen describes
two roles for the evaluation of immigration programs. The first focuses on
identifying the objectives of immigration, multicultural and population poli-
cies, and the means for their attainment. The evaluator might examine, for
example, the numbers and countries of origin of immigrants, and their
reasons for coming. The other role is concerned with examining impacts of
immigration policies. A particular challenge of this sort of work is to generate
the ability to assess outcomes of immigration programs for specific economic,
social, labor market, intake, settlement, environmental, urban infrastructure,
and many other impacts, as well as across all these impacts to obtain an
overall judgment. Nieuwenhuysen describes how solutions to these evalu-
ation problems helped discipline what could otherwise have been an even
more highly charged debate. He specifies seven lessons that intertwine
immigration and evaluation and that should be required reading for any
serious student of this topic.

Josette Murphy gives an account in Chapter 17 of the treatment of gender issues by the World Bank. This chapter is a good complement to Chapter 14, by Robert Picciotto, as it involves one of the kinds of World Bank evaluations (specifically, a self-evaluation) that he describes. Murphy used both quantitative and qualitative methods, with both new data and existing records, to trace the developing treatment of gender issues over the years at the World Bank. The focus on gender reflects an increasing understanding that the World Bank's overarching goal of reducing poverty cannot be achieved without ensuring that women as well as men are fully involved in and benefit from development activities. Murphy asks an ambitious set of questions: What did the Bank say it should do? What did it actually do? Did the Bank meet its goals? Why did things happen the way they did? Her chapter provides a useful model of the valuable interplay that can occur when quantitative and qualitative methods are used together, and in that sense is also in the same spirit as Lois-ellin Datta's chapter later in this volume (Chapter 24).

In Chapter 18, Michael Bamberger describes a specific example of evaluating the long-term impacts of World Bank development projects on women. The example Bamberger uses is from Tunisia, where the World Bank funded a number of projects aimed at women, each of which Bamberger describes. He then devotes the bulk of his chapter to discussion of the methodological problems the evaluation encountered. By far the most prominent problem was determining what would have happened in the absence of the activities generated by the World Bank loans. So Bamberger describes the host of admittedly imperfect methods used in Tunisia to determine what baseline conditions might have been like in the absence of good data about them, and to construct both control sites and control groups that might approximate what might have happened without intervention. All of these notions fall under what is often called the "counterfactual," that is, using some method to discern what would have happened had a treatment not been implemented. The latter concern must inevitably arise and be addressed at some point in a credible impact evaluation, but it is easy to overlook how often the concern is not even recognized by those with relatively little experience in impact assessment. Of course, this is not the only important methodological issue that Bamberger mentions. In particular, his description of difficulties in constructing and gathering information on measures of all kinds—but especially from women themselves in some cultures—is a clear reminder of how little we can take for granted as we move from evaluations in one culture to evaluations in another. And like so many other contributors to this volume who deal with international evaluations, Bamberger notes the importance of developing an infrastructure for evaluation in any newly developing national system of evaluation.

The Honorable Kristina Svensson, member of the Swedish Parliament, relates in Chapter 19 her experiences on a committee to evaluate Sweden's foreign aid policies and programs. With the end of the Cold War, aid is no longer distributed in accord with superpower tensions. Today, donor nations are asking hard questions about whether their aid policies are fostering such goals as economic growth, economic and social equality, economic and political independence, democracy, and sustainable use of natural resources and protection of the environment. Svensson outlines many of the problems that evaluators encounter in studying this problem—especially the difficulties of separating out the effectiveness of donor countries' aid policies and programs from structural and procedural problems in recipient countries that may interfere with effectiveness. She also points to the key but often problematic link between evaluative information and decision making—what might traditionally be called the utilization issue—that donor countries have rarely considered in the past because the effectiveness of aid was often defined in geopolitical terms rather than program outcome terms. Like the issues involved in the evaluation of global environment problems (see, e.g., Chapters 22 and 23) or gender issues in World Bank lending practices (see, e.g., Chapter 17), the evaluation of foreign aid raises new intellectual and practical issues that less global evaluations have rarely had to address.

In Chapter 20, by Kwai-Cheung Chan and Jonathan Tumin, we move to the evaluation of nuclear weaponry. The specific topic is the U.S. nuclear "triad" strategy, or the reliance on land-, air-, and sea-based nuclear delivery systems as part of overall defense strategy. The context was a request to the U.S. General Accounting Office (GAO) by the Congress in 1990 for an evaluation of the nuclear triad. Congress was beginning to deal with mounting U.S. budget problems, and simultaneously was facing suggestions for the further development of new nuclear weapons systems, such as the Midgetman missile. In response, GAO's Program Evaluation and Methodology Division (PEMD) evaluated existing and proposed nuclear systems against seven effectiveness criteria as well as relative costs. The results of this massive effort were fascinating. PEMD found systematic tendencies to overestimate the likely effectiveness of proposed new weapon systems or upgrades, to underestimate the performance of existing systems, and to overstate the likely offensive or defensive threats to current systems by the former Soviet Union. PEMD also found that the operational testing on which the claims about new weapons systems were based was often insufficient and unrealistic; that costs were understated because life-cycle costs were not used; that performance results were incomplete or unrepresentative; that there was a lack of systematic comparison of new systems to the ones they were to replace; and that the rationales for the development of new systems were unconvincing from the very beginning. PEMD concluded that (a) Soviet defensive and offensive threats to all three legs had been systematically overstated, meaning that existing U.S. systems were considerably more robust than popularly believed; (b) the air leg's bombers offered certain flexibility by virtue of being recallable, reusable, retargetable, and available for conventional (i.e., nonnuclear) missions, which was not the case for silos and their ballistic missiles; and (c) the sea leg, overall, was more cost-effective than the land leg, across multiple measures of effectiveness. Chan and Tumin's chapter presents much more detail about these findings, and it is fascinating reading.

In Chapter 21, Vladimir Novikov describes an evaluation of a highly charged technological problem—the 1986 Chernobyl nuclear power plant accident. Because the Chernobyl accident was (one hopes) a relatively unique event, and as the subsequent policy interventions were aimed at reducing the future frequency of such events to zero, any evaluation of those interventions is bound to face unique problems. Novikov first acquaints us with the general issues involved in the safety of nuclear power plants. He then summarizes the results of studies concerned with what caused the Chernobyl accident, what steps were taken to remediate those causes, and the consensus about how effective those solutions are likely to be (after all, the kinds of experiments one can conduct to test these solutions are highly constrained for ethical reasons). Novikov ends with an analysis of the policy issues that surround the present and future use of nuclear power plants as sources of electricity, especially in nations with high electricity needs and relatively smaller budgets with which to meet those needs (nuclear power being cheaper than most alternatives).

W. Haven North gives us another view in Chapter 22 of an international evaluation effort pertaining to the environment in which the World Bank was, this time, a participating partner along with a number of other international agencies, such as the United Nations. The topic was a pilot evaluation of the Global Environmental Facility, an agency funded and governed by representatives from more than 70 countries. North devotes most of his chapter to description of the very complex organization of this pilot phase and the lessons that were learned from it about how the full evaluation ought to be conducted. Such organizational details are familiar in programs of much smaller scope, but at the global level, they represent problems of unprecedented size that all evaluators will encounter when they evaluate programs of worldwide significance that have the involvement of multiple organizations. Such global evaluation efforts are novel to most evaluators for their scale, substantive and organizational complexity, global dimensions, and sometimes the exceptionally sensitive settings of distrust in which they occur. In this context, the lessons from experiences such as the GEF evaluation are increasingly important to document in the professional literature of the field.

In Chapter 23, Charles Zraket and William Clark echo the environmental theme of the preceding two chapters with their analysis of some issues that arise in the evaluation of global environmental change. Their focus is quite different, however. Zraket and Clark point out that the evaluation of policies pertaining to global environmental change, by the very nature of such changes, necessarily involve globally dispersed information systems on a huge array of sometimes interrelated topics. The data gathering and management challenges here are potentially overwhelming. Such a system needs to be able to identify developing changes, assess the risks they present, provide adequate measures of the outcome of ameliorative interventions, and present links to feasible actions. Believing that no single information system is capable of doing all the necessary tasks on all the requisite topics, Zraket and Clark call for integrated evaluation systems at different levels that complement the strengths and weaknesses of each other and that are cheaply and easily accessible to citizens, researchers, evaluators, managers, and policy makers.

William R. Shadish

15

Evaluating Human Rights Violations

Ignacio Cano

In this chapter I will attempt to show how the analysis of massive human rights violations can be treated within the framework of evaluation and social science. This issue is not often conceptualized in this way, yet it can benefit notably from the methodologies developed in these fields. I will review some of the problems usually present in the documentation of human rights violations and make some suggestions about how to confront them.[1] My main aim here is to foster further reflection on these issues, and my main focus is on violations of the most basic civil rights (e.g., the right to life, integrity, and freedom of movement). I will deal with situations where these violations are or have been massive, because in contexts where human rights violations are few, standard juridical practice may suffice.

A wide variety of persons and institutions (e.g., national and international bodies; governmental, nongovernmental, and intergovernmental institutions) engage in documenting past human rights violations. In some cases, analyzing and publicizing past violations may be only a part of an institution's human rights work. For instance, some nongovernmental organizations record violations shortly after they happen, follow up on them, act in court, and try to help victims and their families, while also producing periodic reports on these and other violations. In other cases, institutions have been created with the specific purpose of giving accounts of abuses. They may do so periodically (e.g., the Special Rapporteurs for Human Rights appointed by the United Nations) or they may be intended for the one-time purpose of documenting a certain period of violations in a country. This is typical of political transitions after phases of massive violations or internal armed confrontations. A good example of this is the "Truth Commission," which is charged with writing a report unveiling the reality of particular violations. The mandate of such a commission often includes the formulation of recommendations to avoid the repetition of abuses. Here, the information concerning violations is collected at specific points in time, sometimes long after they happened, rather than "on-line," although it is not unusual for such commissions to benefit from the cases collected by the more stable institutions that record abuses as they happen.

It would seem at first that dealing with human rights violations is a prosecutor's task, and indeed, it should be. Nevertheless, the issue of human rights tends to come to the forefront precisely when the judicial system fails to work properly and may even be used to cover up abuses, thus contributing to the perpetrators' impunity. It can be argued as well that the study of human rights should be carried out by independent lawyers using the same methodology as that used by prosecutors. However, this is usually not feasible because, from a juridical perspective, each case must, by definition, be investigated individually, with a verdict reached for each individual case. Perpetrators, for their part, are judged on each of the individual crimes they may have committed. The search for evidence and proof for each alleged crime requires considerable time and resources, but no lower standard of evidence is admissible to convict. Yet in contexts of massive violations, cases are usually too many and time too short for in-depth investigation of each one of them, even if the political or social climate allows such an investigation at all (it may be prohibited or risky to conduct such an investigation). Hence global judgments and inferences are needed, as, for example, "There was a standard practice by the police of torturing prisoners," or "The human rights situation is improving in the country."

Thus we need the ability to draw broad inferences from vast amounts of data composed by individual cases that cannot be fully investigated. Because this is what social science does, and does well, a wide space opens here for social scientists to assist in this process. In other words, in situations of massive abuses, the study of human rights violations can be considered as social research. Indeed, we can think of it as evaluation. It may in fact involve a concrete program to be evaluated (e.g., a policy designed to reduce abuses, or a new regime that claims to have eliminated them), thus rendering the task equivalent to a traditional evaluation. More commonly, there is no specific program to be evaluated. Rather, we often have to infer the *program* the perpetrator had in mind (i.e., the perpetrator's plan or strategy) from its *outcomes* (i.e., from the violations). A pattern of killings in an area may lead to the conclusion, for example, that the perpetrator intended to eliminate young men in that area (who might join the guerrilla forces), or we may infer that an increasing level of violence against civilian populations located near the border was intended to drive those people to leave the country. In those cases where the documentation of abuses is accompanied by recommendations designed to avoid their repetition—as, for example, in most truth commissions— the process can be conceived as formative evaluation, the aim of which is to improve or generate a "program" to stop the violations.

However, this is an unusual type of evaluation, for several reasons. Stakes are very high, and the stakeholders tend to have strong and opposing views and interests. It is not uncommon for some key stakeholders, such as governments or guerrilla forces, to cooperate reluctantly or not at all, even though they may be compelled to say publicly that they will. In other cases, they may actively oppose the enterprise. These tensions are especially acute when an attempt is made to evaluate violations in periods of armed confrontations, and, particularly, in cases of internal conflicts or civil wars. In these situations, both sides tend to accuse each other of violations, and the field of human rights becomes just another trench in which the conflict is fought.

Although we can conceive the task of studying massive human rights violations as applied research, the process of collecting the information necessary for this task differs and goes beyond standard research for several reasons:

1. Often, cases are or were collected not just to document or make a global judgment about a situation, but with other purposes in mind, for example, to initiate a judicial process or to help a victim and his or her family.

2. Each case has a value in itself beyond its representativeness toward a general process. One would want a representative sample of what happened in the country, but one would also want the names of as many individual victims as possible, regardless of their representativeness. For many victims who were killed and for their families, publishing their names is a way to vindicate their memories and to set the record straight. Also, if some compensation is finally offered to the victims and their families, the documentation and publishing of their cases may be, in the absence of a judicial verdict, a requisite for obtaining such compensation.

3. It is hardly ever possible to choose which subjects or cases to interview. Nearly always, one must wait for informants to decide to come forward. The only way to encourage or hasten this process is through general information campaigns.

4. The process of collecting data is valuable in itself, quite beyond the information gathered. For many victims and their relatives this may be their first opportunity to tell of their experiences outside their inner circle and to look for vindication. In these cases, giving testimony may have a cathartic component and a healing effect for individuals long forced to hide both the facts and their feelings about them. Indeed, the expression of past abuses and suffering may have similar effects at the social level, and may not only reduce the fear of testifying but also help to change the social and political climate for the better.

In short, the purpose of giving an objective account of human rights violations must take into account, and coexist with, the other aims and potential effects (whether intended or not) of the enterprise of gathering reports.

■ *Objectives of Human Rights Violations Studies*

The objectives of these studies can be summarized as follows:

1. *Determine and quantify the existence of human rights violations.* A final figure, or at least an estimate of the total number of violations (and of the violations attributed to each perpetrator), is usually sought.

2. *Examine common features of the violations,* such as the profile of the usual victims and direct perpetrators, the pattern and mode of the violations, and the existence of temporal trends in the number of violations.

3. *Make inferences,* both general and specific (based on the data emerging from the work done for the two previous objectives), about higher responsibilities, intentions, strategies, events that had an impact on the number of violations, and so on.

Some of these objectives can be fulfilled in a fairly straightforward manner from the data collected (e.g., the number of assassinations in a given period); in other cases, more detailed analyses and syntheses are required, and inferences may appear more tentative (e.g., a strategy to kill certain groups of people).

Some Problems in Evaluating Human Rights Violations

First, the question of *source credibility* is an important consideration for the evaluator, given the limited scope for investigating cases individually. The choices range from (a) accepting every case as declared and then presenting the results as "alleged" or "denounced" cases, with no claim as to the authenticity of each, to (b) screening or giving a confidence rating to each case or informant. Accepting every declaration as made carries a risk of distortions or inventions, because the stakes are so high. But screening the cases and rejecting some may open the door to bias, as well as criticism from the least satisfied stakeholders, who may claim that the process was not fair.

A second issue, concerning the *unit of analysis,* is not as straightforward as it may appear. Usually, information is sought and stored about (a) the victim (e.g., identity, social characteristics, group memberships), (b) the violation (e.g., the type of violation, the date and place it occurred), (c) the perpetrator (both at the individual and group levels), and (d) the informant (e.g., identity and relation to the victim). If each victim suffered only one violation at the hands of one perpetrator and this were to be related by one informant, the task would be much simpler. But in reality, one victim may suffer several violations (e.g., arbitrary arrest, torture, and rape), either in succession or in separate incidents. Many victims may suffer the same violations at the same time. Various informants may come independently to report on the same case, and each may report different violations in the same sequence of events. One perpetrator may be responsible for a certain violation but not for others in the same chain of events against the same victim.

Coding, processing, and storing all this information while maintaining its integrity (i.e., which victim suffered which violation at the hands of which perpetrator, testified to by which informant) is far from easy, given that these elements (victim, violation, perpetrator, informant) have multiple links and many possible combinations. Keeping all of them intact in the final database is very time-consuming and labor-intensive, so it is not uncommon to have to compromise and renounce the integrity of some of these links to speed up the process and make it more manageable (e.g., in a case with several informants, the database may not tell exactly which of the violations were reported by each of the informants). There is not even agreement on the most basic unit of storage and analysis. One may refer to the number of victims, to the number of violations (regardless of the number of victims in each), or one may work with the number of victims by violations (i.e., count every time a different person suffers a violation). In order to keep the linkage between violations that occurred to a group of individuals together, in the same place and time, and often precisely because of their group membership (e.g., trade union officials or inhabitants of the same village), the concept of "collective case" is sometimes used. Each individual violation has, apart from its own violation code, also a collective case code if it happened to several victims together.

It is also important to keep the linkage between a sequence of violations happening one after the other to the same victim(s). For example, a person is illegally arrested, taken to a secret location, tortured, and finally executed. This linkage is very relevant to any attempt to reconstruct the patterns in which violations have taken place, and it helps, in turn, to ascertain the intentions of the perpetrators. For this purpose, a concept such as "episode of violations" is sometimes used, with all violations pertaining to the same episode sharing a common code.

The limits for both "collective case" and "episode of violations" have to be defined explicitly, particularly the criteria for deciding when a case or an episode ends. This is usually done in terms of temporal contiguity and succession (e.g., an episode ends when the violations to the victim cease because he or she is either released or killed), but even this is not unproblematic. For example, if a group of persons is captured and tortured and one of them is released only to be captured again a few days later and brought back to the same cell and to the torture sessions, it would have to be determined whether this new entry would start a new case (and a new episode) or whether it would be part of the same collective case.

A third problem that affects both the quantification of human rights violations and the inferences that can be made from these data is *bias*. Although our purpose is to infer something about a universe of violations, we have access to only a sample of them, because many of the abuses may not have been reported. Furthermore, this underreporting will most probably not be random, so our sample will not be random either, and will therefore be subject to biases of various types. Let me mention seven common types of bias, among others that occur.

First is *bias arising from fear of reprisal against people who declare.* This fear may not be random and may affect mostly those persons and groups who are less organized and politically involved and who have a lower (real or perceived) possibility of self-protection.

Second is *bias related to the location where testimonies are taken.* Depending on the system and the places where people give their declarations, it may be easier for people from certain areas (e.g., cities where there may be offices) than for others who may have to travel extensively. This may produce geographic bias.

Third is *bias linked to institutions.* This refers both to the organization that has undertaken the study and to others that may submit their files to the former or that may collaborate in the campaign to promote and encourage informants to declare. Unbiasedness with regard to the various perpetrators is not always easy to attain and demonstrate, because the institutions are important stakeholders and they may be perceived by the public to be biased or to have their own political agenda.

Fourth is *bias related to memory.* Recent, more salient cases will be better remembered than those that happened long ago, so they will be reported more reliably and accurately.

Fifth is *bias related to the social definition of a human rights violation.* Usually, violations are not defined specifically when people are called to testify about abuses, and it is left to them to decide what they should relate. Basically, the main dimension is severity, and the person has to decide whether his or her case is severe enough not only to be defined as a human rights violation, but also to make the effort and risk of reporting it worthwhile. So there is a threshold of minimum severity above which people will decide to testify. This subjective threshold is not necessarily fixed, however, and it tends to vary in different times and social contexts. The tendency, at least in Central America, seems to be that (a) violations that are distant in time will have to be more severe than more recent ones in order to have the same likelihood of being reported and (b) in times and places of massive and extreme human rights violations, relatively minor violations will stand a lower chance of being reported than the same violations would have in periods of fewer and less brutal abuses.

For instance, in the case of the Truth Commission for El Salvador (United Nations, 1993), relatively few reports of torture alone were received for the worst years of violence (1980-1982), whereas more cases were denounced for the period after 1984. During the worst years, tortures were mostly reported if the person was killed afterward, but relatively rarely was torture denounced on its own. These results were interpreted to mean that people did not consider torture alone, in the context of massacres and widespread executions, to be a violation serious enough to require testimony. This bias must be taken into account to avoid the mistaken inference of the absence of relatively minor violations in the hardest times.

Sixth is *bias related to the purpose for which the violation is reported.* Often people report a disappearance to an institution immediately after it has happened, with the purpose of trying to obtain some information. If the victim should reappear alive (or even if the victim's corpse is found), relatives may think they have little to gain from denouncing the case again to other institutions or at a later time.

Seventh is *"perverse" bias, related to the enormity of a crime.* In some cases, the higher the number of victims of a crime, the lower the probability that the crime will be reported at all, or with enough information to identify the victims. Given that informants tend to be close relatives or neighbors of victims, if a whole family or village is killed (or driven to leave), it is less likely there will be an informant of the crime, especially somebody with all the relevant information.

Suggestions for Collecting and Analyzing Information on Human Rights Violations

First, there are different ways to confront the problem of bias. With regard to bias related to the location where testimonies are taken and bias related to the purpose for which the violation is reported, it may be possible for the evaluator to mitigate at least some of these problems. Even though one cannot choose one's informants, one may direct the information campaign and locate resources for collecting testimonies so as to target preferentially those areas and groups where there are more difficulties or less likelihood of receiving reports.

Where bias related to memory is concerned, people can be encouraged to remember, check, and write down details before they come to testify. It is important that interviewers be trained in stimulating people's memories, as, for example, by providing time referents that are known to informants and that can be easily dated (an interviewer may ask whether the events happened before, during, or after a flood, an earthquake, or some other highly memorable event). Also, if it is known that certain areas suffered violations particularly at a distant point in time, these areas may be specially targeted in the campaign and in the data collection effort.

With respect to bias related to the social definition of a violation and the unstable threshold it entails, a rate between less extreme and more extreme violations may be computed (say, the number of tortures divided by the number of executions) and monitored over time to see whether it correlates with the absolute number of executions in each period. The correlation should be negative, as we may predict that the more numerous the extreme violations in a certain period, the less likely it is that less severe violations will be reported. Then, if the rate is indeed higher in the milder periods, this could be used to estimate the number of unreported tortures in the harsher periods, unless there should be complementary information of what went on in those times that would point to a real change in the pattern of violations (e.g., several major detention centers where torture was rampant were closed at the time). Another strategy is to compute the rate between a milder violation alone and this same violation accompanied by another extreme violation in the same episode (say, number of tortures alone divided by number of tortures followed by execution) and carry out a similar analysis to the one just discussed.

An important point to recognize here is that a single dependent variable—that is, the number of violations—may depend on many independent variables. Therefore, the role of qualitative side information about what was happening in the country is essential for correct estimation and interpretation of the results.

In trying to deal with perverse bias, which involves the increased difficulty of obtaining reports of killings when many related people have been killed together, the evaluator should give more value and weight to scarce or even individual testimonies, so as not to favor the perpetrator who purposefully sought to eliminate witnesses. Further, informants should be asked not only about the victims they knew and can identify, but also about how many victims may have suffered violations in a collective case. Thus we would have a count of identified victims and another count of the total estimated number of victims (both identified and unidentified). The latter will logically be closer to the real number of victims. Then we can calculate the rate of identified victims to the total number of estimated victims for each area and period. Particularly low rates may be indicators of massive crimes, where it is harder to get reports from relatives that identify each victim unequivocally, or of special difficulty in getting reports (e.g., people have taken refuge abroad and are therefore unavailable to testify, or there is high fear in the area).

One more element that may be of use in cases of perverse bias is the relationship between victims and informants. Most informants tend to be close relatives of the victims. We can calculate the proportion of informants who correspond to a few of the closest categories (mother, wife, and so on) and then examine how these proportions vary across time and space. A low proportion of close relatives may again be a pointer toward possible massive violations, or special difficulties in getting reports, and the exact proportions may help in the estimation of this unreported figure.

Second, in attempting to quantify the number of violations that have occurred in a certain country over a specific period, it is useful to consider the proportion of cases reported repeatedly, that is, by different independent informants. If there is a high proportion of cases reported several times and very few reported only once, we will probably conclude that the total number of cases may not be considerably larger than our sample. If, on the contrary, most cases are reported just once and only very few are backed by several testimonies, we will surely agree that the total pool of violations must be much larger than the number we have registered. This is the principle used in the "recapture method" used to estimate animal populations in the wild, based on the number of repeated captures of the same individuals at different moments in time. Even though in our case we would probably be violating several assumptions under which the method is based,[2] it might still help us get some kind of bound (a lower or an upper bound) for the final estimation of our figure.

Third, when one is trying to make inferences based on the data collected, it is worth noting again that inferences can usually be made only from the number of violations and their patterns, their geographic distribution, and their evolution over time, unless the evaluator receives confessions or other information from the perpetrators' side (e.g., written orders, plans, instructions). For instance, in El Salvador, the similarity in the pattern of executions and their wide geographic extension during certain phases allowed the Truth Commission to conclude that they were not the product of the excesses of a few lower-ranked officers, but a planned strategy from the top, the aim of which was to wipe out the political enemy or to empty certain areas of population altogether.

A methodological strategy that may be very suitable is to model the series of violations over time and try to analyze them using an interrupted time series approach. This would allow one to check, for example, whether a certain policy designed to reduce abuses did indeed have an effect, or whether the arrival of a new commander in chief in a certain area was followed by a significantly higher or lower number of violations, while controlling for the general level of violations in the country as a whole during that period. In this way, one could analyze the impacts of specific individuals, policies, or events on the level of abuses. On some occasions, the aim is just to conclude whether there has been an improvement or a deterioration in the human rights situation. Time series analysis may also be very relevant for this aim.[3]

It goes without saying that to make inferences from these series of violations to the impacts of different policies or persons, using time series analysis, it is crucial, once again, to have qualitative side information about what was happening in the country in each period, possible factors that may help explain the shifts in the number or pattern of violations, and so forth. Because we are nearly always faced with an overdetermined system with many more possible unknowns (independent variables) than recorded parameters (often just one dependent variable, the number of violations), it is essential to have this side information to be able to sort out competing explanations for the same results.

To summarize, I have argued in this chapter that the study of human rights violations, often carried out within a juridical perspective, can benefit considerably from a social science frame of reference and methodology, particularly in contexts where the massive nature of violations prevents in-depth investigation of each instance. Furthermore, the logic of evaluation research can fruitfully be applied to this field. To demonstrate this, I have reviewed a few common problems in the analysis of human rights abuses and offered some suggestions on how to deal with them.

Moreover, insisting on a strictly juridical methodology may in some cases lead to impoverished results or questionable overall inferences. For instance, this would be the case if one attempted to exemplify a certain pattern of violations or reach inferences on strategies and higher responsibilities just from the criminal investigation of a single allegedly representative case. Instead, one should capitalize on the convergent validity of a wealth of testified yet unresearched cases reported in different times and places and by many independent informants. Hence it is my belief that evaluators with social scientific backgrounds should be involved in the process of collecting and analyzing human rights violations from the outset.

■ Notes

1. Strictly speaking, I will be referring here to violations of human rights by states as well as to violations of international humanitarian law by states or by nongovernmental parties that are bound to abide by such law (e.g., guerrilla forces in internal armed conflicts). For the sake of simplicity, I refer to all of these as *human rights violations.*

2. The method is normally based on the assumptions that the sample of individual units (in this case, violations) is a random sample from the total population (total number of violations) and that the probability of an individual being selected into the sample (a violation being reported) at a certain time is independent of its probability of being selected at another time. These assumptions probably do not hold in this case, because the probability of a case being reported once is not truly independent of its being reported again: There are a limited number of people who know about a given case and they may know of each other's reporting, which may encourage them to report it again or (more commonly) discourage them from reporting it again.

3. A good example of how time series analysis may be used for a related though slightly different purpose is given by William Stanley (1987), who shows that the series of illegal Salvadoran immigrants apprehended in the United States increased significantly after the worst waves of abuses in El Salvador, while controlling for economic migration in the area by introducing into the model the number of illegal Mexican immigrants apprehended. Thus he was able to demonstrate that immigration from El Salvador, contrary to Reagan administration claims, seemed to originate more from people's desire to take refuge against human rights abuses than from economic motivation.

■ *References*

Stanley, W. (1987). Economic migrants or refugees from violence? A time-series analysis of Salvadoran migration to the United States. *Latin American Research Review, 12*(1), 132-154.

United Nations. (1993). *De la locura a la esperanza. Informe de la Comisión de la Verdad para el Salvador.* San Salvador/New York: Annex II.

16

Lessons of Immigration Policy and the Role of Research

John Nieuwenhuysen

This chapter asks two questions: What are some lessons learned from the past 25 years of implementing international and national immigration policies? In particular, how does one establish a research agenda that is designed to inform and drive policy?

■ *Lessons From Implementing International and National Immigration Policies*

Comparisons among the policies of different countries are hazardous at the best of times, but these hazards are multiplied in immigration studies, which are diverse and contentious: Not only do they cover an extraordinary range of disciplines, they also incite very strong feelings. Moreover, immigrant flows to various countries are extremely different in their volume, composition, and nature. Some recipient nations, for example, do not appear to have even the basic policy starting point for determining how many or which people will cross their borders.

Difficulties of comparisons are compounded by enormous differences among nations in political and administrative cultures and traditions: Many institutions do not have counterparts in countries other than their own. And the political lobbying power of competing community groups is of course not identical from one place to another, nor are the attitudes of governments uniform with respect to refugee acceptance.

Despite these problems of comparison, I nonetheless wish to propose here seven lessons on immigration policy. These conclusions are based mostly on the lessons, as I see them, of Australian policy, though the last two are more universal. This is obviously a somewhat confined way of viewing the issue of recent immigration policy lessons, as Australia is an island continent and not readily privy to clandestine entry. I submit, however, that the first five lessons nonetheless remain quite robust. At the least, they have relevance for countries contemplating how best to try to regulate and manage the flow of new arrivals. The last two lessons are broader, with the seventh being indeed international and also probably unattainable, at least in the immediate future.

Australia has achieved basically positive economic and social outcomes from its long-standing immigration program. An enormous flow of people, relative to Australia's population, from a great diversity of backgrounds, has been largely successfully accommodated and integrated, socially and economically, despite public opinion that is generally unfavorable to the program, at least according to some polls. However, as emphasized below in Lesson 6, there is now a dramatic international shift toward greater mobility. The aspirations of many of those with skills who move between rich or industrializing countries are no longer for permanent residence or citizenship but for the ability to work and live temporarily in another country. The great growth of mobility and the speed of communication and change in a trade-liberalizing global economy have created a new order and ethos of need for freedom of movement. In Australia, the volume of any given cohort of temporary visa and other workers and tourists far exceeds, at any point in time, the total permanent settlement for the year.

In my view, the following lessons flow from Australia's experience. They are obviously not generalizable in toto to other countries, although Australian policies do resemble Canadian policies somewhat. Nonetheless, there may be germs of ideas that are of use outside Australia. Indeed, the question of such generalizability is an important one for evaluation research.

Lessons 1 and 2 go together:

■ *Lesson 1:* A policy of laissez-faire in dealing with immigrant settlement issues is not advisable in conditions of relatively high unemployment. It cannot be assumed that, responding to education and training systems in host nations, immigrants will be absorbed into jobs and will adapt to the local culture without friction.

■ *Lesson 2:* Ethnicity-specific settlement and language-training facilities are necessary and should be provided in a coordinated way.

A major foundation for current planned and assisted settlement in Australia was the (Galbally) *Review of Post-Arrival Programs and Services for Migrants* (Australian Government Printing Service, 1978). The Galbally report was commissioned in a decade that began with the effective ending of the White Australia policy and that was characterized by a steady increase in non-English-speaking background (NESB) immigrants, including many from Asia, such as Indo-Chinese refugees.

The review was driven by concern to find an effective means of integrating immigrants from increasingly diverse backgrounds and avoiding the problems sometimes associated with multiracial issues. Equity was also important—notably, working conditions, qualification recognition, and English-language knowledge and training. The report enunciated (para. 1.7) a new and innovative settlement and multiculturalism program based on four key principles:

1. All members of society must have equal opportunity to realize their full potential and must have equal access to programs and services.
2. Every person should be able to maintain his or her culture without prejudice or disadvantage and should be encouraged to understand and embrace other cultures.
3. Needs of immigrants should, in general, be met by programs and services available to the whole community, but special services and programs are necessary to ensure equality of access and provision.
4. Services and programs should be designed and operated in full consultation with clients, and self-help should be encouraged as much as

possible, with a view to helping immigrants to become self-reliant quickly.

The practical outcomes of this assessment were substantive. These included the following:

- formalization of the previous hit-or-miss efforts to cater to the postarrival needs of NESB immigrants, through the implementation of 57 recommendations and through the injection of $50 million for postarrival support services over the next 3 years (a vastly increased sum)
- expansion of a network of migrant hostels acting as highly centralized settlement bureaus—with a focus on provision of accommodation, adult English-language classes, welfare support, child-care services, and information provision (through bilingual officers)
- substantial expansion of adult English-language training, including a radical shift in focus from "general English" grammar-based instruction to "on-arrival courses"
- introduction of a range of language and cultural maintenance initiatives (e.g., an ethnic broadcasting service), as well as free national interpreting services (e.g., Telephone Interpreter Service)

In addition, and following other settlement-related reports, several initiatives have been taken. For example:

- Efforts have been made to ensure the proper recognition of overseas qualifications.
- Advanced occupation-specific English-language training has been introduced.
- Dedicated funding for adult migrant education programs has been considerably increased and now stands at about $124 million a year.
- National and regional multicultural broadcasting networks have been developed.
- A grant-in-aid welfare network has been created, with an enormous diversity of projects.
- A national spread of migrant resource centers has been established.
- The national policy of languages in 1987 provided powerful advocacy for NESB language maintenance in Australia.

These settlement policies in Australia bear comparison with Canadian and Swedish initiatives, each of which supplements general welfare policy with specific measures and reforms specially designed for immigrants. The experiences and attitudes of Australia, Canada, and Sweden may be contrasted with those of other countries, such as Britain and Germany. In Britain, for example, the overall immigrant population is about 8% of the total. The main period of immigration was in the 1950s and 1960s, with immigrants coming mainly from the West Indies, India, and Pakistan. At that time, as Marian FitzGerald (1993) has noted, "central government broadly adopted a 'laissez faire' attitude towards the settlement of immigrants" (p. 5). Later, by the end of the 1980s, "different government departments were not only implementing and developing a range of programmes to promote equality of opportunity for these groups but . . . were beginning routinely to make explicit reference to them in the mainstream of their policies" (p. 5; see also Dummett, 1995; FitzGerald, 1995).

Even though it may have been felt that immigrant minorities in Britain needed to feel secure in their own subcultures, "civil unrest . . . suggested a serious threat to social cohesion if no action was taken . . . and has more recently led to demands for improved " 'targeting' of resources." However, the policy response is neither " 'comprehensive nor coherent,' and underlying it is even a tradition which emphasises the need to be 'racially inexplicit' and to avoid specific reference to the needs of ethnic minorities" (FitzGerald, 1993, p. 6).

The absence of explicit multicultural and settlement policy in Britain no doubt reflects the view that Britain is not a "country of immigration." The same has been said of Germany, even though it has received about 20 million immigrants since 1945. Germany, however, is perceived as a nation that has historically recruited temporary workers. Yet, as Professors Stephen Castles and Mark Miller (1993) have shown, there are great "similarities in the migratory process to Australia and Germany, though there are differences in migration policies and attitude towards permanent settlement." Castles and Miller conclude:

If the architects of the post-war European "guest-worker systems" had studied the migratory processes in their own histories or elsewhere, they would never have held the naive belief that they could turn flows of migrant labour on and off as if with a tap. They would have understood the movement of workers almost always leads to family reunion and permanent settlement. The very fears of permanent ethnic minorities held by some governments turned into self-fulfilling prophecies: by denying legitimacy to family reunion and settlement, government made sure that these processes would take place under the most unfavourable circumstances, leading to the creation of minorities and to deep divisions in society. (p. 123)

■ *Lesson 3:* A welcoming attitude to citizenship, recognition of diversity, and cultivation of security within a multicultural society are desirable.

It is clear that the policy initiatives in Australia that followed the Galbally report have been important, if not instrumental, in creating conditions that enabled Professor Robert Holton to reach the following conclusion based on a survey of the social consequences of immigration:

The experience of Australia's post-Second World War immigration has been characterised by a significant level of social cohesion even amidst rapid, culturally diverse immigration processes. Social cohesion of this kind is not, however, to be equated with social justice or the complete elimination of racist behaviour. In analysing why social cohesion has been maintained, it is important to note that Australia's national identity is a relatively weak one, facilitating both immigrant integration and host-society tolerance . . . The case of Australia, therefore, supports the view that culturally pluralistic and multi-racial immigrant societies can work, especially where national identity is weak, where host society responses are not overwhelmingly antagonistic, and where there is a degree of party political bi-partisanship. (Wooden, Holton, Hugo, & Sloan, 1994, p. 281)

The outcome Holton describes has been achieved in the context of a policy of multiculturalism, which encourages a view that social cohesion does not require abandonment of cultural differences—on the contrary, these differences should be celebrated. And multiculturalism was not merely for immigrants, but for all Australians. This open, welcoming approach is coupled with strong encouragement that immigrants adopt Australian citizenship.

■ *Lesson 4:* An immigration program should be visibly under control, because community confidence that it is not running loose is extremely important.

It is difficult to envisage bipartisan political acceptance of an immigration policy in Australia without the controls that have characterized the post-war period. The main ways in which the intake has been regulated are as follows:

- a federal government Department of Immigration
- fixed arrival intake planning levels, also comprising targets for different immigrant categories
- visible selection principles or rules, including a "points test" for different categories
- a system of Immigration Agreements, overseas-based immigration officers, and settlement-assistance arrangements, in order to encourage potential immigrants (Wooden et al., 1994)

This regulation has permitted widespread consultation by the minister to determine community attitudes toward the overall intake and its component parts. An annual announcement of the planned immigration program gives details of targets under each category, and a sophisticated administrative system has enabled the Department of Immigration and Ethnic Affairs to attain the targets very accurately.

Emphasizing its desire to maintain and to be seen as maintaining its control over the program, the government has taken care to ensure that there is no queue jumping. Consequently, despite some public criticism of processing, a strict policy of disallowing illegal and unjustified entry has been pursued. (Of course, as an island, Australia is better placed than some other countries to manage this.) This insistence on not permitting queue jumping has been coupled with the public and defined nature of the program's regulation.

■ *Establishing a Research Agenda to Drive and Inform Policy*

Lesson 5 brings me to the second issue on which I want to comment—how we can establish a research agenda to drive and inform policy:

- ■ *Lesson 5:* It is necessary to monitor any immigration program's consequences, and to have available good data and analysis for its assessment and evaluation. It should also be possible for society to discuss dispassionately and in open forums the issues, however sensitive, relating to all aspects of the topic.

Immigration is potentially an extremely controversial subject. Feelings can run strong, especially because flows of new people to a society can alter forever its character in a way that is not popular with portions of the host group. Comments by public figures can capture headlines, and arguments based on back-of-the-envelope calculations may enjoy long and misleading lives.

Most immigrant-receiving countries can no doubt point to parts of their history in which emotional debates have persisted with only sparse relevance to full knowledge, statistics, or analysis of the consequences of immigration. In Australia, an episode of heated exchanges in the early to mid-1980s led to an inquiry into immigration that proposed a government-funded Bureau of Immigration Research (Committee to Advise on Australia's Immigration Policies, 1988). The Bureau, established in 1989, has presided over a great expansion in data, analysis, discussion, and the general literature. Its title and province of responsibility have also grown, and now encompass multicultural and population as well as immigration research.

The Bureau is part of a rather unusual genre in the Australian Commonwealth government administrative structure. It is funded by, but largely independent of, the government and the Department of Immigration and Ethnic Affairs, of which it is a division. Its independent function has been created through convention rather than statute. That convention permits the Bureau to decide (after due consultation) its own terms of reference for studies, and to determine (after public advertisement or tender) its authors and whether (after peer review) and how to publish their work.

Professor Graeme Hugo has observed that "recent years [in Australia] have seen a veritable explosion of publication on immigration and settlement issues. Foremost here has been the active publication program of the [Bureau] . . . which alone now constitutes the most comprehensive collection of immigration and settlement research of any nation in the world" (Wooden et al., 1994, p. 1). The Bureau's work has been well accepted in general public, media, government, and academic circles. In 1994 an evaluation of its work included a survey of more than 3,000 of its clients.

Of the 770 respondents, the vast majority rated the Bureau's research as good, very good, or excellent on a range of criteria, as follows: quality, 94.1%; usefulness, 91.2%; credibility, 89.9%; and independence, 82.4% (Australian Government Printing Service, 1994).

■ *Setting a Research Agenda for Evaluating
the Immigration Program*

☐ *Policy Rationale and Reasons for Fluctuation in the Size of the Intake*

A first concern for the Bureau in establishing a research agenda focuses on the objectives of immigration, multicultural and population policies, and the means for their attainment. But the reasons for planned immigration to countries such as Canada, Australia, Sweden, and New Zealand are not always very clearly spelled out. The motivation is part of a shifting historical stream, and it is unusual to have clear, or very detailed, specified objectives with defined means for assessment. The closest explicit statement of objectives that I have been able to find is that for New Zealand, which nominates four strategic objectives for an immigration policy designed to make New Zealand grow economically with social cohesion and become "a better place in which to live—both for the people already here and for new residents": (a) build human capital, (b) strengthen international linkages, (c) encourage enterprise and innovation, and (d) maintain social cohesion. In Australia, the current goals are rather similar, though not always as explicitly drawn together. For policy evaluation purposes, however, it is important to recall that the goals change from year to year.

Parkin and Hardcastle (1990) observe that there was political bipartisanship in Australia over the rationale for the postwar immigration program, which had two main purposes. First, it was considered necessary for Australia to boost its population for defense reasons. Following the Japanese military drive during the war, the government saw a need to increase the country's defense and industrial capacity, and to populate what might otherwise appear to be an invitingly empty continent adjacent to crowded Asia. Second, postwar labor shortages were envisaged, and the government intended that the supply of immigrants' skills would help fill these gaps (though temporary migration was eschewed) and also boost economic growth through the creation of economies of scale.

Evaluation of success thus depends on which historical period is being considered, and four and a half decades later, the defense justification for immigration is hardly ever heard, and the economic case is far more muted. One of the first tasks of the Bureau on establishment was indeed to assess a variety of criticisms of the economic consequences of immigration. Its finding that the economic impact of immigration on Australia was neutral to benign, with a likely positive but small overall effect (Nieuwenhuysen, 1992), showed a substantial shift from perceptions of the immediate postwar period. Moreover, fears of environmental damage arising from rapid population growth, fueled by immigration, have been articulately expressed.

The official present-day rationale for immigration is thus far more complex than that in 1947, but it has been expressed by successive prime ministers at the Bureau's National Outlook Conferences. At the first, in 1990, Prime Minister Bob Hawke stated:

> The economic purpose of immigration from the Government's point of view is not to achieve specific goals such as a lower current account deficit or higher export. . . . There are more efficient arms of policy that can be applied to meet broad macro-economic goals. . . . [The purpose]—in addition to its international humanitarian and family reunion aspects—is to strengthen the productive capacity of the economy. . . . we are creating, through immigration, a much stronger, more powerful, more resilient economy—one that should enable us better to meet the challenges of competitive world markets. And we are also creating a dynamic and cohesive community. (Hawke, 1991, pp. 8-9)

At the second Outlook Conference, in 1992, the new prime minister, Mr. Paul Keating, observed:

> It seemed to me that, for all its great virtues, [the Australia of my youth in Bankstown, Sydney], was missing out on what the world had to offer, and it was offering the world less than it could. Australians in those days tended to believe that you could only keep traditions up by keeping others out. By the 1970s I had begun to see my cause among those who wanted to open Australia up to the outside world. . . . We can draw a parallel between multicultural policy and economic policy in the 1980s. As Treasurer I saw my role as the

necessary one of opening Australia up to the world, making us a player. (Keating, 1993, p. 12)

Indicating broad bipartisanship at the same conference in 1992, the then leader of the opposition, Dr. John Hewson, stated:

> We [in the Coalition parties] have always believed that immigration has been one of the great nation-building influences in the development of Australia. We believe that a well planned, efficiently administered and nondiscriminatory immigration policy is fundamental to Australia's national economic and social development and to our international standing. One of the great strengths of Australian society is its multicultural character. That reality has enriched our country in all aspects of our natural life. (Hewson, 1993, p. 12)

From the viewpoint of evaluation, however, it can be seen that current objectives (such as opening Australia to the world) are by nature general and not easily or finitely assessable. Whatever the perceived general economic or international rationales for persisting with immigration down the years, Australian governments have been extremely pragmatic in determining the size of the fluctuating inflow. A principal explanation of these fluctuations is to be found in several periods of poor economic growth and high unemployment levels, which were associated with lower intake targets. This relationship—low intake levels at times of low economic growth—extends over the whole of Australia's post-World War II economic history, as Figure 16.1 shows. From this figure one can see that in each postwar low-growth period (marked by bars), there was a sharp rise in unemployment and a steep decline in the intake.

Apart from the size of the immigration intake and the country sources supplying it, desirable composition under its different elements—family, skill, and humanitarian—has also been debated and has been the subject of lobbying. Each of these components provides a justification of itself for those supporting an immigration inflow. Family reunion is seen as a human right for those already accepted under the program, the skill segment is viewed as a means of augmenting the quality of the workforce, and the humanitarian part of the intake serves to help satisfy obligations perceived as part of the U.N. High Commission for Refugees and other arrangements. But in recent years in particular, there have been political differences of opinion about the advisable composition of the intake, with

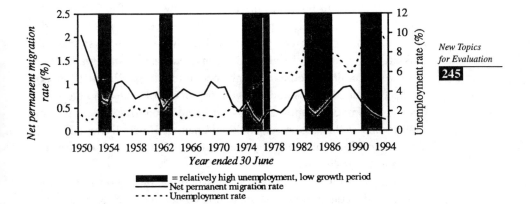

Figure 16.1. Net Permanent Migration Rate and Unemployment Rate, Australia, 1949–1950 to 1993–1994

the opposition coalition parties emphasizing the need for a relatively large skill, rather than family reunion, component.

The policy rationale for immigration to Australia is, therefore, not so explicit as to be easily testable in research, either in its objectives or in its means of attainment. Moreover, because there are differences in emphasis between major political parties, the rather elusive evaluation process is further complicated.

☐ *How the Research Agenda Was Set*

To the rather broad policy justifications for immigration that make evaluation problematic must be added another complexity—the diversity of the subject. Immigration covers an enormous range of issues: demographic and spatial aspects are coupled with economic, social, labor market, intake, settlement, environmental, urban infrastructure, and many other impacts. The task for a research program is therefore to encompass these diverse consequences and to see whether consensus can be discerned in each of the fields as well as overall.

But before an assessment can begin, a stocktaking is necessary. Consequently, the Bureau began by commissioning surveys of the literature that sought to describe the "state of the art" of immigration studies in Australia and to point out the gaps in knowledge. The impact of the surveys was large in highlighting prevailing consensus, as it appeared to authors. Equally important, gaps in the literature could be systematically tackled. For example, the economic consequences of immigration were reviewed overall as well as through special inquiries. Within 18 months of the Bureau's establishment, a general survey of the economic consequences of immigration was published, in addition to volumes on immigration and scale economies, trade and capital flows, living standards, wages and inflation, unemployment, economic status, urban infrastructure, and the environment.

Another important initiative was the publication of a regular series of statistical data on immigration, including community profiles and data on settler arrivals. Based on census figures, a major *Atlas of the Australian People* was produced, which concentrated on ethnicity-related census questions. The regularity and richness of this source of information went a good way toward assisting open and better-documented debate. It made far more difficult the previous possibility, before such easy access to statistics existed, of sensationalist claims. Indeed, a major feature of current public discussion of immigration issues is the way in which Bureau-sponsored authors are proving from their published work to be sources of information and analysis: Controversial themes can no longer be dominated by those able to gain headline media attention through back-of-the-envelope dissertations—the number of players with more fully documented contributions is too large to permit this.

It was not considered sufficient, however, only to produce publications. The Bureau's charter included provision for open public discussion of findings. Consequently, conferences were organized at which results were launched and made available for critical public scrutiny. The major events have been the National Outlook Conferences every second year, which last 3 days and attract crowds of nearly 600 each, as well as enormous media attention. Each conference has featured more than 100 speakers, with many shades of opinion represented.

Several other major conferences and many seminars have also been arranged. Capacity crowds attended conferences on the social impact of immigration, women in immigration, Asia-Pacific migration affecting Australia, and the politics of immigration. The degree of the Bureau's freedom is reflected in the political sensitivity, for the funding government, of many of the issues canvased before the media at these conferences. Perhaps the best illustration was the Politics of Immigration

Conference itself—a professor of political science who addressed it considered that it was extraordinary and remarkable that a government department would give resources for an open public review of the lobbying and other pressures being brought to bear on it, and its response to these. But as I have remarked in the foreword to the book around which the conference was built (Jupp & Kabala, 1993), it was not a courageous move so much as "testimony to the freedom of the environment within which the Bureau is permitted to operate, and the confidence which the Bureau has in exercising this freedom."

The overall outcome of the Bureau's presence and its independent stance, covering sensitive as well as purely factual information topics, has not only been an impact on debate, however. Policy makers have also absorbed many of the messages of research, and cabinet submissions from the Department of Immigration and Ethnic Affairs have been replete with Bureau research conclusions and recommendations.

A question sometimes asked is whether research necessary to inform debate and promote scholarly analysis of immigration, multicultural, and population issues could be better promoted by more diversified funding, that is, by grants to universities. I do not think that spreading the resources without a planned, well-funded central program would have produced the results I have described. At the same time, the Bureau's funding methods—that is, using a wide range of scholars and researchers in universities and the private sector—have capitalized on diversity in the field. Central funding has not resulted in a uniform or restricted, monopolized set of contributors.

■ *Conclusion and Lessons 6 and 7*

Evaluating international and national immigration policies is a difficult task, not merely because of the greatly differing circumstances of nations and their place in international movements of people, but because the criteria for evaluation are so indeterminate, and because governments are not able to specify very clearly the objects of policy. This inability springs from the nature of the subject, and from the way in which policies on and attitudes toward immigration and movements of people are developed. Past historical tradition and inheritance play a part in determining today's conventions and policies, as do obligations accepted under current United Nations refugee programs.

However, applying tests with defined criteria to the policy of one country—Australia—I have suggested in this chapter that planned immigration intakes coupled with careful settlement and welcoming citizenship programs can be successful. In Australia, a proportionally very large intake of people from a multitude of countries in the postwar period has occurred without posing a threat to overall cohesion, and with results that are praised by both major political parties.

The lessons of how this was achieved—and the recent role of research in informing policy and debate—may be difficult to transpose from one country to another. As I have mentioned, I believe the lessons to be robust. But two perspectives on the trend of current events and the likely pattern of future change are sufficiently important to justify the statement of two further futuristic lessons. The first five lessons apply, however, to what some regard as mostly a past age of migration—the permanent settlement of people. That characteristic of earlier periods—especially the notion that a solution to overpopulation in one country was the migration of its people to another—is changing. The new era of migration involves a need for temporary movement in response to the ever-growing globalization of the international economy. The tensions and pressures in this era do not come so much from unwillingness on the part of industrialized countries to accommodate short-term employment stays by those with skills. Rather, the pressures arise from regional inequalities and potential for uncontrollable shifts. The lessons of the next 25 years will be different from those of the past. We cannot easily perceive what these lessons will be, for we are not yet sure of the extent or full nature of the movements the policies will be required to address.

However, there is enough clarity to assert the following further lessons:

■ *Lesson 6:* Temporary movement of people is overshadowing in volume and immediate topical impact the planned immigrant intake programs in Australia and similar countries. And in the international economy generally, globalization is increasing and creating more intense international integration, including that of labor and skill resources.

A study for the Bureau noted:

Changing political economic structures and systems, associated with new technologies which have revolutionised communications and transportation as well as the sociocultural relations between nations, have produced more extensive and varied population flows. The need to respond to these movements in a way which may necessitate changes in existing immigration and population policies is becoming increasingly recognised. (Stahl, Ball, Inglis, & Gutman, 1993, p. xiii)

Lesson 7 is the most difficult to state because it is the hardest to envisage resolving. The events of the 1990s are creating many pressures for the movement of people, for example, in Europe and Africa, and are highlighting the growth of multiethnic tensions and violence in some countries, such as the United States, that have received a strong flow of illegal entries. As Castles and Miller (1993) have remarked:

> Only a minority of the inhabitants of less-developed countries take [the step of trying to move to richer nations] . . . but their numbers still total millions. . . . The perspective of the 1990s and the early part of the next century is that migration will continue to grow [and] . . . ecological and demographic pressure may force many people to seek refuge outside their own countries. (pp. 3-4)

- *Lesson 7:* An ecologically sustainable program of economic development for the international economy at large, but particularly for poorer countries, is a necessary object in its own right. Its consequence would be an increase in the interchange of skills between countries, but it might also partly stem other population flows that would be very difficult to cope with.

This lesson requires, unfortunately, the solution of two problems that have thus far proved intractable—the end of environmental decay and destruction, and a more equal distribution of wealth and economic growth.

■ The Future

The former age of migration entailed the mass movement and permanent settlement of people, especially from war-torn or overpopulated regions to the New World. That age is now past, however—migration is no longer a general solution to problems of overpopulation. The new age of migration in industrialized wealthy countries, and the challenge of future policy, lies in accommodating the flow of people to needs of temporary sojourn, as globalization and trade liberalization expands. And because the option of mass emigration is not available in poorer countries as a solution to overpopulation, the greater challenge is that of ecologically sustainable economic development so as to reduce pressures for exit and fears by richer countries of unwanted influx.

■ *References*

Australian Government Printing Service. (1978). *Review of post-arrival programs and services for migrants.* Canberra: Author.

Australian Government Printing Service. (1994). *Evaluation of the Bureau of Immigration and Population Research.* Canberra: Author.

Castles, S., & Miller, M. (1993). *The age of migration: International population movements in the modern world.* London: Macmillan.

Committee to Advise on Australia's Immigration Policies. (1988). *Immigration: A commitment to Australia.* Canberra: Australian Government Printing Service.

Dummett, A. (1995). British migration policy in the twentieth century. In D. Lowe (Ed.), *Immigration and integration: Australia and Britain.* London: London University, BIMPR and Centre for Australian Studies.

FitzGerald, M. (1993). Integration: The UK experience. In *Migration and international co-operation: Challenges for OECD countries.* Paris: Organization for Economic Development and Cooperation.

FitzGerald, M. (1995). Measuring integration. In D. Lowe (Ed.), *Immigration and integration: Australia and Britain.* London: London University, BIMPR and Centre for Australian Studies.

Hawke, R. J. L. (1991). Building a dynamic and culturally diverse Australia. *BIR Bulletin, 3,* 8-9.

Hewson, J. (1993). Immigration program requires urgent reforms. *BIR Bulletin, 8,* 12.

Jupp, J., & Kabala, M. (Eds.). (1993). *The politics of Australian immigration.* Canberra: Australian Government Printing Service.

Keating, P. J. (1993). Seeking a strong national and international identity. *BIR Bulletin, 8,* 12.

Nieuwenhuysen, J. (1992, November). *An overview of recent research on Australian immigration.* Melbourne: Australian Government Printing Service.

Parkin, A., & Hardcastle, L. (1990). Immigration policy. In C. Jennett & R. Stewart (Eds.), *Hawke and Australian public policy: Consensus and restructuring.* New York: Macmillan.

Stahl, C., Ball, R., Inglis, C., & Gutman, P. (1993). *Global population movements and their implications for Australia.* Canberra: Australian Government Printing Service.

Wooden, M., Holton, R., Hugo, G., & Sloan, J. (1994). *Australian immigration: A survey of the issues.* Canberra: Australian Government Printing Service.

17

Tracing Gender Issues Through Institutional Change and Program Implementation at the World Bank

Josette Murphy

The World Bank is owned today by 180 developed and developing countries. It works with the governments of developing countries to strengthen their economies and improve the quality of life of their people, especially the poorest. This is done in part through loans used for a broad range of investments—from social services to industry—that developing countries could not finance on their own or through commercial banks and private companies. The World Bank's overarching goal is to reduce poverty, and it is well understood today that this cannot be achieved without ensuring that women as well as men are fully involved in and benefit from development activities.

This chapter focuses on mixed methods—the use of qualitative and quantitative data. It is organized around a matrix (see Table 17.1) that

TABLE 17.1 Sources and Types of Data Used

	Type	
Source	*Qualitative*	*Quantitative*
Existing	Cell 1	Cell 2
New	Cell 4	Cell 3

combines the type of data used (quantitative versus qualitative) and the origin of the data (existing data versus data especially created for the study). My discussion of the four cells is based on the experience of a recent study conducted by the Operations Evaluation Department of the World Bank and published under the title *Gender Issues in World Bank Lending* (Murphy, 1995). The study evaluated how the World Bank has addressed the needs of women, and more generally issues related to gender, over the past 25 years.

■ *Study Objectives*

The study addressed four questions:

1. *Concepts and intentions:* What did the Bank say it should do?
2. *Actions:* What did the Bank actually do?
3. *Results:* Did the Bank meet its goals?
4. *Explanation:* Why did things happen the way they did?

The types of data and information that would be needed were derived from these questions, and then the likely sources were identified. The matrix given in Table 17.2 shows how this was done.

☐ *What Did the Bank Say It Should Do? The Evolution of Concepts and Intentions*

Like any institution, the World Bank leaves a paper trail, formal and informal, through which the evolution of thought within the agency can be traced. This is the domain of qualitative information and existing

TABLE 17.2 Study Objectives

	Type		
Source	*Qualitative*	*Quantitative*	
Existing	concepts and intentions?	actions?	
New	explanation?	results?	

TABLE 17.3 Cell 1: Concepts and Intentions

Source	*Type: Qualitative*
Existing	■ formal statements ■ guidelines to staff ■ working documents ■ previous evaluations

records (see Table 17.3). The types of documents and records available include formal statements on policy, guidelines from management to staff, speeches, publications and their various drafts, the minutes of some key meetings, some staffing decisions, work programs of some administrative units, and annual reports. Most of the information was obtained from primary sources (i.e., the original documents). Existing analyses of these documents were also reviewed, as much for what they would reveal about the state of thought at the time the analyses were written as for what they would impart about the documents they analyzed.

Such documents, however, must be placed in the internal and external contexts in which they were written. Because the study focused on one concern among the many issues the World Bank must address—such as poverty, environmental issues, and technological and economic growth—the Bank's general policies and their evolution over time needed careful consideration. A general understanding was also needed of how the concepts of women in development and attention to gender issues were evolving, through a review of the literature and an understanding of what other development agencies had done and when. Thus the matrix includes a third dimension, which shows that all cells must be interpreted in context (see Table 17.4).

TABLE 17.4 Cell 1: Concepts and Intentions in Context

Source	Type: Qualitative	context
Existing	formal statements guidelines to staff working documents previous evaluations	

The study accessed staffing records to determine the number of staff with formal responsibility for promoting attention to gender (not a true measure of the level of effort, but a sign of managers' commitment). The composition of the Bank's delegations at international conferences is telling: In 1975, at the first U.N. International Conference on Women, the Bank was officially represented by two midlevel staff members; at the 1985 Nairobi conference, a department director led the Bank delegation; but in 1995, the president of the World Bank himself gave an address at the fourth such conference in Beijing, and the Bank delegation included several high-level managers.

The information in the first cell grew as the study progressed, influenced by new objectives and work programs emerging from meetings and new documents. A method usually used by anthropologists—that is, participant observation—also serves well for evaluators when they are well enough known and accepted in a group to participate in activities without distorting the results by virtue of their presence. Though I had no authority over the work program or the budget of counterpart Bank units that work on gender issues, I was able to attend meetings in which the general strategy was discussed.

☐ *What Did the Bank Actually Do, Especially in Its Lending Portfolio?*

The Bank has excellent computerized records of basic data on all its loans as well as databases of analytic work on each borrowing country and of its publications. This can be classified as the quantitative domain, which outlines portfolio characteristics and their evolution over time (see Table 17.5). But the study found no ready-made database of projects or analytic work with a high level of attention to gender issues. Some project listings, however, supported various types of action related to gender

TABLE 17.5 Cell 2: Actions

Source	Type: Quantitative	
Existing	■ records, analytic work ■ records, all loans ■ ratings, all loans ■ previous evaluations	

issues, from training more female teachers so that parents would send their girls to school to providing extension services to women farmers. These lists were checked, combined, and added to projects identified through the Cell 1 reviews. Overall, the study identified 615 projects, spanning a 25-year period, as having taken some actions relative to gender. These projects were then compared with the rest of the portfolio, by region, sector, and country income level. This established how the overall level of "good intentions" evolved over the years, showing a clear increase in the late 1980s.

☐ *Did the Bank Meet Its Goals?*

Because this was the first review of the Bank's attention to gender, no attempt was made to evaluate the impact of gender-related activities on the countries and on women. Rather, the study measured whether projects met their objectives. A ready-made tool was available to help identify the results for any completed project: The World Bank Operations Evaluation Department has been building up for 20 years an evaluative database for the entire portfolio of completed projects. All projects are rated at completion for their level of achievement of objectives, their likely sustainability, their institutional impact, and the performance of the Bank and of the borrowers.

The study could therefore extract these quantified evaluation findings for all projects identified with gender-related action, and could thus compare them with the entire portfolio. But, in fact, the database provided little information about the achievements of gender-related actions, which were often a subset of a project component. So the original project files were reviewed to see what was achieved in terms of gender action; this was complemented by interviews with staff members who had been

TABLE 17.6 Cell 3: Results

Source	Type: Quantitative
New	■ file reviews ■ topical ratings ■ new extracts

involved in the projects. Methodologically speaking, the study worked from existing sources of quantitative data, but also created new sets of quantitative data based on qualitative judgment (see Table 17.6). This was done for two samples of projects, looking for evidence of results and types of problems encountered. Qualitative judgments became quantified as all projects were reviewed with the same checklist, established after a pilot review. The approach was iterative, starting with reviews of a few projects, then moving to the identification of key variables to look for and likely categories in each variable; then a qualitative review of all projects using the same standards; and finally a compilation of findings into quantitative tables.

☐ *Why Did Things Happen the Way They Did
(and What Does That Mean for the Future)?*

In a way, everything outlined so far has been a preparatory step for the last cell of the matrix. The focus now returns to the qualitative domain, with the creation of a level of understanding that was not available before and from which lessons and recommendations can be drawn (see Table 17.7).

Once all the facts were established, the study team tried to understand why things happened as they did. The analysis drew on comparisons, timelines showing the sequencing of key steps, and handwritten scribbling on documents cited earlier. In-depth interviews were essential, both with people involved or witness to key steps in the past and with current staff. Tracing people who retired 10 or 15 years ago was achieved with surprising ease. Also surprising was how much the people could remember once they started thinking again about earlier days. Two interviews proved

TABLE 17.7 Cell 4: Explanation

Source	Type: Qualitative
New	■ interviews ■ group discussions ■ participant observation ■ comments on draft ■ (focus groups) ■ (formal survey)

better than one with each person; at the least, providing the interviewees with a thorough explanation when they were first contacted allowed them time to refresh their memories about project details. In fact, many found draft materials and documents in their personal files. A few group discussions were held, and, as noted earlier, attendance at meetings provided opportunities for participant observation.

Finally, the draft of the study was sent for comments to all people concerned. Comments were themselves a source of information, sometimes factual corrections, and often reflections of current opinions. After two rounds of comments, Bank senior managers were asked to prepare a statement on how they would implement the study's recommendations, and both the study and the managers' plans were presented to a committee of the Bank's executive directors, who represent all member countries.

■ *Conclusions*

By necessity, a short chapter oversimplifies. Certainly, there are pitfalls in each cell of the matrix (see Table 17.8). A straight description of intent may be interesting but not very useful. Cell 2 focuses on what is done within the agency, not on results, and by itself is not conducive to learning. Cell 3 looks at immediate results—whether the objectives were achieved—but the great risk here is lack of rigor and comparability across different types of actions, and lack of data on ultimate impact on people. Cell 4 is the one with the most exciting, interesting information, but it is highly vulnerable to bias resulting from the choice of informants.

TABLE 17.8 Pitfalls

	Type	
Source	*Qualitative*	*Quantitative*
Existing	intentions: descriptive history	actions: inputs, not outputs
New	explanation: biased information	results: lack rigor lack comparability

What can be learned from this example? Using both qualitative and quantitative information was much better than using either type alone. The process should be iterative: The evaluator checks back and forth between the cells, and builds them up concurrently (see Table 17.9). There was from the start a tentative, partial quantitative overview of the portfolio for recent years. Official statements announced relevant changes in staff responsibilities and work programs. This search uncovered some cryptic mentions of a quantified database, which, after inquiries, turned out to be still accessible, although unused for years. The study team went back and forth from this database to the (new) reviews of project documents and staff interviews to firm up a database of 615 projects known to have included some clear action related to gender among their objectives. The interviews of staff involved in these projects brought out information not only on the projects themselves, but also on the evolution of staff guidelines and formal statements (answering questions on why a certain step was taken at a given time, when it would have seemed possible much earlier).

Checking and rechecking all data from several sources is a basic evaluation principle (triangulation). In the same manner, the analysis of quantitative data must always be put to the test of qualitative information, and vice versa. Do the numbers make sense? Are the qualitative interpretations plausible given the numbers? Common sense and a good dose of skepticism should always prevail.

Finally, it was essential to place both qualitative and quantitative information in the broader context. What was happening in other agencies

TABLE 17.9 Features of Good Evaluations

■ Combination of methods
■ Use of iterative process
■ Use of triangulation
■ Interpretation of information in context

at that time? How did concepts and analytic frameworks change over time?

In short, this evaluation teaches that much can be achieved through the use of mixed methods, in this case by combining a systematic review of existing records, both qualitative and quantitative, with a limited amount of new data collection and analysis.

■ *Reference*

Murphy, J. L. (1995). *Gender issues in World Bank lending.* Washington, DC: World Bank.

18

Understanding the Impact of Development Projects on Women

The Tunisia Institutional Development Fund Project

Michael Bamberger

In May 1994, the World Bank approved an Institutional Development Fund (IDF) grant to the Ministry of Women's Affairs (MAFF) in Tunisia to establish an Impact Evaluation Cell (CEI) and to assist the cell in developing methodologies for evaluating the long-term impacts of development projects on women.[1] The objective of the 2-year grant was to build an institutional capacity in MAFF to continue to use these methodologies. The grant provided funds for strengthening the CEI staff, conducting impact evaluation studies, contracting with consultants, and developing study tours to visit gender evaluation programs in other countries. The project was a collaborative effort among interested government agencies, with MAFF as facilitator. Conferences and workshops were used to present and discuss different evaluation methodologies. MAFF offered counterpart funds to ministries who were already undertaking impact evaluation work, to permit them to contract with local consultants to integrate gender studies into the existing evaluation frameworks.

The project began with a conference in Tunis in November 1994 to stress the economic rationale for investing in women and to familiarize researchers and line ministries with evaluation methodologies that can be used to assess project impacts on women and other social groups (Institut de Développement Nord-sud, 1995). Interested government agencies in agriculture, housing, employment, and vocational training presented their proposed gender impact evaluation designs, which were discussed in working groups. The evaluation project ended in May 1996 and the results of the studies will soon be available.

■ *Why Study Gender Impacts?*

Despite growing concern to ensure that development projects benefit women, very few studies have examined how development projects differentially affect women and men (Overholt, Anderson, Cloud, & Austin, 1985). Although evidence is accumulating, for example, on the effectiveness of income transfer and other measures for increasing girls' participation in primary and secondary school (World Bank, 1994, 1995), we know little about the long-term economic, social, and demographic benefits of these projects or their impacts on particular groups of women. This is a serious weakness, as it is difficult for policy makers and development planners to select and design projects to produce sustainable benefits for women without having data on the impacts and benefits produced by earlier projects.

Whereas men in most societies have primarily a productive role, women have multiple roles, including reproduction and child care, responsibilities for management of the household (and in rural areas the farm), production, and in many cases community management (Moser, 1993). Because of these different roles, women and men face different constraints and have different needs and potentials with respect to development policies and projects. In all societies, productive roles and access to productive resources and to social services are to lesser or greater degree "gendered," and if these differences are not understood, projects and policies will fail to satisfy the needs of both women and men, and will fail to utilize fully the resources of both sexes. In many cases, male labor and female labor are not interchangeable. Consequently, the success of projects will depend on the availability of both female and male labor of the appropriate kind at the appropriate periods during the production cycle. In addition, significant sectors of the female population may not have full access to project benefits, services, and productive resources, unless projects are specifically designed to respond to their needs and to allow socially acceptable forms of access.

■ *The Projects Included in the Tunisian Evaluation Study and Their Potential Gender Impacts*

☐ *Urban Development Projects*

Three urban development projects were included in the evaluation: one in the capital city of Tunis, one in the capital port zone, and a third in one of the largest interior cities. These projects represented the first efforts in Tunisia to replace slum demolition and forced relocation with the intensive development of existing low-income settlement areas. The largest of these projects, Ettadhamen, is in a natural reception zone for migrants coming from the interior to the capital. Dramatic improvements in housing can be observed since the project began in the mid-1980s, and public infrastructure investments promoted private investments in small enterprises. Despite the dynamism of the area, unemployment has remained around 15%.

A number of hypotheses were explored in the evaluation about how women have been affected by the housing projects. Progressive civil laws have permitted women to own property, and women may have made significant financial contributions to housing, as well as benefiting from the growing rental market, as both landlords and tenants. Women also help manage construction and upgrading of housing and play a significant role in community management. Piped water and modern cooking methods have produced significant savings in women's time, permitting women to start small businesses or to raise animals. Housing projects also give girls easy access to schooling and health services. However, as education is becoming almost universal in Tunisia, the evaluation needed to assess whether or not projects brought education to girls significantly earlier than in other urban areas. The projects have also helped integrate isolated communities into the city, and improved public transport allows women to travel further to work, for example, supplying domestic servants to middle-class areas of Tunis.

☐ *A Rural Development Project*

The rural development project is part of the World Bank's long-term commitment to this resource-poor mountainous region. It provides many small and isolated communities with dirt roads, flood control, drinking water, conservation programs, economic development (dairy improvement, vocational training programs), and health and education. A number of potential gender impacts are to be assessed. The provision of drinking water and modern cooking methods may have freed women for several hours per day, allowing them to pursue economic activities such as poultry and embroidery or to participate in vocational training projects, such as embroidery and textiles. Girls now have easier access to schools. Since the late 1980s, the project has promoted participatory planning and management, and it will be important to assess the extent to which women have benefited from these processes. Extension services have been provided for women, but evidence suggests that resources have been inadequate and impacts less than expected. The improved roads may have benefited women. Women are involved in many economic development programs, but it is not yet clear how much control women have over the extra revenue generated. Finally, as a majority of rural-to-urban migrants have been men, this has further increased women's responsibilities for farm management.

☐ *Job Preparation and Placement Project*

The FIAP (Fonds d'Insertion et d'Adaptation Professionelle) project is part of the government's strategy for adapting the labor market to the needs of a dynamic and liberalizing economy. The project responds to demand for helping companies to organize 4- to 8-month on-the-job training programs. Trainees receive modest allowances and companies recruit promising graduates. Women represent about 75% of trainees, partly because women are concentrated in the industrial sectors, such as textiles, where there is high demand for training. The gender impact evaluation addressed several issues. First, what are the implications of women's being trained for a few traditional employment areas such as textiles? Does this depress wages or limit women's opportunities? The study also assessed the labor productivity and performance of male and female workers. Second, how will the productivity and stability of female labor be assessed? Are there any problems facing female labor that the project does not address? Third, the situation of women who have participated in the project was compared with that of women who have not participated. What differences are there? What problems do women encounter in obtaining and keeping jobs through this project? What impacts does the project have on women's welfare, their control over household income, and time use? Does the project provide women with skills they can use to start their own businesses?

■ *Evaluation Design Issues and How They Were Addressed in the Tunisian Impact Studies*

The nature of the five projects, and the fact that they have been operating for several years, presents difficult challenges for the design of an impact evaluation.

□ *Reconstructing Baseline Conditions and Control Groups*

The urban projects were begun in the early 1980s, and the rural project has a similarly long history. Much basic information, including the disaggregation of data by sex, was not collected when the project began. Consequently, it is difficult to obtain information on the characteristics of women and men at the start of the projects.

Most evaluation designs require comparison between the project population and a control group to evaluate whether observed changes are effects of the project. This is particularly important for multicomponent projects targeting large and diverse populations that are simultaneously affected by other social, economic, political, and cultural changes (Valadez & Bamberger, 1994). The need for a reference group becomes even greater because in Tunisia, essential social and infrastructure services such as primary and secondary education, health and family planning, electricity, water, and roads have become widely available. One result of the availability of these services is a reduction in the time women must spend collecting water and fuel.

The civil code introduced during the 1970s and 1980s greatly affected women's control of property, family status, and political participation. Economic development also increased female labor force participation, particularly in industries such as textiles. The combination of the progressive civil code and the demand for female labor created a high level of social acceptance for women working outside the home. All of these factors greatly complicate efforts to isolate the impacts of the project.

There are fundamental problems in trying to construct a reference group comprising individuals, families, or communities not affected by the project. Within the project area different people receive different levels and quality of services. For example, families nearer to paved roads, footpaths, or water supplies may receive more benefits than families who are farther away. Projects evolve over years, so that some families may have received services longer than others. When participation in a project is voluntary (as in FIAP), significant socioeconomic and motivational differences exist between people who choose to participate and those who do not. Differences in job performance may reflect these initial differences rather than the program.

☐   *Approaches Used in the Studies:*
     Reconstructing Baseline Conditions and Control Groups

Baseline Conditions and Data

Although the evaluations had access to some baseline data from existing studies, this rarely provided an adequate baseline for estimating changes produced by the projects. Socioeconomic data collected for planning purposes treated the family as a group and, except for the FIAP project, sex-disaggregated data were not available. FIAP collected data on the employment history of both male and female participants, but not on the socioeconomic conditions of women.

Several approaches were used to reconstruct baseline conditions. Respondents were asked to recall the social and economic conditions at the time the projects began. In some cases they were asked to link the recall of project impacts to critical incidents, such as marriage, election campaigns, or dramatic events in the community history, that helped them to date changes in their own lives with reference to these easily remembered events. Interviews were conducted with key informants such as community leaders, police, and health and education officials who could provide general information on baseline conditions. Group discussions were conducted using participatory evaluation methods such as timelines and trend analysis (see Butler, 1994; Feldstein & Jiggins, 1994). Secondary sources such as census data and studies conducted by ministries and local authorities were also used.

Control Sites and Groups

Most evaluations included control sites for the ex post study, selected to have conditions as similar as possible to the project areas at the times the projects began. Typical control sites for urban housing projects were low-income areas close to the project sites with similar characteristics but that had not benefited directly from the project. However, these control sites were small (one contained only 50 families), whereas the project might have a population 10 times larger. There also was some contamination, as control families sometimes benefited from project services such as public transport, improved roads, and possibly schools and public water supply.

In rural areas, control villages were identified that had not received many project services. Villages tended to be geographically separated due to the mountainous terrain, and they received distinct packages of services (one might have dirt roads constructed, whereas another received public water fountains), so it was often possible to use a village that had not received a particular service (such as a road) to control for the impacts of this service. This allowed the use of regression models in which a set of services were regressed on an indicator of project impact (changes in household income, number of children in school, or average number of years of girls' education). In the case of FIAP, the control group comprised women working in the enterprises where job training and placement programs were operating, but who had not participated in these programs, and women from the communities where many FIAP participants lived, but who were not in the labor force, were unemployed, or had other employment.

☐ *Developing and Using Impact Evaluation Measurement Tools*

Many women covered by the study had limited education and difficulty in understanding and responding to structured questionnaires. Many communities also limit access to women and girls, so that interviewers may talk only to the "household head," and it may be difficult to meet with the wife or teenage girls in a context in which they feel free to speak openly. Even when women can be reached, they may have difficulty expressing their views to outsiders.

For interviewing the wife and other female members of the household, special instruments were designed with questions on time use, on the impacts of employment, on women's control of household income, and on decision making. Group discussions with women and participant observation of women's role in community activities and within the household were also used.

☐ *Assessing Outcomes and Impacts: Which Were the Right Questions?*

Evaluating women's time usage and how projects affect the distribution of responsibilities and time. Information was obtained on how much time women and girls spent on child care, schooling, household duties, unpaid farm activities, and income earning, and how this was affected by the projects. For example, what was sacrificed when activities such as paid employment were increased? What was the economic value of child care and of the unpaid domestic and farm management activities of women?

Access to benefits. Data were obtained on which groups in the community had access to and used project services. Did men and women and boys and girls have equal access to health, education, and other services, and did they use them equally? Did all groups have equal access to credit and extension services?

Social and cultural impacts of projects. Projects such as housing, which create a new social environment, can have significant impacts on women and girls. Women with easier access to the services of the city through transport and proximity may become exposed to an urban lifestyle. More secure conditions in the community (street lighting, paved streets) may give women and girls greater mobility in the community and surrounding areas. New services such as community centers may expose women to new ideas. Access to water and the use of laborsaving cooking methods can free women from the burdens of carrying water and fuel.

Control of resources. It is important to assess who controls resources, as women may have significantly less control even over resources they help to produce. Did women help decide the design or remodeling of houses or the selection and construction of community facilities? Do women have access to and control over the use of credit and agricultural extension services? Do they control household income? Who decides the use of water and other agricultural inputs?

☐ *Methods Used in the Studies*

Women's time use was studied through a number of complementary methods. Questions in survey instruments asked how much time women spent on domestic and nonpaid farm activities and how time use changed when a woman obtained paid employment. Participant observation was used to examine how girls and women used time in urban and rural communities. The economic value of women's time was estimated by assigning an estimated market wage to different activities and multiplying this by the number of hours spent on each activity. For example, the wages paid to agricultural workers were used to assess nonpaid agricultural labor, and the wages paid to people working in restaurants were used to assess the value of domestic labor. Access to benefits was assessed through questionnaires applied to random samples of project and control groups identifying the types and levels of services they had received. Social and cultural impacts of projects were assessed through questionnaires, participant observation, group discussions, and time-use studies. Participatory evaluation methods were also used. Control of resources was covered through questionnaires that gathered information from women on the proportion of household expenditures they contributed and how this changed if they obtained paid employment directly or indirectly through the projects.

■ Strengthening Local Evaluation Capacity

A number of measures were taken to strengthen local evaluation capacity.
First, the project was managed through MAFF, which coordinated with
the line ministries for the contracting and supervision of the local consulting companies. The international consultants provided on-the-job training
for MAFF research staff by involving them in the studies and by organizing workshops and seminars. Study tours were organized to evaluation
organizations in Canada, and four MAFF staff participated in the International Evaluation Conference in Vancouver in November 1995. Second,
the participating line ministries were actively involved in the selection
and supervision of consultants evaluating their projects. They also participated in and met regularly with the international consultants and World
Bank staff to discuss the progress of the evaluations. Third, all of the
studies were conducted by local consulting firms, with the international
consultants and the World Bank providing technical support. Fourth, an
evaluation handbook is being prepared to present and assess the methods
used in the five evaluations with respect to quasi-experimental designs,
sampling, instrument development, and data analysis.

The capacity-building strategies proved to have both strengths and
weaknesses. One strength was creation of ownership of the studies by
MAFF and participating ministries and national consulting groups. This
was important in Tunisia, where there is strong resentment of international
consultants' being brought in to do—at a higher cost—what could have
been done by local consultants. However, a weakness was that it was
assumed that MAFF would be able to hire a permanent staff for the
evaluation unit early in the project and that this team would work closely
with the international consultants and local research groups. In this way
MAFF staff would receive extensive on-the-job training and would also
provide regular feedback to the international consultants to help them
identify key problems. Unfortunately, administrative difficulties delayed
the hiring of permanent staff, so less training could be provided and less
feedback was obtained on the progress of the evaluations.

The goal of creating local ownership of the studies introduced several
intermediary levels into the design and supervision of the evaluation.
MAFF coordinated with the line ministries, who in turn coordinated with
the research groups. Five independent studies were conducted using four
different local consulting groups, which made it more difficult to ensure

a standard evaluation design. The greater autonomy of the ministries and research groups permitted experimentation with a wider range of evaluation methods, but, on the negative side, reduced comparability among studies.

There was also sensitivity about criticisms by international consultants of the professional capacity of local consultants, and recommendations had to be carefully phrased. International consultants worked successfully with the consulting groups on a one-to-one basis, and these groups seemed anxious to receive technical inputs, but, owing to institutional complications, a proposed activity to bring together all of the research groups to discuss common research problems could not take place.

◼ *Lessons Learned*

Several lessons were learned as a result of this evaluation project. First, it made a wide range of government, research, and nongovernment agencies aware that development projects may have significantly different impacts on women and men. Unless these differences are taken into consideration during project design, and the specific constraints affecting women are addressed, the potential economic and social contributions of women to the project's success are likely to be reduced significantly. Second, almost none of these gender differences were considered during the design of the projects studied. As a result of the evaluation program, the situation may improve for future projects—particularly with respect to the kinds of data collected during project design.

Third, the studies demonstrated the need for better baseline data. As the design phase of most projects includes the collection of significant amounts of social and economic data, it would be relatively simple to produce sex-disaggregated baseline data. This would involve (a) defining the impacts the projects are intended to achieve, defining measurable indicators, and collecting data on them; (b) ensuring that sex-disaggregated data are collected on households; (c) ensuring that surveys cover the whole target population; and (d) obtaining data on control groups. The evaluation studies demonstrated that this can be done. Fourth, cost-effective and relatively simple methods can be used to create a framework for basic impact evaluation studies. And finally, despite some limitations, the institutional development model significantly strengthened gender impact evaluation capacity in Tunisia. In future efforts, several factors should be emphasized. The evaluation team of the local partner agency should be fully in place as early in a project as possible. Although considerable autonomy should be given to participating agencies, procedures should ensure close coordination between the local research groups conducting the studies.

■ *Note*

1. The grant is managed by the Human Resources Division 1, North Africa and Middle East Department of the World Bank, with technical assistance from the Gender Analysis and Policy Group.

■ *References*

Butler, F. C. (1994). Using focus groups with rural women. In H. Feldstein & J. Jiggins (Eds.), *Tools for the field: Methodologies handbook for gender analysis in agriculture.* West Hartford, CT: Kumarian.

Feldstein, H., & Jiggins, J. (Eds.). (1994). *Tools for the field: Methodologies handbook for gender analysis in agriculture.* West Hartford, CT: Kumarian.

Institut de Développement Nord-sud. (1995). *Les méthodologies d'évaluation de l'impact des projets de développement sur les femmes* (Actes d'un séminaire tenu à Tunis en Novembre 1994). Quebec: Pocatière.

Moser, C. (1993). *Gender planning and development: Theory, practice and training.* London: Routledge.

Overholt, C., Anderson, M., Cloud, K., & Austin, J. (1985). *Gender roles in development projects.* West Hartford, CT: Kumarian.

Valadez, J., & Bamberger, M. (1994). *Monitoring and evaluating social programs: Guidelines for policy makers, planners and managers in developing countries.* Washington, DC: World Bank, Economic Development Institute.

World Bank. (1994). *Enhancing the participation of women in economic development.* Washington, DC: Author.

World Bank. (1995). *Toward gender equality: The role of public policy.* Washington, DC: Author.

19

The Analysis and Evaluation of Foreign Aid

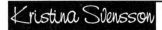

Kristina Svensson

How should the overall evaluation and analysis of development cooperation be performed over the long term? This question was put by the
Swedish government to a committee of researchers, aid experts, and
politicians in 1993. Three issues crystallized as central: (a) the effectiveness of Swedish foreign aid policies in general, (b) the effectiveness of
that aid in achieving particular goals, and (c) the extent to which—and
the ways—aid affects developing countries in general. I participated in
this study as a politician, and in this chapter I present both our deliberations and our conclusions.

■ *Some Historical Background About Aid Policy*

More than 30 years ago, the Swedish Parliament decided that the overriding goal of Swedish aid to developing countries should be "to raise the

standard of living of the poorest people." The specific objectives of aid were economic growth, economic and social equality, economic and political independence, democracy, and sustainable use of natural resources and protection of the environment. There is broad political consensus on these goals.

However, recent years have seen many refinements in our understanding of the overall development process, with the following factors receiving increased emphasis. First, governmental and nongovernmental institutions that function well are a key factor in a recipient country, so there should be an institutional framework, clear ownership structures, an open administration that takes responsibility, and a state governed by law. Second, the state, the market, and civil society must interact in balance with each other. Third, investments in human capital—that is, in education and health services—are important for growth and equality. Fourth, investments in physical infrastructure—to handle communications, the flow of water, and disposal of sewage, for instance—are a central concern. Fifth, openness to foreign investments, free trade, and new technologies are decisive factors for growth. Sixth, good macroeconomic policy is essential, especially a national budget under control, control of inflation, a realistic exchange rate, good market orientation, and a program to make the public sector more effective. Seventh, donors and recipients should have the same objectives for their cooperation. Eighth, the purpose of aid should be to contribute to the better utilization of resources in the recipient country, rather than to further increases in production capacity. Finally, the active interest of the recipient country, along with its assumption of responsibility, is of decisive importance.

At the same time, experience has shown us that cooperation is more complicated than originally imagined. Some complications are related to circumstances on the recipient side. Aid to the poorest countries comes in many projects from many donors with specific conditions, making it difficult for recipients to coordinate the flow of aid. This leads to mismanagement of funds, and opportunities for corruption increase. Few politicians in recipient countries accept the emphasis on poverty stressed by donors, so aid may be channeled in directions that differ from the preferences of donors. Long-term development cooperation agreements have been used by most donors, sometimes leading to recipient countries and their decision makers becoming dependent on aid and making it difficult to pursue policies that lead to independence. Indeed, when aid is very great in relation to a developing country's other international transactions, it can force up the exchange rate to such high levels that exports and competitive imports are unprofitable, further diminishing prospects for independent development. Finally, aid can negatively affect the incentive structure in recipient countries, especially savings and efficient production.

However, other problems that reduce the effectiveness of aid lie primarily with the donor side. For example, donor communities do not adequately coordinate their efforts and are reluctant to reduce and focus the number of aid projects, which makes the absorption of aid difficult. Many donor countries allocate fixed amounts each year to each recipient country, so that spending the allocated amount becomes an end in itself, with less attention paid to the quality and effectiveness of aid. Donor countries are often slow to demand results from development cooperation. In Sweden, for example, there has been reluctance to take a definite position on fundamental issues in the development policies of recipient countries. Aid policy has also been unduly influenced by security and commercial motives that have damaged effectiveness. Finally, donor organizations must improve their ability to learn from mistakes and to correct misjudgments.

■ *Greater Emphasis on the Effectiveness of Aid*

In response to such problems, the international donor community has given greater attention to the effectiveness of aid, fostered even more by apparently growing doubt among the general public about the effectiveness of aid. Facilitating these adjustments will require that the system's readiness for change be strengthened, including greater evaluation capacity and renewed commitment to results-based management. However, a common mistake made in attempts to determine the effectiveness of aid is that countries' choices of development strategies are reviewed, instead of aid and its effects. Such evaluations may unfairly criticize aid and donors for an unsatisfactory state of affairs that lies outside their control, and may fail to influence those decisions that donors do control. Choices of development strategies and the organization of aid programs must be linked, but an understanding that development assistance only marginally affects a country's development strategy is important. It is also important to recall that the goals of aid may conflict. In the Swedish case, for example, it may be difficult to combat poverty, cooperate with recipients, and foster political and economic equality simultaneously. In addition, different parts of aid policy have different motives that may conflict. Swedish motives include pure altruism, solidarity, mutual interest, and commercial self-interest. Aid policy consensus has often been reached through compromises among these motives. All this points to the great importance of evaluating and analyzing the formulation of goals. Of course, different development programs can be effective in different ways. Nevertheless, the most basic question of the effectiveness of aid is, Does it fulfill its purpose? A corollary question concerns the cost-efficiency of aid, measured by placing costs in relation to effects. Finally, any study of the overall effectiveness of an aid program must also ask who has defined the program's aims.

☐ *Concepts of Effectiveness*

Effectiveness issues are dealt with differently by anthropologists, sociologists, political scientists, lawyers, and ecologists. The predominant school of thought in the study of aid programs is the national economic school, in which *effectiveness* and *quality* refer to how much the gross domestic product grows in a recipient country as a result of foreign aid. However, the concept of effectiveness also has other characteristics in the evaluation of aid programs. Evaluators concerned with the *soundness* and *sustainability* of aid programs emphasize the permanence of positive program effects. The *degree of efficiency* concerns whether all effects are included in the evaluation. Finally, *relevance* refers to the degree to which the program corresponds to the priorities of the recipient country.

☐ *Levels of Effectiveness*

In the Swedish aid system, there are also different levels on which evaluations can focus: (a) the goals of aid, both the overriding goal to raise the standards of living of poor people and the five aid policy goals (growth, equality, independence, democracy, and the environment); (b) policies, procedures, and guidelines that direct the preparation, approval, and implementation of aid programs; (c) projects and programs through which aid funds are transferred to the recipient; and (d) organizations that prepare, approve, implement, and follow up specific projects (including both Swedish aid agencies and implementing agencies in Sweden, in the recipient countries, and in the multilateral system). The first two levels should be the subjects of analyses of the effectiveness of aid. At the third and fourth levels, analyses of the effectiveness and cost-efficiency of aid can be made.

☐ *The Quality of Aid*

The concept of quality is central to the improvement of aid programs and should be used as an essential supplement to the effectiveness concept. The *quality of aid* concerns the characteristics that enable projects to satisfy the needs of recipients. Quality is not a fixed characteristic of a product or service, but is more fleeting. It depends on how the product or service is used by recipients, how well it meets needs, how adequate and well adapted it is to the circumstances. If aid is placed at the disposal of the recipient, the recipient's perspective should be of decisive importance in the assessment of quality. Quality also implies a time dimension. A service or a product of good quality serves its purpose not merely for the moment but for as long as the needs require it or until it is replaced by other goods or services. Unfortunately, this attempt to straighten out the concept of quality only shifts the difficulty to the next word—what is meant by *needs*?

This question must be examined concretely on the basis of the special circumstances, the political conditions, and the period that is being studied. One approach is to talk about the present quality of an activity in relation to its previous quality. In this way, quality demands are transformed into a challenge to improve activities in comparison with how they were previously. Possibly this competition with one's own organization and activities could be supplemented with comparisons with other similar activities or the programs of other organizations. In some large companies this has become a normal routine with the use of benchmarking, in which one activity is systematically compared with another. In the international debate, similar discussions have taken place on aid program characteristics that could influence the quality of aid, for example, tied compared with untied aid, projects compared with programs, transfers of funds compared with technical cooperation, bilateral aid compared with multilateral aid, and government organizations compared with nongovernmental organizations.

■ *Linking Effectiveness Evaluations to Decision Making*

Studies and evaluations of effectiveness are often static, answering the question of what happened: Did a certain type of implementation lead to the achievement of the project's goals? Has aid as a whole been successful? The answers to such questions contribute to the ability to implement necessary changes at the right time and with minimum resources. However, such effectiveness studies are not sufficient. Rather, the links of effectiveness studies to decision making and the learning process must be the point of departure. A point of departure is the analysis of the decision-making process, the foundation of which should be management by objectives and results. In this approach, results are measured against goals, and projects are changed on the basis of these measures to achieve better results. Results-based management requires that goals at different levels are logically connected internally so that goal fulfillment at lower levels leads to goal fulfillment at the aggregate level. If this is so, then isolated projects to produce better reports on results, or better project evaluations, are not enough. It is necessary to transform evaluation criticism into action, decisions, and changes. This cannot be achieved solely through central decisions at the ministry or agency level. Rather, another way of thinking and acting at the project implementation level is required. A transition to methods governed by goals and results does not merely require comparing results to goals, but developing and improving the goals themselves. Without this basis, the remainder of the reform will lack a concrete foundation.

The analysis of decision making must focus on the learning process of decision makers who deal with aid projects at all levels. For example, we should not assume that decisions are made on given occasions by identified decision makers in a certain hierarchical order. Rather, in a learning organization, regulated learning via the formal decision-making process is supplemented by searches for information and exchanges of experience outside the formal decision-making process. Analysis must also focus on those factors that affect the willingness of the entire system to change, such as leadership, incentives, human resources management, division of responsibilities, organizational structure, and institutional competition. To direct aid toward greater effectiveness, it is therefore necessary to work on a broad basis in all these areas.

Three links between effectiveness evaluation and decision making are key. The first is the extension of the discussion of goals. Overall goals must be broken down into agency goals, and these, in turn, into goals for programs and projects. The goals should be expressed in terms of quality, volume, cost, and time, the latter two being mostly neglected in present work. Clarifying goals is important because it gives those with program duties and responsibilities a clearer picture of the expectations and conceptions that existed when the activity was planned. Without goals as a starting point, the work will be unclear and mistakes will be repeated. Of course, in a small, stable organization with great continuity, the need for explicit goals is not as great, because the responsible decision maker may remember how he or she thought and learned over time. However, this is rarely the case with aid programs. Aid has a long-term perspective, and it can be years before mistakes become evident. The connection between projects and results is often vague, contradictory, and difficult to assess. Circumstances change rapidly, and work does not proceed as anticipated. Staff turnover is rapid in relation to project implementation. Hence formalizing and documenting goals is necessary.

The second link between effectiveness evaluation and decision making is the reporting of how results compare with goals and criteria in terms of content, time, and cost. Often such reporting is an easy task, but sometimes it can be demanding. Reporting may require extensive presentation of facts with difficult demarcation problems. How, for example, is it possible to determine the outcome of balance-of-payments support? How can the effect of Swedish support be separated from the support of other donors? How do results of aid programs compare with other economic factors?

Finally, there is a third link in the chain: evaluation. The role of evaluation varies depending on which of three functions it serves: learning, results reporting, or management and control. Evaluations of aid policy (policy analysis) concentrate on the learning process, and conclusions aim to help the strategic aid decisions of Parliament and the government. Survey evaluations are conducted to show results—successes and failures. Operations-based, clearly defined, concrete evaluations aim to improve project management. This great range illustrates the importance of attending to the needs of the entire system. Along with consideration of the recipient perspective, the function determines what is evaluated, how it is done, and how results are presented.

The functions of evaluations are closely linked to the reporting of results, in that both require formulation of clear and realistic goals. However, results reporting does not replace evaluation. Evaluations penetrate deeper to assess results from an overall perspective. Hence evaluations are essential for proper reporting of results and for better definition of new goals and working methods. Evaluations are vital to the interplay between goals and results, on which management controls are based, and by which organizations have the capacity for renewal.

During recent years, reporting of results has assumed an increasingly prominent position in public administration, including aid policies. Although such reporting is difficult when aid is provided to distant countries with no automatic feedback mechanisms, an open and honest results report is necessary to a donor's willingness to give aid over the long term. This function of evaluation has assumed even greater importance with the introduction of goal- and results-based management. However, there is a need for better evaluation methods if management and controls are to be a powerful instrument in the aid area.

■ *Necessary Conditions for Evaluations to Play a Role in Aid Work*

If evaluations are to have more importance in aid policies, evaluation activities must be adapted to the changing conditions for aid and changing aid policies. Important shifts have taken place in aid linked to reforms in the recipient countries, sector-based aid, multisector programs (women), new areas (democracies, states governed by law and human rights), and changed goals (sustainable development). The emphasis and methods of evaluations must be similarly renewed so that, for example, countries are transformed into analysis units, sector evaluations are given greater importance, and methods and measurements are devised that reflect progress relating to multisector programs, new areas, and the formulation of goals.

The role of evaluations in aid policies has been affected considerably by recent changes in forms of management and controls in the aid field, especially by results-oriented management and by the introduction of country strategies for management and control of long-term development cooperation. Both factors increase the need for evaluations as a basis for management and controls, especially for in-depth analysis of both a country's general development and prospects and the results of past development cooperation programs with the country. Evaluations are also needed to prepare for international conferences on, for example, specialist areas or the operations of multilateral organizations.

Relevant evaluations of good quality can have difficulty achieving impacts, especially if they advocate comprehensive changes. Good timing and effective presentation can strengthen the acceptance of an evaluation, but the readiness of the management and staff members of the organizations concerned to accept change is crucial. Political pressure, management style, reward systems, and attitudes all influence that readiness. A lack of ability to react to evaluations can also be a problem. Against this background, results-oriented management assumes more importance, for if it is undertaken with energy and skill it can strengthen the readiness to change.

■ *The Role of Recipient Countries in Evaluations*

Ultimately, the readiness for change in recipient countries is decisive for the results of aid, such change being the ultimate aim of aid. The recipient country's perspective must permeate the evaluation, and the goals and values on which the evaluation is based must be shared by the recipient country. The fundamental requirement for evaluation results to be of interest to recipient countries is that those countries accept and support aid projects and assume responsibility for the projects when aid ends. Of course, a recipient may have good reasons not to follow the recommendations of an evaluation, including different values and ways of thinking, domestic policy considerations, or more narrow organizational interests. These reasons, and our respect for the integrity of recipient countries, prompt us to restrain demands that recipient countries take particular actions.

Donor countries have the ultimate responsibility for using aid funds well. A first step is to make aid funds an integral part of the central government budgets of recipient countries. Only then can the governments of recipient countries assume real responsibility for decisions on, for example, investments and overall economic policies, including the use of aid funds. Another step would be for recipient countries to organize the evaluations of aid programs, something that is not a reality for the poorest countries today. Such countries tend to give evaluation low priority, and they generally have few qualified evaluation personnel. They sometimes regard aid as a gift and do not study the value of this gift too carefully, because the alternative to accepting aid seems to them to be to refuse it. They correctly regard evaluation activities of donor organizations as donor controlled, and as concentrating on the reporting of results and on financial accounting. However, evaluation could be, and should be, an instrument that recipient countries can use to improve the management of scarce aid resources. Just as in donor countries, the learning process, the reporting of results, and information for management and control purposes should also be key evaluation functions for recipient countries.

So the effectiveness and cost-efficiency of projects and programs depend on how both donor and recipient act. Both have responsibility for effective utilization of scarce public funds. Donors should ensure that aid is audited in the same way as internal funds, by authorized bodies, in accord with existing regulations, and in a spirit of openness toward the media and the general public in the recipient country. Aid should also help improve or build existing institutions and mechanisms in the country through which the recipient can assume responsibility and participate in the evaluation of aid activities. In particular, evaluators should be selected from developing countries, and preferably from the recipient country, for major evaluations. Donor countries can also help developing countries to obtain existing results and experience at the international level. Aid for public administration can be the common denominator for such projects.

◼ *Statistics on Aid*

Analysis and follow-up of the effectiveness and cost-efficiency of aid by donor countries require appropriate statistics that describe the scope, content, and structure of aid, and that place this information in relation to corresponding information on other donor countries. Aid statistics can be divided into statistics for general information and statistics for use as instruments. General-information statistics aim to meet the needs of an interested general public, the needs of different groups of lobbyists, and the needs of those working with opinion groups. The needs of the Swedish Parliament, for example, fall mainly under this category. Instrumental statistics are those employed to obtain reference data and key ratios for comparative studies, follow-ups, and program analyses. Such uses require flexibility in the grouping of projects and definitions, topicality, and the capacity to break data down into periods of time. In addition, quality aspects of these statistics concern accuracy, availability, and frequency. Most of the statistics discussed here originate from administrative sources, the quality of which varies far too much. Aid statistics need a quality guarantee that should cover examination of project registration as well as reporting on the final use of funds.

The statistics available today on Swedish aid are not appropriate for studies and analyses of the effectiveness of aid. Their shortcomings can be summarized under three main points: (a) Comprehensive and uniform accounting of the final use of aid funds is lacking, (b) the information on disbursements of aid funds is not sufficiently detailed, and (c) the accounting of aid flow does not permit detailed analysis of administrative costs in different parts of the system, which makes analysis of the cost-effectiveness of the system difficult.

■ *Research on Aid*

There is a close connection between evaluation and research. The research world is an important base for the recruitment of evaluators. Research on aid and development helps ensure the quality of evaluation methods and content, and it is, in principle, independent of government agencies and financing structures because it is done by persons located at universities with some permanent sources of financing. These units can be research and educational bodies established within the university system and units that undertake policy research on a commission basis. The results of such research are directed to other researchers and interested parties, such as the Swedish Parliament, lobbyists, and the general public.

Sufficient research capacity is also necessary to use the results of research performed abroad and to involve Swedish research institutions as interested partners in research on aid. Examples of desirable international cooperation are joint evaluations, common methods of working, and common efforts to build up evaluation systems in recipient countries.

Finally, nongovernmental organizations that receive state support must be able to report results, so they should also have an evaluation function in proportion to the aid they receive.

■ *Conclusions*

The committee that I described at the start of this chapter concluded that questions of effectiveness must be given greater attention at all levels of aid policy. We called attention to the role of the recipient countries in evaluations—aid should be an integral part of recipient countries' state budgets, and those countries should have their own systems of evaluation. Donor countries should see that aid flows are examined and accounted for in the same way as domestic resources. Support for building up evaluation functions should be part of development cooperation. The committee also pointed out that scrutiny of results and evaluations carried out on the donor's side should be done in such a way that the recipient's point of view is taken into account; results should be presented so as to be accessible to the recipient; and conclusions should be applicable from the recipient's point of view. The committee also emphasized the importance of international cooperation in evaluation. The considerations of the committee were adopted by Parliament, and in late 1995 the Swedish government appointed a number of internationally known evaluators to implement its recommendations. This will no doubt further the impact of evaluations on Swedish aid policy.

20

Evaluating the U.S. Nuclear Triad

In April 1990, the chairman of the House Foreign Affairs Committee, Representative Dante Fascell, asked the U.S. General Accounting Office (GAO) to assess the major strategic (i.e., nuclear weapons) modernization programs of the Carter, Reagan, and Bush administrations, with the objective of providing a data-based evaluation to assess the strengths and weaknesses of these programs and the determination of which among them appears to be most cost-effective. At the time, these new systems and/or upgrades would have cost an estimated $350 billion. In September 1992, the GAO's Program Evaluation and Methodology Division published a comprehensive evaluation of the strategic nuclear "triad," as it is

AUTHORS' NOTE: The opinions and conclusions expressed in this article are solely our own, and do not represent those of the U.S. General Accounting Office or any other government agency.

commonly referred to, comparing test and operational data on the delivery platforms and warheads of the land, sea, and air legs. To make such comparisons, seven measures of effectiveness were used, along with the life-cycle cost of each leg's systems and proposed or ongoing modernizations. A set of eight reports was published (these reports remain classified and are therefore not available to the public).

Among other findings, the work showed that technological advances had enabled the sea leg's submarine-launched ballistic missiles (SLBMs) to acquire the accuracy, reliability, communications speed, and time-to-target of the land leg's intercontinental ballistic missiles (ICBMs), but without the liability of vulnerability. As a consequence, it is possible to achieve major cost savings, in the billions of dollars, by decommissioning all land-based ICBMs, as well as by reducing the size of the submarine fleet. Further, although the air leg's bombers offered more flexibility than ballistic missiles, there was no need to replace B-52s with B-2s, given that claims that the B-52s were either near the end of their life cycle or highly vulnerable to Soviet air defenses were contradicted by the actual data. Indeed, across all three legs and associated systems, GAO found that the Department of Defense (DoD), before the end of the Cold War, had systematically overstated both the threats to these systems and the likely performance of proposed new systems while understating the capabilities of existing weapons.

Although many specific data in these reports cannot be revealed under classification rules, the key findings can be summarized, as well as the methodology used to produce the studies. In this chapter we will discuss the objectives of the study, its key findings, and the evaluation methodology used to arrive at conclusions that contradicted many of the commonly held public beliefs about the capabilities of the triad legs and that pointed to major potential cost savings without loss of strategic capabilities. However, we will also go beyond the original set of studies to take into account important changes in the world's political and military environment since the reports were issued.

■ *Development of U.S. Strategic Forces*

It is probably useful to review briefly how the strategic triad came about, along with the rationale for the nuclear forces deployed by the United

States for the past 40 years. The nuclear triad, which developed in a largely unplanned way, as ICBMs and SLBMs were tested and deployed, and as other related technological capabilities grew, consists of (a) the original air-based leg, composed of long-range bombers (B-52s and 20 B-2s) as well as the bombs and missiles they carry;[1] (b) a land-based leg, composed of silo-based ICBMs (now limited to 450 aging 3-warhead Minuteman IIIs and 10-warhead Peacekeepers, the latter being retired under START II); and (c) a sea leg, consisting of 18 "Ohio"-class Trident SSBNs, each of which can carry up to 24 D-5 SLBMs, with up to 8 warheads each, for a potential maximum of 192 nuclear warheads on every SSBN.

As U.S. nuclear forces were developed and tested in the 1950s, this triad slowly emerged from what was originally only a force of bombers intended to penetrate Soviet airspace (the first Minuteman ICBMs were not deployed until 1961, and the first Polaris SLBMs in 1962). During the 1960s, when each leg became reasonably robust in terms of deployed delivery platforms and warheads, as well as the communications systems required to assure their control and launch, public impressions about their comparative merits and capabilities became relatively fixed—a conventional wisdom that changed very little over the next three decades.

The bombers were viewed as having the virtue of being recallable once launched, due to their slowness in reaching targets, but also as being deficient precisely because they took so long to get to what was then the Soviet Union. They were also potentially vulnerable at their bases, and so had to be maintained in a state of high alert if they were to survive surprise Soviet ICBM attack, which would not provide more than tactical (i.e., some tens of minutes) warning of detonation on U.S. soil. For this reason, a percentage of the bomber force was always kept "on alert," meaning that it would escape because the bombers would take off after Soviet ICBMs were detected, but before those missiles could reach U.S. bomber bases. Finally, bombers were "flexible" because they could be recalled, or their targets changed en route; they were also reusable, in contrast to silos with ballistic missiles, once launched.

The conventional perception of the land leg's silo-based ICBMs was that they were highly accurate and very prompt, given that they could be launched almost immediately upon receipt of orders to do so. By virtue of being silo based, the ICBMs were seen as being tightly controlled by civilian authority, yet highly responsive to launch orders that could be transmitted via a multitude of redundant means, from buried cables to radio. The major liability of ICBMs was that they were of necessity based at fixed sites that could be easily targeted in advance by the Soviets, and, as Soviet ICBM accuracy increased, so did the hypothetical vulnerability of silo-based ICBMs. This perceived vulnerability led to plans in the 1970s for mobile ICBMs, at potentially staggering expense.

The third leg—nuclear-powered submarines and their SLBMs—was widely believed to be relatively invulnerable to attack (when submerged), but also deficient in terms of both missile accuracy (due to the combination of platform movement and inferior guidance technology compared with ICBMs) and reliability for receiving orders in the midst of a nuclear attack. Hence, although the submerged SSBNs were not vulnerable to surprise attack, they were not seen as providing as lethal or as reliable weapons as the ICBMs. Further, it was widely believed—and ratified in the defense-related press—that it was only a matter of time until the Soviets developed technologies that would permit them to "see" through water, thereby putting the entire SSBN fleet at risk. This provided justification for the land and air legs, which would thus serve as "hedges" against the "inevitable" day of the Soviet technology breakthrough.

As this triad panoply came into being, so too did the rationale for the triad on the basis of "synergy." That is, the "need" for three legs—each with different advantages and liabilities—was justified with the argument that it took these three to assure a synergy that could foil any conceivable Soviet attack, including the most stressful surprise attack that could be hypothesized. With three legs at different locations, there was no way the Soviets could effectively destroy the entire U.S. nuclear force and thereby prevent massive retaliation, even if the Soviets were to use every single one of thousands of weapons at once. This was because (a) wiping out any single leg would still leave two other legs intact; (b) U.S. bomber bases were located sufficiently far from the Soviet Union, and inside the United States, so that Soviet ICBMs could not reach them before there was sufficient warning for the alert bombers to take off; (c) a Soviet attack on U.S. ICBMs first would likewise leave both bombers and SLBMs intact; and (d) no simultaneous Soviet attack on ICBMs and bombers was feasible, due to the problems inherent in hitting targets hundreds of miles apart (and further south) at the same moment. Thus the synergy of the triad assured, first, that no Soviet attack, regardless of size or lack of warning to the United States, could eliminate more than a portion of the U.S. forces; and, second, that a Soviet attack therefore could not prevent massive assured retaliation and destruction of the Soviet homeland.

Similarly, offensive synergy derived from the fact that the deployment of different types of weapons on different platforms makes it essentially impossible to have a single defense technology that can deal with all three types. An air defense optimized against low-altitude bombers cannot deal with ballistic missiles. Moreover, the slowness of bombers means that ballistic missiles could clear a path for them to targets; alternatively, they could launch cruise missiles from outside Soviet borders, before becoming vulnerable to air defenses.

Despite these apparent strengths, by the late 1970s it was widely believed that improvements in Soviet nuclear technologies and air defenses were undermining the U.S. deterrent, even as U.S. weapons improved as well. It was claimed that greater warhead yield and Soviet ICBM accuracy placed more U.S. silos at risk, decreasing the potential number of retaliating ICBMs. The seas were expected to become transparent to some new and advanced technology, and Soviet SSBNs were ever quieter and more likely to reach U.S. coastal waters undetected, putting U.S. bomber bases at greater risk from close-in attack. In response to these perceived threats to U.S. strategic forces, serious consideration was being given to upgrading the triad legs, through such costly modernization programs as putting Peacekeepers on train railcars ("railgarrison"); investing in small (single-warhead) ICBMs, or SICBMs ("Midgetman"); deploying a total of 133 B-2 stealth strategic bombers and additional advanced cruise missiles for them; and development of more lethal warheads for the D-5 SLBM. At this point, responding to Chairman Fascell's request, we evaluated the costs and claimed merits of each of these programs, as well as those of the existing systems they were intended to either replace or enhance. We then assessed all systems under a full range of threat scenarios, moving from total surprise attack to strategic warning (i.e., several hours or more).

■ *Current Nuclear Forces and Arms Control Efforts*

Although the triad study's findings made it clear in late 1991 that a significant restructuring of the nation's strategic triad could be contemplated—prior to the Soviet collapse—there has been little or no movement to do so over the intervening years, *despite* (a) the disappearance of the Soviet Union and the breaking apart of its nuclear capabilities and defense systems among Russia, Ukraine, Kazakhstan, and various other non-Russian republics and now independent nations; and (b) a 40% contraction in the total Russian economy and a cut of at least 70% in weapons modernization, according to 1994 testimony by the Defense Intelligence Agency director (U.S. Senate, Select Committee on Intelligence, 1994, p. 23).

Since late 1991—when the Soviet Union still existed and when President Bush announced the cancellation of two extremely costly undeveloped mobile ICBM systems (Peacekeeper railgarrison and SICBM), as well as taking all U.S. strategic bombers off alert—there have been no further cuts in nuclear warheads below the levels already agreed to in the START II arms control treaty.[2] The Clinton administration accepted DoD's *Nuclear Posture Review,* which largely ratified the status quo, with two exceptions—reducing the nuclear-powered submarine (SSBN) fleet from 18 to 14 boats and cutting the number of B-52 bombers by 28, from 94 to 66 (U.S. Department of Defense, 1994, p. 17). However, these reductions involved no cuts in the number of warheads that were permitted the United States under START II (3,500) and clearly preserved the fundamental three-legged triad of air, land, and sea nuclear delivery systems. Ironically, therefore, by far the greatest cost savings in nuclear forces and operating costs since the Cold War began occurred under the Bush administration, before the Soviet Union disintegrated.

In effect, although the Soviet threat to the United States has disappeared, although the Russian "threat" is vastly reduced compared with that of the former Soviet Union (FSU), and although Russia's defenses against bomber attack are now split among itself and now-independent nations with long histories of hostility toward Russia (in particular, Ukraine), there has been no U.S. action to revisit the issue of whether we can safely reduce nuclear warheads below START II levels or restructure existing strategic forces to save valuable tax dollars at a time of immense spending constraints. This is the more remarkable in view of current efforts to balance the budget and the relevance to those efforts of the findings from the present evaluation.

■ Measures Used to Assess Strategic Systems

We analyzed each major existing strategic system and proposed upgrade or replacement against seven key measures of effectiveness (MOEs), most quantitative and some qualitative. These seven MOEs were as follows:

1. survivability against both offensive and defensive threat systems, for both platforms and weapons (e.g., bombers, gravity bombs, and cruise missiles)

2. delivery system performance (i.e., accuracy, range, and payload—number of weapons carried by a single platform)

3. warhead yield (in kilotons—1 kiloton is equal to 1,000 tons of dynamite) and reliability (the probability the warhead will detonate)

4. weapon system reliability (the combined reliability of all the component processes, from platform launch to warhead detonations)

5. flexibility across a number of dimensions, including retargeting and recall

6. communications (e.g., reliability of connectivity between command authority and platforms; capability to recall)

7. responsiveness (i.e., the percentage of a force that is maintained on alert at any given moment and time-to-target)

In addition to these measures, we collected and analyzed data on the costs of the systems in question, to be able to compare each in terms of 30-year life-cycle costs, across a number of measures: life-cycle cost per warhead; cost per warhead for life-cycle costs remaining for deployed systems (or costs-to-go); and life-cycle costs and costs-to-go per arriving warhead, thereby taking into account system survivability and reliability.

Despite the seemingly quantitative nature of most of the MOEs, our assessment intentionally took into account several important qualitative aspects of the systems under consideration. Among these other factors were evaluation of (a) the potential impact of both existing and proposed strategic systems on arms control efforts; (b) the likely synergistic interactions of the various systems within and among the triad legs, both defensively and offensively; and (c) the possible impact of interactions among the three legs and proposed modernizations on Soviet nuclear force and attack planning. By combining the highly quantitative MOEs with the more qualitative arms control and synergy dimensions, we sought to provide as comprehensive a comparison as possible of all the relevant factors needed to compare the strategic triad systems and modernizations.

We tried hard to find and use the best data available. Toward this end, we included an unprecedented variety and depth of classified data on U.S. systems, collected from several dozen U.S. government agencies and strategic-related entities. These data were gathered from multiple sources, including about 250 major technical reports and more than 200 interviews with military, civilian, and intelligence experts on strategic issues and systems.

Among the data collected and analyzed were the following: the results for every C-4 and D-5 SLBM test up to the time of report processing; every Peacekeeper test; every Minuteman III test; results of warhead detonation and reliability tests and field deployment; operational patrol data on communications to SSBNs; operational data on communications to ICBM silos; data from extensive tests of communications to all three triad legs; and intelligence agency data and analysis on every relevant potential Soviet nuclear weapon system and defense against each of the three legs, from air defense to Soviet nuclear attack submarines and submarine-detection technologies. Among the agencies whose experts we interviewed were the Strategic Air Command; the Central Intelligence Agency; the Defense Intelligence Agency; the Defense Advanced Research Projects Agency; the Johns Hopkins Applied Physics Laboratories; NORAD; the Arms Control and Disarmament Agency; the Institute for Defense Analyses, the Center for Naval Analyses; the Joint Chiefs of Staff and the Office of the Secretary of Defense; the Defense Nuclear, Defense Mapping, and Defense Communications Agencies; the Congressional Budget Office; the Congressional Research Service; and the Office of Technology Assessment; as well as the relevant U.S. Air Force and Navy offices, plus experts at the RAND and MITRE Corporations, the Brookings Institution, Massachusetts Institute of Technology, and others.

The data gathering and analysis proved to be even more daunting than we originally anticipated, considering that DoD had never itself attempted a comparable analysis. This amount of "real" data on the triad had never before been collected by one analytic team anywhere, perhaps because of the scope of the required effort, the classification issues involved, and/or the fact that none of the armed services perceived an incentive to attempt such comparisons.

☐ *Data Analysis Hurdles*

A notable feature of our experience in collecting and examining classified data and analysis on this scale from the Pentagon and intelligence agencies was the amount of distortion we found: There was a pervasive practice in DoD analyses of overestimating the likely effectiveness of proposed new weapon systems or upgrades while underestimating the performance of existing systems and overstating the likely FSU offensive or defensive threats to current systems.

With regard to proposed strategic upgrades, we not only found serious problems in the DoD performance claims, but also discovered that the operational testing (on which the claims were based) was often insufficient and unrealistic, that costs were understated (e.g., by not using life-cycle costs), that performance results were incomplete or unrepresentative, that there was a lack of systematic comparison to the systems they were to replace, and that the rationales for their development were unconvincing from the very beginning (U.S. Senate, Committee on Governmental Affairs, 1993, pp. 42-43).

☐ *Performance Findings*

We reported a number of significant findings, bringing together the data on performance, costs, arms control, and synergy. Among these were (a) that Soviet defensive and offensive threats to all three legs had been systematically overstated, meaning that existing U.S. systems were considerably more robust than popularly believed; (b) that the air leg's bombers offered certain flexibility by virtue of being recallable, reusable, retargetable, and available for conventional (i.e., nonnuclear) missions, which was not the case for silos and their ballistic missiles; and (c) that the sea leg, overall, is more cost-effective than the land leg, across multiple measures of effectiveness.

This last finding was based, in part, on the following data. First, the sea leg's D-5 SLBMs with Mark (Mk) 5 warheads provide a hard-target kill capability not possessed by the Minuteman III ICBMs, due in part to the combination of the former's greater accuracy and kilotonnage (even with less powerful Mk4 warheads, the D-5s are still more accurate), as well as because ICBM performance data were more uncertain on a number of dimensions than expected. Second, the sea leg's SLBMs can reach targets essentially as quickly as silo-based ICBMs: Communications to SSBNs are substantially quicker and more reliable than widely understood and are as prompt as to ICBMs under day-to-day conditions, and almost as prompt under the more stressful—and far less likely—conditions of launching under a surprise attack. Third, the sea leg's submerged SSBNs are vastly more secure than readily targetable silo-based ICBMs, and there is no technological threat, either in the short or long term, that has the capability to locate, much less attack, submerged, deployed SSBNs. Fourth, the sea leg is considerably less costly per warhead, in terms of life-cycle costs, than the land leg's Minuteman IIIs (the latter are 25-40% more costly per warhead, depending on whether a 28-year or 18-year life cycle is assumed). The cost advantage of SSBN warheads may be even greater, under certain attack scenarios, depending on the number of ICBMs that are assumed lost to an attacker (we calculated and presented the life-cycle costs per arriving warheads for all three legs under several war scenarios, but cannot discuss these due to classification).

We also found that a limited strategic role could be identified for the B-2 bomber, but that, contrary to widespread perceptions of obsolescence, the B-52s had reached only the halfway point in their life expectancies, meaning that they would be viable platforms until about the year 2030 (due in part to the very few hours per year that they actually fly). (Unlike conventional fighter aircraft, such as F-15s or F-16s, B-52s are flown relatively fewer hours per year, are much more physically robust, and therefore have much longer planned life cycles.) On the other hand, producing and operating an additional 20 B-2s for 20 years would cost no less than $26 billion, yet these aircraft would carry less than 1% of the nuclear warheads permitted under the START II treaty.[3] Some selected findings are summarized in Tables 20.1-20.3, couched in terms of the beliefs commonly held in these areas. The disparities between some of these beliefs and our own findings occurred over a wide spectrum of issues and were a source of considerable surprise both to ourselves and to the requesting congressional committee.

Some Conclusions From the Findings

The finding that the sea leg was overall more cost-effective than the land leg's ICBMs, and the greatly reduced post-Cold War threat environment, led us to question the advisability of proceeding with the Air Force's planned major life-service upgrades of the aging Minuteman III ICBMs, intended to preserve the force through the year 2020. This recommendation, if followed, would have led to retirement of the ICBMs and reliance on a dyad (rather than a triad) of strategic forces consisting of Trident II

TABLE 20.1 The Strategic Air Leg: Beliefs Versus Findings

	Beliefs	Findings
On air base survivability	Bombers at bases have been vulnerable to surprise attack.	The data show surprise attack to have been extremely unlikely.
On bomber survivability to Soviet air defenses	Air defenses have grown dramatically.	High growth did not occur.
	Soviet defenses are very effective.	Combat experience and intelligence assessments indicate lesser capabilities.
	B-2 is needed to preserve the penetrating bomber role.	The data show B-52s can continue to be survivable penetrators.
On target coverage	Detectability and slowness make the air leg "stabilizing."	Available data support this belief.
	B-2s and B-1Bs have sufficient range for strategic missions.	The data are insufficient to support this; reliable test data are lacking.
On obsolescence	B-52 age mandates replacement.	Air Force data show B-52s as viable for several decades.

SLBMs and strategic bombers, thus saving about $23 billion in projected ICBM life-cycle costs.

We also recommended not buying any B-2s beyond the 20 already in the pipeline, given that only limited strategic missions for them could be identified, their high cost, their minimal potential contribution to total strategic capabilities, and the fact that existing B-52s had been found to have another 30-40 years of operational viability (U.S. Senate, Committee on Governmental Affairs, 1993, pp. 40-44). Our conclusions with regard to the robustness of the sea leg were supported by (then Deputy) Secretary of Defense William J. Perry. In June 1993 testimony before the Senate's Committee on Governmental Affairs on our triad study, Perry stated that he agreed that the sea leg was the "dominant leg of the triad," and that he was prepared to give it "quite a bit more emphasis" than the other two

TABLE 20.2 The Strategic Land Leg: Beliefs Versus Findings

	Beliefs	*Findings*
On survivability	Silo-based ICBMs have been highly vulnerable to massive, surprise Soviet attack.	Claims were based on worst-case estimates of Soviet ICBM capabilities, as well as other questionable assumptions.
On Soviet defenses	ICBMs face no effective defenses.	Available data support this belief.
On performance	ICBM communications are prompt, reliable, and redundant.	Available data generally support this perception.
	Peacekeeper (MX) is very reliable.	Confidence in estimates reduced by DoD's denial of data.
	Railcar Peacekeepers and mobile SICBMs would be as accurate and reliable as ICBMs in silos.	Insufficient data to support this belief.
	ICBMs can launch promptly after receipt of attack orders.	Available data support this but are based on test-silo launches and simulated electronic launch tests.

legs in future post-Cold War force readjustments. Further, whereas he was opposed to eliminating the air and land legs, he noted that "it would be a different question" if we were now to think about building a strategic force "from scratch," with regard to the non-sea legs (U.S. Senate, Committee on Governmental Affairs, 1993, pp. 26-27).

■ *Further Potential Strategic Force Reductions*

In the years since the triad reports were published, the strategic threat to the United States has further diminished, given the disappearance of the

TABLE 20.3 The Strategic Sea Leg: Beliefs Versus Findings

	Beliefs	*Findings*
On survivability	A technology breakthrough will eventually threaten the detectability of submerged SSBNs.	No current, near-, or far-term detection technology would be effective in reliably locating a single submerged, deployed SSBN, much less the entire fleet.
On performance	Communication to SSBNs is much slower and less reliable than to ICBMs in silos.	Data show communications to be about as prompt and as reliable as to ICBMs, under a wide range of conditions.
	SLBMs cannot be used against time-urgent targets due to slow communication and launch procedures.	No operationally meaningful difference in time-to-target compared with ICBMs was found.
	SLBMs cannot effectively attack the hardest (most reinforced) targets due to insufficient accuracy.	Test data show that D-5 SLBMs do in fact have this capability.
	Range and deployment area limitations may weaken sea leg accuracy and survivability.	SSBN patrol areas and D-5 range and accuracy impose no such limitations.

Soviet Union; the splitting up of FSU strategic weapons among Russia, Kazakhstan, Belarus, and Ukraine, and air defenses among even more (i.e., in addition, Lithuania, Latvia, and Estonia); and drastic decreases in Russian defense spending and military readiness. We believe, therefore, that our initial recommendations with regard to further potential reductions in U.S. strategic forces not only stand but could be expanded upon. Such actions are reflected to a limited degree by DoD's decision to reorient the entire B-2 force toward conventional missions and to cap the force at 20 bombers; to take all bombers off alert; and to "detarget" the ICBMs so that none is aimed at the FSU. However, as noted above, DoD's

1994 *Nuclear Posture Review,* which followed GAO's triad study by two years, recommended no reduction in the number of START II warheads, or major force reductions or restructuring, beyond cutting the planned SSBN force from 18 to 14 boats.

In line with the recommendations of its "Roles and Mission Commission" report, DoD has now decided to conduct major reassessments of U.S. defense needs, presumably including strategic forces, on a quadrennial basis. These reviews are intended to reassess U.S. defense needs in light of changes in the threat environment. GAO's eight-report triad study demonstrated that it is possible to conduct a comprehensive evaluation of America's complex strategic weapons systems, and the models for comparison now exist for use by DoD's analysts and others. Defense Secretary William Perry testified in 1993 that he had found the GAO report "valuable" and that "it will be an important and well-studied input in our restructuring of the strategic force" (U.S. Senate, Committee on Governmental Affairs, 1993, p. 19). Given the steady diminution of the strategic threat—to the point that smuggling of nuclear materials by terrorist groups may be a more likely threat to the lives of Americans or their allies than is a Russian nuclear attack—it is permissible to hope that the issue of achieving further cost savings from nuclear weapon retirements will one day be revisited.

■ Notes

1. The bombs are "gravity" bombs, which, as the name implies, are released from the aircraft and fall onto the target without benefit of further guidance, such as from a laser or other guiding device. The missiles are cruise missiles, which can be released hundreds of miles from the target.

2. The paper that was the basis for this chapter was delivered in November 1995, 3 months before the Senate's approval of ratification, which did not occur until January 26, 1996, 3 years after the treaty was signed by the United States and Russia. It was approved by a vote of 87-4 as part of a legislative agreement involving the fiscal year 1996 DoD authorization bill—after Russia made it clear that it would not continue adhering to the more modest reductions of the earlier START I treaty unless funding for an anti-ballistic missile defense program were excised from the defense authorization bill.

3. According to a Congressional Research Service analysis of START II, the B-2s were intended to carry 16 warheads each, or a total of 320 out of the 3,500 limit (equal to just under 1% of the total). The life-cycle cost per warhead for 20 B-2s beyond the 20 already ordered would be about $81 million each (assuming $750 million for each off-the-shelf B-2, annual operating costs of about $545 million for 20 B-2s, 16 bombs per aircraft, and a 20-year

life cycle), or more than 150% higher than comparable ICBM costs per warhead, and more than double the sea leg costs (before losses from an attack and then from Soviet defenses) (U.S. Air Force, 1995, p. 3; Woolf, 1993, p. 26).

■ *References*

U.S. Air Force. (1995, July). *Fact sheet 95-05, B-2 Spirit* [On-line]. Available WWW: search "B-2"

U.S. Department of Defense. (1994). *Nuclear posture review* [briefing slides] (press/public version).

U.S. General Accounting Office, Program Evaluation and Methodology Division. (1992, September). *US strategic triad: Final report and recommendations*; *US strategic triad: Modernizing strategic bombers and their missiles*; *US strategic triad: ICBM vulnerability*; *US strategic triad: SSBN vulnerability*; *US strategic triad: A comparison of ICBMs and SLBMs*; *US strategic triad: Costs and uncertainties of proposed upgrades*; *US strategic triad: Strategic relocatable targets*; *US strategic triad: Current status, modernization plans, and doctrine of British and French nuclear forces* (C/PEMD-92-1 through 8). Washington, DC: Author.

U.S. Senate, Committee on Governmental Affairs. (1993, June 10). *Evaluation of the U.S. strategic nuclear triad, testimonies of Eleanor Chelimsky and William J. Perry* (S. Hrg. 103-457). Washington, DC: Government Printing Office.

U.S. Senate, Select Committee on Intelligence. (1994, January 24). *Current and projected national security threats to the United States and its interests abroad* (S. Hrg. 103-630). Washington, DC: Government Printing Office.

Woolf, A. F. (1993, June 30). *The START and START II arms control treaties: Background and issues* (Congressional Research Service 93-617 F). Washington, DC: Government Printing Office.

21

Evaluation, Nuclear Power Plant Remediation and Redesign, and Russian Policy Making After Chernobyl

Vladimir Novikov

The accident at the nuclear power plant in Chernobyl on April 26, 1986, has been extensively evaluated both to determine its causes and to prevent similar catastrophes from occurring in the future. In this chapter I examine both of these issues, focusing first on nuclear power development in the former Soviet Union (FSU) before 1986, then on the factors responsible for the Chernobyl accident and the actions taken directly after the event, on the continuing rationale for nuclear power in the FSU, and finally, on the goals and objectives of advanced designs now being planned to deliver nuclear energy safely and effectively.

■ Background

□ *Nuclear Power Development Before Chernobyl*

The date of birth for nuclear power in the FSU was June 27, 1954, when the first nuclear power plant was put into operation in Obninsk, near Moscow. Figure 21.1 illustrates the rate of nuclear power growth reached in the mid-1980s by the FSU. The figure shows that the index for the FSU was at about the same level as for countries that had been able to establish nuclear power capacity faster. The average annual increase was 4-5 electric gigawatts, unit power was 1-1.5 gigawatts, and the nuclear share of electricity production reached 35-40% in some large regions.

Although the FSU had vast coal, oil, gas, and hydro resources, the majority of these resources were and are in the eastern sections of the FSU, rather far from the densely populated European areas. Because this posed a huge and expensive transportation problem for organic fuel, it was a major reason for intensive nuclear power development.

This development was facilitated and encouraged by the existence in the FSU of a large nuclear fuel cycle infrastructure, and also by the fact that centrally planned economies favor consistent program implementation; nuclear programs especially benefited from this. In such economies, once the technical and economic studies have been performed and the political decisions made, the government authorities in all the related economic sectors have the obligation to support the implementation of the approved policy and programs (Semenov, Dastidar, & Bennett, 1993). Table 21.1 describes the state of nuclear power capacity in the FSU and in Eastern European countries (as of 1994) that have used Soviet nuclear power plant designs.

□ *Characteristics of Nuclear Power Plants in the FSU*

Nuclear power in the FSU and Eastern European countries is based on Soviet-made designs of nuclear reactors, which are of two types: the VVER (water-cooled, water-moderated energy reactor) and the RBMK (water-cooled, graphite-moderated channel reactor). Both of these types have undergone three generations of development.

The RBMK is often called the Chernobyl reactor; it is unique to the FSU. All three generations of RBMKs were designed primarily in the

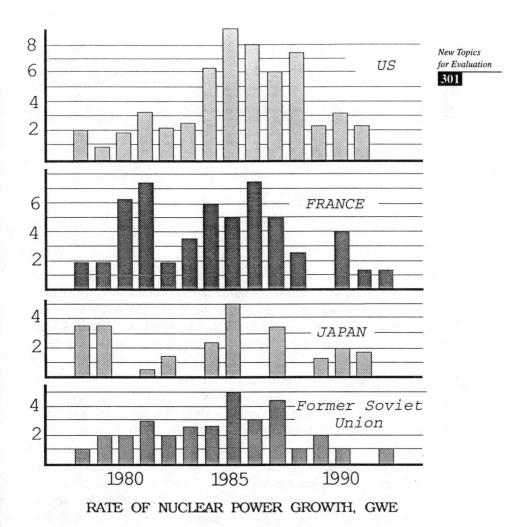

RATE OF NUCLEAR POWER GROWTH, GWE

Figure 21.1. Rates of Nuclear Power Growth in the United States, France, Japan, and the Former Soviet Union (in gigawatts)

1960s. There are 15 such reactors in operation in the countries of the FSU. Two 1,500 megawatt units, the world's largest nuclear power plants, are operated in Lithuania; eleven 1,000 megawatt units are in Russia, and two

TABLE 21.1 Nuclear Power Capacity in the Former Soviet Union and Eastern
European Countries (as of 1994)

Country	Installed Capacity		Nuclear Share of Electricity Generation (% of total)
	Number of Units	Gigawatts	
Bulgaria	6	3.5	34
Czech and Slovak Republics	8	3.3	29
Hungary	4	1.6	48
FSU[a]	45	34.7	13

a. Includes Lithuania, Russia, and the Ukraine.

are at Chernobyl in Ukraine. Experts generally agree that these RBMK
reactors are the ones requiring the most urgent attention. They have no
Western-style containment structure and their safety has been a matter of
continuing international concern since the Chernobyl incident.

The first generation of the VVERs was developed in the 1960s; this
is the 440/230 model. All the VVER plants are located in Bulgaria, the
Slovak Republic, and Russia. Six others have been shut down: two in
Armenia for seismic reasons (but these may be restarted for economic
reasons) and four at Greifswald by West German safety authorities,
shortly after German reunification in 1990. The design has many problems, including lack of containment, limited emergency core cooling
capability, almost total lack of redundancy and separation of safety
equipment, deficient instrumentation and control systems, and serious
deficiencies in fire protection.

The second generation of VVERs—the 440/213 model—was designed between 1970 and 1980 to improve upon the first generation.
Further, the second-generation development coincided with the first uniform safety requirements drawn up by Soviet designers. There are some
fourteen second-generation VVERs in operation today in Russia, two in
Ukraine, four in Hungary, two in the Czech Republic, four in the Slovak
Republic, and two in Finland that have been modernized with Western
technology and equipment. Construction of four units was stopped at
Greifswald in the former East Germany. The design deficiencies of the

230s were addressed in the second-generation 213s; that is, the containment was upgraded and improved and emergency core-cooling systems were enhanced. However, plant instrumentation and controls still do not meet international standards.

The largest of the VVERs is the third-generation 1000 model, of which there are nineteen operating in Russia, Ukraine, and Bulgaria. They were developed between 1975 and 1985, based on the requirements of a new Soviet nuclear standard that incorporated some international practices, particularly in the area of plant safety. This model has been viewed as one that could replace the old VVER and RBMK models because many of their design deficiencies have been addressed in the VVER-1000. Overall, the safety concept of this model is similar to that of the pressurized-water reactor in Western-designed plants and it possesses steel-lined and prestressed concrete containment structures that conform to Western counterparts. Steel design has improved safety standards over the previous generations. However, at an International Atomic Energy Agency (IAEA) meeting in 1992, important continuing safety problems with VVER-1000 plants were identified, including core power stability, instrumentation and control, and the integrity of steam generators (IAEA, 1993a).

■ Factors Responsible for the Chernobyl Accident and Efforts Made to Remediate Them

Evaluation of the Chernobyl experience reveals that there were two main factors in the development of the accident. The first of these was the positive reactivity void coefficient (that is, in the RBMK, when bubbles—or voids—form in the water coolant, the power of the reactor increases, whereas in VVERs, as in Western water-cooled reactors, voids lead to a decrease in power). The second factor involved drawbacks in the design of the reactor control and protection system (IAEA, 1993b). These findings caused designers and operators to introduce "urgent measures" within 6 to 8 weeks after the accident for improving reactor shutdown systems and to make additional modifications aimed at a reduction of the positive void coefficient and at mitigation of its effects under accident conditions.

☐ *Factor Remediation*

With respect to both factors, the following modifications were made: Approximately 80 additional fixed absorbers were introduced; an increased operational reactivity margin (ORM) and increased minimum ORM were set; 21 to 24 fast-acting control rods were introduced, constituting a fast "scram" system with an insertion time of 2.5 seconds; the number of bottom-inserted rods, all of which are now inserted when the scram occurs, was increased; control rod design was modified to eliminate the positive scram that contributed to the Chernobyl accident; speed of control rod insertion was increased from about 19 seconds to 12 seconds; calculation of ORM was made more frequent, every 5 minutes instead of every 15 minutes; improvements were made in the computational capabilities of core physics codes; administrative procedures were strengthened; fuel enrichment was increased from 2.0% to 2.4%; modified control rods were installed in first-generation plants; and the control and instrumentation system was modernized.

All of the modifications that have been made to the reactor control and protection system and the operational reactivity margin appear to be good ones in that they should result in the improvement of RBMK reactor safety. However, although these design changes should increase the safety of the reactors in many respects, it is not evident that they will increase safety margins in other respects. Three-dimensional analyses are needed to evaluate properly the real trade-offs between competing and interacting design modifications.

☐ *The Absence of a Containment Structure*

Because RBMK reactors have no containment structure, the protection of the reactor cavity against overpressurization becomes an important safety issue. Excessive cavity pressure can lift the upper shield assembly, break the reactor seal, break (simultaneously) the pressure tubes, and affect the operation of other safety features. The existing overpressure protection system has capacity for two or three channel tube ruptures (for first- and second-generation units, respectively), which reflects a safety margin over the design basis accident of one channel tube rupture. Thus the improvements of RBMK overpressure protection systems made after

Chernobyl were mainly directed toward increasing the capacity of these systems.

A modest increase in capacity was achieved by adding two vent valves to existing cavity steam discharge pipes at the top of the reactor. A further increase in capacity to simultaneous rupture of nine tubes is achieved by the addition of a new 600 mm steam discharge pipe into the cavity. This pipe also has two atmospheric vent valves, and is additionally routed to bubbler/condenser pools, where these exist. New buildings containing bubbler/condenser pools in sealed areas are planned for first-generation units. When existing, the 600 mm steam discharge line will be routed to these pools, eliminating the need for atmospheric vent valves.

It is apparent that the modifications being implemented significantly increase the capacity of the overpressure protection system (up to 9 simultaneous tube failures). However, this is still small compared with the number of channel tubes passing through the cavity (more than 1,600) and small as well compared with the minimum number of channel tubes (43) supplied from a common header. Thus the adequacy of the upgrade must be judged against accident sequences having the possibility of resulting in multiple tube ruptures.

■ Effects of the Chernobyl Accident on Nuclear Power Policy in the FSU and Eastern European Countries

□ Immediate Changes in Nuclear Power Policy

Following the incident at Chernobyl, the entire policy and strategy of nuclear power development in the FSU and Eastern European countries was reviewed several times. This resulted in a set of urgent measures (discussed above) for the safety improvement of nuclear power plants in operation, as well as a particular emphasis on the need to design and build safer reactors. A first policy consequence of the Chernobyl disaster (a consequence also of the major political and economic changes taking place in the region between 1986 and 1992) was a practically total stoppage of new power plant construction. For 5 years after Chernobyl, nuclear power growth was only 5 gigawatts. This change in policy, moving toward drastic curtailment of the program, proceeded not only through rejection of the construction of nuclear power plants already ordered, but also through suspension of work on those that were almost completed. Overall, survey activities and plant construction were stopped at 39 sites, for a total design capacity of 109 gigawatts. Among these are sites in Tatarstan, Rostov, Crimea, Minsk, and Odessa. Other examples of this change in nuclear power policy are the Ukrainian Parliament's decision to decommission the Chernobyl nuclear power plant; the antinuclear movement in Lithuania against the Ignalina plant, which uses a "Chernobyl-type" nuclear reactor; a delay in nuclear programs in Poland and in the Czech and Slovak Republics; the cancellation of four nuclear units in the former East Germany; and the shutdown of two Armenian nuclear power plants (although in this case, an earthquake in Armenia may have been an even stronger motivation for safety precautions than the Chernobyl accident).

In short, by 1992, the policy of nuclear power development appeared dead or frozen in the region. And to some extent, fears resulting from the Chernobyl accident were exacerbated by fears about the FSU's military nuclear legacy, as expressed by strong public concern and requests for thorough analysis of current operating nuclear power plants and the region's nuclear industry in general.

☐ *More Recent Factors Affecting Nuclear Power Policy*

On the other hand, the deep economic motivations that gave rise in the first place to the policy of nuclear power development have not disappeared. Indeed, the need for a nuclear component within the fuel/power balance is actually growing over time. Systematic studies on the specific reduced cost of nuclear- over coal-fired electricity production in the member states of the Organization for Economic Cooperation and Development (1989) indicate a stable nuclear power advantage over the whole period of the 1980s. Studies for the FSU confirm a similar tendency, and the replacement of coal by oil or gas increases nuclear power competitiveness even more (Novikov, Wahlstrom, Lebedev, et al., 1991).

Further, organic fuel, which was always a source of hard currency for the Soviet Union, has now become even more important for the successor states of the FSU. For Russia, which is one of the richest countries in the world in terms of fossil fuel deposits, it is easy to sell coal, gas, and oil for hard currency while using nuclear sources for domestic electricity production. For Ukraine and Lithuania, however, which must import oil and gas from Russia at "world-level" prices, nuclear power has a different economic significance. The largest part of the cost of nuclear power plant production of electricity is the capital cost, and this became free to these countries as a result of the Soviet Union's disintegration. These Soviet-made nuclear power plants thus represent huge gifts, even if involuntarily bestowed, from Russia. Lithuania, in fact, exemplifies the policy effects of this situation. Nuclear generating capacity there constitutes approximately 48% of all electricity-generating capacity, but as of 1993, nuclear-generated electricity accounted for 60% of the total electricity supplied. Neither the Lithuanian government nor that nation's population is raising concerns any longer about the Ignalina nuclear power plant, which currently produces more than 78% of Lithuania's electricity. (It is worth noting that, in 1995, Lithuania led the world in the percentage of total electricity generated by nuclear power.)

In short, existing nuclear power plants now appear to be serving as islands of stability in the vulnerable national economies of the FSU nuclear successors, and to some extent in Eastern European countries. This, together with increasing public recognition of the ecological risks involved in organic fuel burning and a growing understanding of the need for energy in environmental cleanup, makes it possible that the beginning of the new century could also be a new beginning for nuclear power.

■ *The Future*

Today, Russian policy calls for both allowing current reactors to run for their design lives of 30 years (or even longer) and making plans for new reactors of advanced design.

□ *The Viability of Current Reactors*

Although some deficiencies still remain, considerable work has been done to improve the safety of nuclear power plants with reactors of current designs. This was the basis for the Russian policy decision that twelve first-generation nuclear plants will be permitted to operate for their intended design lives of 30 years (MacKenzie, 1995). These plants include four small graphite reactors at Bilibino, four RBMK reactors at St. Petersburg and Kursk, and four VVER 440/230s at Kola and Novovoronezh. In contrast to the Russian stance, the Ukrainian government, which had previously decided to keep the Chernobyl reactors open for their design life and to replace them with nuclear plants, has now changed its view and will shut down Chernobyl, replacing it with a gas-fired plant, but on condition that the West finds $3 billion to pay for it.

☐ *Advanced Nuclear Reactor Designs*

In addition to the backfitting done after the Chernobyl accident to enhance the safety of operating and soon-to-be-established nuclear power plants, work began on new advanced nuclear reactor designs soon after the first shock of the accident had subsided. It was intended that these designs should be applied to new-generation nuclear power plants to be built in the area of FSU influence, as well as in some developing countries.

The major policy goals for advanced nuclear reactor design are public acceptability, very large improvement in stability against severe accidents, increased economic viability, operational effectiveness, and a smooth and quasi-continuous transition from current policy to that based on advanced nuclear power plants. There are two principal approaches to meeting these goals: *evolutionary approaches,* which seek further improvement and extension of traditional active safety means, more extensive use of passive and inherent safety features, and reduction in some specific indices of the power unit along with increases in the stability margins; and *innovative approaches,* which rely on self-protectiveness and inherent safety features.

Given these goals and approaches, a strategic line clearly seen now in Russia is the orientation of nuclear power policy toward light-water reactors in the coming century. The following designs are now under consideration: the VVER-92 for large power plant projects, and the VVER-500/600 and the VPBER-600 (an innovative design) for medium-sized power plant projects. Many of the policy decisions being made are in harmony with world safety enhancement standards and tendencies. Others, however, are more likely based on the domestic experience of creating and successfully operating nuclear installations, and on the further development of some solutions perfected in nuclear district heating plant designs. If successful, such designs may pave the way for nuclear power development in the near future and provide a reasonable transition from the current status to power based on advanced nuclear power plants.

Still, there is some way to go, given the uncertainties of political and economic developments, the volatility of public acceptance, and the fact that a number of the new safety systems now being developed still require both theoretical analysis and experimental validation.

■ Conclusions

The Chernobyl tragedy of 1986 led to many changes: political, technical, and economic. The various evaluations of the accident have shown major weaknesses in reactor design and operations. Subsequent to the breakup of the Soviet Union, policy decisions in several of the elements of the FSU attempted to forgo the use of nuclear power, but they have modified this position based on their pragmatic need for electricity. Russia has joined with the IAEA to evaluate the many Soviet reactor designs. Although technical analysis has identified serious weaknesses in the RBMK (Chernobyl-type) reactors and in the earlier light-water reactors, economic necessity has kept these plants operating. However, some safety improvements have been made, and new designs promising improved safety have been developed. Funding is the obstacle to further improvement of the safety of existing reactors, replacement of the least-safe reactors, and the building of new ones. This is a clear case in which pragmatic policy decisions have been made that run counter to the technical analyses conducted.

■ References

International Atomic Energy Agency (IAEA). (1993a). *International assistance to upgrade the safety of Soviet-designed nuclear power plants* (Publication No. IAEA/PI/A39E). Vienna: Author.

International Atomic Energy Agency (IAEA). (1993b). *Safety assessment of proposed improvements of RBMK nuclear power plants* (Report of the IAEA Extrabudgetary Programme on the Safety of RBMK Nuclear Power Plants, IAEA-TECDOC-694). Vienna: Author.

MacKenzie, D. (1995, May 27). Pleas to shut risky reactors. *New Scientists,* p. 10.

Novikov, V. M., Wahlstrom, B., Lebedev, O. G., et al. (1991). *Economic aspects of ecological risk due to nuclear- and coal-fired electricity production* (Collaborative Paper CP-91-004). Laxenburg, Austria: IIASA.

Organization for Economic Cooperation and Development. (1989). *Projected cost of generating electricity from power stations for commissioning in the period 1995-2000.* Paris: Author.

Semenov, B. A., Dastidar, P., & Bennett, L. L. (1993). Electricity supply in Central and Eastern European countries: The role of nuclear energy. *IAEA Bulletin, 35,* 2-7.

22

The Independent Evaluation of the Global Environment Facility Pilot Phase

W. Haven North

The Global Environment Facility (GEF) was established in 1991 to achieve worldwide environmental benefits in the areas of climate change, biological diversity, pollution of international waters, and ozone depletion. The governing body—known at that time as the Participants, with 70 representatives from industrial and developing country governments— initiated a 3-year pilot phase of the effort, to run from June 1991 to June 1994. The management of GEF operations was assigned to three implementing agencies (IAs): the World Bank, the United Nations Development Program (UNDP), and the United Nations Environment Program (UNEP). The World Bank was entrusted with responsibility for the Global Environment Trust Fund and with chairmanship of the facility. During this pilot period, the GEF funded as grants 112 projects of direct assistance in

63 countries, for a total of about $712 million, with additional funds for special studies and project design services. The evaluation of the pilot phase of the GEF took place between March and December 1993, when the final report was submitted to the Participants.

■ *The Evaluation Setting*

Before considering the task of the evaluation itself, it is important to have in mind several circumstances that provided an unusual setting in which the evaluators had to operate. First, the Participants were determined not to create a new international organization but rather to make use of three existing international development agencies to manage and implement the GEF functions. The World Bank was in the dominant role as trustee and as the main implementing agency, and the director of the Environment Department of the World Bank served as the chairman of the facility and chaired the meetings of the Participants. A small secretariat was formed to assist the chairman with his coordinating responsibilities but without independent authority. In addition, UNEP set up the independent Science and Technology Advisory Panel (STAP), which provided technical guidance to the three IAs and the Participants. In such an arrangement, the three IAs—with very different volumes of funding and scales of operations, areas of expertise, organizational cultures, and management structures—were expected to work cooperatively. Decisions concerning policy guidance, funding allocations, and project reviews and approvals were to be undertaken jointly by means of the Implementation Committee, whose chair (initially under the World Bank) rotated among the principals of the three agencies. The guidance and expectations of the Participants emphasized consensus building and informal arrangements, with a minimum of formal agreements. However, the World Bank's dominant role was not well accepted by the other agencies. Although a great deal was accomplished, the relatively loose administrative setting, with few agreed-upon rules and procedures, resulted in considerable tension as the agencies competed for resources, reviewed each others' projects, and developed policies and strategies largely on the go.

Second, the Participants placed the IAs under substantial pressure to "move the money" in advance of well-thought-out strategies, project approaches, and a monitoring and evaluation system. A common GEF project database and monitoring procedure that would have facilitated the evaluation of the 63-nation program had not been set up. Although moving quickly had benefits for GEF's credibility over the short run, these pressures generated a number of problems that will continue to trouble the program.

Third, the evaluation was initiated at a time when very few projects were being implemented. Although many projects had been endorsed by the Participants (project approval was an IA responsibility following Participant endorsement), they were still in the design and approval process or only just beginning to be implemented in the developing countries. As a consequence, the evaluators were not able to assess project performance and results for the most part. The emphasis was placed on "upstream" project cycle and process considerations relating to the identification, design, review, and approval phases. The project cycle was more complex for the GEF than is customary for development agencies, as there were steps in the project cycle leading up to the Participants' endorsements followed by steps leading to agency approval. In addition to the extended number of steps, the evaluators had to take into account the different approaches to the project cycle of the three agencies.

Fourth, the GEF was challenged to address the global environmental dimensions of development issues for which there was limited experience to build on. It confronted major technological, economic, social, and institutional issues of policy and practice that had to be worked through in concept and field operations—thus the importance of the pilot nature of the GEF during this initial period. Added to this task was the challenging international setting for global environmental questions. The GEF serves as the financing and program instrument for the Conventions of the Parties for Climate Change and Biodiversity and, to a lesser degree, for Ozone Depletion. These conventions are the policy-making and governing bodies for addressing global environmental concerns. Their organizations, policies, and requirements were emerging at the same time the GEF was developing its pilot phase.

Fifth, the evaluation had to proceed in the highly charged political setting of the GEF, which, as a consequence, affected the evaluation process itself. An atmosphere of tension and distrust hung over the GEF and the evaluation like a dark cloud. Most of this was centered on the

World Bank, which at that time was being criticized for its insensitivity to environmental problems. A number of environmentally active nongovernmental organizations (NGOs) were particularly vehement in their opposition to the GEF's lack of autonomy from World Bank management. Some of the main donors had intended and preferred that the World Bank have the dominant role and receive the bulk of the GEF funding, but the other IAs and many NGOs did not accept this role for the World Bank and were outspoken in their objections. Also, the availability of substantial "additional" grant funds generated tensions as the IAs and countries competed for this attractive new source of funds. At the same time, the developing countries that received GEF assistance were also concerned about the close association with the World Bank. Although they were eager to obtain the GEF's grant funds, they feared the imposition of conditions tied to GEF funding that were customary in regular World Bank lending. More broadly, the GEF was created by the donor community as a response to the UNCED Conference in 1992, in part as a counter to the moves of some of the developing countries to create separate green funds under their own control. Among the Participants themselves there were fears that either the developed or developing countries would have too much control over policies and resource allocations—an issue that would be central in the design of voting arrangements for the "restructured" (or next-phase) GEF.

Overarching these conditions was, of course, the fact that the GEF was a new venture in international development addressing issues that cut across the traditional sector orientations of most development activity. The distinctive organizational arrangement—the "no new organization" principle—was an experiment in cooperative action by major international organizations and a test of their ability to collaborate on a global development problem. As a consequence, the GEF staffs in the IAs and secretariat were caught up in rapidly evolving policies and procedures. The GEF experienced the inevitable start-up problems of a new program under pressure to move quickly, as well as those difficulties inherent in its structure. The officials involved were severely strained in this situation, despite their best efforts and intentions.

This setting for the GEF pilot phase is of particular interest for the evaluation, because the evaluation process itself reflected the GEF organizational structure and operating tensions, as will become evident.

■ The Approach to an Independent Evaluation

In December 1992, the Participants at their general (Ivory Coast) meeting requested an independent evaluation of the GEF pilot phase to be completed in time for their meeting in December 1993. They also wished to have an interim evaluation report for their meeting in September 1993. This timing was set in order to provide evaluative information to assist the Participants in preparing the next phase of the GEF (now known as GEF1) to start in June 1994. Preparations included questions concerning restructuring of the GEF and, most important, replenishment of its funding for the 3 years following the pilot phase.

□ The Terms of Reference

The terms of reference (TOR) were prepared by staff in the Operations Evaluation Department of the World Bank and reviewed by the Participants at their March 1993 meeting in Rome. The purposes of the independent evaluation were (a) to assess the progress, prospects, and potential outcomes of the pilot phase and its relevance to overall GEF objectives; (b) to examine GEF policies, procedures, and processes and their probable impact on GEF resource use and the achievement of objectives; and (c) to make recommendations about the actions to be taken by each of the partner agencies and GEF Participants to ensure an effective and efficient use of GEF resources. The focus of the project-related aspect of the evaluation would be on the upstream phases of the GEF project cycle for the operations approved before June 30, 1993, and the outcomes of this phase. The appropriateness of the portfolio in terms of lessons to be learned would be a special focus of the evaluation.

The Participants accepted the outline as proposed, but they also "felt that the Terms of Reference should have greater specificity and scope" and thus provided a list of additional topics that should be covered. These included responsiveness of the GEF to country needs and participants' expectations; integration of GEF projects with country priorities and strategies; how projects are identified and selected, and the pace of project preparation and implementation; the extent to which projects have identified and specified global benefits; how local participation has been encouraged; the catalytic role (if any) played by GEF in affecting regular activities of the implementing agencies; the different experiences with core, co-, and parallel financing, and how activities funded from these various sources have matched the objectives of the GEF; a critical analysis of the project cycle level of disbursements; the level of additionality represented by the GEF contributions; success of GEF in leveraging additional resources; absorptive capacities of recipient countries and implementing agencies for GEF projects; the role of STAP; and impact on project design of comments by STAP and participants. The Participants also urged that field interviews be a stronger component of the evaluation.

In their comments, the Participants also stressed the importance of having the results of the evaluation available for their September meeting, "so that its results can feed into the replenishment and restructuring process." This expanded TOR and tight time frame presented a major challenge to the evaluators, most of whom at that time had not been identified and had not had the opportunity to review and comment on the scope and timing of the evaluation.

☐ *The Organization of the Evaluation*

From the outset, the Participants had specified that the evaluation units in each of the IAs would conduct evaluations of their agencies' operations separately. (None of the three agencies would agree to an evaluation led by one of the other agencies.) The reports of the three separate evaluations plus a fourth—the assessment of the GEF Trust Fund and related management issues—would then be combined in a synthesis. The Participants were especially concerned about the organization of the evaluation, its management, and the selection and supervision of the evaluators. The chairman's summary of the Participants' discussion of the TOR included the following statement:

> There were a number of expressions of respect for the competence and objectivity of the agencies' evaluation units. But there was wide agreement that, in order to assure the appearance and reality of independence and objectivity, the proposed international panel of experts must be strengthened and made more central to the evaluation process.

As this quote suggests, there were concerns about the independence of the evaluation units within the IAs; thus the Participants were determined to have also an independent international panel of experts to report directly to them. The issue of the independence of the evaluators was a continuing undercurrent of contention throughout the evaluation process and was not laid to rest until the final report was submitted.

In this setting, the organization of the evaluation was worked out approximately as illustrated in Figure 22.1. Apart from the formal lines of authority and responsibility between the team leaders and the managers, the arrangement was relatively fluid and evolving as the evaluation progressed. Of the three managers, only the Director General of the Operations Evaluation Department of the World Bank was directly concerned with institutional evaluations and had no other responsibilities that were associated with the GEF operations. The other two managers included under their administration the units responsible for the GEF operations in their agencies. The three managers operated on the basis of consensus, with the Director General of Operations Evaluation acting as chief facilitator. However, as was evident from time to time, they addressed issues of common concern but did not question the evaluation activity of each others' teams, such as the selection of team members (although informally the suitability of some of the team members was raised) and the administration of the evaluation budgets. The evaluation units of the UNDP and UNEP did not participate—for one agency, because of its small size and limited capacities, and for the other, because of its decision not to be involved in a shared evaluation responsibility. Each manager selected his evaluation team leader and approved the choice of team members proposed by the team leaders. The managers were in an awkward and ambiguous position, as they were obliged to keep some distance from the evaluators' work and conclusions while being responsible for the evaluators' performance and the quality of the results.

The team members were for the most part hired on a part-time basis to carry out specific assignments. However, the team leaders and coordinator worked largely full-time from May until the next December. In two instances the team leaders changed. The role of the coordinator/synthesizer was ambiguous and evolving. As noted in Figure 22.1, there was, at the start of the evaluation, no position for an overall leader of the evaluation—no one person was in charge. This original arrangement was

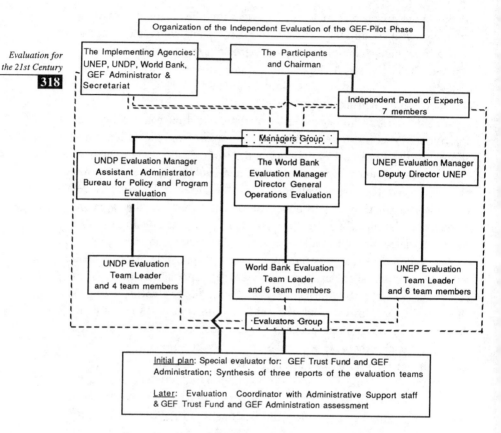

Figure 22.1. Organization of the Independent Evaluation of the GEF Pilot Phase

a clear reflection of the GEF's unique organizational structure and the determination of the IAs not to be dominated by the World Bank (the coordinator/synthesizer was working under a contract with the World Bank's Operations Evaluation Department, but had no special relationship with the Bank). When the idea of a coordinator was suggested in the first meeting of the IAs' evaluation team leaders with the independent panel of experts and the evaluation managers, it was a point of contention and was not formally resolved until later.

Fortunately, the evaluation team members were individuals with high professional qualifications, possessing substantial experience in various combinations of operations management, technical knowledge of at least one of the focal areas, and experience with evaluation processes. They made up a group with strongly held views about the environment and the agencies they were evaluating (not always positive). As the evaluation progressed, however, they were able to work well together to develop consensus on the processes and results of the evaluation. During the course of the evaluation, particularly at the beginning, various members of the teams were criticized by outside groups and individuals for one reason or another bearing on their ability to be objective and independent—concerns that were not well founded and that were disturbing to the team members, who considered themselves fully independent.

The independent panel of experts (IPE) was an unusual requirement of the Participants, reflecting their lack of certainty about the independence of the evaluation managers and the evaluation team members. The seven members of the IPE included two who represented their countries as Participants, two who were associated with governments and experienced with evaluations, and three from nongovernmental organizations or private firms. Four of the panel members were from developing countries and GEF recipients; three were from developed countries. They were all professional people in their own right, holding significant positions in public and private life; they had definite views about the GEF and the outcome of the evaluation. And because of their role and visibility, they were sensitive to their important "political" responsibility as a liaison with outside groups and their direct line to the Participants in providing credibility to the evaluation process and report. They also believed they were responsible for voicing their own substantive views about the GEF even if these views were not consistent with the evaluation's conclusions and recommendations. As is evident from the TOR for the IPE, it was expected to carry out its own assessment of the GEF as well as of the evaluation process and report to the Participants as a parallel activity.

The relationships of managers and evaluation teams were complicated by their different physical locations. The World Bank team and the coordinator and support staff were located in Washington, the UNDP manager and team were in New York, and the UNEP manager and team were variously in Nairobi and Geneva. There were strong feelings that all of the meetings on the evaluation should not take place in Washington at the World Bank; thus some were held in New York. Although there was pressure from the UNEP group to meet in Nairobi or Geneva, cost considerations eventually ruled that out.

☐ *Developing Working Relationships*

The task of building working relationships among people and institutions caught up in the evaluation process was particularly intricate. Each of the main groups involved had to create its own suitable working relationships. The evaluation managers had to establish a working rapport among themselves, taking account of the determination of their agencies to maintain their separate identities. In the early stages of planning for the evaluation, there were concerns that the World Bank's evaluation staff had moved ahead on their own. Also, the managers had to be mindful of the importance, in substance and appearance, of not influencing the evaluators' work, while being responsible for the delivery of the reports and the quality of the process. Similarly, the members of the IPE had to work out their relationships and identify the areas of the GEF operations on which they should focus. They were not all of a mind on their role and their views. Most important, the three team leaders had to establish a degree of teamwork within each of their teams, as is common to most evaluations, with the team leaders of the other teams, and with the coordinator's functions. Altogether, there were 22 evaluators active in the evaluation, most of them working part-time.

The web became more complex as these three groups with their separate responsibilities for the evaluation had to interact with each other and with the GEF program coordinators and staff in each of the IAs and the staff of the GEF secretariat. Also, there was a continuous interaction, mostly informal and ad hoc, with the NGO community and other organizations and individuals who had interests in one or another of the focal areas and wished to have their strongly held views heard. With each country visit, there were numerous groups and individuals with special interests in GEF projects. Periodic feedback from the Participants and their demands were ever present.

In such a setting, sensitivity to the need to keep all parties up-to-date, in the loop, and aware of what the others were planning, doing, or saying was a critical feature of the evaluation process. This was particularly the case owing to the acute sensitivities of the people engaged, reflecting, in part, the nature of the GEF structure and the history of difficult relationships among the various interested parties.

☐ *Evaluation Methodology*

The evaluation methodology and instruments, exceptional only for the volume of data gathered, included questionnaires, country visits (involving 31 projects in 22 countries), reviews of project files, staff interviews, and meetings with NGO representatives. Six sets of questionnaires were tailored specifically for the Participants, IA staff in headquarters and the field, recipient country officials, UNEP country representatives, and members of the STAP. The overall response rate was 41%. To ensure a broad response from nongovernmental organizations, questionnaires were sent out over the ECONET and through a global newsletter with some 40,000 subscribers worldwide. There was little response to these latter two initiatives. However, the country visits provided opportunities to obtain the views of local NGOs and communities. The list of projects to be visited reflected a fair representation by type among the four focal areas, a regional distribution, IA participation, and stages in the project cycle. In addition, to obtain a greater understanding of project cycle issues and to examine questions of design and innovation, the teams conducted in-depth reviews of more than half of the projects that had been endorsed by the Participants. Interview guides were prepared for the country visits and numerous staff interviews.

Most important to the evaluation was a complete and accurate database of the projects. Although the GEF secretariat had much of this information, it was not complete or fully accurate in coverage of projects, their classifications, their funding, and their evolution in the project cycle. This last characteristic was particularly important, as the TOR called for a careful examination of the "upstream" project cycle processes. The development of the profile of the GEF pilot phase was a key component of the evaluation, both to guide the evaluation process and to provide the audiences with a comprehensive picture of the GEF as a whole.

■ The Evolution of the Evaluation Process

It was expected that the two products of the evaluation—the September interim report and the December final report—would be syntheses of the separate evaluation reports of the three IAs plus the report on the Trust Fund and GEF administration. However, it was apparent as the chapters of the two synthesis reports took shape that this approach would not be successful. An attempt at a synthesis would be frustrated by the lack of common treatment and data among the three separate IA reports. Clearly some subjects, such as the internal project cycle processes of each agency and GEF administration, would require separate treatment. But there was a need for comparable and balanced analyses for the syntheses. Some of the topics, such as those related to the four focal areas, the GEF's policy framework, and developing country perspectives, required an integrated view. Also, time factors became important: The preparation of fully developed IA reports would take too long and prevent timely completion of the two syntheses.

As a result of these concerns, the character of the evaluation process shifted to one with a more integrated approach. The separate IA evaluation reports, although maintained, were de-emphasized as key documents and became working papers. Arrangements were made to have the country visits of the various team members cover all GEF projects in those countries regardless of the IA sponsors. This measure was more efficient and also promoted cross-agency appraisals and comparisons, which helped to moderate single-agency biases among the evaluators.

The chapter outline for the interim and final reports provided the essential guide for the evaluation, replacing the three separate outlines prepared by each of the team leaders. Responsibilities for preparing the various chapters were then assigned among the three teams and supporting evaluation staff. The coordinator's role was to keep this process moving, add inputs for each chapter, integrate comments as the chapter drafts were reviewed by each team leader, work out differences of views and facts, prepare the assessment of the Trust Fund, and address concerns about fairness and balance in the treatment of the IAs.

In addition to the (repeated) sharing of drafts of the chapters among the team leaders for comment, the integrated approach was further facilitated by all the participating evaluators meeting together in special sessions to develop consensus on the main analyses, findings, conclusions, and recommendations. It was important that an effort be made to have the reports reflect a common view and be owned by the evaluation teams and not be undercut by "minority" positions or subsequent challenges by team members. This task was complicated by the widely dispersed situation of team members in the United States, Europe, Latin America, and Africa and their differing levels of involvement. Special meetings were organized to bring the team members together to examine drafts and develop conclusions and recommendations. This may not seem unusual for evaluations, but in this case the numbers of people involved, the costs, and time pressures worked against holding such sessions.

An essential step in the evaluation process was the opportunity for those being evaluated—the staffs of the IAs and secretariat—to comment on the drafts concerning accuracy, coverage, and fairness of interpretation. This review step was handled through both a joint session of evaluators with the GEF staff principals and written, page-by-page comments. Without jeopardizing the independence of the evaluators' positions, this step made the process more participatory, dealt with a number of factual questions, and moved the reports toward some common understanding of the recommendations and their intent.

The interim and final reports covered many topics in considerable detail. As a consequence, the preparation of an assessment overview and recommendations chapter as the first substantive part of the report served a useful purpose. This chapter provided a general overview followed by a series of major issues, with their analyses and recommendations. Its drafting became the focal point for the development of consensus among the evaluators, the IPE, and evaluation managers. The chapter then became the basis for discussions with the IAs and, finally, a readable agenda of issues and recommendations for the Participants.

☐ *The Evaluators, Evaluation Managers,*
    and Independent Panel of Experts

Throughout the evaluation process, the evaluators had to be mindful of the views and concerns of their managers and the IPE. The managers served an important role in dealing with conflicts and controversies from within and outside the evaluation structure, providing resources—funds and support staff—and decisions to keep the process on track, and putting the brakes on the evaluators from time to time as their desire for more coverage, time, and expenditure grew. As noted, their role was a delicate balancing of guidance, support, and responsibility without becoming substantively involved. At the same time, the evaluators were concerned about being overly managed and guided and worked to preserve an arms-length but cooperative relationship.

The IPE was a particularly controversial and demanding dimension of the evaluation process because of its responsibility to report directly to the Participants in parallel with the evaluation and its mandate to obtain the views of a wide spectrum of organizations, particularly from the NGO community. The IPE met four times alone and with the evaluators and evaluation managers, and, at the end, with the IA staffs. The IPE also held a special meeting with the 22 representatives of the NGO community, which, for the most part, seemed to calm the NGOs' fears about the independence of the evaluation process. However, when the IPE preempted the leadership of this meeting that the evaluators had envisioned for themselves, the evaluators missed an opportunity to probe in depth the issues and criticisms the NGOs were voicing. Moreover, some of the NGOs were carrying out their own evaluations of the GEF, concurrent with the independent evaluation.

At various stages during the evaluation process, the IPE gave its views on the evaluation plan and methods, with particular attention to the topics that should be covered and proposed and other topics that would have broadened the scope of the evaluation. The main thrust of the comments was to ensure that the report would be forthright, clear, and not watered-down. The need to be responsive to the IPE added a substantial workload of special reports and meetings for the evaluators. The IPE reported separately on the evaluation process and the quality of the independent evaluation, its views of the overall assessment and recommendations, and its own recommendations for the GEF and for further evaluations.

In the end, the IPE may well have shielded the evaluators from external pressures intended to influence the conclusions of the report, although not from some of the members of the IPE itself. The IPE assured the Participants that the report was carried out in a professional manner. The IPE's participation also gave its members the opportunity to make their own recommendations on the GEF derived from their own experiences. The question remains whether the evaluators needed the oversight of an independent panel of experts. Given the highly charged and sensitive political circumstances surrounding the evaluation, the prevailing view is that it was needed and served its purpose satisfactorily.

◼ *Recommendations of the Independent Evaluation*

The final report, *Global Environment Facility: Independent Evaluation of the Pilot Phase, United Nations Development Programme, United Nations Environment Programme, and the World Bank,* was completed in November 1993. It provided an assessment overview and six issues with recommendations. The overview stressed:

> The GEF is a promising, and presently the only significant, mechanism for funding programs relevant to the protection of the global environment. However, the promise of this significant new fund will not be realized unless there are fundamental changes in the GEF strategies, the functions and relationships of its organizational components, and operating procedures.

The issues and recommendations related to the articulation of the GEF raison d'être, objectives, and strategies; program leadership and management of the GEF as a global program facility; capacities and procedures within the implementing agencies for managing the GEF portfolio; engagement of country- and community-level participation; the involvement of nongovernmental organizations; and the need for a sound monitoring and evaluation system. The recommendations concluded with a firm statement that the GEF should not proceed with the review and approval of new projects for the next phase (GEF1) without having a clear program strategy and criteria in place.

◼ *The Presentation*

In December 1993, the several dimensions of the evaluation process came together in a meeting with the 70 members of the Participants in Cartagena, Colombia. Over a period of 2 to 3 hours, the Participants heard reports about the evaluation from the evaluation managers, the representatives of the IAs, a representative of the NGO community, the chair of the IPE, and, finally, the evaluation coordinator and three team leaders. The Participants probed the findings and recommendations and methodologies of the evaluation. Overall, the reception was positive. The Participants then turned to efforts to achieve agreement on the restructuring and replenishment of the GEF—a process that had been going on in parallel with the evaluation for some months. With the approval of the Participants, the GEF1 now involves more than 100 countries in 200-300 projects, with commitments, including the pilot phase, projected at $3 billion.

Although some of the report's conclusions were reflected in the work on restructuring, it is clear that the full impact of the report will have to emerge over time. Work on the recommendations is under way, with varying prospects for their outcomes. One recommendation from the report of particular interest to evaluators was the proposal to create an evaluation unit in the GEF secretariat and an evaluation program for the GEF, including a complete project database and systematic project monitoring. The Chelimsky/North report on an evaluation program for the GEF was submitted to the Participants in the spring of 1995. A senior evaluation specialist was appointed in February 1996 to lead this work. An interesting feature of this report is the recommendation to balance the need for a comprehensive assessment of the GEF's performance—to address outcomes as well as opinions on process—while recognizing the need for each of the IAs to maintain its own evaluation operations. The idea of a central unit that would evaluate IA performance continues to be sensitive, generating opposition to developing significant evaluation capacity in the secretariat.

■ *What Are the Lessons From This Experience?*

Certainly, the independent evaluation of the GEF pilot phase was unique in its scale, substantive and organizational complexity, and global dimensions. Most important, the evaluation was carried out in an exceptionally sensitive setting of distrust among those involved in the GEF and its mission and the independence of the evaluation process. However, as programs of worldwide significance call for the involvement of multiple organizations, a brief description of some of the lessons learned from the experience of the GEF evaluation may be useful:

1. The attempt to undertake parallel evaluations organized along the lines of the separate agencies working on a common program is unlikely to provide a basis for a useful synthesis. Instead, a common script, as in a report outline, that covers the topics of the TOR should serve as the basis for designing the various subtasks required, including separate working papers on topics that may be unique to individual participating organizations.

2. Similarly, it is essential to have an evaluation coordinator who is acceptable to all parties, with the authority and responsibility for selecting the evaluation team members, overseeing the evaluation design and processes, and producing the report. The evaluation coordinator should be selected (in addition to professional qualifications) for skills as a facilitator and consensus builder. He or she should be someone who will avoid the tendency to get out front—who will take more of a sheep dog role than head of the pack.

3. Panels of experts can be useful if they are structured to work within the evaluation process and do not have a separate competing evaluation role and line of authority. Panels can serve as useful sounding boards or as technical advisers for areas that are especially complex or technologically difficult.

4. The absence of a well-developed database with common standards and procedures can result in costly and time-consuming efforts for evaluators. As is true for all programs, a sound database that defines the situation at the outset of the program is critical to measuring its performance. Where the concern is the impact on the environment of global development initiatives, such a baseline is vital for judging the contribution of massive investments in environmental protection. This task is extremely complex, owing to the difficulties of measuring changes in biodiversity and climate and their causes.

5. An essential companion to monitoring and evaluation systems is the importance of systematic dissemination of experience and lessons learned in forms and techniques that facilitate learning and application in policy and practice.

6. Finally, trust and mutual respect among the evaluators and in evaluators' relationships with stakeholders (those who are being evaluated and those who have vested interests in the results of the evaluation) are matters of

importance in all evaluations, but especially so in evaluations of global programs that involve multiple international and national implementing organizations (public and private) and diverse cultural settings. Addressing the matter of trust should start from the outset of the evaluation with openness and participation in developing the terms of reference and selecting the evaluators and their management arrangements. Team building is also desirable, as frequently evaluators are not known to each other at the outset and their roles and responsibilities are inadequately defined. Accenting the value of a mutual learning process can smooth the way to more effective results.

23

Environmental Changes and Their Measurement

What Data Should We Collect and What Collaborative Systems Do We Need for Linking Knowledge to Action?

Charles A. Zraket
William Clark

The need to integrate knowledge with action is nowhere greater than in the area of global environmental change, a field with linkages to a broad range of planning, monitoring, and evaluation issues. Today, the term *global environmental change* is used to refer to changes in many areas: climate, biological diversity, natural resource use and management, air quality, water resources, toxic and hazardous substances, and natural disaster reduction. Especially notable in the environmental changes facing humankind are the degradation and depletion of agricultural land, forests, water resources, and fish. Among the social effects already engendered by this destruction have been scarcities, adverse population movements, and violent conflict.

To address the amelioration and prevention of these problems, policies and measures are needed to promote widespread and continuous interaction between the global environmental change research communities and the policy-evaluation communities. Such interaction has heretofore never been achieved, but it is essential if such environmental issues are not to be thrown "over the wall" from one community to the other to deal with. Public information networks and monitoring systems are required to provide the data needed for collaborative policy and treaty assessments, and for environmental analyses and evaluations of the destruction of resources and of the effectiveness of amelioration and prevention measures intended to deal with them at local, regional, and global levels. The challenge now is to collect, create, and distribute usable knowledge for managing responses to global environmental change. This challenge is compounded by the difficulty of effectively managing and making use of the vast quantities of information to be collected about the global environment, its changes, and their impacts on the earth and society.

We need to address four interrelated questions:

1. Which environmental changes are we dealing with now worldwide, and which must we deal with, in what sequence, in the future?

2. How can we achieve better assessments of global environmental risks, of the policy options to deal with them, and of past management performance in environmental matters? We should note here that assessment is the bridge between science and policy; it is very difficult to make the transition from good scientific research to policy-relevant assessment. There are limits to what science can determine, and the needs of the various assessment communities throughout all sections of society are rarely well defined and clearly articulated. We use *assessment* here to include policy formulation and analysis, as well as evaluation.

3. What kinds of data must be collected for policy and other kinds of assessment? Today there is a massive international effort going on to collect scientific data on "how the earth works" through the Global Change Research Program, the World Climate Research Program, the International Geosphere-Biosphere Program, the Human Dimensions Program, and the Man and Biosphere Program. Understanding global changes will require complete synoptic observations of the total earth

system, as well as high-quality, long-term data sets in each of the earth sciences. But these scientific data will be in the possession of government agencies, separate research organizations, and individual researchers around the world. Somehow, these data and the information systems in which they are embedded will need to be joined together in a complex interdisciplinary research process that can culminate over the coming decades in new scientific knowledge about the global changes that are occurring.

4. How can we achieve collaborative information systems for linking knowledge to action in environmental matters?

The assessment communities in all sectors of the economy at local, regional, and worldwide levels require access not only to this scientific knowledge about how the earth system works but also to vast amounts of demographic, social, and economic data in order to determine impacts and risks. To say the least, then, assessment and evaluation of environmental changes will be an information-intensive activity.

In the next section we address some aspects of the first three questions by discussing the changes in the past 25 years in environmental issues leading to the current situation. These changes involve an evolution from acute to chronic problems (e.g., toxic wastes), from local to global issues (e.g., whaling), and from simple to complex issues (e.g., climate change). In the final section, we offer some recommendations that address the problems of access and interpretation posed by the fourth question.

■ *The Dynamic Nature of Environmental Issues*

Some simple, back-of-the-envelope socioeconomic calculations have driven us to reject the notion of unbounded future growth toward a loosely defined vision of "sustainable development." By the year 2050, the global population is projected to increase by a factor of 2, agricultural consumption by a factor of 4, energy consumption by a factor of 6, and economic turnover by a factor of 8. The cumulative impacts of these estimates in terms of chemical flows are that carbon dioxide emissions will increase by 25%, sulfur emissions by 100%, sediment flows by 300%, water withdrawals by 400%, lead use by 18,000%, and synthetic organic compounds by 70,000%. In terms of ecosystems, fertile soils will decrease by

10%, forested land by 20%, and wetlands by 50%, not to mention unknown impacts upon biodiversity.

Our challenge is to navigate successfully the transition from unbounded growth to sustainability, through research, technology, policy assessment, and critical ex post evaluation of our successes and failures to date. These tools must be brought to bear upon a set of environmental issues that has changed substantially in the past 25 years.

On one dimension, we have addressed many of the acute decisions that we faced in the early 1970s. Rivers such as the Cuyahoga no longer spontaneously combust, and we no longer face the need to relocate entire communities, as we did in the cases of Love Canal and Times Beach. Instead, we face a range of less sensational but more pervasive issues, such as having to deal with increasing quantities and varieties of toxic wastes, decreasing reserves of landfill capacity, and freshwater scarcity. As a result, the United States now spends in the neighborhood of 2% of its gross national product on environmental protection and remediation. Congress is currently in the midst of reevaluating the U.S. framework for environmental policy as a whole, and the sheer number of individual decisions that have to be made suggests that they will be operationalized at lower bureaucratic levels.

Second, the scale of environmental issues has changed—in terms of both geography and time. Backyard issues have given way to regional and global issues for three basic reasons: (a) Pollutants travel over great distances across numerous jurisdictional boundaries (this is most apparent with issues such as watershed protection, tropospheric ozone, and acid rain); (b) in cases such as salmon and whaling, it is the resources we are trying to protect that travel over great distances; and (c) changes in the yield of essentially localized resources, such as the Georges Bank and the Peruvian anchoveta fisheries, have global economic consequences.

In parallel to this expansion of geographic scale, the timescale of major environmental issues has significantly lengthened for three basic reasons: (a) It may take decades before the environmental effects of substances become known, as in the case of chlorofluorocarbons; (b) the investment horizons for large infrastructure projects with significant environmental impacts (such as power plants, dams, and reservoirs) span decades, and thus efforts to reduce acidifying SO_x and NO_x emissions must be implemented over similar timescales; and (c) in cases in which there is significant background variability, as with global warming and stratospheric ozone depletion, we require long observational records to distinguish anthropogenic change from natural change.

Third, environmental issues are increasingly interrelated with one another and with the universe of socioeconomic policy issues in general. These linkages add significant complexity to scientific analyses and policy responses required to address environmental concerns adequately. Two examples make this point. First, we now know that the issues of acid rain, stratospheric ozone depletion, and climate change are inexorably linked. Chlorofluorocarbons are both major stratospheric ozone depletants and an important greenhouse gas. NO_x and SO_x are major sources of acidifying deposition and, in the short term, counteract the warming effects of greenhouse gases. Second, negotiations during the Montreal Protocol process and the U.N. Conference on Environment and Development institutionalized the notion that environmental protection is inextricably connected to the broader issue of international development.

The evolution of all these changes and their dynamic interrelationships make it clear not only that problem resolution is embedded in a sea of data, but also that close—and possibly new—ties will need to be forged among the analysts and users of these data and the developers of information systems worldwide.

■ Collaborative Information Systems for Linking Knowledge to Action

The need to promote broad use of information about environmental change in the assessment and decision-making communities is well recognized by both the research and policy communities. Investment in better information and new knowledge for policy and assessment purposes will not be realized until it is also used for decision making.

In a recent study that we chaired at Harvard on this subject, the study group envisioned a self-organizing complex of worldwide, autonomous, interdependent information systems that will enable more effective assessments of global environmental change. These interdependent systems, centers, and communication networks would be both government and market driven. The many such information systems emerging worldwide to support analysis of global environmental change must be designed and implemented in a manner that is consistent with and encourages the collaborative, pluralistic, information-intensive, and unpredictable characteristics of successful assessments by many professional communities. The Internet, for example, would be an appropriate model for the exchange of such information.

An example of what we mean by this kind of information system is the Earth Observation Satellites Data and Information System (EOSDIS) being developed by NASA for the Mission to Planet Earth, and the Global Change Research Program (GCRP) in general. The EOSDIS design started out in 1990 as a centralized system to be built as a package and delivered 7 years later to the GCRP community. This design architecture was changed in 1993, and today the EOSDIS design is a more evolutionary, scalable, and logically distributed system consisting of active and archiving centers serving a variety of users. In response to criticisms this year by the U.S. Congress, NASA is again changing the design architecture to allow for privatization of some of the information centers of the EOSDIS network in order that a newly named Earth Sciences Information Partners System (ESIPS) can be implemented as a federation consisting of all the responsible parties—government and private—who will develop, operate, and use the system. ESIPS will operate on the Internet and can be accessed by libraries, public schools, and others. Thus a major source of information, the GCRP database, will be available worldwide for research, assessment, education, and other uses.

For assessment purposes, the complex of information systems on global environmental change that is evolving worldwide should support a broad base of user communities. Four broad categories of assessment should be targeted:

1. large-scale governmental assessments performed by international government organizations and individual national governments
2. smaller-scale governmental assessments performed at regional and local levels
3. independent professional assessments performed by academic researchers, industry, consultants, and public interest groups
4. "concerned citizen" assessments performed by nongovernmental agencies, citizens' grassroots groups, journalists, students, and others

Another desirable characteristic of such information systems is that they should leverage their efforts through existing and emerging information brokers such as libraries, Internet servers, and other on-line information services. Also, access mechanisms analogous to those refined over the years for scientific and technical literature should be developed for new forms of environmental change information resources. Traditional access mechanisms such as catalogs, abstracts, citation indexes, and full text search and retrieval should be augmented, for example, with electronic journals and enhanced software services that dynamically index and rank the relevance of large bodies of textual and numerical information according to user specifications.

Finally, government-produced information, such as that derived from the GCRP, should be provided to all classes of users according to a single-tier pricing strategy. For example, the GCRP states: "Data should be provided at the lowest possible cost to global change researchers in the interest of full and open access to data. This cost should, as a first principle, be no more than the marginal cost of filling a specific user request." This policy should be extended to all users of the data and to all information systems for global environmental change data, recognizing that value-added services will cost more than the core data furnished by the government, but that these services will grow and pay for themselves.

In short, the immediate task is to ensure that the development of knowledge and strong (national and international) policy based on that knowledge are not impeded by unnecessary problems of access to data. The second task involves developing a new basis for collaboration between the knowledge-creating and policy-making functions, which may require new forms of networking across researchers, evaluators, managers, and policy makers.

PART VI

A Sampler of the Current Methodological Tool Kit

*A*s Cook points out in Chapter 2 of this volume, evaluators have probably focused more attention on the methods they use than on any other topic. Volumes have been written about such diverse methods as experiments, case studies, surveys, and the statistical armamentarium often used to analyze quantitative data. In Part VI, we present a sampler of some of these evaluation methods, highlighting both some presumably well-known older methods (e.g., time series) as well as newer ideas about methods that may be less familiar (e.g., cluster evaluation). We begin with chapters that describe broad multi-method strategies and gradually narrow the focus through multimethod strategies that nonetheless have somewhat more narrow interests in, say, empowerment or causation, through some very specific methods that evaluators can use. The aim is not to endorse or criticize any one of these methods, but rather to portray the breadth of methodology that our experience has shown must necessarily characterize the methodological tool kit of the evaluation profession.

In Chapter 24, Lois-ellin Datta argues persuasively for the frequent superiority of multimethod evaluations for answering many evaluation questions. A multimethod evaluation can combine any two or more methods (e.g., a survey and an experiment), but here Datta focuses on the benefits that might accrue from mixing other methods with case study methods. She adopts the U.S. General Accounting Office (GAO/PEMD) definition of the case study evaluation as a method for learning about a complex instance, based on a comprehensive understanding of that instance, obtained by extensive description and analysis of that instance, taken as a whole and in its context. The methods used to understand the case are primarily qualitative, such as participant observation and ethnography. Datta then presents a very interesting and convincing example of how case study methods contributed unique and critical new knowledge to PEMD's multimethod evaluation of a migrant farmworker program.

Among the more valuable parts of Datta's chapter are the two tables (Tables 24.2 and 24.5) that present criteria for evaluating the quality of case study and mixed-method evaluations, respectively. Although these brief tables necessarily leave some important questions unanswered (e.g., What are the strengths and weaknesses of different methods? By what criteria are we to judge which methods are more appropriate for which questions?), they nonetheless do evaluation a great service by summarizing a very plausible if initial set of quality criteria to use in judging the implementation of these methods. Finally, Datta emphasizes two of the primary lessons we have learned in evaluation over the past three decades: Qualitative methods must be a part of the evaluator's tool kit, and multimethod evaluations are quite frequently the highest goal to which we can aspire.

The next two chapters in this section pertain to the same topic, research synthesis—a set of techniques that rely in part on quantitative methods for synthesizing the results of multiple studies addressing the same issue. In Chapter 25, Judith Droitcour describes the development of cross-design synthesis in the U.S. General Accounting Office (GAO/PEMD) as a method that potentially allows researchers to capture the strengths and compensate for the weaknesses of studies with quite different designs. The example she uses is breast cancer treatment, in particular the comparison of breast conservation to mastectomy. In this area, two sources of data are available, each with different strengths and weaknesses. On the one hand, in controlled clinical trials where patients are assigned one of the two treatments at random, the results have higher internal validity (high fidelity of causal inference about treatment effectiveness) but often lower external validity (generalizability), because, for example, of the highly selected nature of patients often admitted to these trials (e.g., only those in a narrow age range). On the other hand, certain large databases that track thousands of cancer clients for 5 years are stronger in external validity because they include a large fraction of the universe of patients, but are weaker in internal validity because the assignment of these patients to particular treatments may have been due to confounding factors that may have influenced outcomes in ways that mimic treatment effects. Cross-design synthesis allows the researcher to study results from both kinds of studies and then to examine whether the results are similar. If they are similar, both the internal validity and the external validity of the conclusions about therapy effectiveness are enhanced.

In Chapter 26, Michael Stoto presents two examples of how research synthesis has been used at the Institute of Medicine in the U.S. National Academy of Sciences (NAS). In the first example, the concern was with determining the health effects on veterans of exposure to Agent Orange and other herbicides in Vietnam. The second example involved the question of whether childhood vaccinations produce harmful effects in addition to all the positive effects for which they are justly well-known and used. In both cases, the U.S. Congress specifically asked NAS to synthesize what was known about these questions, and NAS used research synthesis techniques to do so. The results were particularly politically charged, because compensation to harmed children or veterans was at stake. Stoto describes the NAS process as starting from a neutral position, assuming neither that any relationships existed nor that they did not exist. The methods used in this synthesis were partly quantitative and partly qualitative. The evaluation concluded that there does appear to be a link between exposure to the herbicides used in Vietnam and a few diseases, and that rare adverse effects may be caused by childhood vaccines. These results were then given to Congress for use in its deliberations about whether or not to compensate individuals who might have experienced these adverse effects. Droitcour's research synthesis was somewhat more quantitative than was Stoto's research synthesis, but both clearly relied on synthesizing results from different kinds of designs. Both chapters also help us understand the need for multiple designs with diverse strengths and weaknesses to generate evaluative inferences that stand up to stringent inspection. In their own ways, therefore, they reinforce the general message of this part of the book—that the evaluator's tool kit must include a wide array of methods.

In the early 1990s, David Fetterman presented another multimethod approach to evaluation that he termed empowerment evaluation, which he reviews in Chapter 27. Empowerment evaluation is not so much a method as an overall strategy for approaching evaluation, a strategy that combines many different methods. In fact, Fetterman describes empowerment evaluation as the use of evaluation concepts, techniques, and findings to foster improvement and self-determination, employing both qualitative and quantitative methodologies. Its aim is to help people help themselves and improve their programs using a form of self-evaluation and reflection. The outside evaluator serves as a coach or additional facilitator, depending on internal program capabilities. To illustrate the approach, Fetterman describes how empowerment evaluation has been applied to accreditation in higher education. An interesting feature of this approach is the particular twist that it puts on the use of evaluation. Use is frequently taken to refer to what happens to the results of the evaluation—are the results used to make a change in the program, to change how people think, or for some other purpose? In empowerment evaluation such uses are still important, but equal emphasis is put on the use of the process of evaluation—How does the very act of doing an evaluation change what happens in the program being evaluated? The distinction is important, and too often overlooked. Fetterman's chapter also foreshadows an issue addressed by Robert Stake and Michael Scriven in Chapters 32 and 33 of this volume, about the relative roles played in evaluation by advocating for a program, on the one hand, and telling the truth about a program on the other. In some situations, of course, the two goals may be entirely compatible; but in many situations some conflict between the two goals will emerge. Stake makes the case for at least occasional advocacy, and Scriven for the primacy of truth. Fetterman addresses this issue briefly in his chapter, but that brevity inevitably leaves room for continued argument about the terms of the debate. This generic issue seems to us to be an important emerging challenge for evaluators to clarify.

In Chapter 28, James Sanders describes another strategic multimethod approach to evaluation: cluster evaluation. Cluster evaluation is appropriate for projects that have a common mission but have local procedural autonomy, and where the funders of those projects want evaluations of the results obtained from their investment. It asks whether desired changes have occurred associated with the project, and searches for insights that can explain, sustain, and expand those changes. Sanders notes that cluster evaluation bears closer resemblance to naturalistic and case study evaluation than to many other kinds of evaluation. However, it differs from them in that it is holistic and outcome oriented, it seeks generalizable learning, and it involves frequent communication and collaboration among the partners—with the emphasis on generalizable learning about outcomes being the presumably important differentiator. To his credit, Sanders writes not only about the strengths of cluster evaluation, but also about its weaknesses, something done too infrequently by advocates of particular approaches. He notes, for instance, that the outcome data from a cluster evaluation may be less certain than data from controlled experiments, and that the risk that the cluster evaluator will lose his or her independence is a real concern. As proposed new strategies such as empowerment evaluation and cluster evaluation emerge, we hope that evaluators will begin not only to follow Sanders's lead in analyzing both strengths and weaknesses of the approach they advocate, but also extend their discussions to additional historical and conceptual analyses of how these new approaches resemble and differ from those of the past.

Ray Pawson and Nick Tilley argue in Chapter 29 for an approach to evaluation that they call scientific realist evaluation, where the central issue is causation, especially causal explanation. They begin by noting that social programs are embedded social systems that can be understood only through examination of the social rules and institutions within which they are embedded. A given program embedded in different contexts—with different people, different institutions, different providers, different settings, and so on—will play out differently, with potentially different effects. As Pawson and Tilley put it, a program is its personnel, its place, its past, and its prospects. This leads them to postulate a fundamental formula for explanation in scientific realist evaluation: Outcome = Mechanism + Context. That is, they prefer to see evaluators search for the causal mechanisms that lead to program outcomes, but with the critical caveat that those mechanisms are likely to be context specific (although they acknowledge that it may eventually prove possible to classify contexts in some more general way). After describing their theory in general terms, they give an example of the use of video surveillance cameras to deter the theft of cars from parking lots. No matter what one's views on causation (or scientific realism), the examples they give of searching for alternative explanations are worth emulating in many evaluations.

In Chapter 30, Mansoor Kazi describes how social workers in the United Kingdom have adapted single case study methodologies (commonly known in some quarters as ABAB designs) to cope with increased demands for social

worker accountability initiated by the National Health Service and Commu-
nity Care Act of 1990 and the Children Act of 1989. Of course, Kazi uses the
phrase single case study methodology quite differently from Datta, for Kazi
is appealing to a tradition steeped in causal inference and quantitative
measures, like that in behavioral psychology, compared with Datta's empha-
sis on qualitative methods more in the tradition of anthropology and quali-
tative sociology. With Kazi's version of the design, a client's problem is
measured and tracked over time, and problem responsiveness to interventions
is then plotted. Kazi describes a practical implementation experience that
will be familiar to many evaluators. That is, social workers found they had
to adapt these designs in three important ways to make them practical: (a)
The designs had to be simplified when more complex designs proved imprac-
tical; (b) the ideal measure of a problem was rarely available, so evaluators
often had to make due with available approximations of desired measures;
and (c) the design had to be applied flexibly so that it could be adapted over
time as circumstances changed even within the same case. Kazi presents a
large number of examples of the design's application, showing how it can be
used not only to track client outcome but also to monitor program implemen-
tation. In this setting, with these particular kinds of evaluation problems, this
design makes sense as one part of the methodological tool kit—especially
when it is used as one part of a multimethod evaluation, something Kazi
explicitly advocates at the end of his chapter.

Robert Orwin discusses in Chapter 31 the interrupted time series design,
one closely related to the single case study methodology discussed by Kazi
but usually conducted at a different level of aggregation entirely (e.g., the
nation rather than the person). In one form or another, time series designs
are used to study many different topics where it is possible to retrieve (or
create) archives of data repeatedly gathered at the same intervals over time.
Yet few of these applications reflect the rich array of design variations that
can enhance the inferential power of these designs. Orwin gives a host of
examples, including not only the basic simple interrupted time series design,
but also designs that add either control groups or control variables, that use
switching replications, and that use other series as covariates. He illustrates
these possibilities with nine vivid examples of how the design has actually
been used to study topics as diverse as agricultural economics, managerial
incentive payments, penalties for driving while intoxicated, and the effects of
television on crime. His chapter is heavy on illustration and light on statis-
tical issues, but Orwin offers just enough explanation for the reader to know

what the statistical issues are, and where to look to find further guidance. The time series design is probably one of the most underutilized designs in the evaluator's repertoire, and we hope that Orwin's lucid explanation will promote its more frequent use.

William R. Shadish

24

Multimethod Evaluations

Using Case Studies Together With Other Methods

Lois-ellin Datta

Lessons learned from multimethod evaluations using case studies are twofold. First, with appropriate selection, due care, and realistic expectations, multimethod designs can lead to better evaluations. Second, without appropriate selection, due care, and realistic expectations, choosing monomethod studies may be the better part of valor. I will illustrate these points in this chapter by discussing some evaluations in which case studies were an integral part of the design.

■ *Multimethod Evaluations Are Eclectic Works*

Studies mixing types of data, such as test scores, parent surveys, and placement records, are now commonplace. Considerable work remains to be done in such methodological matters as establishing clearer standards

TABLE 24.1 Types of Mixes and Their Acceptance in Evaluation

Type of Mix	Acceptance in Evaluation
Data (for example, using test scores, surveys, interviews, observations, and documents in the same evaluation)	High, but with recognition of some questions, such as weight given to different data sources.
Analysis (for example, using descriptive and various kinds of inferential statistics in the same evaluation)	High, but with recognition of some questions, such as best ways to "cancel out" biases in different techniques.
Methods (for example, using time series designs and case studies in the same evaluation)	Moderately high, particularly when different methods are used to answer different evaluation subquestions, but with recognition of considerable remaining work on such matters as defining quality in multi-method studies.
Paradigms (for example, using the frameworks of experimentation and of phenomenologically based evaluation theories in the same evaluation)	Moderate, when the study design is strongly grounded in evaluation theory, to low, when the design is not so grounded. Practical pragmatists, however, mix paradigms freely.
Nested (for example, using mixes of different types in the same evaluation for questions dealing with different organizational or social levels, such as classrooms, schools, districts, and states)	Moderate to low, reflecting concerns for the types of mixes summarized above.

of excellence, weighting results, avoiding overanalysis of data, and dealing with nonconvergent findings. This kind of eclecticism is, however, noncontroversial. What is more controversial, and not so easy to do well, is completing a single evaluation whose design calls for mixing methods, such as cost-benefit analyses, survey research, quasi-experimental designs, research syntheses, and case studies. At considerable issue among some theorists is the extent to which mixing methods from different traditions or paradigms, particularly case studies, leads to mixed-up methods. Table 24.1 summarizes the kinds of mixes that have been discussed. The focus of this chapter is on multimethod studies involving true case studies.

■ A Definition of Case Study Evaluations

A case study evaluation is not a site visit. It is not a small-*N* evaluation based on one or fewer instances. For the purposes of this chapter, a case study evaluation is defined as "a method for learning about a complex instance, based on a comprehensive understanding of that instance, obtained by extensive description and analysis of that instance, taken as a whole and in its context" (U.S. General Accounting Office, 1990, p. 14). As such, this method is often expensive because it is highly labor-intensive. It places demands on the audience beyond the sound bite and the executive summary, because it can yield rich understanding difficult to compress into a few words. Until recently, the trustworthiness of a case study was difficult to assess. There were few explicit standards of quality and relatively few evaluators formally trained in case study evaluations.

Happily, the first concerns are being remedied through many now-classic books and articles. These include, for example, Halpern (1983) on auditing case studies, Miles and Huberman (1984) on analyzing qualitative data, Yin (1994) on case study research, and LeCompte and Goetz (1982) on issues of validity and reliability in ethnographic research. Fine new articles and books such as those by Stake (1995) and Van Rizyn (1995) continue to improve the state of the art. The second concern—the scarcity of adequately prepared and experienced evaluators—is fading with the expansion of diversified evaluation graduate programs. Further, some, and possibly many, of an impressive new generation of evaluators are experienced in qualitative as well as quantitative paradigms and methods.

■ Theorists Vary, Whereas Practicing Evaluators Seem to Like Multimethod Evaluations That Include Case Studies

Theorists vary in their views on multimethod evaluations (Datta, 1994). Some argue that the best evaluations are grounded in a guiding paradigm or theory about such matters as the nature of reality, the role of evaluation in society, and the derivation of specific methods, although they recognize and want to give due place to increasing the array of methods available to evaluators. As examples, evaluators have made closely reasoned, eloquent cases for the stakeholder perspective and qualitative paradigms (e.g., Guba, Lincoln, and Fetterman) and for empirical, more experimental approaches (e.g., Sechrest, Sidani, and Boruch). Other theorists, however, argue for the compatibility of multiparadigm and multimethod evaluations (see, for example, Reichardt & Rallis, 1994) while recognizing the need to grapple with some difficult issues of combining methods (see, for example, Caracelli & Riggin, 1994; Greene, Caracelli, & Graham, 1989).

Practical evaluators, however, have been conducting multimethod evaluations for more than three decades. As defined, instances of such evaluations using case studies date from the 1960s. Consider, for example, the first national evaluations of the Head Start Planned Variation experiments. These included in their design, data collection, and reporting case studies of the development of individual children based on intensive observations over the Head Start year. Ethnographic case studies were part of a multimethod study of an alternative program for low-income youth and of other educational evaluations (Fetterman & Pitman, 1986). Many of the earlier large-scale national evaluations, particularly in human services areas, incorporated case studies as defined in their designs (see, for example, Herriott, 1977; Hi/Scope Educational Research Foundation, 1972-1976; Maxwell & Sandlow, 1986). Among many more recent instances are Niemiec and Walberg's (1993) collection on Chicago school reform and Murphy's (1995) internal evaluation of gender issues in World Bank lending (see Murphy, Chapter 17, this volume).

The applications of multimethod designs for answering formative, process, descriptive, and implementation questions are numerous. It has become almost standard to look to case studies combined with document analysis in evaluating implementation, for example. The applications for answering summative, outcome, results, and effects questions are less frequent. That is, although it is now commonplace to include qualitative evidence such as interviews and document analysis in evaluations, close integration of a full case study with other methods is not. Even in some of the instances cited above, the case studies were more freestanding than fully integrated with other methods in the evaluations of which they were part, although this was not the original conceptualization. In other instances, although case studies were nominally part of the design, they seem to be silent partners in the analyses and reports. Again, this was not part of the original conceptualization. Case studies may be drawn on to add zip to a discussion of findings, or for explanations of problems in the data, such as differential enrollment in presumably randomized designs. They are not, however, apparently central to the analyses. For example, an extraordinarily carefully designed national evaluation of a program intended to serve homeless individuals with multiple problems included case studies. A fine report on this effort focused, however, on the efforts to achieve a randomized experiment and on the quantitative data.

Nonetheless, there are approaches to combining case studies with other methods that suggest useful lessons. In the following sections, I will first discuss a specific example and then present more general observations. For illustrative purposes, I have selected a study completed in 1988 at the U.S. General Accounting Office (GAO/PEMD, 1989).

■ *The Evaluation of the H-2A Program*

The broad issue is an old one and not unique to the United States. To compete, prices need to be low. Low wages contribute to lower prices. Where a resident (legal) population is too small or is unwilling to work for low wages or in poor working conditions, producers want to bring in foreign labor willing to do so. However, the interests and welfare of resident workers must be protected. Whatever adjustments are made ideally would enable producers to compete but not undercut or unfairly treat resident workers.

Agriculture is a widely known case in point. To reduce U.S. farmers' harvest-time temptation to hire illegal immigrants, the H-2A program makes it possible for them to request special temporary immigration permits for legal farmworkers. The farmers must show that the labor necessary for a harvest is unavailable from legal workers already in the United States. At issue in the evaluation was the effectiveness of H-2A provisions intended to protect wage and working conditions for U.S. citizens and legal immigrants. Congress requested a study of these questions by the U.S. General Accounting Office, to be completed prior to program reauthorization and other pending immigration legislation.

The overall design had three key elements. First was an in-depth understanding of the history and context of the H-2A program. Second was a thorough critical review of the technical quality of the U.S. Department of Agriculture (USDA) surveys used to establish what are considered fair hourly wages and fair piecework wages for agricultural workers.

This review examined in depth all aspects of technical quality, from underlying concepts such as prevailing wages, through the design of the USDA survey instruments, to a thorough observational study of how these surveys were actually carried out, coded, analyzed, and reported. The third element was an examination, in depth, of how the wage and working condition protections were actually working (or not) through an entire agricultural season.

The evaluation plan combined traditional auditing methods, economic analyses, social science methods, research syntheses, and case studies. Specific techniques included historical analysis, using documentation and informants; secondary analysis of existing data from records of the prevailing fair market wages; critical reviews of administrative data quality and of measurement constructs; analysis of documents such as applications for the permits and advertisements for workers; interviews with farmers and immigration officials; and studies of selected industries, with one in-depth case study. The tobacco industry was selected for the in-depth case study, based on two factors: First, this industry accounted for a considerable portion of the H-2A permits issued; and second, it was possible to locate two tobacco-producing counties, side by side although in different states, one of which had high H-2A permit issuances and the other of which had low issuances.

■ *A Better Study Than a Monomethod Design Could Have Produced*

Reliance primarily on the interviews, surveys, economic data, and documents would have shown a program with some flaws in reporting that essentially was working as intended. For example, the USDA survey was regarded as technically sound but flawed by lack of information on the precision of estimates, so the data were potentially unreliable. GAO advised that routine production of sampling estimates could fix this problem. The technical adequacy of the prevailing wage survey was judged less acceptable (the observers found, for example, that in some instances, the nicely drawn sampling plans were not carried out in the field). Again, some of the troubling practices were seen as readily correctable.

The ethnographic studies showed, however, a more complex picture. On receiving the grower labor requests, the local USDA staff put enough effort into recruiting to meet legal requirements for checking out the local labor market, but not much more. They called the U.S. Employment Office, for example, and referred anyone listed as a farmworker to the grower. There were few such workers available for referrals. Follow-up on the few referrals showed that the local workers believed the farmers did not want them. If they were nominally hired, working conditions would be such as to "run them off the farm." For example, one worker hired in response to an ad for tobacco leaf loaders was told to muck out cow barns, whereas the workers hired under H-2A opportunities were assigned relatively lighter work. Follow-up on the small number of local U.S. workers referred and hired appeared to confirm this. For instance, some workers were asked to do heavier tasks than they signed up for, and some fights ensued.

With regard to nonlocal U.S. workers, the conditions of farmwork were not sufficiently attractive to bring a reliable labor force to less populated rural areas. Harvesting some crops, such as tobacco, can be very hard work; tobacco leaves can inflict constant deep cuts, and the work of stripping them from the plant is backbreaking. Temporary housing can be sparse, and housing facilities may lack running water and indoor toilets. Thus, with some exceptions, farmers fairly readily received the H-2A permits requested. The labor force in the immediate vicinity was not adversely affected in a technical sense because whoever was willing to work for the prevailing wages could make connections easily.

Farmers often had well-established arrangements to bring in workers from villages in Central American countries. The villagers expected the yearly trek to the United States. A legal permanent resident from each village lived in the U.S. county. Legal U.S. residents from various villages formed the connection from the farmers to the villagers. These young, strapping men offered a reliable, docile, and relatively easy-to-access labor force. Further, they were more productive than the mostly older, mostly female U.S. workers who lasted the season. With some exceptions, the effort required for the farmer was filing each year essentially the same application used in previous years. The local federal offices responsible for verifying labor needs expected to receive these applications and routinely approved them.

The U.S. workers were not layabouts or welfare cheats. Most were working at minimum-wage or slightly higher-paid jobs with considerably better working conditions than stripping tobacco. And the apparent paradox of side-by-side tobacco counties with differing rates of H-2A permits was not due to local labor force differences. In the county with the lower number of H-2A permits, the evolved pattern was said to be to hire illegals.

The evaluation could document these evolved patterns of accommodation but was not designed to speak directly to the underlying—and very old—policy issue. The findings from the tobacco worker in-depth case study were congruent with those of the information from other industries gathered in this evaluation and reported in the literature. As noted earlier, without access to special-permit immigrant workers or with a crackdown on illegals, farmers would have had to change working conditions to attract the large unskilled labor force from urban areas, plus take on different supervisory and training responsibilities. The costs of attracting, training, and supervising the larger U.S. unskilled labor pool might raise prices too high, even with federal price supports, for some of the industries using the H-2A program to compete with imported products. The GAO report observed that an intermediate step would be to require more extensive recruiting within the United States. At least a somewhat wider pool of nearby workers willing to take on the seasonal agricultural work could have a fairer shot at the jobs than was then possible.

Subsequent changes in immigration laws, responding to many factors, including this and scores of other studies, have included greater employer accountability for documenting the legal status of all workers. These changes were intended to improve work opportunities, wages, and working conditions for legal farmworkers.

With some exceptions, the farmworkers evaluation case study meets the guidelines for assessing the quality of case study reports shown in Table 24.2. These include presenting the evaluation questions clearly and explicitly, presenting the basis for case selection, selecting appropriate information sources, and presenting arguments for and against various resolutions of evaluation questions. Among the exceptions, where feasibility overruled ideal practice, were the guidelines in the table labeled A3, B2, and E2. Ideally, time would have permitted a longitudinal and perhaps participant observer design rather than the cross-sectional

TABLE 24.2 A Checklist for Reviewing the Quality of Case Study Reports

Area	Guideline	
A. Design	A1.	The evaluation questions are stated clearly and explicitly.
	A2.	The type of case study application (illustrative, normative, results, etc.) is clearly described.
	A3.	The time span of the study is long enough to address the core issues fairly.
	A4a.	The basis (convenience, random, extremes, best case, etc.) for case selection is presented.
	A4b.	The basis is appropriate for the purpose of the case study.
B. Data collection	B1a.	The methods for data collection are presented.
	B1b.	The methods are appropriate for the purpose of the case study.
	B2.	If more than one investigator collected the data, all evaluators were properly selected, trained, and supervised.
	B3a.	The information sources are described fully and clearly.
	B3b.	The sources are appropriate for the purpose of the case study.
C. Database information and data analysis techniques	C1a.	The procedures for database formation are described.
	C1b.	The procedures are appropriate.
	C2a.	The techniques of data gathering and processing are explicitly described.
	C2b.	The techniques are appropriate.
	C3a.	Any differences in interpretation between evaluators are presented.
	C3b.	How the differences were resolved is explained.
	C4.	The results of other studies relevant to the issue are presented and reconciled with the case study findings, to permit cumulative knowledge on the issue.
D. Reporting	D1.	The methodological strengths and limitations are identified clearly.
	D2.	Arguments for various resolutions of the evaluation questions are presented.
	D3.	Arguments against various resolutions of the evaluation questions are presented.
	D4a.	The study identifies factors explaining what happened (observed phenomena).
	D4b.	The study clearly states whether identification of these factors was based on insight and recognition, on quantitative techniques, or both.
E. Impartiality and generalizability	E1.	Proper safeguards were taken to ensure the competence and impartiality of the investigators.
	E2.	Comments on the draft report by stakeholders are available in the report or readily available elsewhere.
	E3a.	Adequate information is provided to judge generalizability (such as detailed information on the basis for selecting the instances beyond a tag like "purposive").
	E3b.	Appropriate limitations to generalizations have been presented.

SOURCES: Gilbert (1982, pp. 138-139), U.S. General Accounting Office (1990, pp. 99-106), and Yin (1994, pp. 140-145).

TABLE 24.3 Some Interesting Features of the Farmworkers Evaluation

Feature	Comments
Depth	The findings from each of the approaches were reported in approximately equal depth and detail, with the thoroughness needed for understanding of the results. However, the richness of the ethnographic data could have been more fully presented in a longer, possibly separate report.
Methodological equity	The team included a highly experienced agricultural ethnographer, economists, "traditional" auditors, and social science analysts. The best way to answer the evaluation questions drove selection of methods, and thus the diversity of the team. The final analyses and conclusions gave equal weight to the different methods. This was not a qualitative study with quantitative embellishments, or vice versa, but more of a partnership among equals.
Transparency of findings from all methods	For each method, the report provided approximately equal depth and detail on the techniques of data collection and data reduction, with the thoroughness needed for assessing the credibility of the results.

observer studies. Ideally, the principal agricultural ethnographer would have had the support of other equally well-trained observers instead of social science analysts trained to a "second eyes and ears" level. Ideally, the farmworkers and farmers, as well as relevant agency and other officials, would have commented on the draft report.

Turning to other qualities, Table 24.3 summarizes features that make this evaluation methodologically interesting. These include depth, methodological equity, and transparency. The common theme across these features is methodological equity, rather than methodological dominance. That is, the value added of each method, including the case studies, to answering the evaluative questions was well established in the design phase and adhered to in analysis and reporting.

In some multimethod evaluations, the final report suggests that the evaluators regard one approach or another as more trustworthy in reaching conclusions. The findings from this favored approach are featured in the last chapter and in the summaries. The rationale and procedures for the favored method get more space in the body of the report and in the technical sections. Treatment of the findings from other methods tends to

TABLE 24.4 Some Problems Encountered and Lessons Learned From the Farmworkers Evaluation

Problems	Lessons
Management time was underestimated, and there were delays in getting access. Access to information was easier for some methods than others. This was anticipated as fully as possible in the design. However, the management time required for readjustments to maintain design integrity was underestimated.	If maintaining design integrity is crucial, get the best possible estimate of time required for management of access and double it!
Illegal activity was uncovered. The ethnographic case studies uncovered some violations of immigration laws. This was anticipated, and the evaluators thought within-agency issues had been worked out to permit certain data to be collected under assurance of confidentiality. When the final report was drafted, however, it took a lot of management time to resolve exactly what this meant. There are places in the report where the words walk on eggshells.	Agencies with legal responsibilities for acting on information about illegal activities need to provide extremely clear guidelines in case study evaluations about what is focal and what is peripheral to a specific study.
The element of judgment and interpretation was not easily assimilated into auditing standards. Quality control in auditing requires a clear track from initial observations through all steps of data reduction, conclusions, and recommendations. An independent reviewer called a *referencer* must be convinced that each statement in the report is documented and plausible. Finding a meeting place between ethnographic procedures, particularly under time pressures during fieldwork and referencing procedures, took more time and anguish than anticipated.	Unsure. Perhaps with experience, the procedures would become better defined and the task no more arduous than for any other method. At the least, organizations using internal referencing procedures for quality control before evaluations are presented need to allow for a considerable learning curve for some case study methods.
The agricultural ethnographer left before the report was completed. A very senior position was offered to the ethnographer, who appropriately took it. This placed a considerable burden on other project staff to complete the report and maintain the desired methodological balance. Because the ethnographer was not available during the referencing process, the report was less rich than it might have been. Economists, auditors, and social science analysts could have been more readily replaced.	"Rent" an ethnographer (or a person in any other discipline needed) on a contract basis for the duration of the study if the organization does not have sufficient depth in a given discipline. This can be done on a retainer if there is sufficient coordination throughout to prepare the understudy. Case study evaluations may be particularly sensitive to loss of experienced staff.

be both separate and unequal. To some extent and in some cases, this is appropriate. For example, in some studies, the best way to answer the evaluative questions is determined at the design stage to be reliance primarily on one method, supplemented by other methods. In such instances, the emphases in analyses and reporting appropriately reflect the initial design decisions. In other cases, however, the design stage calls for a fully integrated multimethod approach. Here the integrity of the design requires an equal partnership, and a report that depends on the tripod falls, methodologically, if most of the weight is put on one leg.

Challenges encountered may teach some useful lessons, too, about multimethod evaluations. Table 24.4 summarizes some of the problems encountered in the H-2A evaluation and suggests some possible lessons about dealing with each problem.

■ *Appropriate Selection, Due Care, and Realistic Expectations in Combining Case Studies With Other Methods in Evaluation*

What are the lessons learned from multimethod evaluations using case studies? There probably will be considerable commonality in what is considered good practice. This reflects well on the development of evaluation as a field. As noted elsewhere, both qualitative and quantitative methods have a long way to go before some troubling, significant issues are resolved. Both, however, are moving steadily toward establishing standards of excellence that can guide new designs and the trustworthiness of new reports.

Of particular interest are calls for getting on with three important tasks. One is to articulate the logic and theoretical structure of a third paradigm specific to multimethod evaluations (Lincoln & Guba, 1994; Reichardt & Rallis, 1994; Sechrest, Babcock, & Smith, 1993). Another task is to establish explicit quality guidelines for multimethod studies (see Table 24.5, which is derived from an exploratory study by Caracelli & Riggin, 1994). And the third task is to develop new methodologies that solve some of the problems of multimethod (and monomethod) evaluations.

In contrast to what may be broad agreement on what makes a multimethod evaluation exemplary, problems encountered may be more situ-

TABLE 24.5 Quality Criteria Specific to Mixed-Method Evaluations

Feature		Illustrative Items
A. Design	A1.	In triangulation, methods are implemented independently.
	A2.	Applicable rules of evidence are applied to data from the method types.
	A3.	Methods are selected to minimize shared bias.
	A4.	Strengths and weaknesses of the different method types are considered in the evaluation design.
	A5.	The use of multimethods matches the stated purpose for combining the method types.
B. Data quality and analysis	B1.	Analysis of data from different method types is conducted systematically.
	B2.	Analysis techniques are appropriate to data collected from different method types.
	B3.	Use of qualitative data to elaborate quantitative findings is appropriate.
C. Bias	C1.	Conceptual framework guides selection of qualitative and quantitative methods.
D. Interpretation	D1.	When data from different method types are combined in analysis, weights are assigned that reflect any disparities.
	D2.	The weights given to inferences from different methods reflect the relevance of the measures to the construct.
	D3.	Convergent findings are not the result of shared bias between the methods.
	D4.	Interpretation of data collected by different methods considers the biases (shared or divergent) of the methods.
	D5.	Mixed methods used for complementary purposes enable a more comprehensive evaluation (e.g., both process and outcome are considered).
	D6.	The inclusion of data from quantitative and qualitative methods enhances the interpretability of findings.
E. Resources	E1.	Differential vulnerabilities to resource problems require exceptional resources, exceptional management skills, exceptional flexibility in completing the evaluation, and some major trade-off decisions when problems arise.
F. Stakeholders	F1.	The manner of reporting findings from the method types maximizes interest of stakeholders in the evaluation.
	F2.	The combination of methods informs changes in policy/progress.
G. Reporting	G1.	A rationale for combining methods is provided.
	G2.	Nonconvergent findings are plausibly explained.

SOURCE: Adapted from Caracelli and Riggin (1994, Table 2, pp. 145-149).

ation specific. Concern about uncovering illegalities, for instance, may be unique to a few agencies. Concern about staff turnover, particularly in a multiyear evaluation, may be more widespread. How would the coin land on the issue of decisions in the face of scarce resources? It is by no means clear in such situations that more is better.

For example, a recent evaluation of statewide systemic change had many aims and few resources. The design combined, among many techniques, economic analysis and case studies. The staff time available for nested individual, class, and school case studies over seven sites totaled about 40 days over a 5-year period. The better choice might be to answer the top-priority question thoroughly through a monomethod evaluation rather than to spread staff thinly over a broader range of issues. In other instances, so little use appears to have been made of the case study data—or of the non-case study data—that, again, a better choice might have been a monomethod study, focused on a smaller number of questions. In yet other instances, data from the different methods are clearly in conflict, yet resources and time have not permitted the gathering of additional data needed for an adequate resolution. Here again, a better choice might have been either an exploratory-level study or a monomethod.

Yin (1994) is among the methodologists who draw on rich experience with actual completed evaluations to suggest many design alternatives to the concurrent use of multiple methods. For example, in some instances, case study results are the basis for designing later surveys, using the efficiency and representativeness of the latter to assess the generalizability of insights from the former. In other examples, secondary analyses and evaluation syntheses are used to reach broad conclusions, with subsequent case studies to follow up on reasons, processes, and dynamics. In still other instances, the design is conceptualized from the beginning as a sort of federation of substudies.

■ *In Conclusion*

In an evaluation context, combining case studies with other methods can lead to better evaluations for results as well as descriptive, normative, and implementation questions, *if* the following conditions are met:

■ Selection of methods is *parsimoniously* appropriate to the evaluation questions, particularly checking to be sure resources are not being stretched too thinly. A key issue is deciding what kind of case study best meets the needs, looking at the wide array of types and sequencing of case studies.

■ Due care—actually, *exquisite* care—is used in anticipating threats to the integrity of the multimethod design, data collection, analysis, and reporting, including ethical concerns and quality assurance procedures.

■ Expectations are *pitilessly* realistic concerning the value added of case studies and every other method examined to the overall design.

Where these considerations are not carefully applied, combining case study methods with other approaches to evaluation of results, effects, and impacts may be ill-advised indeed.

■ *References*

Caracelli, V. J., & Riggin, L. J. C. (1994). Multimethod evaluation: Developing quality criteria through concept mapping. *Evaluation Practice, 15,* 139-152.

Datta, L.-e. (1994). Paradigm wars: A basis for peaceful coexistence and beyond. In C. S. Reichardt & S. F. Rallis (Eds.), *The qualitative-quantitative debate: New perspectives* (pp. 53-70). San Francisco: Jossey-Bass.

Fetterman, D. M., & Pitman, M. A. (Eds.). (1986). *Educational evaluation: Ethnography in theory, practice, and politics.* Beverly Hills, CA: Sage.

Gilbert, J. R. (1982). Guidelines for reporting large case studies. In D. C. Hoaglin et al. (Eds.), *Data for decision information: Strategies for decision makers.* Cambridge, MA: Abt Associates.

Greene, J. C., Caracelli, V., & Graham, W. F. (1989). Toward a conceptual framework for multimethod evaluation designs. *Educational Evaluation and Policy Analysis, 11,* 255-274.

Halpern, E. S. (1983). *Auditing naturalistic inquiries: Some preliminary applications.* Paper presented at the annual meeting of the American Educational Research Association, Toronto.

Herriott, R. E. (1977). Ethnographic case studies on federally funded multi-disciplinary policy research: Some design and interpretation issues. *Anthropology and Education Quarterly, 9,* 106-115.

Hi/Scope Educational Research Foundation. (1972-1976). *National Home Start evaluation.* Ypsilanti, MI: Author.

LeCompte, M. D., & Goetz, J. P. (1982). Problems of reliability and validity in ethnographic research. *Review of Educational Research, 152,* 31-60.

Lincoln, Y. S., & Guba, E. G. (1994). RSVP: We are pleased to accept your invitation. *Evaluation Practice, 15,* 179-192.

Maxwell, J. A., & Sandlow, L. J. (1986). Combining ethnographic and experimental methods in educational evaluation: A case study. In D. A. Fetterman & M. A. Pitman (Eds.), *Educational evaluation: Ethnography in theory, practice, and politics.* Beverly Hills, CA: Sage.

Miles, M. B., & Huberman, A. M. (1984). *Qualitative data analysis: A sourcebook of new methods.* Beverly Hills, CA: Sage.

Murphy, J. L. (1995). *Gender issues in World Bank lending.* Washington, DC: World Bank.

Niemiec, R. P., & Walberg, H. J. (Eds.). (1993). *Evaluating Chicago school reform.* San Francisco: Jossey-Bass.

Reichardt, C. S., & Rallis, S. F. (Eds.). (1994). *The qualitative-quantitative debate: New perspectives.* San Francisco: Jossey-Bass.

Sechrest, L., Babcock, J., & Smith, B. (1993). An invitation to methodological pluralism. *Evaluation Practice, 14,* 227-235.

Stake, R. E. (1995). *The art of case study research.* Thousand Oaks, CA: Sage.

U.S. General Accounting Office. (1989). *The H-2A Program: Protections for U.S. farmworkers* (GAO/PEMD-89-3). Washington, DC: Author.

U.S. General Accounting Office. (1990). *Case study evaluations* (GAO/PEMD-10.1.9). Washington, DC: Author.

Van Rizyn, G. C. (1995). Cluster analysis as a basis for purposive sampling of projects in case study evaluations. *Evaluation Practice, 16,* 109-119.

Yin, R. K. (1994). *Case study research* (2nd ed.). Thousand Oaks, CA: Sage.

25

Cross-Design Synthesis
Concept and Application

Judith A. Droitcour

■ *Concept of Cross-Design Synthesis*

Cross-design synthesis (Droitcour, Silberman, & Chelimsky, 1993; U.S. General Accounting Office [GAO/PEMD], 1992) builds on recent work in meta-analysis (notably, Rubin, 1990) and on cross-design comparisons in health research (e.g., Hlatky, 1991). It involves three key ideas. The first is simply that, for some evaluation questions, no single design is ideal. The second is that it can be useful to synthesize results from studies with dramatically different, complementary designs.[1] The third is that a specific strategy is needed to capture the diverse strengths of different designs—and to minimize the impact of study weaknesses on synthesis results.

□ *When No Single Design Is Ideal*

Cross-design synthesis was initially developed to evaluate the effectiveness of alternative treatments in medical practice. Although randomized studies are deemed the "gold standard" for testing causal hypotheses, they are vulnerable with respect to external validity. Thus the results of randomized studies may not generalize to (a) the full range of subjects/

AUTHOR'S NOTE: The views expressed in this chapter are my own, and do not necessarily reflect the position of the U.S. General Accounting Office.

patients or (b) typical treatment implementations in day-to-day medical practice. Indeed, when different types of patients are relevant and implementations vary with respect to quality as well as type, randomized studies may cover only a small portion of the patient-treatment domain represented by medical practice.

Some analysts believe that the key constraints on the size, number, and scope of randomized studies are cost factors and inadequate funding, and that increased funding for larger randomized studies ("large simple trials" that encompass a broad range of patients) represents the solution. However, in reviewing breast-conservation studies, my colleagues and I found that coverage was limited by factors other than funding.

First, we found that in randomized studies with long-term follow-up, investigators who include elderly patients face the prospect of a sizable portion of the sample's dying of unrelated causes during the study. Thus, although breast cancer becomes more prevalent with age, some studies have explicitly excluded all patients over age 70—and those studies that have, enrolled only token numbers of elderly women (GAO, 1994, Table I.3, p. 33).

Second, we found that patients who prefer one of two alternative treatments may not enroll in randomized studies. In the breast-conservation area, both a Scottish study (see McDonald, 1991; Stewart & Robinson, 1984) and an English study (Lucas, Mitchell, & Lee, 1984; Peckham, Tobias, & Houghton, 1984) were scrapped because too few patients accepted randomization. And because of difficulties in enrolling women in a large multicenter U.S. randomized study (the National Surgical Adjuvant Breast Project, known as the NSABP; Fisher et al., 1985; Stablein, 1994), a new form of randomization was introduced: so-called prerandomization (here, the physician enrolls a breast cancer patient and obtains her random assignment before telling her about the study; Zelen, 1979).[2] A related problem is that when the results of early randomized studies are reported, patients as well as physicians may become aware of the results; this can lessen willingness to enroll in subsequent studies.[3]

Finally, with respect to treatment implementation factors, a degree of physician judgment and skill is involved in some (but not all) treatments. When judgment and skill are involved—as they apparently are for breast-conservation therapy[4]—the quality of the implementation can affect generalizability to day-to-day practice, because the typical practitioner's abilities may not match those of physicians in randomized studies. Fur-

TABLE 25.1 Complementary Strengths and Weaknesses of Two Study Designs

Study Design	Primary Strength	Primary Weakness
Randomized studies	INTERNAL VALIDITY (controlled comparison; random assignment to alternate treatments)	EXTERNAL VALIDITY (potential lack of generalizability)
Database analysis	EXTERNAL VALIDITY (potential for full coverage of patients/subjects and implementations)	INTERNAL VALIDITY (uncontrolled comparison; selection bias)

ther, unlike day-to-day practice, randomized studies (a) require physicians to follow "protocols" (detailed written procedures) and (b) may be conducted at leading medical centers, which feature state-of-the-art medical equipment and well-trained support staff.[5]

Considering, then, that potential limitations on the generalizability of randomized studies' results may not be due only to funding constraints, but also to patient attributes, preferences, and knowledge, as well as treatment implementation factors, one must conclude that increasing funding does not always represent a solution. And when it does not, a cross-design synthesis may help.

☐ *A Complementary Set of Designs*

By definition, complementary designs provide different strengths. A design complementary to randomized studies would be one that inherently provides greater coverage of patients or treatment implementations—or both. Certain large-scale databases capture the full range of relevant patients and typical treatment implementations (see Table 25.1). An example is the National Cancer Institute's SEER (Surveillance, Epidemiology, and End Results) database, which includes treatment and survival information on almost all cancer patients living in five states and four metropolitan areas (Hankey, Ries, Miller, & Kosary, 1992). An analysis of such a database could describe outcomes for patients who received specified treatments—thus depicting the results of the full range of implementations occurring in day-to-day practice. Of course, such an analysis is vulnerable with respect to internal validity because patients were not randomly assigned to alternative treatments; thus the goal of a database analysis must be to elucidate and minimize selection bias.

☐ *Strategies for Combining Results*

Drawing upon studies with complementary strengths can potentially provide improved information relative to relying upon a single study—or even multiple studies that share the same weakness(es). Of course, one cannot simply assume that it is justifiable to average together results from studies with different designs: There is no reason to expect that this would magically preserve the strengths of the different designs while counteracting their varied weaknesses (Staines, 1974). On the contrary, a successful cross-design synthesis requires the development of an appropriate strategy. The specific strategy will vary according to the goal(s) of the synthesis. For example, the main goal of a synthesis may be to expand patient coverage beyond that provided in existing randomized studies (see GAO, 1992). Alternatively, the main goal might be to extend coverage of treatment implementations to the typical treatments given in day-to-day practice, as was the case in the breast-conservation application (GAO, 1994). A more complex synthesis might expand coverage of both patients and treatment implementations.

■ *Four-Step Strategy in the Breast Cancer Application*

The GAO (1994) study of breast conservation versus mastectomy provides an illustration of synthesis strategy. Here, the generalizability issue concerned the quality of breast-conservation therapy in day-to-day practice. The basic approach was to summarize existing randomized studies in a meta-analysis and compare results to a new analysis of the SEER database. The goal was to minimize cross-design differences except for differences in the quality of treatment implementation—thus isolating the impact of any difference in quality on patient survival. The specific strategy consisted of the following four steps.

□ *Step 1: Defining the Synthesis Domain*

Step 1 defined a limited "synthesis domain" so that the SEER analysis and the meta-analysis would focus on the same type of treatments, similar patients, and the same outcome measure.[6] An initial literature review indicated that the dominant form of breast-conservation therapy consisted of lumpectomy plus nodal dissection plus radiation;[7] GAO limited the synthesis to studies comparing this form of breast-conservation therapy with mastectomy.[8] Six randomized studies met this domain requirement, as well as additional criteria.[9] Three were single-center studies and three were multicenter studies—a relevant distinction, because quality may differ. Notably, single-center studies may be conducted at premier institutions (such as the National Cancer Institute), whereas multicenter studies can involve "community surgeons." [10]

Figure 25.1 summarizes the coverage provided by the six randomized studies. The synthesis aimed to extend the randomized studies' results to unshaded areas of the figure—in particular, to cells under the heading "average quality: day-to-day practice." SEER cases appropriate for the analyses covered most—but not all—of the patient groups included in the randomized studies. The synthesis domain was therefore limited to patient groups covered by both types of studies (see cells marked "SEER - yes" in Figure 25.2).[11] With respect to length of follow-up, only 5 years were available for SEER lumpectomy patients; follow-up was longer in randomized studies. A common end point for the synthesis was selected: 5-year survival.

In sum, Step 1 ensured that the synthesis would include only those patients, treatments, and outcome measure(s) that were adequately covered *both* in randomized studies and in the SEER analysis. Thus, provided that selection bias could be minimized in the database analysis, a *difference* between the treatment effects observed in the meta-analyses and in the database analysis would suggest that implementation of breast-conservation therapy in day-to-day practice differed from that of randomized studies—and affected patient survival. By contrast, *similar* effects in the meta-analyses and the database analysis would support the generalizability of the randomized studies.

With respect to conclusion criteria, it was recognized, first, that the probabilistic nature of medical studies precludes proving identical effects; second, that very large samples are required to detect very small differ-

Types of Patients/ Subjects	Treatment Implementation: Differing Type and Quality			
	Breast conservation = lumpectomy + nodal dissection + radiation			Other types
	Single-center studies (Potentially highest quality)	Multi-center Studies (Presumably high quality)	Average quality: day-to-day practice	
age 30 to 70				
tumor =< 2 cm				
tumor 2+ to 4 cm				
node-negative				
node-positive				
age > 70				
tumor > 4 cm				

Figure 25.1. Randomized Studies' Coverage of Patients and Treatments
NOTE: The shaded cells represent the "patient-treatment domain" covered by an existing set of randomized studies.

ences in survival rates; and third, that the sample sizes of available studies are limited.[12] Thus the GAO report avoided terming results "identical" and instead used the word "similar" or the phrase "no appreciable difference." Even these terms were used only when the observed difference in survival rates was both (a) not statistically significant and (b) of an absolute value smaller than 1.5 percentage points (GAO, 1994, pp. 28-30).

Types of Patients/ Subjects	Treatment Implementation: Differing Type and Quality			
	Breast conservation = lumpectomy + nodal dissection + radiation			Other types
	Single-center studies (Potentially highest quality)	Multi-center Studies (Presumably high quality)	Average quality: day-to-day practice	
age 30 to 70			SEER - yes	
tumor =< 2 cm			SEER - yes	
tumor 2+ to 4 cm			SEER - yes	
node-negative			SEER - yes	
node-positive	no	no	SEER - no	
age > 70	NA	NA		
tumor > 4 cm	NA	NA		

Figure 25.2. Coverage in the Breast Conservation Synthesis

☐ *Step 2: Meta-Analyses of Randomized Studies*

Step 2 included meta-analyses for the six randomized studies and for two subgroups of studies that might differ in terms of quality of treatment implementation (see Table 25.2).[13] In each of these meta-analyses, the odds ratio proved to be not significant and the actual difference in 5-year survival (following the two treatments) was never as large as 1.5 percent-

TABLE 25.2 Meta-Analyses: Treatment Effects for Single- and Multicenter Studies

	5-Year Survival Rates[a] for		Difference in Rates	Common Odds Ratio[b]	
	Breast-Conservation Patients (%)	Mastectomy Patients (%)	Breast Conservation Minus Mastectomy (%)	Estimate	Confidence Interval
Single-center studies					
U.S.-NCI, Milan, France	93.7	93.7	0.0	1.00	.55 to 1.79
Multicenter studies					
Denmark, EORTC, U.S.-NSABP	89	88	1	1.07	.79 to 1.44
Omitting U.S.-NSABP	88	88	0	1.05	.72 to 1.53
All six studies	90	90	0	1.05	.81 to 1.38
Five studies (omitting NSABP)	91	90	0[c]	1.03	.75 to 1.42

SOURCE: U.S. General Accounting Office (1994, Table 3, p. 9), node-negative patients only.

a. Weighted average survival rate. In calculating this rate for breast-conservation patients, the size of the total study (relative to the total size of all relevant studies) was used as the weight; the same is true for the weighted average for mastectomy patients. For three studies, "effective *ns*" were used (U.S. General Accounting Office, 1994, App. I). When survival rates for all component studies were available to the nearest tenth of a percentage point, the survival estimate is reported to the nearest tenth of a percent. Survival rates for one study were available only to the nearest whole percentage; survival estimates involving this study are rounded to the nearest whole percentage.

b. The odds ratio is defined here as the odds of surviving (to not surviving) for breast-conservation therapy divided by the odds of surviving (to not surviving) for mastectomy. A ratio below 1 favors mastectomy; a ratio larger than 1 favors breast-conservation therapy.

c. Before being rounded to the nearest whole percentage, the 5-year survival estimates for the five studies combined were 90.5% and 90.3%, with a difference of 0.2% These figures rounded to 91%, 90%, and a difference of 0 percentage points.

age points. Thus randomized studies' results for the two treatments were deemed "similar."

☐ *Step 3: SEER Database Analysis*

In Step 3 (the database analysis), the main goal was to elucidate and minimize the impact of "selection bias." This step began with prediction of which patients would select/receive breast conservation and which would select mastectomy. A logistic regression defined the "propensity score" (Rosenbaum & Rubin, 1984) for each patient, that is, her propensity to receive breast conservation. Patients most likely to receive breast conservation were younger, had smaller tumors, and resided in areas (such as San Francisco) where lumpectomies were relatively common. Patients least likely to receive breast conservation were older, had larger tumors, and resided in "low lumpectomy" areas.

The propensity scores defined 5 quintiles of patients (Rosenbaum & Rubin, 1984)—with quintile 1 consisting of those who were least likely to receive breast conservation and quintile 5 consisting of those most likely to receive it. Within each quintile, breast-conservation patients were similar to mastectomy patients—at least in terms of measured variables that affect selection.

For each quintile, Table 25.3 shows (a) the 5-year survival rate for breast-conservation patients and (b) the corresponding rate for mastectomy patients. The bottom row shows survival rates "adjusted across quintiles." The "adjusted across quintiles" estimate of 86.3% was obtained by averaging the separate quintile survival estimates for breast-conservation patients—with each quintile receiving a one-fifth weight (although there were fewer breast-conservation patients in quintile 1 than quintile 5). Analogous procedures were used to calculate the adjusted mastectomy survival rate of 86.9%. The adjusted rates differ by less than 1.5 percentage points, and the odds ratio (.94) is not significant (GAO, 1994, p. 13).

Factors that argue for the minimization of bias in the SEER database analysis include the following: (a) the relative homogeneity of the patients included in the synthesis domain (node-negative, nonelderly, with tumors 4 cm or less), (b) the statistical controls (quintiles), and (c) the fact that the decision between breast conservation and mastectomy seems, in many cases, to be determined mainly by patient or physician preferences (see Tarbox, Rockwood, & Abernathy, 1992). Thus GAO deemed average 5-year survival in day-to-day practice to be "similar" after breast conservation and mastectomy.[14]

☐ *Step 4: Cross-Design Comparisons*

Step 4 consisted mainly of the cross-design comparison of treatment effects. As detailed in the GAO (1994) report, the odds ratios calculated

TABLE 25.3 Treatment Effect Estimated for SEER Cases, by Quintile

Quintile	Treatment	Number of Node-Negative Patients	5-Year Survival (%) Estimate[a]	Standard Error[b]
1	breast conservation	56	85.6	4.7
	mastectomy	1,008	86.7	1.1
2	breast conservation	106	82.8	3.7
	mastectomy	964	83.4	1.2
3	breast conservation	193	85.2	2.6
	mastectomy	866	88.8	1.1
4	breast conservation	289	88.7	1.9
	mastectomy	778	87.3	1.2
5	breast conservation	462	89.0	1.4
	mastectomy	604	88.5	1.3
Adjusted across quintiles[c]	breast conservation	1,106	86.3	1.4
	mastectomy	4,220	86.9	0.5

SOURCE: U.S. General Accounting Office (1994, Table 5, p. 12).

a. Each estimate shown for a specific treatment and quintile represents a weighted average, calculated to adjust for minor differences between breast-conservation and mastectomy patients within each quintile (see U.S. General Accounting Office, 1994, App. I).

b. Standard errors were calculated as specified in Mosteller and Tukey (1977).

c. The "adjusted across quintiles" survival estimate for breast-conservation patients (86.3%) was obtained by averaging the survival estimates for breast-conservation patients in the five quintiles—with each of the five estimates receiving an equal (one-fifth) weight. The corresponding estimate for mastectomy patients (86.9%) was obtained in the same way.

for the randomized single-center and multicenter studies were not significantly different from the odds ratio from the SEER analysis; also, the *difference* between survival rates for the breast-conservation and mastectomy patients in randomized studies and the *difference* for the SEER patients were within 1.5 percentage points of each other.

Also in Step 4, survival rates were calculated with both treatment groups combined. These "overall" rates were then compared. The result was that rates for day-to-day practice (SEER) and for multicenter randomized studies met GAO's criteria for "similar" results in the two types of studies. However, the highest survival rates were found for patients in single-center randomized studies.

■ Conclusion

There are two main conclusions. First, with respect to breast cancer therapy, the evidence available for this synthesis pointed toward the similarity of average patient survival following breast conservation and mastectomy—in day-to-day practice as well as in randomized studies. Second, with respect to the new and still evolving method of cross-design synthesis, it is clear that, in certain instances, drawing on more than one type of study can tell us more about how well treatments work than a single type of study can.

■ Notes

1. Two designs are complementary if the strength of one occurs in an area where the other is weak, and vice versa.

2. Under prerandomization, at the same time the physician tells the patient about the study, he or she specifies which treatment the patient will receive if she participates. This appeared to help enrollment a great deal (Fisher et al., 1985), but perhaps not enough. In 1994, one center of that large U.S. study was charged with fraud, and the fraud at issue concerned letting women into the study who technically did not qualify. At least one European randomized study of breast cancer surgery also used prerandomization (Blichert-Toft et al., 1992). Prerandomization has been criticized on ethical and scientific grounds (Ellenberg, 1984).

3. When the results of a large U.S. study of breast conservation had been published, patients as well as physicians learned of the results—and a large German study dropped its randomization component because patient recruitment had become too difficult (Rauschecker et al., 1990, 1992).

4. "Breast-conservation therapy involves a number of physician decisions not required for mastectomy" (GAO, 1994, p. 2).

5. Of course, such factors do not apply to all treatments—for example, a centrally produced pill or a drug administered at a specified dose in a hospital. In such cases, the generalizability issue would logically pertain mainly (or only) to the patient/subject dimension.

6. Here, the type of treatment is considered separately from the quality of the treatment implementation.

7. *Nodal dissection* refers to the removal of lymph nodes beneath the arm adjacent to the breast with the cancer. Radiation is directed to the breast on which the lumpectomy is conducted.

8. This form of breast conservation was recommended by an NIH Consensus Conference (National Institutes of Health, 1991).

9. The main additional criteria were as follows: randomization; the absence of confounding treatments, such as administration of an additional therapy to one treatment group but not the other; and the availability of 5-year survival rates by treatment group among node-negative patients. Few cases in these studies were lost to follow-up over the years; those that were, were handled through actuarial estimates (see GAO, 1994, Table 2, n. c, p. 7).

10. In addition, one expert points to potential problems of research quality control in multicenter studies, as contrasted to single-center studies (Pocock, 1983). Thus there appears to be a possibility of higher treatment quality in single-center studies compared with multicenter studies.

11. Node-positive patients were excluded because SEER did not record the number of lymph nodes to which the cancer had spread; control for "number of positive nodes" was not possible.

12. Almost 2,500 node-negative patients were included in the randomized studies and more than 5,000 node-negative patients were included in the SEER database analysis. However, much larger numbers are required for very small differences to be found "statistically significant." That is, the power to detect a relatively small difference, using conventional statistical criteria, would be fairly low.

13. GAO's meta-analyses of randomized studies used Mantel and Haenszel's (1959) method, the variance estimation method of Robins, Breslow, and Greenland (1986), and the STAT XACT program produced by Cytel Software of Cambridge, Massachusetts. All odds ratios were based on 5-year survival results obtained for each study.

14. Inspection of the quintile-by-quintile results in Table 25.3 suggests the possibility that some of the patients who were less likely to receive lumpectomy may have fared better with mastectomy; however, none of the differences are significant.

■ *References*

Blichert-Toft, M., Rose, C., Anderson, J. A., Overgaard, M., Axelsson, C. A., & Anderson, K. W. (1992). Danish randomized trial comparing breast conservation therapy with mastectomy: Six years of life-table analysis. *Journal of the National Cancer Institute Monographs, 11,* 19-25.

Droitcour, J. A., Silberman, G., & Chelimsky, E. (1993). Cross design synthesis: A new form of meta-analysis for combining results from randomized clinical trials and medical-practice databases. *International Journal of Technology Assessment in Health Care, 9,* 440-449.

Ellenberg, S. S. (1984). Special report: Randomization designs in comparative clinical trials. *New England Journal of Medicine, 310,* 1404-1408.

Fisher, B., Bauer, M., Margolese, R., Poisson, R., Pilch, Y., & Redmond, C. (1985). Five-year results of a randomized clinical trial comparing total mastectomy and segmental mastectomy with or without radiation in the treatment of breast cancer. *New England Journal of Medicine, 312,* 665-673.

Hankey, B. F., Ries, L. A. G., Miller, B. A., & Kosary, C. L. (1992). Overview. In B. A. Miller, L. A. G. Ries, B. F. Hankey, C. L. Kosary, & B. K. Edwards (Eds.), *Cancer statistics review, 1973-1989* (NIH Publication No. 92-2789) (pp. I.2-I.17). Bethesda, MD: National Institutes of Health.

Hlatky, M. A. (1991). Using databases to evaluate therapy. *Statistics in Medicine, 10,* 647-652.

Lucas, M. J., Mitchell, A., & Lee, E. C. G. (1984). Failure to enter patients to randomized study of surgery for breast cancer. *Lancet, 2,* 921-922.

Mantel, N., & Haenszel, W. (1959). Statistical aspects of the analysis of data from retrospective studies of disease. *Journal of the National Cancer Institute, 22,* 719-748.

McDonald, C. (1991). [Letter to the editor]. *British Medical Journal, 302,* 1271.

Mosteller, F., & Tukey, J. W. (1977). *Data analysis and regression.* Reading, MA: Addison-Wesley.

National Institutes of Health. (1991). Early-stage breast cancer: NIH consensus conference. *Journal of the American Medical Association, 265,* 391-395.

Peckham, M. J., Tobias, J. S., & Houghton, J. (1984). Recruitment to breast cancer trials [Letter to the editor]. *Lancet, 2,* 1460.

Pocock, S. (1983). *Clinical trials: A practical approach.* New York: John Wiley.

Rauschecker, H. F., Gatzemeier, W., Sauer, R., Seegenschmiedt, M. H., Schauer, A., & Ummenhofer, L. (1992). Erste ergebnisse des projekts der Deutschen Brustkrebs-Studerngruppe (GBSG) zur "Brusterhaltenden therapie des kleinnen mammacarcinoms." *Chirurg, 63,* 495-500.

Rauschecker, H. F., Gatzemeier, W., Schumacher, M., Sauerbrei, W., Schmoor, C., & Sauer, R. (1990). The German breast preservation trial: Concept and first results related to structural relationship of various prognostic factors. *Tumordiagnostik und Therapie, 11,* 243-248.

Robins, J., Breslow, N., & Greenland, S. (1986). Estimators of the Mantel-Haenszel variance consistent in both sparse data and large-strata limiting models. *Biometrics, 42,* 311-323.

Rosenbaum, P. R., & Rubin, D. B. (1984). Reducing bias in observational studies using subclassification on the propensity score. *Journal of the American Statistical Association, 79,* 516-524.

Rubin, D. B. (1990). A new perspective. In K. W. Wachter & M. L. Straf (Eds.), *The future of meta-analysis.* New York: Russell Sage Foundation.

Stablein, D. M. (1994). *A reanalysis of NSABP Protocol B06: Final report.* Potomac, MD: Emmes Corporation.

Staines, G. L. (1974). The strategic combination argument. In W. Leinfellner & E. Kohler (Eds.), *Developments in the methodology of social science.* Boston: Reidel.

Stewart, H. J., & Robinson, S. M. (1984). Recruitment to breast cancer trials. *Lancet, 2,* 1096-1097.

Tarbox, B. B., Rockwood, J. K., & Abernathy, C. M. (1992). Are modified radical mastectomies done for T1 breast cancers because of surgeons' advice or patients' choice? *American Journal of Surgery, 164,* 417-422.

U.S. General Accounting Office (GAO). (1992). *Cross design synthesis: A new strategy for medical effectiveness research* (GAO/PEMD-92-18). Washington, DC: Author.

U.S. General Accounting Office (GAO). (1994). *Breast conservation versus mastectomy: Patient survival in day-to-day medical practice and in randomized studies* (GAO/PEMD-95-9). Washington, DC: Author.

Zelen, M. (1979). A new design for randomized clinical trials. *New England Journal of Medicine, 300,* 1242-1245.

26

Research Synthesis for Public Health Policy

Experience of the Institute of Medicine

Michael A. Stoto

In two recent examples, the Institute of Medicine of the U.S. National Academy of Sciences has developed and applied new techniques for research synthesis to help clarify politically charged policy issues. In both cases, the U.S. Congress has acted based on concern that people are dying, in one case because of exposure to chemicals and in the other because of vaccines.

For nearly three decades, concerns have lingered over the health effects of veterans' exposure to Agent Orange and other herbicides used in the Vietnam War. More than 19 million gallons of herbicides were sprayed over South Vietnam between 1962 and 1971 before reports of health effects in laboratory animals ended the spraying. Since that time, some of the 3 million Americans who served in or near Vietnam have come to suspect that their exposure to herbicides caused them to develop cancer or their children to have birth defects. Their concern has spawned thousands of scientific studies on the health effects of herbicides and of dioxin, which contaminated two-thirds of the herbicides used in Vietnam. Yet veterans and their families face continuing uncertainty about whether exposure to herbicides has led to past health problems or could lead to problems in the future. Recognizing this uncertainty, the U.S. Congress passed the Agent Orange Act of 1991. That legislation required the National Academy of Sciences to review the available scientific and medical evidence regarding this issue. Based on the review, the Department of Veterans Affairs (DVA) was charged with determining whether any Vietnam veterans should receive compensation for diseases related to their military service.

Childhood immunization has been one of the most effective public health measures of the twentieth century. It prevents many diseases that in the past accounted for staggering morbidity and mortality. However, serious neurological side effects and even death in some children in the early 1980s led some parents to refuse vaccinations for their children. Some parents sued vaccine manufacturers, which led some companies to curtail vaccine research, development, and production. In response, Congress passed the National Childhood Vaccine Injury Act (NCVIA) in 1986 to encourage vaccine production by creating a no-fault compensation program for children who are injured by vaccines. To inform decisions about which injuries should be compensated, the NCVIA called upon the Institute of Medicine to study the evidence bearing on the adverse effects of childhood vaccines.

■ The Role of the Institute of Medicine

In both these cases, the Institute of Medicine (IOM) was called upon by government agencies that must decide whether to compensate individuals who feel they have been harmed. As a nongovernmental agency, the IOM cannot decide compensation, but it can assess and summarize the existing scientific evidence to inform the federal agencies charged with these decisions. In both projects the IOM used meta-analysis for combining statistical information wherever possible. The IOM's responses to these two congressional mandates are contained in four reports (Institute of Medicine, 1991, 1993, 1994, 1996).

The National Academy of Sciences (NAS) is a unique private institution charged with advising the U.S. government on matters of science and public policy. It was originally chartered by Congress in 1863 to provide a mechanism for eminent scientists and engineers to "investigate, examine, experiment, and report upon any subject of science or art" requested by the government. The IOM was chartered in 1970 by the NAS to enlist distinguished medical and other professionals to study issues that affect public health. Like NAS, the IOM conducts studies on particular topics and has a distinguished elected membership.

All IOM studies are carried out by expert volunteer committees appointed specifically for that purpose. Committee members are chosen to avoid conflicts of interest relative to the subjects of particular reports. These committees generally meet in closed sessions to consider the evidence and prepare findings and recommendations. All findings must be fully documented in written reports, and an appointed panel of expert reviewers ensures that the findings are consistent with the data in the reports. This process preserves the committee's independence and produces clear thinking about the problem.

■ *The IOM's Approach to Evaluating the Evidence*

For both Agent Orange and vaccines, there was scientific evidence to establish the plausibility of the health risks in question. Some herbicides used in Vietnam contained dioxin. Dioxin's potential to cause a skin disease called chloracne was recognized in 1957, and in the early 1970s, animal studies showed that the drugs caused reproductive problems. Toxicological data showed that dioxin caused a variety of cancers in different species, and that it had strong hormonal effects. Data also showed that a cellular receptor for dioxin in animals and humans was responsible for most of the effects of dioxin. The toxicologic data did not prove that Vietnam veterans' exposure to the herbicides caused the particular cancers and other health effects that they were experiencing. Similarly, studies indicated that adverse effects of childhood vaccines were plausible, but did not establish causality. The most politically compelling evidence concerning both herbicides and vaccines came from the reports of individual veterans and children (or their families, friends, and physicians) who believed their illnesses were due to Agent Orange or vaccines.

Both committees did systematic searches of the scientific literature bearing on their charges. In addition, the interested groups that carefully followed both issues were asked to submit material. Given the need to make statements about health effects in particular individuals, both committees focused on epidemiological data rather than animal data. The vaccine committee also systematically identified and interpreted individual case reports.

For a few disease and adverse events, the committees could identify enough studies to use quantitative meta-analytic techniques. Mostly, however, the nature and level of exposure (to herbicides, dioxin, or vaccines) and the health outcomes varied too much over studies to allow quantitative combination of results. Unlike most scientific reviews, the committees started from a neutral position, presuming neither that there is no association unless proven nor that there is an association unless disproved. They found that the best approach to synthesizing the available research for policy makers was to construct categories of outcomes for which the strength of the evidence was similar, and present the results in these terms.

☐ *Agent Orange Results*

After reviewing thousands of studies, the Agent Orange committee focused on about 265 epidemiological studies. Most of these were not of Vietnam veterans but of people exposed to herbicides or dioxin on their jobs or through the environment, for example, because of a nearby industrial accident. The legislation calling for the Agent Orange study set out a standard for the DVA to use in deciding compensation and a process for making such determinations after the IOM report was completed. The standard was that if credible scientific evidence for an *association* outweighed that against an association, the DVA should determine that a disease was service connected and thus deserved compensation. To integrate the results of the review and to present clear, policy relevant results, the committee presented its findings in four categories:

■ *Sufficient evidence of an association.* Evidence is sufficient to conclude that there is a positive association between herbicides and the outcome in studies in which chance, bias, and confounding could be ruled out with reasonable confidence. For example, several small studies that are free from bias and confounding and that show an association that is consistent in magnitude and direction may be sufficient evidence for an association. The committee found sufficient evidence of association between exposure to herbicides or dioxin and soft-tissue sarcoma, non-Hodgkin's lymphoma, Hodgkin's disease, and chloracne, an acnelike skin disorder.

- *Limited/suggestive evidence of an association.* Evidence is suggestive of an association between herbicides and the outcome but is limited because chance, bias, and confounding could not be ruled out. For example, at least one high-quality study shows a positive association, but other studies are inconsistent. The committee found limited or suggestive evidence of association between exposure to herbicides and respiratory cancers, prostate cancer, multiple myeloma, and spina bifida.

- *Inadequate/insufficient evidence to determine whether an association exists.* Available studies are of insufficient quality, consistency, or statistical power to infer the presence or absence of an association. For example, studies fail to control for confounding, have inadequate exposure assessment, or fail to address latency. Most of the outcomes fell into this category.

- *Limited/suggestive evidence of no association.* Several adequate studies, covering the levels of exposure that humans encounter, all fail to show a positive association between exposure to herbicides and outcome. A conclusion of "no association" is inevitably limited to the conditions, level of exposure, and length of observation covered by available studies. The committee found that a sufficient number and variety of well-designed studies exist to conclude that there is limited or suggestive evidence of no association between the herbicides or dioxin and gastrointestinal tumors, bladder cancer, and brain tumors.

The assignment of diseases to one of these categories required substantial judgment and group deliberation in which the committee compared diseases in the same group and considered whether the evidence was similar. The committee focused on the evidence as a whole rather than on each specific study, although the quality of all relevant studies was reviewed, and better studies were given more weight.

Most of the evidence the committee reviewed came from studies of people exposed in their jobs or by industrial accidents. These exposures often were at high levels and for long periods of time. Getting a clear picture of the health risks for Vietnam veterans was hard because the levels of exposure were extremely wide-ranging. Indeed, whereas most veterans probably had low exposure, some may have experienced levels as high as that of occupational or agricultural exposure. It is uncertain how many and which veterans were exposed to higher levels.

☐ *Vaccine Safety Results*

The charge to the vaccine safety committee concerned causality more than association. The committee judged whether each of a set of adverse events was caused by exposure to a particular vaccine. These judgments have quantitative and qualitative aspects. They reflect the nature of the exposures, events, and populations at issue; the characteristics of the evidence examined; and the approach taken to evaluate that evidence. The exposures—vaccinations—are widespread in the population, so absence of exposure may itself require explanation in interpreting studies. The adverse events under consideration by the committee are mostly rare in the exposed population, and can occur in the absence of vaccination. Some are clinically ill defined, or without known causes. Such features raise difficulties for the investigation and evaluation evidence.

The committee considered three kinds of causal questions about adverse events that may be caused by a vaccine:

1. *Can the vaccine cause the event, at least in certain people and circumstances?* This question was the main focus of the committee's work. The committee examined controlled epidemiological studies, using standard criteria for assessing causality: strength of association, analytic bias, biological gradient (dose response), statistical significance, consistency, and biological plausibility and coherence.

2. *In a vaccine recipient who developed the event, did the vaccine cause it?* This question came into play rarely in the few instances in which carefully prepared individual case reports provided convincing evidence.

3. *Will the next vaccine recipient develop the event? Or, how frequently will vaccine recipients develop the event?* The committee addressed this question as the data permitted.

The committee assigned each vaccine-adverse event pair to one of the following five categories, according to the strength of the evidence that this relationship is causal:

1. There is no evidence (other than biological plausibility).
2. The evidence is inadequate.
3. The evidence favors rejection of causal relation
4. The evidence favors acceptance of causal relation.
5. The evidence establishes a causal relation.

The committee found that available evidence established a causal relation between anaphylaxis and vaccines for pertussis, measles and mumps, hepatitis, and tetanus toxoid; between protracted, inconsolable crying and pertussis vaccine; between acute arthritis and rubella vaccine; between thrombocytopenia and the vaccine for measles, mumps, and rubella; and between polio and polio vaccines or these vaccines' recipients' contacts. The committee also found evidence that favors the acceptance of a causal relation between diphtheria, pertussis, and tetanus vaccine (DPT) and acute, and in some cases chronic, encephalopathy. These adverse events were rare, however. The committee also found that data on DPT and sudden infant death syndrome favored rejection of a causal relation.

◼ Conclusions

The Institute of Medicine did not make judgments about individual injuries or appropriate compensation for Vietnam veterans or vaccine recipients. Rather, the committees provided information that government agencies could use to do so. For most of the health effects studied, the committees felt that the evidence was not sufficient to determine whether associations exist. The committees did not take the standard scientific approach, which usually starts from the assumption of no relation and asks that an association be proved. Nor did they take the approach often taken by people who feel that they are the victims of some toxic exposure and ask that the responsible parties disprove the putative association. By adopting the approach they used, the committees were able to concentrate on evaluating the science—which was their expertise—rather than applying their values to the question of whether people deserved compensation. Because the evidence remains uncertain in many cases, decisions about compensation are inevitably, and appropriately, social and political.

Over the years, extreme views have evolved on Agent Orange and vaccine safety. The IOM committees found a middle ground, developed through an extensive review of the scientific literature, that there does appear to be a link between exposure to the herbicides used in Vietnam and a few diseases, and that rare adverse effects may be caused by childhood vaccines. One way that the IOM was able to achieve this was by choosing committees with appropriate disciplinary expertise but no commitments to prior positions in studying dioxin, Agent Orange, or adverse vaccine effects. The IOM has been criticized for excluding scientists with experience in studying these subjects. It does involve such scientists in hearings, testimony, and other venues; but those scientists have not resolved these controversies in other settings, and achieving consensus (a hallmark of IOM committees) would have been difficult if they had been included. I believe that the IOM's results support the validity of its approach, as does the acceptance of the report by both the government agencies and the concerned parties. The IOM's reports are comprehensive, scientific reviews of available evidence. They will not end these controversies, but perhaps they can provide an agreed-upon base of information from which research and policy can proceed.

■ *References*

Institute of Medicine. (1991). *Adverse effects of pertussis and rubella vaccines.* Washington: National Academy Press.

Institute of Medicine. (1993). *Adverse events associated with childhood vaccines: Evidence bearing on causality.* Washington: National Academy Press.

Institute of Medicine. (1994). *Veterans and Agent Orange: Health effects of herbicides used in Vietnam.* Washington: National Academy Press.

Institute of Medicine. (1996). *Veterans and Agent Orange: Update 1996.* Washington: National Academy Press.

27

Empowerment Evaluation
and Accreditation in
Higher Education

David M. Fetterman

One measure of the power and credibility of an evaluative approach is the degree to which it is adopted in high-stakes assessments and forms of accountability. This chapter highlights a case in point. I begin with an overview of empowerment evaluation and then present a brief case study of this approach as it has been adopted in an accreditation self-study. This accreditation study was considered a high-stakes event in higher education for all parties involved, including the accrediting agency. I conclude the discussion with a few additional considerations, including the relationship between internal and external evaluation.

■ *Empowerment Evaluation*

Empowerment evaluation is an innovative approach to evaluation. It has been adopted in higher education, government, inner-city public education, nonprofit corporations, and foundations throughout the United States and abroad. Many program and policy sectors use empowerment evaluation, including those involving substance abuse prevention, HIV prevention, crime prevention, welfare reform, battered women's shelters, agriculture and rural development, adult probation, adolescent pregnancy prevention, tribal partnership for substance abuse, self-determination for individuals with disabilities, doctoral programs, and accelerated schools. Descriptions of programs that use empowerment evaluation appear in *Empowerment Evaluation: Knowledge and Tools for Self-Assessment and Accountability* (Fetterman, Kaftarian, & Wandersman, 1996).[1]

Empowerment evaluation is the use of evaluation concepts, techniques, and findings to foster improvement and self-determination. It employs both qualitative and quantitative methodologies. Although it can be applied to individuals, organizations,[2] communities, and societies or cultures, the focus is usually on programs. Empowerment evaluation has an unambiguous value orientation—it is designed to help people help themselves and improve their programs using a form of self-evaluation and reflection. Program participants—including clients—conduct their own evaluations; an outside evaluator often serves as a coach or additional facilitator, depending on internal program capabilities.

Empowerment evaluation is necessarily a collaborative group activity, not an individual pursuit. An evaluator does not and cannot empower anyone; people empower themselves, often with assistance and coaching. This process is fundamentally democratic in the sense that it invites (if not demands) participation, examining issues of concern to the entire community in an open forum.

As a result, the context changes: the assessment of a program's value and worth is not the end point of the evaluation—as it often is in traditional evaluation—but is part of an ongoing process of program improvement. This new context acknowledges a simple but often overlooked truth: that merit and worth are not static values. Populations shift, goals shift, knowledge about program practices and their value changes, and external forces are highly unstable. Through the internalization and institutionalization of self-evaluation processes and practices, a dynamic and responsive approach to evaluation can be developed to accommodate these shifts. Both value assessments and corresponding plans for program improvement—developed by the group with the assistance of a trained evaluator—are subject to a cyclical process of reflection and self-evaluation. Program participants learn to assess their progress continually toward self-determined goals, and to reshape their plans and strategies according to this assessment. In the process, self-determination is fostered, illumination generated, and liberation actualized.

Value assessments are also highly sensitive to the life cycle of the program or organization. Goals and outcomes are geared toward the appropriate developmental level of implementation. Extraordinary improvements are not expected of a project that will not be fully implemented until the following year. Similarly, seemingly small gains or improvements in programs at an embryonic stage are recognized and appreciated in relation to their stage of development. In a fully operational and mature program, moderate improvements or declining outcomes are viewed more critically.

■ *Pursuit of Truth and Honesty*

Empowerment evaluation is guided by many principles. One of the most important of these is a commitment to truth and honesty. This is not a naive concept of one absolute truth, but a sincere intent to understand an event in context and from multiple worldviews. The aim is to try to understand what is going on in a situation from the participant's own perspective as accurately and honestly as possible and then proceed to improve it with meaningful goals and strategies and credible documentation. There are many checks and balances in empowerment evaluation, such as having a democratic approach to participation—involving participants at all levels of the organization, relying on external evaluators as critical friends, and so on.

Empowerment evaluation is like a personnel performance self-appraisal. You come to an agreement with your supervisor about your goals, strategies for accomplishing those goals, and credible documentation to determine whether or not you are meeting your goals. The same kind of agreement is made between evaluator and clients in empowerment evaluation. In a personnel performance self-appraisal, if the data are not credible, you lose your credibility immediately. If the data merit it at the end of the year, you can use them to advocate for yourself. Empowerment evaluation applies the same approach to the program and community level. Advocacy, in this context, becomes a natural by-product of the self-evaluation process—if the data merit it. Advocacy is meaningless in the absence of credible data. In addition, external standards and/or requirements can significantly influence any self-evaluation. To operate without consideration of these external forces is to proceed at one's own peril. However, the process must be grounded in an authentic understanding and expression of everyday life at the program or community level. A commitment to the ideals of truth and honesty guides every facet and step of empowerment evaluation.

■ Facets of Empowerment Evaluation

In this new context, training, facilitation, advocacy, illumination, and liberation are all facets—if not developmental stages—of empowerment evaluation. Rather than additional roles for an evaluator, whose primary function is to assess worth (as defined by Scriven, 1967; Stufflebeam, 1994), these facets are an integral part of the evaluation process. Cronbach's developmental focus is relevant: The emphasis is on program development, improvement, and lifelong learning (Cronbach et al., 1980; see also Patton, 1994).

■ Steps of Empowerment Evaluation

There are several pragmatic steps involved in helping others learn to evaluate their own programs: (a) taking stock or determining where the program stands, including strengths and weaknesses; (b) focusing on establishing goals—determining where the program wants to go in the future, with an explicit emphasis on program improvement; (c) developing strategies and helping participants determine their own strategies to accomplish program goals and objectives; and (d) helping program participants determine the type of evidence required to document progress credibly toward their goals.

Dynamic Community of Learners

Many elements must be in place for empowerment evaluation to be
effective and credible. Participants must have the latitude to experiment,
taking both risks and responsibility for their actions. An environment
conducive to sharing successes and failures is also essential. In addition,
an honest, self-critical, trusting, and supportive atmosphere is required.
Conditions need not be perfect to initiate this process. However, the
accuracy and usefulness of self-ratings improve dramatically in this
context. An outside evaluator who is charged with monitoring the process
can help keep the effort credible, useful, and on track, providing additional
rigor, reality checks, and quality controls throughout the evaluation.
Without any of these elements in place, the exercise may be of limited
utility and potentially self-serving. With many of these elements in place,
the exercise can create a dynamic community of transformative learning.

The Institute: A Case Example

The California Institute of Integral Studies has adopted an empowerment
evaluation approach as a tool to institutionalize evaluation as part of the
planning and management of operations. Empowerment evaluation is a
form of self-evaluation that is designed to foster program improvement
and self-determination (instead of dependence). It has two parts: The first
is focused on examining and assessing the merit of a unit; the second is
designed to establish goals and strategies to improve program practice.
This second stage is part of strategic planning and is built on the foundation of program evaluation.

All units in the Institute—including academic, governance, and administrative units—have conducted self-evaluations. The purpose of
these self-evaluations is to improve operations and build a base for
planning and decision making. In addition to focusing on improvement,
these self-evaluations contribute to institutional accountability.

Workshops were conducted throughout the Institute to provide training in evaluation techniques and procedures. All unit heads attended the
training sessions, which were held over 3 days. They served as facilitators
in their own groups. Training and individual technical assistance were
also provided throughout the year for governance and other administrative

groups, including the Office of the President and the Development Office (see the appendix to this chapter for additional detail).

The self-evaluation process required thoughtful reflection and inquiry. The units described their purposes and listed approximately 10 key unit activities that characterized their units. Members of the units democratically determined the top 10 activities that merit consideration and evaluation. Then each member of each unit evaluated his or her unit's key activities by rating the activities on a scale of 1 to 10. Individual ratings were combined to produce a group or unit rating for each activity and one for the total unit. These ratings were reviewed by unit members. Figure 27.1 provides a sample matrix to illustrate how this process was implemented.

Unit members discussed and dissected the meanings of the activities listed in the matrix and the ratings given to each activity. This exchange provided unit members with an opportunity to establish norms concerning the meaning of terms and ratings in an open and collegial atmosphere. Unit members were also required to provide evidence or documentation for each rating and/or to identify areas in which additional documentation was needed. These self-evaluations represent the first baseline data about program and unit operations concerning the entire Institute. This process is superior to survey methods, for example, for three reasons: First, unit members determine what to focus on to improve their own programs—improving the validity of the effort and the buy-in required to implement recommendations; second, all members of the community are immersed in the evaluation experience, making the process of building a culture of evidence and a community of learners as important as the specific evaluative outcomes; and third, there is a 100% return rate (compared with typically low return rates for surveys).

These self-evaluations have already been used to implement specific improvements in program practice. This process has been used to place old problems in a new light, leading to solutions, adaptations, and new activities for the future. It has also been used to reframe existing data from traditional sources, enabling participants to give meaningful interpretation to data they already collect. In addition, self-evaluations have been used to ensure programmatic and academic accountability. For example, the Psychology Program decided to discontinue its Ph.D. program as part of the self-evaluation process. This was a significant WASC (accreditation agency) and Institute concern of long standing. The empowerment

Sample Self-Evaluation Worksheet

	Activities	EK	KK	YT	DE	BH	MT	EG	DF	JA	MC	CJ	PPV	CLS	GJ	Subtl	Average	
1	Building Capacity	7	5	7	5	5	7	5	6	7	8	8	6	7	6	89	6.357	
2	Teaching	5	6	8	8	8	8	8	8	8	9	8	6	5	na	97	7.461	
3	Research (activist)	5	7	7	3	6	6	3	8	7	6	4	5	5	na	72	5.538	
4	Attract Students	4	5	6	6	7	7	8	6	7	7	7	4	6	6	86	6.142	
5	Attract Staff/Fac	4	5	9	6	7	7	6	6	6	5	8	7	6	7	89	6.357	
6	Retain Students	7	5	7	8	7	6	5	6	6	5	8	4	6	8	88	6.285	
7	Retain Staff/Fac	4	6	7	6	5	6	5	6	6	6	7	4	6	8	82	5.857	
8	Transformative Learning	8	6	6	6	7	7	9	7	7	8	8	8	6	7	97	6.928	
9	Infrastructure STL	5	6	8	6	7	8	8	6	8	5	7	5	6	6	91	6.500	
10	Infrastructure STL/CIIS	5	4	8	6	5	8	8	6	6	5	6	6	6	4	81	5.785	
11	Dissemination - scholarly	3	6	7	4	6	6	5	8	5	5	6	5	5	8	79	5.642	
12	Enhance health relationship CIIS	7	6	8	6	6	8	6	7	5	7	8	4	7	5	89	6.357	
13	Community Building	6	6	7	6	7	7	6	6	6	8	8	5	6	6	88	6.285	
14	Curriculum dev/refin/eval	8	6	7	7	7	7	8	8	8	8	8	7	6	7	102	7.285	
15	Experimental pedagogy	8	6	9	8	8	8	8	8	8	9	8	8	8	7	110	7.857	
16	Diversity	5	4	8	6	5	7	5	4	4	6	8	4	6	6	78	5.571	
	Subtotal	91	89	119	96	99	113	102	106	104	107	117	84	100	91	1418	102.2	Subtotal
																88.63	6.388	Average (activity)
	Average	5.7	5.6	7.4	6	6.2	7.1	6.4	6.6	6.5	6.7	7.3	5.3	6.3	6.5	89.44	6.388	Average (person)
																	6.388	Unit Average

Figure 27.1. Sample Self-Evaluation Worksheet

387

evaluation process provided a vehicle for the Institute to evaluate the program in light of scarce resources and make an executive decision to discontinue the program. Similarly, the all on-line segment of one of the Institute's Ph.D. programs has been administratively merged with a distance learning component of the same program as a result of this self-evaluative process. This was done to provide for greater efficiencies of scale, improved monitoring and supervision, and more face-to-face contact with the Institute (for description of one of these on-line educational programs, see Fetterman, 1996a, 1996b).

The second stage of an empowerment evaluation is to build plans for the future based on these evaluations. All units at the Institute have completed their plans for the future, and these data will be used to design an overall strategic plan. This process ensures the involvement of the entire institutional community as well as its commitment to the effort, generating a plan that is grounded in the reality of unit practice. The provost has institutionalized this process by requiring self-evaluations and unit plans on an annual basis to facilitate program improvement and contribute to institutional accountability.

■ *Conclusion*

Empowerment evaluation is fundamentally a democratic process. The entire group—not a single individual, not the external evaluator or an internal manager—is responsible for conducting the evaluation. The group thus can serve as a check on its own members, moderating the various biases and agendas of individual members. The evaluator is a coequal in this endeavor, not a superior and not a servant; as a critical friend, the evaluator can question shared biases or groupthink.

As is the case in traditional evaluation, everyone is accountable in one fashion or another and thus has an interest or agenda to protect. A school district may have a 5-year plan designed by the superintendent; a graduate school, as in this case, may have to satisfy requirements of an accreditation association; an outside evaluator may have an important but demanding sponsor pushing either timelines or results, or may be influenced by training to use one theoretical approach rather than another. Empowerment evaluations, like all other evaluations, exist within contexts. However, the range of intermediate objectives linking what most people do in their daily routines and macro accreditation goals is almost infinite. People often feel empowered and self-determined when they can select meaningful intermediate objectives that are linked to larger, global goals.

Despite its focus on self-determination and collaboration, empowerment evaluation and traditional external evaluation are not mutually exclusive—on the contrary, they enhance each other. In fact, the empowerment evaluation process produces a rich data source that enables a more complete external examination. In the empowerment evaluation design described above, which was developed in response to a school's accreditation self-study requirement, a series of external evaluations were planned to build on and enhance self-evaluation efforts. A series of external teams were invited to review specific programs. They determined the evaluation agenda in conjunction with department faculty, staff, and students. However, they operate as critical friends, providing a strategic consultation rather than a compliance or traditional accountability review. Participants agreed on the value of an external perspective for adding insights into program operation, serving as an additional quality control, sharpening inquiry, and improving program practice. External evaluators can also help determine the merit and worth of various activities. An external evaluation is not a requirement of empowerment evaluation, but external evaluation and empowerment evaluation are certainly not mutually exclusive. Greater coordination between the needs of the internal and external forms of evaluation can provide a reality check concerning the external needs and expectations of insiders and a rich database for external evaluators.

A matrix or similar design to further systematize internal evaluation activity facilitates comparison and analysis on a larger scale. One type of matrix is presented here in Figure 27.1 to highlight the empowerment evaluation process at the Institute. Another design involves a more colorful approach, using green and red dots to signify progress or deterioration concerning specific topics of concern. The dots have a strong visual impact and can be quantified. Any system can work if it provides participants with straightforward, user-friendly tools to make credible judgments about where they are at any given point in time; provides consistent patterns (including those with strong visual impact) that are meaningful to them; facilitates comparison—across individuals, categories, and programs; and stimulates constructive activity to improve program practice.

Finally, it is my hope that empowerment evaluation will benefit from the artful shaping of evaluators' combined contributions rather than follow any single approach or strategy. As Cronbach et al. (1980) urged more than a decade ago: "It is better for an evaluative inquiry to launch a small fleet of studies than to put all its resources into a single approach" (p. 7).

■ APPENDIX
California Institute of Integral Studies 1994–1995 Unit Self-Evaluation Workshops for Unit Heads

■ TIMES AND PLACES
February 7, 4:00-6:00, 4th-floor conference room
February 9, 4:00-6:00, 4th-floor conference room
February 12, 12:00-2:00, All Saints' Church

■ WORKSHOP FACILITATORS
David Fetterman, Karine Schomer, Mary Curran

■ AGENDA

1. Introduction

   □ Purpose of unit self-evaluation; how it will feed into academic program review; the WASC self-study

   □ Unit-based strategic planning

2. Timelines and deadlines, report formats

3. The self-empowerment evaluation method: purpose, process, product

4. Overarching institutional WASC issues and themes

5. Conducting a demonstration "taking stock" session with a volunteer unit

   □ PART I

   a. Volunteer unit members describe their units, their units' missions or purposes, and their relationship to the Institute's mission.

b. They list their units' key activities.

c. They rate the quality and/or effectiveness of the top 10 key activities.

d. They list documentation/evidence to support the ratings.

e. They do an overall rating of their units.

□ PART II: BREAKOUT PERIOD

a. Volunteer unit members discuss among themselves their ratings of key activities: Why did each person rate as he/she did? What did the ratings mean to each person? How did the unit achieve the rating given? How could it achieve a higher rating? Should ratings be adjusted in view of the discussion?

b. Meanwhile, other workshop participants form small groups. Each person writes a description of his or her unit, lists five key activities, rates these activities and the unit as a whole, and lists supporting documentation. Then all this is reported and discussed in the group.

c. Small group discussions are shared in a large group.

□ PART III

a. Volunteer unit members adjust their ratings of units' key activities.

b. They adjust their overall ratings of their units.

c. They prioritize the key activities they have rated.

d. They list two or three preliminary recommendations for future courses of action: major goals, objectives related to the goals, strategies to achieve the objectives, documentation/evidence that would demonstrate success.

6. Instructions for unit tasks after completion of the "taking stock" session

a. Unit head writes up preliminary unit self-evaluation report based on the "taking stock" session, including unit mission/purpose, overall unit rating, rating of key activities, prioritization of key activities, list of documentation/evidence to support ratings, and preliminary recommendations for future courses of action.

b. Minisessions of the unit to review the report, discuss and adjust ratings, and build consensus about what the ratings mean and what everyone thinks about the unit.

c. Unit gathers and analyzes supporting documentation.

d. Unit head completes and submits final draft of the unit self-evaluation report and supporting documentation.

☐ *1994–1995 Unit Self-Evaluation Report*

- Note 1: Form is available on disk from the Office of the Provost. (Please supply your own disk.)
- Note 2: A single report format is being used for academic, administrative, and governance units. Some items may therefore not be applicable to all units. They should be marked N/A.
- Note 3: Reports and supporting documentation should be reviewed by person whom unit head reports to before submission to Office of the Provost.
- Note 4: Reports should be distributed as widely as possible within unit and to other relevant units.
- Name of unit:
- What larger unit does it belong to? Academic/Administrative/Governance (circle one).
- Name and title of unit head:
- To whom does unit head report? (Title):

Part I: Unit Description

1. Mission or purpose of unit (narrative)
2. Relationship to Institute mission
3. Organizational structure of unit (narrative)
4. List of 10 key activities performed by unit, prioritized (from "taking stock" session)
5. Other ongoing activities of unit (narrative)
6. Special projects of unit (list)
7. Direction of unit development over past 3 years (narrative)
8. Current three major goals and objectives related to goals, strategies being used to achieve objectives, and documentation/evidence that demonstrates success (narrative)
9. Number and names of core faculty by % time
10. Number and names of adjunct faculty
11. Number and names of staff, by title and % time

12. Number of students (persons) over 3 years 1992–1993 1993–1994 1994–1995 (est.)

13. Number of students (FTE) over past 3 years 1992–1993 1993–1994 1994–1995 (est.)

14. Number of class enrollments over 3 years 1992–1993 1993–1994 1994–1995 (est.)

15. Operational budget for past 2 years and current year 1992–1993 1993–1994 1994–1995 (rev.)

    Revenue expense (Note: Please footnote any figures requiring significant explanation.)

16. Institutional issues and themes of particular relevance to unit (refer to Strategic Directions)

17. WASC issues and themes of particular relevance to unit (refer to WASC Recommendations, WASC Standards, WASC Self-Study Themes)

Part II: Unit Self-Evaluation

1. Names of participants in unit self-evaluation process (F = faculty, S = student, AS = administrative staff)

2. Date(s) of "taking stock" session

3. Dates and purpose of follow-up minisessions

4. Narrative of self-evaluation process

5. Overall rating of unit:

   Range   Average

6. Rating of prioritized 10 key activities (list)

Item	Range	Average
1		
2		
3		
4		
5		
6		
7		
8		
9		
10		

7. List of documentation/evidence used to support ratings (attach documentation in appendix).

8. Discussion of findings (narrative based on overall ratings and ratings of prioritized 10 key activities). Describe the key activities and how they are related to the mission or purpose of the unit. Explain what the individual and overall ratings mean. Explain the relevance of the documentation used. Summarize the overall strengths and weaknesses of the unit and progress made over the past 3 years.

9. Preliminary recommendations for two or three future courses of action: major new goals, objectives related to the goals, strategies to achieve the objectives, and documentation/evidence that would demonstrate success.

10. Evaluation and feedback on the unit self-evaluation process.

■ Notes

1. *Empowerment Evaluation* (Fetterman et al., 1996) provides additional insight into this new evaluation approach, including information about how to conduct workshops to train program staff members and participants to evaluate and improve program practice (see also Fetterman, 1994a, 1994b). This approach is consistent with the spirit of the standards developed by the Joint Committee on Standards for Educational Evaluation (1994; see also Fetterman, 1995). This approach has also been institutionalized within the Empowerment Evaluation Institute. In addition, the Collaborative, Participatory, and Empowerment Evaluation Topical Interest Group was created within the American Evaluation Association by evaluators who share a commitment to exploring these forms of evaluation and sharing tools that work in this new and somewhat uncharted territory.

2. See Stevenson, Mitchell, and Florin (1996) for a detailed explanation about the distinctions concerning levels of organizations. See also Zimmerman (in press) for more detail about empowerment theory focusing on psychological, organizational, and community levels of analysis.

■ References

Cronbach, L. J., & Associates. (1980). *Toward reform of program evaluation.* San Francisco: Jossey-Bass.

Fetterman, D. M. (1994a). Empowerment evaluation: Presidential address. *Evaluation Practice, 15,* 1-15.

Fetterman, D. M. (1994b). Steps of empowerment evaluation: From California to Cape Town. *Evaluation and Program Planning, 17,* 305-313.

Fetterman, D. M. (1995). In response to Dr. Daniel Stufflebeam's Empowerment evaluation, objectivist evaluation, and evaluation standards: Where the future of evaluation should not go and where it needs to go. *Evaluation Practice, 16,* 179-199.

Fetterman, D. M. (1996a). Ethnography in the virtual classroom. *Practicing Anthropology, 18*(3): 2, 36-39.

Fetterman, D. M. (1996b). Videoconferencing: Enhancing communication on the Internet. *Educational Researcher, 25*(4).

Fetterman, D. M., Kaftarian, S., & Wandersman, A. (1996). *Empowerment evaluation: Knowledge and tools for self-assessment and accountability.* Thousand Oaks, CA: Sage.

Joint Committee on Standards for Educational Evaluation. (1994). *The program evaluation standards.* Thousand Oaks, CA: Sage.

Patton, M. Q. (1994). Developmental evaluation. *Evaluation Practice, 15,* 311-319.

Scriven, M. S. (1967). The methodology of evaluation. In R. E. Stake (Ed.), *Curriculum evaluation.* Chicago: Rand McNally.

Stevenson, J. F., Mitchell, R. E., & Florin, P. (1996). Evaluation and self-direction in community prevention coalitions. In D. M. Fetterman, S. Kaftarian, & A. Wandersman (Eds.), *Empowerment evaluation: Knowledge and tools for self-assessment and accountability.* Thousand Oaks, CA: Sage.

Stufflebeam, D. L. (1994). Empowerment evaluation, objectivist evaluation, and evaluation standards: Where the future of evaluation should not go and where it needs to go. *Evaluation Practice, 15,* 321-338.

Zimmerman, M. A. (in press). Empowerment theory: Psychological, organizational, and community levels of analysis. In J. Rappaport & E. Seldman (Eds.), *Handbook of community psychology.* New York: Plenum.

28

Cluster Evaluation

James R. Sanders

One of the new developments in program evaluation over the past decade has been a creative and evolving approach called cluster evaluation. The request for cluster evaluation comes from funders of projects that have a common mission but have local procedural autonomy; these funders want an evaluation of the results obtained from their investments.

The label of *cluster evaluation* was first used in 1988 by Dr. Ronald Richards, director of evaluation for the Kellogg Foundation at the time. The label described a design specified in a contract for an external evaluation of a W. K. Kellogg Foundation-funded health initiative. Since then, cluster evaluations have been commissioned by the Kellogg Foundation in science, education, agricultural health and safety, youth development, public health, health professions education, public policy education, food systems professions education, youth exchanges, and leadership development. In addition, others outside the Kellogg Foundation have been doing cluster evaluation under other names or have adapted or extended the ideas behind cluster evaluation to start a literature on cluster evaluation methodology (Barley & Jenness, 1993, 1995;

Campbell, 1994; W. K. Kellogg Foundation, 1992, 1995; Parsons, 1994; Sanders, 1995; Worthen & Matsumoto, 1994). In addition, many cluster evaluation technical reports have been prepared for the Kellogg Foundation since 1990.

In 1994, the Topical Interest Group on Cluster Evaluation was created within the American Evaluation Association by evaluators who wanted to share ideas and information. In this chapter I will describe the fundamentals of cluster evaluation and discuss its strengths and limitations. Future development of cluster evaluation methodology will depend on program evaluators' sharing their cluster evaluation experiences.

■ *Fundamentals of Cluster Evaluation*

Cluster evaluation is one kind of program evaluation. It is evaluation of a program that has projects in multiple sites aimed at bringing about a common general change. Examples of such changes include increasing adult literacy in science or in agricultural safety, improving the health practices of parents in rural communities, and increasing the participation of rural citizens in public policy formulation. Projects are relatively autonomous. Each project develops its own strategy to accomplish the program goal, uses its own human and fiscal resources to carry out its plan, and has its own context.

□ *Questions Addressed*

The questions that cluster evaluation addresses are as follows:

1. Overall, have changes occurred in the desired direction? What is the nature of these changes?
2. In what types of settings have what types of change occurred, and why?
3. Are there insights to be drawn from the program failures and successes that can inform future initiatives?
4. What is needed to sustain desired changes?

Cluster evaluation is one of several approaches to program evaluation that can be used to address these questions. Other approaches include analyses of project-level evaluations and use of site visits to make judgments about individual programs. Such approaches are common in program evaluation, but they address the above questions in ways very different from cluster evaluation.

☐ *Audiences*

Cluster evaluations serve two primary audiences: program directors at the parent organization who are responsible for current and future programming decisions, and project staff who are responsible for local programming decisions. Secondary audiences include the administration and board of the parent organization, professionals working in the program area outside of the cluster being evaluated, and policy leaders who may use the insights supplied by cluster evaluation to shape organizational or governmental policy.

☐ *Relationships*

A basic assumption underlying the design of a cluster evaluation is that it does not dictate how projects plan and conduct either their operations or their evaluations. The cluster evaluator becomes part of a team that includes (a) the sponsor/funder/parent organization, (b) the project staffs (including the project evaluators), and (c) the cluster evaluator. The dynamics of this tripartite relationship bear directly on the success of cluster evaluation. This relationship leads to the development and use of a shared vision/goal/mission for the program. If the parent organization representative lacks conceptual clarity, the cluster evaluation will be affected. The same will be true if representatives of projects or the cluster evaluator lacks an understanding of the mission of the program. The productivity of the cluster evaluation is affected even more if more than one of the three parties lacks conceptual clarity about the program. Thus shared vision among participants is one factor that can affect cluster evaluation. Other relationship factors affecting cluster evaluation include the following:

■ *Role definitions:* Cluster evaluation requires a partnership among three groups. There are costs involved in time and expenses when collaboration is expected.

- *Cooperation:* If any member backs out of the partnership, it will be weakened; parity among the partners is important.

- *Conflict resolution:* Communication is especially important in any disagreement, especially when a request by one or more of the partners negatively affects the work of the others.

- *Trust:* Information shared in confidence is to be protected.

- *Credit:* Giving credit where credit is due is important when instruments, information, and ideas are being shared in the partnership.

□ *Design*

Cluster evaluation has taken various forms, but it has certain basic characteristics: (a) It is holistic, (b) it is outcome oriented, (c) it seeks generalizable learning, and (d) it involves frequent communications and collaborations among the partners. Cluster evaluation can be either formative or summative, but it has most frequently been both. Typically, a cluster evaluation project will involve the following steps.

Site visits by the cluster evaluators. These visits include introductions, orientation to the cluster evaluation, role definitions, orientation to the local project, collection of documents, arrangement for the first networking conference, and identification of evaluation issues.

Analysis of project and program documents. This analysis includes the search for commonalities and uniqueness in outcome objectives across projects in the program, development of categories for project strategies, and efforts to understand the program mission and establish conceptual clarity.

Networking conferences. Project and program directors plan to meet as a cluster group for a day or two every 6 months. The first conference might be dedicated to project presentations of intended outcomes and strategies, mapping each project onto a list of possible program outcomes and associating alternative strategies with each outcome. Subsequent conferences could focus on sharing evaluation plans, instruments, and findings, so as to begin identifying operational definitions and assessment techniques for outcomes and activities that have been tried and appear promising as well as activities that have been tried and have not worked.

Outside speakers or consultants might be invited to stimulate new ways of thinking about the program or about evaluation methods. Later conferences might focus on discussions and debate of tentative evaluative conclusions, with a look at existing and missing documentation, alternative frameworks for judging the program, and gaining outside interpretations of cluster evaluation data.

Collection and analysis of data. This is a continuous process during the life of the cluster evaluation. It includes refining evaluation questions, taking stock of existing data, using working hypotheses (Glaser & Strauss, 1967) to test and refine tentative conclusions, examining data needs and who is in the best position to gather needed information, seeking cooperation in data collection, developing new instruments and data collection plans that are needed, scheduling and supervising data collection (including naturalistic observations at sites), analyzing data as they become available, and using results to refine future data collection and analyses.

Interpretation and reporting. Like data collection and analysis, interpreting and reporting data are continuous processes. Cluster evaluation draws from a diversity of perspectives (including methodological) to arrive at conclusions. Multiple interpretations of data early in the cluster evaluation process will allow for the testing of certain interpretations over time in the projects. Networking conferences are valuable forums for interpretations of early cluster evaluation findings.

Confirmation of findings. Final conclusions are reviewed for accuracy and conceptual integrity by participants at each level of the cluster evaluation.

The elements of cluster evaluation as a continuous process are depicted in Figure 28.1. The stages of inquiry reflected in cluster evaluation design are not unique to cluster evaluation. Starting with the classic work of Glaser and Strauss (1967), there is a strong and well-documented tradition of the methodology used in cluster evaluation found in the literature under such labels as *qualitative methods, case study methods,* and *naturalistic methods.* What is unique about cluster evaluation is the combination of the four characteristics listed above: (a) It is holistic, (b) it is outcome oriented, (c) it seeks generalizable learning, and (d) it involves frequent communications and collaborations among the partners.

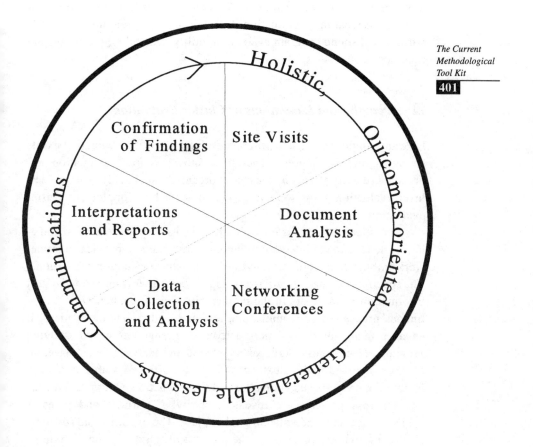

Figure 28.1. The Elements of Cluster Evaluation

It is an approach to evaluation that is intrusive and affects the thinking and practices of project staff, the parent or funding organization, and the cluster evaluator along the way. It does not seek to establish causation through controlled comparative designs, but instead depends on natural-istic observations of many people to infer and test logical connections. The underlying paradigm is one of argumentation and rules of evidence, such as those found in our legal system. It strives for documentation and logical conclusions that have been tested as fully as possible given resources, time, and methodological constraints of the evaluation. In terms of *The Program Evaluation Standards* (Joint Committee on Standards for Educational Evaluation, 1994), it places a premium on all four attributes of sound program evaluation: utility, feasibility, propriety, and accuracy.

■ *Strengths and Limitations of Cluster Evaluation*

Like any single approach to program evaluation, cluster evaluation has its strengths and limitations. Therefore, other program evaluation approaches (e.g., site visits by the parent organization or analysis of project-level evaluations) are sometimes recommended to supplement cluster evaluation.

The strengths of cluster evaluation are its responsiveness to stakeholder needs and the interactions among participants. It provides a framework within which both formative and summative evaluation can be done. The specifics of data collection develop as the partners interact and digest information from others in the partnership. Cluster evaluation is a continuous process of communication, learning, and reshaping of ideas. It engages many minds and perspectives in strengthening and studying program effectiveness. As ideas are shared and learning takes place, all of those involved in the cluster evaluation are affected. Capacity is built in both the program subject matter and the evaluation. Contextual differences across projects are revealed, clarity of purpose and plans is achieved, and new understanding takes place. The overall value added by cluster evaluation consists of the insights that go beyond individual project experiences.

The limitations of cluster evaluation can be very serious, depending on one's philosophical orientation toward evaluation methodology and the performance of the cluster partners. A characteristic of cluster evaluation is that it is continuously evolving, and the program that is being evaluated is also continuously evolving, being shaped by the cluster evaluation. The program itself is also a product of contextual differences across projects. Given these circumstances, those who would rely on controlled comparative designs to establish program impact, for example, will be disappointed with the cluster evaluation approach to program evaluation. Further, the potential for cluster evaluators to lose their independence through the cluster evaluation process is a very real con-

TABLE 28.1 Summary of Strengths and Limitations of Cluster Evaluation

Strengths	Limitations
Contributes in the formative role and allows logical inferences about attribution within the summative role	Includes no controls
	Has potential for co-optation
Evolves	Does not evaluate individual projects
Is continuous	Has time limits for looking at change over the long term
Is collaborative/participatory	
Builds capacity	Depends on goodwill, communication, coordination, and relationships across three partners
Brings information beyond individual project evaluations (e.g., contextual differences)	Depends on stability of cluster membership
Focuses on broad issues	Depends on conceptual clarity/shared vision by partners
Provides synergy	
Involves an outcome orientation/ documentation and logical explanation of outcomes, as well as a push toward clarity	Cannot establish causal attribution between results and interventions
Includes multiple perspectives	

cern, and one not to be taken lightly. Employment of a metaevaluation panel to oversee the cluster evaluation is one way to address this concern. The opportunity to look for long-term change is often missing in cluster evaluations, and funding or parent organizations need to look at the feasibility of conducting follow-up cluster evaluations beyond the initial study period. Finally, the success of cluster evaluation is dependent on all of the partners performing as expected over the life of the cluster evaluation. All partners need to take seriously their responsibilities for sharing information, responding to reasonable requests from the others, listening to the others, keeping the same personnel assigned to the program, and keeping the mission of the program in the forefront as plans are refined. A summary of the strengths and limitations of cluster evaluation is provided in Table 28.1.

■ Conclusion

Cluster evaluation is in its infancy and will continue to be shaped by the ideas and experiences of evaluators using it as an approach to program evaluation. As more experience is gained by program evaluators who are doing cluster evaluation, we can expect to see a growing literature on cluster evaluation practices and methodology.

■ References

Barley, Z. A., & Jenness, M. (1993). Cluster evaluation: A method to strengthen evaluation in smaller programs with similar purposes. *Evaluation Practice, 14*, 141-147.

Barley, Z. A., & Jenness, M. (1995). *Guidelines for the conduct of cluster evaluations.* Paper presented at the annual meeting of the American Evaluation Association, Vancouver.

Campbell, J. L. (1994). *Emerging issues in cluster evaluation: Issues of cluster evaluation use.* Paper presented at the annual meeting of the American Evaluation Association, Boston.

Glaser, B. G., & Strauss, A. L. (1967). *The discovery of grounded theory: Strategies for qualitative research.* Chicago: Aldine.

Joint Committee on Standards for Educational Evaluation. (1994). *The program evaluation standards.* Thousand Oaks, CA: Sage.

W. K. Kellogg Foundation. (1992). *Cluster evaluation information.* Battle Creek, MI: Author.

W. K. Kellogg Foundation. (1995). *Cluster evaluation model of evolving practices.* Battle Creek, MI: Author.

Parsons, B. A. (1994). *Relationship and communication issues posed by cluster evaluation.* Paper presented at the annual meeting of the American Evaluation Association, Boston.

Sanders, J. R. (1995, March). Cluster evaluation: A creative response to a thorny evaluation issue. *Newsletter of the AEA Nonprofits and Foundations TIG,* p. 5.

Worthen, B. R., & Matsumoto, A. (1994). *Conceptual challenges confronting cluster evaluation.* Paper presented at the annual meeting of the American Evaluation Association, Boston.

29

An Introduction to Scientific Realist Evaluation

Claiming to be a "realist" can sometimes feel like choosing to bat on the side of the "good." Too many people, in too many walks of life, have argued for their cause under the banner of "realism" for the concept to perform any wonders of clarification. We find the epithet to be irresistible, nonetheless, because the roots of the *scientific realist evaluation* perspective, which we seek to introduce here, can be traced directly back to the influential realist tradition in European philosophy of science, as identified in the writing of Hesse (1974), Lakatos (1970), Bhaskar (1975), and Harré (1972). Without going into the details, we can say that realism has sought to position itself as a model of scientific explanation that avoids the traditional epistemological poles of positivism and relativism. Realism's key features are its stress on the mechanics of explanation and its attempt to show that certain explanatory strategies can lead to a progressive body of scientific knowledge. In social science there have been a number of attempts to make the leap from scientific realist explanation to realist social explanation. In a forthcoming book, we attempt to spread the word to evaluation (Pawson & Tilley, in press); this chapter serves as a brief introduction to the key explanatory ideas.

■ Social Reality, Social Causation, and Social Change

What are social programs? It is useful to begin with such a stunningly simple question because much misunderstanding about the nature of the change engendered by programs has followed from an overly simple understanding of how such initiatives are themselves constituted. For us, there is no particular mystery about what one might term the *ontology* of the policy initiative. Social programs are undeniably, unequivocally, unexceptionally social systems, and they are composed, as is any social system, of the interplay of individual and institution, of agency and structure, of micro and macro social processes. Much is to be learned from inspecting the "social nature" of programs. Realism has a standard set of concepts for describing the operation of any social system, and our main purpose in this chapter is to draw parallels across from them into the explanation of program systems. We attempt this under four (sub)headings: embeddedness, mechanisms, contexts, and outcomes.

☐ Embeddedness

Realists refer to the embeddedness of all human action within a wider range of social processes as the *stratified nature of social reality*. Even the most mundane actions make sense only because they contain in-built assumptions about a wider set of social rules and institutions. Thus, to use a favorite realist example, the act of signing a check is accepted routinely as payment, only because we take for granted its place within the social organization known as the banking system. If we think of this in causal language, it means that causal powers do not reside in particular objects (checks) or individuals (cashiers), but in the social relations and organizational structures that they form. One action leads to another because of the actions' accepted place in the whole. It is precisely because of this need to explain human actions in terms of their location within different layers of social reality that realists shun the *successionist* view of causation as a relationship between discrete events (i.e., cause and effect).

This simple principle is our starting point for understanding program systems. What we want to resist here is the notion of programs as uniform "dosages" targeted at individual subjects. Think of the delivery of a "treatment" for offenders such as a cognitive skills program. At one level, it can be understood simply as a "curriculum," a specific set of ideas and skills introduced into the minds of the prisoners. The ideas, however, are delivered in classroom interaction, and so are forged within a wider web of expectations about how prisoners should be treated. Programs are thus also "work." The instructor will be bound by one set of rules of behavior, the prisoner another. The instructor will have one set of aims, the inmate may choose another. Programs are also about "people." Practitioners have one particular set of backgrounds, experiences, and loyalties, inmates another; and the nature and success of the exchange of ideas will in turn be mediated by these characteristics. Programs, moreover, carry "histories." Prisoners and instructors will fetch into and out of the program a wider set of social resources and cultural expectations customarily given over to the treatment of the "criminal classes." Programs inevitably assume a "future," and the impact of any initiative will depend on a rigid pattern of opportunities and constraints awaiting the inmate on release. We would submit that all social programs are encapsulated in a like manner, a proposition we can embody in the aphorism, "A program *is* its personnel, its place, its past, and its prospects."

□ *Mechanisms*

This vision of a stratified reality leads directly to the next and most characteristic tool of realist explanation, which is the notion of the *explanatory mechanism.* One image that realists use to express the idea is that of the "underlying" mechanism (Bhaskar, 1975; Sayer, 1984). This is a useful metaphor because it captures the idea that we often explain how things work by going beneath their surface (observable) appearance by delving into their inner (hidden) workings. We can never understand how a clock works by examining only its face and the movement of its hands; rather, we examine the works, and so a proper understanding requires us to master the construction of the balanced spring or the oscillation of cesium atoms.

When it comes to explaining *social* outcomes, uniformities, and regularities, most social scientists would allow for the causal potential of *both* micro and macro social mechanisms. For example, if we think of the granddaddy of all sociological tasks, that is, the explanation of suicide rates, we see that social constitution is a matter for both individual action and social constraint. Durkheim (1897/1951), while accepting that the decision to commit suicide is, of course, a matter of the individual's misery, desperation, isolation, and so on, was able to show that such dispositions are socially structured and thus vary with the social cohesion and social support that different communities are able to bring to marginalized members. Social mechanisms are thus about people's *choices* and the *capacities* they derive from group membership.

This idea of calling on different layers of reality in social explanation has vital implications for the way we think about causation. When we say that the mechanism that explains an outcome is located at a different *layer* of social reality, we employ a quite distinctive and *generative* conception of causality. Again, the terminology is vital. To *generate* is to "make up," to "manufacture," to "produce," to "form," to "constitute." Thus when we explain an outcome generatively, we are not coming up with variables or correlates that associate one with the other; rather, we are trying to explain how the association itself comes about. The generative mechanisms thus actually *constitute* the outcome; they *are* the outcome.

Figure 29.1 is an attempt to portray the difference between this and the notion of successionist causation. When realists say that the constant conjunction view of one event producing another (model a) is inadequate, they are not attempting to bring further "intervening" variables into the picture. So the idea is not that there might be a further unforeseen event that brings about a spurious relationship between the original variables (model b), or that the original relationship is "indirect" and works through an intervening variable (model c). The idea is that the mechanism is responsible for the relationship itself (model d). A mechanism is thus not a variable but an account of the makeup, behavior, and interrelationships of those processes that are responsible for the outcome. A mechanism is thus a theory—a theory that spells out the potential of human resources and reasoning.

We can now draw some parallels across to evaluation research, which, in some of its foundational statements, has itself been rather $X \rightarrow Y$ fixated (Cook & Campbell, 1979, chap. 1). Mechanisms carry the

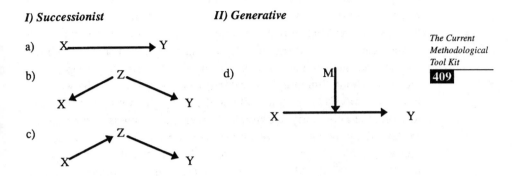

Figure 29.1. Models of Causation

weight of realist explanations, as they must in our understanding of evaluation research. It is through the notion of *program mechanisms* that we take the step from asking whether a program works to understanding *what it is about a program* that makes it work. So far, we have developed three key identifiers of a "mechanism." Thus of program mechanisms, we would expect them (a) to reflect the embeddedness of the program within the stratified nature of social reality, (b) to take the form of propositions that will provide an account of how both macro and micro processes constitute the program, and (c) to demonstrate how program outputs follow from the stakeholders' choices and their capacity to put these into practice.

We can provide a brief illustration by thinking across from suicide research to those rates that tend to be of interest to program evaluators, such as crime rates. If we consider police "neighborhood patrol" programs, the realist investigator would begin by thinking about the mechanisms through which they might work. Identifying mechanisms involves the attempt to think through how a program actually changes behavior, and the basic realist claim is that initiatives always work in a "weaving process" that binds choices and capacities together. One such mechanism within the contact program might be an "empowerment" process. Thus if we think of the patrols as providing a new resource in that community, this capacity could work its way into people's reasoning by developing mutual trust, so that the newly empowered members of the community increase their own surveillance, crime reporting, and self-protection. A recognition of these new choices and increased community resources might in turn induce the potential criminal to think again and recalculate

the risk of operating in that neighborhood. Alternatively, the increased contact capacity might fire off a "reassurance" mechanism in which the simple presence of the "cop on the beat"—combined, perhaps, with messages about "lightning not striking twice"—might work its way into the reasoning of residents to build confidence, which might in turn lead to increased neighborly activity, so further increasing assuredness. The reader will appreciate that we are merely outlining processes that are not mutually exclusive and not complete in the way the above descriptions might imply. What we hope to have demonstrated, however, is something about the nature of all mechanisms. Programs will always work through a process of weaving resources and reasoning together, and without this being the first item on the research agenda, all subsequent work on outcomes will remain a mystery.

☐ *Contexts*

Our next task is to introduce mechanism's partner concept—the notion of *context,* which can be evoked via another standard realist proposition that posits that *the relationship between causal mechanisms and their effects is not fixed, but contingent* (see Sayer, 1984, p. 107). A favorite physical science example for the realist is gunpowder, which has within it the causal potential to explode, but whether it does so depends on it being in the right conditions. The same explanatory structure will write directly across into social science. We invoke the identical propositional form when we say that the unemployed have the power to work even when economic conditions prevent them from doing so. Our previous illustration of the "banking system" provides another fine example and one that is somewhat closer to the policy field. Within such a system there would be little evidence (and conceivably much denial) of any formal rule that forbids the advancement of loans to single parents, mortgages to the unskilled, and so on. However, the contextual conditions that bring about such a state of affairs are there aplenty. In order to survive as commercial concerns, banks and building societies have to make a profit on their transactions. One of the simplest ways of failing to make a profit is to have a significant rate of default on the repayment of advances. Transactions are thus judged against a perceived level of risk, which may well be judged excessive for the aforementioned groups. If one multiplies this little chain of reasoning a thousandfold, it is not difficult to see the sedimentation of a monolithic, cautionary, asset-sensitive culture. The promotion of any specific policy initiative (We loan to lone parents!) will thus involve a wrestling match with the reproduction of longer-term financial convention.

All social programs wrestle with prevailing contextual conditions. Programs are always introduced *into* preexisting social contexts, and these prevailing social conditions are of crucial importance when it comes to explaining the successes and failures of social programs. By *social context,* we do not refer simply to the spatial or geographic or institutional locations into which programs are embedded. So although indeed programs are initiated in prisons, hospitals, schools, neighborhoods, and car parks, it is the prior set of social rules, relations, and cultural systems gathered in these places that sets limits on the efficacy of program mechanisms. We have no hesitation in pointing to this lack of attention to the social conditions that preexist and endure through programs as one of the great omissions of evaluation research. What we have in mind are sets of basic, broadly accepted conventions that place limits on appropriate behavior in particular institutions or localities.

Programs work by introducing new ideas and/or resources into existing sets of social relationships. A crucial task of evaluation is to include (via hypothesis making and research design) investigation of the extent to which these preexisting structures "enable" or "disable" the intended mechanism of change. Recall the contact patrol example. In the above section on mechanisms, we mentioned a couple of potential mechanisms through which they *might* work, namely, empowerment and confidence building. It is not too difficult to imagine circumstances where these would *not* work. For instance, in terms of the latter mechanism, messages of reassurance from the community constable are likely to fall on deaf ears if the local crime rates remain static and repeat victimization continues to bite. The use of an adverse example of context is no accident here, for it highlights the fact that positive conditions in which a program *will* work might be relatively rare. Conditions that have been responsible for a crime-producing mechanism might well prove inhospitable to a crime-reducing one.

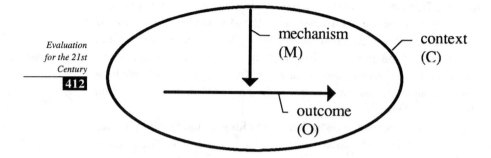

Figure 29.2. Basic Ingredients of Realist Social Explanation

□ *Outcomes*

We now move to the goal of realist explanation. No surprises in store here, for we pick up on a task that is held in common with most explanatory paradigms. That is to say, the objective of realist inquiry is to explain social "outcomes," "uniformities," "regularities," "rates," "associations," "patterns." What is unique to realism, however, is a rather precise prescription about the explanatory propositions that will meet this goal. Explanans and explanandum are related according to the following formula: Outcome = Mechanism + Context. Rendering this into prose, we are now in a position to summarize the basic logic of realist explanation in the following statement (and in Figure 29.2):

> The basic task of social inquiry is to explain interesting, puzzling, socially significant outcomes (O). Explanation takes the form of positing some underlying mechanism (M) that generates the regularity and thus consists of propositions about how the interplay between structure and agency has constituted the outcome. Within realist investigation there is also investigation of how the workings of such mechanisms are contingent and conditional, and thus only fired in particular local, historical, or institutional contexts (C).

Although the (M,C,O) terminology here will be new to many evaluators, it actually evokes a challenge that is well-known to them. Recall Palmer's (1975) famous retort to the "nothing works" controversy. Look closely and you will see realism incarnate: "Rather than ask 'What works for offenders as a whole? (O),' we must increasingly ask, 'Which methods (M) work best for which types of offenders (C) and under what conditions (C) or in what types of settings (C)?' " (p. 150). Programs cannot be considered as some kind of external, impinging "dosage" to which subjects "respond." Rather, programs "work" if subjects choose to make them work and are placed in the right conditions to enable them to do so. In reality, programs offer complex sets of choices that will vary markedly in feasibility according to the circumstances of the subject. Realists attempt to capture this process of "constrained choice" by generating sets of M,C,O propositions. Research has the task of testing, refining, and adjudicating among these hypotheses. The realist approach can thus be seen as a family member of the "theory-driven" perspective on evaluation (Chen, 1990). Alas, that approach is often bedeviled by a family argument about the exact scope and content of the theory required. Realism delivers a precise prescription for theory development based on the time-honored explanatory ingredients of mechanisms, contexts, and outcomes.

■ *Realism in the Car Park*

Thus far we have adopted a sprinkling of illustrations in making our case for realism, and it is high time we took on a developed example. We choose as our example of realist theory in action a programming area that is seemingly mundane and mechanical. We want to look at car parks. More specifically, we wish to examine the problem of car park crime and attempts to reduce it through the installation of closed-circuit television (CCTV). Such programs, in fact, share a key characteristic with all social initiatives, in that there is nothing about CCTV in car parks that intrinsically inhibits car crime. Although it may appear to offer a technical solution, CCTV certainly does not create a physical barrier that makes cars impenetrable. A moment's thought has us realize, therefore, that the cameras must work by instigating a chain of reasoning and reaction. Realist evaluation is all about turning this moment's thought into a comprehensive theory of the mechanisms through which CCTV may enter the potential criminal's mind and the contexts needed if these powers are to be realized. We begin with mechanisms:

1. *The "caught in the act" mechanism.* CCTV could reduce car crime by making it more likely that present offenders will be observed on-screen, detected instantly, and then arrested, removed, punished, and deterred.

2. *The "you've been framed" mechanism.* CCTV could reduce car crime by deterring potential offenders who will not wish to risk investigation, apprehension, and conviction by the evidence captured on videotape.

3. *The "nosey parker" mechanism.* The presence of CCTV may lead to increases in usage of car parks, because drivers feel less at risk of victimization. Increased usage could then enhance natural surveillance, which may deter potential offenders who feel they are at increased risk of apprehension in the course of criminal behavior.

4. *The "effective deployment" mechanism.* CCTV may facilitate the effective deployment of security staff/police officers toward areas where suspicious behavior is occurring. They then act as a visible presence that might deter potential offenders. They may also apprehend actual offenders red-handed and disable their criminal behavior.

5. *The "publicity" mechanism.* CCTV and signs indicating that it is in operation could symbolize efforts to take crime seriously and to reduce it. Potential offenders may be led to avoid the increased risk they believe to be associated with committing car crimes in car parks and so be deterred.

6. *The "time for crime" mechanism.* Those car crimes that can be completed in a very short space of time may decline less than those that take more time, as offenders calculate the time taken for police or security officers to come or the probability that panning cameras will focus in on them.

7. *The "memory jogging" mechanism.* CCTV and notices indicating that it is in operation may remind drivers that their cars are vulnerable, and they may thereby be prompted to take greater care to lock them, to operate any security devices, and to remove easily stolen items from view.

8. *The "appeal to the cautious" mechanism.* It might be that cautious drivers, who are sensitive to the possibility that their cars may be vulnerable and are habitual users of various security devices, use and fill those car parks with CCTV and thereby drive out those who are more careless, whose vulnerable cars are stolen from elsewhere.

It is clearly possible that more than one of these mechanisms for change may operate simultaneously. Which (if any) mechanisms are fired turns on the context in which CCTV is installed, and this may vary widely. Consider the following:

- *The "criminal clustering" context.* A given rate of car crime may result from widely differing prevalences of offending. For example, if there are 1,000 incidents per annum, these may involve anywhere from a single (very busy) offender to as many as 1,000 offenders, or still more if they operate in groups. A mechanism leading to disablement of the offender (as in mechanism 1, above) holds potential promise according to the offender/offense ratio.

- *The "style of usage" context.* A car park may have an enormous influx of vehicles early in the morning, when it becomes full. It may then empty between 5:00 and 6:00 in the evening. If the dominant CCTV-fired mechanism turns out to be increased confidence and usage (as in mechanism 3 or 8, above), then this will have little impact because the pattern of usage is already high with little movement, dictated by working hours, not fear of crime. If, however, the car park is little used, but with a very high per user car crime rate, then the increased usage mechanism may lead to an overall increase in numbers of crimes but a decreased rate per use.

- *The "lay of the land" context.* Cars parked in the CCTV blind spots in car parks will be more vulnerable if the mechanism is increased chance of apprehension through evidence on videotape (as in mechanism 2, above), but not if it is through changed attributes/security behavior of customers (as in mechanism 7 or 8, above).

- *The "alternative targets" context.* The local patterns of motivation of offenders, together with the availability of alternative targets of car crime, furnish aspects of the wider context for displacement to car crimes elsewhere, whatever crime reduction mechanisms may be fired by CCTV in the specific context of a given car park.

- *The "resources" context.* In an isolated car park with no security presence and the police at some distance away, the deployment of security staff/ police as a mobile and flexible resource to deter car crime (as in mechanism 4, above) is not possible.

- *The "surveillance culture" context.* As the usage of CCTV surveillance spreads through all walks of life and features in extensive media portrayals of "modern policing," then the efficacy of the publicity given to CCTV in car parks (as in mechanism 5, above) may be enhanced or muted, according to the overall reputation of such surveillance.

We do not claim that these listings of potential contexts and mechanisms are mutually exclusive or exhaustive. What we trust they reveal instantly, however, is that a bit of lateral thinking in the realm of hypothesis making requires that we trudge well off the beaten track in the search for supporting empirical evidence. A series of studies would be required to sift, sort, and adjudicate which of the various mechanism/context permutations is active, a task we can summarize with the following highly abbreviated list of investigative tacks:

■ As well as checking for reductions in crime rate following CCTV installation, it would be important to check on *convictions* attributable to CCTV, for this would reveal whether direct detection or taped evidence (as in mechanisms 1 and 2, above) is actually capable of generating the outcome. Further evidence on these detection mechanisms could be compiled through actual inspection of the *technical capabilities* of systems in respect to whether their resolution power is great enough to identify individuals and how quickly they can home in on an offense. Tilley (1993) has reported on highly limited performance in terms of both conviction and technique, inclining him to the belief that the remaining, indirect, risk-perception mechanisms are more crucial.

■ Before-and-after data, again not just on changing rate, but on changes in *type* of crime and of *criminal opportunities,* may be a crucial next step, but, as far as we are aware, one that has not been utilized with respect to these programs. A survey ascertaining changes in numbers of cars left locked and in the extent to which attractive goods were left on display would allow some test of the appeal-to-the-cautious and memory-jogging mechanisms. This could be complemented with data on the changing pattern of thefts from cars, including the sorts of items stolen and where they were in the cars, to test the time-for-crime mechanism. Without the prior theory, it is by no means obvious that actually examining unmolested parked cars would constitute an important part of the evaluation process.

■ Another important body of evidence would concern the location within the car park of crimes committed. If these had some spatial concentration, it would demonstrate that the potential thief had a (perhaps sophisticated) understanding of camera angles, panning times, blind spots, escape routes, response times, and so on. Thinking through the local geography of the outcomes would allow us to test aspects of the lay-of-the-land context as well as features of the aforementioned mechanisms 2, 4, 6, and 7. These would in turn produce good process-evaluation data for the refinement of CCTV installations.

■ Data on the *temporal* patterning of crime, cross-referenced perhaps to information on the amount of *capacity* in use at any time would be the obvious material to test the influence of the style-of-usage context. As well as informing us on whether the potential offender feared natural surveillance more or less than CCTV surveillance, a more elaborate investigation of outcomes across a range of types of car parks (long-stay, short-stay, commuter, rail, shopper, and so on) will provide some evidence of the pattern of perceived risks associated with different sites, as well as intelligence on the most beneficial CCTV locations.

■ Hard evidence on the publicity mechanism and surveillance culture context is probably the most difficult to ascertain. A start on this could be made with the pursuit of some variations in the publicity attendant to the arrival of the CCTV cameras to see if the specifics of the message make a discernible difference on outcomes. A periodic reworking/refreshing of publicity could also be undertaken in order to detect whether the over-time car crime rate was responsive. As with all of the risk-perception mechanisms, the most potentially valuable data may well come from the potential risk takers themselves. In this respect, we hit a standard catch-22 of criminological research, in that the greater the success of a publicity deterrent, the greater the difficulty in the construction of a sample of the very respondents one needs (the deterred).

Ultimately, realist evaluation should be mechanism and context driven, rather than program led. To follow through the same example, we could anticipate a broadening of the scope of inquiry to include investigation of the use of CCTV in other areas of crime control, and even other forms of surveillance altogether. There is no reason to suppose an entirely different set of mechanisms and contexts condition the effectiveness of stadium cameras or store detectives. Although the terrain may differ, we are confident that transferable lessons could eventually be learned about, say, the lay of the land (as context) in the high-rise building or on Main Street (on the latter, see Brown, 1995). We leave our example with a restatement of what we trust is the main transferable lesson of this chapter: Without a theory of why CCTV may be effective, and a theory of the conditions that promote this potential, research into its usage is blind. And thus it is in all evaluation.

■ References

Bhaskar, R. (1975). *A realist theory of science.* Brighton: Harvester.

Brown, B. (1995). *CCTV in town centres: Three case studies* (Police Research Group, Crime Prevention Unit Series Paper No. 68). London: Home Office.

Chen, H. (1990). *Theory-driven evaluations.* Newbury Park, CA: Sage.

Cook, T. D., & Campbell, D. T. (1979). *Quasi-experimentation: Design and analysis issues for field settings.* Chicago: Rand McNally.

Durkheim, E. (1951). *Suicide.* London: Routledge & Kegan Paul. (Original work published 1897)

Harré, R. (1972). *The philosophies of science.* Oxford: Oxford University Press.

Hesse, M. (1974). *The structure of scientific inference.* London: Macmillan.

Lakatos, I. (1970). Falsification and the methodology of scientific research programmes. In I. Lakotos & A. Musgrave (Eds.), *Criticism and the growth of knowledge.* Cambridge: Cambridge University Press.

Palmer, T. (1975). Martinson revisited. *Journal of Research in Crime and Delinquency, 23,* 133-152.

Pawson, R., & Tilley, N. (in press). *Realistic evaluation.* London: Sage.

Sayer, A. (1984). *Method in social science.* London: Hutchinson.

Tilley, N. (1993). *Understanding car parks, crime and CCTV* (Police Research Group, Crime Prevention Unit Series Paper No. 42). London: Home Office.

30

Single-Case Evaluation in British Social Services

Mansoor A. F. Kazi

This chapter reports on the growing use of single-case evaluation methodology in social work in Britain. This methodology was introduced to social work largely in the past two decades as part of the movement toward scientifically based practice. Experience has led to significant methodological shifts to accommodate the needs of social work practice. In the following pages I present a number of examples from social work practice within health and education settings based on the evaluation activities at the Center for Evaluation Studies at the University of Huddersfield (Kazi, 1996a). The center advocates single-case evaluation in combination with other evaluation methodologies to serve the needs of social work practice.

◾ *Single-Case Evaluation*

Single-case evaluation refers to the use of single-case designs by practitioners to evaluate client progress (Robinson, Bronson, & Blythe, 1988).

419

Single-case design refers to a specific research methodology designed for systematic study of a single client or system. Continuous assessment over time is used as a basis for drawing inferences about intervention effects. The *Encyclopedia of Social Work* describes single-case design as "a research methodology that allows a social work practitioner to track systematically his or her progress with a client or client unit. With increasingly rigorous applications of this methodology, practitioners can also gain knowledge about effective social work interventions, although this is a less common goal" ((Blythe, 1995, p. 2164). A fundamental requirement of this methodology is the measurement of the subject's target problem (i.e., the object of the intervention or treatment) repeatedly over time. In all cases, the resulting data will enable the systematic tracking of progress. In some cases, it is also possible to draw inferences as to whether the treatment program was responsible for the observed changes in the subject's condition. However, such judgments can be made only if the outcome measure is used before, during, and/or after the treatment program is implemented, allowing comparisons to be made between the treatment and no-treatment phases (Bloom, Fischer, & Orme, 1995; Thyer, 1993). Single-case designs are usually categorized by their phases, usually referred to as A, B, C, and so on. A is the baseline phase, that is, when the independent variable or intervention either has not yet been introduced or has been withdrawn. B, C, D, and so on usually denote intervention phases (Bloom & Fischer, 1982). In a B design, the measurement begins and ends at the same time as the intervention; in an AB design, a baseline phase is followed by an intervention phase; and so on.

◼ *The Complex Nature of Social Work and Accountability*

The increased use of single-case evaluation in Britain is the result of a growing demand for social work to be accountable. Parton (1994) elaborates that, in the British context, the National Health Service and Community Care Act of 1990 and the Children Act of 1989 reflected a move away from therapeutic/medical models of casework toward social workers acting as care managers, coordinating both formal and informal networks, through care packages based on assessment of individual need and monitoring and evaluation of the effects of such packages. According to Cheetham, Fuller, McIvor, and Petch (1992), a useful working definition of effectiveness is the extent to which social work achieves its intended aims.

■ *Flexible Applications of Single-Case Evaluation*

Blythe (1995) acknowledges that early attempts at single-case design emphasized the more rigorous designs "without really knowing whether such designs could be implemented in routine social work practice. Unfortunately, this meant that practice was made to fit the confines of rigorous research designs and was not allowed to evolve naturally" (p. 2164). Examples include withdrawal designs, the requirement of equal phase lengths, and the use of standardized measures with proven reliability. This emphasis led to concerns that attempts to fit practice into a particular methodology may distort practice.

Blythe and Rodgers (1993) note three ways in which single-case designs have been changed methodologically in light of experience in practice. First, emphasis has shifted from more rigorous designs to simpler ones, such as the AB design. Second, the exact nature of the design is not determined at the outset—rather, it falls into place as practice unfolds. Finally, some of the research requirements have been relaxed, for example, the use of less rigorous measures such as self-anchored scales and rating scales. These three changes have improved the fit between single-case designs and social work practice. Our British experience with regard to these methodological shifts is in keeping with that of our American colleagues. The following three examples illustrate the British experience of using single-case evaluation.

■ *Example 1:*
The Kirklees Project—An Agencywide Application

The catalyst that led to the establishment of the Center for Evaluation Studies was the completion of a research project titled "Measuring Outcomes in Direct Client Services" in the Kirklees Education Social Work Service (Yorkshire, England). The service is aimed at schoolchildren, their families, and their teachers, to help resolve both home- and school-based problems. This project's central aim was to enable social workers

Client: AC   Observer: Parents

Date	What Happened Before	Behavior	What Happened After
8/5 10:00 a.m.	Asked AC to fetch extension and unroll it	Banged on floor, trying to break it Ran into the house & slammed the door, calling mother "silly cow"	Told to put it down and leave it Sent to bed for ½ hour
12/5 4:30 p.m.	Asked to go to friend's house and told "no"	Told me she was going anyway	Told to stay in garden or go to bed
14/5 8:25 p.m.		Set alarm off	Sent to bed
15/6 5:45 p.m.	Asked to go to friend's house and told "no"	Being cheeky	Ignored her

Figure 30.1. Excerpts From the ABC Chart Kept by AC's Parents

to become practitioner-evaluators, using single-case designs on an agencywide basis. In this example, 21 social workers used single-case evaluation in 83 cases (Kazi, 1994a, 1994b, 1996b; Kazi & Wilson, 1993, 1996).

☐ *Case Illustration 1: AC*

At the request of her mother, AC—a primary school student aged 8 years—was referred to the social worker for help with management of aggressive and destructive behavior at home. In order to make these global descriptions more precise, the social worker asked both parents to log all significant incidents of the girl's bad behavior, using a chart to log not only the behaviors, but also the antecedents and consequences (hence this

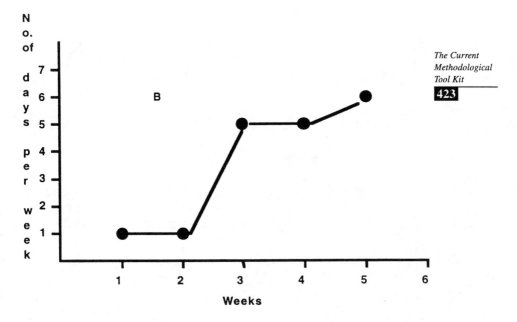

Figure 30.2. Number of Days per Week When Bad Behavior Did Not Occur

is called an ABC chart). At the same time, an intervention program consisting of advice and support for both parents was initiated to enhance their skills for managing AC's behavior. Figure 30.1 illustrates some excerpts from AC's ABC chart, essentially a qualitative measure used by AC's parents. The data from this measure are quantified in Figure 30.2 as the number of days per week when bad behavior did not take place.

Figure 30.2 illustrates a B design; that is, no baseline measurements were available and the target problem was measured during the intervention program. This design is at the bottom end of the experimental continuum. The only inference that can be drawn is that behavior improved in the course of the 6 weeks. No further conclusions can be drawn with regard to the extent to which the intervention program itself was responsible for the changes observed. Nevertheless, the B design can provide useful information on progress to both the worker and the client. This case is an example of how qualitative and quantitative data can be combined to provide such information.

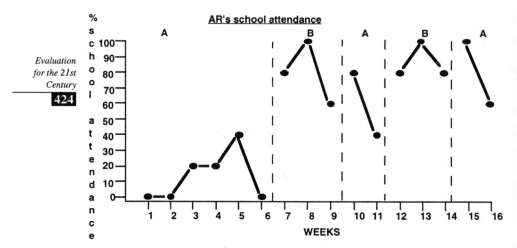

Figure 30.3. AR's School Attendance

NOTE: A represents baseline periods; B represents intervention phases.

☐ *Case Illustration 2: AR*

AR, aged 14 years, was referred by the high school for persistent absenteeism. The intervention (B phases in Figure 30.3) consisted of counseling for both AR and his family, building better home-school links, and providing encouragement for AR in school. The measure used was the school attendance register, in which attendance is recorded twice a day; AR's actual attendance is represented in Figure 30.3 as a percentage of the total possible attendance per week.

Figure 30.3 illustrates an ABABA design, which is stronger than the classical ABAB experimental design because it ends with a further "return to baseline" phase A. The first (retrospective) baseline indicates that attendance varied from nil to 40%. At the onset of the first intervention phase B, an immediate improvement took place. When the intervention was withdrawn, attendance once again deteriorated, but improved dramatically when the intervention was reintroduced. The follow-up phase A at the end indicates that although attendance was deteriorating, it was still higher than the baseline.

This design allowed addressing whether the intervention was responsible for the changes because of the four successive "coincidences." Using the principle of "successive coincidences" (Thyer, 1993) it can be concluded with increased confidence that the intervention program was responsible for the improvements in attendance. The withdrawal phases occurred naturally due to the social worker's caseload management.

The Kirklees project's basic strategy was to enable the exact nature of the designs to be determined by practice considerations (and therefore the needs of the clients) rather than research considerations. Training was provided for practitioners in breaking down global target problems into measurable component parts (or indicators), selecting appropriate measures, and then proceeding with practice, allowing single-case design to be determined naturally. This position has since been corroborated by Blythe and Rodgers (1993). The social workers began with the use of standardized measures from Corcoran and Fischer (1987) and Bloom and Fischer (1982), and frequently supplemented them with their own measures for client problems such as school attendance, behavior, feelings, and attitudes.

The project demonstrates that the full range of single-case designs is available to the social worker. The B design was used most frequently (47 times), followed by the AB design (26 times). Four AB designs were replicated across clients with the same target problem, and another three across target problems with the same client. Withdrawal—or return to baseline conditions—was used in 19 designs, including an ABABC design (i.e., baseline, intervention B, baseline, intervention B, combined with another C) replicated across four clients with the same target problem. These replicated designs occurred naturally in the course of practice and allowed stronger causal inferences to be made in those cases.

It is also worth noting the use of both qualitative and quantitative measures (Bostwick & Kyte, 1993; Brennan, 1992). The use of qualitative measures such as the ABC chart (client self-log) enriched the evaluation process for both the social workers and their clients, particularly in cases where both qualitative and quantitative measures were used. Further, the use of single-case designs supplemented the normal qualitative process recording that takes place in the agency.

■ Example 2: Truancy and Disaffection Projects in Kirklees Metropolitan Council

Single-case evaluation is being used to evaluate a number of school-based projects (known as GEST 20) jointly funded by the government's Department for Education and Employment and Kirklees Metropolitan Council

(Kazi, Craven, & Wilson, 1995). In 1994-1995, there were eight projects involving problems of truancy and disaffection from school, and single-case procedures were used in 79 individual cases. For the purposes of this chapter, two of these projects are considered to illustrate flexible use of single-case evaluation to fit the needs of practice and the use of this methodology in combination with others to provide a fuller description of reality.

☐ *Project 1: Whitcliffe Mount School*

The school-based project at Whitcliffe Mount School consisted of a teacher (Elizabeth Ineson) and a social worker (Stuart Haigh) who aimed to identify persistent absentees and reintegrate them into school. This process included investigating reasons for nonattendance and implementing interventions to deal with those reasons. Specific targets were agreed upon with individual pupils and parents, and educational support was provided within the school to help with reintegration. The project staff worked with 15 pupils and their parents, constructing personal achievement charts for each pupil and using single-case evaluation to monitor progress.

For each case, the measure was percentage attendance per school week. The baseline consisted of the first few weeks immediately preceding the first contact made with the pupil and/or parent. The changes in the levels of attendance following each contact demonstrate both whether progress was made and the extent to which such progress can be attributed to the work of the project team. The designs used in this project were an application of the "periodic treatment elements design" as described by Barlow, Hayes, and Nelsen (1984, p. 210). If a consistent pattern emerges between the periodicity of intervention elements and the periodicity of behavior change, then inferences are strengthened regarding the effectiveness of the intervention. The following examples are taken from this project.

Case Illustration 1: DK

The baseline attendance was a stable zero, but considerable progress was achieved in raising attendance levels to 50%, 100%, and 90% in the weeks following the intervention. Figure 30.4 demonstrates that contacts

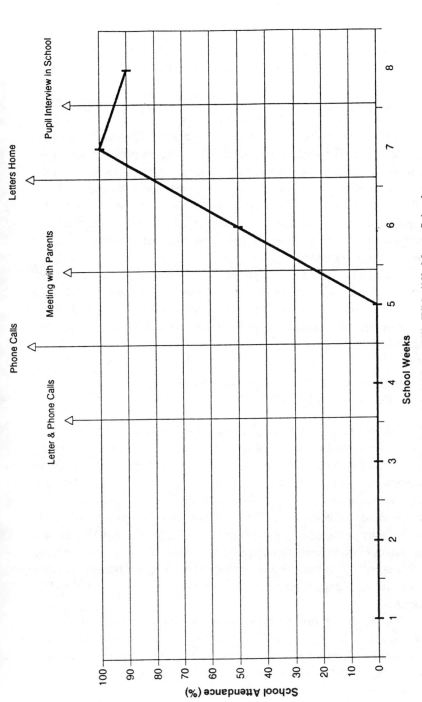

Figure 30.4. DK's School Attendance (%), Whitcliffe Mount School

made were immediately followed by progress on three occasions, indicating that this progress was likely to be attributable to the intervention.

Case Illustration 2: PW

The baseline phase A in Figure 30.5 indicates attendance of between 30% and 70%. The subsequent contacts made by the project team (intervention phase B) actually led to a deterioration in attendance. It was not until the meeting was arranged at the local authority's Attendance Panel (phase C) that considerable progress was made. It can be concluded that progress was made and that it was slightly attributable to the efforts of intervention B followed by the panel meeting, intervention C (where contracts were agreed upon).

The 15 cases in which the project team was involved in some depth were all successful in achieving higher levels of attendance. There is substantial evidence that this project was effective in its work, and that the intervention programs were successful in helping pupils achieve higher levels of attendance.

☐ *Project 2: Truancy and Disaffection Project at Fartown High School*

The project at Fartown High School involved a teacher (Fran Perry) and an education social worker (Sarah Adams). The aims were to raise awareness of the importance of good attendance and to provide incentives for improving school attendance, through group work that included separate personal and social skills training and English lessons taught in small groups. Students were allocated to the group following parental approval. Tokens were awarded for good behavior, leading to other rewards, including letters of commendation and trips to a center for motorcycle riding. Community placements were also provided at Deighton Junior School, at the technical college's textile department, and at a day center for older people.

Additional support was provided by the education social worker for the pupils, their siblings, and their parents. Approval was sought and gained from all parents for inclusion in the group, following extensive discussions with the education social worker. Regular home visits were made to report on progress and to clarify school issues with parents.

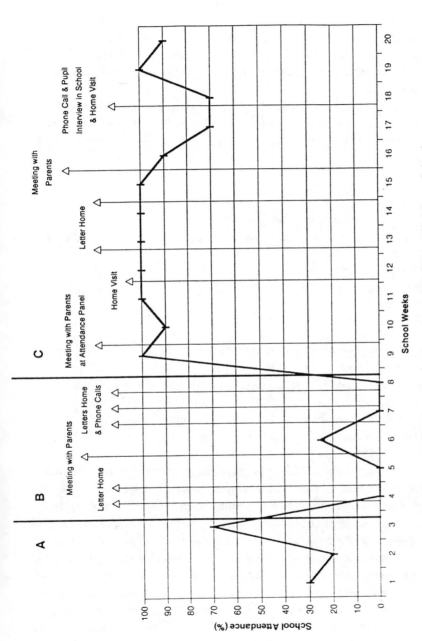

Figure 30.5. PW's School Attendance (%), Whitcliffe Mount School

Single-case evaluation was used with the 15 pupils who became regular participants of the group, which began in September 1994 and terminated in January 1996. The measures used were the school attendance register and qualitative data of the parents' perceptions obtained from semistructured meetings with parents at home following the termination of the group work.

Every family involved in the group work project was visited at home following the termination of the intervention. The unanimous response from all parents was that their children had benefited from this intervention. Comments made included the following:

> "I could not get him out of bed . . . now he's up without me shouting."
>
> "He couldn't wait to get a 'good boy' letter."
>
> "It's been good getting nice letters from school. . . . He always used to be in trouble."
>
> "He now has friends and likes school more."
>
> "He's much more pleasant at home, is more confident, and talks positively about school."

Single-case design charts were constructed and shared with each of the 15 participants. Two of these appear here as Figures 30.6 and 30.7. The measure used was the percentage of attendance at school per month. The resulting single-case evaluation design was the ABA design, the first phase A being the baseline before the intervention, the second phase B being group work, and the third phase A representing the return to baseline following the end of the intervention.

The figures show that the intervention phase was followed by immediate progress in 11 of the 15 cases (as in Figure 30.6), whereas attendance actually deteriorated in the 4 remaining cases (as in Figure 30.7). In the 11 cases where progress was made, attendance immediately dropped somewhat when the group work ceased in 9 cases, indicating that the improvement in attendance was probably attributable to the group work. In the other 2, attendance did not drop immediately after the group work ceased, indicating that there may have been alternative explanations for the progress in the B phase, and therefore the progress is only slightly attributable to the group work in these 2 cases. When combined with the qualitative data of the parents' perceptions of progress, these results make

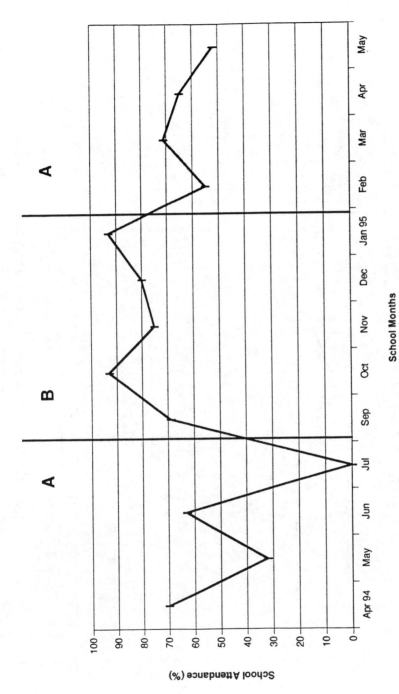

Figure 30.6. SS's School Attendance (%), Fartown High School

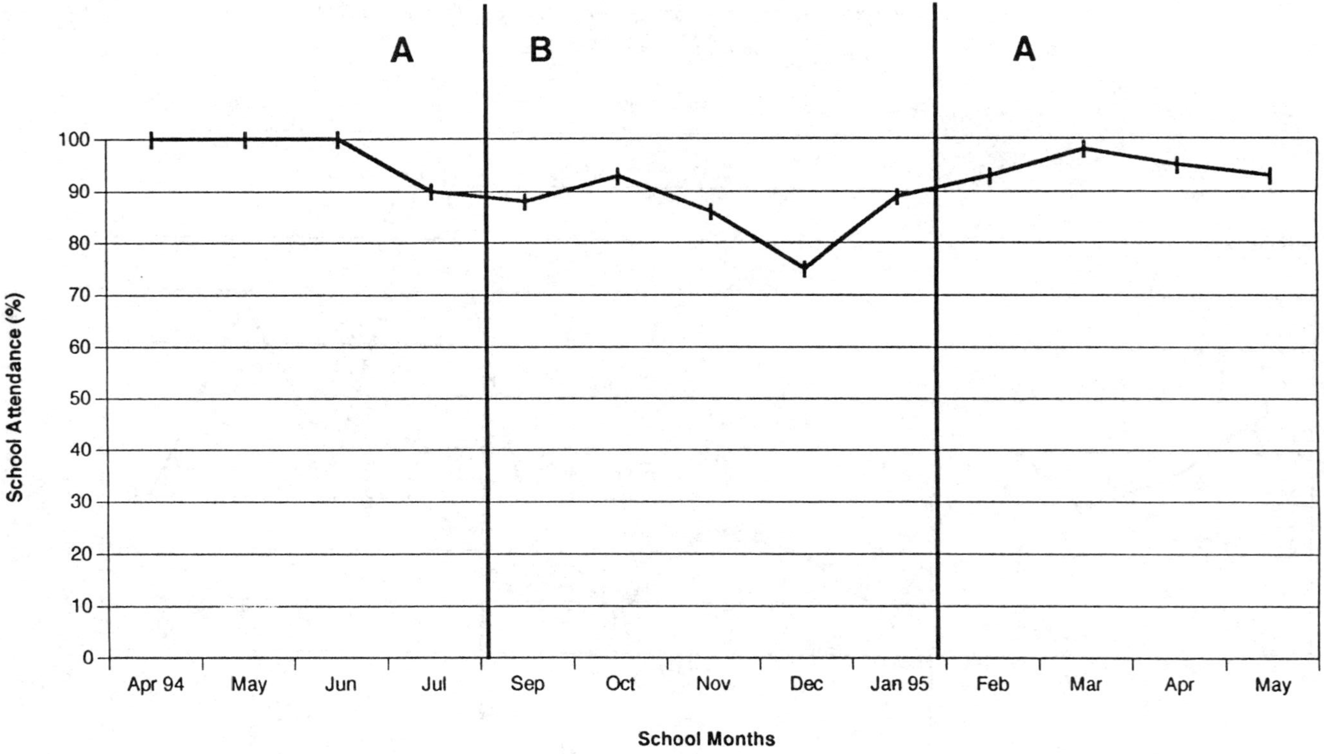

Figure 30.7. CJ's School Attendance (%), Fartown High School

it possible to conclude that the group work was effective in achieving its stated aims.

■ *Example 3: Social Work in Health Settings*

The final examples from the Center for Evaluation Studies's activities involve social work with older people in health settings, particularly in the provision of services to people aged 65 years and over. This setting has seen many changes in the past few years, with the implementation of the 1990 National Health Service and Community Care Act, which aims to empower service users to make informed choices, to enable people to be cared for in their own homes where appropriate, and to provide seamless service where both social services and health authorities are involved (Audit Commission, 1992).

☐ *Project 1: A Community Care Project*

The implementation of the 1990 act led to the creation of a number of joint initiatives involving both health and social services in England. The Center for Evaluation Studies has completed the evaluation of one project and is involved in the evaluation of three others. The first project's evaluation was commissioned when the project had ceased to provide services, and therefore the evaluation was completed retrospectively (Kazi, Craven, & Weavill, 1995). This evaluation consisted of a combination of research methods, influenced in particular by program evaluation (Hornick & Burrows, 1988), single-case evaluation (Bloom & Fischer, 1982; Thyer, 1993), and pluralistic evaluation (Smith & Cantley, 1988). The perspectives of all the relevant parties involved in the project were included, namely, the referring agents (health and social services staff in the locality), the project staff, the users (and their caregivers) who received the project's services, and the project's management group.

The project was jointly funded and managed by health and social services, providing an integrated service to older people who required both nursing and social care following acute conditions and who had prognoses for independent living. The project's services were provided 24 hours a day, 7 days a week, and the records were very detailed. Each user was assessed, and a care plan was formulated to promote rehabilitation and independent living; daily records were kept of progress. The quality of these records enabled the retrospective use of single-case evaluation procedures (Bloom & Fischer, 1982).

The measures used in the project's cases were selected from case records. First, variables of independent living were identified from the care assessments, plans, and reviews. Second, the daily records of the community care assistants were used to determine the progress of each of these variables. For each variable (e.g., dressing, preparing meals, changing catheter bags), the user either performed the activity independently or did not. The occasions when the client had received help from project staff or other caregivers were not counted. These were then converted into a frequency count of the number of times per week each variable was done independently, expressed as a percentage.

Case Illustration 1: Mr. F.M.

Mr. F.M., aged 81 years, was admitted to hospital in March 1994 with a suspected stroke (right side, upper-limb weakness). The community care officer completed an assessment in May 1994, immediately prior to Mr. F.M.'s discharge home. The variables for independent living were identified from the case records as follows:

1. preparation of snacks and drinks (including breakfast and tea)
2. preparation, cooking, and serving of main meal
3. undressing
4. dressing

Mr. F.M.'s chart (Figure 30.8) shows the daily progress made with the above variables. Assistance was provided by community care assistants, but sometimes also by relatives and friends. However, in this chart only the occasions when Mr. F.M. completed the activities totally independently are counted. Good progress was made against all of the above four variables. Figure 30.8 illustrates a B design for each variable; that is, the measurement started at the same time as the intervention. Mr. F.M. and his daughter-in-law were interviewed at a follow-up in October 1994, and they expressed satisfaction with the services provided by the project,

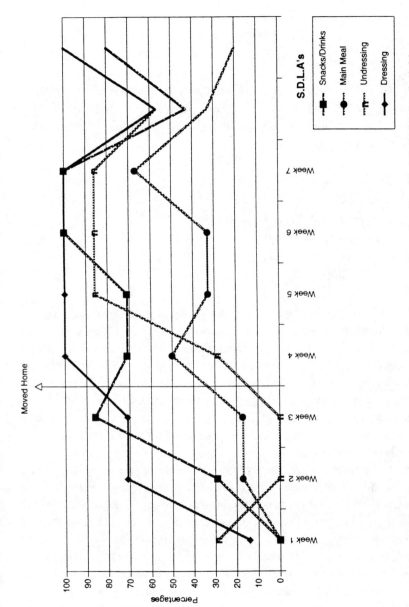

Figure 30.8. Percentage of Time per Week Mr. F.M. Was Able to Carry Out Specified Daily Living Activities

describing it as "a big help." They noted, "It gives you a breathing space. They need extra help at the beginning."

Case Illustration 2: Mr. F.K.

Mr. F.K., aged 87 years, was admitted to the hospital with right-sided pneumonia. The community care officer completed an assessment in May 1994. The variables for independent living were identified from the case records as follows:

1. washing/dressing
2. preparation, cooking, and serving of the main meal
3. preparation of drinks and snacks
4. emptying catheter bag
5. changing catheter bag
6. undressing

Mr. F.K.'s chart (Figure 30.9) shows that progress was made against all of the above variables, even though there were problems with a skin infection that required daily medication and a chest infection that required hospital treatment for one night. In the follow-up, Mr. F.K. expressed satisfaction: "I would like to express my thanks to the ladies who have looked after me for the last few weeks since my discharge. Nothing has been too much for them and their kindness and patience in dealing with an old man is very much appreciated. In fact I am at a loss to find the . . . words. Many thanks."

As in the charts for Mr. F.M. and Mr. F.K., the resulting single-case designs for all other cases were B designs (in most cases, several for each patient). The construction of baselines was not possible, as the archival records used began at the same time as the intervention programs. Despite these limitations, the single-case evaluation procedures provided a more complete picture of reality when combined with other evaluation methods. The perceptions of the users and caregivers were obtained with the use of semistructured, qualitative interviewing techniques that corroborated the data in the single-case evaluations. The single-case evaluation of all eight cases where services were provided by the project indicated that progress was made in the specified daily living activities in six cases,

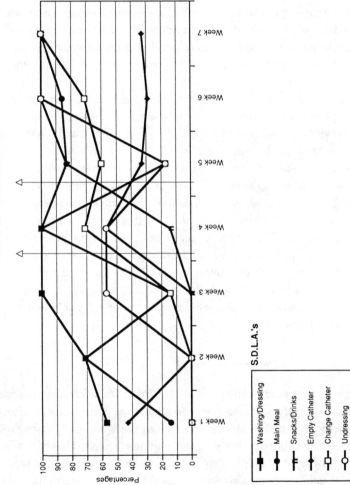

Figure 30.9. Percentage of Time per Week Mr. F.K. Was Able to Carry Out Specified Daily Living Activities

437

and the follow-up interviews of the clients (and, where involved, care-givers) indicated that progress was being maintained and that all the service users were pleased with the project's services. The survey of referrers (health and social work staff) to the project found that 74% were also satisfied with the services their clients had received.

A needs analysis found that the criterion that potential service users should be in receipt of both nursing and social services was too restrictive and in part explained why the project was underused. A survey of potential referrers found that, of those who responded to the survey questionnaire, only half were aware of the referral process, which may also account for the project's underuse.

Staff members were asked to provide semistructured written reports of their perception of interagency collaboration between the health and social services. Results showed that they were confident and felt they were achieving their goals with the clients, but they also felt undervalued because of problems in their conditions of service that were changed when they transferred from the social services to the health authority.

Program evaluation, based on data from the regular reports provided to the management group, suggested that the project was indeed conducted as planned. These approaches to evaluation from the perspectives of the different parties involved in the project were influenced by pluralistic evaluation (Smith & Cantley, 1988). When combined with single-case evaluation in this project, this multimethod approach enabled the evaluation to provide data that would not have been possible with the use of any one method alone.

☐ *Project 2: The Oakes Villa Project*

The project being conducted at the Oakes Villa has the purpose of rehabilitating patients so that they can reenter the community. The evaluation methods used are similar to those in the community care project described above, but this project is still ongoing. The staff has been trained in the application of single-case evaluation and other methods from the project's inception. Learning from the first project, the staff (managed by project leader Kathleen Firth) created a rating scale for measuring the extent to which progress is made with each client's activities of daily living (ADL). The scale ranges from 1 to 6 as follows: 6 = independent, 5 = independent with equipment, 4 = receiving enabling assistance (i.e., setting the scene), 3 = receiving slight assistance (i.e., finishing off with partial help), 2 = receiving moderate assistance (i.e., needing quite a bit of help to do the task), and 1 = totally dependent (i.e., requiring someone else to undertake the task).

The project's staff are enhancing reliability by providing specific examples for each point on the scale and by agreeing on the definitions as precisely as possible within the staff team. Each specified activity is assessed daily against the scale and then expressed as a weekly percentage: % = (total of actual scores in the week)/(maximum possible in the week) × 100. This scale is used in conjunction with another 6-point scale to measure each client's feelings at one point in time in the latter part of each day, indicated by the number of beans the client places in a pot (0 = terrible to 6 = excellent). These measures are combined with follow-up assessment when the clients are rehabilitated in their own homes, including a semistructured customer survey of the services provided by the project.

Case Illustration: Mrs. J.

Mrs. J., 83 years old, was admitted into the project's rehabilitation unit in July 1995. She had been in the hospital for 11 days with chronic bronchitis, cervical myopathy, and peripheral vascular disease. Her main problems were poor mobility and reduced ability with daily living activities due to poor manual dexterity and generally reduced self-confidence. The daily living tasks identified in the community care assessment and plans were getting up and going to bed, washing, dressing, toileting, eating, transfers (e.g., from chair to bed), mobility, and medication. All of these variables were assigned scores on the ADL scale, expressed in weekly percentages.

Mrs. J.'s chart (Figure 30.10) shows that progress was made against all the variables. The project's objective was to build up her self-confidence and ability to undertake daily living tasks, with the overall aim of enabling her to return to her own home. This aim was achieved 6 weeks later, and a follow-up assessment and consumer survey were being arranged at the time of writing. Mrs. J.'s chart represents eight B designs with the same client; that is, the rehabilitation unit's interventions are evaluated across eight target problems. The first week in the unit could be considered a baseline, and the resulting design could be AB, but in this

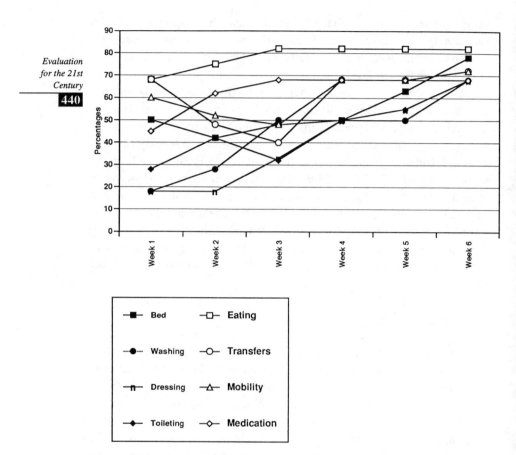

Figure 30.10. Percentage of Time per Week Mrs. J. Was Able to Carry Out Specified Daily Living Activities

case maturation could not be ruled out, as Mrs. J. did have a medical prognosis for improvement following the period of acute illness.

■ *Conclusion*

The above examples from the activities of the Center for Evaluation Studies illustrate the methodological shifts in single-case evaluation as outlined by Blythe and Rodgers (1993). The designs need not be experimental, the designs unfold with practice, and requirement of the use of standardized measures can be relaxed. These developments in the application of the methodology enable a better fit with social work practice, which is itself a complex activity. Single-case evaluation can be used with other methods, including qualitative methods—descriptive, subjective perceptions and feelings can be combined with more objective measures. Single-case evaluation can be part of a pragmatic, methodologically pluralist strategy—the development of each method can be achieved without having to destroy another. These improvements have led to an increased use of the single-case evaluation methodology in British social services.

■ *References*

Audit Commission. (1992). *The community revolution: Personal services and community care.* London: Her Majesty's Stationery Office.

Barlow, D. H., Hayes, S. C., & Nelsen, R. O. (1984). *The scientist practitioner.* New York: Pergamon.

Bloom, M., & Fischer, J. (1982). *Evaluating practice: Guidelines for the accountable professional.* Englewood Cliffs, NJ: Prentice Hall.

Bloom, M., Fischer, J., & Orme, J. (1995). *Evaluating practice: Guidelines for the accountable professional* (2nd ed.). Boston: Allyn & Bacon.

Blythe, B. J. (1995). Single-system design. In R. L. Edwards et al. (Eds.), *Encyclopedia of social work* (19th ed., Vol. 3, pp. 2164-2168). Silver Spring, MD: National Association of Social Workers.

Blythe, B. J., & Rodgers, A. Y. (1993). Evaluating our own practice: Past, present, and future trends. *Journal of Social Service Review, 18,* 101-119.

Bostwick, G. J., Jr., & Kyte, N. S. (1993). Measurement in research. In R. M. Grinnell, Jr. (Ed.), *Social work research and evaluation* (4th ed., pp. 174-197). Itasca, IL: F. E. Peacock.

Brennan, J. (Ed.). (1992). *Mixing methods: Qualitative and quantitative research.* Aldershot: Avebury.

Cheetham, J., Fuller, R., McIvor, G., & Petch, A. (1992). *Evaluating social work effectiveness.* Milton Keynes, UK: Open University Press.

Corcoran, K., & Fischer, J. (1987). *Measures for clinical practice: A source book.* New York: Free Press.

Hornick, J. P., & Burrows, B. (1988). Program evaluation. In R. M. Grinnell, Jr. (Ed.), *Social work research and evaluation* (3rd ed., pp. 400-424). Itasca, IL: F. E. Peacock.

Kazi, M. A. F. (1994a, November). *Single-case evaluation in improving services.* Paper presented at the autumn research conference of the Association of Directors of Social Services, Stafford, England.

Kazi, M. A. F. (1994b, December). *Single-case evaluation in the public sector.* Paper presented at the conference of the European Evaluation Society, the Hague, Netherlands.

Kazi, M. A. F. (1996a). The Center for Evaluation Studies at the University of Huddersfield: A profile. *Research on Social Work Practice, 6,* 104-116.

Kazi, M. A. F. (1996b). Single-case evaluation in the public sector. *Evaluation, 2,* 85-97.

Kazi, M. A. F., Craven, M., & Weavill, C. (1995). *Evaluation of the Chickenley Project based at Dewsbury District Hospital.* Huddersfield, England: University of Huddersfield, Center for Evaluation Studies.

Kazi, M. A. F., Craven, M., & Wilson, J. T. (1995). *Evaluation of the Kirklees GEST 20 Program: Truancy and disaffection.* Huddersfield, England: University of Huddersfield, Center for Evaluation Studies.

Kazi, M. A. F., & Wilson, J. T. (1993). *Applying outcome measures in direct client services.* Huddersfield, England: University of Huddersfield, Center for Evaluation Studies.

Kazi, M. A. F., & Wilson, J. T. (1996). Applying single-case evaluation methodology in a British social work agency. *Research on Social Work Practice, 6,* 5-26.

Parton, N. (1994). The nature of social work under conditions of (post) modernity. *Social Work and Social Sciences Review, 5*(2), 93-112.

Robinson, E. A. R., Bronson, D. E., & Blythe, B. J. (1988). An analysis of the implementation of single-case evaluation by practitioners. *Social Service Review, 62,* 285-301.

Ruckdeschel, R. A., & Farris, B. E. (1981). Assessing practice: A critical look at the single-case design. *Social Casework, 62,* 413-419.

Smith, G., & Cantley, C. (1988). Pluralistic evaluation. In J. Lishman (Ed.), *Evaluation* (pp. 118-136). London: Jessica Kingsley.

Thyer, B. A. (1993). Single-system research designs. In R. M. Grinnell, Jr. (Ed.), *Social work research and evaluation* (4th ed., pp. 94-117). Itasca, IL: F. E. Peacock.

31

Twenty-One Years Old and Counting

The Interrupted Time Series Comes of Age

Robert G. Orwin

The two quasi-experimental designs long considered to best approximate true experiments in terms of strength of causal inference are the regression-discontinuity (RD) design and the interrupted time series (ITS) design.[1] Deemed among the most generally interpretable quasi-experiments in Cook and Campbell's (1979) seminal book on quasi-experimentation, they were described much the same way 15 years later by Marcantonio and Cook (1994) as the "two that stand out because of the high quality of causal inference they often engender" (p. 134).

RD designs have been offered as an attractive alternative to true experiments when the latter are not feasible.[2] Despite its attractive features and continual refinement (see Trochim, 1990), the RD design has infrequently been used outside of compensatory education evaluation.[3] The ITS design has enjoyed somewhat more success. Still, it is less often used than it could be (Cook & Shadish, 1994; Marcantonio & Cook, 1994).

As the name implies, a time series is a sequence of data points from a single variable measured at multiple points in time. Time series have many uses outside of program evaluation, such as economic forecasting and industrial quality control. Within evaluation, a time series is said to be interrupted when an external event occurs that potentially alters it. The ITS quasi-experiment has a minimum of one time series and one interruption, but, as discussed below, the basic design can be augmented in a number of ways. As in all quasi-experimentation, the analyst's task is to employ these enhancements (where available) in the manner that most persuasively rules out alternative explanations to the intervention.

In this chapter I will present a brief overview of the basic design and analysis of the ITS quasi-experiment, describe some design enhancements that increase its inferential power, review recent technical developments that have expanded its utility, and speculate on future applications.

■ The Simple ITS Design

In its simplest form, the ITS design requires (a) a naturally occurring event or planned intervention occurring at a known time point and (b) repeated observations of an aggregate outcome measure both before and after the event. The more preprogram data points, the better; most texts on time series analysis recommend having at least 50 observations at equal intervals for stable parameter estimates (Glass, Wilson, & Gottman, 1975; McCleary & Hay, 1980). Conceptually, the analysis is straightforward. The preprogram trend, seasonality, and error structure of an aggregated indicator are analyzed in order to project the counterfactual condition—that is, What would have happened in the absence of the program? This projected trend is then compared with the actual postprogram trend to estimate the net program effect. The simple ITS strategy does not rule out all threats to internal validity, but it is easily the strongest of the "full-coverage" designs (Rossi & Freeman, 1993) that do not include comparison groups because the programs being evaluated are delivered to all, or nearly all, eligible recipients. The source of ITS's strength is that one can assess several major threats to validity, such as maturation, prior to the program onset by analyzing the multiple pretest waves.

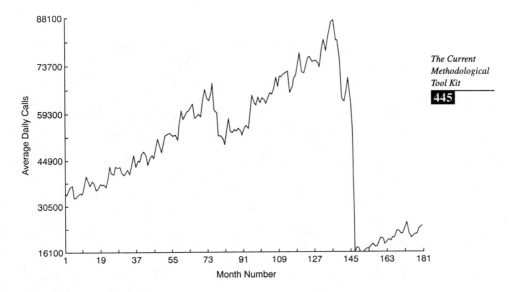

Figure 31.1. Average Daily Number of Calls to Cincinnati Directory Assistance
SOURCE: Data from McSweeny (1978).

A classic example of a simple ITS design is McSweeny's (1978) analysis of the effect of Cincinnati Bell's decision to begin charging for local directory assistance calls (see Figure 31.1). Looking at the timing and size of the effect, skeptics would be hard-pressed to pose a plausible alternative explanation. Similarly, few would argue that the McSweeny data need a comparison series of directory assistance calls in, say, Cleveland to support an interpretation that the fee-for-service plan was responsible for the observed change. The McSweeny example is literally a "textbook case," reprinted repeatedly over the years. A more recent example of a dramatic intervention effect can be found in Rogers's (1992) study of the volume of dollar-denominated accounts held in Mexican banks. The Mexican government adopted various measures in 1982 to try to discourage the use of such accounts. As shown in Figure 31.2, the effects are again unmistakable.

Other time series show dramatic intervention effects in both onset and decay. In 1982, for example, China and Great Britain began talks concerning the 1997 expiration of Britain's 99-year lease on the so-called New Territories off the coast of Hong Kong. The island of Hong Kong per se

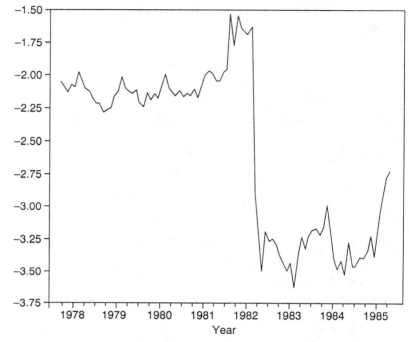

Figure 31.2. Log of the Peso Value of Dollar-Denominated Bank Accounts
in Mexico to the Peso Value of Peso-Denominated Bank Accounts in Mexico,
1978–1985
SOURCE: Data from Rogers (1992).

was not supposed to be at issue, having been permanently ceded by the
Chinese to the British in 1842 (Wei, 1990). However, the new Chinese
government argued that the treaties ceding the entire territory of Hong
Kong were unequal and unjust, and on July 16, 1982, announced its first
proposal for the eventual reversion of Hong Kong to Chinese sovereignty
and administration. The reaction of the Hong Kong stock market to the
announcement can be seen easily in Figure 31.3. On that day (day 260 in
the figure), the market hit its lowest point since the Arab oil embargo of
1973. Other indicators (e.g., the value of the Hong Kong dollar on foreign
exchange markets) behaved similarly. Clearly, it is possible to make

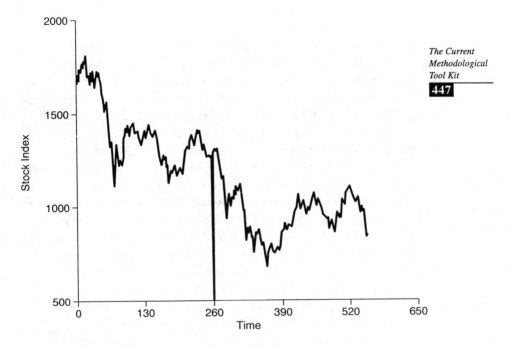

Figure 31.3. Hang Seng Index of Hong Kong Stock Prices From July 16,
1981, to September 31, 1983
SOURCE: W. W. S. Wei, *Time Series Analysis: Univariate and Multivariate Methods,* © 1990 Addison-
Wesley Publishing Company, Inc. Reprinted by permission of Addison-Wesley Longman Publishing
Company, Inc.

causal attributions to such events without sophisticated statistical techniques.

■ Analysis Considerations

More commonly, the effects measured in time series data are smaller, more
gradual, or otherwise less clear-cut, and require appropriate (and often
sophisticated) statistical analysis to estimate. For example, although visual means were sufficient to detect the immediate, short-term effects of
the Chinese announcement on Hong Kong stock prices in Figure 31.3,

they are less able to ascertain long-term effects. Using an approach called autoregressive integrated moving average (ARIMA) analysis (described below), Wei (1990) detected no significant long-term effects. As shown in Figure 31.3, a long-term downward trend was in fact established well before the Chinese government's announcement, and the large variance of the stock index meant that any detectable long-term effect of the announcement would also have to be reasonably large.

The key to valid ITS analysis or any other use of time series data (e.g., forecasting) is an understanding that each observation of the series is statistically dependent on prior observations. The true underlying process of the dependent relationship is rarely known, and therefore must be carefully modeled. As noted by Box and Tiao (1975) in the article that first wed ARIMA modeling with intervention analysis, standard methods such as ordinary least squares (OLS) and even generalized least squares (GLS) regression "lack memory"; that is, they ignore or make unverified assumptions about interobservational dependence over time.

Historically, there have been two distinct yet related approaches to time series analysis: structural modeling and ARIMA modeling. In the former approach (traditionally favored by econometricians), the error structure is modeled on the basis of prior research and/or theory. In the latter, it is identified empirically from the data. In practice, the two approaches are more convergent than this simple description implies (McCleary & Hay, 1980), yet each has its adherents (e.g., see Harvey & Durbin, 1986). For better or worse, the ARIMA approach appears to have emerged as the approach of choice among applied social researchers (including program evaluators) other than economists, so ARIMA modeling is the focus of this chapter.

The ARIMA analysis begins by "whitening" the time series—that is, reducing it to random error or "white noise." The analyst typically starts by removing any secular trend and/or seasonality by differencing the series at appropriate lag points. The process may also include a nonlinear transformation (e.g., a log transform) to counteract increasing or decreasing heterogeneity. Finally, an ARIMA "noise" model is fit, which includes the specification of one or more autoregressive (AR) and/or moving average (MA) parameters to remove the remaining serial correlation. These parameters are specified through an iterative process of identification, testing, and diagnosis (for details, see Box, Jenkins, & Reinsel, 1994; McCleary & Hay, 1980). The iterative process keeps the analyst "in the loop" from beginning to end. In principle, the decision rules are all laid out, so the process should be entirely replicable. In practice, analysts must frequently make decisions while "in the cracks" between one rule or another, making replicability an issue.[4] One obvious way to boost confidence is to test replicability empirically by subjecting the data to an independent reanalysis by a second time series analyst.[5] Practically speaking, it is probably sufficient to verify that the substantive results replicate, even if some of the interim decisions (e.g., whether to add additional lag terms to the noise model) do not.

Once the series has been whitened, it is ready for the intervention assessment. The general approach is to fit a model that describes the expected response and apply a set of diagnostic tests. Optimally, the initial model selection is guided by knowledge of the intervention or available theory about the implementation of the intervention and its expected effects. For example, is the effect expected to be immediate or gradual, permanent or temporary? Each potential variation is represented by different mathematical models. As with the noise model, if the diagnostics show lack of fit, the model is modified and rediagnosed until no serious model inadequacies remain.[6] ARIMA-based ITS has been used to estimate the effects of a wide variety of interventions, from its maiden application in an assessment of the impact of air pollution controls on ozone levels in downtown Los Angeles (Box & Tiao, 1975) to the effects of the Arab oil embargo on electricity consumption (Montgomery & Weatherby, 1980), the impact of television on crime rates (Hennigan et al., 1982), the effects of the saccharin warning label on national diet soft drink sales (Orwin, Schucker, & Stokes, 1984), and numerous others.

Perhaps the most famous problem to which a simple ITS analysis has been applied is the impact of the 1965 New York City blackout on birthrates. On November 9, 1965, most of New York City was plunged into darkness by a massive power failure. On the following August 10, the front-page headline of the *New York Times* read, "Births Up 9 Months After Blackout." The next day, a somewhat more cautious follow-up article appeared (this one on page 35, however): "Theories Abound on Birth Increase—Possible Link Will Not Be Determined for Two More Weeks." A week later, the British magazine *New Scientist* reported on the "apparent sharp rise in births in New York City," and a year later the respected medical journal *Lancet* described New Yorkers' "vigorous procreative urge stimulated . . . by the stygian darkness of electric-power cuts." Articles continued to appear in the professional as well as popular literature (e.g., a 1968 article in the *American Journal of Obstetrics and Gynecology* "confirming" that the blackout had indeed caused an increase in births 9 months later). By the 1970s, the "blackout babies" story was an accepted part of American folklore. Noting various omissions and erroneous assumptions in earlier analyses, Izenman and Zabell (1981) used ARIMA modeling to analyze the New York birthrate data.[7] After fitting the appropriate noise model (which included terms for both trend and seasonality), the parameter estimate for the blackout effect was clearly nonsignificant ($t = 0.67$, C.I. $= -0.06 < \beta < 0.11$). Alternative analyses using different assumptions (e.g., alternative centerings of the gestational interval distribution) also revealed no effects.[8]

■ *Time Series With Multiple Interruptions*

The ITS design can also be used to assess the impacts of multiple interventions.[9] In the first known ITS analysis that used ARIMA modeling, Box and Tiao (1975) assessed the effects of two discrete events on ozone levels in downtown Los Angeles between 1955 and 1973: (a) in January 1960, the implementation of a new law that reduced the allowable proportion of reactive hydrocarbons in locally sold gasoline, and (b) in January 1966, the implementation of regulations requiring engine design changes in new cars that were expected to reduce the production of ozone. After fitting the noise model, event 1 was modeled as an abrupt permanent effect (step function), whereas event 2 was modeled as a gradual permanent effect, reflecting annual increases in the proportion of new-design vehicles in the total car population. The final model indicated an immediate reduction in ozone levels from event 1, whereas event 2 was associated with a progressive reduction in summer ozone levels, with little if any change in winter levels.[10]

■ *Enhancements of the Basic Design*

The inferential power of the simple ITS design can be further bolstered by additional design enhancements. These are particularly helpful when, as is often the case, effects are gradual rather than abrupt. Gradual

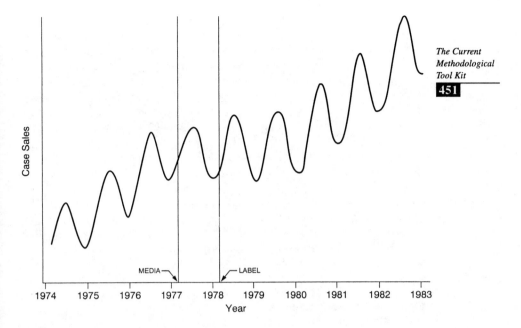

Figure 31.4. Diet Soft Drink Case Sales, 1974–1983
SOURCE: Orwin et al. (1984).

implementation of the intervention further complicates the detection of gradual effects. Such effects are virtually impossible to interpret in the context of a single time series unless a substantive theory can clearly predict the delay interval. This section describes some common ways of enhancing the basic design.

☐ *Adding Other Input Series as Covariates*

ITS analyses can use additional time series as covariates, just as standard regression analyses use pretest scores or demographic characteristics.[11] An example of the use of a covariate series is provided by the Food and Drug Administration's analysis of the effect of the saccharin warning label on diet soft drink sales (Orwin et al., 1984).[12] The bimonthly diet soft drink sales series (smoothed) is shown in Figure 31.4. After sufficiently whitening the sales series, the researchers included a term for diet soft drink price to increase the precision of the estimates of

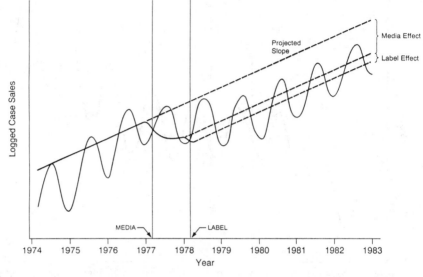

Figure 31.5. Superimposition of Effects Over Diet Soft Drink Series
SOURCE: Orwin et al. (1984).

the intervention components. (In an earlier GLS regression analysis of the same data set, diet soft drink price had the largest net effect of any substantive predictor.) Price was adjusted by the nonalcoholic Consumer Price Index to capture the competitive price of diet soft drinks relative to potential beverage substitutes, including nondiet soft drinks. This relative price term was then appropriately differenced and added to the noise model as a covariate. After obtaining an acceptable model fit, the price coefficient was significant (albeit marginally) and in the expected direction. It was therefore retained for the fitting of the intervention components: the onset of media coverage in February 1977 and the implementation of the warning label in February 1978. The best fit for media coverage was a gradual permanent effect, whereas the best fit for the label was an abrupt (albeit smaller) permanent effect. Figure 31.5 shows the effects of the two interventions superimposed on the data. The figure clearly shows the label effect as "over and above" the media effect alone. The estimated effect of the label was a 4% decrease in sales, which was statistically significant.

☐ Adding a Comparison Series

As noted by Cook and Shadish (1994), plausible threats to validity are best ruled out through the use of additional time series. The most straightforward is a comparison group series that is not expected to produce the hypothesized change in level, slope, or variability of the outcome series.[13] Campbell (1976) presents numerous examples of ITS designs with comparison series covering welfare reform, traffic safety, Medicaid and physician visits, agricultural advances in Mexico, and other topics. In each, the effect of the intervention on the target series is clearly brought into relief by the presence of one or more comparison series. For example, Figure 31.6 illustrates the impact of introducing a particular type of wheat to Mexico, with Argentina and Chile used as controls.

☐ Adding a Switching Replication

In this variant, there are two independent groups. First, one group receives the intervention and the other does not. Later, their roles are reversed. Marcantonio and Cook (1994) note that the switching-replications design is particularly useful when effects are expected to be gradual rather than immediate. The logic is that if approximately the same lag time appears in independent groups at different points in history, then attribution of the effect to the intervention is more credible. An example of the switching-replications design is Hennigan et al.'s (1982) analysis of the impact of the introduction of television on certain types of crime. The study capitalized on the fact that television was not introduced uniformly throughout the United States, which serendipitously created the opportunity for a "natural experiment." The Federal Communications Commission froze the issuance of new broadcasting licenses from late 1949 through mid-1952. This permitted the construction of two groups of cities: prefreeze and postfreeze. Under the switching-replications design, the prefreeze group was the initial treatment and the postfreeze group served as their controls. After the freeze was lifted, the group roles were reversed. Results for larceny thefts are shown in Figure 31.7. As illustrated, during the freeze the prefreeze cities show an increase relative to the postfreeze cities, and the difference is statistically significant. During the postfreeze period, the difference disappears as the postfreeze cities appear to "catch up." The merits of the switching-replications design are clear: Were only

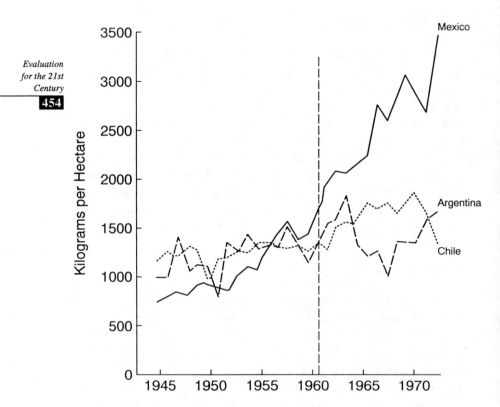

Figure 31.6. Introduction of Semi-Dwarf HYV Wheat in Mexico, With
Argentina and Chile Presented as Control Series
SOURCE: Campbell (1976). Copyright 1976 by D. Reidel Publishing Co., Dordrecht, Holland. Reprinted
by permission of Kluwer Academic Publishers.

one group's data available, the effect of television on larceny thefts would
be (a) more difficult to detect and (b) more vulnerable to alternative
explanations.

☐ *Adding a Nonequivalent Dependent Variable*

Another way to strengthen causal inference is by adding a time series
on a second dependent variable, specifically one that will not be affected
by the intervention in the manner predicted for the first. Perhaps the
best-known application is Ross, Campbell, and Glass's (1970) study of

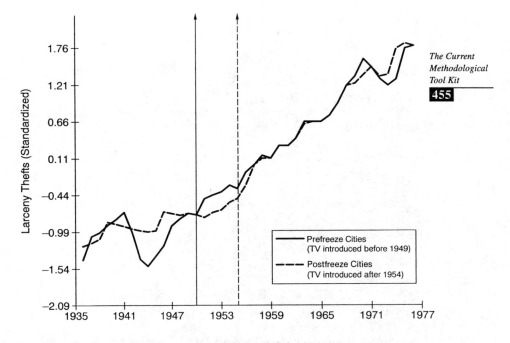

Figure 31.7. Larceny Thefts for Selected Cities, 1936–1976
SOURCE: K. M. Hennigan et al., "Impact of the Introduction of Television on Crime in the United States: Empirical Findings and Theoretical Implications," *Journal of Personality and Social Psychology, 42* (1982), 461-477. Copyright © 1982 by the American Psychological Association. Reprinted with permission.

the British Breathalyzer crackdown of 1967.[14] Use of the Breathalyzer was an attempt to reduce drunken driving, in the hope that this in turn would decrease serious traffic accidents. The study capitalized on a feature of British drinking laws that restricts the hours that pubs can be open. On the assumption (well borne out anecdotally) that predriving drinking in Britain is primarily a social event taking place in pubs, Ross et al. disaggregated the total traffic casualties series into hours when pubs are open (specifically weekend nights) and hours when pubs are closed. The closed-hour series could then serve as a control for the open-hour series, on the premise that the Breathalyzer crackdown would have little or no impact during the hours when pubs are closed. As shown in Figure 31.8, the results were exactly as predicted. As with the switching-replications example, numerous alternative explanations were neutralized by the use of this design enhancement.

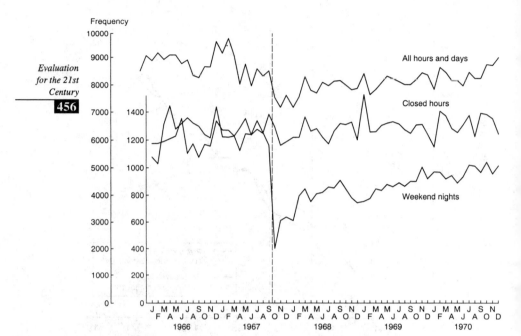

Figure 31.8. British Casualties (Fatalities Plus Serious Injuries) Before and
After the British Breathalyzer Crackdown of October 1967
SOURCE: Data from Ross et al. (1970).

☐   *Adding Multiple Enhancements*

Consistent with the quasi-experimental tradition (Cook & Campbell,
1979), the above discussion of design enhancements as separate entities
is not intended to suggest that multiple enhancements cannot be creatively
combined to increase confidence in causal attributions. Two excellent
examples of recent multiple-enhancement designs are found in the work
of Wagner, Rubin, and Callahan (1988) and West and Hepworth (1989).

Wagner et al. (1988) used ITS to examine productivity changes in a
unionized iron foundry following the introduction of nonmanagerial
incentive payments. Combining a nonequivalent dependent variables
design with covariate series, the researchers used three series in addition
to productivity: labor costs, number of employees, and grievance data.
Labor costs—serving as the nonequivalent dependent variable series—

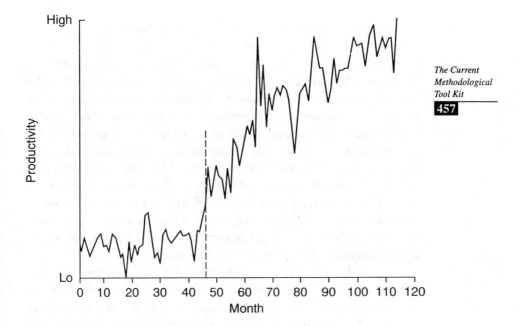

Figure 31.9. Incentive Payment and Productivity
SOURCE: Wagner (1988). Copyright 1988 by Academic Press. Reprinted by permission.

were used to examine the possibility that observed changes in productivity might have occurred due to general changes in payment magnitude rather than incentive payments contingent upon performance. The number of employees, or employee count, was used as a covariate series to factor out the effects of exogenous economic conditions (recessions, changes in market conditions, and so on) over the 114-month period that data were collected. The grievance data were used not to support causal inferences regarding productivity, but to check on side effects, or—in the language of economists—externalities. Specifically, they served to assess the possibility that observed increases in productivity came with unacceptable human costs. Wagner et al. had hoped also to use a nonequivalent comparison group from another foundry, but for a variety of reasons that proved impossible. In addition to acquiring the time series data, however, they conducted interviews with several key informants from both management and labor to establish the sequence of events in the development and implementation of the incentive structure.

The ARIMA analysis of the Wagner et al. productivity series (shown in Figure 31.9) indicated that the best-fitting form for the intervention was a gradual but steady increase that decelerated over time (technically known as a "power function" approaching an asymptotic limit). Labor costs (the nonequivalent dependent variable) fell over the course of the incentive plan, supporting the conclusion that the increase in productivity was not due to pay increases received by the workforce as a whole. The grievance rate remained stable throughout most of the series, giving no indication that the incentive payment introduced unacceptable human costs. In the absence of a comparison group, Wagner et al. examined the plausibility of the three main internal validity threats that ITS does not rule out—instrumentation, selection, and history artifacts—in painstaking detail. They concluded that none of these were plausible alternatives to the intervention as explanations of the observed results.

West and Hepworth (1989) combined a switching-replications design with the use of a no-treatment comparison group, nonequivalent dependent variables, and covariate series. In evaluating the effect on vehicular fatalities of an Arizona law that mandated severe penalties for driving while intoxicated (DWI), these authors analyzed fatalities from three localities: Phoenix, where the state law went into effect in July 1982; San Diego, where a similar California law went into effect in January 1982; and El Paso, where no such state or local laws were applicable. The nonequivalent dependent variables were citation rates for moving and parking violations in Phoenix, which were not expected to change as a function of the DWI law. Because traffic safety data are affected by changes in the number of miles driven, data were obtained on annual gasoline consumption and the estimated miles per gallon of all vehicles in Arizona for use as covariate series.

Results showed reduced vehicular fatalities in Phoenix and San Diego at their respective postintervention time points, and no changes in El Paso corresponding to implementation of the Arizona or California laws. They also showed no change in the nonequivalent dependent variables. This exemplary study also included a daily quantification of preimplementation media coverage, as represented by the number of square inches on the subject in the highest-circulation Phoenix morning newspaper, and qualitative interviews with two key informants (a judge and a police spokesperson) on their perceptions as to how the law had worked. As in

Orwin et al. (1984), the media effect was sizable, and the interviews were particularly informative on unintended effects—for example, a dramatic increase in the percentage of DWI cases carried through to trial rather than pled out (30% before the law, 90% after).

■ Recent Technical Developments in ITS

The ARIMA-based ITS technology has seen important technical advances since its introduction in 1975. These developments are important to evaluators and policy makers because they expand the range of time series to which ITS analysis can be applied. Consequently, they expand its utility and versatility in addressing policy questions as they arise.

☐ Missing Values and Unequal Time Intervals

The standard ARIMA model assumes complete sets of observations with each observation taken at regular intervals. Modest departures from these assumptions can be ignored (e.g., different lengths of months), but more marked ones cannot. Recently, however, techniques have been developed to accommodate these in the parameter estimation process.[15] Interpolations of the missing values themselves and their corresponding error variances can also be derived. The same process handles both irregularly spaced series and regularly spaced series with missing values.

☐ Fractional Differencing

Differencing has traditionally been confined to integers (e.g., lag 1 for secular trend, lag 12 for seasonality in monthly data), under the implicit assumption that secular and/or seasonal differencing is sufficient to induce a level series ("stationarity"). Yet in some instances, fractional differencing using a lag period < 1 may be more appropriate as a way of removing apparent nonstationarity.[16]

☐ *Robust Estimation*

Extreme observations (i.e., outliers) may have considerable and disproportionate influence on standard ARIMA estimation procedures. "Robust smoother-cleaners" are now available that identify and adjust extreme observations (Martin & Yohai, 1985). The resulting estimators lack some large-sample properties, but this is typically outweighed in practice by the ability to avoid bias from extreme outliers (Kendall & Ord, 1990).

☐ *Nonlinear Models*

Finally, standard ARIMA models rely on the assumption that time series processes are linear, which will not always be the case. Kendall and Ord (1990) describe several ways in which nonlinear processes can now be modeled, and also present the mathematical underpinnings of multidimensional processes (e.g., processes defined spatially as well as, or in place of, the time dimension).[17]

■ *Future Opportunities for ITS in Policy Evaluation*

Despite their strength in causal hypothesis testing, ITS designs are still used relatively infrequently in evaluation (Cook & Shadish, 1994; Marcantonio & Cook, 1994). Clearly, part of the reason stems from technical constraints: the need for relatively long series (50 or more observations) and the limited availability of appropriate, high-quality archival data for use as time series. (The latter is less of a concern when the evaluators can get out in front of an intervention and select the measures themselves.) Cook and Shadish (1994) also cite the general lack of familiarity of social scientists with ARIMA modeling, but note that researchers can quickly learn these methods once they have applications that call for them. Then there is the reality that ITS analysis will not always yield unambiguous confirmation or disconfirmation of a treatment effect. As a general rule, weak, diffusely implemented interventions whose expected effects are gradual or temporary are not good bets, particularly in the absence of applicable theory to predict lag times. For such effects to be detected and attributable to the intervention, one or more of the above-described design enhancements is probably essential. Even in these instances, the ITS quasi-experiment still affords a better shot at projecting the counterfactual than its alternatives, and it clearly warrants "a special status among quasi-experimental designs whenever they are feasible" (Cook & Shadish, 1994, p. 563).

As we approach the millennium, it is easy to envision increasing opportunities for the use of ITS. The following list presents a mere handful of the potential possibilities:

1. The present thrust in the U.S. Congress to "reform" entitlements by granting more autonomy to state and local governments will not only create the potential for state-level ITS quasi-experiments, but could create a "natural laboratory" of switching replications throughout the country. State governments could choose to stage the introduction of certain reforms across localities, thereby building switching-replications designs into their evaluation plans a priori, rather than relying on the cooperativeness of uncontrolled variation.

2. The 1993 Government Results and Performance Act (P.L. 103-62) requires each U.S. government agency to, among other things, establish performance indicators to be used in measuring or assessing the relevant outputs, service levels, and outcomes of each program activity. State and local government agencies are also under increased pressure to take performance monitoring seriously.

3. The managed care movement in the U.S. health care industry also cries out for ITS, given all the ways in which managed care initiatives are expected to affect the cost, availability, and quality of health care, not to mention patient outcomes.

4. The myriad post-Cold War international agreements (e.g., NAFTA, GATT) present still more source material for ITS. Potential outcome series are not limited to economic variables, but could include social ones as well (e.g., legal immigration).

5. Events expected to affect worldwide environmental changes can also be assessed—for example, the impact of economic aid to developing nations on rain forest depletion rates.

And, as noted above, technical advancements such as the accommodation of unequal intervals and missing data points will also expand the availability of time series suitable for ITS. In sum, the design's future looks promising, and we may expect that, as familiarity increases, more evaluators, policy analysts, and funding agencies will consider ITS for their research and evaluation purposes.

■ Notes

1. In a 1975 article in the *Journal of the American Statistical Association,* statisticians G. E. P. Box and G. C. Tiao laid the statistical foundations of modern interrupted time series analysis. (The conceptual foundation of the ITS quasi-experiment is of course considerably older; see Campbell & Stanley, 1963.)

2. RD employs an assignment process based on participants' scores on pretreatment measures. The theory is that because the source of the nonequivalence between treatment and comparison groups is known—namely, the cutoff rule used to assign participants to groups—analyses can correctly model selection and produce unbiased estimates of the treatment effect, even without random assignment (Trochim, 1984, 1990). The especially attractive feature is that the choice of assignment measures may include clinical ratings about a prospective participant's suitability or need for the program. Therefore, regression-discontinuity designs come closest to randomized experiments in the ability to produce unbiased effect estimates and remove a common practitioner objection to random assignment in field settings.

3. In the health area, for example, a MEDLINE search conducted a few years back by Williams (1990) turned up no medical or health services studies that used the RD design. I searched through back issues of *Evaluation Review* and concluded that the RD literature may contain more methodological debates about the design than actual applications of the design.

4. A sample paragraph from Orwin et al. (1984) illustrates the problem:

> Spikes at lag 16 were observed in both the ACF [autocorrelation function] and PACF [partial autocorrelation function] from the original twice-differenced series. Only the PACF had the semblance of a spike at lag 32, once again suggesting that a MA model was most appropriate. Like Model 1, Model 2 passed both minimum requirements, but left no significant spike in either the ACF and PACF and yielded a significantly improved residual mean square (RMS). However, the lag 6 MA structure was still apparent in the ACF and PACF from the Model 2 residuals. Therefore, a 3rd model was identified that combined the first two. Model 3 met the minimum requirements, had no significant spikes in the ACF or PACF, and had a lower RMS than either Models 1 or 2. The parameter estimates themselves, however, were no longer significant. The initially suspected reason was correlation between the estimates, but examination ruled this out. As both parameters had been significant when tested separately and multicollinearity was not an issue, it was not clear why both parameters were reduced to nonsignificance when combined, particularly because combining them better whitened the residuals. Both terms were therefore tentatively retained on the premise that if either was still nonsignificant after the inclusion of intervention components, it would then be dropped from the model. (p. 808)

Rereading the above paragraph for the first time in 12 years (and others like it sprinkled throughout the article), I cannot help but wonder about replicability within analysts—that is, would I have made all the same decisions today?

5. This practice has in fact been followed in the GAO as part of the standard prepublication quality control process when ARIMA modeling was used. For example, see U.S. General Accounting Office (1984).

6. As elsewhere, a good fit does not itself demonstrate a causal relationship between the intervention and the time series, only that the data are consistent with one.

7. For a discussion of the shortcomings of prior attempts, see Izenman and Zabell (1981).

8. Evidence notwithstanding, the story of the blackout babies is apparently just too appealing to go away; as recently as March 17, 1996, I heard it recalled as fact by a highly reputable commentator on National Public Radio. The conclusion drawn by Izenman and Zabell in 1981 is no less true today: The New York blackout babies story "is now one of those innumerable facts that everyone 'knows' " (p. 298).

9. Theoretically, the number of intervention events included in the model is limited only by the number of observations in the time series. Practically, the individual effects become difficult to isolate if there are more than three or four, or if any two are precisely or nearly concurrent. Too many effect parameters complicate model identification and make for disappointing results, particularly when the series are short (Kendall & Ord, 1990).

10. Because the net effect expected in winter, when oxidant pollution is low, was different from that expected in summer, when it is high, event 2 was represented by two parameters: one each for winter and summer.

11. In the language of time series analysis, input series (including covariates) are called *transfer functions*. In the broader context of time series forecasting and control, the interventions modeled in ITS are a special class of transfer functions represented by dichotomous indicator variables (e.g., presence/absence).

12. A brief history: In early 1977, the FDA concluded from a series of animal studies that saccharin is carcinogenic, and announced that it would ban the use of the substance in food and beverages. The so-called Delaney clause of the Food, Drug, and Cosmetic Act (Section 409[c][3]) prohibited the use in foods of any ingredient shown to cause cancer in animals or humans. The decision did not please the food and beverage industry, or for that matter the public, which blanketed the FDA with about 40,000 protest letters in the first month after the announcement. This led Congress to place an 18-month moratorium on the ban (later extended indefinitely) and to mandate that saccharin-containing products bear a conspicuous warning label that read: "Use of this product may be hazardous to your health. This product contains saccharin, which has been determined to cause cancer in laboratory animals."

13. The Orwin et al. study described above could have benefited from a comparison series, the obvious choice being sales of nondiet soft drinks. However, these data were not made available at the time. Fortunately, the best-fitting warning-label effect was of the least ambiguous type: abrupt and permanent. Had it been gradual or temporary, coming as it did on the trailing edge of the much larger media onset effect, interpretability would have suffered.

14. Note that this study predates the use of ARIMA modeling in ITS, yet is very much within the quasi-experimental tradition of ruling out validity threats by design.

15. For technical details, see Kendall and Ord (1990), Jones (1985), and Box et al. (1994).

16. For details on applying fractional differencing, see Hosking (1981) and Kendall and Ord (1990).

17. For further technical details on nonlinear models in time series analysis, see Subba Rao (1983), Tong and Lim (1980), and Ord and Young (1989).

References

Box, G. E. P., Jenkins, G. M., & Reinsel, G. C. (1994). *Time series analysis: Forecasting and control* (3rd ed.). Englewood Cliffs, NJ: Prentice Hall.

Box, G. E. P., & Tiao, G. C. (1975). Intervention analysis with applications to economic and environmental problems. *Journal of the American Statistical Association, 70,* 70-79.

Campbell, D. T. (1976). Focal local indicators for social program evaluation. *Social Indicators Research, 3,* 237-256.

Campbell, D. T., & Stanley, J. C. (1963). *Experimental and quasi-experimental designs for research.* Chicago: Rand McNally.

Cook, T. D., & Campbell, D. T. (1979). *Quasi-experimentation: Design and analysis issues for field settings.* Chicago: Rand McNally.

Cook, T. D., & Shadish, W. R. (1994). Social experiments: Some developments over the past fifteen years. *Annual Review of Psychology, 45,* 545-580.

Glass, G. V, Wilson, V. L., & Gottman, J. M. (1975). *Design and analysis of time series experiments.* Boulder, CO: Associated Universities Press.

Harvey, A. C., & Durbin, J. (1986). The effects of seat belt legislation on British road casualties: A case study in structural time series modelling. *Journal of the Royal Statistical Society, 149,* 187-227.

Hennigan, K. M., Del Rosario, M. L., Heath, L., Cook, T. D., Wharton, J. D., & Calder, B. G. (1982). Impact of the introduction of television on crime in the United States: Empirical findings and theoretical implications. *Journal of Personality and Social Psychology, 42,* 461-477.

Hosking, J. R. M. (1981). Fractional differencing. *Biometrika, 68,* 165-176.

Izenman, A. J., & Zabell, S. L. (1981). Babies and the blackout: The genesis of a misconception. *Social Science Research, 10,* 282-299.

Jones, R. H. (1985). Time series with unequally spaced data. In E. J. Hannan, P. R. Krishnaiah, & M. M. Rao (Eds.), *Time series in the time domain.* Amsterdam: North Holland.

Kendall, M., & Ord, J. K. (1990). *Time series* (3rd ed.). London: Edward Arnold.

Marcantonio, R. J., & Cook, T. D. (1994). Convincing quasi-experiments: The interrupted time series and regression-discontinuity designs. In J. S. Wholey, H. P. Hatry, & K. E. Newcomer (Eds.), *Handbook of practical program evaluation.* San Francisco: Jossey-Bass.

Martin, R. D., & Yohai, V. J. (1985). Robustness in time series and estimating ARIMA models. In E. J. Hannan, P. R. Krishnaiah, & M. M. Rao (Eds.), *Time series in the time domain.* Amsterdam: North Holland.

McCleary, R., & Hay, R., Jr. (1980). *Applied time series analysis for the social sciences.* Beverly Hills, CA: Sage.

McSweeny, A. J. (1978). Effects of response cost on the behavior of a million persons: Charging for directory assistance in Cincinnati. *Journal of Applied Behavior Analysis, 11,* 47-51.

Montgomery, D. C., & Weatherby, G. (1980). Modeling and forecasting time series using transfer function and intervention methods. *AIEE Transactions, 12,* 289-307.

Ord, J. K., & Young, P. (1989). *Model building for technological forecasting* (Working paper). University Park: Pennsylvania State University, Department of Management Science.

Orwin, R. G., Schucker, R. E., & Stokes, R. C. (1984). Evaluating the life cycle of a product warning: Saccharin and diet soft drink sales. *Evaluation Review, 8,* 801-822.

Rogers, J. H. (1992). The currency substitution hypothesis and relative money demand in Mexico and Canada. *Journal of Money, Credit, and Banking, 24,* 300-318.

Ross, H. L., Campbell, D. T., & Glass, G. V (1970). Determining the social effects of legal reform: The British "Breatholizer" crackdown of 1967. *American Behavioral Scientist, 13,* 493-509.

Rossi, P. H., & Freeman, H. E. (1993). *Evaluation: A systematic approach* (5th ed.). Newbury Park, CA: Sage.

Subba Rao, T. (1983). On the theory of bilinear time series models. *Journal of the Royal Statistical Society B, 43,* 244-255.

Tong, H., & Lim, K. S. (1980). Threshold autoregression, limit cycles and cyclical data (with discussion). *Journal of the Royal Statistical Society B, 42,* 245-292.

Trochim, W. M. (1984). *Research design for program evaluation: The regression-discontinuity approach.* Beverly Hills, CA: Sage.

Trochim, W. M. (1990). The regression-discontinuity design. In L. Sechrest, E. Perrin, & J. Bunker (Eds.), *Research methodology: Strengthening causal interpretations of nonexperimental data.* Washington, DC: U.S. Department of Health and Human Services.

U.S. General Accounting Office. (1984). *An evaluation of the 1981 AFDC changes: Initial analyses* (GAO/PEMD-84-6). Washington, DC: Author.

Wagner, J. A., III. (1988). *Incentive payment and productivity: An interpreted time series analysis of magnitude and trend.* Orlando, FL: Academic.

Wagner, J. A., III, Rubin, P. A., & Callahan, T. J. (1988). Incentive payment and nonmanagerial productivity: An interrupted time series analysis of magnitude and trend. *Organizational Behavior and Human Decision Processes, 42,* 47-74.

Wei, W. S. (1990). *Time series analysis: Univariate and multivariate methods.* Reading, MA: Addison-Wesley.

West, S. G., & Hepworth, J. T. (1989). An evaluation of Arizona's July 1982 drunk driving law: Effects on the city of Phoenix. *Journal of Applied Social Psychology, 19,* 1212-1237.

Williams, S. V. (1990). Regression-discontinuity design in health evaluation. In L. Sechrest, E. Perrin, & J. Bunker (Eds.), *Research methodology: Strengthening causal interpretations of nonexperimental data* (pp. 145-149). Washington, DC: U.S. Department of Health and Human Services.

PART VII

An Enduring Argument About the Purpose of Evaluation

*T*he final part of this book contains two chapters that discuss an enduring theoretical issue in evaluation. We suspect this repetition is due partly to the importance of the issue itself, and partly to its likely intractability. The issue concerns the relative weight that ought to be given in evaluation to advocacy versus truth. In various guises, this issue has been with evaluation for many years, for example, in House's (1980) suggestions about the role that social justice ought to play in evaluation. Extending this tradition, Robert Stake argues eloquently in Chapter 32 for the desirability of the evaluator as advocate for the program. One of his more interesting premises—one that will resonate with many readers in today's world—is that advertising, salesmanship, politics, and campaigning are far more persuasive than teaching, fact-finding, and research, so much so that the authority of the discipline of evaluation has been overcome by the power of advocacy. Stake believes that the evaluator's ideological bent inevitably influences the evaluation in at least some ways, and so he aims to legitimate that bent by making advocacy *an acceptable value among evaluators—indeed, he believes it already is accepted by many evaluators. He gives a personal example of the advocacy he engaged in for the Chicago Teachers Academy, an institution he believed was doing a very good job in a very difficult environment, and one that needed support more than it needed the public criticism that might make its work even more difficult. Consequently, the final report stated the good achievements of the Academy, but did not speak "persistently" of its weaknesses, and "misdirections" were conveyed only privately to the Academy rather than publicly for all to hear. At the same time, however, Stake values truth (veridical representation) in evaluation and wishes to minimize or resist advocacy, expressing regret that evaluators sometimes get caught up in promotionalism. At the end of his chapter he calls for more extensive and careful study not only of the process of valuing in evaluation, but also of the poverty of the processes often used in evaluation to expose ideology and prevent misrepresentation in evaluation reports. Clearly Stake's advocacy of advocacy is complex, continuing to develop, not extremist, but still a challenge to all evaluators to think about this issue.*

In Chapter 33, Michael Scriven does exactly that. He takes as a starting point that many arguments in favor of advocacy proceed by attacking the conceptual viability of the notions of truth and objectivity. He acknowledges that such notions have come under attack from some philosophers, but notes that the attacks have not led philosophers to a new, consensually agreed-upon alternative position. Lacking that, Scriven argues for continuing to rely on the commonsense notions of truth and objectivity that we all use in everyday life on a regular basis. Scriven suggests that the evaluator should be distanced from the thing being evaluated, and he offers ways to foster this distance. He acknowledges that such distancing has its price, but argues that the alternative is to lose the validity of the evaluation entirely. Scriven's sweep is broad, criticizing not only advocacy approaches such as that of Stake, but the related class of evaluation approaches, such as Fetterman's (see Chapter 27) empowerment evaluation. Yet Scriven also acknowledges that such actions—advocacy, empowering clients, and so on—are legitimate in their own right on many grounds, such as free speech. Hence he distinguishes between the evaluator and the evaluation consultant. The evaluator's job is to make judgments about merit or worth, and that job requires giving precedence to truth and objectivity over advocacy. The evaluation consultant, however, is an evaluator who chooses to render evaluation-relevant services but not to make any evaluative judgments; the consultant is free to engage in some advocacy in that role. Scriven argues against mixing these roles in most circumstances, however. He prefers that the evaluator's slogan be "To tell the truth, the whole truth, and nothing but the truth." Anything less, he claims, risks the destruction of evaluator credibility for the profession as a whole.

William R. Shadish

■ Reference

House, E. R. (1980). *Evaluating with validity.* Beverly Hills, CA: Sage.

32

Advocacy in Evaluation

A Necessary Evil?

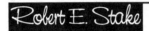

I find it aesthetically pleasing and methodologically enabling to honor personal experience and postmodern insight, to recognize multiple realities and constructivist knowledge—but at such a cost! Obscuring the lines between fiction and fact, between evidence and opinion, we discover ourselves more transparently caught up in advocacy for or against our clients, usually for. Advocacies, our own as well as those of our sponsors, no longer can be expected to be caught in the sieve of objectivity. Honoring personal construction of knowledge leads to denial that anything important can be known that is not value laden and advocative.

What should be the place of advocacy in program evaluation studies? Most clients hope to use evaluation findings in advocacy for program continuation. Given supportive findings, they expect the evaluator to testify in their behalf. Jennifer Greene, stepping off in a different direc-

AUTHOR'S NOTE: This chapter is a revised version of a panel presentation made at Evaluation '95, Vancouver, November 4, 1995. Members of the panel were Jennifer Greene, Linda Mabry, Michael Scriven, and myself.

tion, has taken the position that evaluators should actively advocate for the program's target groups—who are sometimes allied with their clients, but sometimes not. Greene (1995) states: "Evaluation inherently involves advocacy, so the important question becomes advocacy for whom. The most defensible answer to this question is that evaluation should advocate for the interests of program participants" (p. 1). Michael Scriven (1994) has urged evaluators to reject the advocate role. There is a choice to make, but sometimes we find little freedom to make the choice.

Part of the educational evaluator's plight is that of being caught in a field losing its authority. Most educational programs engaged in formal evaluation are under increasing scrutiny, their accountability challenged; for many, the future is cloudy. Education remains a championed virtue, but educators everywhere are under fire. We seldom allow it to rise into consciousness, but unconsciously we are aware that advertising is a far more persuasive medium than teaching or research. Salesmanship sells better than teaching teaches. Politics broaches, often with deceit. Campaigns and legislation push the boundaries of disregard for the facts. Advocacy has overcome Authority.

Given *our* causes, many of them noble, evaluative research increasingly mimics the media world of sound bites. We seek the quotable quote, the executive summary, the deciding graphic, the bottom-line indicator, even the cartoon, to stand for Quality in each constantly moving, complex, and contextual evaluand. We ourselves are reluctant to separate epistemology from ideology, findings from yearnings. We consciously seek those expressions of findings that persuade the reader to our points of view. We too are advocates, some more than others. Linda Mabry (1995) points out that "natural variation among evaluators along these dimensions guarantees that proactive advocacy must always be an uneven current in our field, even if we could agree [that advocacy is] acceptable" (p. 7).

■ One Instance

With my CIRCE (Center for Instructional Research and Curriculum Evaluation at the University of Illinois) colleagues, I have just completed the Year II evaluation report of the Chicago Teachers Academy for Mathematics and Science.[1] It is a freestanding professional-development institution devoted to improved teaching and reform in Chicago's elementary schools. Our findings told of good curricular and pedagogical bases in Academy workshops for teachers in the 60+ participating schools. We told of changes in some classrooms. We told of a School Improvement Unit (department) dedicated to helping schools resolve to define and solve their problems themselves—but also giving them too little help connecting with problem-solving efforts at other schools and with the "change literature" (Little, 1993; Newmann & Clune, 1992). And on— But it is not findings I want to discuss here, but rather the ideological stance to be found in our report.[2]

The Chicago Teachers Academy existed in a fragile state financially, not greatly buttressed by cross-institutional support. I saw the Academy as a positive force for education in Chicago, notwithstanding occasional mistakes, inefficiencies, and political indulgences. It clearly was a positive force for assisting teachers—and without a serious competitor institution, without a successor, in sight.

Many will find the ideology paternalistic, protectionist. It grew over time and familiarity with the teachers and schools that we case studied. The ethic is stated this way: "We try not to allow our evaluation study to make it more difficult for the staff to discharge its responsibilities." In practice, it means resisting judgment about important practices in the schools, especially of those not directly the responsibility of the evaluand. Contractually, we were not evaluating the teachers, the classrooms, and the schools, but the Academy. We saw ourselves as guests in the schools we visited, inquiring sometimes into the teachers' personal affairs. We wanted to do our work with empathy and care, with discretion.

Yet we are evaluators. We work to find and understand quality. We do not come to assist in remediation. We do not think of ourselves as collaborators in reform. We promised to help the Academy staff understand itself, particularly in terms of the quality of its operations. We provided details of merit and shortcoming. We interpreted and discussed the issues.

Among the ideological positions discernible in our report are the following:

■ Teaching that emphasizes problem solving, experiential learning, and constructivist epistemology is generally more educationally valuable than direct teaching of basic skills.

- Professional development programs basically dependent on face-to-face teaching by expert instructors seldom extend to the bulk of teachers needing it; thus the traditional in-servicing strategy is inadequate.
- Reform standards and expectations for Chicago schools set by central authorities, however popular and legitimate, actually divert schools and teachers from improvements that they and the Academy desire.

And there are others. It should be noted that these positions, these standards of quality for Academy operation, are not agreed upon. Although shared by many educators and evaluators, they are not endorsed by many others. In using these standards in our evaluation we are expressing a parochial ideology and promoting reform as we define it.

Where responsibility to schools ends and responsibility to the Academy begins is not clear. Operating under an ethic of minimized disruption, and given an Academy rationale with curricular values we share, we have emphasized Academy strengths in our reporting. Weaknesses we have not as persistently stated. Of misdirections, we have spoken more privately. Good moves we have repeated to more distant listeners. Going beyond the stated ethic, we have tried not to author a final report that, if distributed, might add to the Academy's insecurity.

Scriven and Kramer (1995) have advised that after the evaluation is done, the evaluator may "advocate on the merits of the case." But when subsequent evaluation work is anticipated, as it was here, the report-distributing evaluator is not newly free to advocate. And does "advocate on the merits" mean one can downplay shortcomings? What is advocacy if it is not to apply a favorable gloss?

■ *Value Resolution*

How should an evaluation study be culminated? In "The Final Synthesis," Scriven (1994) makes a strong plea for dispassionate, analytic resolution of value claims. He urges the evaluator to be empiricist and logician, identifying and weighing the criteria of quality. He berates the evaluator who puts empowerment of clients or other advocacy groups above straightforward pursuit of merit. Rejecting postmodern relativism, he insists that the value of a program, its superiority, can be discerned independent of personal opinion, as not merely a matter of credibility.

In education, the dispassionate analytic mechanism for value resolution is not even on today's drawing boards. Our program evaluations are infused with ideology, perhaps always will be. Ideology is closely connected to each evaluation standard. Even with extensive inquiry and careful logic, ultimately evaluators must rely on their sense of what is good. The evaluator may draw upon a great range of resources but eventually must decide what counts. In the panel at AEA, Scriven outlined that responsibility and rejected intuitive resolution of the claims.

I yearn for the certainty running through Scriven's advocacy even though I doubt it can be attained. I envy his confidence in that certainty and would like to keep something of it in the new inquiry. Finding no way herself to separate advocacy from veridical representation, Jennifer Greene (1995) urges us to get on with the decision as to whose advocacy to join. I don't agree. I feel that our stance should be to resist advocacy, to minimize advocacy, even though it is ever present, to help to recognize worthy and unworthy advocacies but to resist joining them. But, then, aren't each of my cases an Academy? As Linda Mabry (1995) concludes, "Our field lies within the intersection of demands for credible science, ambiguous and conflicting responsibilities, and the quicksand of postmodernity and post-structuralism."

■ *Checks and Balances*

Whatever the epistemological stance, what sadly is missing in present practice is rigorous challenge to our standard-setting processes. During our 2 years at the Academy, we sought disconfirming evidence and counteradvocates, but the press of time and unavailability of opponents severely limited the triangulation. External checks and balances were happenstance at best. We presented the Academy findings to our client, its directors, almost upon completing the spell check.

Science has had traditional mechanisms for validation, for exposing ideology and purging misrepresentation. But today, in evaluation reporting, we are not drawn tight by publication editors and reviewers, by faculty panels, by debate within learned societies. It is seldom that an evaluation report is challenged at our professional meetings. For the Chicago Teachers Academy, we finished our annual report and that was it. No one asked to see our data. No one seemed troubled by our advocacies.

Advocacy within program evaluation is not new. Twenty years ago,
Ernest House urged us to think of program evaluation as argumentation. Regularly unchallenged, we have been safe making arguments for objectivity, explication, historical perspective, and rational thinking, each traditionally considered a virtue in research, even an obligation. Advocacy for educational reform, curricular remediation, and pedagogical change has been almost as common. Those advocacies are fundamental to our work. We have long been sympathetic to the values of our colleagues and our clients. But we seem to be moving further and further into advocacy of little-agreed-upon values. And of course we know that some advocacies are not acceptable. Are we justified in vigorous protection of teachers, opposition to home schooling, and tolerance of kids' dropping out of school? As of now, we have few guidelines for examining distinctions between advocacies good and bad.

Until the recent legitimation of qualitative evaluation methods, we thought that we could enumerate the threats to validity. We could speak with confidence of inference procedures and confirmation of findings. Now, with postmodern insight, validity is methodologically unimportant, epistemologically destabilized. Without the backing of positivist authority, we evaluators are caught in the web of advocacy and have become unwittingly, sometimes willingly, simply a party to promotionalism.

■ Notes

1. The report, titled "Restructuring," was an internal document submitted by us to the Chicago Teachers Academy in July 1995.

2. I hasten to withdraw indictment of my colleagues, for it is I, principal investigator, senior evaluator, mentor, and chief author of the report, who vouchsafed the ideological standards.

■ References

Greene, J. (1995, November). *Evaluators as advocates.* Paper presented at the annual meeting of the American Evaluation Association, Vancouver.

Little, J. W. (1993). Teachers' professional development in a climate of educational reform. *Educational Evaluation and Policy Analysis, 15,* 129-151.

Mabry, L. (1995). *Advocacy in evaluation: Inescapable or intolerable?* Unpublished manuscript.

Newmann, F. M., & Clune, W. H. (1992). *When school restructuring meets systemic curriculum reform* (Brief to Policymakers No. 3). Madison: University of Wisconsin, Center on Organization and Restructuring of Schools.

Scriven, M. (1994). The final synthesis. *Evaluation Practice, 15,* 367-382.

Scriven, M., & Kramer, J. (1995, January). Risks, rights, and responsibilities in evaluation. *Australasian Journal of Evaluation,* p. 15.

33

Truth and Objectivity in Evaluation

Michael Scriven

In evaluation practice today, the abstract concepts of truth and objectivity have come to take on particular importance, because the usual interpretations of them are under fire. Because these interpretations are under fire, certain standard practices in evaluation—crucial practices designed to protect objectivity in investigating and truth in reporting—have also come under fire. I will argue here that the grounds for these attacks are mistaken. One way to argue this would be on the basis of an exhaustive analysis of the abstract concepts, and this is sometimes thought to be the only way one can defend them. However, these attacks are not based on any such analysis and can be repelled without one, for an interesting reason.

The reason is perhaps best understood in terms of an analogy. We regularly engage in legal disputation, and our legal system works quite well despite this, indeed, partly because we have developed a system for including it. One reason the system works is that it contains many

AUTHOR'S NOTE: My thanks to John Hattie for good suggestions about an earlier draft of this chapter.

procedures for self-correction. From time to time, the concept of legal truth has come under attack in the academic halls where the philosophy of law is discussed. In some sense, these have been attacks on the foundations of every legal decision. But we do not suspend legal process while the force of the attacks is considered. For good pragmatic reasons, we continue as we have before until the philosophers come up with some specific recommendations for change that we can appraise for their pragmatic significance—and that they never do. The same is true about the great attacks on the foundations of mathematics, for example, by the intuitionists. The same is true about the perpetual attacks on the foundations of ethics—we do not abandon our everyday discussions of the rights and wrongs of allowing drug squads to use money from their sale of confiscated property, for example, and the decisions we make based on those discussions.

The general point is simply this: Until one of two conditions is met, we cannot sensibly abandon good working practices. Either the philosophers must bring to the table some suggestions for altering practice about which they are reasonably well agreed, or, at the very least, one school of philosophers must bring to the table some practical considerations that flow from its views, which can then be evaluated in practical terms for costs and benefits.

It is not sensible to suppose that merely waving one philosophical argument in the air is grounds for practitioners to change practice. From the practitioners' point of view, there are no reasons to suppose that one position is superior to the opposing philosophical position, which they well know is widely supported. They think that these matters should be left to the philosophers until the philosophers can come up with something that goes beyond philosophy. That is surely a sensible position.

Practitioners understand that analyzing epistemological issues is a lifetime's work and see no reason to make it the work of their own lifetimes, because doing the philosophical work does not seem to lead to any conclusions that pass the modest test of agreement among equally well qualified philosophers. If every discipline had first to cover all the epistemological issues that bear on it before starting or continuing work, nothing else would ever get done, especially because most practitioners lack both natural predilection and thorough training for that task.

The usual counterargument to this pragmatic approach suggests that we need to halt "proceedings as usual" because to go ahead without a satisfactory resolution of the key epistemological problems is to build on sand and/or to trust to oft-duped authority. (It is sometimes added that defending the status quo is an unprogressive or moribund or inhumane position, but I will restrict myself here to the basic complaint.)

My response is to say that it is better to build on what *might conceivably be sand but has so far given no signs of weakness* than not to build at all. It is exactly the solution we follow in everyday life, where we do not let epistemological speculations overpower common sense—until they can be given decisive commonsense support. Entranced by the arguments of Plato or others who make a case against the possibility of direct knowledge of the real world, we may come to worry about the entire foundation of knowledge—but we do not let such arguments persuade us to ignore furniture that appears to be in our path on the way to the front door. Analogously, in evaluation, it is a waste of time to try to solve the problems of epistemology before getting on with the job. Nevertheless, we can properly tackle any specific problems *at the level of practical methodology* that are said to arise from deep epistemological concerns. To these we can apply common sense and the refinements of common sense that make up logic and scientific method. These serve us well as stabilizers to prevent philosophical giddiness.

Of course, as the philosophically besotted are quick to point out, these stabilizers in turn depend on deep philosophical assumptions about their own validity. Indeed they do, but until those fail us by leading to errors that we can see or show at the commonsense level, they continue to earn their place in the armamentarium of practical wisdom. So the fundamental question is whether our previous practice is getting us into demonstrable—rather than hypothetical—trouble, by comparison with the practices recommended by those taking a different epistemological tack.

Now, attacks based on epistemology are sometimes very successful, especially in the early days of a discipline's development and especially when they accord with the private prejudices of the practitioners. The attitude toward the work of women scientists has been an obvious example. Specific to our own discipline was the bad epistemology—specifically, the value-free doctrine—that provided the official basis for banning the birth of a discipline of evaluation throughout most of this century. During this time, of course, evaluation was continually *practiced* by those enforcing the ban—with the usual mixed success that is the lot of poorly thought-out practice. Eventually this theory/practice schizophrenia became or was made obvious. The very history of evaluation thus exhibits both the power of bad epistemology and the triumph of common sense. Today it is not evaluation's *prima facie* legitimacy, but certain approaches to it that are at stake—although the two positions are closely connected—because it is the legitimacy of the fundamental concepts of truth and objectivity in evaluation that is under fire.

■ *Objectivity and Truth*

The first dispute we take up concerns objectivity and some aspects of practical methodology that the new epistemological concerns allegedly affect. These aspects involve the extent to which interaction with personnel being evaluated undermines objectivity. The interactions in question range from discussion of the evaluation design or preliminary results to public postevaluative advocacy. The second dispute concerns truth, and the particular issue is the extent to which evaluators have the right—or, as some see it, the duty—to modify an evaluation report in light of what they see as its possible consequences.

The notion of truth used here is the usual one, on which even those attacking the possibility of truth rely without realizing it, given that they wish to claim that their position is true. There is some sense to the notion that truth is a social construct, but not much significance, because its usually intended implication—that truth is *merely* a social construct, and hence not something one can rely on—is self-refuting. Truth is what makes beliefs into knowledge, and we all know a million truths. The fact that we are sometimes mistaken about one or a few is no basis for seriously doubting them all, only for commonsense caution.

The notion of objectivity is here taken to mean "with basis and without bias." The phrase *with basis* is present to exclude the case of random assertions, which are without bias but hardly make up objective accounts. Bias is *systematic* error or disposition to error, basically in humans, although the measurement textbooks tend to use inaccurate thermometers as an example. We all know how to distinguish some cases of objective commentary from mere partisanship, by checking the correctness and completeness of claims, and we know the kind of evidence that bears on demonstrating the existence of bias, for example, systematic unfairness in assessing or describing some groups of humans. Among the sources of bias with which we are familiar are those stemming from personality clashes, personal attraction, and other personal feelings; dictionaries usually list these as the paradigmatic examples of bias, sometimes along with racial or religious prejudice. These basic examples support the *prima facie* case for minimizing personal interaction between evaluator and evaluee, to the extent this can be done without a greater loss of the information required to provide a sound basis for the evaluation.

It is likely enough that all of us have biases of these kinds about something or other; it is commonsensically obvious that we don't all have such biases about everything. Only philosophical neuroticism leads us to think that everything is biased, that there is really no such thing as objectivity, at all, anywhere, for anyone, on any topic. Common sense says (a) that there is a very important distinction between biased reporting and objective accounts, (b) that we can often—sometimes with great certainty—identify where the difference shows up, and (c) that we can reduce it by critical interaction and further research—and, in the long run, by better training and more learning. The distinction is no less important for not always being easy to make—after all, that's the nature of the difference between right and wrong—and for having a gray area between the two extremes (these are two different properties of the distinction).

☐ *Terminology*

For the most part, the language here refers to external evaluators doing program evaluation, but most of the points transfer immediately to personnel evaluation per se (of course, some personnel evaluation is commonly part of program evaluation), and many of them transfer to policy evaluation, product evaluation, and other branches of the discipline. The extent to which they apply to internal (and hybrid) evaluators is discussed in the course of the chapter.

■ *External* (as in "an external evaluator") means "not on the regular payroll of the program (or whatever) being evaluated." Often this means that the evaluator is paid and commissioned by a third party, typically the agency funding the program to be reviewed. It may also mean that the program itself has commissioned an external evaluation, usually but not necessarily for formative purposes. Or it may mean that the program has commissioned the evaluator for general evaluation-related services, which may or may not include an actual evaluation of the program.

■ The term *client* is used here to refer to the client for the evaluation, that is, the person or group actually commissioning an evaluation (not to the group, if any, that caused someone—who might or might not be in their employ—to commission an evaluation).

■ The term *consumer* is used to refer to anyone affected by the services of the program (or whatever) being evaluated, including the immediate recipients and those indirectly affected. Thus the people referred to by a clinic as clients are here referred to as consumers. This rejection of a standard usage is the lesser evil, in order to enable discussion of all fields of evaluation without having constantly to make an exception for clinical programs.

■ A *payer* is one of those who pays the bills for the program, often including taxpayers in general. Payers are of course affected by a program, but in a different sense from consumers. Payers are affected by the expense of starting up a program and keeping it running; consumers are affected by the program's creation and continued existence. Payers are upstream of the program's services, in the causal flow; consumers are downstream. Payers cause it to exist (and continue to exist); changes in consumers are caused by it.

■ A *stakeholder* is someone who has made a significant investment in the program, either financial or psychological. Taxpayers *qua* taxpayers are usually below the threshold of significance, unless there has been high visibility and much political discussion (e.g., the space program). Program staff are stakeholders. (A school board that told a superintendent to get an evaluation done of some program in the district is a stakeholder, not a client.)

■ An *audience* is a group of parties to whom an evaluation report is made, or made accessible, or to whom it should be made available. Parents of young students or patients are typical audiences; professional peers are sometimes an audience.

These terms are not mutually exclusive, and none of them is a subset of any other.

Whereas one purpose of this chapter is to assist evaluators in deciding on a proper course of action, another is to warn prospective clients and other audiences about sources of bias that they may not have recognized as such.

■ Objectivity and Distancing

To what extent should an evaluator stay at arm's length from those being evaluated, during the process of the evaluation? "Distancing" of this kind was part of the classical ideal of objectivity maximization, but along with and perhaps because of the current attack on the possibility of objectivity—an attack associated with but not restricted to deconstructionists and critical theorists—distancing is also under heavy fire. In fact, from the earliest days of the new era in program evaluation, beginning circa 1969, there has been a strong group arguing against distancing—for example, those advocating "transactional evaluation."

It is my contention, however, that both distancing and objectivity remain correct and frequently achievable ideals for the external evaluator, ideals to which we must try to adhere as closely as possible even when circumstances put full realization beyond our grasp. The closer we come to them, the more accurate our conclusions are likely to be, other things being equal. When other things are not equal, we should try to give as little ground as possible, and that solely in the interest of improving the validity, credibility, and comprehensibility of the evaluation. The costs of deviations from this policy, although partially offset by significant advantages on occasion—for example, decreasing the painful or destructive impact of an evaluation, or improving data adequacy, or increasing the extent to which the evaluation is accepted—are far too high, across the board, to make any alternative general policy acceptable. Tempering validity with mercy (or the like) is a violation of validity—and validity is the highest professional imperative of the evaluator, as of the radiologist or engineer or historian. Now, this recommendation does not mean that nothing useful can be done when distancing is sacrificed. It does mean that some—and sometimes too much—validity is sacrificed.

Throughout the discussion that follows, it should be kept in mind that weakening the subject-investigator links, or in some other way weakening the effects that such interactions can have on interpretation, is a pervasive and well-justified feature of modern scientific method. One great paradigm of research on human subjects—the double-blind experimental design—is aimed mainly at reduction of any possible human bias at the point where the investigator or the investigator's agent interacts with the subject. It would be bizarre to suggest that the double-blind design is a symptom of failure of trust; it is a well-justified refinement of what would now be regarded as subscientific work, except where double-blind conditions cannot be met. The basic practical point is that many thousands of lives, and many millions of dollars that would be spent on nostrums, are saved by the use of double-blind designs. Nor is this just an analogy; it is an example from evaluation research.

Distancing can be thought of as a scale on which a number of points are of particular interest to the practicing evaluator. At one end of the scale is complete distancing, as when a program (person, policy, or whatever) is evaluated on the basis of extant data alone. At the other end is ownership or authorship of the program, usually conceded to be a poor basis for objective evaluation of it. Moving from the totally distanced end of the scale toward increased amounts of interaction with the evaluees (those whose work is being evaluated), an early and important point is the one representing interviewing of program staff. Although it is better in principle to use extant data, it is often the case that one needs more, and the risks attendant on personal involvement must be undertaken. There is no doubt that the risks are sometimes severe enough to compromise the validity of the evaluation, for example, when an interviewee is extremely hostile or particularly inspirational or attractive. In personnel evaluation, the research on the interview makes clear how common and serious the problems are; some experts believe that even when the sole issue is the merit of the individual being interviewed, the interview should be dispensed with entirely in favor of performance data (see Eder & Ferris, 1989). In any case, interviews should be avoided or minimized if that is possible without reduction of the amount of valuable information below the critical mass level. If used, their use should be preceded by a substantial degree of preliminary structuring of the evaluation based on noninterview data, and should involve supervised, task-specific training of interviewers. As we all know, staff interviews are often a valuable source of data; we are too often overwhelmed by that conviction and use them to go fishing without due care about the traps they involve, and without looking carefully into the possibility of doing without them. We lose data by not allowing the dispenser of medicine to know whether a placebo is being administered, but that consideration is trivial compared with the improvement in the power of the design to answer the primary question about effectiveness.

There are many ways to do distanced evaluations, but it is perhaps worth mentioning that in goal-free evaluation, which works very well in many circumstances, the evaluator not only never talks to program staff at all, but never reads the program rationale documents. Heavy interviewing is done, but only with consumers—and sometimes a selection of stakeholders—and the results of these interviews are combined with observations of process and the analysis of relevant extant data, possibly also with the results of tests. Of course, the extant data need to be weighed for bias, too, as do the procedures for analyzing them. Observations, too, are possible sources of bias, and control procedures should be discussed (e.g., use of audiotapes only).

When an evaluation has been completed and turned over to the client, it is commonly appropriate for evaluators to spend some time with the evaluees, explaining the report's significance and evidential basis. That interaction has nothing to do with the problem at hand, because it cannot affect the evaluation. It is a good feature of good evaluations. However, at a slightly earlier point on the timeline, when a draft of the evaluation is complete but not yet turned in, many evaluators (myself included) like to arrange a meeting (or phone call or correspondence) to discuss it, at least with the director of a program if not with all the staff. Sometimes, of course, this is expressly forbidden by the contract, and there can be good reasons for such restrictions (avoiding staff stress at a critical time and so on). In general, however, it is an opportunity to pick up errors in the evaluation and to give early warning to the director (if the evaluation is highly critical) that will enable him or her to prepare a defense against any criticisms. One may in fact offer to attach the response to the final report.

The risks in this process are many, some more apparent than others. Given that this interaction is going to occur, the evaluator may tone down criticisms that are well deserved in order to avoid hostile confrontation. At the meeting, the evaluator may encounter threats and bribes of various kinds, presented with varying degrees of subtlety. For obvious reasons, we are a little short of data on the success rate of these maneuvers. But the possibility of their success is another good reason some clients abjure such interactions. Again, there are procedures and training that can control the risks to some extent—for example, having a colleague present, or concurrently putting the premeeting draft into escrow for the client's later perusal. However, the evaluator needs to consider very carefully whether the correction of errors should not be left to the further interactions between the evaluee and the client (assuming these are different entities).

At this point on the distancing scale, it seems that we are dealing with an option that is risky and often dispensable, although it can offer benefits in some circumstances.

What of the ethical issues here? Does not a project director have a right to see evaluations done of his or her project? Some clients are unwilling to commit to allowing their project staff to see these evaluations. There may be, as noted above, good reasons for this policy—to those already mentioned, we can add, Why allow access to what may be an erroneous and extremely negative report? Why provide access to what is just one input to decisions about the project when others cannot be made public—such as the views of board members? We can also add a number of invalid reasons. This issue is becoming more complex as some directors are beginning to threaten lack of cooperation with evaluators unless they are guaranteed access to the final report. All in all, however, it is hard to see a clear moral imperative about the "preview" approach, and there is no doubt that it risks compromising the independence of the evaluation. If the project staff will definitely have the right to see and reply after the report is turned in, then the evaluator may just have to take the risk of errors (because they will be corrected) in order to avoid the risk of compromise.

A much more densely populated point on the scale, and one that is much closer to full involvement, concerns meeting with project or program staff to discuss a proposed evaluation design. One of the problems here is that the evaluator needs to get some cooperation in order to do the forthcoming evaluation, so staff members have a powerful source of pressure they can use to move the design toward one biased positively (e.g., with respect to choice of interviewees, types of comparisons to be made). But of course there is also the ever-present hazard of the emergence of personal likings and dislikings that can affect the objectivity of the evaluation. On the whole, it seems desirable to avoid such meetings, replacing them, if at all, with a design submitted to the project director, who may or may not circulate it and may or may not call for and pass on comments. So-called participatory design, part of the empowerment movement, is about as sloppy as one can get, short of participatory authoring of the final report (unless that report is mainly done for educational or therapeutic purposes). To say that is not in tension with saying that (noninteractive) feedback on the design from the staff is often, perhaps typically, highly desirable.

An even more serious kind of involvement occurs when the evaluator role temporally overlaps with the helping/teaching/recommending role. Here we have essentially the case of a coauthor reviewing a book. The success of the program has become partly a matter of the quality of the services provided by the evaluator, who can hardly be regarded as an objective judge of those services. A related case occurs when the program rejects the services offered by the evaluator; here, the influence of "rejected suitor" bias cannot be dismissed.

Relatedly, the role of the internal evaluator is a very difficult one, because the program not only is the paymaster but also represents the social environment in which the evaluator has worked for some time. Still, the label is not an oxymoron; such a position is a great challenge for an evaluator, and the difficulties can be overcome to a remarkable degree. However, we'll never know to what degree they are overcome if all we have is the internal evaluator's report, or the report of an external evaluator who has done his or her best to become internal.

Many evaluators reading this will throw up their hands at what they see as the suspicious or standoffish or generally unhelpful attitude inherent in much of it. For these friendly folks, interaction is the essential means by which they build trust, without which they feel they will get little insight into the working of the organization and its problems—and still less chance of implementation of recommendations. For them, and for many of their clients, staff endorsement and improvement are the outcomes prized above all others.

Of course, there is the serious problem of what counts as improvement. If the evaluator's judgment is impaired by interaction, he or she may not see where the deepest and most serious problems lie. If the pharaohs' failing was a belief in their omnipotence, the interactive evaluators' failing is the belief in their incorruptible objectivity—that is, their ability to retain objectivity and sensitivity to problem/strength (and side-effect) identification. Perversely, the opposite belief amounts to the same thing— that is, the belief that there is no objectivity, that everyone is biased, and no biases are provably worse than any others (I understand both Bob Stake and Jennifer Greene to support this position). On either of these assumptions, interaction poses no threat. However, the public is less naive and thinks that regulatory agencies that socialize with those they regulate should be viewed with suspicion, as judges think the same about jurors socializing with defense attorneys. Whether or not evaluators are serving in an accountability role in a particular case is unimportant; in either that role or the formative evaluation role, the experts' value depends on the validity of their evaluation, and that validity is compromised by social interaction. As is agreed here, distancing has its price; but involvement risks the whole capital.

Dismissing the relativist view of bias as naive is not in itself an argument—the same might be said of the distanced ideal. But the reference to naïveté is meant to remind the reader of the theme argument here: One must not let epistemological speculations overpower common sense—until they can be given overwhelming commonsense support.

Concerns about objectivity's objectivity are no justification for thinking that the SAT is on a par with a random teacher's assessment of a random student's achievement level; depth does not in general offset independence, and quoting examples where it does is irrelevant to the general claim. The distanced evaluator has a substantial advantage—even if sometimes it is not a net advantage—over the interactive evaluator. Opposition to the use of performance indicators in evaluation is often justified because they are often invalid; but a generic opposition, to which Bob Stake lends some support, presupposes a generic advantage of the depth approach over the distanced approach, and that is questionable.

Many of the concerns of the evaluator who prefers the interactive role are really due to role confusion. The evaluation consultant (to be discussed below) must indeed interact with staff, should be concerned with winning their confidence, and so on. Evaluators per se should do so only to the minimum extent necessary, in order to avoid losing the edge on the one gift they bear—the distanced view—the nearest possible approach to a true view of the program's merit or worth.

Finally, we turn to latent reality. A kind of involvement that is particularly destructive of objectivity is not actual during the evaluation, but is only prospective. It has the same corrupting effect as the high-paying jobs with Defense Department contractors that were routinely offered to high-ranking military personnel in charge of the evaluation of weapons and other procured materiel. That "revolving-door" situation was eventually attacked by the passage of federal legislation imposing a multiyear interval between service in the armed forces and any such job. Today, in program evaluation, a very similar approach is being touted as "empowerment evaluation." The most objectionable aspect of this is the notion that it can be entirely proper for the evaluator to switch roles to that of paid advocate after the evaluation is complete. The moment such a possibility is legitimated, it will be present as a latent possibility in every case, and is of course likely to lead the evaluator interested in such further employment to improve the argument that he or she will then have to present—that is, sweeten the evaluation. (Note that whereas postevaluation advocacy done without pay or favor is of course within the free speech rights of an evaluator, there are some circumstances, even there, in which certain types of advocacy would still be inappropriate, e.g., if the evaluator has not had the opportunity to examine competing programs or other alternatives with equal care.)

Weaker forms of the same latent bias occur when it is supposed that the evaluator is going to, or may be going to, become (a) a teacher of evaluation skills to the program staff; (b) someone who will help the staff evaluate their own program; (c) someone who will subsequently seek to identify ways to improve the program, that is, a recommender (some recommendations may occur naturally in the course of the evaluation); or (d) a helper with the process of implementing the recommendations made in the evaluation (or in the process referred to in c) or in other ways helping to improve the program. The problems with these roles are not merely weak versions of the problems with the advocacy role. To give just one example of a further problem, if there is the slightest possibility that one could legitimately provide training workshops to the staff of the program (or whatever) being evaluated, at a later date, as an employee of the program, there is a temptation—conscious or not—to make some recommendation that indicates a need for training of this kind, even if there are no objective reasons for it.

In passing, I should note that even the future role of continuing as an evaluator after a midstream evaluation has been seen by program staff is not without its risks (resulting from hostile or subservient or friendly responses). Here we see a third reason for nondisclosure, reluctant though I am to support that practice in general.

The activities referred to in this section are seen by many evaluators as routine and proper parts of their evaluation service, most notably in Australia and New Zealand, but also by many who are attracted to the "empowerment" guidon. As these activities are indeed highly proper in their own right, it is essential for us to distinguish between "doing evaluation" and "providing evaluation-related services."

■ *Evaluators and Evaluation Consultants*

We will say here that someone simply doing evaluation (i.e., trying to determine the worth, merit, or significance of something) is, in that role, serving as *an evaluator,* whereas someone providing evaluation-related services is serving as *an evaluation consultant.* One may in principle do either or both, even on the same contract (as long as the contract allows both). My argument here is about the advisability and risks involved with trying to do—or even considering doing at a later date—the second if one's contract calls for doing the first.

I take the useful term *evaluation consultant* from Michael Quinn Patton, who says that he increasingly favors describing himself in that way, contrasting the term with *evaluator* (personal communication). Serving consistently in the former role, as he now does, he avoids making any direct evaluative claims—at least, about the program he is serving. Now, to be an evaluation consultant, it seems clear that one must be *capable* of doing evaluations, even if one does not normally do them (the converse claim, however, is not correct). Hence it is entirely sensible to refer to Patton as an evaluator, in the general sense of someone who is not only capable of doing evaluation, but is professionally engaged in evaluation-related activities. But it is not correct to refer to his role, or to him, as the evaluator of a project for which he is serving simply as an evaluation consultant.

How do other evaluators fit into this distinction? The situation is similar for several who, like Marv Alkin, see evaluation as the process of gathering and synthesizing data to support decisions, but not as drawing evaluative conclusions. In this role, they are not serving as evaluators; if that had been the only role they had ever adopted, it is not clear that they would ever have acquired the skills involved in true evaluation, and so it would not be clear that they could be referred to even loosely as evaluators. They are evaluation consultants, pure and simple. In general terms, this role is one that many well-rounded social scientists could do; it has nothing evaluation specific about it.

Rossi and Freeman's *Evaluation* (1993) in fact defines evaluation as a branch of applied social science. This is no nearer the truth than the claim that evaluation is a branch of logic or ethics: All put important tools in the tool kit of the evaluator, but no more. It is not surprising that such terms as *ethics* and *values* do not turn up in Rossi and Freeman's index;

it is equally telling that *needs assessment, personnel, synthesis,* and *grading* are also on the missing list.

Bob Stake, in his "rich description" phase, was also pulling the punches, as I would put it; providing an inkblot in which the client and other audiences are supposed to see some truth portrayed. But what truth? Too often, I fear, the one they want to see—or one they fear, sometimes without justification. In the recent evaluation on which he reports in Chapter 32 of this volume, he saw part of his role as trying "not to make it more difficult for the staff to do their job," and took that to cover deleting some negative content in the draft report before releasing it. The best of motives, indeed, but did the clients really request censorship of the released version? Did that censorship really benefit them (as opposed to reducing short-term discomfort)? This is the evaluator *in loco parentis,* too close to being *in loco God* for my taste and, I suspect, for the taste of most clients. Even telling the program staff the bad news, but keeping it out of the official report to an external client or public—as occurred in this case—is quite simply the fast road to the destruction of evaluator credibility. To make it possible for critics to quote just one example of this being done and advocated by a leading evaluator, supported or condoned by others, seems to be a fearful setback for professional standards in evaluation. This is surely, in the long run, a more serious cost than the possible benefit of temporarily saving a program here or there.

Professional ethics is part of a profession's contract with society, in return for which professionals are granted a reasonable degree of autonomy. For this reason, the society is a kind of client for everything we do, especially because it nearly always involves some use of public money. We need to study what that relationship implies.

It is sometimes suggested that the push for distance is itself an attempt to be superior, external, an attempt to play God the Judge. On the contrary, it is part of the simple and sensible human effort to get things right, to uncover and report the truth, the effort that is an ideal of every scientist, historian, ethicist, and better journalist. Deciding when and to what extent to withhold those findings from those who paid for them is the "doing what's good for you, not what you asked me to do" step, the step over the border between expertise and censorship/parenting.

To serve only as an evaluation consultant, although thinking of that role as an evaluator's role—or allowing the client to think of one as an evaluator per se—is often to mislead, with the risk of serious consequences. We are currently in an intermediate stage in the development of evaluation as a major social service, and in this stage both evaluators and clients are more inclined toward the evaluation consultant role. It is to be hoped that this will change, and that both parties will come to see the importance of separating the roles. There is no reason to think this is any more expensive in terms of front-end costs, and it offers the prospect of large savings in the long run (through avoidance of unnecessary changes and costs, improvement of outcome quality with attendant increase in numbers served with attendant economies of scale, and so on).

When serving as an evaluation consultant to a project, or hoping to so serve, one is severely handicapped as an evaluator for the reasons outlined above, and should not undertake the latter role. Conversely, when serving as an evaluator of a project, one should absolutely rule out any possibility of later serving as an evaluation consultant in the employ of the same project. It should, in my view, be one of the ethical principles governing professional evaluation practice that the two roles are mutually exclusive, at least for a period of some years. Taking on both lays one open to a charge of conflict of interest; not as crass as some such conflicts, but nevertheless improper.

One of the forces that makes the doctrine expressed in the previous paragraph difficult to accept is economic. As a New Zealand evaluator pointed out to me over the Internet recently, it is hard to make a living as an evaluator unless one takes on the evaluation consultant role as well. However, there is no need to separate the two roles at the career level, only at the project level. One must, however, take some steps to avoid a revolving-door situation. I have normally said that I will not provide services to a program I am evaluating for at least 3 years after the evaluation is concluded; there may be better arrangements with the same effect. In many situations, this commitment is itself quite expensive, but as one builds up a practice, it is not as serious as restricting oneself forever to one or the other role.

Another force that pushes us toward role blending is the wish to help; related to this is the drive for efficient use of resources. Now, there is one situation in which some role-doubling in these interests is entirely acceptable. It occurs when the evaluator volunteers to take on some further helper role after the evaluation is complete, as a pro bono activity. Many of us do this, and it may be something that deserves some study and discussion in training programs.

Can there ever be a justification for bending the tough rules laid out above? Perhaps the best case can be made when (a) an evaluator does a modest amount of helping some small components of a large project, (b) if this occurs for a brief part of the time occupied by a long evaluation, and (c) if this is encouraged by the (third-party) client and (d) involves no extra pay for so doing, and (e) the evaluator has committed to avoiding any further work of this kind after the evaluation is complete that would be paid for by the evaluees or any other sources. All these qualifications are aimed at one or another causes of bias, and there are no doubt some loopholes in them. The idea here is to give some practical guidance that follows from the general principles being put forward, and to indicate that it is rather complicated to do so. Some further discussion of borderline cases is offered below. These very limited cases are the ones where we can best experiment and learn more about the risks and how to avoid them, if experiment we must. It should be clear that even if we make exceptions as here, they would be few in number and small in benefit. Risking them, absent serious studies, is not a good bet; and jumping into the deep end of full-scale consulting as a normal concomitant of evaluation is quite a different matter.

The claim here is that free-for-all mixed-role commitments are serious compromises with proper procedure. Plenty of evaluators will feel that the compromise is an acceptable trade-off for the extra good they are able to do, and plenty of clients will feel the same. But the evaluators are hardly unbiased judges of this, and the clients rarely know much about the costs of role doubling. It is certainly desirable for the profession to push for funding for some metaevaluations of role-doubled projects, beginning with the marginal ones. Until those results point incontrovertibly in the opposite direction, evaluators should follow the principles here if for no other reason than that they need credibility as well as validity, and the concerns raised here are the fairly simple commonsense concerns that tend to affect credibility. My view is that they also affect validity, but it must be agreed that we do not know the extent of that effect.

Jennifer Greene, who prefers the term *border-crossing* to *role blending* or *role doubling,* thinks that increased familiarity with program staff improves the validity of the evaluation to an extent that more than offsets the possible loss due to personal likings and dislikings. If this were true, a mother would be the best judge of her son's character, a view that few of us, particularly parole officers and family court judges, find well supported in practice. More seriously, the argument is closely parallel to the one legislators have used for years to head off any legal impediment to their free use of airplanes and hunting lodges offered by lobbyists.

One might suppose that the normal role of the teacher is a counterexample to the doctrine proposed here. A teacher normally serves as both evaluator and helper, switching roles all the time. Good teachers handle this very well; others have great difficulty. A leading problem is the difficulty of flunking students who fail to achieve minimum competence, because of the direct stress that it occasions for the students and the indirect repercussions from parents and—all too often—principals. This fault has made possible the massive grade inflation of the past few decades, which contrasts sharply with the functional illiteracy of a substantial proportion of the graduates from these schools. Recognition of this fault has provided much of the continued support for external testing. Swarthmore College, which arguably provides the best undergraduate education in the country, has long felt it essential to pay the bill for completely external evaluations of all students in its honors program, following the example of Oxford and Cambridge—and many other institutions. So the ideal is to separate the helping and the evaluating roles, the teaching from the testing. But the analogy leaves open the possibility that one can combine the roles and still do a good, if not ideal, job.

Before evaluators get too encouraged by that possibility, it would be well to remember that this case is unlike program evaluation in important respects. For example, there are several independent measures for determining whether students are harmed by teachers' playing the double role (e.g., the SAT, the views of employers and subsequent teachers). In most cases, program evaluators who are role-doubling are often the only judges of the success of the program, a fact of which they are well aware. No doubt, if teachers' own tests and test results were the only ones available, we would be more optimistic about successful role doubling by them.

Matching the weaknesses of teachers forced to role-double is the frequently poor performance of principals in proceeding against incompetent teachers. Here again we have the problem of the double role. The teachers are, after all, the people with whom the principals have to live every day, and whom they are supposed to inspire and instruct in matters pedagogical. Many of them prefer to have the roles separated, as they are in inspectorate systems in other countries. The same lesson has been well learned in the product field, where using noncompany evaluators for the so-called beta version (the last preproduction version) is a sine qua non for quality assurance. All these cases support the distanced ideal.

Notwithstanding the above, many readers may still feel that it is surely sometimes better to have an evaluator role-double than have no one provide services sorely needed by the program under review. (Granted that if anyone else can provide these services with approximately equal competence, that is the preferable alternative.) What is lost on the swings of evaluator objectivity is surely sometimes gained on the roundabouts of troubles avoided and benefits increased. This is especially likely to be true in some multiyear projects, because of the problem of cumulative effects of nonhelping, and when the intervention is very small compared with the scale of the project. Even in such cases, there is one catch: How can the evaluator—or a third-party client—be sure that the resulting conflict of interest does not have serious results? Neither is free from interest in the matter, so the judgments are tainted to an unknown degree.

Having succumbed to the temptation on more than one occasion, for what seemed good reasons at the time (less so in retrospect), I can suggest four procedural conditions that should be met in order to objectify the decision (in addition to the restrictions to small interventions in multiyear projects). First, such interventions cannot be planned in advance (or else they establish the bias of coauthorship from the beginning). Second, they should not be considered until a first evaluation report has been done that uncovers some need for them (of course, this precaution creates the risk of inventing the need). Third, provision of them by some other source, not the evaluator, should be explicitly advocated in discussions with the funder, the client, and the project director before the possibility of the evaluator's doing them is considered (the issue here is not whether the evaluator could do it best, but whether the evaluator's doing it would weaken the evaluation). Fourth, the evaluator should try to invoke the assistance of a metaevaluator in making the decision and following up on its effects. In general, the complications required to justify this small intervention, and the loopholes in them, suggest that a straight prohibition is the better principle.

What I have just been discussing might be called remedial role doubling. It leaves us with the question of whether it is ever appropriate to commission or participate in a study in which the evaluator is, from the beginning, seen as providing support services—planned role doubling. Of course, there will be some cases where this does work out, even though it is intrinsically undesirable. Especially with very-low-budget operations, it may even be a defensible although undesirable bet if an experienced and hard-nosed evaluator is involved. But with operations where a staff of more than a half-time person is involved in evaluation-related activities, across a period of more than half a year, it is hard to see any possible justification for it, because division of labor becomes feasible and greatly superior. That is, one can identify one (part-time) person to serve as evaluator and another to provide evaluation consulting services. Interaction between the evaluator and the project should be limited, and so too should interaction between the evaluator and the evaluation consultant, but the latter interaction should be enough to enable the consultant to serve as explainer and assistant implementer.

■ *The Truth, the Whole Truth, and Nothing But the Truth*

There are many social scientists and evaluators today who think that the slogan that heads this section is impossibly naive. On the contrary, it is better than any alternative, good enough for the courts, and clear enough, in whole and in every part, for anyone to understand. This is because native speakers understand in context, not because they can reply to a demand for an acontextual definition of "truth." What other formula should the courts use when swearing in an expert witness, in order to avoid the alleged naïveté? Something along the lines of "I swear to tell what strikes me as the truth, at least as much of it as seems appropriate, leavened with whatever else seems called for"? That's exactly what the oath as now administered is designed to avoid.

An evaluator is an expert witness, and should be bound by exactly the standard oath. The evaluation consultant, on the other hand, has other roles, including that of psychotherapist, and in those other roles may well wish to soften the blow of unexpurgated criticism. Such censorship on the part of evaluators is essentially never justified, and amounts to an abandonment of their commitment to expertise. Courts and clients call on experts to get expert opinion, not psychotherapy or edited or bowdlerized testimony. It seems clear that the muddying of the role of the evaluator that has occurred with the introduction of evaluation-related activities has led to the muddying of the obligations of the evaluator to the client and other audiences.

Of course, we are here talking about substantial censorship and unwarranted icing on the cake, not the minor—although sometimes psychologically significant—nuances involved in the phrasing or starkness of an evaluation report. In those respects, kindness and charity have their place. Moreover, other things being equal, evaluators should be interested in the acceptance of their findings, and that will be facilitated by the avoidance of unnecessary grounds for resentment and rejection. But the other things that have to be equal include strict adherence to the slogan above.

The entire social role of the expert, an exceedingly valuable one not only in the administration of justice but in the determining of policy, depends on the expert's willingness to set aside, as a task for others, the role of weighing and balancing the legal and social impacts of the expert's view. Of course, experts have to weigh and balance various considerations within their own fields, and these considerations can include, for evaluators, many weighty ethical issues (such as program racism). That has nothing to do with the point here, which concerns the social impact of the result of their deliberations.

The classic microexample of this corruption of the evaluator's role occurred a couple of years ago in the Adele Jones case in Suffolk County, Virginia, where a teacher was fired for flunking 30% of her Algebra II class, this being the precollege class, where grades are supposed to give an extrapolable preview of college standards. Checking with Ms. Jones's former students who had gone on to college made clear that the standards were fully justified; if anything, they were a little lenient. The principal defended the firing on the grounds that the low grades "discouraged the students from taking mathematics." His standing instructions to his staff were that no student should get less than 55% on any test. Of course it is true that low grades discourage students—but that does not provide any justification for firing the teacher who gives such grades, when the grades are justified by the students' work (as they were in this case). For the expert to give high grades where they are not warranted is to lie—and lie on a crucial matter for which the students and their parents need sound expert advice, even if they would rather have favorable lies.

A common version of ignoring the "whole truth" part of the expert's imperative consists in reporting only or mainly on the parts of a program that can still be changed. After all, the rationalization goes, what is the point of saying that some things about the program are bad when it is too late to change them? The point is that the evaluator's obligation is to provide the whole truth, which is required in order to get a correct perspective on the program; and that perspective may affect major decisions that were not foreseen when the evaluation was commissioned or completed.

Will this straight-arrow line really hold up in the limit? A favorite case of Bob Stake's is one in which condemning a program in a final report, although deserved, will be likely to result in its being closed (so he judges), with the result that needy consumers will not (so he judges) receive services at all. In such a case, he will not condemn the program. The position taken here is that he should condemn it, and that his going beyond this into domains where he is not expert about social effects and not requested to render a judgment is inappropriate, a case where good intentions produce bad results. This is closely analogous to an oncologist's deciding not to tell a patient that he has terminal cancer because to do so may adversely affect the patient's spirits. Whereas the family physician might discuss this option with close relatives, if there are any, the specialist is surely abrogating a duty to report accurately, if hired by the family. Concealing the true state of affairs impedes efforts to improve matters in the large; so, in the interests of improving society, censorship may have the opposite effect.

■ *Formative and Summative Evaluation*

The preceding remarks are not just about summative evaluation, but also about formative evaluation. Lately, there has been a tendency to think that formative evaluation necessarily involves various helping and hand-holding activities that are appropriate for the evaluation consultant. This is completely incorrect; the terms were defined as referring to different roles for evaluation, not different kinds of process—both are simply best efforts to determine and inform about merit or worth or significance, in different contexts. Formative evaluation is, to a large extent, best designed as summative evaluation of an early version, with particular attention to components or dimensions rather than a holistic account (because this facilitates improvement), and provided directly to the program director or staff rather than to external decision makers. It should be contrasted with a midcourse summative evaluation, on which continuance is often dependent. The latter can be holistic and is reported to an external client, who may or may not reveal it to the evaluees. For both, a high degree of distancing is desirable; for both, if possible, a complementary evaluation consultant is useful, for the program's sake.

Where role doubling has been forced (e.g., in the case of the teacher), the formative evaluation may be softened or rosied up in order to produce desired effects on self-esteem and so on—but at considerable risk, because misrepresentation often has bad effects later.

It is a mistake to think that formative evaluation needs to involve evaluation consultant activities—in fact, it should try not to do this—and it is a mistake to think that formative evaluation must involve recommendations for improvement. It may or may not involve these, depending on whether they are in or are logical consequences of what is in an analytic evaluation, for example, the identification of improperly functioning components such as discrimination in personnel policies. Very often, recommendations require a great deal more information about the ambient circumstances (e.g., local politics and funding sources) than are available to the evaluator, or they may require more knowledge of technical matters (e.g., which programming language to use for setting up new procedures in the admissions department) than the evaluator of a college, school, or hospital can reasonably be expected to possess.

The role of formative evaluation is to provide feedback on midstream merit, as a service to assist program improvement, and given that the program itself is constantly evaluating midstream merit in an informal way, what the professional independent evaluator brings to the party is a fresh eye and some technical skills. It is not smart to muddy that eye by getting into bed or a brawl with someone on the program staff, and hence not smart to engage in activities that may lead to that kind of situation or its weaker relations.

Finally, a few clarifications and disclaimers. First, although it is true that any evaluation, properly so-called, concludes with evaluative claims the truth of which it of course advocates, this kind of "advocacy" has nothing to do with program advocacy. Hence one cannot argue, as she appears to do, that evaluators are per se committed to advocacy in the sense talked about here. Even in the weakest sense of program advocacy—advocating that the program be continued—the evaluator often takes the opposite position, and may make no recommendations at all. In the usual sense of program advocacy, we are talking about representing the program in public forums, coauthoring proposals for funding it, and any support for it when on its payroll.

I should also stress that no assumption is made here that clients will respond rationally or in any other way to evaluation reports. The expert witness in court makes no assumption that the jury—or for that matter the judge—will use the testimony rationally. He or she must nevertheless give it as fully, clearly, and truly as possible. The duty of the evaluator precludes distortion, whether for good motives or for bad ones.

■ *References*

Eder, R. W., & Ferris, G. R. (Eds.). (1989). *The employment interview: Theory, research, and practice.* Newbury Park, CA: Sage.

Rossi, P. H., & Freeman, H. E. (1993). *Evaluation: A systematic approach* (5th ed.). Newbury Park, CA: Sage.

Index

ABAB designs, 341-342. *See also*
    Single-case evaluation; Single- case
    study methodologies
Abernathy, C. M., 368
Accountability, social work and, 420-421
Accountability evaluators, 22, 70
    criticism of knowledge evaluators, 19
    working in institutions, 20
    working in think tanks, 20
Accountability perspective in evaluation,
    5, 6, 10, 16, 22
    acceptability of to clients/users, 21
    auditors and, 11
    description of, 11
    donors to international organizations
        and, 11
    evaluator role re client in, 21
    government sponsors of evaluation
        studies and, 11
    independence of, 21
    methods used, 11-12
    objectivity of, 21
    position of under policy debate, 21
    purpose of, 21
    typical uses of, 21
Action research-based evaluations, 183

Advocacy:
    as acceptable value among evaluators,
        468
    as unacceptable value among
        evaluators, 471
    in evaluation studies, 471-475
    in program evaluation, 475
    over authority, 471
    power of, 467
    program, 499-500
    versus truth in evaluation, 467
Affholter, D. P., 130
AGA Task Force report, 115
Agency for Health Care Policy and
    Research, 63, 66
Agent Orange Act of 1991, 374
Aid-giving agencies, joint evaluation
    between, 166
Albæ, E., 178, 179, 180, 185, 187
Alchian, A., 193
Alkin, Marv, 490
Alvesson, M., 186
American Evaluation Association (AEA),
    32, 44, 397
American Public Health Association
    (APHA), 32, 44

American Society for Public Administration, 125, 132
Government Accomplishment and Accountability Task Force, 131
Anderson, J. A., 370
Anderson, K. W., 370
Anderson, M., 261
Anthony, R. N., 125
Asian Development Bank, 173
Association for Public Policy Analysis and Management (APPAM), 32, 44
Association of Government Accountants, 115
Attkisson, C. C., 121
Audit agencies, adoption of evaluation by national, 6, 54
Audit Commission, 93, 94, 102, 433
Auditing:
    evaluation in, 8
    origin of, 88, 112
    traditional methods, 349
    versus evaluation, 69, 70, 88-90
    See also specific types of auditing
Auditor General Act (Canada), 73, 75
Auditor General of Canada, Office of, 72
    encouraging evaluation development in Federal government, 75-77
    evaluation in work of, 73-74
    obtaining information re effectiveness of government programs, 74-75
    oversight responsibility of, 174
Auditors, 7, 86-87, 89
    as change agents, 87
    evaluation and performance assessment and, 6
    versus evaluator methodology, 98-99
    versus evaluators in choosing topics, 91
    versus evaluators securing funding, 92
Audits, results-based, 74
Austin, J., 261
Australian Government Printing Service, 236, 242
Australian National Audit Office, 94
Autoregressive integrated moving average (ARIMA) analysis, 448, 458. *See also* Interrupted time series (ITS) design
Axelsson, C. A., 370

Babcock, J., 355
Ball, R., 249
Bamberger, M., 264
Barklund-Larsson, U., 87
Barley, Z. A., 396
Barlow, D. H., 426
Bauer, M., 361, 370
Behn, R. B., 132
Benchmarking, 276
Bennett, L. L., 300
Bhaskar, R., 405, 407
Black-box task, 32
Blackstone, T., 66
Blank, R. M., 42
Blichert-Toft, M., 370
Bloom, M., 420, 425, 433, 434
Blythe, B. J., 419, 420, 421, 425, 441
Boll Hansen, E., 181, 182
Bostwick, G. I., Jr., 425
Botner, S. B., 110
Bourn, J., 102
Box, G. E. P., 448, 449, 450, 463
Brandl, J., 113, 118
Brennan, J., 425
Breslow, N., 371
British Evaluation Society, 54
Bronson, D. E., 419
Brown, B., 417
Brown, J. R., 110
Bryant, C., 181
Bureau of Immigration Research (Australia), 241, 242, 243, 245
    charter, 246
    degree of freedom of, 246
    National Outlook Conferences, 243-244, 246
    research conclusions/recommendations, 247
    study, 248-249
Burrows, B., 433
Bush, George, 289
Bush administration, nuclear weapons modernization program of, 284
Butler, F. C., 266
Buxton, M., 97

Calder, B. G., 449, 453, 455
California Institute of Integral Studies:

as case example of empowerment
evaluation, 385-388
unit self-evaluation workshops for unit
heads, 390-394
Callahan, T. J., 456, 458
Campbell, D. T., 34, 35, 45, 408, 443, 453,
454, 456
Campbell, J. L., 397
Canada:
evaluation as government function in,
69, 72-79
policy evaluations in, 80
See also Auditor General of Canada,
Office of
Canadian International Development
Agency, 166
Cantley, C., 433, 438
Caracelli, V. J., 347, 355, 356
Carter administration, nuclear weapons
modernization program of, 284
Case studies, 24, 27, 131-132, 337, 338,
345, 347-348, 349, 357
accountability perspective and, 11
conditions needed when using with
other methods, 358
criteria for evaluating quality of, 338
definition of, 346
developmental evaluators and, 14
developmental perspective and, 13
ethnographic, 347, 350
example of combining with other
methods, 348-349
in large-scale national evaluations, 347
multimethod designs and, 344,
346-348, 358
Case study reports, guidelines for
assessing quality of, 351-353
Castles, S., 4, 17, 238, 249
Caudle, S. L., 130
Center for Evaluation Studies, University
of Huddersfield, 419, 421, 433, 440
Cheetham, J., 420
Chelimsky, E., 41, 46, 47, 88, 194, 360
Chen, H.-T., 47, 178, 413
Chernobyl nuclear power plant accident,
299, 309
absence of containment structure and,
304-305
economic changes due to, 309

factor remediation after, 304
factors responsible for, 303
nuclear power policy in FSU and
Eastern Europe after, 305-307
political changes due to, 309
technical changes due to, 309
Chicago Teachers Academy, 468
evaluation report of, 471-472, 474-475
Chief Financial Officers Act of 1990, 125,
128
Children Act of 1989 (U.K.), 342, 420
Children's rights, evaluation and, 3
China, People's Republic of, 146
banking and evaluation in, 172-173
bilateral development organizations in,
173
demand for evaluation in, 176
evaluation as new in, 170, 172-173
loan portfolio of, 176
multilateral development organizations
in, 173
reform movement, 171
tasks to be undertaken, 174-176
World Bank and, 176
See also State Planning Commission
(SPC) [PRC]; China International
Engineering Consulting
Company (CIECC)
China International Engineering
Consulting Company (CIECC), 172,
173
Cicirelli, V. G. & Assoc., 38
Citizen's Charter program (U.K.), 122,
137, 138-139, 143
results of, 138-139
Clinton administration, 289
Cloud, K., 261
Clune, W. H., 472
Cluster evaluation, xiii, 23, 337, 340-341
accuracy and, 402
and frequent
communications/collaborations
among partners, 399, 400
as creative approach, 396
as evolving approach, 397
as holistic, 399, 400
as intrusive, 401
as outcome oriented, 399, 400
as program evaluation, 397

audiences served by, 398
case study evaluation and, 340
collaboration and, 341
conflict resolution in, 399
cooperation in, 399
credit in, 399
design of, 399-402
developmental perspective and, 13
elements of, 401
feasibility and, 402
fundamentals, 397-402
generalizable learning and, 341
limitations of, 402-403
metaevaluation panels and, 403
naturalistic evaluation and, 340
origins of, 396
outcome data, 341
propriety and, 402
questions addressed by, 397-398
role definitions in, 398
seeking generalizable learning, 399
steps in, 399-400
strengths of, 402, 403
team relationships in, 398-399
trust in, 399
underlying paradigm of, 401
utility and, 402
Coase, R., 193
Cognitive mapping, 100
Cohen, D., 103
Colby, J., 33
Collective case codes, 226
Columbia (S.A.):
   Law 115 of 1994, 196
   Law 60 of 1993, 196
   National Development Plan, 197
   National System of Evaluation, 197
   strategic evaluation program of, 197,
     198
   See also Developing countries;
     Developing countries, evaluation
     in
Committee to Advise on Australia's
   Immigration Policies, 241
Community settings, globalization and:
   challenges posed for evaluation in,
     161-165
Comparative analysis, SAI use of, 99

Competing for Quality program (U.K.),
   122, 137, 139-140
Complementary designs, 362-363
Comptroller and Auditor General (U.K.),
   91
Comptroller General of the United States,
   111, 112, 113
Conceptual evaluations, 28
Congressional Budget Office, 129, 131
Content analysis, 74
Contexts, 410-411
   definition of, 410
   examples of, 415
   social, 411
Controlled designs, accountability
   perspective and, 11
Cook, T. D., 34, 35, 36, 38, 39, 42, 44, 47,
   89, 130, 408, 443, 444, 449, 453,
   455, 456, 460, 461, 462
Cooper, H., 36, 38
Corcoran, K., 425
Cordray, D. S., 36, 38
Cost-benefit designs, 345
   accountability evaluators and, 14
   knowledge evaluators and, 14
Cost-effectiveness, policy:
   evaluation and, 5
Cost-effectiveness, program:
   evaluation and, 5, 8
Cost-effectiveness designs:
   accountability evaluators and, 14
   accountability perspective and, 11
   knowledge evaluators and, 14
Craven, M., 426, 433
Credibility testing, 167
Critical reviews, 349
Cronbach, L. J. & Associates, 46, 47, 55,
   56, 384, 390
Cross-case "lesson learned" analysis, 132
Cross-design synthesis, 338-339
   and complementary set of designs,
     362-363
   as evolving, 370
   as new, 370
   comparisons of treatment effects,
     368-370
   concept of, 361-363
   example of, 363-370
   key ideas, 361

strategies for combining results, 363
when to use, 361-362
See also GAO breast conservation
versus mastectomy study

Danish evaluation research:
areas covered by, 177
criticisms of, 186
general interest in, 186
growth of, 177
major features in development of,
180-185
political interest in, 186
social policy and social science in,
179-180
See also Danish evaluations
Danish evaluations, 177
action research-based, 147, 181,
183-184, 186
development of theory in, 147, 181
external, 181
internal, 147, 181, 184-185, 186-187
Social Development Programme
(SUM), 181-183
survey-based, 147, 181, 185
theory-oriented, 183, 185-186
See also Danish evaluation research
Danish National Institute for Social
Research (SFI), 179, 181, 184
Dastidar, P., 300
Data base analysis:
primary strength of, 362
primary weakness of, 362
Datta, L.-e., 346
Decision making, effectiveness
evaluations and, 277-279
Defense policy, evaluation of, xii
Del Rosario, M. L., 449, 453, 455
Democratic reform, evaluation and, 6
Demsetz, H., 193
Denmark, evaluation research in. *See*
Danish evaluation research
Denmark, evaluations in. *See* Danish
evaluations
Derlien, Hans Ullrich, 80
Developing countries:
fiscal decentralization in, 147, 189,
190, 192

new spending priorities in, 147, 189,
190, 192
political decentralization in, 147, 189,
190, 192
privatization drives in, 147, 189, 190,
191-192
reform programs, 189
Developing countries, evaluation in:
challenges for, 194-197
economics and, xii, 3
external competitive environment and,
196
reform agenda role of, 145, 147,
190-192
interventionist, 194
nominal performance compliance
versus real, 195-196
strategic, 196-197, 198-199
Developmental evaluators, 70
Developmental perspective in evaluation,
16, 22, 23
acceptability of to clients/users, 21
advocacy and, 21
flexibility of, 12
beneficiaries' opinions and, 12
capacity builders and, 12
cooperation among collaborating
agencies and, 12
data systems and, 12
evaluator role re client in, 21
formative methods used, 13
government reformers and, 12
independence in, 21
institutional effectiveness and, 12
institutional performance and, 12
institutional responsiveness and, 12
methods used, 13
need for use of to fulfill purpose, 21
objectivity of, 21
organization activities and, 12
outcome designs and, 13
position of under policy debate, 21
process designs and, 13
project/demonstration designs and, 12
project implementation and, 12
public managers and, 12
purpose of, 21
research agendas and, 12

specific questions asked evaluators in,
    12-13
typical uses of, 21
Development assistance:
    evaluation and donor accountability, 7
    evaluation and organizational learning
        process, 8
    evaluation in, 8
Development cooperation agreements,
    273-274
Development process:
    factors receiving emphasis in, 273
Development projects, reasons for
        studying gender impacts of, 261-262
Direct observation, World Bank use of, 205
Disciplinary theories, substantive base in,
    48-50
Document analysis, 349
Droitcour, J. A., 360
Drucker, P., 161
Dryfoos, J., 49
Dudden, A. P., 67
Dummett, A., 238
Durbin, J., 448
Durkheim, E., 408

Economic analyses, 349
Economic models, construction of, 98
Economies:
    evaluation and globalization of local, 3
    evaluation and globalization of
        national, 3
Economies of scale, 243
Eder, R. W., 484
Edin, K., 39
Education evaluators, 49
Effectiveness evaluations, decision
        making and, 277-279
    agency goals, 278
    evaluation, 278-279
    program goals, 278
    project goals, 278
    reporting results, 278
Elderly people's rights, evaluation and, 3
Eliot, T. S., 55
Ellenberg, S. S., 370
Embeddedness:
    as stratified nature of social reality, 406

Empowerment evaluation, xiii, 381-383
    accountability in, 388
    advocacy as facet of, 384
    and dynamic community of learners,
        385
    as collaborative group activity, 382
    as democratic process, 388
    criticism of, 488-489
    definition of, 340, 382, 385
    developmental perspective and, 13
    evaluator's role in, 388
    external evaluation and, 389
    external evaluators and, 389
    facilitation as facet of, 384
    focus of, 382
    guiding principles of, 383
    honesty as guiding principle of, 383
    illumination as facet of, 384
    institutions using, 382
    liberation as facet of, 384
    participatory design and, 486
    steps of, 384
    training as facet of, 384
    truth as guiding principle of, 383
    value assessments and, 382-383
    versus personnel performance
        self-appraisal, 383-384
    See also California Institute of Integral
        Studies
Enlightenment use, knowledge evaluators
        and, 17-18
Environmental change (global):
    definition of, 329
    social effects of, 330
Environmental change (global),
        assessment/evaluation of:
    as information-intensive activity, 331
    collaborative information systems for,
        333-335
Environmental interventions, evaluation
        of, xii, 3, 8
Environmental issues:
    backyard, 332
    dynamic nature of, 331-333
    global, 332
    interrelation of, 333
    regional, 332
    socioeconomic policy issues and, 333
    timescale of, 332-333

Episode of violations, 226
Escobar, S., 197
European Commission, 54
European Evaluation Society, 54
Evaluability assessment, accountability
   evaluators and, 14
Evaluation:
   accountability and, 72
   adaptations, 25
   as applied social science, 490
   ascertaining communicability of, 166
   as eclectic enterprise, 25
   as interactive learning, 89
   as international, xi-xii
   as transnational, xii
   decision-oriented models of, 46
   definition of, xii, 112-113
   development of as discipline, xi
   development of as profession, xi
   enlightenment use of, 43
   fourth-generation, 89, 183
   fractionation of, 28
   future of, 77-79
   globalization of, 23
   government programs and, 72
   honesty in, 23
   importance of, 54-55
   informed decision making and, 72
   instrumental use of, 28, 32, 41
   international use of, 28, 145
   method concerns and, 43-44
   methodological diversity of, xiii, 339
   origins of, 88, 112, 215
   political environment of, 28-29
   tensions in, 23
   theoretical issues in, 467
   trends, 194
   versus auditing, 69, 70, 88-90
   See also specific types of evaluation
Evaluation consultants, 468-469
   versus evaluators, 468, 488, 490-496
Evaluation diversity, xii
Evaluation journals, professional, 28
Evaluation methods, 27-29. *See also*
   specific evaluation methods
Evaluation methods, qualitative, 27, 31,
   32, 33, 34, 35, 43, 50, 338, 355
   legitimizing, 33
   rationale for, 34

versus quantitative, 35, 50
Evaluation methods, quantitative, 27, 31,
   34, 43, 337, 355
   advocates of, 33
   criticism of, 33, 35
   dominance of, 33
   versus qualitative, 32-33, 50
Evaluation perspectives:
   blurring of, 22
   commonalities among, 14-15
   complementarity among, 22
   differences among, 14-15
   See also Accountability perspective in
      evaluation; Developmental
      perspective in evaluation;
      Knowledge perspective in
      evaluation
Evaluation process, internationalization of,
   165-168
Evaluation purposes, 9, 10
   for accountability, 10, 11-12
   for development, 10, 12-13
   for knowledge, 10, 13-14
Evaluation research:
   in Denmark, 177-178
   in United States, 178
   postpositivist, 183
   versus other applied social research,
      178-179
Evaluation Research Society, 30
Evaluation societies, professional, 28
Evaluation studies, value resolution in,
   473-474
Evaluation synthesis, 74, 75, 357
Evaluation theory:
   need for better, 44-47
   need for more, 44-47
Evaluation use:
   as criterion for developmental
      evaluation, 17
   differing views about, 15-26
   purpose and, 15-18
Evaluator role, 29
   advocacy and, 19-20
   criticisms of, 18
   in accountability perspective, 18
   in developmental perspective, 18
   in knowledge perspective, 18
   in 21st century, 25-26

See also Evaluators
Evaluators, 86-87
  assembling skilled teams, 94
  contacting evaluation subjects, 95
  interactive, 487
  role of internal, 487
  tasks for, 147-148
  versus auditor methodology, 98-99
  versus auditors in choosing topics, 91
  versus auditors securing funding, 92
  versus evaluation consultants, 468, 488,
    490-496
  See also specific types of evaluators;
    Evaluator role
Experimenting society, 45
Experiments, 27, 337
External evaluation in United Kingdom, 7

Fascell, Dante, 284
Feldstein, H., 266
Ferris, G. R., 484
Fetterman, D. M., 347, 382, 388, 394
Financial auditing, 112
Financial Management Initiative of 1982
  (U.K.), 121, 122, 135, 141
Finnish State Audit Office (SAO), 87, 90,
  91, 92, 94, 95, 96
  and timing of audit report publishing,
    101
  audit criteria, 102
  clearance arrangements of, 100
  guidelines, 103
  professional criticism of, 96
  substantive audits by, 97
Fischer, F., 87
Fischer, J., 420, 425, 433, 434
Fisher, B., 361, 370
FitzGerald, M., 238
Flex, K., 181, 182
Florin, P., 394
Focus groups, 74
Foreign aid policy:
  and recipient countries' role in
    evaluations, 280-281
  conditions for evaluations to play role
    in, 279-280
  effectiveness issues and, 275
  emphasis on effectiveness of, 274-277

  evaluation of, xii, 8
  general information statistics and,
    281-282
  instrumental statistics and, 282
  quality of, 276-277
  research on, 282-283
Forester, J., 87
Formative evaluations, 498-499
  role of, 499
Foss Hansen, H., 183
Freeman, H. E., 444, 490
Freeman, H. F., 112
Fukuyama, F., 164
Fuller, R., 420
Funkhouser, M., 110

Gaebler, T., 125
GAO breast conservation versus
  mastectomy study:
  as example of synthesis strategy, 363
  defining synthesis domain in, 364-365
  meta-analyses of randomized studies in,
    366-367
  SEER database analysis and, 367-368
  specific strategy used in, 363-370
Gatzemeier, W., 370
GEST 20 project (U.K.), single-case
  evaluation and, 425-433
Glaser, B. G., 400
Glass, G. V., 444, 454, 456
Global Environmental Facility (GEF),
  220, 311
  implementing agencies for management
    of, 311
  origins of, 311
  Trust Fund, 316, 322
  See also Global Environmental Facility
    (GEF) pilot evaluation
Global Environmental Facility (GEF) pilot
  evaluation, 219
  approach to independent, 315-321
  developing working relationships in,
    320-321
  evaluation managers, 323, 325
  evaluators, 323-325
  evolution of process of, 322-325
  independent panel of experts, 323-325
  lessons learned from, 327-328

methodology, 321
number of evaluators, 320
organization of, 316-320
presentation of, 325-326
recommendations of, 325
setting, 312-314
Globalization of local community,
149-150. *See also* Japan, Oguni
Goetz, J. P., 346
Gore, A., 125, 128
Gottman, J. M., 444
Governmental reform, evaluation and, 6
Government Management Reform Act of
1994, 125, 128
Government Performance and Results Act
of 1993 (U.S.), 121, 122, 124, 125,
127-129, 461
implications of for evaluation practice,
129-132
performance plans, 126
program performance reports, 126-127
purposes, 127
strategic plans, 126
Graham, W. F., 347
Green, A., 110
Greenberg, D., 89
Greene, J. C., 182, 183, 186, 187, 347,
470, 471, 474, 487, 493
Greenland, S., 371
Groszyk, W., 127
Guba, E. G., 33, 35, 89, 178, 183, 355
Guerrero, P., 190
Gutman, P., 249

Haenszel, W., 371
Halpern, E. S., 178, 346
Hankey, B. F., 362
Hardcastle, L., 242
Hargreaves, W. A., 121
Harré, R., 405
Harrison, S., 98
Hartmann, H., 36, 38
Harvey, A. C., 448
Havel, V., 57, 58
Hawke, R. J. L., 243
Hay, R., Jr., 444, 448
Hayes, S. C., 426
Head Start, first evaluation of, 38, 347

Health Care Financing Administration, 66
Heap, J. L., 34, 35
Heath, L., 449, 453, 455
Hedges, L. V., 36, 38
Hellstern, G.-M., 91
Hencke, D., 96
Henkel, M., 90, 93, 95, 104
Hennigan, K. M., 449, 453, 455
Hepworth, J. T., 456, 458
Her Majesty's Treasury, 136
Herriott, R. E., 347
Hesse, M., 405
Hewson, J., 244
High-stakes events, 24
Hi/Scope Educational Research
Foundation, 347
Historical analysis, 349
Hlatky, M. A., 361
Holmquist, J., 87
Holton, R., 239, 240, 241
Hornick, J. P., 433
Horowitz, M. J., 121
Hosking, J. R. M., 463
Houghton, J., 361
House, E., 47, 178, 179, 185, 467, 475
H-2A program, evaluation of, 348-355
checklist for reviewing quality of,
352-353
combination of methods used in, 349
industry studied in, 349
interesting features of, 353
lessons learned from, 354-355
problems encountered in, 354-355
specific techniques used in, 349
Huberman, A. M., 346
Hugo, G., 239, 240, 241
Human rights violations:
documenting, 222
evaluating, xii, 3, 8, 223-224
problems in evaluating, 225-228
study of as social research, 223
suggestions for collecting/analyzing
information on, 229-232
types of, 221
Human rights violations studies:
bias problem in, 227-228
confronting bias problem in, 229-230
interrupted time series approach in, 231
objectives of, 224-225

source credibility problem in, 225
unit of analysis problem in, 225-227
using different independent informants,
230-231
Hunter, D. J., 98
Huntington, S., 164

Immigration policy, Australian:
Bureau of Immigration Research
(Australia), 241, 242, 243
establishing research agenda for policy,
240-242
evaluation and, 8
Galbally report and, 239
lessons learned from implementing,
235-240
multiculturalism and, 239
setting research agenda for evaluating,
242-247
versus Canadian immigration policy,
238, 242
versus German immigration policy, 238
versus New Zealand immigration
policy, 242
versus Swedish immigration policy,
238, 242
versus United Kingdom immigration
policy, 238
Immigration policy, future of, 249-250.
See also Immigration policy,
Australian
Informal surveys, World Bank use of, 205
Information:
access, 63-64
brokering, 166
classification of, 63
classified, 63, 64f
trading, 166
unclassified, 63
Inglis, C., 249
Institut de Développement Nord-sud, 261
Institute of Local Government Studies
(AKF) [Denmark], 181, 184
Institute of Medicine (IOM):
and Agent Orange results, 376-378
and childhood vaccine safety results,
378-379
conclusions of, 379-380

evaluating evidence re childhood
vaccinations, 375-379
evaluating evidence re Agent Orange,
375-379
purpose of, 375
studies, 375
use of research synthesis by, 339,
373-380
Institutional development, evaluation and,
6
Institutional learning, evaluation and, 6
Institutions:
as key link between information and
markets, 193
Instituto Colombiano de Bienestar
Familiar, 196
Instrumental positivism, 181
Internal evaluation:
bias and, 15
developmental evaluators and, 14
developmental perspective and, 13
in Denmark, 147, 181, 184-185
loss of control and, 15
quality of information and, 15
International Atomic Energy Agency
(IAEA), 309
1992 meeting of, 303
International Evaluation Conference,
1995, 1-2, 269
attendees, 54
purpose of, 1
topics of, 1
Interrupted time series (ITS) design, 231,
342, 443, 444
adding comparison group series to, 453
adding multiple enhancements to,
456-459
adding nonequivalent dependent
variable to, 454-455
adding switching replication to, 453-454
analysis considerations, 447-450
ARIMA-based, 449, 450, 458, 459, 460
classic example of simple, 445
enhancements of basic, 450-459
famous problem applied to, 449-450
future policy evaluation applications
for, 460-461
recent technical developments in,
459-460

simplest form of, 444-447
using additional time series as
        covariates in, 451-452
with multiple interruptions, 450
Interventionist evaluations, 194
Interviews, 349
    SAI use of, 98-99
    structured, 74
    World Bank use of, 205
Izenman, A. J., 450, 463

Jæger, B., 181
Japan, Oguni, 146, 150-155, 163
    as designated depopulated area, 151
    as reservoir of industrial labor, 150
    case studies on, 161
    crisis of identity in, 159
    crisis of intergenerational succession,
        159-160
    drastic alteration of age structure in, 151
    economic activity in, 150
    global changes affecting life in, 156-158
    global issues observed in, 155-161
    global orientation in
        community-building effort, 160
    government-supported farming, 151
    outflow of youth from, 150
    planning mechanism of, 164
    Yuki Village Development Scheme in,
        152-155, 160, 163, 168
Japan International Cooperation Agency,
    166
Jencks, C., 39
Jenkins, G. M., 448, 463
Jenness, M., 396
Jensen, M. K., 181, 182
Jiggins, J., 266
Joint Committee on Standards for
    Educational Evaluation, 402
Joint evaluation exercises, 166
Jones, R. H., 110, 463
Jupp, J., 247

Kabala, M., 247
Kaftarian, S., 382, 394
Kanter, R. M., 150
Kazi, M. A. F., 419, 422, 426, 433

Keating, P. J., 243, 244
Keen, J., 97
Keiretsu, 164
Kellogg Foundation, 54, 396
    cluster evaluations by, 396
Kendall, M., 460, 463
Kirklees Project (U.K.), single-case
    evaluation and, 421-425
Kirlin, J. J., 132
Knowledge building, evaluation and, 6
Knowledge evaluators, 22, 70
    working in institutions, 20
    working in think tanks, 20
Knowledge perspective in evaluation, 14,
    16
    academic researchers and, 13
    acceptability of to clients/users, 21
    description of, 13
    evaluator role re client in, 21
    independence in, 21
    methods used, 14
    objectivity of, 21
    position of under policy debate, 21
    purpose of, 14, 21
    questions addressed by, 13-14
    research teams and, 13
    typical uses of, 21
Knowledge sharing, evaluation and, 6
Koch-Nielsen, I., 181, 182
Kosary, C. L., 362
Koskinen, J. A., 131
Kramer, J., 473
Krueger, A., 199
Kyte, N. S., 425

Ladd, E. C., 56
Lakatos, I., 405
Lateef, S., 207
Lawrence-Lightfoot, S., 44
Lebedev, O. G., 306
LeCompte, M. D., 346
Lee, E. C. G., 361
Leeuw, F. L., 103, 179, 185
Legislative auditing, development of
    in Minnesota, 110
    in New York, 110
Legislative audit offices, role of
    evaluation in, 77-79

Le Grand, J., 99
Lending practices of multinational institutions, evaluation of gender issues in, 145
Leviton, L. C., 42, 44, 47, 89
Light, R. J., 36, 38
Lim, K. S., 463
Lincoln, Y. S., 33, 35, 89, 178, 183, 355
Lindblom, C., 103
Lipsey, M. W., 37, 38, 42, 49
Lipton, D., 38
Little, J. W., 472
Longdon, P., 93
Louis, T. A., 36, 38
Lucas, M. J., 361
Lykketoft, Mogens, 184

Mabry, L., 471, 474, 499
MacKenzie, D., 307
Malek, F. V., 125
Management, good:
    evaluation and, 5, 6
Management, public:
    evaluation in, 8
Management by objectives, 125
Mandell, M., 89
Mantel, N., 371
Marcantonio, R. J., 130, 443, 444, 453, 460
Margolese, R., 361, 370
Market Testing initiatives, 143
Marnoch, G., 98
Martin, R. D., 460
Martinson, R., 38
Matsumoto, A., 397
Matt, G. E., 37, 39
Maxwell, J. A., 347
Mayer, S., 39
McCleary, R., 444, 448
McDonald, C., 361
McIvor, G., 420
McNamara, Robert, 203, 204
McSweeny, A. J., 445
Mechanisms, 407-410
    examples of, 414
    explanatory, 407
    as tool of realist explanation, 407
    as underlying mechanism, 407
    program, 409-410

social, 408
Medical technology, evaluation of, xii
Mega-Cities Group, 150
Meta-analysis, 37-38
Metaevaluation, 178
Methodological equity, 353
Micro-intrainstitutional evaluations, 196
Miles, M. B., 346
Military technology, evaluation of, xii
Miller, B. A., 362
Miller, M., 4, 17, 238, 249
Miller, T. I., 130
Minnesota Office of the Legislative Auditor, 118
Mitchell, A., 361
Mitchell, R. E., 394
Modeling, 74
Monitoring, developmental perspective and, 13
Monnier, E., 89
Montgomery, D. C., 449
Montreal Protocol process, 333
Moser, C., 261
Mosteller, F., 36, 38, 369
Moynihan, D. P., 56
Multimethod evaluations, 338, 340
    analysis mixes, 345
    as eclectic, 344-345
    criteria for evaluating quality of, 338
    data mixes, 345
    evaluators' views on, 346-347
    importance of, 338
    lessons learned from, 344
    method mixes, 345
    nested mixes, 345
    paradigm mixes, 345
    quality criteria specific to, 356
    theorists' views on, 346-347
    using case studies, 344, 347
Multiple evaluations, syntheses of, 28
Murphy, J. L., 252, 347

National Academy of Public Administration, 125, 129, 132
National Academy of Sciences, 374
    description of, 374-375
National Audit Office (U.K.), 90, 92, 96, 98, 102, 140, 141

National Cancer Institute, 364
National Cancer Institute's SEER study:
    database, 362, 363
    database analysis, 367-368
National Childhood Vaccine Injury Act
    (NCVIA), 374
National Health Service and Community
    Care Act of 1990 (U.K.), 342, 420
    purpose of, 433
National Institute of Education,
    meta-analyses commissioned by, 42
National Institutes of Health, 371
National Performance Review, Clinton
    Administration, 128
    initiatives, 128
National Planning Department (DNP)
    [Columbia], 196, 197
National State Auditors Association
    (NSAA) peer review process, 111
National Surgical Adjuvant Breast Project
    (NSABP), 361
Navarro, A. M., 37
Nelsen, R. O., 426
Neoinstitutional economics, 193
Netherlands Court of Audit, oversight
    responsibility of, 174
Nevada State Auditor's Office, 113
New Jersey Income Maintenance
    Experiment, 38
Newmann, F. M., 472
New public management, 6
Next Steps Executive Agencies program
    (U.K.), 122, 137-138, 141
    impact of performance measurement
        on, 138, 143
Niemiec, R. P., 347
Nieuwenhuysen, J., 243
"No new organization" principle, 314
Nongovernmental organizations (NGOs),
    161
North, D., 193
Novikov, V. M., 306
Nuclear power, development of
    pre-Chernobyl, 300
Nuclear power plant accidents, evaluation
    of, xii, 8. *See also* Chernobyl nuclear
    power plant accident
Nuclear power plants:
    advanced designs of, 308-309

characteristics of FSU, 300-303
evolutionary approach to design of, 308
innovation approach to design of, 308
viability of current, 307-308
See also Chernobyl nuclear power plant
    accident
Nuclear triad, U.S.:
    current, 288-289
    evaluating, 284-285, 288-297
    evolution of, 285-288
    See also Strategic systems (U.S.),
        assessing
Nunn, Sam, 41

Objectivity:
    and distancing, 483-489
    bias and, 480
    in evaluation practice, 477, 480-481
Ocampo, J. A., 197
Office of Management and Budget, 128
Office of Public Service, 139
Olsen, R., 131
Operations Evaluation Department (OED),
    World Bank, 203, 210, 211, 212
Ord, J. K., 460, 463
Organization for Economic Cooperation
    and Development, 306
Orme, J., 420
Orwin, R. G., 449, 451, 452, 459, 462
Osborne, D., 125
Ostrom, E., 193
Outcomes, 412-413
Output budgeting, 135
Overgaard, M., 370
Overholt, C., 261

Packwood, T., 97
Palmer, T., 412
Palumbo, D., 103
Parkin, A., 242
Parsons, B. A., 397
Participant observation, 27
Participatory analyses, 10
Parton, N., 420
Patton, M. Q., 33, 179, 384, 490
Pawson, R., 406
Peckham, M. J., 361

People's Construction Bank of China (PCBC), 172
Performance auditing, 86, 87
  assembling skillful team for, 92-93
  definition of, 112
  methodology, 98-99
  preliminary investigation phase of, 95
  recent expansion of, 90
  See also State audit institutions (SAIs)
Performance evaluation, 86
  See also Performance measurement
Performance measurement, 74
  accountability and, 142
  developmental perspective and, 13
  in mental health field, 121
  management decisions and, 142
  purpose of, 142
Performance measurement practitioners, evaluation and, 6-7
Performance measurement problems, audit viewpoint of, 140-141
Performance partnerships, 128, 129
Perlman, J., 150
Perry, William J., 294, 297
Personnel evaluation, xii, 484
Petch, A., 420
Pilch, Y., 361, 370
Pillemer, D. B., 36
Pitman, M. A., 347
Plowden, W., 66
Pocock, S., 371
Poisson, R., 361, 370
Policy analysis, 125, 278
Policy debates:
  accountability evaluators and, 20
  developmental evaluators and, 20
  knowledge evaluators and, 20
Policy evaluation, 481
Policy use, 31, 54
  accountability evaluations and, 18
  knowledge evaluators and, 17
Political environment:
  ideology and, 56-57, 63, 67
  incrementalism and, 56-58, 63
  understanding, 55-58
  See also Political environment, implications of for evaluation
Political environment, implications of for evaluation, 58-65

access to data, 63-64, 65
  courage, 59-60, 65
  credibility, 58-59, 65
  disseminating strong findings, 60-61, 65
  improving evaluator training, 64-65
  linking disciplines, 61-63, 65
  linking with basic research, 61-63, 65
Political prisoners, evaluation of treatment of, 3
Pollitt, C., 88, 91, 98
Pollution, evaluation and, xii
Power, M., 89, 90, 97
Prerandomization, 361
Process evaluations:
  accountability perspective and, 11-12
  in institution building, 12
Product evaluation, xii, 481
Program analysis and review (PAR), 135
Program evaluation, 125, 483
  as argumentation, 475
  origin of, 112
  See also Evaluation
Program evaluators, 494
  role-doubling by, 494
Programs and policies:
  evaluation of, xii
  political context of, 40-43
Project evaluation, 167
  in Japan, 166
Proud'homme, R., 192
Public Health Service, 63
Public management environment, U.S., 124
Public management reform initiatives, 124, 125
Public programs, blended approach to assessment of, 70-71
  in Minnesota, 71
Pyhrr, P., 125

Quasi-experimental designs, 345
Quesnel, J., 193

Rallis, S. F., 347, 355
Randomized studies/clinical trials, 9, 24, 43, 361
  accountability perspective and, 11
  design complementary to, 362

primary strength of, 362
primary weakness of, 362
Rauschecker, H. F., 370
Rayner scrutinies, 134
Reagan administration, nuclear weapons
    modernization program of, 284
Redmond, C., 361, 370
Rees, A., 38
Regression analysis, 74
Regression-discontinuity (RD) design, 443
Reich, R., 161
Reichardt, C. S., 34, 347, 355
Reinsel, G. C., 448, 463
Researchers, basic, 62
Research synthesis, 24, 31, 50, 62, 338,
    345, 349
    accountability perspective and, 11
    developmental evaluators and, 14
    developmental perspective and, 13
    for public health policy, 339, 373-380
    growth in use of, 36
    validity of, 36
Richards, Ronald, 396
Ries, L. A. G., 362
Riggin, L. J. C., 347, 355, 356
Rist, R. C., 179, 185
Rivlin, A. M., 125, 128
Roberts, S., 91
Robins, J., 371
Robinson, E. A. R., 419
Robinson, R., 99
Robinson, S. M., 361
Rockefeller Foundation, 54
Rockwood, J. K., 368
Rodgers, A. Y., 421, 425, 441
Rogers, J. H., 445, 446
Role doubling, evaluator:
    forced, 499
    planned, 495
    remedial, 495
Rose, C., 370
Rosenbaum, P. R., 368
Rosenthal, A., 116
Ross, H. L., 454, 456
Rossi, P. H., 46, 112, 178, 444, 490
Rubin, D. B., 360, 368
Rubin, P. A., 456, 458

Sanders, B. A., 397
Sandlow, L. J., 347
Sauer, R., 370
Sauerbrei, W., 370
Sayer, A., 407, 410
Schauer, A., 370
Scheirer, M. A., 130
Schmoor, C., 370
Schorr, L. B., 49
Schroeder, L., 193
Schucker, R. E., 449, 451, 452, 459, 462
Schumacher, M., 370
Schumpeter, J. A., 210
Schwandt, T. A., 178
Scientific realist evaluation, 341
    causation and, 341
    example of, 413-417
    key features of, 405-406
    origins of, 405
    See also Contexts; Embeddedness;
        Mechanisms; Outcomes
Scriven, M., xii, 44, 45, 47, 384, 471, 473
Sechrest, L., 355
Secondary analysis, 349, 357
Seegenschmiedt, M. H., 370
Self-evaluation, 22
    bias and, 15
    developmental evaluators and, 14
    loss of control and, 15
    quality of information and, 15
Semenov, B. A., 300
Shadish, W. R., 34, 35, 44, 47, 89, 444,
    453, 460, 461
Shweder, R. A., 33
Silberman, G., 360
Simulation, 74
Single-case design, 420, 421
Single-case evaluation, 419-420
    examples of British experience with,
        421-440
    flexible applications of, 421
    See also ABAB designs; Single case
        study methodologies
Single-case study methodologies, 341-342.
    See also ABAB designs; Single-case
    evaluation
Skjöldberg, K., 186
Sloan, J., 239, 240, 241
Sloan, N., 91, 94

Smith, B., 355
Smith, G., 433, 438
Social programs:
  as social systems, 406
  definition of, 406
Social science methods, evaluation and,
  xiii, 349
Sonnichsen, R. C., 179, 184, 185
Sorenson, J. E., 121
Spain, D.M., 66
Special interests, fighting, 66
Stahl, C., 249
Staines, G. L., 363
Stake, R. E., 33, 346, 487, 488, 491, 498
Stakeholder evaluation, 22
Stanley, J. C., 462
Stanley, W., 233
State auditing and evaluation units (U.S.),
  119
  blended approach of, 114-115
  budget making and, 117-118
  flexibility of, 120
  in Minnesota, 111, 118
  in Mississippi, 111
  in Virginia, 111
  in Wisconsin, 111
  key success factors, 119-120
  legislative oversight and, 116-117
  number of, 110, 111
  policy making and, 118-119
  professionalism of, 119
  responsiveness of, 119-120
State audit institutions (SAIs), 87, 88, 89,
  95
  audit criteria, 102-104
  choosing topics to audit, 90-92
  clearance arrangements, 100-101
  contacting evaluation subjects, 94-95
  delays and, 99-100
  methodology used by, 98-99
  preliminary investigation by, 95-98
  reports versus academic evaluations, 99
  securing funding and personnel, 92
  tension between audiences and, 101
  timing problems, 101
  versus evaluation units, 104-106
  See also NAO; SAO; U.K. Audit
    Commission

State Audit Office (Finland), 90, 91, 92,
  94, 96, 103
State Development Bank, 173
State legislatures:
  auditing versus evaluation units in,
    110-111
  evolution of, 109-110
  See also Legislative auditing
State Planning Commission (SPC) [PRC],
  172, 173
Stevenson, J. F., 394
Stewart, H. J., 361
Stewart, J., 142
Stigler, G., 193
Stiglitz, J., 193
Stokes, R. C., 449, 451, 452, 459, 462
Strategic evaluations, 196-197, 198-199
Strategic systems (U.S.), assessing,
  289-293
  and potential further reductions,
    295-297
  agencies consulted in, 291
  conclusions from findings, 293-295
  measures of effectiveness (MOEs) used
    in, 290
Strauss, A. L., 400
Stufflebeam, D. L., 384
Subba Rao, T., 463
Substantive audits, 97
Suchman, E., 32
Summa, H., 97
Summative evaluations, 498
Survey evaluations, 278, 345
Surveys, 24, 27, 74, 337
  customer satisfaction, 98
  in Denmark, 181
  opinion, 98
Sustainable development, 331, 332
Sweden:
  development of evaluation in, 80-82
  evaluation during fiscal expansion
    versus contraction in, 83-85
  evaluation in, 70
  Expert Group on Public Finance in, 84
  government agencies as evaluation
    institutions in, 84-85
  policy evaluations in, 80
  See also Swedish National Audit Office
Swedish foreign aid policy:

general effectiveness of, 272
effectiveness of for specific goals, 272
effects of on developing countries, 272
evaluations on, 283
history of, 272-274
levels of effectiveness for evaluations
  of, 275-276
problems with, 273-274
See also Foreign aid policy
Swedish National Audit Office, 82
auditors, 87
evaluation and, 82-83
evaluation example from, 85
oversight responsibility of, 174
Systemic audits, 97

Tarbox, B. B., 368
Technology, adoption of new:
evaluation and, 2-3
Terrorism, spread of:
evaluation and, 3
Texas State Auditor's Office, 113
Theory-oriented evaluations, 183
Third Sector, 166
as beneficiary of international transfer
  of evaluation practice, 168
Thyer, B. A., 420, 424, 433
Tiao, G. C., 448, 449, 450
Tilley, N., 406, 416
Time series, definition of, 444
Time series analysis:
ARIMA modeling approach to, 448
structural modeling approach to, 448
Time series design, 337, 342-343. *See also*
  Interrupted time series (ITS) design,
  231, 342
Tobias, J. S., 361
Tong, H., 463
Topical Interest Group on Cluster
  Evaluation, 397
Total quality management, 125
Training evaluators, 64-65
Transactional evaluation, 483
Trochim, W. M., 443, 462
Trosa, S., 137
Truth:
in evaluation practice, 477, 480
versus advocacy in evaluation, 467, 468

Truth seeking, alternative cultural models
  of, 41
Tukey, J. W., 369
Tullock, G., 199
Tunisia:
Ministry of Women's Affairs (MAFF),
  260, 261, 269
See also Tunisia Institutional
  Development Fund Project
Tunisia Institutional Development Fund
  Project, 260-271
assessing control of resources for
  women, 268
assessing outcomes and impacts,
  267-268
assessing social/cultural impacts on
  females, 267-268
assessing women's access to benefits,
  267
assessing women's time usage, 267
gender impact of job preparation and
  placement project, 263-264
gender impact of rural development
  project, 263
gender impact of urban development
  projects, 262-263
lessons learned from, 270-271
methods used in, 268-270
reconstructing baseline
  conditions/control groups in,
  264-267
strengthening local evaluation capacity,
  269-270

U.K. Audit Commission, 87, 90, 96, 136
audit criteria, 102
consulting with specialists, 93
U.K. Contributions Agency, 139
U.K. National Audit Office (NAO), 87, 91,
  92, 95, 96, 122, 139, 140, 143
audit criteria, 102
clearance arrangements, 100
"good practice" as criteria, 102
hiring expert consultants, 93
methodology, 98
Pergau Dam project audit, 95-96
study, 141
substantive audits, 97

systemic audits, 97
U.N. Conference on Environment and
Development, 333
U.N. International Conference on Women:
1985, 254
1994, 254
1975, 254
U.S. Air Force, 298
U.S. Congress, Senate, Committee on
Governmental Affairs, 121, 129, 131
U.S. Defense Intelligence Agency, 289
U.S. Department of Agriculture (USDA),
technical quality of surveys by,
348-349
U.S. Department of Defense, 29, 63, 64,
285, 289, 291, 292, 296, 297
Nuclear Posture Review, 289
U.S. Department of Justice, 63
U.S. Department of Veterans Affairs
(DVA), 374, 376
U.S. General Accounting Office (GAO),
26, 63, 66, 70, 129, 218, 284, 285,
297, 346, 348, 352, 360, 361, 363,
365, 367, 368, 369, 370, 371, 463
definition of case-study evaluation, 338
development of cross-design synthesis
in, 338-339
multimethod evaluation of migrant
farmworkers, 338, 348-349, 351
oversight responsibility of, 174
Program Evaluation and Methodology
Division (PEMD), 36-37, 41, 57,
218, 219, 284
See also GAO breast conservation
versus mastectomy study
U.S. Office of Management and Budget
(OMB), 127, 129
U.S. Office of Personnel Management, 132
U.S. Senate, Committee on Governmental
Affairs, 292, 294, 295, 297
U.S. Senate, Select Committee on
Intelligence, 289
Ummenhofer, L., 370
United Kingdom, performance
measurement in, 134-144
future developments, 142-143
new public management and, 135
origins of modern, 134-135
output budgeting in, 135

policy level, 136-137, 143
program analysis and review (PAR) in,
135, 143
United Kingdom evaluation techniques,
uses for, 7
United Kingdom Overseas Development
Administration, 173
United Nations, 145, 219, 228
United Nations Development Program
(UNDP), 54
management of GEF, 311, 312, 317, 319
United Nations Environmental Program
(UNEP), 54
management of GEF, 311, 317, 319
United Nations High Commission for
Refugees, 244
United Nations Special Rapporteurs for
Human Rights, 222

Valadez, J., 264
Value analysis, 100
Value-for-money (VFM) audit work, 73,
76, 92, 135, 140
auditors, 143
Van Rizyn, G. C., 346

W. K. Kellogg Foundation, 397
Wagner, J. A., III, 456, 457, 458
Wahlstrom, B., 306
Walberg, H. J., 347
Walsh, K., 142
Wandersman, A., 382, 394
War, evaluation and, 3
Watts, H. W., 38
Weatherby, G., 449
Weavill, C., 433
Wei, W. S., 446, 447, 448
Weiss, C., 46, 47, 105
West, S. G., 456, 458
West Germany, policy evaluations in, 80
Wharton, J. D., 449, 453, 455
Wheat, E. M., 110
Wholey, J. S., 45, 46, 47, 121-122, 130,
147
Wiesner, E., 192, 193, 194
Wildavsky, A., 56
Wilkins, J., 38

Williams, S. V., 462
Williamson, O. E., 193
Wilson, D. B., 37, 38, 42
Wilson, J. T., 422, 426
Wilson, V. L., 444
Winter, S., 178, 179, 180
Wittmann, W. W., 37
Women, role of:
  evaluation and, xii
Women's rights, evaluation and, 3
Wooden, M., 239, 240, 241
Woolf, A. F., 298
World Bank, 54, 145, 146, 148, 173,
    201-202, 217, 260, 261
  areas of special emphasis, 207
  business processes of, 205
  country assistance reviews by, 205
  country program assessments by, 204
  developing countries and, 202
  Economic Development Institute of,
    202
  escalating evaluation demands and,
    206, 207-208
  evaluation instruments of, 204-206
  evolution of evaluation function of,
    208-210
  goal of, 251
  global/regional policy reviews by, 204
  impact evaluations by, 204-205
  independent evaluation function, 201,
    212
  institutional development activities of,
    211-212
  Institutional Development Fund (IDF)
    grant, 260
  International Development Association
    of, 202
  investment project participation and,
    212
  loan programs evaluation, xii
  management of GEF, 311, 312,
    313-314, 319

Operations Evaluation Department
    (OED), 148, 203, 204, 205, 206,
    210, 252, 255, 315, 317, 318
  origins and scope of evaluation
    function, 203-204
  ownership of, 251
  performance audits by, 204
  portfolio, 205
  process evaluations by, 204
  project-level evaluation activities, 203
  public sector management activities,
    212
  sector studies by, 205
  self-evaluation by, 212
  sustainability as criterion in World
    Bank evaluation, 210
  See also World Bank, study on gender
    and lending practices of
World Bank, study on gender and lending
    practices of, 218, 252
  actions of, 254-255
  concepts and intentions of, 252-254
  explanation of, 256-257
  methodology used in, 251-252, 256,
    258-159
  objectives of, 252-257
  results of, 255-256
World Trade Organization, 156
Worthen, B. R., 397
Wynne, S., 193

Yin, R. K., 346, 352, 357
Yohai, V. J., 460
Young, P., 463

Zabell, S. L., 450, 463
Zelen, M., 361
Zero-base budgeting, 125
Zimmerman, M. A., 394

About the Editors

Eleanor Chelimsky is an independent consultant for evaluation policy and methodology. Between 1980 and 1994, she was Assistant Comptroller General for Program Evaluation and directed the U.S. General Accounting Office's Program Evaluation and Methodology Division, whose mission was to serve the Congress through evaluations of government policies and programs and through the development and demonstration of methods for evaluating those policies and programs. She also helped many other countries—Canada, China, Colombia, France, Germany, Malaysia, Pakistan, Poland, Sweden, the United Kingdom—institute their own evaluation organizations. From 1970 to 1980, she worked at the MITRE Corporation, where she directed work in evaluation, planning and policy analysis, criminal justice, and research management. From 1966 to 1970, she was an economic analyst for the U.S. mission to NATO, and before that she was a Fulbright Scholar in Paris. She received the 1982 Myrdal Award for Government Service from the Evaluation Research Society, the 1985 GAO Distinguished Service Award, the 1987 GAO Meritorious Executive Award for 1987, the 1991 Comptroller General's Award (GAO's top honor), and a 1994 National Public Service Award. She was 1980 President of the Evaluation Research Society and 1994 President of the American Evaluation Association, and was elected a Fellow of the National Academy of Public Administration in 1994. She is a member of the Advisory Boards for the University of Chicago's School of Social Service Administration and for Carnegie Mellon's John Heinz School of Public Policy. She is a member of the editorial review board for the Sage Research Series in Evaluation and serves on the editorial boards for *Policy Studies Review, Policy Studies Review Annual,* the book series New Directions for Program Evaluation, and the new international journal, *Evaluation.*

William R. Shadish is Professor of Psychology at the University of Memphis, where he is Director of the Center for Applied Psychological Research and Director of the Research Design and Statistics doctoral training program. He received his bachelor's degree in sociology from Santa Clara University in 1972, and his M.S. (1975) and Ph.D. (1978) degrees from Purdue University in clinical psychology. He completed a postdoctoral fellowship in methodology and program evaluation at Northwestern University from 1978 to 1981. His current research interests include experimental and quasi-experimental design, the empirical study of methodological issues, the methodology and practice of meta-analysis, and evaluation theory. He is author (with T. D. Cook and L. C. Leviton) of *Foundations of Program Evaluation*; coeditor of five other volumes, including *Guiding Principles for Evaluators* (with D. Newman, M. A. Scheirer, and C. Wye) and *Evaluation Studies Review Annual* (Volume 12, with C. Reichardt); and the author of numerous articles and chapters. He is President-Elect (1996) of the American Evaluation Association, winner of the 1994 Paul F. Lazarsfeld Award for Evaluation Theory from the American Evaluation Association, winner of the 1994 and 1996 Outstanding Research Publication Awards from the American Association for Marriage and Family Therapy, and a past editor of the book series New Directions for Program Evaluation.

About the Contributors

Inga-Britt Ahlenius was appointed Auditor General of the Swedish National Audit Office in 1993. Previously, she worked for the Ministry of Finance as Head of the Budget Department, 1987-1993. On her appointment as Auditor General, she also assumed the position of Chairman of the Governing Board of the European Organization for Supreme Audit Institutions. In addition, she is a member of a number of governing boards in Sweden, primarily in the area of commerce and industry. During her career in the Ministry of Finance, she also served as Head of Ministerial Department during 1980-1987, responsible for issues related to education, agriculture, environment, energy, and the judiciary. Her work in the Ministry of Finance, where she served from 1975 to 1980, began with the position of Head of Section in the International Department and in the Budget Department. Her public employment started in 1968 in the Ministry of Commerce and Industry, where she was engaged in the program of cooperation among the Nordic countries and participated in the negotiations and preparations for Sweden's free trade agreement with the European Economic Community. Her public career has been founded on experiences in the private financial sector. From 1962 to 1968, she worked in the economic secretariat of Sweden's largest commercial bank, Svenska Handelsbanken. During 1963-1964, she was granted a leave of absence to work at the Société Tunisienne de Banque in Tunisia, where she was employed in the department for medium-term credits. Her education includes humanities and languages, and she holds a degree in business administration from the Stockholm School of Economics.

Michael Bamberger is Senior Sociologist in the Gender Analysis and Policy Group of the Poverty and Social Policy Department of the World Bank. He has a Ph.D. in sociology from the London School of Economics (1965). Previous positions he has held in the World Bank include Coordinator of the Policy Alleviation Training Program for the Economic Development Institute and Adviser on Monitoring and Evaluation for the Urban Development Department. Prior to joining the World Bank he lived in Latin America for 13 years, working in urban community development and social research. His current research activities include designing monitoring and evaluation systems to assess the impacts of development programs on women and using gender analysis and participatory assessment methods to make development policies and programs more responsive to the concerns of both women and men. In May 1996 he completed a 2-year institution-building project in Tunisia to develop capacity in the Ministry of Women's Affairs to promote gender planning and gender impact assessment in all major development sectors. His recent publications include *Monitoring and Evaluating Social Programs in Developing Countries: A Handbook for Policymakers, Managers, and Researchers,* with Joseph Valadez (1994), and two chapters in *Policy Evaluation,* edited by Ray C. Rist (1995).

Roger A. Brooks is Deputy Legislative Auditor for Program Evaluation for the state of Minnesota, a position he has held since March 1984. Prior to his appointment as Deputy, he was a Program Evaluation Specialist, Senior (1978-1981), and Program Evaluation Specialist, Principal (1981-1984), for the Office of the Legislative Auditor. Under his direction, his office has conducted more than 100 evaluations of state programs. Before joining the Auditor's Office, he was Assistant Professor of Political Science at Macalester College, specializing in comparative policy analysis. He has also taught at the University of Florida, Michigan State University, Augsburg College, Mankato State University, and the University of Minnesota, both in the Political Science Department and in the Hubert H. Humphrey Institute of Public Affairs. He received an A.B. degree from the University of Michigan, an M.A. and Ph.D. in political science from Michigan State University, and a certificate in program evaluation from the Massachusetts Institute of Technology. He also spent a year at the University of Strathclyde in Glasgow while conducting research on Scottish nationalism. He has been a Woodrow Wilson Fellow, an NDEA Fellow, and a recipient of a European Parliament Study Grant. He is a biographee of *Who's Who in the Midwest* and *Who's Who in American Education,* and a member of the American Evaluation Association, the Association for Public Policy Analysis and Management, and the American Political Science Association. He has served as Chairman of the National Legislative Program Evaluation Society and as a member of the editorial board of the book series New Directions for Program Evaluation.

Ignacio Cano is a postdoctoral fellow at the University of Arizona, where his work focuses on the areas of program evaluation and data analysis. He completed a degree in sociology at the Universidad Complutense de Madrid (Spain) in 1985 and a Ph.D. in social psychology at the same university in 1991. From 1991 to 1993 he worked in El Salvador in refugee relief, mental health, and human rights. He was a member of the United Nations Truth Commission for El Salvador, which analyzed the violations of human rights during the civil war in that country. In 1994 he was a research fellow at the University of Surrey (U.K.), where he did work related to the social perception of environmental change, and at the University of Michigan. He has recently been involved in projects related to analysis of human rights violations in Guatemala and Haiti. His research interests include program evaluation and data analysis, human rights, social perception and cognition, and social and economic development. His publications are related to these last three areas. He is now a researcher at the Instituto de Estudos da Religiao (Institute of Studies on Religion) in Rio de Janeiro, where his focus so far is on research on violence, criminality, and police work.

Kwai-Cheung Chan is currently the Director of Program Evaluation in Physical Systems Areas in the Program Evaluation and Methodology Division in the U.S. General Accounting Office. He is responsible for leading GAO's program evaluation work in national defense; transportation; agriculture and natural resources; environment, environmental health, and energy; and aging and public health. He manages and works with some 25 highly skilled social scientists and physical scientists and others working on about 20 ongoing projects. Prior to joining GAO in 1978, he was a research analyst in the executive branch for 7 years with the Institute for Defense Analysis, which serves the Joint Chiefs of Staff and the Office of the Secretary of Defense. Prior to that he was a Senior Electronics Engineer with General Dynamics Corporation for 5 years and taught in the Graduate School of Applied Mathematics at the University of Rochester, New York, for 3 years. He has a bachelor of science degree from Hobart College in Geneva, New York; a master's degree in mathematics from McGill University in Montreal; and a master's degree in statistics from George Washington University. He received PEMD ACG's Awards in 1982 and 1985, GAO's Meritorious Service Award in 1985, and GAO's Distinguished Service Award in 1992, and in 1993 he achieved the rank of Meritorious Executive in the SES.

William Clark is the Sidney Harman Professor of International Science, Public Policy, and Human Development at Harvard University's John F. Kennedy School of Government. He is Vice Chairman of the University Committee on Environment and served as Director of the School's Center for Science and International Affairs in 1993-1994. His current research focuses on the sources of long-term social learning to cope with the policy issues arising through the interactions of environment, development, and security concerns in international affairs. In particular, he has studies under way on the development of better assessment frameworks for use in the management of global environmental change and on the problems of monitoring and evaluating progress toward sustainable development. His previous research has included policy analysis for resources and environmental management, work on understanding societal risk-taking behavior, evaluation of human development strategies being pursued in the Third World, and basic research and modeling studies on the stability and resilience of ecological systems. He is coauthor of *Redesigning Rural Development: A Strategic Perspective* (1982) and *Adaptive Environmental Assessment and Management* (1978), editor of the *Carbon Dioxide Review* (1982), and coeditor of *The Earth Transformed by Human Action* (1990), *Sustainable Development of the Biosphere* (1986), and *Learning to Manage Global Environmental Risks* (1996).

Thomas D. Cook is Professor of Sociology, Psychology, Education, and Public Policy at Northwestern University, where he has been since 1968.

He was educated at Oxford University and Stanford University, receiving his Ph.D. at the latter in 1967. He was an Academic Visitor at the London School of Economics in 1973-1974, a Visiting Scholar at the Russell Sage Foundation in 1987-1988, and has been invited to be a Fellow at the Center for Advanced Study for Behavioral Sciences. He has been the recipient of the Myrdal Prize for Science of the Evaluation Research Society and of the Donald T. Campbell Prize for Innovative Methodology of the Policy Sciences Organization. He has served on many federal committees and scientific advisory boards. He has two major research interests. The first is in routes out of poverty for racial minorities in particular, with special emphasis on how material and social resources activate self-help activities. He is currently studying a program developed by Dr. James Comer to improve the social and academic climate of schools, foster academic achievement, and reduce social problems. He is also exploring how families in poor neighborhoods manage children's behavior so as to link them to opportunities and prepare them against street dangers. His second line of research is methodological, dealing with design and execution of quasi-experiments, methods for promoting causal generalization through both meta-analysis and explanation of causal processes, and the theory of the practice of evaluation. In these contexts he has written or edited the following books: *"Sesame Street" Revisited*; *Evaluation Studies Review Annual* (Vol. 3); *Quasi-Experimentation: Design and Analysis Issues for Field Settings*; *Qualitative and Quantitative Methods in Evaluation*; *Foundations of Program Evaluation: Theories of Practice*; *Meta-Analysis for Explanation: A Casebook*; and *Losing Generations*.

Lois-ellin Datta, now President of Datta Analysis, previously was Director of Program Evaluation in the Human Services Area at the U.S. General Accounting Office's Program Evaluation and Methodology Division. She also has served as Director for Teaching, Learning and Assessment at the U.S. Department of Education's National Institute of Education, as National Director of Evaluation for Project Head Start and the Children's Bureau, and as Research Fellow at the National Institutes of Health. She received her Ph.D. in comparative and physiological psychology from Bryn Mawr College. She is currently Editor in Chief of the series New Directions for Evaluation, and her research interests and publications include case study methodology and, more recently, evaluations in nontraditional settings.

L. Denis Desautels has been Auditor General of Canada since 1991. His association with the Office of the Auditor General dates back to the 1970s, when he worked for several years on various assignments at the Office on Executive Interchange. At the time of his appointment, he was a senior partner in the Montreal Office of Ernst & Young (formerly Clarkson Gordon), Regional Director of Consulting Services for the Province of Quebec and the National Capital Region. He was born in St. Bruno, Quebec, and attended schools in Montreal and earned a bachelor of commerce degree from McGill University in 1964. He joined the firm of Clarkson Gordon in Montreal and became a chartered accountant in 1966. In addition to a distinguished career in the private sector, he has had extensive experience in public sector auditing and accounting at the federal, provincial, and municipal levels. For his noteworthy service to the auditing and accounting professions, he was awarded the designation Fellow by the Order of Chartered Accountants of Quebec in 1986, and by the Institute of Chartered Accountants of Ontario in 1991. He has been a lecturer at McGill University and the University of Ottawa, Ontario; Chairman of the Advisory Committee to the Accounting Chair of École des Hautes Études Commerciales (Montreal); and Chairman of the Audit Committee of the École Nationale d'Administration Publique (Quebec). He is currently a member of the Board of Governors of the Canadian Comprehensive Auditing Foundation and a member of the Board of Trustees of the Ottawa Général Hospital.

Judith A. Droitcour is Assistant Director in the Advanced Studies and Evaluation Methodology Group of the U.S. General Accounting Office. She received her Ph.D. in sociology (with a concentration in research methods) from the George Washington University; her B.A. is from Wellesley College. Before joining GAO, she was a Senior Scientist at the Social Research Group at George Washington University, where she worked on the National Household Survey on Drug Abuse and was coinvestigator on methodology-development grants from the National Institute on Drug Abuse and the National Institute of Justice. She was also a lecturer in the university's Sociology Department. Her main research interest is in assessing the methods used to produce policy-relevant information and, as needed, developing new research strategies that will yield improved information. Her work at GAO has spanned varied fields, including assessing the research program at the Health Care Financing

Administration, evaluating projections of the size of the AIDS epidemic, and devising a revised methodology for estimating "visa overstays." She also developed the strategy of "cross-design synthesis" and applied it in the area of breast cancer therapy. Her current work includes examining the barriers to collecting systematic data on illegal aliens and other immigrants, and identifying potential solutions or ways around those barriers; she has also recently begun an examination of crime-related statistics. She is coauthor of "Cross Design Synthesis: A New Form of Meta-Analysis for Combining Results From Randomized Clinical Trials and Medical Practice Databases" (*International Journal of Technology Assessment in Health Care,* 1993) and "The Item Count Technique as a Method of Indirect Questioning: A Review of Its Development and a Case Study Application" (in *Measurement Errors in Surveys,* edited by P. Biemer et al., 1991).

David M. Fetterman is Professor, Director of Research at the California Institute of Integral Studies, Director of the M.A. Policy Analysis and Evaluation Program at Stanford University, and a member of the faculty at Sierra Nevada College. He was formerly a Principal Research Scientist at the American Institutes for Research and a Senior Associate and Project Director at RMC Research Corporation. He received his Ph.D. from Stanford University in educational and medical anthropology. He has conducted fieldwork in both Israel (including living on a kibbutz) and the United States (primarily in inner cities across the country). He works in the fields of evaluation, ethnography, and policy analysis, and focuses on programs for dropouts and gifted and talented education. He is a past president of the American Evaluation Association and the American Anthropological Association's Council on Anthropology and Education. He has been elected a Fellow of the American Anthropological Association and the Society for Applied Anthropology. He received the Myrdal Award for Evaluation Practice, one of the 1990 Mensa Education and Research Foundation Awards for Excellence, and the George and Louise Spindler Award for outstanding contributions to educational anthropology as a scholar and practitioner. He is the general editor for the book series Studies in Education and Culture, and he has contributed to a variety of encyclopedias, including the *International Encyclopedia of Education* and the *Encyclopedia of Human Intelligence.* He is also the author of *Empowerment Evaluation: Knowledge and Tools for Self-Assessment and*

Accountability; *Speaking the Language of Power: Communication, Collaboration, and Advocacy; Ethnography: Step by Step; Qualitative Approaches to Evaluation in Education: The Silent Scientific Revolution; Excellence and Equality: A Qualitatively Different Perspective on Gifted and Talented Education; Educational Evaluation: Ethnography in Theory, Practice, and Politics;* and *Ethnography in Educational Evaluation.*

Finn Hansson is a sociologist from the University of Copenhagen (1975); he is currently working as a Subject Specialist and Research Librarian at the Copenhagen Business School Library. Previously, he was a Research Fellow at the Institute of Sociology, University of Copenhagen. He has published several works in Danish on critical Marxist sociology, the welfare state and social policy in Scandinavia, and recently on evaluation research and sociology. He is coeditor of books on sociology of law (1988) and the history of Danish sociology (1996). He has been involved in library evaluation projects, and his current research interest is the development of evaluation theory and the social functions of evaluation as a part of the functions of expert knowledge in modern society.

Hong Houqi was born in Jiangxi Province, China, and studied mathematics at East China Normal University, Shanghai, from 1980 to 1984. After graduation, he became interested in economics and management and earned his M.B.A. and Ph.D. degrees in management from Tsinghua University, Beijing, in 1987 and 1992, respectively. He is now Section Chief and Economist in the World Bank Department, Ministry of Finance, People's Republic of China, responsible for management of World Bank loans to infrastructure and industrial sectors in China. He has worked as project manager for about 25 World Bank loan development projects and a World Bank grant project on establishment of evaluation capacity in China, and he has taught in the School of Economics and Management at Tongji University, Shanghai. His active research on project management and technological innovation resulted in about 20 publications in journals and edited volumes, including a recently coauthored book titled *Post Evaluation of Public Investment: Mechanisms, Policies, and Methods.* Currently his research interests are mainly in financing and management of development projects and development economics, as well as project evaluation.

Mansoor A. F. Kazi is Senior Lecturer in Social Work and Applied Social Studies at the University of Huddersfield in England. He is also Director of the Center for Evaluation Studies based at the university. Following graduation from the London School of Economics, he went to complete an M.A. in social work at the University of Hull. His previous position was Service Manager of Rochdale Education Welfare Service and Team Leader of the local education authority's Performance Review Team. He is currently involved in a number of evaluation projects in social work, health, and education settings in both public and voluntary sectors.

Caroline Mawhood is an Assistant Auditor General at the U.K. National Audit Office, where she is responsible for personnel corporate policy, including the development of performance measurement at the NAO, the development of the NAO's role in auditing European transactions, and leading the financial audit technical team as well as submitting to Parliament and managing the overall budget of the NAO. She graduated from the University of Bristol with a B.Sc. honors upper second class degree in geography. She then undertook training for the professional qualification of the Chartered Institute of Public Finance and Accountancy. In her final examinations she came top of her year in the NAO and received the CIPFA prize for this achievement. At the NAO she has had experience in delivering quality value-for-money studies that include performance measurement. In particular, she has completed acclaimed studies covering job creation in Wales, roads programs, and ship safety and pollution. Also, as a secondee to the Office of the Auditor General in Canada, she was a key player in a review team responsible for examining program evaluation, involving the research of international comparisons and identifying ways of making program evaluation more effective. She remains closely involved with the development of public accountancy standards in the United Kingdom. She has been a member of several CIPFA technical/audit committees and represented the NAO and CIPFA on the joint accountancy bodies' Auditing Practices Committee.

Josette Murphy joined the World Bank in 1985 and is currently a Senior Evaluation Officer with the Operations Evaluation Department. Her previous affiliations include the International Service for National Agricultural Research, the U.S. Agency for International Development, and Purdue University. Throughout her career, she has focused on two main objectives: to promote the integration of social factors into evaluation practices, and to help build the capacity of less developed countries to set up monitoring and evaluation mechanisms that meet their information needs. Her recent publications include *Gender Issues in World Bank Lending: An Overview* (1995) and *The Development of Cooperatives and Other Rural Organizations: The Role of the World Bank* (1994). She holds a Ph.D. in cultural anthropology from the University of California, Santa Barbara, and undergraduate degrees in history and biology.

Masafumi Nagao is Chief Program Officer for the Sasakawa Peace Foundation. He directs the foundation's program to promote international networking among researchers, civic groups, and community organizations for new knowledge creation and information sharing on problems and concerns commonly shared across national boundaries. The program has addressed a wide range of issues, such as management of megacities, renewal of rural communities in postindustrial society, examination of the evolving public character of enterprise, promotion of multilateral cooperative action at the people's level among neighboring countries (e.g., China, Japan, South Korea, and Russia), and improvement of Asia-Africa links for the sharing of development experience. Before joining the foundation in 1987, he worked for 12 years as Economic Affairs Officer for the United Nations Conference on Trade and Development, carrying out research on technology policy issues for Third World countries. He prepared many UNCTAD secretariat documents on transfer and development of technology, especially in energy and capital goods sectors, including one that he coauthored for outside publication titled *Capital Goods Production in the Third World* (1983). His academic training started at Carleton College in Northfield, Minnesota, where he obtained his B.A. in economics, and was continued at Hitotsubashi University (Japan), from which he received his M.A. in economic policy. His current research interests lie in identifying issues and action possibilities raised by the globalization of the perspectives of local communities, NGOs, and micro-level agents, and the increased interactions among these entities.

John Nieuwenhuysen was the Foundation Director of the Bureau of Immigration, Multicultural and Population Research from 1989 to 1996. The bureau is an independent research agency within the Department of Immigration and Ethnic Affairs. He is now Chief Executive Officer of the

Committee for Economic Development of Australia, which is an independent apolitical organization mainly made up of business leaders who have an interest in and commitment to Australia's economic and social development, through undertaking objective discussion and research into issues affecting Australia's growth. He was previously Reader in Economics, University of Melbourne, and Research Director at CEDA. He has worked at the International Labour Office, Geneva; the British Department of Trade and Industry in London; the University of Pittsburgh; and the University of Natal. He holds an M.A. degree (Natal) and a Ph.D. (London). He was chairman of two major state government inquiries in Victoria—a review of the Liquor Control Act (1984-1986) and a committee of inquiry into revenue raising (1982-1983). His report on the Victorian Liquor Control Act delivered in 1986 formed the foundation for the reforming 1987 Liquor Act. During 1991, he was commissioned by the Secretary General of the Organization for Economic Cooperation and Development to provide a report titled *A Possible Migration Research Program for the OECD*. Also during 1991 and 1992, he served as chair of the Victorian Government's Committee for Multiculturalism in the Arts. He has been an adviser in national wage hearings and trade practices matters, has undertaken many government and private sector consultancies, and has written extensively on subjects as diverse as wages, competition, and price policy; international trade; the economics of social opportunity; the economic status of Australian Aborigines; industry economics; and Australian economic growth.

W. Haven North served with the U.S. Agency for International Development for 37 years, largely on African development programs. He lived and worked in Ethiopia, Nigeria, and Ghana for 15 years and in Ghana served as the Mission Director for U.S. Agency for International Development (1970-1976); he also served as Deputy Assistant Administrator for the Africa Bureau (1976-1982) and as the Associate Assistant Administrator and Director (founder) of USAID's Center for Development Information and Evaluation (1983-1989). From 1985 to 1988 he was also Chairman of the OECD/DAC Expert Group on Aid Evaluation. As an independent consultant to USAID, UNDP, IFC, IDB, and the World Bank, he conducted studies and evaluations of management of technical cooperation, strategies for capacity building in developing countries, strengthening aid coordination (LDCs and, recently, Vietnam), UNDP management of

HIV/AIDS control programs, strategies for development information dissemination and use, and assessments of evaluation systems. He was coordinator of the evaluation of the Global Environment Facility's pilot phase, and he also undertook a review of DAC principles for the evaluation of development assistance and an evaluation of UNDP's noncore resources and cofinancing modalities. He has a B.A. in history from Wesleyan University and an M.A. in history from Columbia University. His most recent publication is "Sustainability of the Danfa Group of Health Projects: A 26-year Overview," with Julius S. Prince and Alfred K. Neumann (in *Sustainable Development in Third World Countries: Applied and Theoretical Perspectives,* edited by Valentine Udoh James, 1996).

Vladimir Novikov joined the Radiation Safety of the Biosphere (RAD) Project in the International Institute for Applied Systems Analysis (IIASA) in 1994 to undertake a feasibility study on the RAD Project and to take part in its management. He is now in charge of the Evaluation Study of the RAD Project and the management of its contacts with the Russian network of experts participating in the project. He previously took part in the IIASA Social and Environmental Dimensions of Technology Project and the Risk Analysis and Policy Project within the framework of the cooperation between IIASA and the Russian Research Center's Kurchatov Institute. He studied physics at Moscow State University and received his first degree from the International Institute for Nuclear Research. He was awarded his Ph.D. in physics and mathematics from the Atomic Energy Institute in Moscow. He is currently Chief of the Nuclear Power Problems Laboratory at the Russian Research Center's Kurchatov Institute and Professor of Physics at Moscow State University. His professional activities include research in nuclear physics and transport theory, administration, teaching, and consulting. His special research interests include the sustainable evolution of nuclear industry and the ecological and social aspects of the nuclear legacy of the Cold War. He is an observer in the Contact Expert Group for International Cooperation on Nuclear Waste Management in the Russian Federation. His recent publications include "Progress Report on IIASA RAD-Project" (in *International Co-Operation on Nuclear Waste Management in the Russian Federation,* 1995); "Development of a Sophisticated Computer Based Data System for Evaluation of the Radiation Legacy of the FSU," with N. N. Egorov and N. P. Laverov (in *Proceedings of WM '96,* 1996); and "Chernobyl, 10 Years Later" (*Environment,* 1996). He is a recipient of the Kurchatov Award in Science.

Robert G. Orwin received his Ph.D. in psychology from Northwestern University in 1982. He currently serves as Research Director and Program Area Developer at R.O.W. Sciences, Inc., a health research and information services firm in Rockville, Maryland. Apart from time series analysis, his research interests include the evaluation of alcohol, drug abuse, and mental health treatment and prevention programs; issues in the design and conduct of multisite evaluations; quantitative synthesis; and the integration of process and outcome evaluation. His recent publications include "Evaluation of Alcohol, Drug Abuse, and Mental Health Services," with Howard H. Goldman (in *Mental Health Services: A Public Health Perspective,* edited by Bruce L. Levin and John Petrila, 1995); "Pitfalls in Evaluating the Effectiveness of Case Management Programs: Lessons From the NIAAA Community Demonstration Program," with L. Joseph Sonnefeld, Roberta Garrison-Mogren, and Nancy G. Smith (in *Evaluation Review,* 1994); and "Judicious Applications of Randomized Designs," with David S. Cordray and Robert B. Huebner (in *Critically Evaluating the Role of Randomized Experiments in Evaluation,* edited by K. J. Conrad, 1994).

Ray Pawson (B.A., University of Essex, U.K.; Ph.D., University of Lancaster, U.K.) is a Senior Lecturer in the School of Sociology and Social Policy at the University of Leeds, U.K. He is a Senior Research Fellow of the U.K. Economic and Social Research Council. His main research interest is in social science methodology, and he has written about methodological issues—philosophical and practical, pure and applied, qualitative and quantitative. He is the author of *A Measure for Measures: A Manifesto for Empirical Sociology* (1989) and coauthor, with Nick Tilley, of *Realistic Evaluation* (1997). He is currently President of the Research Committee on Logic and Methodology of the International Sociological Association. Recently he has served much time in prison (for research purposes), being the U.K. Director of the International Forum for the Study of Education in Penal Systems.

Robert Picciotto is Director-General, Operations Evaluation, in the World Bank. He reports to the Board of Executive Directors and oversees the activities of the Bank's Operations Evaluation Department and IFC's Operations Evaluation Group. An Italian citizen, he obtained his civil engineering degree from the École Nationale Supérieure de l'Aéronautique in Paris. After an assignment with Exxon Research, he obtained a master's degree in public affairs at Princeton University. He joined the World Bank Group in 1962. His first position was in the International Finance Corporation, where he worked as a Development Finance Company Analyst. He transferred to the Bank in 1964 and has since held a variety of positions in the organization. He spent 2 years in New Delhi (1967-1969) as Agriculture Economist and then, on his return to headquarters, headed the Agriculture Industries Division. In 1970, he took over a Special Projects division dealing with what was then East Pakistan and later became Bangladesh. In 1972 he became Assistant Director, Agriculture and Rural Development in the Asia Region. From 1976 to 1986 he was Director of Regional Projects Departments, and in 1987 he was appointed Director of Planning and Budgeting. In 1990 he was promoted to Vice President, Corporate Planning and Budgeting. He assumed his current position in 1992. He is the author of several essays and articles on institutional economics and development evaluation. Along with Ray Rist, he coedited *Evaluating Country Development Policies and Programs: New Approaches for a New Agenda* (1994).

Christopher Pollitt, M.A. (Oxon.), Ph.D. (LSE), is Professor of Government at Brunel University in West London. He is also Co-Director of Brunel's Centre for the Evaluation of Public Policy and President of the European Evaluation Society (1996-1998). He is the author of many books and articles in the field of public management and evaluation, and his current research concerns the nature of performance audit and its relationship to the "new public management." He is working with Hilkka Summa and others on a five-country comparative study. In the past he has undertaken consultancy for the U.K. Treasury, the Organization for Economic Cooperation and Development, the European Commission, the Finnish Ministry of Finance, and a number of other public bodies. His recent publications include *Quality Improvement in European Public Services,* with Geert Bouckaert (1995), and *Managerialism and the Public Services* (2nd edition, 1993).

Ray C. Rist is Director of the Center for Policy Studies, Graduate School of Education and Human Development, George Washington University, a position he has held since 1993. He is also Professor of Educational Leadership and of Sociology. He was previously Director of Operations for the General Government Division, U.S. General Accounting Office. He was also GAO's Director of the Case Studies Program and Deputy Director of the Program Evaluation and Methodology Division. During 1991-1992, he was the first person to hold the Leon Sachs Chair in Public Policy at the Johns Hopkins University. From 1977 to 1981, he was National Director of the Youthwork National Policy Study on youth employment and training programs and a Professor at Cornell University. He worked from 1974 to 1976 with the National Institute of Education (NIE). He left NIE in 1976 to accept an appointment as Senior Fulbright Fellow at the Max Planck Institute in Berlin, West Germany. From 1968 to 1974, he was a sociology professor, first in Illinois and then in Oregon. He earned his Ph.D. in sociology and anthropology in 1970 from Washington University (St. Louis). His 21 books include *Policy Evaluation* (1995), *Can Governments Learn?* (1994), *The Democratic Imagination* (1994), *Program Evaluation and the Management of Government* (1990), *Policy Studies Review Annual,* Volume 9 (1989), and *Finding Work: Cross-National Perspectives on Employment and Training Policy* (1987). He has lectured in more than 30 countries, consulted to many national and international organizations, and testified on multiple occasions for the U.S. Congress.

James R. Sanders is Professor of Education and Associate Director of the Evaluation Center at Western Michigan University. He received his Ph.D. in educational research and evaluation methodology from the University of Colorado. He is author or coauthor of five books and numerous articles and technical reports in the area of program evaluation. His most recent book, *Program Evaluation* (in press) is coauthored with Drs. Blaine Worthen and Jody Fitzpatrick. He is Chairman of the Joint Committee on Standards for Educational Evaluation and has served on the board of directors for the American Evaluation Association. His current professional interests are in capacity building in evaluation.

Michael Scriven has degrees in mathematics and philosophy and has taught in those departments as well as departments of psychology and education. He was on the faculty of the University of California, Berkeley, for 12 years, is a former president of the AERA, and was the first president of one of the two organizations that merged to become the American Evaluation Association as well as founding editor of its journal (now *Evaluation Practice*). He has received the AEA's Lazarsfeld Award for contributions to evaluation theory and has been a Fellow of the Center for Advanced Study in the Behavioral Sciences at Palo Alto, a Whitehead Fellow at Harvard, and a Senior AERA Fellow in Evaluation at the National Science Foundation. He has served on the editorial boards of 36 journals in 10 fields, editing 6 (2 on microcomputers), and his 300 publications include the *Evaluation Thesaurus,* now in its fourth edition.

Robert E. Stake is Professor of Education and Director of the Center for Instructional Research and Curriculum Evaluation at the University of Illinois. Since 1963 he has been a specialist in the evaluation of educational programs. Among the evaluative studies he has directed have been works in science and mathematics in elementary and secondary schools, model programs and conventional teaching of the arts in schools, development of teaching with sensitivity to gender equity, education of teachers for the deaf and for youth in transition from school to work settings, environmental education and special programs for gifted students, and the reform of urban education. He is the author of *Quieting Reform,* a book on Charles Murray's evaluation of Cities-in-Schools; two books on methodology, *Evaluating the Arts in Education* and *The Art of Case Study Research*; and *Custom and Cherishing,* a book with Liora Bresler and Linda Mabry on teaching the arts in ordinary elementary school classrooms in the United States. Recently he led a multiyear evaluation study of the Chicago Teachers Academy for Mathematics and Science. For his evaluation work he received in 1988 the Lazarsfeld Award from the American Evaluation Association and, in 1994, an honorary doctorate from the University of Uppsala, Sweden.

Michael A. Stoto, Ph.D., is Director of the Division of Health Promotion and Disease Prevention of the Institute of Medicine of the National Academy of Sciences. He received an A.B. in statistics from Princeton University and a Ph.D. in statistics and demography from Harvard University, and was formerly Associate Professor of Public Policy at Harvard's John F. Kennedy School of Government. A member of the Institute of Medicine staff since 1987, he directed the IOM's effort in support of the U.S. Public Health Service's Healthy People 2000 project and has worked on IOM projects addressing a number of issues in public health, health statistics, health promotion and disease prevention, vaccine safety and policy, environmental health, and AIDS. He served as study director for the IOM committee that produced *Veterans and Agent Orange: Health Effects of Herbicides Used in Vietnam* and *Veterans and Agent Orange: Update 1996*. He also led the staff responsible for *HIV and the Blood Supply: An Analysis of Crisis Decisionmaking*. He is coauthor of *Data for Decisions: Information Strategies for Policy Makers* and numerous articles in statistics, demography, epidemiology, health policy, science policy, risk assessment, and other fields. His research interests include decision making under uncertainty and research synthesis. He is an active member of the American Public Health Association, the American Statistical Association, the International Union for the Scientific Study of Population, the Population Association of America, and other organizations.

Hilkka Summa is a Senior Counselor in the Public Management Department of the Finnish Ministry of Finance. Her current work includes evaluation of public management reforms and development projects in the field of financial management and public accountability. She holds a doctorate in political science and she lectures at the University of Helsinki on public management. As a researcher she is engaged in a comparative study of the role of audit institutions and performance audit in the context of new public management (in a project led by Professor Christopher Pollitt). Her research interests also include political rhetoric and argumentation as an approach to studying political and administrative phenomena. She is the author of articles in the field of political rhetoric appearing in *The Rhetorics of Bureaucracy in Tracing the Semiotic Boundaries of Politics,* edited by P. Ahonen (1993), and in *The Language of Efficiency: Applied Social Science as Depoliticization in Writing the Social Text,* edited by R. H. Brown (1992).

Kristina Svensson has been a member of the Swedish Parliament since 1985. She is currently posted in Burundi to launch a Swedish program on conflict prevention, democracy, and human rights. She is a member of the Standing Committee of Foreign Affairs and also a member of the Swedish Security Council, and is President of the Swedish Delegation to the OSCE

Parliamentary Assembly. She has been monitoring elections in El Salvador, Russia, Kazakhstan, Latvia, Lithuania, Burundi, and Peru. She was a member of the Swedish delegation to the United Nations in 1990-1991. Before being elected to Parliament, she was the principal of a college for adult education. She has a university degree in literature and Scandinavian languages from the University of Lund, Sweden. She has published a number of articles on political and educational issues, and she has also coedited reports for the Swedish government on Swedish bilateral aid to developing countries, on the multilateral aid agencies, and on evaluation of Swedish development cooperation.

Nick Tilley is Professor of Sociology at the Nottingham Trent University, England, where he is also Director of the Crime and Social Research Unit. He spent 1992-1994 with the Home Office Police Research Group in London, where he still spends two days a week as a Research Consultant. He has published widely in criminology and in evaluation studies, both for practitioners and for academics. In the academic field he has most recently contributed to the *British Journal of Criminology*; *Knowledge and Policy*; *Crime and Justice: A Review of Research*; *Evaluation*; and the *European Journal on Criminal Policy and Research.* His current research projects include an examination of police uses of forensic science, an evaluation of a program aiming to reduce crime against small businesses, and participation in an action project aiming to implement problem-oriented policing in Leicestershire.

Jonathan R. Tumin is a Senior Social Science Analyst in the Program Evaluation and Methodology Division of the U.S. General Accounting Office, the investigative arm of the Congress. Since he joined GAO in 1986, his work has been primarily in the defense area. He has completed a number of major studies, including reports on flaws in the developmental and operational testing of the "Bigeye" chemical nerve gas bomb, on the strengths and weaknesses of the three legs of U.S. strategic forces, and on the air campaign in Operation Desert Storm, the war against Iraq. In addition to these reports, he contributed to an analysis of U.S. aid provided to postcommunist Hungary for democracy building. He is currently analyzing the assumptions underlying the recommendations of the Defense Department's 1993 "Bottom-Up Review," which is the basis for current U.S. defense strategy. He received his Ph.D. in 1979 from the Department of Government at Harvard University. He worked in several positions for the Congress over a period of 5 years before beginning at PEMD/GAO, including 3 years as the Foreign Policy/Defense Analyst for the Democratic Study Group in the House of Representatives.

Joseph S. Wholey is Professor of Public Administration at the University of Southern California. His research focuses on the use of strategic planning, performance measurement, and evaluation to improve policy decision making, public management, and public confidence in government. He is author, editor, coauthor, or coeditor of eight books, including the *Handbook of Practical Program Evaluation* (1994, coedited with Harry Hatry and Kathryn Newcomer). He is a Fellow of the National Academy of Public Administration, a Principal in the Council for Excellence in Government, and cofounder of the American Evaluation Association. Over the past 6 years, he has assisted Congress and executive agencies in development and implementation of the Government Performance and Results Act and other performance-related initiatives. He has served as Senior Adviser to the Deputy Director for Management at the U.S. Office of Management and Budget, Deputy Assistant Secretary for Planning and Evaluation in the U.S. Department of Health and Human Services, Director of Program Evaluation Studies at the Urban Institute, and Director of Evaluation in the U.S. Department of Health, Education, and Welfare. He received his B.A. from Catholic University, Phi Beta Kappa, and his Ph.D. from Harvard.

Eduardo Wiesner is Senior Partner in Wiesner and Associates in Bogotá, Colombia. His work focuses on public economics and institutional development. He has been a Professor at the University de los Andes in Bogotá, and he has served as Minister of Finance as well as Director of the Planning Department of Colombia. In Washington, D.C., he was Director of the Western Hemisphere Department at the International Monetary Fund and member of the Executive Board of the World Bank. He received his M.A. degree in economics from Stanford University. He writes and publishes extensively on decentralization, evaluation, and institutional reform. He has been a consultant for the World Bank, the Inter-American Development Bank, the government of Colombia, and Coopers and Lybrand.

Charles A. Zraket is Adjunct Research Scholar at the Center for Science and International Affairs, Kennedy School of Government, Harvard University, and a Trustee and retired President and Chief Executive Officer of the MITRE Corporation (a nonprofit research and systems engineering organization serving government agencies). At CSIA, he studies national and international security, global environmental change information policy, and the impact of science and technology on U.S. public policy and economic development. At MITRE, where he worked since 1958, he managed MITRE's activities in systems research, engineering, and the acquisition of large-scale electronic systems for defense, intelligence, space, air traffic control, and other civil information systems; and for energy generation and environmental control and remediation systems. He is a member of the National Academy of Engineering and a Fellow of the American Academy of Arts and Sciences, the American Association for the Advancement of Science, the American Institute of Aeronautics and Astronautics, and the Institute of Electrical and Electronic Engineers. He has a B.S.E.E. from Northeastern University, an S.M.E.E. from the Massachusetts Institute of Technology, and an honorary Doctorate of Engineering from Northeastern University. He is Chairman of the Committee on International Security Studies of the American Academy of Arts and Sciences and a Member of the American Association for the Advancement of Science Committee on Science and International Security. He is a member of the Earth System Science and Applications Advisory Committee of the NASA Advisory Council; the National Research Council Committee on the Physical Sciences, Mathematics, and Applications; and the Visiting Committee for Research at MIT. He has been awarded the Department of Defense Medal for Distinguished Public Service, the American Institute of Aeronautics and Astronautics Reed Aeronautics Award for 1993, and the Air Traffic Control Association Medallion Award for Outstanding Contributions to the Science of Air Traffic Control. He is a Trustee of MITRE, Northeastern University, and the Hudson Institute; Chairman of the Computer Museum; a Director of Alpha Industries and the Wyman-Gordon Corporation; and a retired Director of the Bank of Boston and Boston Edison.